2nd edition

Korean made easy • Intermediate

Korean made easy • Intermediate 2nd edition

Written by Seung-eun Oh
Translated by Tyler A. Lau, Isabel Kim Dzitac
Illustrated by Byung-chul Yoon

1st Published January, 2015
2nd Edition April, 2022
2nd Printing August, 2023
Publisher Kyu-do Chung
Editor Suk-hee Lee, Ji-hee Han, Ji-eun Oh, Isabel Kim Dzitac
Designer Na-kyoung Kim, Soo-jung Koo, Hyun-ju Yoon
Voice Actor So-yoon Shin, Rae-whan Kim, Toosix Media

DARAKWON Published by Darakwon Inc.
Darakwon Bldg., 211 Munbal-ro, Paju-si, Gyeonggi-do
Republic of Korea 10881
Tel : 82-2-736-2031 Fax : 82-2-732-2037
(Marketing Dept. ext.: 250~252, Editorial Dept. ext.: 420~426)

ISBN : 978-89-277-3289-1 14710
978-89-277-3272-3 (set)

http://www.darakwon.co.kr
http://koreanbooks.darakwon.co.kr

※ Visit the Darakwon homepage to learn about our other publications and promotions and to download the contents in MP3 format.

Seung-eun Oh

Preface

〈Korean Made Easy〉 시리즈는 제2언어 혹은 외국어로서 한국어를 공부하는 학습자를 위해 집필되었다. 특히 이 책은 시간적·공간적 제약으로 인해 정규 한국어 교육을 받을 수 없었던 학습자를 위해 혼자서도 한국어를 공부할 수 있도록 기획되었다. 〈Korean Made Easy〉 시리즈는 초판 발행 이후 오랜 시간 독자의 사랑과 지지를 받으며 전 세계 다양한 언어로 번역되어 한국어 학습에 길잡이 역할을 했다고 생각한다. 이번에 최신 문화를 반영하여 예문을 깁고 연습문제를 보완하여 개정판을 출판하게 되었으니 저자로서 크나큰 보람을 느낀다. 한국어를 공부하려는 모든 학습자가 〈Korean Made Easy〉를 통해 효과적으로 한국어를 공부하면서 즐길 수 있기를 바란다.

시리즈 중 〈Korean Made Easy - Intermediate (2nd Edition)〉는 중급 학습자가 혼자서도 한국어를 공부할 수 있도록 고안한 책으로, 〈Korean Made Easy for Beginners (2nd Edition)〉의 다음 단계의 책이라고 할 수 있다. 하지만 중급 책은 초급 책과 형식을 달리하여 언어적 다양성과 의사소통을 강조하였다. 중급 학습자는 문법을 정확히 이해하고 적절한 상황에서 활용하는 능력과 함께 각기 다른 상황에서 다양한 어휘 사용 능력을 발휘하는 것이 중요하기 때문에 초급과 다른 형식이 필요했다. 더욱이 혼자 공부할 때 가장 어려울 수 있는 의사소통을 펼칠 수 있는 활동도 중급 책에서 강화되어야 한다고 판단했다.

〈Korean Made Easy - Intermediate (2nd Edition)〉는 일상생활에서 접할 수 있는 15가지 주제가 과로 구성되어 있다. 이 책에서는 중급 학습자가 어휘와 문법을 주어진 맥락에 맞게 어떻게 활용할 수 있는지 보여 주는 것을 최우선 과제로 삼았기에, 각 주제별로 3개의 담화 상황을 설계하여 어휘와 문법이 제시, 연습, 확장되도록 구성하였다. 또한 해당 주제와 문맥에 맞게 어휘와 문법을 사용하여 의사소통 할 수 있도록 말하기 활동을 포함하였다. 아울러, 어휘의 짜임을 이해할 수 있도록 중급 어휘에 필수적인 한자의 음을 의미별로 묶은 어휘망을 제시하였다. 마지막으로 관용어 표현 및 속어, 줄임말 등 문화 속에 반영된 어휘를 배움으로써 한국 문화를 엿볼 수 있도록 하였다.

이 책을 완성하기까지 많은 사람의 관심과 도움, 격려가 있었다. 먼저 훌륭한 번역을 해 주신 타일러 라우 씨와 명확한 교정으로 개정판을 완성시켜 주신 이사벨 킴 지탁 씨께 감사의 말씀을 전하고자 한다. 또한 한국어 책 출판을 든든하게 지원해 주시는 ㈜다락원의 정규도 사장님과, 저자의 까다로운 요구를 마다하지 않고 근사한 책으로 구현해 주신 한국어출판부 편집진께 마음을 다해 감사드린다. 마지막으로, 항상 저를 응원해 주시며 매일 기도하기를 잊지 않으시는 어머니와, 딸의 출판을 어느 누구보다 기뻐하셨을 돌아가신 아버지께 이 책을 바치고 싶다.

오승은

The *Korean Made Easy* series was written for learners who are studying Korean as a second or foreign language. In particular, this book was designed so that learners who cannot receive regular Korean language education can study Korean on their own. The *Korean Made Easy* series has been loved and supported by readers since its initial publication. It has been translated into various languages around the world, and I believe that it has served as a guide to learning Korean. As an author, I feel very rewarded to publish a revised version that offers example sentences and supplement practice questions to reflect the latest cultural developments. I hope that all learners who want to study Korean can enjoy studying Korean effectively through *Korean Made Easy*.

Korean Made Easy - Intermediate (2nd Edition) is a book designed for intermediate learners to study Korean on their own. This intermediate version emphasizes linguistic diversity and communication in a different format from *Korean Made Easy for Beginners (2nd Edition)*. Intermediate learners need a format different from that of beginners because it is important for intermediate learners to correctly understand grammar and use it in appropriate situations, along with the ability to use a variety of vocabulary in different situations. Furthermore, activities that develop communication, which can be the most difficult when studying alone, have been included in the intermediate version.

Korean Made Easy - Intermediate (2nd Edition) consists of 15 chapters that draw upon experiences encountered in daily life. The top priority of this book is to show intermediate learners how to use vocabulary and grammar in a given context. As such, three discourse situations were designed for each topic and the vocabulary and grammar were presented, practiced, and expanded. In addition, speaking activities were included to enable communication by incorporating vocabulary and grammar appropriate to the subject and context. Furthermore, in order to understand the structure of the vocabulary, a word web is presented in which the sounds of Sino-Korean syllables, which are essential for intermediate vocabulary, are grouped by meaning. Finally, by learning vocabulary reflected in cultures, such as idioms, slang, and abbreviations, it is possible to get a glimpse of Korean culture.

Many people's interest, help, and encouragement assisted in the completion of this book. First and foremost, I would like to express my utmost gratitude to Tyler Lau for translating the first edition and Isabel Kim Dzitac for completing the revised version. Their contributions as both translator and proofreader were impeccable. In addition, I would like to express my heartfelt gratitude to the CEO of Darakwon, Kyu-do Chung, who provided immense support for the publication of Korean books, and to the editors of the Korean editorial team, who did not shy away from my demands and made the following into a wonderful book. Lastly, I would like to dedicate this book to my mother, who always supports me and does not forget to pray every day, and to my late father, who would be happier than anyone else about the publication of this book.

Seung-eun Oh

How to Use This Book

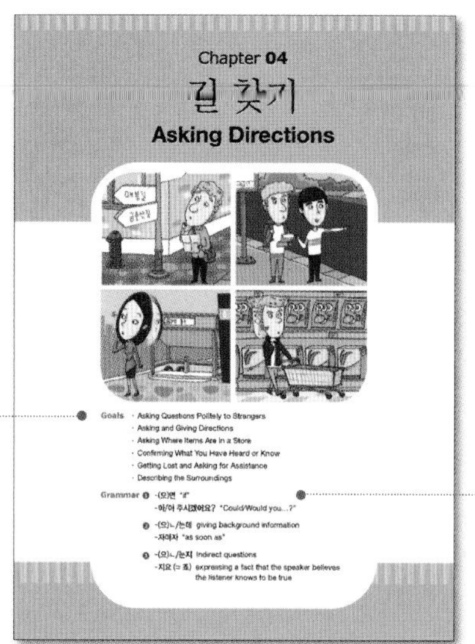

Goals

Each chapter begins by introducing the linguistic skills that the learner will be able to perform after studying the chapter. The vocabulary, grammar, and the final goals of the chapter are laid out for the learner.

Grammar

This section lays out the grammar necessary to perform the linguistic skills that are introduced. Each chapter is made up of three conversations, and each conversation introduces two grammar points, totaling six grammar points per chapter.

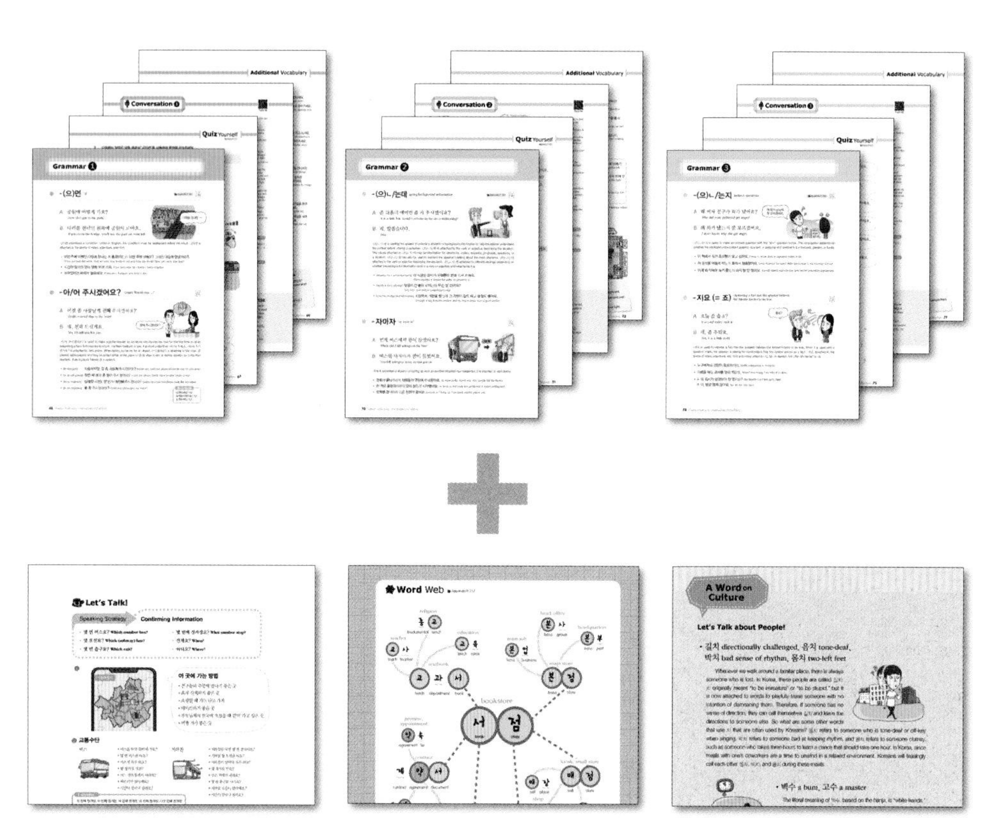

Grammar

This section uses example sentences to present the meaning and key uses of the grammar points. Through seeing the illustrations in combination with the example sentences, it will be easy to intuitively understand the conversations, situations, and associated grammar. The grammar points that appear at the end of a sentence are split into those that end in 1) -다 (ex. -고 있다, -(으)려고 하다, etc.) and those that end in 2) -요 (ex. -(으)시겠어요?, -지요, etc.). Remember that grammar points that end in -다 may be used in both speech and writing, while those that are conjugated and end in -요 may only be used in speech.

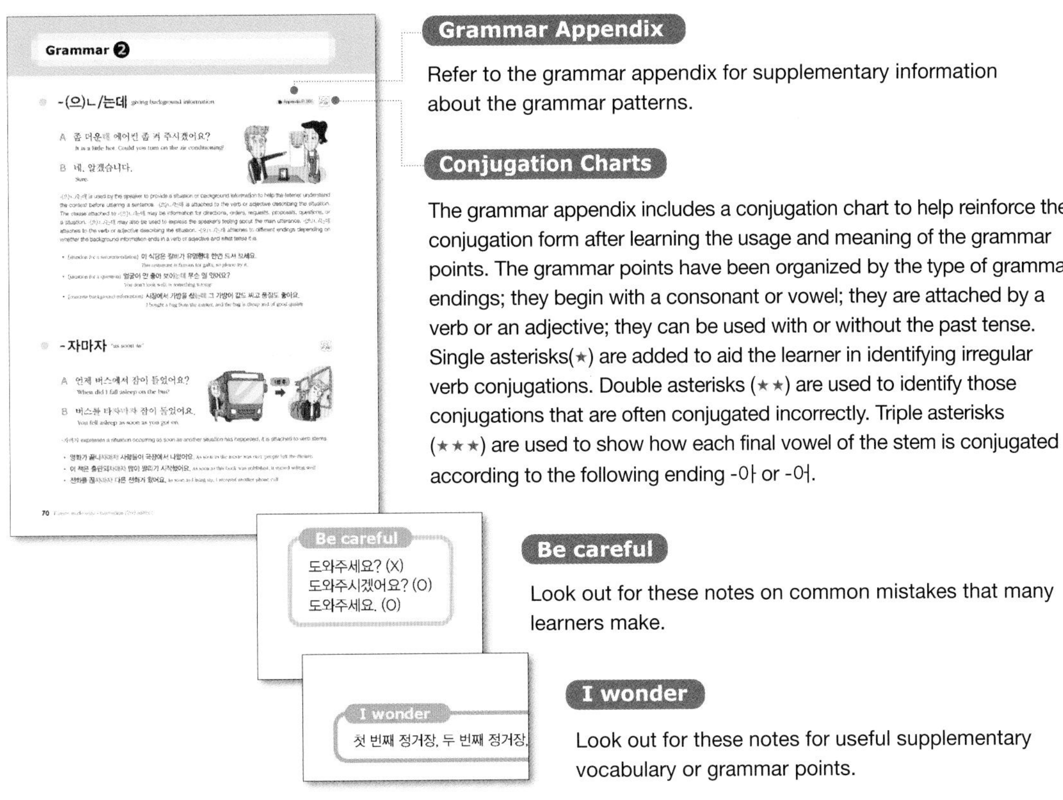

Grammar Appendix

Refer to the grammar appendix for supplementary information about the grammar patterns.

Conjugation Charts

The grammar appendix includes a conjugation chart to help reinforce the conjugation form after learning the usage and meaning of the grammar points. The grammar points have been organized by the type of grammar endings; they begin with a consonant or vowel; they are attached by a verb or an adjective; they can be used with or without the past tense. Single asterisks(★) are added to aid the learner in identifying irregular verb conjugations. Double asterisks (★★) are used to identify those conjugations that are often conjugated incorrectly. Triple asterisks (★★★) are used to show how each final vowel of the stem is conjugated according to the following ending -아 or -어.

Be careful

Look out for these notes on common mistakes that many learners make.

I wonder

Look out for these notes for useful supplementary vocabulary or grammar points.

Quiz Yourself

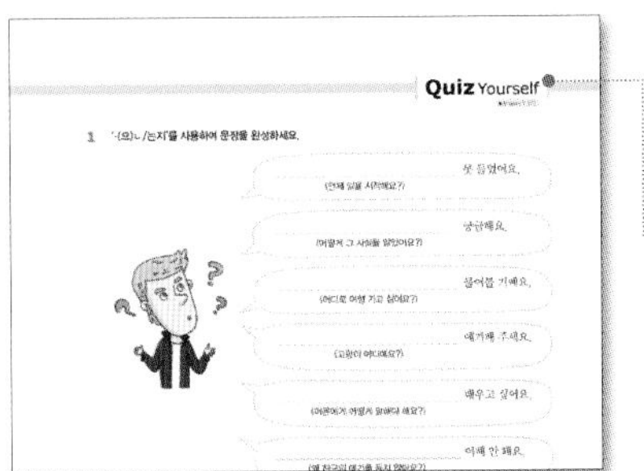

The learner may quiz him/herself on the grammar points. This section uses the grammar points in a variety of structures to help the learner understand the usage.

Answers

The answers are listed in the Appendix.

Conversation

The key vocabulary in each chapter is inserted into the conversations along with illustrations. The conversations are longer than those at the beginner level and are designed, not for the learner to memorize, but rather to follow along and approach proficiency.

Each conversation is accompanied by a QR code so that the learners can practice pronunciation and intonation.

Tips

This section provides additional explanations for non-key grammar points that appear in the conversation. Each conversation is accompanied by two tips.

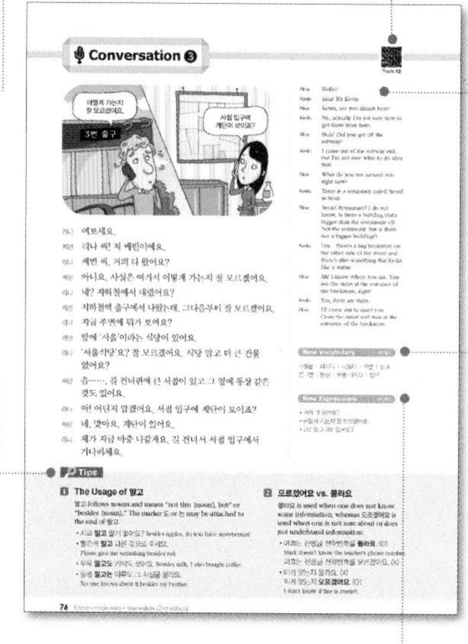

Translation

Each conversation has been translated into English to help the learner with comprehension. However, the translation is not word-for-word, but a natural translation, with necessary literal translations appearing in parentheses.

New Vocabulary

The English translations of new vocabulary learned in each conversation may be found in the Appendix.

New Expressions

This section introduces three expressions that are commonly used by Koreans. The English translations of new expressions may be found in the Appendix as well.

Additional Vocabulary

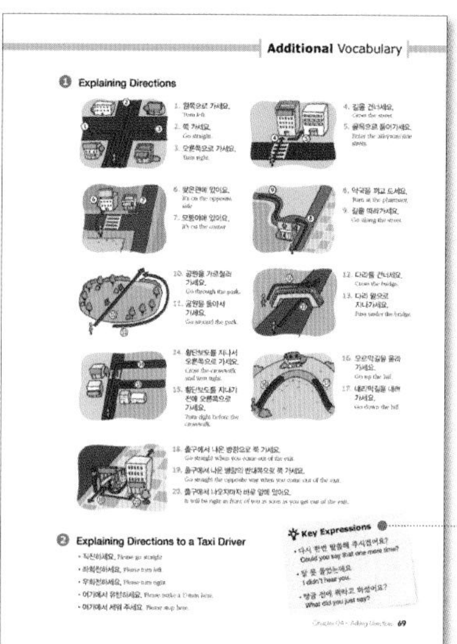

Extra vocabulary that is related to the conversation has been categorized by meaning and provided to aid the learner in expanding his/her vocabulary. Focus on this section when utilizing the key points learned in each chapter to diversify and improve your vocabulary.

Key Expressions

Look out for this note and keep these key expressions in mind in order to improve your command of vocabulary.

Let's Talk!

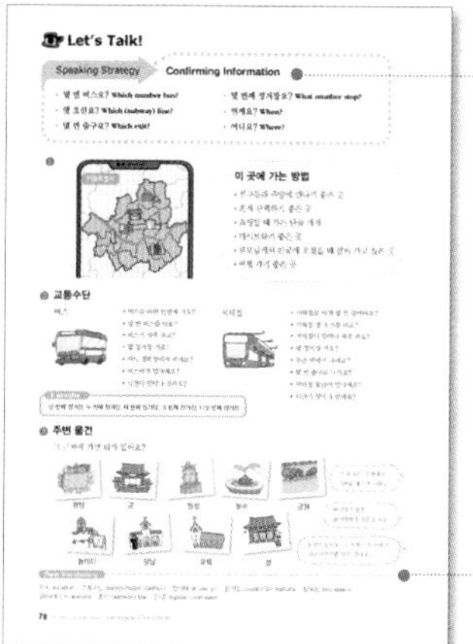

This section is designed to help the learner interact in real-life conversations using the grammar and vocabulary that has been learned. The learner is encouraged to utilize this section with a Korean speaker or a Korean learner to practice free flowing speech.

Speaking Strategy

This section lays out expressions pertinent to specific situations. The learner should practice these expressions to effectively attain naturalness in speech.

New Vocabulary

Each "Let's Talk!" section includes Korean new vocabulary and English translations facilitate the understanding in everyday real-life conversations.

Word Web

One Sino-Korean word has been picked from each chapter and has been broken down by the syllable and connected to other Sino-Korean syllables in order to facilitate understanding of the meaning of specific Sino-Korean syllables in certain compounds. Here, it is not important to be able to actually read or write the corresponding Hanja (Chinese character), but to remember and have a better grasp of the meanings of Sino-Korean words based off the syllables. Thus, the Chinese characters themselves are not shown but rather just the meaning. The Sino-Korean syllables are laid out in the "Word Web Appendix with Hanja" section of the Appendix, such that the learner can distinguish between each Sino-Korean syllable that sound the same in Korean, but in actuality differ due to a different Chinese character.

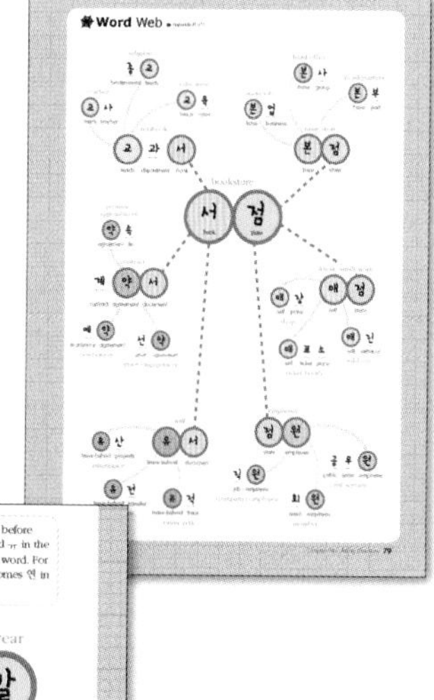

Sino-Korean syllables that are pronounced differently from the original form are explained in the notes.

A Word on Culture

Through introducing idioms and slangs used in specific situations, rather than just vocabulary words that can be looked up in a dictionary, the learner will be able to understand the Korean language through a cultural lens.

Appendix

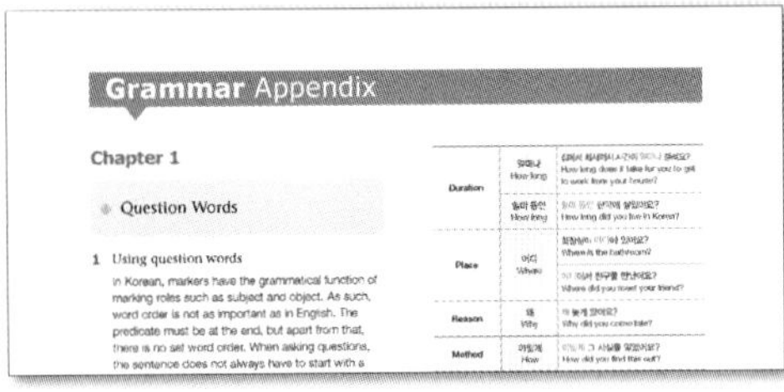

Grammar Appendix

Chapter 1

Question Words

1 Using question words

In Korean, markers have the grammatical function of marking roles such as subject and object. As such, word order is not as important as in English. The predicate must be at the end, but apart from that, there is no set word order. When asking questions, the sentence does not always have to start with a

Grammar Appendix

This section describes the grammar points learned throughout the book in greater detail.

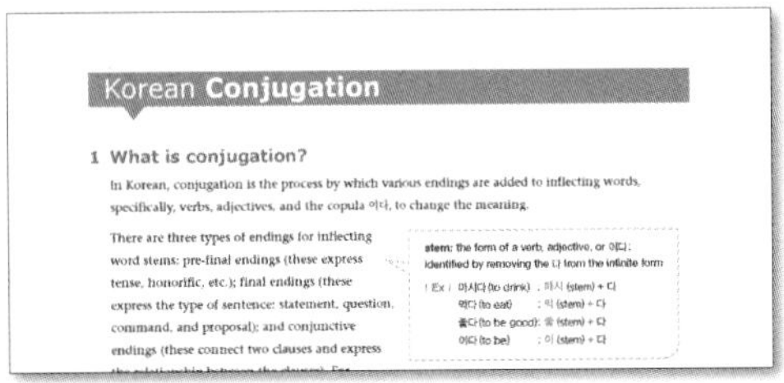

Korean Conjugation

1 What is conjugation?

In Korean, conjugation is the process by which various endings are added to inflecting words, specifically, verbs, adjectives, and the copula 이다, to change the meaning.

There are three types of endings for inflecting word stems: pre-final endings (these express tense, honorific, etc.); final endings (these express the type of sentence: statement, question, command, and proposal); and conjunctive endings (these connect two clauses and express

Korean Conjugation

This section explains what Korean conjugation is and how it works to aid learners in understanding Korean.

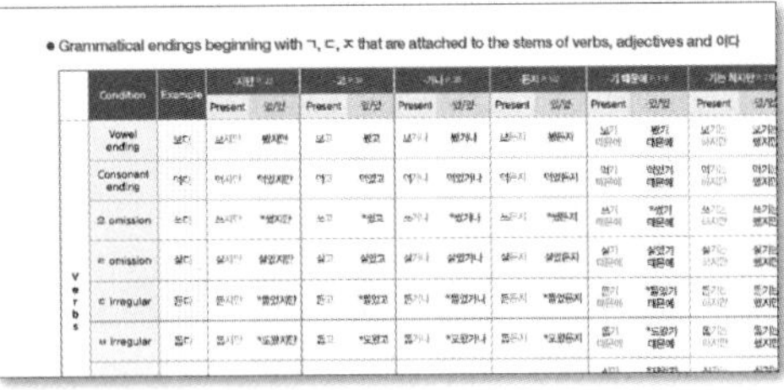

Conjugation Charts

This section lays out both regular and irregular conjugations in a clear, organized format.

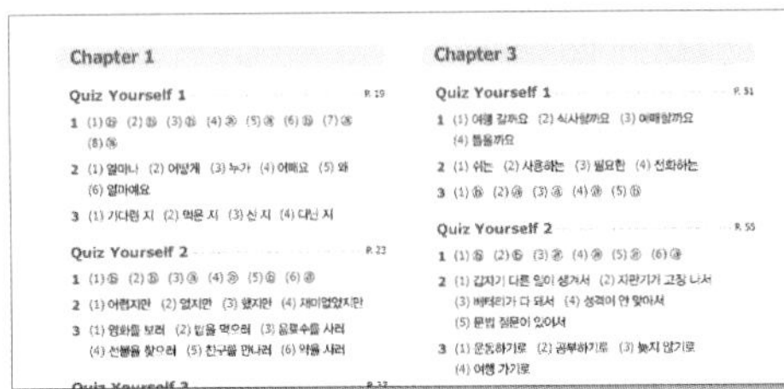

Answers

This section provides the answers to the questions from "Quiz Yourself".

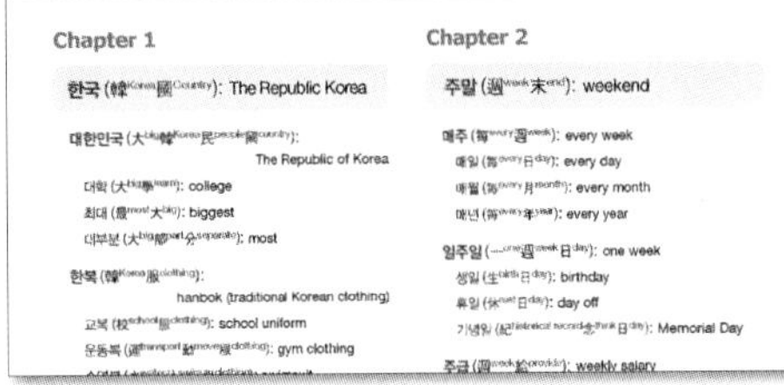

Chapter 1

한국 (韓國): The Republic Korea

Chapter 2

주말 (週末): weekend

Word Web Appendix with Hanja

This section provides Hanja (Chinese characters) and its meaning with Sino-Korean syllables learned through a Word Web.

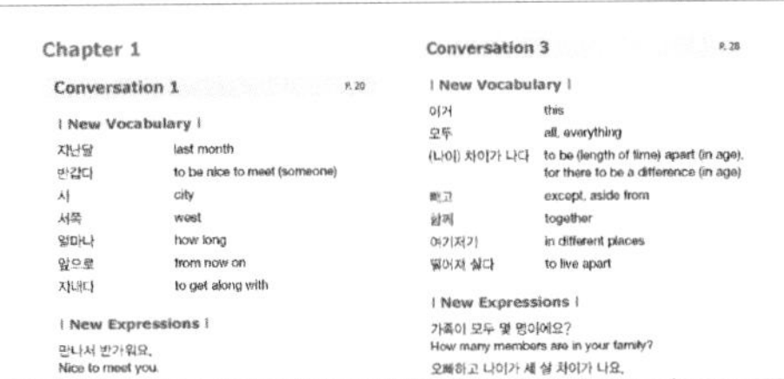

Chapter 1

Conversation 1

| New Vocabulary |

지난달	last month
반갑다	to be nice to meet (someone)
시	city
서쪽	west
얼마나	how long
앞으로	from now on
지내다	to get along with

| New Expressions |

만나서 반가워요.
Nice to meet you.

Conversation 3

| New Vocabulary |

이거	this
모두	all, everything
(나이) 차이가 나다	to be (length of time) apart (in age), for there to be a difference (in age)
빼고	except, aside from
함께	together
여기저기	in different places
떨어져 살다	to live apart

| New Expressions |

가족이 모두 몇 명이에요?
How many members are in your family?

New Vocabulary & New Expressions

This section lays out the new vocabulary and expressions learned in "Conversation".

Contents

Table of Contents

Additional Vocabulary 2	Grammar 3	Additional Vocabulary 3	Let's Talk!	Speaking Strategy	A Word on Culture
• Name • Occupations	• Reading Native Korean Numbers • The Possessive Marker 의	• Siblings • Parents' Siblings • In-Laws • Younger Generation; Children	Speaking about Family and Myself	Finding Commonalities	Who Can I Use 언니 and 오빠 with?
• Doing Chores • Frequency	• -(으)ㄴ 후에/다음에: "after" • -기 전에: "before"	• Time Expressions • Reading Time • Expressing an Action Occurring During a Period of Time	Speaking about Daily Routines	Making Comparisons to Others	English Words in Korean: 컴퓨터하다 터프하다 에어컨 핸드폰
• Appointments: Active and Passive Expressions • Appointment-Related Verbs • 잘못: Expressing a Mistake • Adverbs Expressing Length of Time	• -(으)니까: "because" • -는 게: patterns using -는 것 -는 게 어때요? "How about…?" -는 게 좋겠어요 "It would be good to…"	• Two Meanings of 뭐/누가/어디/언제 • Differentiating Meanings of Related Compound Verbs	Speaking about One's Thoughts about a Promise	Vague Expressions	Expressions Involving Waiting: 눈이 빠지게 목이 빠지게 바람맞다 약속을 칼같이 지키다
• Expressing Floor Numbers • Pointing Out an Object in a Display • Describing a Location	• -(으)ㄴ/는지: indirect questions • -지요 (= 죠): expressing a fact that the speaker believes the listener knows to be true	• Actions Done on the Street	Describing How to Get from One Place to Another	Confirming Information	Let's Talk about People!: 길치, 음치, 박치, 몸치 백수, 고수 술고래
• Vegetables • Fruits • Meat • Seafood • Fish • Other • Ingredient States	• -(으)ㄴ 적이 있다: "having done something before" • -고 있다: "to be doing"	• Cooking Methods • Eating Methods • Describing a Restaurant	Speaking about One's Food Preferences	Agreeing	The Nuances of Describing Taste: 시원하다 느끼하다 고소하다
• Comparing Actions with Static States • Describing Static States	• -(으)면 안 되다: "may not" • -네요: expressing realization	• Before Finding a Job • Hanja Vocabulary Related to Work • Commonly Used Vocabulary in the Workplace	Providing Useful Information about Living in Korea	Comparing Korea with My Country	Korean Cultural Awareness: 눈치가 없다 눈치를 채다 눈치를 보다
• Describing Conditions at Home	• -거든요: expressing and emphasizing a reason • -지 그래요?: expressing a gentle suggestion	• Common Home Problems	Describing the Pros and Cons of a Living Space	Revising What One Has Said	Let's Learn How to Use 방 (Room) and 집 (House)!: 노래방, 찜질방, 만화방 꽃집, 빵집, 떡집, 술집, 고깃집

Chapter	Topic	Goals	Grammar 1	Additional Vocabulary 1	Grammar 2
8	쇼핑 Shopping	• Asking and Answering about Products • Talking about Pros and Cons of Products • Making Comparisons • Buying Products • Requesting Product Exchanges • Explaining Product Problems • Asking about the Listener's Intent • Explaining One's Reasons for Exchanging Products • Explaining Item Return Procedures	• -(으)ㄴ/는데: "but"; contrasting • -는 동안에: "during", "while"	• Describing Products	• -(으)니까: expressing the realization of something after having done a certain action • -(으)시겠어요?: "Would you...?"
9	한국 생활 Living in Korea	• Comparing When You First Came to Korea with the Present • Talking about Mistakes • Expressing Feelings • Expressing One's Difficulties in Studying Korean • Asking and Giving Advice • Talking about One's Current Job and Future Goals	• -(으)ㄹ 때: "when" • -겠-: the speculative suffix	• Expressions of Emotion from Hanja Attached to 하다 • Native Korean Expressions of Emotion with 하다 • Expressing Feelings about a Person or Object	• -아/어도: "even if", "even though" • -아/어지다: "to become", "to get more"
10	문제 Problems	• Asking and Replying about Problems • Making Requests • Accepting Requests • Concerns about the Weather • Suggesting New Ideas • Bringing up Obligations • Speaking about Decisions	• 반말: "banmal" (casual speech) • -(으)ㄴ/는데요?: Question ending asking more detail	• Verbs Pertaining to Using Items	• -(으)ㄹ 줄 알다: "to know how to" • -(으)ㄹ까 봐: "I'm afraid that..."
11	사람 People	• Describing People's Appearances • Talking about Transitions and Changes of State • Describing People's Outfits • Expressing Vague Questions • Confirming Information • Talking about One's Wishes • Talking about the Goals of One's Actions	• -(으)ㄴ/는: noun modifier • -아/어 보이다: "to look like"	• Facial Features • Hair • Physique and Age • First Impressions	• -(으)ㄹ까요?: expressing vague questions • -잖아요: reminding the listener of a fact he/she knows
12	건강 Health	• Relating News • Confirming What One Has Just Heard • Making Conjectures • Making Vague Guesses • Confirming Rumors • Inquiring After and Saying Hello to People • Explaining Reasons for Injuries and Illnesses	• -다고 하다: indirect quotations • -다고요?: "Did you say...?"	• Parts of the Body • Verbs Related to Body Parts	• -(으)ㄴ/는 것 같다: "to seem" • -(으)ㄹ지도 모르다: "might"
13	관심사 Interests	• Speaking about One's Plans • Making Proposals • Expressing Worries • Giving Encouragement • Expressing One's Opinions Politely • Giving Advice	• -(으)ㄹ 테니까: "since (someone) will probably...", "I will, so..." • -(으)ㄹ래요: "I will", "I want"	• Fields of Interest	• -(으)ㄹ까 하다: "I might", "I am thinking of" • -(으)ㄹ수록: "The more..."
14	여행 Travel	• Making Conjectures • Talking about Misunderstandings • Talking about Trip Memories • Asking and Answering about Travel Experiences • Talking about Habitual Actions • Making Excuses • Talking about Regrets	• -나 보다: "to look (like)" • -(으)ㄴ/는 줄 알았다 "to have thought that"	• Identifying a Person's Location • Pointing Out a Location in a Photograph • Common Descriptions of Photographs	• -던: the retrospective modifier • -곤 하다: "usually", "used to"
15	관계 Relationships	• Explaining One's Actions • Asking One's Opinion • Reprimanding Someone for Not Doing Something They Should Have Done • Making Excuses • Making Official Apologies • Rejecting Requests • Guessing Future Events • Describing Another Person	• -다가: "while ...ing", "in the middle of ...ing" • -(으)ㄴ/는데도: "even though", "even if"	• Making Reservations • Using the Telephone	• -았/었어야지요: "You should have..." • -았/었어야 했는데: "should have..., but..."

Additional Vocabulary 2	Grammar 3	Additional Vocabulary 3	Let's Talk!	Speaking Strategy	A Word on Culture
• Problems with Clothing • Problems with Electronics • Problems with Furniture	• -(스)ㅂ니다: formal speech • -는 대로: "as soon as"	• Verb Related to Money • Hanja Referring to Money • Payment Methods	Speaking about Shopping Experience	Expressing Surprise	Expressions Used When Shopping: 바가지 쓰다 대박 싸구려
• Expressions of Emotion Attached to 나다 • Expressions of Emotion Using 되다 • Other Expressions of Emotion	• -(으)려고: "in order to", "so that" • -(으)려면: "if one intends to", "if one wants to"	• Noun + 있다: "to be", "to have" • Noun + 많다: "for many/much to exist" • Noun + 나다: "to be emitted" • Noun + 되다: "to become", "to happen" • Other	Discussing about Experiences in Korea	Reacting to Another's Feelings	Interjections Commonly Used by Koreans: 아이고! 깜짝이야! 맙소사! 세상에! 이야~!
• Weather Vocabulary • Weather Descriptions	• -아/어야지요: "You should" • -아/어야겠다: "I think I should..."	• Common Problems	Providing Advice about a Problem	Giving Advice	When Can You Say 너?
• Wearing Clothing • Describing Products	• -았/었으면 좋겠다: "I wish", "I hope", "It would be nice if" • -도록: "such that", "so that"	• Contrasting Personal Traits • Other Personality Traits	Introducing Someone and Attributing Personal Characteristics	Describing People	Let's Talk about Personality!: 통이 크다 통이 작다 뒤끝이 있다 뒤끝이 없다
• Expressions Using 아프다 with Body Parts • Expressions Using the Hanja 통 (pain) with Body Parts • Expressions of Body Ailments and Injuries Using the Verb 나다 • Expressions Using 걸리다 or 있다 to Describe Specific Conditions • Other	• -다면서요?: "I heard... Is that true?" • -(으)ㄹ 뻔하다: "almost"	• Injuries • Reasons for Injuries • Treating an Injury or Sickness • Types of Medicine	Talking about Illnesses, Injuries, and Health	Expressing One's Opinions in a Roundabout Manner	Idioms Involving the Body Part 애: 애타다 애태우다 애쓰다 애먹다
• Opposite Adverbs • Common Expressions	• -기는 하지만: "It is..., but" • -군요: expressing recognition and understanding of a newly learned fact	• Demographics • Comparing Metrics • Reading Graphs	Talking about Hobbies and Interests	Recalling Information	Let's Talk about People!: 괴짜, 왕따, 컴맹, 몸짱
• Packing for Trips • Travel Preparations • Travel Destinations • Travel Duration • Types of Trips • Travel Expenses	• -느라고: "because (of doing something at the time)" • -(으)ㄹ 걸 그랬다: "should have"	• Adverbial Expressions • Travel Issues	Speaking about Travel Experiences	Hesitating in Speech	Let's Talk about Food!: 파전, 막걸리, 김밥, 짜장면, 치맥
• 받다: Encoding the Passive Meaning	• -(으)ㄹ 텐데: expressing conjectures, hopes, and hypothetical situations: "will probably...", "I hope", "I wish" • -(으)려면 참이다: "to be about to"	• Describing Conversations	Discussing about Social Interactions	Agreeing and Disagreeing	Let's Learn Some Contractions!: 남친, 여친, 샘, 알바, 화욜

Main Characters

진수 Jinsu
Korean

College student about to graduate,
Worried about his career,
Classmate of Rina

리나 Rina
Korean

College student,
Highly interested in international culture,
Classmate of Jinsu

마크 Mark
American

Exchange student,
Korean studies major,
Highly interested in Korean culture

새라 Sarah
Korean-American

Studying Korean in order to be able to speak with her Korean relatives,
Friend of Mark

케빈 Kevin
Australian

English teacher at a Korean elementary school,
Working while studying Korean

유키 Yuki
Japanese

Enjoys Korean dramas and songs,
Started studying Korean as an interest

웨이 Wei
Singaporean

Working in a Korean company with Koreans,
Friend of Ling Ling,
Colleague of Minho

링링 Ling Ling
Chinese

Exchange student who has come to Korea in order to enter a Korean college,
Friend of Wei

민호 Minho
Korean

Employee at a trading company,
Colleague of Wei

Chapter **01**

첫 만남

Meeting Someone for the First Time

Goals
- Meeting and Greeting
- Asking and Answering about One's Hometown and Length of Stay
- Speaking about One's Goals in Coming to Korea
- Speaking about One's Life in Korea
- Asking and Answering about One's Occupation and Contact Information
- Speaking about One's Family
- Speaking about Age Differences

Grammar

❶ Question Words
-(으)ㄴ 지 "It has been (length of time) since"

❷ -지만 "but"
-(으)러 "in order to"

❸ Reading Native Korean Numbers
The Possessive Marker 의

Grammar 1

Question Words

Appendix P. 258

A 어디에서 왔어요?
Where are you from?

B 미국에서 왔어요.
I'm from America.

In English, word order expresses a word's grammatical function (subject, object, etc.), but in Korean, the grammatical function is expressed by markers (이/가, 을/를, 에/에서, etc.). As shown in the above example, Korean questions are arranged in the same order as statements with markers following question words. In contrast, English questions require a different word order from statements. In the example below, in order to ask who Jinsu is meeting, the marker 를 is attached to 누구 and the resulting 누구를 does not appear at the beginning of the question, as it does in English, but rather in the same place as it does in a statement.

- A 진수가 누구를 만나요? Who is Jinsu meeting?
  B 진수가 친구를 만나요. Jinsu is meeting a friend.
- A 그 얘기를 누구한테서 들었어요? From who did you hear about it?
  B 그 얘기를 친구한테서 들었어요. I heard about it from a friend.

-(으)ㄴ 지 "It has been (length of time) since"

Appendix P. 259

A 한국어 공부를 시작한 지 얼마나 됐어요?
How long has it been since you began studying Korean?

B 6개월 됐어요.
It's been 6 months.

-(으)ㄴ 지 is used to express how long an action or situation has been occurring. -(으)ㄴ 지 is attached to verb stems. When asking how much time has passed, 얼마나 is used in the question.

- 그 친구를 만난 지 꽤 됐어요. I've known him for quite a while.
- A 진수를 안 지 얼마나 됐어요? How long have you know Jinsu?
  B 2년쯤 됐어요. It's been about two years.
- 밥 먹은 지 1시간도 안 됐어요. 그런데 배고파요. It hasn't even been 1 hour since I last ate. But I am hungry.

1 알맞은 답을 고르세요.

(1) ⓐ 어디에 / ⓑ 어디에서 왔어요?

(2) 이 가방이 ⓐ 누가 / ⓑ 누구 거예요?

(3) 이 음식 중에서 ⓐ 뭐가 / ⓑ 뭐를 제일 좋아해요?

(4) 이번에 ⓐ 누가 / ⓑ 누구 승진했어요?

(5) 어제 ⓐ 누구를 / ⓑ 누구한테 도와줬어요?

(6) 친구들이 ⓐ 어디에 / ⓑ 어디에서 기다려요?

(7) 그 사람은 성격이 ⓐ 어떤 / ⓑ 어느 사람이에요?

(8) 좋아하는 음식이 ⓐ 뭐예요? / ⓑ 뭐 있어요?

2 대화를 완성하세요.

(1) A 회사까지 시간이 ____________ 걸려요?

B 1시간 넘게 걸려요.

(2) A 그 사실을 ____________ 알았어요?

B 친구한테서 들었어요.

(3) A ____________ 전화했어요?

B 회사 동료가 전화했어요.

(4) A 한국 생활이 ____________?

B 재미있어요.

(5) A ____________ 늦게 일어났어요?

B 어젯밤에 늦게 잤어요. 그래서 늦게 일어났어요.

(6) A 월세가 ____________?

B 50만 원이 조금 안 돼요.

3 다음에서 알맞은 답을 골라서 '-(으)ㄴ 지'를 사용하여 문장을 완성하세요.

다니다	기다리다	먹다	살다

(1) 그 사람의 소식을 ____________ 한참 됐어요. 그런데 아직 연락도 없어요.

(2) 밥을 ____________ 얼마 안 됐어요. 그래서 지금 배 안 고파요.

(3) 이 집에 ____________ 오래됐어요. 그래서 이웃들을 잘 알아요.

(4) 이 회사에 ____________ 한 달밖에 안 됐어요. 그래서 회사에 대해 아직 잘 몰라요.

Conversation 1

Track 01

리나 안녕하세요? 저는 리나예요. 이름이 어떻게 되세요?
마크 마크예요. 여기 학생이세요?
리나 네, 지난달부터 여기에서 공부해요. 만나서 반가워요.
마크 저도 만나서 반가워요.
리나 마크 씨는 어디에서 오셨어요?
마크 미국에서 왔어요.
리나 미국 어디에서 오셨어요?
마크 뉴저지에서 왔어요.
리나 뉴저지요?
마크 뉴욕 알죠? 뉴저지는 뉴욕 시의 서쪽에 있어요.
리나 그래요? 한국에 온 지 얼마나 되셨어요?
마크 1년 됐어요.
리나 그렇군요. 우리 앞으로 잘 지내요.
마크 네, 잘 지내 봐요.

Rina Hello. I'm Rina. What's your name?
Mark I'm Mark. Are you a student here?
Rina Yes, I've been studying here since last month. Nice to meet you.
Mark Nice to meet you too.
Rina Where are you from, Mark?
Mark I'm from the US.
Rina Where are you from in the US?
Mark I'm from New Jersey.
Rina New Jersey?
Mark You know New York, right? New Jersey is west of New York City.
Rina Ah, is that so? How long has it been since you came to Korea?
Mark It's been one year.
Rina I see. I look forward to seeing you again (lit. Let's get along well from now on).
Mark I look forward to seeing you again as well.

New Vocabulary ▸P. 322

지난달 | 반갑다 | 시 | 서쪽 | 얼마나 | 앞으로 | 지내다

New Expressions ▸P. 322

- 만나서 반가워요.
- 그렇군요.
- 우리 앞으로 잘 지내요.

Tips

1 Subject Omission

As in this conversation, there are many cases in Korean in which the subject is omitted if it is clear who the subject is based on the context. Omitting the subject is especially natural in speech. In this conversation as well, "I" and "you" are omitted because it is clear that the subject is "you" for the question and "I" for the answer.

- 마크 **(리나 씨는)** 점심을 뭐 먹었어요?
  What did you (Rina) have for lunch?
  리나 **(저는)** 냉면을 먹었어요.
  (I) Ate naengmyeon.

2 Honorific Question

When asking someone about their personal information, for example, their name, family, age, hobbies, contact information, etc. in honorific speech, the marker 이/가 is attached after the noun, and the phrase 어떻게 되세요? follows.

- (취미)가 **뭐예요**? What is your hobby?
  → (취미)가 **어떻게 되세요**?
- (연락처)가 **몇 번이에요**? What is your contact number?
  → (연락처)가 **어떻게 되세요**?
- 나이가 **몇 살이에요**? How old are you?
  → 나이가 **어떻게 되세요**?

❶ Nationality & Background Information

1. 국적 Nationality

[country name + person]: Nationality is expressed by 사람 or 인 following a country's name.

동양인
Asian

- 한국인 Korean
- 중국인 Chinese
- 일본인 Japanese
- 태국인 Thai

서양인
Westerner

- 미국인 American
- 영국인 British
- 호주인 Australian
- 프랑스인 French

2. 배경 Background

• 태어나다 to be born	영국에서 태어났어요. I was born in Britain.
• 자라다 to grow up	호주에서 자랐어요. I grew up in Australia.
• 이민 가다 to emigrate	6살 때 미국으로 이민 갔어요. I emigrated to the US when I was 6.
• 교포 overseas Korean	저는 교포예요. 부모님이 모두 한국인이에요. I am an overseas Korean. My parents are both Korean.
• 혼혈 person of mixed descent	저는 혼혈이에요. 아빠가 프랑스 사람이고 엄마가 태국 사람이에요. I am of mixed descent. My father is French and my mother is Thai.
• 입양되다 to be adopted	4살 때 입양됐어요. I was adopted when I was 4.

❷ Location

1. 동 East, 서 West, 남 South, 북 North

- 동유럽 Eastern Europe
- 서유럽 Western Europe
- 남미 South America
- 북극 North Pole
- 동북아시아 Northeast Asia
- 동남아시아 Southeast Asia
- 중앙아시아 Central Asia
- 중동 Middle East

2. When expressing a wide area

북부 지방 The North
서부 지방 The West
중부 지방 The Center
동부 지방 The East
남부 지방 The South

3. Places

도시 city

교외 suburb

시골 countryside

국경 border
경계선 boundary Line

- 우리 집은 남산 북쪽에 있어요. Our home is on the north side of Namsan.
- 저는 미국의 동부에서 왔어요. I am from the east side of the US.
- 저는 시골에서 태어났지만 지금은 도시에서 살아요.
  I was born in the countryside, but now I live in the city.
- 우리 집은 미국하고 캐나다 국경 지역에 있어요.
  Our home is at the border of the US and Canada.

Key Expressions

- 저는 서울 출신이에요.
  My hometown is Seoul.
- 홍대 근처에 살아요.
  I live near Hongdae.

Grammar 2

-지만 "but"

A 날씨가 어때요?

How is the weather?

B 집 밖은 덥지만 집 안은 시원해요.

It is hot outside but cool in the house.

-지만 is used to connect two clauses whose contents are in opposition to each other. -지만 is attached to the stem of verbs, adjectives, and 이다. -았/었- or -겠- can also be attached in front of -지만. As in the above example, the marker 은/는 can be used to show contrast (as in between 밖 and 안). -지만 is also used to introduce a topic in a roundabout manner.

- 이 음식은 비싸지만 맛이 없어요. (= 이 음식은 비싸요. 하지만 맛이 없어요.)
  This food is expensive but tasteless. (= This food is expensive, but it doesn't taste good.)
- 친구를 만났지만 오래 얘기하지 못했어요. I met a friend, but I didn't talk for long.
- 이 얘기를 하면 놀라겠지만 말할게요. You'll be surprised if I tell you this, but I'll tell you.
- 죄송하지만, 길 좀 가르쳐 주세요. Excuse me, but could you please show me the way?

-(으)러 "in order to"

Appendix P. 260

A 왜 한국에 왔어요?

Why did you come to Korea?

B 일하러 왔어요.

I came to work.

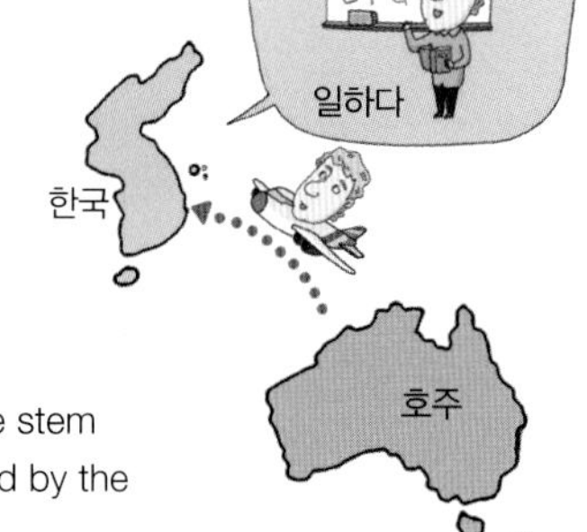

-(으)러 is followed by action verbs, such as 가다, 오다, and 다니다, and expresses the purpose of moving somewhere. -(으)러 may be attached to the stem of a verb to express this purpose. The destination of the movement is followed by the marker 에 and may be before or after -(으)러.

- 우리 집에 집을 구경하러 한번 오세요. Please come over to see my house
- 다음 주에 친구 만나러 제주도에 갈 거예요. I'm going to Jeju Island next week to see my friend.
- 어제 저녁 먹으러 친구 집에 갔어요. I went to a friend's house for dinner yesterday.

▸Answers P. 312

1 **알맞은 답을 고르세요.**

(1) 음식을 많이 먹었지만 ⓐ 배불러요. / ⓑ 배고파요.

(2) 저 사람은 부자지만 돈을 ⓐ 많이 써요. / ⓑ 안 써요.

(3) 이 건물은 오래됐지만 시설이 ⓐ 좋아요. / ⓑ 나빠요.

(4) 많이 아프지 않지만 병원에 ⓐ 갔어요. / ⓑ 안 갔어요.

(5) 여행을 떠나고 싶지만 돈이 ⓐ 많아요. / ⓑ 없어요.

(6) 그 친구를 자주 만나지 않지만 저하고 정말 ⓐ 친해요. / ⓑ 안 친해요.

2 **'-지만'을 사용하여 대화를 완성하세요.**

(1) A 일이 어려워요?
B 네, 일은 ________________ 재미있어요.

(2) A 열이 있어요?
B 아니요, 열은 ________________ 콧물이 나요.

(3) A 숙제 다 했어요?
B 네, 숙제는 다 ________________ 집에 놓고 왔어요.

(4) A 그 영화가 재미있었어요?
B 아니요, 영화는 ________________ 배우 연기가 좋았어요.

3 **다음에서 알맞은 답을 골라서 '-(으)러'를 사용하여 문장을 완성하세요.**

밥을 먹다	영화를 보다	약을 사다
선물을 찾다	친구를 만나다	음료수를 사다

(1) 내일부터 새 영화가 시작해요. ________________ 극장에 같이 가요.

(2) 아침을 못 먹었어요. 그래서 ________________ 식당에 가는 중이에요.

(3) 목이 말라요. 그래서 편의점에 ________________ 가요.

(4) 내일 친구 생일이에요. 그래서 ________________ 밖에 나갔어요.

(5) 친구가 한국에 왔어요. 그래서 ________________ 공항에 마중 나갔어요.

(6) 아침부터 머리가 아팠어요. 그래서 ________________ 약국에 갔어요.

Conversation ❷

Track 02

유키	케빈 씨, 왜 한국에 오셨어요?
케빈	일하러 왔어요.
유키	무슨 일 하세요?
케빈	한국 사람한테 영어를 가르쳐요.
유키	그러세요? 일은 재미있으세요?
케빈	네, 재미있어요.
유키	한국 생활은 어떠세요?
케빈	언어 때문에 조금 힘들지만 재미있어요.
유키	한국어 공부는 시작한 지 얼마나 되셨어요?
케빈	1년 됐지만 아직 잘 못해요.
유키	잘하시는데요. 연락처가 어떻게 되세요? *(while saving on her phone)*
케빈	010-4685-9234예요.
유키	이름을 이렇게 써요?
케빈	네, 맞아요.

Yuki	Kevin, why did you come to Korea?
Kevin	I came to work.
Yuki	What kind of work do you do?
Kevin	I teach English to Koreans.
Yuki	Really? Is your work enjoyable?
Kevin	Yes, it's enjoyable.
Yuki	How do you find life in Korea?
Kevin	It's a little difficult because of the language, but it's fun.
Yuki	How long has it been since you began studying Korean?
Kevin	It's been one year, but I still cannot speak it well.
Yuki	But you do speak it well. What's your phone number (lit. contact information)? *(while saving on her phone)*
Kevin	It's 010-4685-9234.
Yuki	Is your name written like this?
Kevin	Yes, that's right.

New Vocabulary ▸P. 322

가르치다 | 생활 | 언어 | 때문에 | 힘들다 | 아직 | 못하다 | 잘하다 | 연락처

New Expressions ▸P. 322

- 무슨 일 하세요?
- 한국 생활은 어떠세요?
- 아직 잘 못해요.

Tips

1 The Marker 한테

In Korean, grammatical markers differ depending on whether they follow animate or inanimate nouns. Even with the same animate noun, the marker may differ depending on whether formal or informal speech is being used.

- 한테 (animate noun, informal):
  가족**한테** 편지를 썼어요. I wrote a letter to my family.
- 에게 (animate noun, formal):
  회사 사람들**에게** 인사했습니다. I greeted my company colleagues.
- 에 (inanimate noun):
  사무실**에** 전화했어요. I called the office.

2 The Topic Marker 은/는

The marker 은/는 follows a topic that is currently being discussed or is used when a new topic is introduced. 은/는 plays the role of "pointing" to the topic that is currently being discussed. 은/는 is also used to introduce oneself, another person, or an object as the topic of the discussion. In this conversation, 은/는 is used after each change in the discussion (일, 한국 생활, 한국어 공부).

1 Name

1. 성 (famliy name) and 이름 (given name)

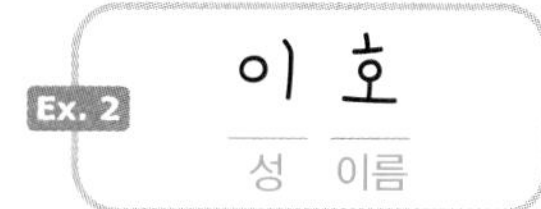

Generally, Korean names, such as Example 1, are made up of three characters, with the first character being the family name and the following two being the given name. Occasionally, there are also names such as Example 2 that have one-character family names and one-character given names, and names such as Example 3 that have two-character family names and one-character given names.

2. Spelling one's name

(1) When you are confused about which letters are in (the characters of) someone's name, such as in the characters 전 and 정

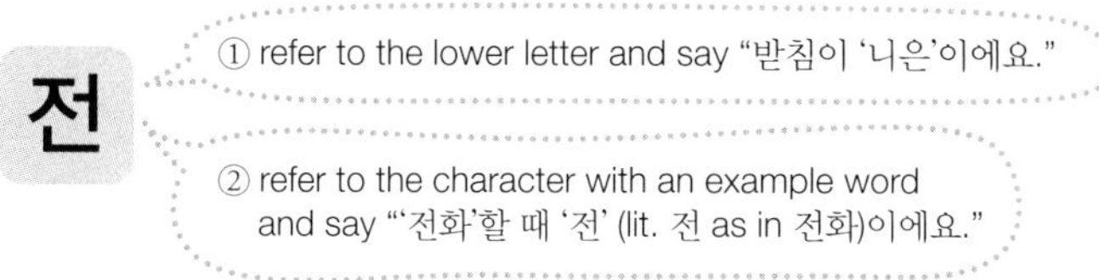

(2) When you are confused between 'ㅐ' and 'ㅔ' such as in 재 and 제

pronounce 'ㅐ' as "아이."

pronounce 'ㅔ' as "어이."

2 Occupations

The following Sino-Korean suffixes are used in many occupations.

OO사 Attached to occupations respected by society	교사 teacher, 의사 doctor, 수의사 veterinarian, 간호사 nurse, 약사 pharmacist, 변호사 lawyer, 회계사 accountant, 요리사 chef
OO원 Attached to general, unspecialized occupations	회사원 company employee, 공무원 civil servant, 연구원 researcher, 은행원 teller
OO가 Attached to occupations related to a particular art or skill, such as a craftsman	음악가 musician, 작곡가 composer, 작가 author, 화가 painter, 예술가 artist, 사업가 businessman
OO관 Attached to administrative occupations that work for the country	경찰관 policeman, 소방관 fireman
OO 직원 Refers to an employee working in a certain location or specialized field	식당 직원 restaurant employee, 대사관 직원 embassy employee
기타 Other	배우 actor, 가수 singer, 운동선수 athlete, 군인 soldier, 정치인 politician, 기자 reporter

Key Expressions

- [회사명]에 다녀요.
  I go to [company name] (to work).
- [지역명] 지사에서 일해요.
  I work at the [place name] branch.

Grammar 3

Reading Native Korean Numbers

Appendix P. 260

A 나이가 몇 살이에요?
How old are you?

B 스물한 살이에요.
I am 21.

In the Korean numerical system, there are Sino-Korean numbers and native Korean numbers. When counting numbers, the native Korean system is used. The classifier that follows depends on the noun that is being counted. When expressing one's age, the following native Korean numbers are used with 살, with the exception of the numbers from 1 to 4, as well as 20. In the spoken language, 살 is sometimes omitted following ages that are above 40 or 50.

1	2	3	4	5	6	7	8	9	10
하나	둘	셋	넷	다섯	여섯	일곱	여덟	아홉	열

11	12	13	14	15	16	17	18	19	20
열하나	열둘	열셋	열넷	열다섯	열여섯	열일곱	열여덟	열아홉	스물

10	20	30	40	50	60	70	80	90	100
열	스물	서른	마흔	쉰	예순	일흔	여든	아흔	백

- 아버지는 예순다섯 살이고 어머니는 쉰일곱 살이에요.
  My father is sixty-five years old and my mother is fifty-seven years old.
- 동생하고 세 살 차이가 나요. My brother and I are three years apart.
- 선생님의 실제 나이는 마흔이 넘었어요. The actual age of the teacher was over forty.

The Possessive Marker 의

Appendix P. 261

A 친구의 회사가 어디에 있어요?
Where is your friend's company?

B 시청 근처에 있어요.
It is near City Hall.

The marker 의 is used between nouns to express a possessive relation. The subject precedes 의, while the possessed noun follows it. 의 is generally used in writing and it is often omitted in speech. When reading the possessive marker 의, it is often pronounced [에]. When following pronouns, it is almost always contracted with a pronoun.

- 친구의 부탁(= 친구 부탁)을 거절 못 했어요. I couldn't refuse my friend's request.
- 선생님의 전화(= 선생님 전화)를 못 받았어요. I didn't answer the teacher's call.
- 혹시 저의 안경(= 제 안경)을 못 보셨어요? Have you not seen my glasses?

Quiz Yourself

▸Answers P. 312

1 **알맞은 답을 고르세요.**

(1) 시골에 2번 (ⓐ 이 번 / ⓑ 두 번) 갔다 왔어요.

(2) 제 사무실은 7층 (ⓐ 칠 층 / ⓑ 일곱 층) 에 있어요.

(3) 학교에서 집까지 1시간 (ⓐ 일 시간 / ⓑ 한 시간) 걸려요.

(4) 우리 아들은 올해 5살 (ⓐ 오 살 / ⓑ 다섯 살) 이에요.

(5) 1달 (ⓐ 일 달 / ⓑ 한 달) 전에 한국에 처음 왔어요.

(6) 6개월 (ⓐ 육 개월 / ⓑ 여섯 개월) 후에 고향에 돌아갈 거예요.

2 **다음에서 알맞은 답을 골라서 문장을 완성하세요.**

곡　　마디　　마리　　군데

(1) 우리 집에는 개가 세 (　　　)이/가 있어요.

(2) 노래방에서 노래 두 (　　　)을/를 불렀어요.

(3) 그 사람에게 말 한 (　　　)도 하지 마세요.

(4) 오늘 친구의 선물을 사러 가게를 세 (　　　) 갔어요.

3 **그림을 보고 보기 와 같이 문장을 완성하세요.**

잔　　장　　개　　봉지　　켤레　　상자

보기 사과 한 개 이/가 있어요.

(1) 커피 ________ 을/를 주문했어요.

(2) 표 ________ 을/를 예매했어요.

(3) 신발 ________ 밖에 없어요.

(4) 사과 ________ 을/를 사 왔어요.

(5) 포도 ________ 을/를 선물로 보냈어요.

Conversation ❸

Track 03

진수 이거 새라 씨의 가족 사진이에요?

새라 네, 제 가족 사진이에요.

진수 가족이 모두 몇 명이에요?

새라 할머니하고 부모님, 오빠, 남동생, 그리고 저, 여섯 명이에요.

진수 오빠는 지금 무슨 일 하세요?

새라 회사원인데 친구의 회사에서 일해요.

진수 그래요? 오빠하고 나이가 몇 살 차이가 나요?

새라 3살 차이가 나요.

진수 동생은요?

새라 동생은 저보다 2살 어려요.

진수 새라 씨 빼고 다른 가족들이 함께 살아요?

새라 아니요, 여기저기 떨어져 살아요. 할머니하고 부모님은 시애틀에 사세요. 오빠는 일 때문에 시카고에 살아요. 그리고 동생은 학교 때문에 보스톤에 살아요.

Jinsu Is this a picture of your family?

Sarah Yes, it's a picture of my family.

Jinsu How many members are in your family?

Sarah My grandmother, my parents, my older brother, my younger brother, and me, so six people.

Jinsu What's your older brother's job now?

Sarah He's an employee at his friend's company.

Jinsu Really? How many years apart are you and your older brother?

Sarah We're three years apart.

Jinsu And your younger brother?

Sarah My younger brother is two years younger than me.

Jinsu Aside from you, does your family live together?

Sarah No, we all live separately (lit. apart in different places). My grandma and parents live in Seattle. My older brother is in Chicago because of work and my younger brother is in Boston because of school.

New Vocabulary ▸P. 322

이거 | 모두 | (나이) 차이가 나다 | 빼고 | 함께 | 여기저기 | 떨어져 살다

New Expressions ▸P. 322

- 가족이 모두 몇 명이에요?
- 오빠하고 나이가 3살 차이가 나요.
- 여기저기 떨어져 살아요.

Tips

1 Noun + 인데

When preparing to describe a noun in detail, 인데 is attached after the noun. The specific information may be expanded upon after 인데. For example, when introducing someone, 인데 is used after the person's name, occupation, or nationality and then followed by detailed information.

- 이곳은 인사동**인데**, 외국인이 기념품을 사러 많이 가요.
  This is Insadong, and a lot of foreigners go to buy souvenirs there.
- 이분은 우리 이모**인데**, 지금 대학교에서 일하세요.
  This is my aunt, and she works at the university now.

2 The Plural Suffix 들

In Korean, the suffix 들 is attached to nouns (for example as in 친구들) to express a plural. However, because 들 is generally limited to countable or proper animate nouns, it is not used with inanimate nouns.

- 학생들이 가방을 2개씩 들었어요.
  The students picked up two bags each.
  가방들을 (X)

1 Siblings

Depending on whether the speaker is a male or a female, what a sibling is called differs.

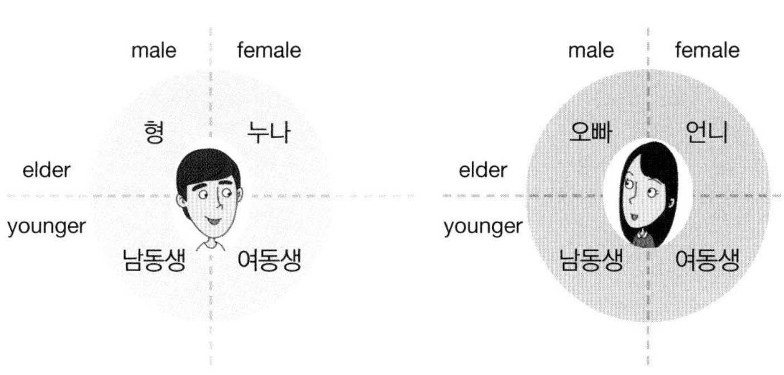

- 형제: 형과 남동생
  자매: 언니와 여동생
- When there are two brothers (for a male):
  큰형 first elder brother
  작은형 second elder brother
- When there are three or more brothers (for a male):
  첫째 형 first elder brother
  둘째 형 second elder brother
  셋째 형 third elder brother
  ⋮
  막내 형 youngest elder brother

2 Parents' Siblings

	Father's siblings			Mother's siblings	
Parent's siblings	큰아버지 father's older brother (married)	작은아버지 father's younger brother (married)	고모 father's sister	외삼촌 mother's brother	이모 mother's sister
Parent's siblings' spouse	큰어머니 father's older brother's wife	작은어머니 father's younger brother's wife	고모부 father's sister's husband	외숙모 mother's brother's wife	이모부 mother's sister's husband

★ 삼촌 uncle: an unmarried brother of one's father

3 In-Laws

Referring to One's Wife's Family		Referring to One's Husband's Family
장인 father-in-law	아버지 father	시아버지 father-in-law
장모 mother-in-law	어머니 mother	시어머니 mother-in-law
처남 older brother-in-law	형 older brother	시아주버니 older brother-in-law
처형 older sister-in-law	누나 older sister	시누이 older sister-in-law
처남 younger brother-in-law	남동생 younger brother	시동생 younger brother-in-law
처제 younger sister-in-law	여동생 younger sister	시누이 younger sister-in-law

★ What a married man directly calls his wife's parents: 장인어른! 장모님!

★ What a married woman directly calls her husband's parents: 아버님! 어머님!

★ 형 (오빠 is used when the speaker is a woman.), 누나 (언니 is used when the speaker is a woman.)

4 Younger Generation; Children

Son's Side	아들 son, 며느리 daughter-in-law 친손자 grandson, 친손녀 granddaughter
Daughter's Side	딸 daughter, 사위 son-in-law 외손자 grandson, 외손녀 granddaughter

Key Expressions

- 아들과 딸 한 명씩 있어요.
  I have one son and one daughter.
- 제가 셋 중에서 막내예요. I am the youngest of three.
- 제가 외동딸이에요. I am an only daughter.

Let's Talk!

Speaking Strategy — **Finding Commonalities**

- When remarking about a similarity
  저도 그래요. **Me too.**
  제 경우도 같아요. **My situation is similar too.**
- When remarking about a difference
  저는 안 그래요. **Not for me. Not me.**
  제 경우는 달라요. **That's not what my situation is like.**

Family

1 □ 우리 가족은 가까이 살고 있어요.
□ 우리 가족은 멀리 떨어져 살고 있어요.

2 □ 나는 형제와 사이가 좋은 편이에요.
□ 나는 형제와 사이가 좋지 않은 편이에요.

3 □ 나는 친척하고 자주 모여요.
□ 나는 친척하고 거의 연락하지 않아요.

4 □ 나는 아버지하고 외모가 많이 닮았어요.
□ 나는 아버지하고 외모가 안 닮았어요.

5 □ 나는 아버지하고 성격이 많이 닮았어요.
□ 나는 아버지하고 성격이 안 닮았어요.

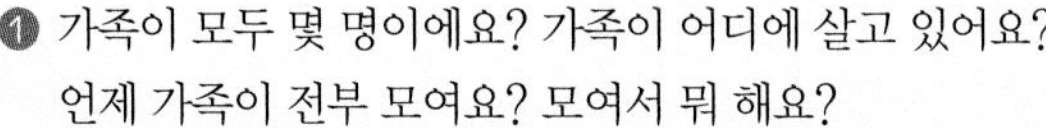

❶ 가족이 모두 몇 명이에요? 가족이 어디에 살고 있어요?
언제 가족이 전부 모여요? 모여서 뭐 해요?

❷ 형제나 자매가 있어요? 여러분과 몇 살 차이가 나요?
형제하고 사이가 좋아요? 어떤 형제하고 더 친해요? 왜요?

❸ 친척이 많이 있어요? 어디에 살아요?
친척과 많이 친해요? 누구하고 제일 친해요?

❹ 가족 중에서 누구하고 외모가 닮았어요? 어디가 많이 닮았어요? 아버지와 어머니 중에서 누구하고 더 닮았어요?

❺ 가족 중에서 누구하고 성격이 비슷해요? 어떤 점이 비슷해요?
가족 중에서 누구하고 성격이 잘 맞아요?

Myself

□ 나는 태어난 곳과 자란 곳이 같아요.
□ 나는 태어난 곳과 자란 곳이 달라요.

□ 나는 어렸을 때 자주 이사를 다녔어요.
□ 나는 어렸을 때 이사를 다니지 않았어요.

□ 나는 한국에 아는 사람이 많이 있어요.
□ 나는 한국에 아는 사람이 별로 없어요.

□ 나는 한국의 문화에 관심이 있어요.
□ 나는 한국의 문화에 관심이 없어요.

□ 나는 문법 때문에 한국어 공부가 어려워요.
□ 나는 단어 때문에 한국어 공부가 어려워요.

❶ 어디에서 태어났어요? 어디에서 자랐어요?

❷ 어렸을 때 자주 이사했어요? 어디에서 학교를 다녔어요?

❸ 한국에 아는 사람이 몇 명 있어요?
그 사람을 어떻게 알게 됐어요? 그 사람하고 자주 연락해요?

❹ 한국에 대한 것 중에서 무엇에 관심이 있어요?
왜 관심을 갖게 됐어요?

❺ 어떻게 한국어를 공부해요? 뭐가 제일 어려워요?

New Vocabulary

가까이 nearby | 멀리 faraway | 사이가 좋다 to have good relations | 친척 relatives (extended family) | 모이다 to gather | 거의 almost | 외모 appearance | 닮다 to look similar | 성격 personality | 태어나다 to be born | 자라다 to grow up | 이사를 다니다 to move around (다니다 may mean to attend, but it generally refers to the action of doing a movement verb multiple times (ex. 돌아다니다 "to go around", 찾아다니다 "to look around for") | 아는 사람 acquaintance | 별로 not really | 문화 culture | 관심을 갖다 to take interest

Word Web

Appendix P. 316

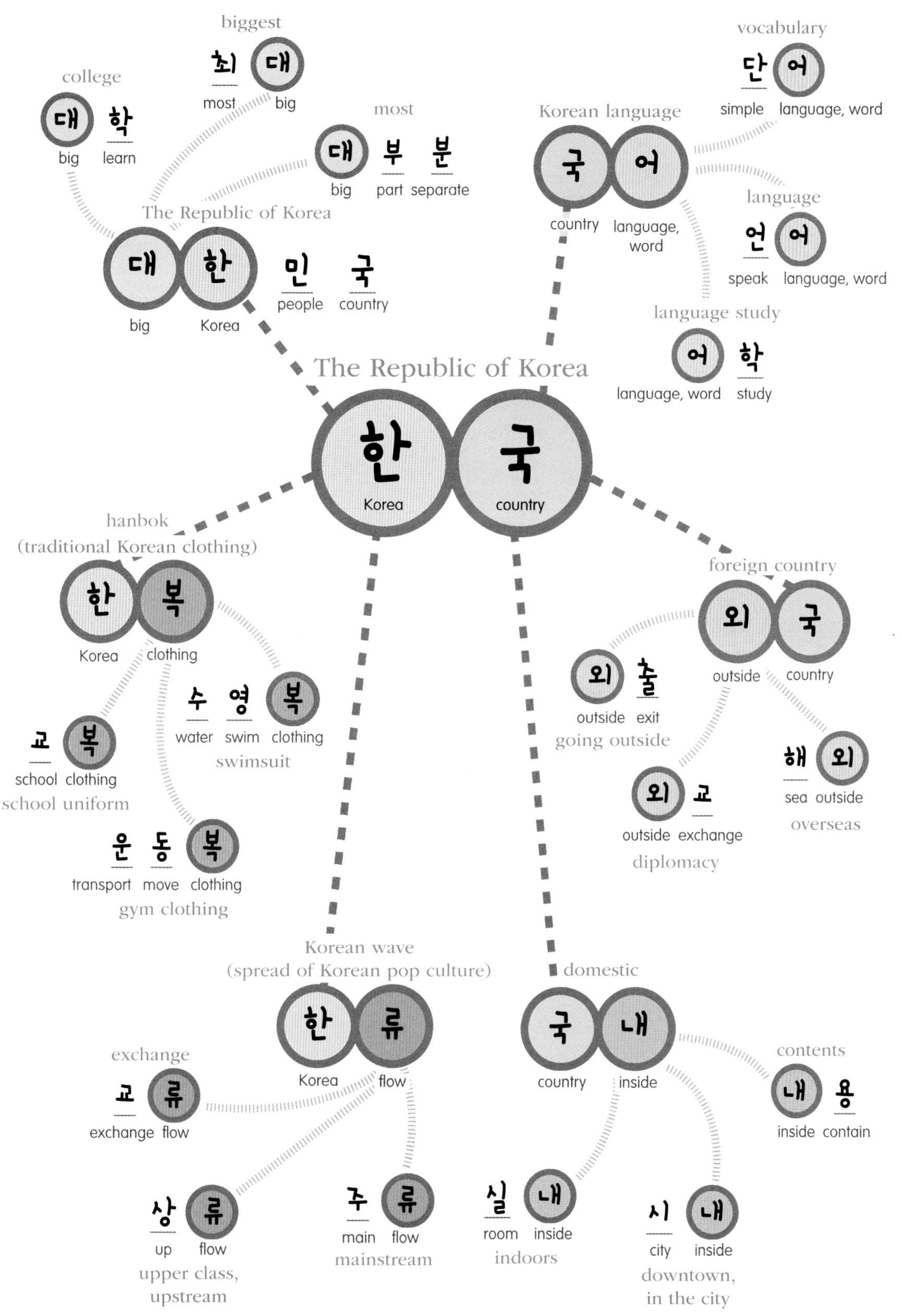

A Word on Culture

Who Can I Use 언니 and 오빠 with?

• 언니

Because it is rude to call someone who is older or of higher status by name in the age- and rank-based society of Korea, you should call people by a title rather than by name if they are older than you, even if the difference is as little as one year.

The common title 언니 was originally used as a household name by females to refer to an older sister, but it may also be used with older females to whom you feel close in environments such as school clubs or churches. If you have a formal relationship with someone older, such as a coworker, from a formal setting it is better to call her 선배 or by her office title than to call her 언니.

However, nowadays, it is also not uncommon to see people calling someone 언니 when meeting them for the first time. If you are female and meet a female employee at a store who looks to be of similar age to you, it is perfectly fine to call her 언니. When you are meeting someone for the first time, it is clear that there is no close relationship, and since you cannot confirm her age, you may be calling someone younger than you 언니. As it is inappropriate to call a stranger "you" in Korean, it is permissible to call someone 언니 in an informal situation, even when the age is uncertain, so long as there is the intent of approaching her in a friendly manner.

For the same reason, female shopkeepers may also call a customer 언니 instead of 손님 (customer) to express familiarity and friendliness. It is common to see in markets, such as in Namdaemun or Dongdaemun, female shopkeepers in their forties or fifties calling women in their twenties or thirties, who are ten or more years younger, 언니. In these situations, the age difference is overlooked. In cases where there is no appropriate title and 아줌마 would upset the person you are calling, as in cases when the person is a younger, middle-aged woman, use 언니.

• 오빠

오빠 was initially used by females to refer to an older male sibling. Like 언니, 오빠 is also a title of familiarity. Therefore, 오빠 is also one way to express closeness. However, unlike 언니, 오빠 is never used with strangers. Instead, it is often used with older males to who one feels close. The usage of 오빠 implies a very intimate and personal relationship.

In many cases, 오빠 is also used to refer to famous singers or movie stars in popular culture. In these cases, the age difference is not considered, but rather it is a familiarity expressed by fans. Therefore, even when these stars reach the age of fifty or sixty, devoted fans still call them 오빠 regardless of age.

Chapter **02**

일상생활

Everyday Life

Goals
- Talking about Daily Life
- Talking about Interests
- Talking about Leisure Activities
- Talking about the Frequency of Doing Hobbies
- Talking about One's Daily Routine

Grammar

❶ -고 "and"
-(으)면서 "while"

❷ -거나 "or"
-(으)ㄴ/는 편이다 "relatively", "sort of"

❸ -(으)ㄴ 후에/다음에 "after"
-기 전에 "before"

Grammar 1

-고 "and"

▶ Appendix P. 261 

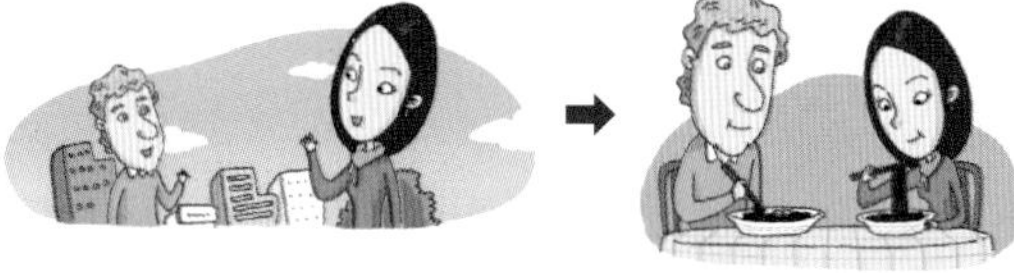

A 보통 주말에 뭐 해요?
What do you usually do on weekends?

B 친구를 만나서 저녁을 먹고 커피를 마셔요.
I meet my friends to eat dinner and drink coffee.

-고 has two main functions. One is to connect actions or states without regard to chronological order, as in the first example below. In this case, -고 is attached to the stems of verbs, adjectives, and 이다. -고 is also used to connect actions occurring in chronological order, as in the second example below. In this case, because the order is important, the order of verbs cannot be switched. Also, this usage of -고 is attached only to the stems of verbs. If the action of the first clause directly leads to that of the second clause, as in the third example below, -아/어서 is used instead of -고.

- 이 식당은 음식이 맛있고 값이 비싸요. = 이 식당은 값이 비싸고 음식이 맛있어요.
  This restaurant has delicious food and is expensive. = This restaurant is expensive and the food is delicious.
- 얼굴을 씻고 자요. ≠ 자고 얼굴을 씻어요. I wash my face and go to bed. ≠ I go to bed and wash my face.
- 지난 주말에 친구 집에 가서 놀았어요. Last weekend I went to a friend's house and played.
  (If the action of playing took place at the friend's house, 가서 is used rather than 가고.)

-(으)면서 "while"

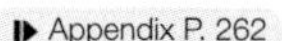

A 주말에 집에서 뭐 해요?
What do you do at home on the weekends?

B 음악을 들으면서 책을 읽어요.
I read books while listening to music.

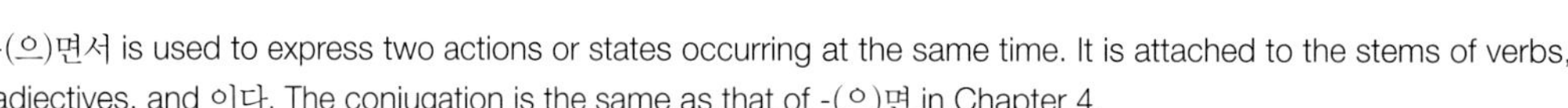

-(으)면서 is used to express two actions or states occurring at the same time. It is attached to the stems of verbs, adjectives, and 이다. The conjugation is the same as that of -(으)면 in Chapter 4.

- 텔레비전을 보면서 밥을 먹어요. I eat while watching television.
- 이 스피커는 작으면서 소리가 좋았어요. These speakers are small and the sound is great.
- 이 호텔은 전통적이면서 멋있어요. This hotel is traditional while nice.

1 **그림을 보고 보기 와 같이 질문에 답하세요.**

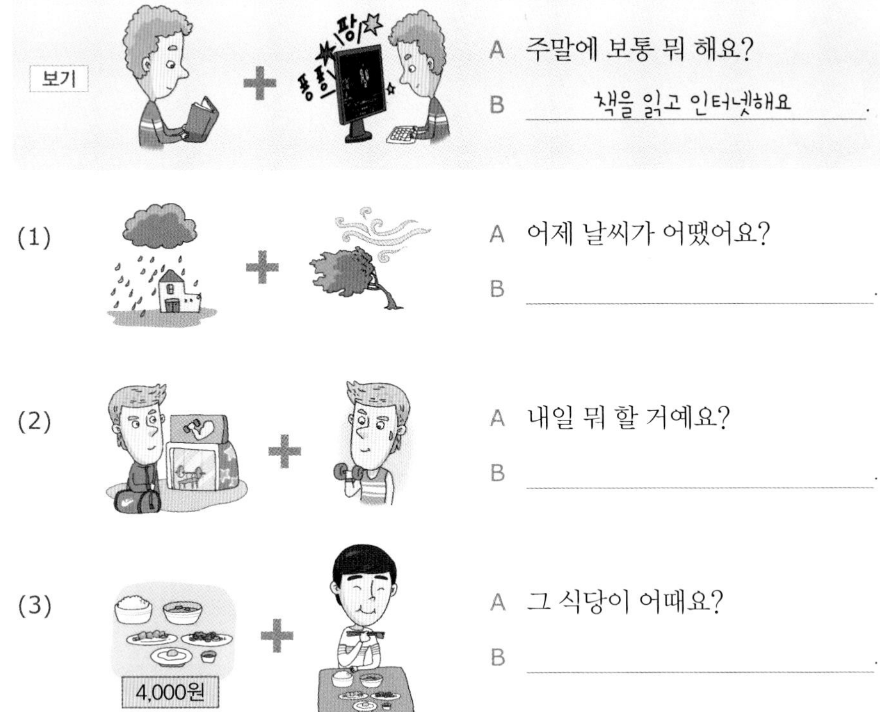

보기
A 주말에 보통 뭐 해요?
B 책을 읽고 인터넷해요.

(1)
A 어제 날씨가 어땠어요?
B ______________________.

(2)
A 내일 뭐 할 거예요?
B ______________________.

(3)
A 그 식당이 어때요?
B ______________________.

2 **알맞은 답을 고르세요.**

(1) 먼저 손을 ⓐ 씻고 / ⓑ 씻어서 요리를 시작해요.

(2) 아침에 일찍 ⓐ 일어나고 / ⓑ 일어나서 운동할 거예요.

(3) 친구에게 ⓐ 연락하고 / ⓑ 연락해서 회사 전화번호를 물어볼게요.

(4) 어제 버스를 타지 ⓐ 않고 / ⓑ 말고 지하철을 탔어요.

(5) 너무 많이 걱정하지 ⓐ 않고 / ⓑ 말고 자신감을 가지세요.

(6) 여기는 제 방이 ⓐ 않고 / ⓑ 아니라 동생 방이에요.

3 **다음에서 알맞은 답을 골라서 '-(으)면서'를 사용하여 문장을 완성하세요.**

낮다　　　일하다　　　운전하다　　　좋다

(1) 그 사람은 낮에 ______________ 밤에 공부해요.

(2) 이 집은 시설이 ______________ 월세가 싸요.

(3) ______________ 전화하지 마세요.

(4) 이 음식은 칼로리가 ______________ 맛있어요.

Conversation 1

Track 04

리나 보통 일이 몇 시에 끝나요?

케빈 저녁 7시쯤 끝나요.

리나 일이 끝나고 뭐 해요?

케빈 집에 돌아가서 저녁 먹고 쉬어요.

리나 그리고요?

케빈 핸드폰하면서 이메일도 확인하고 친구의 블로그도 봐요.

리나 어떤 블로그를 봐요?

케빈 저는 여행에 관심이 있어요.
그래서 주로 여행에 대한 블로그를 봐요.

리나 운동은 안 해요?

케빈 주중에는 시간이 없어요.
하지만 주말에는 토요일 아침마다 운동해요.

리나 무슨 운동을 해요?

케빈 주로 한강 공원에서 음악 들으면서 자전거 타요.

리나 어떤 음악을 자주 들어요?

케빈 이것저것 다양하게 들어요. 가끔 한국 가요도 들어요.

Rina What time does your work usually end?

Kevin It ends at 7 PM.

Rina What do you do when you're done with work? (lit. Work finishes and then what do you do?)

Kevin I return home, eat dinner, and rest.

Rina And then?

Kevin I check my email and read my friend's blogs while on my phone.

Rina What kind of blogs do you read?

Kevin I'm interested in travel, so I mostly read blogs about travel.

Rina Do you not exercise?

Kevin I don't have time on weekdays, but on weekends, I exercise every Saturday morning.

Rina What kind of exercise do you do?

Kevin I mostly bike along the Han River while listening to music.

Rina What kind of music do you usually listen to?

Kevin I listen to all kinds of music. Sometimes I even listen to Korean music.

New Vocabulary ▸ P. 322

돌아가다 | 쉬다 | 확인하다 | 관심이 있다 | 주로 | 에 대한 | 주중 | 마다 | 이것저것 | 다양하게 | 가요

New Expressions ▸ P. 322

- 저는 여행에 관심이 있어요.
- 토요일 아침마다 운동해요.
- 이것저것 다양하게 들어요.

Tips

1 에 대해 vs. 에 대한: "about"

The English word "about" is translated in Korean as 에 대해 or 에 대한. 에 대해 is used in front of verbs while 에 대한 is used in front of nouns. In this conversation, 에 대한 was used because it follows the noun "blog."

- 한국 역사**에 대해** 얘기했어요.
  I spoke about Korean history.
- 한국 역사**에 대한** 책을 샀어요.
  I bought a book about Korean history.

2 The Marker 마다: "each", "every"

The marker 마다 is attached to a noun and means "each" or "every."

- 일요일**마다** 교회에 가요. Every Sunday I go to church.
- 사람**마다** 성격이 달라요.
  Every person has a different personality.
- 지역**마다** 음식 맛이 달라요.
  Every district's food tastes different.
- 학생**마다** 책을 한 권씩 받았어요.
  Every student received one book each.

1 Using a Computer

• (타자를) 치다
to type

• 저장하다
to save (a document)

• 삭제하다
to delete

• 이메일을 보내다
to send an email
• 첨부 파일을 보내다
to send an attachment

• 이메일을 받다
to receive an email
• 첨부 파일을 받다
to receive an attachment

• 이메일을 읽다
to read an email
• 첨부 파일을 읽다
to read an attachment

• 제 친구는 저보다 두 배 빠르게 **타자를 칠** 수 있어요. My friend can type twice as fast as I can.
• 서류를 만들 때 꼭 파일을 **저장하고**, 필요 없는 파일은 **삭제하세요.**
When you make documents, you must save your files and delete files that you don't need.
• 이메일로 신청할 때 신청서를 **다운로드한** 후 **첨부 파일**로 보내세요.
When you apply by email, send the application as an attachment after downloading it.

2 Using the Internet

1. 자료를 검색하다
to search for information
2. 동영상을 보다
to watch a video clip
3. 블로그를 방문하다
to visit a blog
4. 채팅하다
to chat
5. 다운로드하다
to download
6. (글/사진)을 올리다
to upload (a post/picture)
7. 댓글을 달다
to write a comment
8. 인터넷 쇼핑하다
to shop online/on the Internet
9. 컴퓨터 게임하다
to play computer games

• 시간이 날 때마다 재미있는 **동영상을 보거나** 관심 있는 분야의 **블로그를 방문해요.**
When I have time, I watch a fun video clip or visit a blog about things I'm interested in.
• 저는 친구하고 자주 **채팅하지만**, 인터넷에 **글을 올리거나 댓글을 달지** 않아요.
I chat with my friends often, but I don't upload posts or write comments on the Internet.
• **자료를 검색할** 때 인터넷을 사용하지만 **인터넷으로 쇼핑하지 않아요.**
When I search for information, I use the Internet, but I don't shop on the Internet.

3 Adverbs Expressing Frequency

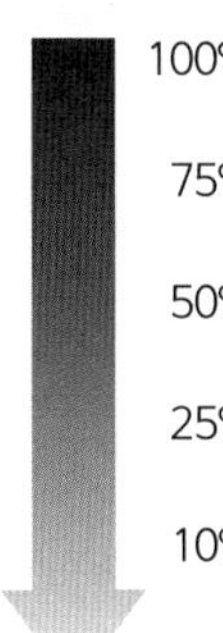

100% 항상 / 언제나 / 늘 always
75% 자주 often
50% 가끔 / 이따금 / 때때로 / 종종 sometimes
25% 별로 + (안) rarely, not really
10% 거의 + (안) almost (never)
0% 전혀 + (안) never

• 저는 **항상** 아침에 이메일을 확인해요.
I always check my email in the morning.
• 친구는 약속 시간에 **자주** 늦어요.
I am often late for appointments with my friends.
• 보통 지하철을 타지만 **가끔** 버스를 타요.
I usually take the subway, but sometimes I take the bus.
• 고기를 **별로** 많이 먹지 않아요. I don't really eat meat.
• 저는 핸드폰으로 게임을 **전혀** 하지 않아요.
I never play games on my cell phone.

Be careful

Low frequency words such as 전혀, 별로, and 거의 must be used with negative forms of verbs.

Key Expressions

• (A)와/과 (B) 둘 다 사용해요. I use both (A) and (B).
• (A)와/과 (B) 둘 다 사용 안 해요. I don't use (A) or (B).

Grammar 2

-거나 "or"

▶ Appendix P. 263

A 저녁은 어디에서 먹어요?
Where do you eat dinner?

B 친구하고 사 먹거나 집에서 간단하게 해 먹어요.
I buy it with friends or simply make it at home.

-거나 expresses a choice between two or more actions, just as in the English word "or." -거나 is attached to the stems of verbs and adjectives.

- 밤에 큰 소리로 얘기하거나 전화하지 마세요. Do not speak loudly or call at night.
- 저녁에 1시간쯤 책을 읽거나 텔레비전을 봐요. I read a book or watch TV for about an hour in the evening.
- 몸이 아프거나 피곤해요? 그럼, 이 약을 드세요. Are you sick or tired? Then, take this medicine.

-(으)ㄴ/는 편이다 "relatively", "sort of"

▶ Appendix P. 263

A 동생이 키가 커요?
Is your little sister tall?

B 아니요, 제 동생은 키가 작은 편이에요.
No. My little sister is rather short.

-(으)ㄴ/는 편이다 is used to talk about a fact being fairly true, rather committing to it being fully true. In the first example below, Jinsu is on the more talkative side in his group of friends. -(으)ㄴ 편이다 is attached to adjective stems, while -는 편이다 is attached to verb stems.

- 진수는 말이 많은 편이에요. 그래서 진수를 만나면 저는 보통 진수 얘기를 들어요.
  Relatively speaking, Jinsu talks quite a lot. That's why, when I meet him, I usually listen to him speak.
- 운동을 잘하는 편이니까 금방 배울 수 있어요.
  Relatively speaking, because you are rather good at sports, you can learn it quickly.
- 저는 일찍 일어나는 편이 아니니까 아침 회의는 정말 힘들어요.
  Relatively speaking, because I don't wake up early very often, morning meetings are very difficult.

▸Answers P. 312

1 보기 와 같이 '-거나'를 사용하여 대화를 완성하세요.

보기 A 보통 주말에 뭐 해요?
B 장을 ___보거나___ 빨래해요. (보다)

(1) A 거기에 어떻게 가요?
B 택시를 ________ 15분쯤 걸으세요. (타다)

(2) A 보고서는 어디에 내요?
B 사무실에 직접 ________ 이메일로 보내세요. (내다)

(3) A 보통 언제 음악을 들어요?
B 스트레스가 ________ 피곤할 때 음악을 들어요. (많다)

2 보기 와 같이 '-(으)ㄴ/는 편이다'를 사용하여 글을 완성하세요.

진수는 건강이 보기 ___안 좋은___ 편이에요. 왜냐하면 생활이 불규칙해요. 보통 진수는 잠을 (1) ________ 편이고 아침에 (2) ________ 편이에요. 진수는 요리를 좋아해요. 하지만 집에서 (3) ________ 편이 아니에요. 그래서 주로 밖에서 음식을 사 먹어요. 진수는 영화에 관심이 없어서 (4) ________ 편이에요.

3 알맞은 답을 고르세요.

(1) 서울은 6월에 장마가 있어요. 그래서 비가 ⓐ 안 오는 / ⓑ 많이 오는 편이에요.

(2) 겨울에는 일이 별로 없어요. 그래서 ⓐ 바쁜 편 않아요. / ⓑ 바쁜 편이 아니에요.

(3) 날씨가 안 좋아요. 일주일 내내 비가 와요. ⓐ 거나 / ⓑ 아니면 눈이 와요.

(4) 친구를 사귀고 싶어요. ⓐ 친절하거나 / ⓑ 친절한 이나 착한 친구를 소개해 주세요.

Conversation 2

Track 05

진수 보통 주말에 뭐 해요?

새라 밖에서 친구 만나거나 집에서 쉬어요.

진수 친구를 자주 만나요?

새라 자주 만나는 편이에요. 한 달에 2-3번 정도 만나요.

진수 친구 만나서 보통 뭐 해요?

새라 같이 영화 보고 저녁 먹으면서 얘기해요.

진수 영어로 얘기해요?

새라 아니요, 영어하고 한국어로 반반씩 해요.

진수 집에서는 뭐 해요?

새라 책 읽거나 집안일 해요.

진수 어떤 책을 읽어요?

새라 주로 소설이나 역사 책을 자주 읽는 편이에요.

진수 집안일은 자주 해요?

새라 아니요, 저는 좀 게으른 편이에요.
그래서 집안일은 가끔 해요.

Jinsu What do you usually do on weekends?

Sarah I meet friends outside or rest at home.

Jinsu Do you meet your friends often?

Sarah I meet them rather often. I meet them about two or three times a month.

Jinsu What do you usually do when you meet your friends? (lit. You meet your friends and what do you usually do?)

Sarah We watch movies together and chat while eating dinner.

Jinsu Do you talk to your friend in English?

Sarah No, we talk half in English and half in Korean.

Jinsu What do you do at home?

Sarah I read books or do chores.

Jinsu What kind of books do you read?

Sarah I generally read novels or historical books.

Jinsu Do you often do chores?

Sarah No, I'm rather lazy. So, I only occasionally do chores.

New Vocabulary ▸P. 323

밖 | 정도 | 반반씩 | 집안일 | 소설 | 역사 | 게으르다 | 가끔씩

New Expressions ▸P. 323

- 한 달에 2-3(두세) 번 정도 만나요.
- 영어하고 한국어로 반반씩 해요.
- 집안일은 가끔 해요.

Tips

1 When Markers Can Be Omitted

In speech, the subject marker 이/가, the object marker 을/를, and the possessive marker 의 are often omitted. However, markers like 에, 에서, and (으)로 are not omitted even in speech.

- 토요일**에** 시간~~이~~ 있어요?
  Do you have time on Saturday?
- 우리~~의~~ 집**에서** 밥~~을~~ 먹어요.
  We eat rice at our home.

2 The Marker (으)로

The marker (으)로 is used to express a means or method. In this conversation, (으)로 is attached to "English" and "Korean" to express the means of communicating.

- 부산에 기차**로** 갔다 왔어요?
  Did you go and come back from Busan by train?
- 지도를 핸드폰**으로** 보낼게요.
  I'll send you the map on my mobile phone.
- 종이에 이름을 연필**로** 쓰세요.
  Write your name on the paper with a pencil.

❶ Doing Chores

• 장을 보다
to go grocery shopping

• 음식을 만들다
to make food

• 상을 차리다
to set the table

• 상을 치우다
to clear the table

• 설거지하다
to do the dishes

• 물건을 정리하다
to arrange objects

• 청소하다
to clean

• 쓰레기를 버리다
to throw away the trash

• 빨래하다
to do laundry

• 다리미질하다
to iron

• 아기를 돌보다
to take care of a baby

• 집을 고치다
(= 수리하다)
to fix the house

• 아내가 **상을 치우고 설거지하는** 동안에 보통 남편은 대충 **청소를 하고 쓰레기를 버려요.**
While the wife clears the table and does the dishes, the husband hastily cleans (the house) and throws away the trash.

• 주말에는 아내와 남편 둘 다 **집안일을 하지만** 주중에는 둘 다 집안일을 못 해요.
On weekends, both the wife and husband do chores, but on weekdays, neither of them can do the chores.

❷ Frequency

1. When expressing frequency in Korean, the length of time is written first before the frequency, unlike in English.

length of time + 에 + frequency

• 일 년에 1(한) 번
• 일주일에 1-2(한두) 번
• 한 달에 2(두) 번
• 하루에 3-4(서너) 번

2. When expressing an approximate value, words like 정도, 쯤, 한, and 약 (all meaning "approximately") are used. However, be careful because each word appears in a different position.

[informal]		[formal]
한 2번**쯤** about twice	=	**약** 2번 **정도** about twice

• **한 달에 한 2번쯤** 친구를 만나러 나가요.
I go out to meet my friends about twice a month.

• **일 년에 약 3번 정도** 해외로 출장을 갑니다.
I go on business trips abroad about three times a year.

Key Expressions

• 남편하고 아내가 돌아가면서 집안일해요.
The husband and wife take turns doing chores.

• 남편하고 아내가 반반씩 집안일해요.
The husband and wife each do half the chores.

Grammar ❸

-(으)ㄴ 후에/다음에 "after"

C.C P. 304

A 언제 취직했어요?
When did you find a job?

B 졸업한 후에 바로 취직했어요.
I found a job right after graduating.

-(으)ㄴ 후에 expresses an action or state happening after the completion of another action or state. -(으)ㄴ 후에 may also be replaced with -(으)ㄴ 다음에 or -(으)ㄴ 뒤에. -(으)ㄴ 후에 attaches to verb stems, but it cannot attach to -았/었-. 후에 may also be attached to nouns, but 다음에 or 뒤에 cannot.

- 자료를 본 후 다시 연락할게요. I'll call you after looking at the data.
- 손을 씻은 다음에 식사하세요. Eat after washing your hands.
- 친구가 한국을 떠난 뒤 저도 회사를 그만뒀어요. After my friend left Korea, I also quit the company.
- 수업 후에 뭐 할 거예요? What are you going to do after class?

-기 전에 "before"

C.C P. 298

A 언제 전화해요?
When should I call you?

B 출발하기 전에 전화해 주세요.
Call me before you leave.

-기 전에 is used to express an action or matter occurring before another one has finished. -기 전에 is attached to verb stems but cannot be attached to -았/었- or -겠-. Adverbs, such as 바로 (just) or 한참 (a while), may be used before 전에. 전에 may be attached to nouns.

- 밥 먹기 전에 드라마가 시작했어요. The TV drama began before we ate.
- 자기 바로 전에 전화가 왔어요. The phone rang just before I went to sleep.
- 회의 시작하기 전에 잠깐 만나서 얘기합시다. Before the meeting starts, let's meet and talk a little.
- 발표 전에 다시 한번 확인하세요. Please check it one more time before the presentation.

1 그림을 보고 보기 와 같이 질문에 답하세요.

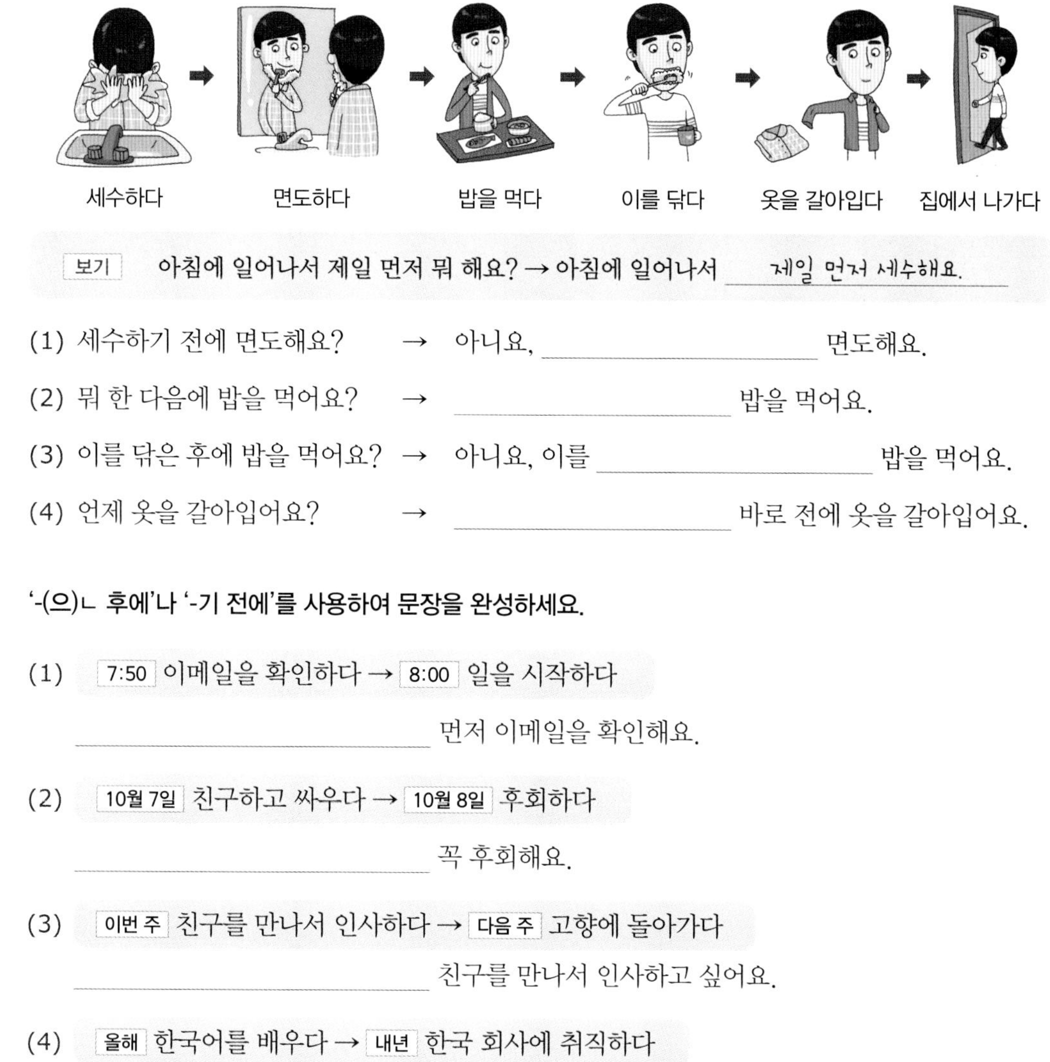

보기 아침에 일어나서 제일 먼저 뭐 해요? → 아침에 일어나서 제일 먼저 세수해요.

(1) 세수하기 전에 면도해요? → 아니요, ________________ 면도해요.

(2) 뭐 한 다음에 밥을 먹어요? → ________________ 밥을 먹어요.

(3) 이를 닦은 후에 밥을 먹어요? → 아니요, 이를 ________________ 밥을 먹어요.

(4) 언제 옷을 갈아입어요? → ________________ 바로 전에 옷을 갈아입어요.

2 '-(으)ㄴ 후에'나 '-기 전에'를 사용하여 문장을 완성하세요.

(1) 7:50 이메일을 확인하다 → 8:00 일을 시작하다

________________ 먼저 이메일을 확인해요.

(2) 10월 7일 친구하고 싸우다 → 10월 8일 후회하다

________________ 꼭 후회해요.

(3) 이번 주 친구를 만나서 인사하다 → 다음 주 고향에 돌아가다

________________ 친구를 만나서 인사하고 싶어요.

(4) 올해 한국어를 배우다 → 내년 한국 회사에 취직하다

________________ 한국 회사에 취직하고 싶어요.

3 다음에서 알맞은 답을 골라서 문장을 완성하세요.

사다 식다 비가 오다 끝나다

(1) ________________ 후에 날씨가 추워졌어요.

(2) 음식이 ________________ 전에 따뜻할 때 드세요.

(3) 물건을 ________________ 전에 한 번 더 생각해 보세요.

(4) 경기가 ________________ 후에 선수들과 사진을 찍었어요.

Conversation ❸

Track 06

마크 보통 아침에 일찍 일어나요?

유키 네, 저는 일찍 자고 일찍 일어나는 편이에요.

마크 몇 시에 자요?

유키 보통 저녁 먹고 씻은 후에 바로 자요.
9시가 되기 전에 자고 새벽 4시쯤 일어나요.

마크 그렇게 일찍 자고 일찍 일어나요?

유키 학생 때부터 쭉 그랬어요. 마크 씨는요?

마크 저는 생활이 불규칙한 편이에요.
저녁 먹기 전에 자기도 하고, 해가 뜬 후에 자기도 해요.

유키 잠은 푹 자요?

마크 그때그때 달라요. 보통 평일에는 4–5시간씩 자고 주말에는 하루 종일 자요.

유키 피곤하지 않아요? 그러면 건강에도 안 좋아요.

마크 네, 알아요. 하지만 습관이 쉽게 고쳐지지 않아요.

유키 그렇긴 해요.

Mark Do you usually wake up early in the morning?

Yuki Yes, I generally sleep early and wake up early.

Mark What time do you go to bed?

Yuki I usually sleep right after eating dinner and washing up. I go to bed just before 9 and wake up at dawn around 4.

Mark You sleep that early and wake up that early?

Yuki I've been doing that ever since becoming a student. What about you, Mark?

Mark My daily routine is rather irregular. Sometimes I go to bed before eating dinner and sometimes I go to bed after the sun rises.

Yuki Do you sleep soundly?

Mark It depends on the day. I usually sleep for four or five hours a day on weekdays and all day on weekends.

Yuki Don't you get tired? If you do that, it's also bad for your health.

Mark Yes, I know, but it's hard to fix (bad) habits.

Yuki That's true.

New Vocabulary ▸P. 323

씻다 | 바로 | 새벽 | 때 | 쭉 | 불규칙하다 | 해가 뜨다 | 푹 | 평일 | 하루 종일 | 건강 | 습관 | 고쳐지다

New Expressions ▸P. 323

- 학생 때부터 쭉 그랬어요.
- 그때그때 달라요.
- 그렇긴 해요.

Tips

1 Expression of -기도 하다: "sometimes", "as well as"

When -기도 하다 is attached to verb stems, it expresses the verb being done sometimes. When it is attached to adjective stems, it implies that the adjective is a special trait.

- 주말에 집에서 쉬**기도 하고** 등산 가**기도 해요**.
  On weekends, I rest at home sometimes and go hiking sometimes.
- 영화가 무섭**기도 하고** 재미있**기도 했어요**.
  The movie was both scary as well as fun.

2 Negative Question: -지 않아요?

-지 않아요? is attached to the stems of verbs, adjectives, and 이다 to express a negative question, which is used to confirm something that one is sure is true. The past form is -지 않았어요?

- 날씨가 덥**지 않아요?**
  Isn't the weather hot?
- 어제 힘들**지 않았어요?**
  Wasn't it difficult yesterday?

❶ Time Expressions

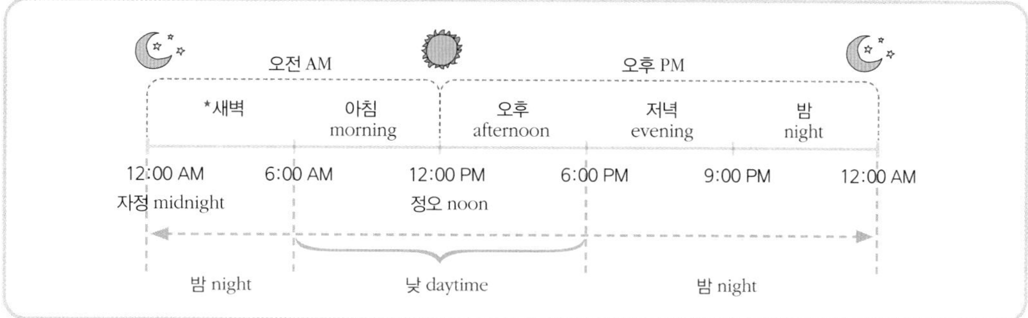

★ 새벽 dawn, hours from midnight to sunrise

> **Be careful**
> 아침 일찍 early in the morning
> 밤늦게 late at night

❷ Reading Time

• 3시 5분 전 = 2시 55분
five to 3 = 2:55

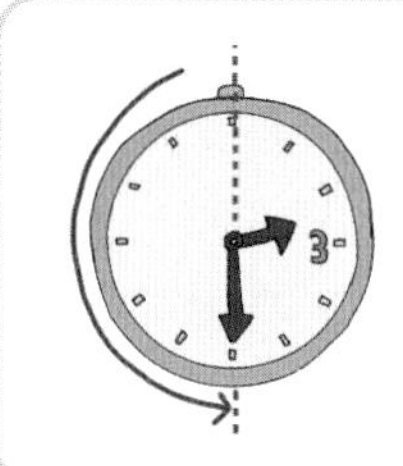

• 3시 30분 전 = 2시 30분
thirty minutes before 3 = 2:30
(3시 반 전 is incorrect.)

1. 5분 일찍 끝나요. We end five minutes early.
   30분 늦게 시작해요. We begin thirty minutes late.
2. 7시 이후에 after 7
   9시 이전에 before 9
3. 3시 직후에 just after 3
   5시 직전에 just before 5

❸ Expressing an Action Occurring During a Period of Time

Noun expressing period of time + 내내 throughout : continuously throughout that period of time

• 여름 **내내** 비가 왔어요.
It rained all summer.

• 일년 **내내** 더워요.
It is hot all year.

• 한 달 **내내** 축제를 해요.
We celebrate all month.

• 회의 **내내** 졸았어요.
I dozed off throughout the entire meeting.

> **Be careful**
> 하루 종일 (all day) and 밤새 (all night) are exceptions.
> Ex. 하루 내내 (X) → 하루 종일 (O) all day
> Ex. 밤 내내 (X) → 밤새 (O) all night

Key Expressions

• 시험을 보는 내내 많이 긴장했어요.
I was nervous the whole time I was taking the test.

• 시험 내내 많이 긴장했어요.
I was nervous throughout the whole test.

Let's Talk!

Speaking Strategy **Making Comparisons to Others**

- 저는 다른 사람**보다** 통화를 많이 해요. I use the phone a lot **compared to** other people.
- 저는 다른 사람**만큼** 통화를 해요. I use the phone just **as much as** other people.
- 저는 다른 사람**만큼** 통화를 하**지 않아요**. I **don't** use the phone **as much as** other people.

컴퓨터

> 저는 하루에 3시간 정도 컴퓨터를 하는데, 주로 유튜브에서 동영상을 보거나 친구하고 채팅해요.

1 ☐ 나는 하루에 1시간 이상 컴퓨터를 한다.
2 ☐ 나는 하루에 이메일을 10개 이상 받는다.
3 ☐ 나는 이메일을 받으면 바로 답장한다.
4 ☐ 나는 컴퓨터 없이 일이나 공부를 하기 어렵다.

❶ 보통 하루에 어느 정도 컴퓨터를 해요?
❷ 주로 컴퓨터로 뭐 해요?
❸ 보통 언제 이메일을 확인해요?
❹ 보통 인터넷으로 무엇을 검색해요?

핸드폰

1 ☐ 나는 매일 친구와 문자를 주고받는다.
2 ☐ 나는 하루에 5통 이상 전화를 받는다.
3 ☐ 나는 친구와 통화보다 문자를 더 많이 한다.
4 ☐ 나는 핸드폰으로 통화보다 다른 것을 더 많이 한다.

❶ 하루에 통화나 문자를 얼마나 많이 해요?
❷ 친구하고 문자로 무슨 얘기를 해요?
❸ 핸드폰으로 통화 이외에 주로 무엇을 해요?
❹ 핸드폰 사용료가 한 달에 얼마나 나와요?

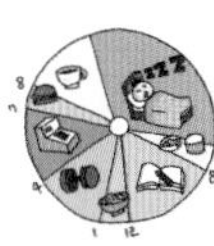

하루 일과

1 ☐ 나는 일찍 자고 일찍 일어나는 편이다.
2 ☐ 나는 식사를 거르지 않는다.
3 ☐ 나는 종종 늦게까지 일할 때가 많다.
4 ☐ 나는 평일에는 규칙적으로 생활한다.

❶ 항상 같은 시간에 자고 같은 시간에 일어나요?
❷ 규칙적으로 식사해요?
❸ 집에 돌아오자마자 제일 먼저 뭐 해요?
❹ 계획을 세우고 잘 지켜요?

주말

1 ☐ 나는 주말에 집에서 아무것도 안 하고 쉰다.
2 ☐ 나는 주말에 여기저기 많이 돌아다닌다.
3 ☐ 나는 가능하면 주말에 친구들과 어울려 지낸다.
4 ☐ 나는 주말에 가족과 함께 시간을 보낸다.

❶ 보통 주말을 어떻게 보내요?
❷ 무슨 요일을 제일 좋아해요? 제일 싫어해요?
❸ 주말에 집에 있을 때 뭐 해요?
❹ 주말에 친구들하고 뭐 하면서 놀아요?

New Vocabulary

채팅하다 to chat | 답장하다 to reply | 검색하다 to search (Internet) | 문자 text message | 통화 telephone conversation | 이외에 besides (that) | 사용료 usage fee | (식사를) 거르다 to skip/miss (a meal) | 종종 occasionally | 규칙적으로 regularly | 계획을 세우다 to make a plan | 계획을 지키다 to keep one's plan | 돌아다니다 to go around | 어울리다 to go well with

Word Web

▶ Appendix P. 316

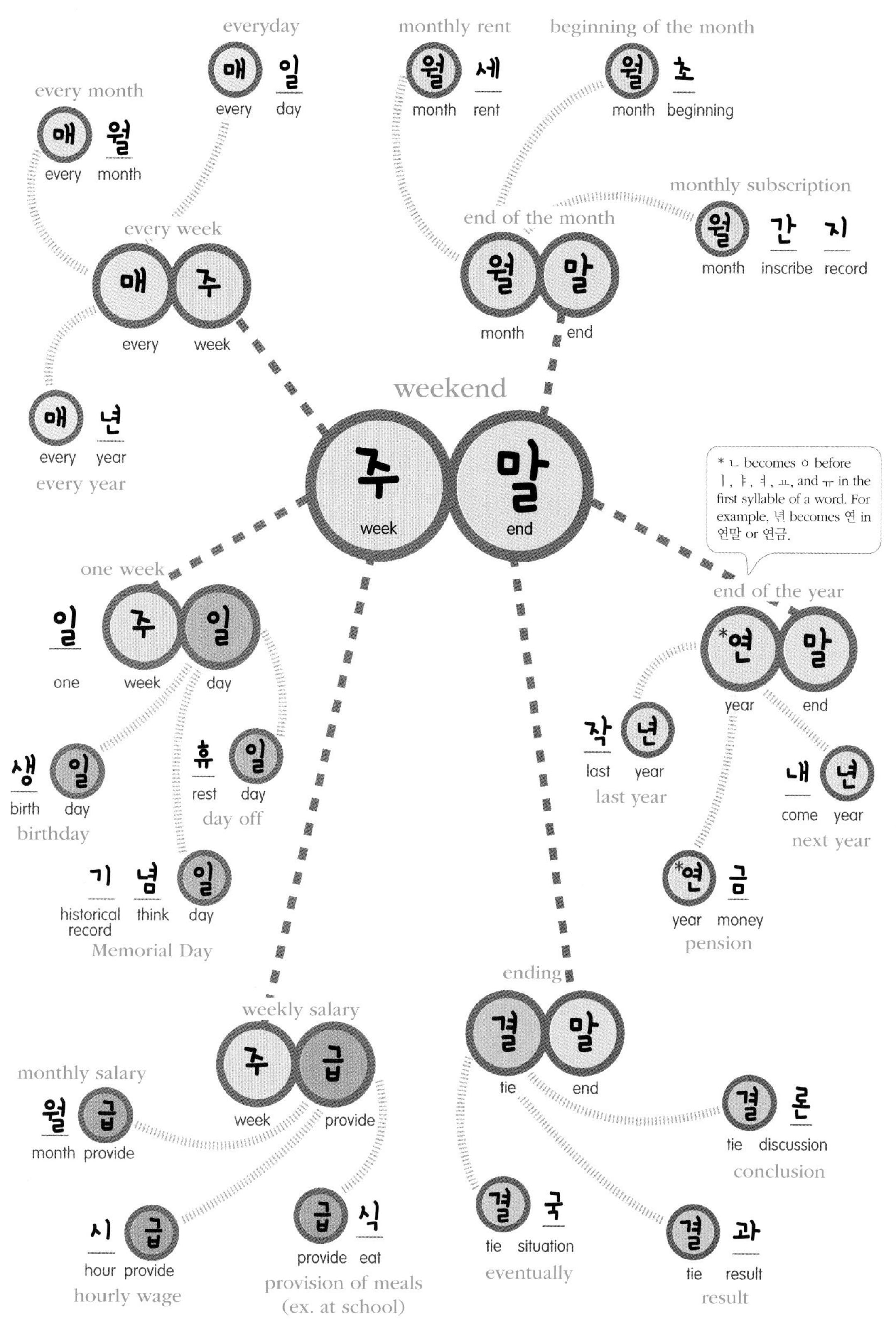

English Words in Korean

A fair number of foreign words in Korean are from English, many English expressions have been changed to fit into Korean. Because the pronunciation or usage may be very different from English, it is sometimes difficult to understand the meaning. But, remember that you must pronounce these words in the Korean way for Koreans to understand.

• Attaching 하다 to English nouns

English Word + 하다

하다 is attached to many concepts from the West, which do not have a matching word in Korean. Representative examples are 컴퓨터 (computer), 인터넷 (Internet), 이메일 (email), 게임 (game), and 블로그 (blog). Recently, the verbs 컴퓨터하다, 인터넷하다, 이메일하다, 게임하다, and 블로그하다 have appeared to express the action of using these objects. 하다 may also be attached to initially Western daily life concepts that are not necessarily related to modern technology but are commonplace, such as 데이트 (date), 드라이브 (drive), and 쇼핑 (shop) to create verbs such as 데이트하다, 드라이브하다, and 쇼핑하다.

• Attaching 하다 to English adjectives

There are quite a few English adjectives that are used by Koreans to describe people or objects, although they are not considered standard Korean. These words are mixed English-Korean phrases and involve English words such as "tough," "sexy," and "luxury" attached to 하다 to make 터프하다 (to be tough), 섹시하다 (to be sexy), and 럭셔리하다 (to be luxurious). Because these English adjectives are seen as nouns, they can be seen as similar to the process above of adding 하다 to nouns to create verbs.

• Shortened words

These words are shortened from long English words. The majority of them express objects with long names that have come from foreign countries. Examples are "air conditioner" or "remote control," which are too long, so the syllables after "con" have been dropped to make 에어컨 and 리모컨. "Apartment" is also shortened to 아파트 and the "accelerator" on a vehicle has been shortened to 액셀. Although Koreans use many English words, those with more than five letters are difficult to pronounce and are also too long to use in Korean.

• Examples made from new words "Konglish"

There are many examples of words that are not shortened from the original English word. The interesting thing about these words is that many Koreans are unaware that many of these words are not used with these meanings in English-speaking countries. Try to remember these words as it will otherwise be difficult to understand what Koreans are talking about.

- **핸드폰(handphone → cell phone)**이 고장 나서 **에이에스(AS: after service → customer service)** 맡겼어.
  Because my cell phone broke, I entrusted it to customer service.
- **아이쇼핑(eye shopping → window shopping)**하러 명동에 갔는데 유명한 배우를 만나서 **사인(sign → autography)**받았어.
  I went to Myeongdong to window shop when I saw a famous actor there, and I got his autograph.
- **원샷(one-shot)**합시다. Bottoms up!
- **파이팅(fighting)!** Good luck! (to someone else before an event)

Eye shopping??

Chapter **03**

약속

Appointments

Goals
- Speaking about One's Preferences
- Proposing Ideas
- Making Appointments
- Giving Reasons
- Changing Appointments
- Cancelling Appointments
- Politely Beginning Conversations
- Revising Opinions

Grammar

❶ -(으)ㄹ까요? "Shall I/we...?"
-(으)ㄴ/는 것 changing verbs to nouns ("...ing")

❷ -아/어서 "because"
-기로 하다 "to decide to"

❸ -(으)니까 "because"
-는 게 patterns using -는 것: -는 게 어때요? "How about...?"
-는 게 좋겠어요 "It would be good to..."

Grammar 1

(으)ㄹ까요? "Shall I/we...?"

A 차 한잔 마실까요?
Shall we drink a cup of tea?

B 좋아요.
Sure.

-(으)ㄹ까요? is used to ask the listener his or her intention or to suggest something to do together. It may be used to politely propose an idea. -(으)ㄹ까요? is attached to verb stems. The intonation rises at the end of a sentence.

- A 오늘 저녁에 만날까요? Shall we meet this evening?
  B 좋아요. 저녁에 만나요. Sounds good. Let's meet in the evening.
- A 내일 같이 점심 먹을까요? Shall we have lunch together tomorrow?
  B 미안해요. 내일은 시간이 없어요. Sorry. I don't have time tomorrow.

-(으)ㄴ/는 것 changing verbs or adjectives to nouns ("...ing")

Appendix P. 264

A 취미가 뭐예요?
What is your hobby?

B 제 취미는 여행 기념품을 모으는 것이에요.
My hobby is collecting travel souvenirs.

-(으)ㄴ/는 것 has the function of making verbs, adjectives, or phrases into nouns when they are in a subject, object, or other position of a sentence in which nouns may appear. -는 것 is attached to verb stems to express a present situation, -(으)ㄴ 것 is attached to verbs to express the past tense verbs, and -(으)ㄴ 것 is attached to adjectives. In colloquial speech, the form with the subject marker 것이 is often contracted to 게 and the form with the topic marker 것은 to 건. 것이에요 is contracted to 거예요 in colloquial speech.

- 한국 문화를 이해하는 것이 한국 생활에서 필요해요.
  Understanding Korean culture is necessary for the Korean lifestyle.
- 친구와 약속을 지키는 게 (= 것이) 중요해요. It's important to keep your promises with your friends.
- 사람마다 성격이 다른 건 (= 것은) 알고 있어요. I know that everyone has a different personality.

1 그림을 보고 '-(으)ㄹ까요?'를 사용하여 대화를 완성하세요.

(1) A 오늘부터 휴가예요. 이번 주말에 같이 ______________?
B 그래요. 같이 여행 가요.

(2) A 좋은 식당을 알아요. 오늘 같이 ______________?
B 미안해요. 벌써 식사했어요.

(3) A 같이 영화 보고 싶어요. 제가 표를 ______________?
B 아니에요. 이번에는 제가 표를 예매할게요.

(4) A 좋은 음악이 있어요. 같이 음악을 ______________?
B 좋아요. 같이 음악을 들어요.

2 다음에서 알맞은 답을 골라서 문장을 완성하세요.

사용하다 필요하다 전화하다 쉬다

(1) 밖에 나가지 마세요. 피곤하면 집에서 ______________ 게 필요해요.

(2) 단어를 외우는 것보다 단어를 ______________ 것이 더 어려워요.

(3) 한국어 공부할 때 가장 ______________ 것은 자신감이에요.

(4) 어제 너무 정신이 없어서 ______________ 것을 잊어버렸어요.

3 알맞은 답을 고르세요.

(1) 김치냉장고는 한국인들이 집집마다 많이 ⓐ 사용한 / ⓑ 사용하는 것이에요.

(2) 제가 졸업한 후 하고 ⓐ 싶은 / ⓑ 싶는 것은 세계 여행이에요.

(3) 어제 제가 ⓐ 본 / ⓑ 보는 것이 생각이 안 나요.

(4) 음식을 직접 만드는 ⓐ 게 / ⓑ 걸 사 먹는 것보다 훨씬 맛있어요.

(5) 주말에 집에서 혼자 음식을 만드는 ⓐ 게 / ⓑ 걸 좋아해요.

Conversation 1

Track 07

마크 리나 씨, 운동하는 것을 좋아해요?

리나 저는 직접 운동하는 것보다 운동 경기 보는 것을 더 좋아해요.

마크 그래요? 어떤 운동 경기를 자주 봐요?

리나 야구나 축구 같은 거 좋아해요.

마크 저도요. 그럼, 이번 주말에 같이 야구 경기 보러 갈까요?

리나 좋아요. 몇 시요?

마크 토요일 오후 2시 어때요?

리나 경기가 몇 시에 시작해요?

마크 6시 반에 시작해요.
그러니까 같이 점심 먹고 시간 맞춰서 경기장에 가요.

리나 그래요. 2시에 어디에서 볼까요?

마크 종합운동장역 5번 출구에서 봐요.

리나 알겠어요. 표는 어떻게 할까요?

마크 표는 제가 예매할게요.

리나 그래요. 그럼, 그때 봐요.

Mark Rina, do you like exercising?

Rina I like watching sporting events rather than exercising.

Mark Really? What kind of sporting events do you usually watch?

Rina I like sports such as baseball or soccer.

Mark Me too. Would you like to go see a baseball game this weekend?

Rina Sure. What time?

Mark How's Saturday at 2?

Rina What time does the game start?

Mark It starts at 6:30, so let's eat lunch and get to the game before it starts (lit. so let's eat lunch and arrive before the game starts.)

Rina Sure. Where shall we meet at 2?

Mark Let's meet at exit 5 in the Sports Complex station.

Rina Sure. What should we do about tickets?

Mark I'll reserve the tickets.

Rina Okay. See you then.

New Vocabulary ▸P. 323

직접 | 경기 | 시간 맞추다 | 경기장 | 출구 | 예매하다

New Expressions ▸P. 323

- 야구나 축구 같은 거 좋아해요.
- 오후 2시 어때요?
- 그때 봐요.

Tips

1 Ways to Give Examples

When providing examples of what one is talking about, the examples must come before the topic.

- 저는 과자 **같은 거** 안 좋아해요.
  I do not like things like cookies.
- 불고기나 갈비 **같은 것**을 자주 먹어요.
  I often eat things like bulgogi or galbi.
- 경복궁, 인사동 **같은 곳**에 가고 싶어요.
  I want to go to places like Gyeongbok Palace and Insadong.

2 Two Meanings for 그래요

In this dialogue, the first 그래요? expresses surprise at the other speaker's comment, while the second 그래요 expresses acceptance of the suggestion.

- **그래요?** 저는 그 사실을 몰랐어요.
  Really? I didn't know that.
- **그래요**. 같이 밥 먹어요.
  Sounds good. Let's eat a meal together.

❶ Time Expressions

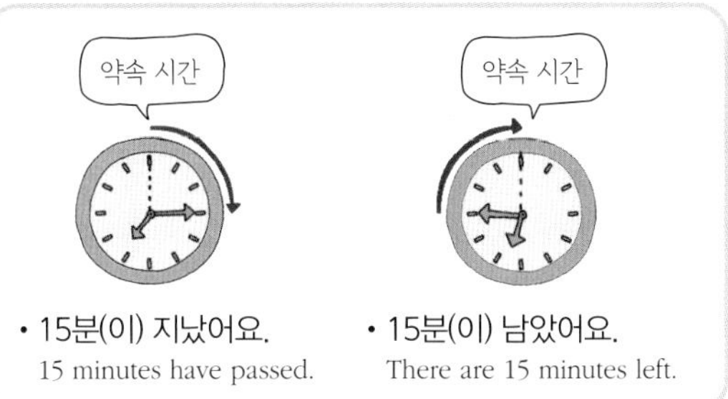

- 15분(이) 지났어요.
  15 minutes have passed.
- 15분(이) 남았어요.
  There are 15 minutes left.

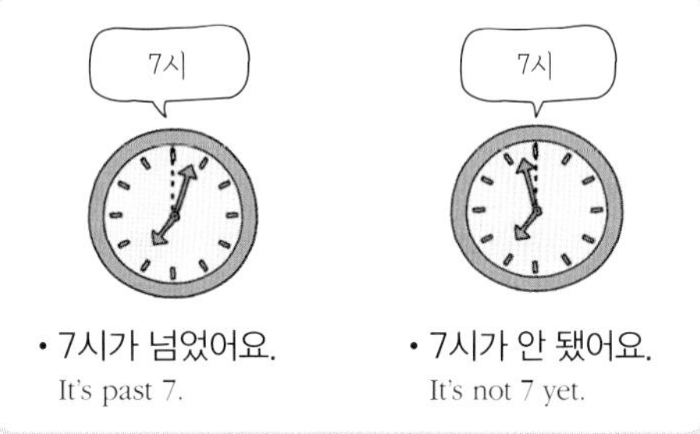

- 7시가 넘었어요.
  It's past 7.
- 7시가 안 됐어요.
  It's not 7 yet.

- 약속 시간까지 30분 **남았으니까** 시간은 **충분해요.** 서두르지 마세요.
  You have thirty minutes left until your appointment, so there's enough time. Don't rush.
- 약속 시간이 15분 **지났어요.** 서둘러도 이미 늦었어요. 시간이 **부족해요.**
  Fifteen minutes have passed since your appointment time. Even if you rush, you'll be late. There isn't enough time.
- 벌써 7시가 **넘었으니까** 아마 회의가 끝났을 거예요. It's already past 7, so the meeting may have finished already.
- 아직 7시도 **안 됐으니까** 한참 기다려야 할 거예요. It's not 7 yet, so we'll have to wait for a little while.

❷ Time-Related Wording

- 시간이 나다 to have time
- 시간을 보내다 to spend time
- 시간을 절약하다 (= 아껴 쓰다) to budget time
- 시간을 내다 to make time
- 시간을 쓰다 to spend time
- 시간을 낭비하다 to waste time

- 오랜만에 휴가지요? 즐거운 **시간 보내세요.**
  It has been a while since you last went on a vacation, right? I hope you have a great time.
- **시간이** 안 **나겠지만** 내일 잠깐이라도 **시간을 내** 보세요.
  Although you might not have a lot of time, please set aside a little time.
- 시간은 되돌아오지 않아요. 이렇게 **시간을 낭비하지** 말고 **아껴 쓰세요.**
  Time isn't renewable. Don't waste your time like this. Budget it.

❸ Appointment Time Expressions

- 시간 맞춰 오다
  to arrive on time
- 정각에 오다
  to arrive exactly on time
- (다른 사람)하고 시간을 맞추다
  to match schedule to (another person's)
- (다른 사람)하고 시간이 맞다
  for one's time to match up with (another person's)
- 시간을 늦추다
  to delay the time

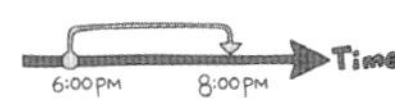

- 시간을 앞당기다
  to move the time up

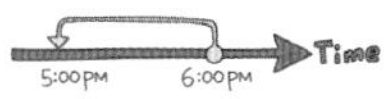

- 딱 **시간 맞춰** 왔어요. 영화가 곧 시작할 거예요. We came right on time. The movie is starting soon.
- 사장님은 항상 회의 시작 **정각에** 오세요. The president always comes exactly when the meeting starts.
- 친구하고 **시간이 안 맞아서** 퇴근 **시간을 앞당겼지만** 결국 못 만나게 됐어요.
  I left work earlier to try to meet my friend (lit. Because my schedule didn't match up with my friend's, I moved up the time I would leave work), but in the end, we weren't able to meet.
- 친구하고 퇴근 **시간을 맞춰** 만나려고 했지만 일이 안 끝나서 약속을 2시간 후로 **늦췄어요.**
  I timed when I would leave work to meet my friend, but because I didn't finish my work, I had to delay my meeting time by two hours.

Key Expressions

- 밤 11시가 넘어서 도착했어요.
  I arrived after 11 at night.
- 아침 8시도 안 돼서 도착했어요.
  I arrived before 8 in the morning.
- 아침 9시에 맞춰서 도착했어요.
  I arrived promptly at 9 in the morning.

Grammar 2

-아/어서 "because"

A 왜 늦게 왔어요?
Why did you come late?

B 길이 막혀서 늦게 왔어요.
I came late because there was traffic.

-아/어서 expresses an event or situation as a cause. -아/어서 is attached to the clause that contains the reason, which must always precede the effect of the cause. -아/어서 attaches to the stems of verbs and adjectives. If -아/어서 is attached to 이다, it is changed to (이)라서. -아/어서 may not be preceded by -았/었- or -겠-.

- 요즘 바빠서 운동을 못 해요. (= 요즘 바빠요. 그래서 운동을 못 해요.)
  I can't exercise these days because I am busy. (= I am busy. Therefore, I can't exercise.)
- 어제 시간이 없어서 전화 못 했어요.
  I couldn't call you yesterday because I had no time.
- 반찬이 무료라서 처음에 깜짝 놀랐어요.
  I was surprised at first because the sidedishes were free.

-기로 하다 "to decide to"

A 리나 씨하고 무슨 얘기를 했어요?
What did you talk with Rina about?

B 아침마다 같이 운동하기로 했어요.
We decided to exercise together every morning.

-기로 하다 is used when the speaker has decided to do something or has made a promise with the other speaker. -기로 하다 is attached to verb stems. In place of 하다, verbs like 약속하다, 결정하다 (or 정하다), or 결심하다 may be used. -기로 했다 may be used if the decision is made prior to the conversation, but -기로 하다 is used if the decision is made at the time of speaking.

- 이번에 회사를 그만두기로 결정했어요. This time, I decided to quit the company.
- 건강을 위해서 담배를 끊기로 결심했어요. I decided to quit smoking for my health.
- 우리 이제부터 서로에게 거짓말하지 않기로 해요. From now on, we decided not to lie to each other.

▸Answers P. 312

1 알맞은 답을 고르세요.

(1) 점심을 ⓐ 먹어서 / ⓑ 못 먹어서 너무 배고파요.

(2) 색이 마음에 ⓐ 들어서 / ⓑ 안 들어서 물건을 바꾸고 싶어요.

(3) 스트레스를 많이 ⓐ 받아서 / ⓑ 받지 않아서 회사를 그만뒀어요.

(4) 한국 역사에 관심이 ⓐ 있어서 / ⓑ 없어서 역사 책을 샀어요.

(5) 지난주에 늦게까지 ⓐ 일해서 / ⓑ 일했어서 이번 주에 일찍 집에 가요.

(6) 요즘 많이 살이 ⓐ 쪄서 / ⓑ 쪘어서 운동을 시작할 거예요.

2 다음에서 알맞은 답을 골라서 '-아/어서'를 사용하여 문장을 완성하세요.

성격이 안 맞다
배터리가 다 되다
문법 질문이 있다
자판기가 고장 나다
갑자기 다른 일이 생기다

(1) ________________ 약속을 취소했어요.

(2) ________________ 음료수를 못 샀어요.

(3) ________________ 지금 충전하고 있어요.

(4) ________________ 여자 친구하고 헤어졌어요.

(5) ________________ 친구한테 전화해서 문법에 대해 물어보려고 해요.

3 보기 와 같이 '–기로 하다'를 사용하여 문장을 완성하세요.

마크 내일 7시에 만나요.
리나 좋아요.

보기 리나하고 내일 7시에 만나기로 했어요.

이제부터 매일 꼭 운동할 거예요.

(1) 이제부터 매일 꼭 ________________ 결심했어요.

앞으로 한국어를 열심히 공부할 거예요.

(2) 앞으로 한국어를 열심히 ________________ 마음 먹었어요.

진수 미안해요. 앞으로 늦지 않을게요.
리나 알겠어요.

(3) 진수가 리나한테 앞으로 ________________ 약속했어요.

유키 휴가 때 같이 여행 갈까요?
링링 그래요. 같이 가요.

(4) 휴가 때 친구하고 같이 ________________ 정했어요.

Conversation 2

Track 08

케빈 여보세요. 저 케빈인데요.
유키 안녕하세요. 케빈 씨, 그런데 웬일이에요?
케빈 우리 다음 주 금요일 7시에 만나기로 했죠?
유키 네, 그런데 왜요?
케빈 그날 회사에 일이 생겨서 7시까지 못 가요.
유키 그럼, 몇 시까지 올 수 있어요?
케빈 글쎄요, 잘 모르겠어요.
혹시 약속을 다른 날로 미룰 수 있어요?
유키 어떡하죠? 다른 사람들한테 벌써 다 연락해서 지금 약속을 바꿀 수 없어요.
케빈 그렇군요. 그럼, 미안하지만 저는 이번에 못 가요.
유키 알겠어요. 다음에 만나기로 해요.
케빈 그래요. 다른 사람들한테도 안부 전해 주세요.
유키 그럴게요. 다음에 봐요.
케빈 네, 끊을게요.

Kevin Hello. This is Kevin.
Yuki Hi, Kevin. What's up?
Kevin We made plans to meet next Friday at 7, right?
Yuki Yes, why?
Kevin I can't go at 7 that day because something came up at work.
Yuki Then by what time can you make it?
Kevin Well, I'm not sure. Could we maybe postpone our meeting to a later day?
Yuki What should we do? I already called everybody, so I can't change the time.
Kevin Is that so? Well, I'm sorry but I can't make it this time.
Yuki I understand. Let's meet next time.
Kevin Okay. Say hi to the others for me (lit. Pass on the greetings to the others as well).
Yuki I'll do that. See you next time.
Kevin Yes, goodbye.

New Vocabulary ▸P. 323

그날 | 일이 생기다 | 혹시 | (약속을) 미루다 | 벌써 | 바꾸다 | 안부 | 전하다

New Expressions ▸P. 323

- 웬일이에요?
- 안부 전해 주세요.
- 끊을게요.

Tips

1 The Marker 까지: "until", "by"

The marker 까지 expresses the endpoint of a time or space ("until" or "by"). When referring to time, 부터 … 까지 is used and when referring to a spatial extent, 에서 … 까지 is used.

- 월요일부터 금요일**까지** 문을 열어요.
  It's open from Monday until Friday.
- 다음 주 월요일**까지** 숙제를 내세요.
  Submit your homework by next Monday.
- 여기**에서** 공원**까지** 너무 멀어요.
  It's too far from here to the park.
- 여기**까지** 해야 해요. I have to get until here.

2 The Usage of the Marker 도

The marker 도 cannot be used together with the subject marker 이/가 or the object marker 을/를, but it may be used with other markers (Ex. 에, 에서, 한테, etc.). In these cases, 도 is attached at the very end.

- 영화**도** 좋아하고 음악**도** 좋아해요. (을/를 is omitted.)
  I like movies and I like music.
- 다음 주말에**도** 다시 올게요.
  I'll be back next weekend.
- 동생한테**도** 말하지 마세요.
  Don't even tell your younger sibling.

1 Appointments: Active and Passive Expressions

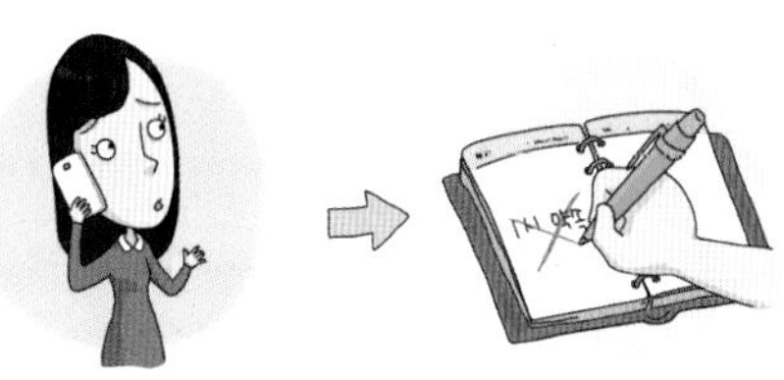

- 약속을 잡다 / 약속이 잡히다
  to make an appointment / for an appointment to be made
- 약속을 바꾸다 / 약속이 바뀌다
  to change an appointment / for an appointment to be changed
- 약속을 취소하다 / 약속이 취소되다
  to cancel an appointment / for an appointment to be cancelled
- 약속을 미루다 (= 연기하다) / 약속이 미뤄지다 (= 연기되다)
  to push back an appointment (= to postpone) / for an appointment to be pushed back (= to be postponed)
- 약속 시간을 늦추다 / 약속 시간이 늦춰지다
  to change an appointment time to later / for an appointment time to be changed to later
- 약속 시간을 앞당기다 / 약속 시간이 앞당겨지다
  to move an appointment time up / for an appointment time to be moved up

- 수요일에 만나기로 **약속 잡았는데**, 갑자기 일이 생겨서 **약속을 바꿨어요.**
  I made an appointment to meet on Wednesday, but something suddenly came up so I changed my appointment.
- 친구와 영화 보기로 했는데 시간이 안 맞아서 약속을 **취소했어요.**
  I decided to watch a movie with my friend, but our schedules didn't match up so I cancelled the appointment.
- 금요일 **약속을** 일요일로 **미룰** 수 있어요? 아니면 수요일로 **앞당길** 수 있어요?
  Can we push back the appointment from Friday to Sunday? Or can we move it up to Wednesday?

2 Appointment-Related Verbs

- 약속을 확인하다 to confirm an appointment
- 약속을 지키다 to keep an appointment
- 약속이 겹치다 for an appointment to overlap
- 약속을 어기다 to break/miss an appointment

- **약속을 확인**하니까 금요일에 **약속 두 개가 겹쳤어요.** 그래서 약속 한 개를 취소했어요.
  After confirming my appointment, I realized that I double-booked (lit. two of my appointments overlapped) for Friday, so I cancelled one.
- **약속을 안 지키는** 사람은 그다음에도 계속 **약속을 어길** 거예요. 기대하지 마세요.
  A person who doesn't keep appointments will keep missing them. Don't expect anything.

3 잘못: Expressing a Mistake

- 약속 시간을 잘못 알다 to mistake the appointment time
- 약속 장소를 잘못 듣다 to mishear the appointment location
- 약속 날짜를 잘못 보다 to mistake the appointment date (when looking)

- 제가 3시 약속을 4시로 **잘못 알아서** 친구가 저를 오래 기다렸어요.
  My friend waited for me for a long time because I thought our three o'clock meeting time was four o'clock.
- 약속 장소를 **잘못 들어서** 다른 데로 갔어요. I went to another place because I misheard where we were meeting.

4 Adverbs Expressing Length of Time

for time to be longer

- 잠깐 a moment
- 한참 awhile
- 오래 a long time

- 친구를 **한참** 기다렸는데 친구가 오지 않아요.
  I waited awhile for my friend, but he didn't come.

Key Expressions

- 아직 시간 남았어요. 천천히 하세요.
  There's still time. Take your time.
- 벌써 시간이 다 됐네요. 서두르세요!
  Time's already up. Hurry up!

Grammar ❸

(으)니까 "because"

▶ Appendix P. 264 

A 약속 시간에 늦었어요. 어떡하죠?

We're late for our appointment. What should we do?

B 길이 막히니까 지하철로 갑시다!

Let's go by subway because there's traffic!

The meaning of -(으)니까 we will introduce is the one used to express the reason or basis for a situation. -(으)니까 is attached to the stems of verbs, adjectives, and 이다. -았/었- may also precede -(으)니까. While -아/어서 is also used to express a reason, it is not used when the sentence ends in a command or proposal. In these situations, -(으)니까 must be used.

- 오늘 수업이 없으니까 학교에 안 갔어요. I didn't go to school because I didn't have class today.
- 여기는 도서관이니까 음식을 가지고 들어가면 안 돼요.
  This is a library, so you are not allowed to bring food inside.
- 회의가 끝났으니까 같이 식사하는 게 어때요? Since the meeting is over, how about eating together?

-는 게 patterns using -는 것: -는 게 어때요? "How about…?" / -는 게 좋겠어요 "It would be good to…"

▶ Appendix P. 264 

A 같이 선물하는 게 어때요?

How about getting a gift together?

B 제 생각에는 따로 선물하는 게 좋겠어요.

I think it would be good to get gifts separately.

Here we will introduce two uses of -는 게 patterns. First, -는 게 어때요? may be used to make a polite suggestion. Second, -는 게 좋겠다 expresses the speaker's subjective opinion. It is generally used to express the speaker's personal opinion or to politely give advice. Both are attached to verb stems.

- 그 사람과 먼저 얘기를 하는 게 어때요? Why don't you talk to that person first?
- 건강을 위해서 담배를 피우지 않는 게 좋겠어요. I'd rather not smoke for the sake of health.
- 계속 비가 오니까 오늘 약속은 취소하는 게 좋겠어요.
  It's constantly raining, so it's better to cancel today's appointment.

▸Answers P. 312

1 알맞은 답을 고르세요.

(1) 배가 ⓐ 고파서 / ⓑ 고프니까 일단 식사부터 할까요?

(2) 어제 ⓐ 바빠서 / ⓑ 바쁘니까 전화 못 했어요.

(3) 친구가 안 ⓐ 와서 / ⓑ 오니까 연락해 보는 게 어때요?

(4) 작년에 여행 안 ⓐ 갔어서 / ⓑ 갔으니까 올해에 여행 가고 싶어요.

(5) 친구가 벌써 일을 다 ⓐ 해서 / ⓑ 하니까 저는 하나도 일을 안 했어요.

(6) 정시에 ⓐ 출발해서 / ⓑ 출발하니까 늦게 오지 마세요.

2 다음에서 알맞은 답을 골라서 '-(으)니까'를 사용하여 대화를 완성하세요.

보다	맛있다	끝나다	불편하다	잠이 들다

(1) A 왜 비싼 식당에 가요?
B 비싸지만 ______________ 그 식당에 가끔 가요.

(2) A 왜 높은 구두를 안 신어요?
B 높은 구두는 ______________ 보통 편한 신발을 신어요.

(3) A 이 영화를 볼까요?
B 이 영화는 벌써 ______________ 다른 영화 봅시다.

(4) A 음악 소리를 키울까요?
B 아이가 조금 전에 ______________ 음악 소리를 줄여 주세요.

(5) A 회의실에 들어갈까요?
B 아직 회의가 ______________ 지금은 회의실에 들어가지 마세요.

3 문장을 완성하도록 알맞은 것끼리 연결하세요.

(1) 비가 올 수도 있으니까 •	• ⓐ 조금 일찍 출발하는 게 어때요?
(2) 요리 솜씨가 좋지 않으니까 •	• ⓑ 우산을 가져가는 게 좋겠어요.
(3) 길이 막힐 수도 있으니까 •	• ⓒ 저녁에 커피를 마시지 않는 게 좋겠어요.
(4) 잠이 안 올 수도 있으니까 •	• ⓓ 식사는 밖에서 사 먹는 게 좋겠어요.

Conversation ③

Track 09

민호 오늘 저녁에 같이 뭐 좀 먹으러 가요.

새라 그래요. 그런데 뭐 먹을까요?

민호 우리 회사 근처에 한정식 집이 있어요. 값도 적당하고 음식도 맛있으니까 거기 가는 게 어때요?

새라 좋아요. 몇 시요?

민호 저녁 7시쯤 어때요?

새라 제가 7시 넘어서 일이 끝나요. 좀 더 늦게 저녁 먹는 건 어때요?

민호 저는 언제든지 괜찮아요. 새라 씨는 몇 시가 좋아요?

새라 보통 7시 30분쯤 일이 끝나니까 8시 이후에 보는 게 좋겠어요.

민호 그래요. 넉넉하게 8시 반으로 예약할게요.

새라 어디에서 봐요?

민호 제가 오늘 차를 가지고 왔으니까 새라 씨를 데리러 갈까요?

새라 그러면 좋지요. 일이 끝나고 바로 연락할게요.

민호 전 괜찮으니까 서두르지 마세요.

새라 네, 이따가 봐요.

Minho Let's go eat something together tonight.

Sarah Okay. What should we eat?

Minho There's a place near our office that does Korean cuisine. The price is reasonable (lit. just right) and the food is good, so why don't we go there?

Sarah Sure. What time?

Minho How about around 7 tonight?

Sarah I finish work after 7. How about eating a little later?

Minho Any time is fine for me. What time is good for you?

Sarah I generally finish work around 7:30 so anytime after 8 would be good for me.

Minho Okay. To be safe, I'll make a reservation for 8:30 (lit. So we'll have an ample amount of time, I'll make a reservation for 8:30).

Sarah Where should we meet?

Minho I drove my car today, so shall I pick you up?

Sarah That would be great if you could do that. I'll call you right after I get out of work.

Minho I'll be fine, so don't rush.

Sarah Okay. See you later.

New Vocabulary ▸P. 324

뭐 | 한정식 | 값 | 적당하다 | 넘어서 | 언제든지 | 이후 | 넉넉하게 | 가지고 오다 | 데리러 가다 | 연락하다 | 서두르다

New Expressions ▸P. 324

- 저는 언제든지 괜찮아요.
- 그러면 좋지요.
- 서두르지 마세요.

Tips

1 Two Meanings of 뭐

In this conversation, the first 뭐 refers to a nonspecific object (something), whereas the second 뭐 is a question word (what).

- **뭐** 좀 얘기할 게 있어요.
  I have something to tell you.
- **뭐** 얘기했어요? What did you talk about?

2 Way to Connect Two Adjectives

-고 is used to link two adjectives or adverbs with the meaning of "and."

- 예쁜하고 멋있는 (X) → 예쁘**고** 멋있**는** 여자 (O)
  a pretty and fashionable girl
- 친절하게 하고 예의 있게 (X) → 친절하**고** 예의 있**게** 말했어요. (O)
  He spoke kindly and politely.

1 Two Meanings of 뭐/누가/어디/언제

	Question Word	Indefinite Meaning (adding -ㄴ가 adds uncertainty)	
뭐/무엇	**뭐** 먹을래요? **What** do you want to eat?	얼굴에 **뭐가** 났어요. There's **something** on my face.	**뭔가** 이상해요. **Something** is strange.
누가/누구	**누가** 찾아왔어요? **Who** came looking (for me)?	**누가** 찾아왔어요. **Someone** came looking (for someone).	**누군가** 밖에 있는 것 같아요. It looks like **someone** is outside.
어디	**어디가** 좋겠어요? **Where** would be good?	**어디** 가서 얘기 좀 해요. Let's go talk **somewhere**.	**어딘가에서** 소리가 나요. There's a sound coming from **somewhere**.
언제	**언제** 모여요? **When** should we gather?	**언제** 한번 같이 가요. Let's go together **sometime**.	**언젠가** 다시 만날 수 있을 거예요. We'll be able to meet again **sometime**.

2 Differentiating Meanings of Related Compound Verbs

1.

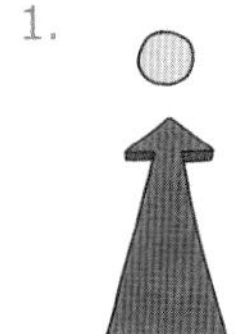

Object
가지러 가다 to go to get

Person (normal)
데리러 가다 to go to pick up

Person (honorific)
모시러 가다 to go to pick up

2.

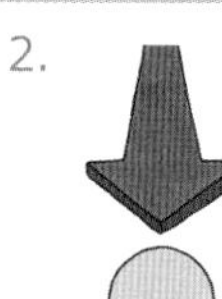

Object
가지러 오다 to come to get

Person (normal)
데리러 오다 to come to pick up

Person (honorific)
모시러 오다 to come to pick up

3.

Object
가지고 가다
to take (something in a direction away from the speaker)

Person (normal)
데리고 가다
to take (a person in a direction away from the speaker)

Person (honorific)
모시고 가다
to take (a person in a direction away from the speaker)

4.

Object
가지고 오다
to bring (something in a direction toward the speaker)

Person (normal)
데리고 오다
to bring (a person in a direction toward the speaker)

Person (honorific)
모시고 오다
to bring (someone as a favor for someone)

5.

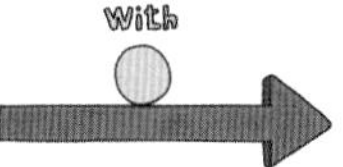

Object
가져다주다
to bring (something as a favor for someone)

Person (normal)
데려다주다
to bring (someone as a favor for someone)

Person (honorific)
모셔다드리다
to bring (someone as a favor for someone)

6. 마중 나가다 to go out to meet (generally for the purpose of picking someone up)

7. 마중 나오다 to come out to meet (generally for the purpose of picking someone up)

8. 배웅하다 to see off

Key Expressions

- 언제든지 상관없어요. I don't mind whenever.
- 아무 때나 괜찮아요. Anytime is fine.
- 편한 대로 하세요. Do as you wish.

Let's Talk!

Speaking Strategy — Vague Expressions

- 그런 편이에요. **(Someone) is rather like that.**
- 그때그때 달라요. **It depends on the time.**
- 상황에 따라 달라요. **It depends on the situation.**

다음 중 어떤 것이 더 좋아요? 왜 그렇게 생각하세요?

1 □ 내가 약속 시간과 약속 장소를 정한다.
□ 친구가 약속 시간과 약속 장소를 정하게 한다.

- 보통 언제 친구를 만나요? 얼마나 자주 만나요?
- 어디에서 친구를 만나요? 보통 친구를 만나서 뭐 해요?

2 □ 나는 친구를 만나기 전에 미리 계획을 세운다.
□ 나는 친구를 만나서 생각나는 대로 한다.

- 공연이나 식당을 예약/예매를 할 때 보통 누가 해요?
- 친구를 만나기 전에 좋은 장소를 미리 찾아요?

3 □ 나는 약속을 잘 바꾸지 않는다.
□ 나는 약속을 잘 바꾸는 편이다.

- 약속을 잘 바꾸는 것에 대해 어떻게 생각해요?
- 언제 약속을 취소하거나 연기해 봤어요?

4 □ 약속 시간에 딱 맞춰서 나간다.
□ 약속 시간보다 조금 일찍 나간다.

- 약속에 늦었을 때 어떻게 변명해요?
- 친구가 약속에 늦었을 때 어떻게 해요?

5 □ 친구 한 명씩 만나는 것을 좋아한다.
□ 친구 여러 명을 함께 만나는 것을 좋아한다.

- 왜 그렇게 해요?
- 한 명 만날 때 뭐 해요? 여러 명을 만날 때 뭐 해요?

6 □ 친구를 만날 때 옷에 신경을 쓴다.
□ 친구를 만날 때 옷에 신경을 쓰지 않는다.

- 친구를 만날 때 어떤 것에 신경을 써요?
- 친구를 만날 때 어떤 것에 신경을 안 써요?

7 □ 식사한 후 음식값을 반반씩 낸다.
□ 친구와 돌아가면서 음식값을 낸다.

- 친구와 만날 때 돈을 어떻게 내요?
- 보통 돈을 얼마나 써요?

New Vocabulary

상황 situation | 정하다 to decide | 미리 in advance | 변명하다 to make an excuse | 신경을 쓰다 to pay attention | 예매하다 to book

Word Web

Appendix P. 316

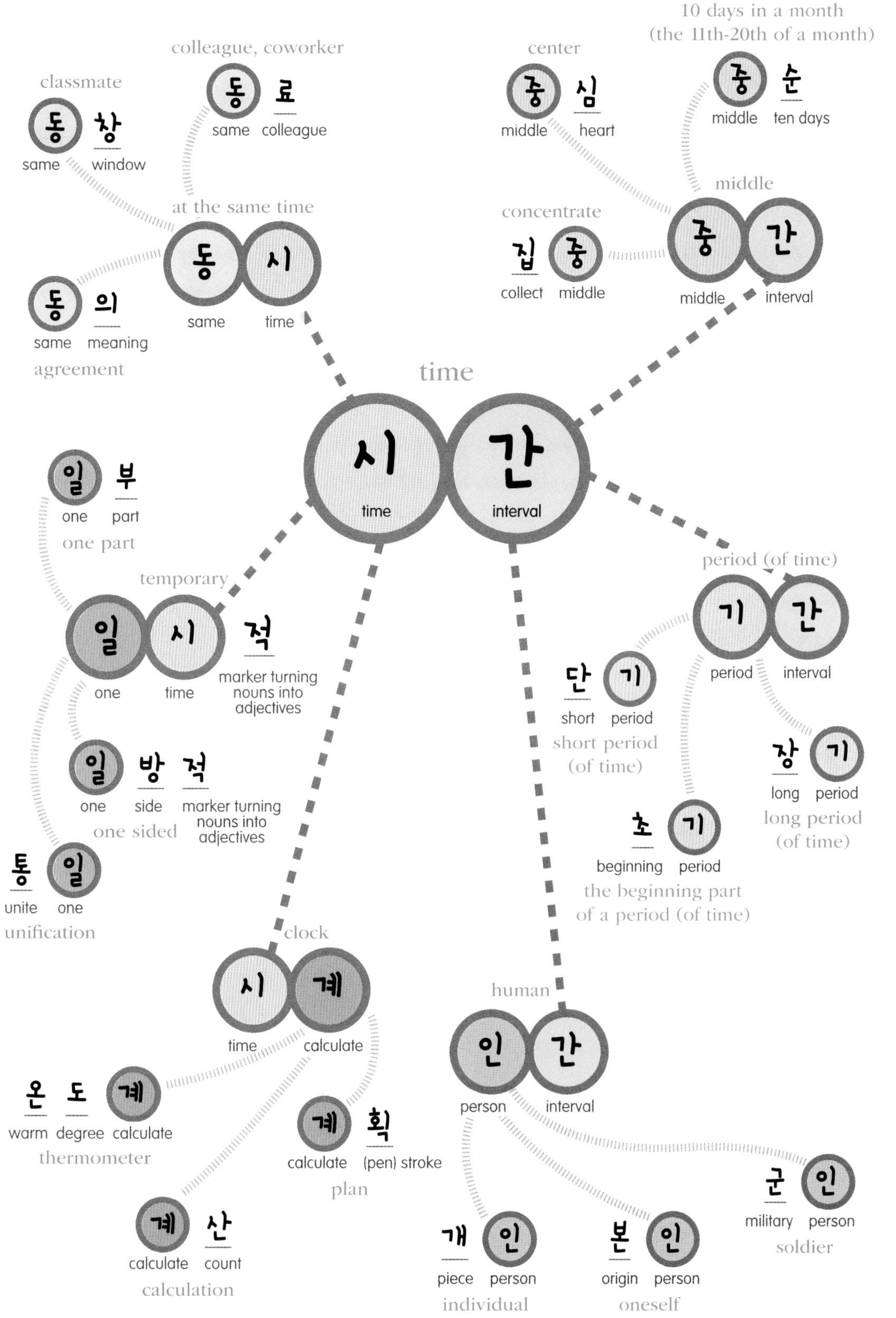

A Word on Culture

Expressions Involving Waiting

- **눈이 빠지게 until one's eyes fall out, 목이 빠지게 until one's neck falls off**

What kind of meaning related to waiting could 눈이 빠지게 or 목이 빠지게 have? These expressions exaggerate the effort it takes to wait for someone for a long time. They are derived from the action of waiting to greet someone at the entrance of a village while staring until one's "eyes fall out" and stretching one's neck to look for the person coming from far away until his "neck falls off." In other words, it means to wait anxiously. This expression captures the anxious feeling that people would feel in the past when news could not be easily communicated by phone and of waiting for someone without the promise that they would ever come. For example, it may be used when waiting for a notice of passing or failing one's exam to enter college or when waiting to hear about the news of whether a family member will live or pass away.

- **바람맞다 to be stood up**

If someone you have made plans with does not show up, you may use 바람맞았다. Why is the "wind" involved? You can remember this expression by the thought of the wind blowing on your face as you wait for the other person. Or perhaps, by the dictionary meaning of 바람 as "stroke," it could be expressing that the feeling of waiting for the other person is similar to having a stroke! The etymology of the expression is unclear, but 바람맞다 is now used to express being stood up more so than becoming sick. 바람맞혔다 may be used if you stood someone up.

- **약속을 칼같이 지키다 to arrive at appointments precisely on time**

Before clocks were introduced by Western culture, Korea had sundials and water clocks. Most people roughly divided time using these instruments by watching the height and movement of the sun. This culture is retained in this expression because a person who keeps an appointment to the exact minute and second is metaphorically called a "knife." A knife cleanly cutting a cross-section is the metaphor used for arriving at meetings precisely on time. In the same manner, getting out of work at precisely six without doing overtime is called 칼퇴근 (lit. knife leaving work).

Chapter **04**

길 찾기

Asking Directions

Goals
- Asking Questions Politely to Strangers
- Asking and Giving Directions
- Asking Where Items Are in a Store
- Confirming What You Have Heard or Know
- Getting Lost and Asking for Assistance
- Describing the Surroundings

Grammar

❶ -(으)면 "if"
-아/어 주시겠어요? "Could/Would you...?"

❷ -(으)ㄴ/는데 giving background information
-자마자 "as soon as"

❸ -(으)ㄴ/는지 indirect questions
-지요 (= 죠) expressing a fact that the speaker believes the listener knows to be true

Grammar 1

-(으)면 "if"

▶ Appendix P. 265 

A 공원에 어떻게 가요?
How do I get to the park?

B 다리를 건너면 왼쪽에 공원이 보여요.
If you cross the bridge, you'll see the park on your left.

-(으)면 expresses a condition. Unlike in English, the condition must be expressed before the result. -(으)면 is attached to the stems of verbs, adjectives, and 이다.

- 이번 주에 바쁘면 다음에 만나는 게 좋겠어요. (= 이번 주에 바빠요? 그러면 다음에 만날까요?)
  If you are busy this week, shall we meet next week? (= Are you busy this week? Then, let's meet next time.)
- 시간이 있으면 같이 영화 보러 가요. If you have time, let's watch a movie together.
- 외국인이면 비자가 필요해요. If you are a foreigner, you need a visa.

-아/어 주시겠어요? "Could/Would you…?"

A 이것 좀 사장님께 전해 주시겠어요?
Could you tell this to the boss?

B 네, 전해 드릴게요.
Yes, I'll tell him for you.

-아/어 주시겠어요? is used to make a polite request of someone whom one has met for the first time or when requesting a favor from someone whom one feels hesitant to ask. It is more polite than -아/어 주세요. -아/어 주시겠어요? is attached to verb stems. When asking someone for an object, 주시겠어요? is attached to the noun. 좀 (please) adds respect and may be added either in the place of 을/를 after nouns or before adverbs as in the third example. A short pause follows 좀 in speech.

- [to strangers] 죄송하지만, 길 좀 가르쳐 주시겠어요? Excuse me, could you please tell me the way (to a location)?
- [to an old person] 잠깐 제 얘기 좀 들어 주시겠어요? Could you please briefly listen to what I have to say?
- [to an employee] 실례합니다만, 한 번 더 확인해 주시겠어요? Excuse me, could you please check this once more?
- [to an employee] 물 좀 주시겠어요? Could you please give me water?

Be careful

도와주세요? (X)
도와주시겠어요? (O)
도와주세요. (O)

1 다음에서 알맞은 답을 골라서 '-(으)면'을 사용하여 문장을 완성하세요.

읽다 늦다 마시다 물어보다

(1) 직원에게 ________________ 물건 위치를 알려 줄 거예요.

(2) 내일도 그 사람이 약속에 ________________ 저는 화가 날 거예요.

(3) 매일 30분씩 책을 ________________ 한국어 실력이 좋아질 거예요.

(4) 따뜻한 차를 꾸준히 ________________ 감기가 금방 나을 거예요.

2 그림을 보고 알맞은 답을 고르세요.

(1)
ⓐ 불을 켜 주시겠어요? ☐
ⓑ 불을 꺼 주시겠어요? ☐

(2)
ⓐ 소리를 키워 주시겠어요? ☐
ⓑ 소리를 줄여 주시겠어요? ☐

(3)
ⓐ 접시 좀 갖다주시겠어요? ☐
ⓑ 접시 좀 치워 주시겠어요? ☐

(4)
ⓐ 물건을 넣어 주시겠어요? ☐
ⓑ 물건을 빼 주시겠어요? ☐

3 알맞은 것끼리 연결하세요.

(1) 다른 사람의 말을 이해할 수 없으면 • • ⓐ 좀 크게 말씀해 주시겠어요?

(2) 너무 작게 말해서 목소리가 안 들리면 • • ⓑ 계산서 좀 갖다주시겠어요?

(3) 다른 옷을 더 보고 싶으면 • • ⓒ 다시 한번 설명해 주시겠어요?

(4) 식사를 끝낸 후 식당에서 나가고 싶으면 • • ⓓ 다른 것으로 보여 주시겠어요?

Conversation 1

Track 10

마크 저, 실례합니다. 길 좀 가르쳐 주시겠어요?

행인 어디 가세요?

마크 동대문시장요. 여기에서 어떻게 가요?

행인 동대문시장은 이쪽이 아니라 저쪽이에요.

마크 네? 저쪽요?

행인 네, 이 길을 건너서 왼쪽으로 쭉 가면 오른쪽에 있어요.

마크 죄송하지만, 좀 자세히 설명해 주시겠어요?

행인 알겠어요. 처음부터 다시 말할게요. 여기 횡단보도를 건너서 왼쪽으로 쭉 가면 오른쪽에 약국이 보여요.

마크 약국요? 그다음에는요?

행인 그 약국을 끼고 오른쪽으로 돌아서 쭉 가면 시장 입구가 보여요.

마크 여기서 걸어서 갈 수 있어요?

행인 그럼요, 10분만 걸으면 돼요. 잘 모르겠으면 약국 근처에 가서 다른 사람에게 또 물어보세요.

마크 네, 감사합니다.

Mark Excuse me. Could you give me some directions?

Pedestrian Where are you going?

Mark (I'm going to) Dongdaemun Market. How can I get there from here?

Pedestrian Dongdaemun Market isn't this way. It's that way.

Mark Huh? That way?

Pedestrian Yes. If you cross this street, make a left and walk straight ahead, it will be on the right.

Mark I'm sorry, but could you tell me more specifically?

Pedestrian Sure. I'll say it again from the beginning. If you cross the crosswalk here, make a left and walk straight ahead, you will see a pharmacy on the right.

Mark A pharmacy? And then?

Pedestrian Turn right at the pharmacy (lit. Walk along the pharmacy and turn right). If you go straight, you'll see the entrance to the market.

Mark Can I walk there from here?

Pedestrian Of course. It will only take about ten minutes. If you're not sure, ask someone near the pharmacy.

Mark Okay. Thank you.

New Vocabulary ▸ P. 324

이쪽 | 저쪽 | 건너다 | 자세히 | 설명하다 | 처음 | 횡단보도 | 보이다 | 끼고 돌다 | 또 | 물어보다

New Expressions ▸ P. 324

- 저, 실례합니다.
- 이쪽이 아니라 저쪽이에요.
- 좀 자세히 설명해 주시겠어요?

Tips

1 Passive Expressions: 보이다, 들리다

As in the conversation above, 보이다 (to be seen) rather than 보다 (to see) is used when giving directions as the focus is on the location. In the same way, when talking about a sound, it is also made the focus of the sentence so 들리다 (to be heard) is used instead of 듣다 (to hear).

- 글자가 안 **보여요**. 좀 크게 써 주세요.
  I can't see the text. Please write a little bigger.
- 소리가 안 **들려요**. 좀 크게 말해 주세요.
  I can't hear the sound. Please speak a little louder.

2 The Direction Marker (으)로

When using movement verbs such as 가다, 오다, the marker (으)로 is used after the destination. For verbs that express existence such as 있다/없다, the marker 에 is used.

- 동쪽**으로** 100미터쯤 걸어가면 돼요.
  Walk about 100 meters to the east.
- 지하철역은 동쪽**에** 있어요.
  The subway station is on the east side.

1 Explaining Directions

1. 왼쪽으로 가세요.
   Turn left.
2. 쭉 가세요.
   Go straight.
3. 오른쪽으로 가세요.
   Turn right.

4. 길을 건너세요.
   Cross the street.
5. 골목으로 들어가세요.
   Enter the alleyway/side street.

6. 맞은편에 있어요.
   It's on the opposite side.
7. 모퉁이에 있어요.
   It's on the corner.

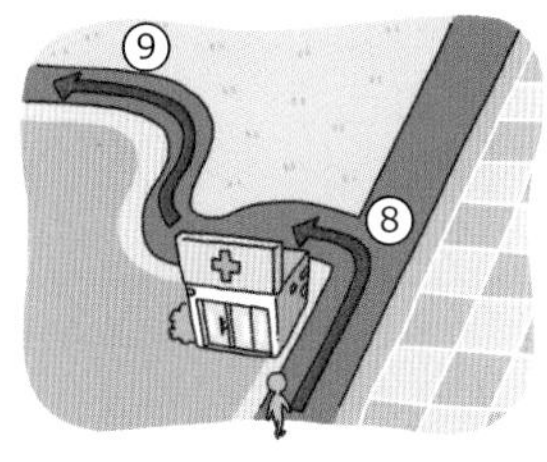

8. 약국을 끼고 도세요.
   Turn at the pharmacy.
9. 길을 따라가세요.
   Go along the street.

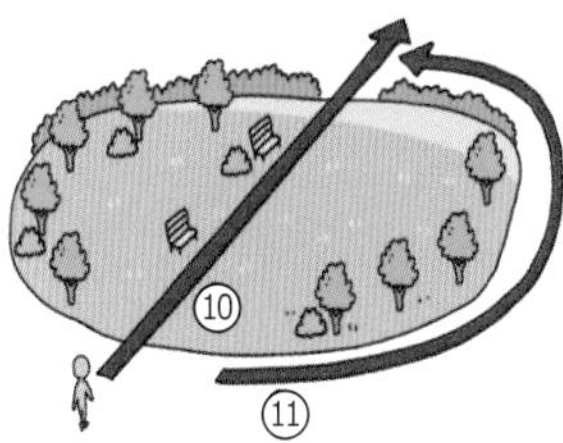

10. 공원을 가로질러 가세요.
    Go through the park.
11. 공원을 돌아서 가세요.
    Go around the park.

12. 다리를 건너세요.
    Cross the bridge.
13. 다리 밑으로 지나가세요.
    Pass under the bridge.

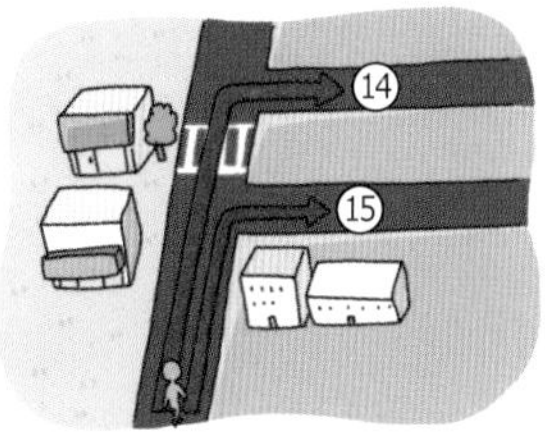

14. 횡단보도를 지나서 오른쪽으로 가세요.
    Cross the crosswalk and turn right.
15. 횡단보도를 지나기 전에 오른쪽으로 가세요.
    Turn right before the crosswalk.

16. 오르막길을 올라 가세요.
    Go up the hill.
17. 내리막길을 내려 가세요.
    Go down the hill.

18. 출구에서 나온 방향으로 쭉 가세요.
    Go straight when you come out of the exit.
19. 출구에서 나온 방향의 반대쪽으로 쭉 가세요.
    Go straight the opposite way when you come out of the exit.
20. 출구에서 나오자마자 바로 앞에 있어요.
    It will be right in front of you as soon as you get out of the exit.

2 Explaining Directions to a Taxi Driver

- 직진하세요. Please go straight.
- 좌회전하세요. Please turn left.
- 우회전하세요. Please turn right.
- 여기에서 유턴하세요. Please make a U-turn here.
- 여기에서 세워 주세요. Please stop here.

Key Expressions

- 다시 한번 말씀해 주시겠어요?
  Could you say that one more time?
- 잘 못 들었는데요.
  I didn't hear you.
- 방금 전에 뭐라고 하셨어요?
  What did you just say?

Grammar 2

-(으)ㄴ/는데 giving background information

▶ Appendix P. 265

A 좀 더운데 에어컨 좀 켜 주시겠어요?
It is a little hot. Could you turn on the air conditioning?

B 네, 알겠습니다.
Sure.

-(으)ㄴ/는데 is used by the speaker to provide a situation or background information to help the listener understand the context before uttering a sentence. -(으)ㄴ/는데 is attached to the verb or adjective describing the situation. The clause attached to -(으)ㄴ/는데 may be information for directions, orders, requests, proposals, questions, or a situation. -(으)ㄴ/는데 may also be used to express the speaker's feeling about the main utterance. -(으)ㄴ/는데 attaches to the verb or adjective describing the situation. -(으)ㄴ/는데 attaches to different endings depending on whether the background information ends in a verb or adjective and what tense it is.

- [situation for a recommendation] 이 식당은 갈비가 유명한데 한번 드셔 보세요.
  This restaurant is famous for galbi, so please try it.
- [situation for a question] 얼굴이 안 좋아 보이는데 무슨 일 있어요?
  You don't look well, is something wrong?
- [concrete background information] 시장에서 가방을 샀는데 그 가방이 값도 싸고 품질도 좋아요.
  I bought a bag from the market, and the bag is cheap and of good quality.

-자마자 "as soon as"

A 언제 버스에서 잠이 들었어요?
When did I fall asleep on the bus?

B 버스를 타자마자 잠이 들었어요.
You fell asleep as soon as you got on.

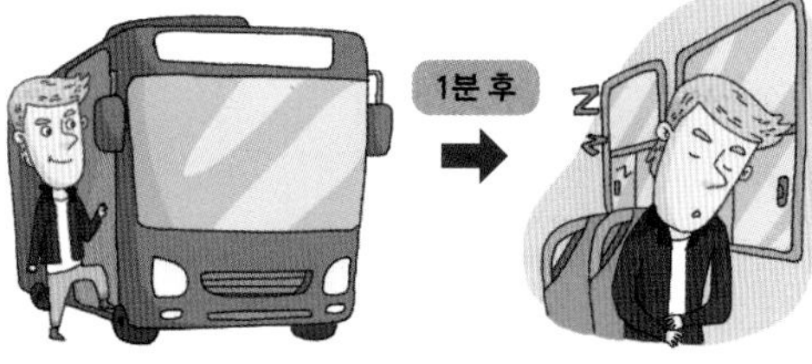

-자마자 expresses a situation occurring as soon as another situation has happened. It is attached to verb stems.

- 영화가 끝나자마자 사람들이 극장에서 나왔어요. As soon as the movie was over, people left the theater.
- 이 책은 출판되자마자 많이 팔리기 시작했어요. As soon as this book was published, it started selling well.
- 전화를 끊자마자 다른 전화가 왔어요. As soon as I hung up, I received another phone call.

▸Answers P. 312

1 문장을 완성하도록 알맞은 것끼리 연결하세요.

(1) 수업에서 설명을 들었는데 •
(2) 친구에게 여러 번 전화했는데 •
(3) 우리 전에 한 번 만났는데 •
(4) 이번에 불고기를 먹었는데 •
(5) 한국 친구가 한 명 있는데 •
(6) 냉장고에 아무것도 없는데 •

• ⓐ 혹시 저 기억하세요?
• ⓑ 요즘은 바빠서 만날 수 없어요.
• ⓒ 음식을 배달시키면 어때요?
• ⓓ 친구가 전화를 안 받았어요.
• ⓔ 아직도 잘 모르겠어요.
• ⓕ 전보다 훨씬 맛있었어요.

2 알맞은 답을 고르세요.

(1) 배가 고픈데 ⓐ 음식을 만들었어요. / ⓑ 음식이 없었어요.

(2) 책을 사고 싶지만 돈이 없는데 ⓐ 책을 살 수 없어요. / ⓑ 친구가 빌려줬어요.

(3) 머리가 아픈데 ⓐ 약이 없어요. / ⓑ 약을 먹었어요.

(4) 제주도에 여행 갔는데 ⓐ 바닷가에서 수영했어요. / ⓑ 바다에서 수영할 수 없었어요.

3 보기 와 같이 '-자마자'를 사용하여 대화를 완성하세요.

보기 A 언제 집에 가요?
B 수업이 끝나자마자 집에 가요. (수업이 끝난 다음에 바로)

(1) A 언제 한국에 왔어요?
B ____________________ 한국에 왔어요. (대학교를 졸업하고 바로)

(2) A 언제 진수 집에 갔다 왔어요?
B ____________________ 진수 집에 갔다 왔어요. (소식을 듣고 바로)

(3) A 언제 핸드폰이 고장 났어요?
B ____________________ 고장이 났어요. (핸드폰을 산 다음에 바로)

(4) A 언제 여행 떠날 거예요?
B ____________________ 떠날 거예요. (숙소를 찾은 다음에 바로)

(5) A 언제 저한테 전화할 거예요?
B ____________________ 전화할게요. (집에 들어간 다음에 바로)

Conversation ❷

Track 11

새라 저기요, 휴지를 못 찾겠는데, 휴지가 어디에 있어요?

직원 휴지요? 휴지는 지하 1층에 있어요.

새라 지하 1층 어디요? 여기 좀 복잡해서 잘 모르겠는데, 더 자세히 말해 주시겠어요?

직원 알겠습니다. 저기 에스컬레이터 보이죠?

새라 네, 보여요.

직원 저 에스컬레이터로 내려가자마자 바로 오른쪽에 있어요.

새라 내려가자마자 오른쪽요?

직원 네.

새라 그럼, 거기에 와인도 있어요?

직원 아니요, 와인은 2층에 있어요. 이쪽 계단으로 올라가면 음료수 코너가 보여요. 와인은 그 맞은편에 있어요.

새라 감사합니다.

직원 또 필요한 거 없으세요?

새라 아니요, 이제 없어요.

Sarah Excuse me, I can't seem to find the toilet paper. Where are they?

Employee Toilet paper? The toilet paper is located on floor B1.

Sarah Where is floor B1? I'm not sure because it's a little confusing here. Could you tell me more specifically?

Employee Sure. You see the escalator over there, right?

Sarah Yes, I see it.

Employee As soon as you get off the escalator, it's just on the right side.

Sarah Just on the right side as soon as I get off the escalator?

Employee Yes.

Sarah So, is there wine too?

Employee No, wine is on the second floor. If you go up the stairs here, you'll see the beverage section. Wine is on the other side.

Sarah Thank you.

Employee Is there anything else you need? (lit. Is there nothing else you need?)

Sarah No, that's it.

New Vocabulary ▸ P. 324

휴지 | 지하 | 복잡하다 | 내려가다 | 계단 | 음료수 | 코너 | 맞은편 | 이제

New Expressions ▸ P. 324

- 더 자세히 말해 주시겠어요?
- 저기 (noun) 보이죠?
- 또 필요한 거 없으세요?

Tips

1 Two Meanings of 저기

In the conversation above, the first 저기 expresses "excuse me." It is used to catch a person's attention. The second 저기 means "there" and is used to point out a place that is far from both the speaker and the listener.

- **저기**요, **저기** 갈색 가방이 얼마예요?
  Excuse me, how much is that brown bag over there?

2 Two Meanings of 바로

바로 has many meanings in Korean. As a time word, it means "soon" or "right away" while as a location word, it emphasizes the proximity of a noun to a certain place (right there).

- 문제가 생기면 **바로** 연락하세요.
  If there is a problem, call me right away.
- 출구에서 나오면 버스 정류장이 **바로** 앞에 있어요.
  When you come out of the exit, the bus stop will be right in front of you.

1 Expressing Floor Numbers

1. 옥상 roof
2. 5층 fifth floor
3. 4층 fourth floor
4. 3층 third floor
5. 2층 second floor
6. 1층 first floor
7. 지하1층 B1
8. 지하2층 B2

- 이 엘리베이터는 **1층**부터 **4층**까지만 운행합니다.
  This elevator only goes from the first floor to the fourth floor.
- 여기는 **3층**인데요. 전자제품은 **한 층** 더 올라가야 됩니다.
  This is the third floor. You have to go up one more floor for electronics.
- 주차장은 이 건물의 **옥상**에 있습니다.
  The parking lot is on the roof of this building.

2 Pointing Out an Object in a Display

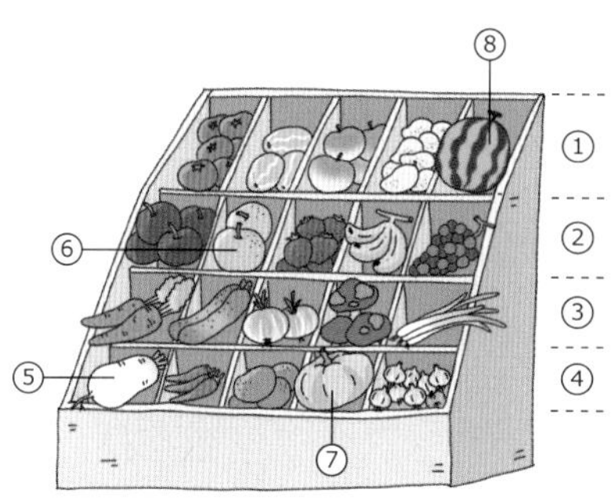

1. 맨 윗줄 top row
2. 위에서 두 번째 줄
   second row from the top
3. 밑에서 두 번째 줄
   second row from the bottom
4. 맨 밑의 줄 bottom row
5. 맨 밑의 줄에서 맨 왼쪽 칸
   leftmost compartment in the bottom row (bottom left)
6. 두 번째 줄의 왼쪽에서 두 번째 칸
   second compartment from the left of the second row
7. 맨 밑의 줄의 오른쪽에서 두 번째 칸
   second compartment from the right in the bottom row
8. 맨 윗줄의 맨 오른쪽 칸
   rightmost compartment in the top row (top right)

- 과일은 **맨 윗줄**에 있고 채소는 **아래 두 줄**에 있습니다. The fruits are in the top row and the vegetables are two rows from the bottom.
- 수박은 **맨 윗줄**의 **맨 오른쪽 칸**에 있습니다. The watermelon is in the rightmost compartment of the top row.
- 당근은 **세 번째 줄**의 **맨 왼쪽 칸**에 있습니다. The carrots are in the leftmost compartment of the third row.
- 감자는 **맨 밑의 줄**의 **가운데 칸**에 있습니다. The potatoes are in the middle compartment of the bottom row.

3 Describing a Location

1. 카트 cart
2. 주차장 garage
3. 보관함 locker
4. 입구 entrance
5. ATM
6. 계산대 cash register
7. 고객 센터 customer center
8. 화장실 bathroom
9. 입구 쪽 toward the entrance
10. 입구의 반대쪽
    the opposite side of the entrance

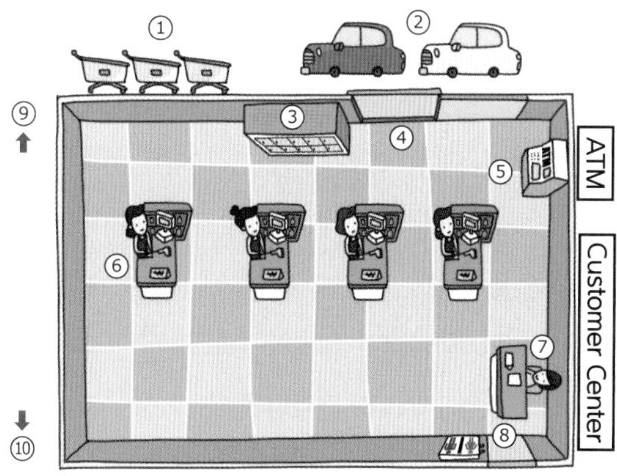

- 보관함이 **입구 쪽**에 있어요.
  The locker is near the entrance.
- 화장실이 **입구 반대쪽**에 있어요.
  The bathroom is on the opposite side of the entrance.
- 건전지가 **계산대 근처**에 있어요.
  The batteries are near the cash register.
- ATM은 계산대 **오른쪽**에 있어요.
  The ATM is to the right of the cash register.
- 카트는 주차장으로 나가는 문 **밖**에 있어요.
  The carts are outside the door leading to the garage.

Key Expressions

- 다음 칸에 있어요. It's in the next compartment.
- 다음다음 칸에 있어요. It's two compartments over.
- 한 층 내려가면 오른쪽에 있어요.
  If you go down one floor, it will be on your right.

Grammar 3

(으)ㄴ/는지 indirect questions

Appendix P. 266

A 왜 여자 친구가 화가 났어요?
Why did your girlfriend get angry?

B 왜 화가 났는지 잘 모르겠어요.
I don't know why she got angry.

-(으)ㄴ/는지 is used to make an indirect question with the "wh-" question words. The conjugation depends on whether the predicate of the indirect question is a verb or adjective and whether it is in the past, present, or future.

- 이 책에서 뭐가 중요한지 알고 싶어요. I want to know what is important in this book.
- 이 음식을 어떻게 먹는지 몰라서 당황했어요. I was flustered because I didn't know how to eat this type of food.
- 어제 왜 약속에 늦게 왔는지 아직 말 안 했어요. You still haven't said why you were late for yesterday's appointment.

-지요 (= 죠) expressing a fact that the speaker believes the listener knows to be true

A 오늘 좀 춥죠?
It is cold today, isn't it?

B 네, 좀 추워요.
Yes, it is a little cold.

-지요 is used to express a fact that the speaker believes the listener knows to be true. When it is used with a question mark, the speaker is asking for confirmation that the listener knows as a fact. -지요 attaches to the stems of verbs, adjectives, and 이다 and it may attach to -았/었-. In speech, it is often shortened to -죠.

- 누구에게나 건강이 중요하지요. Health is important to everyone.
- 어렸을 때는 과자를 많이 먹었죠. When I was young, I ate a lot of cookies.
- A 이 김치가 생각보다 안 맵지요? This kimchi is not that spicy, right?
  B 네, 별로 맵지 않아요. Yes, it's not very spicy.

Quiz Yourself

▸Answers P. 312

1 '-(으)ㄴ/는지'를 사용하여 문장을 완성하세요.

__________________ 못 들었어요.
(언제 일을 시작해요?)

__________________ 궁금해요.
(어떻게 그 사실을 알았어요?)

__________________ 물어볼 거예요.
(어디로 여행 가고 싶어요?)

__________________ 얘기해 주세요.
(고향이 어디예요?)

__________________ 배우고 싶어요.
(어른에게 어떻게 말해야 해요?)

__________________ 이해 안 돼요.
(왜 친구의 얘기를 듣지 않아요?)

2 알맞은 답을 고르세요.

(1) 그 친구와 언제 처음 ⓐ 만나는지 / ⓑ 만났는지 생각이 안 나요.

(2) 왜 생선을 ⓐ 먹지 않은지 / ⓑ 먹지 않는지 설명할게요.

(3) 어디에서 만나기로 ⓐ 하는지 / ⓑ 했는지 생각 났어요.

(4) 어떤 서류가 ⓐ 필요한지 / ⓑ 필요하는지 미리 얘기해 주세요.

3 '-지요'를 사용하여 대화를 완성하세요.

(1) A 이 가게가 값이 __________?
B 네, 싸요.

(2) A 날씨가 __________?
B 네, 더워요.

(3) A 한국어 공부가 __________?
B 네, 쉽지 않아요.

(4) A 밥을 __________?
B 그럼요, 벌써 먹었죠.

(5) A 아이들이 책을 많이 __________?
B 네, 많이 읽어요.

(6) A 고향이 __________?
B 맞아요, 부산이에요.

Conversation ❸

Track 12

리나 여보세요.

케빈 리나 씨! 저 케빈이에요.

리나 케빈 씨, 거의 다 왔어요?

케빈 아니요, 사실은 여기서 어떻게 가는지 잘 모르겠어요.

리나 네? 지하철에서 내렸어요?

케빈 지하철역 출구에서 나왔는데, 그다음부터 잘 모르겠어요.

리나 지금 주변에 뭐가 보여요?

케빈 앞에 '서울'이라는 식당이 있어요.

리나 '서울식당'요? 잘 모르겠어요. 식당 말고 더 큰 건물 없어요?

케빈 음……, 길 건너편에 큰 서점이 있고 그 옆에 동상 같은 것도 있어요.

리나 아! 어딘지 알겠어요. 서점 입구에 계단이 보이죠?

케빈 네, 맞아요. 계단이 있어요.

리나 제가 지금 마중 나갈게요. 길 건너서 서점 입구에서 기다리세요.

Rina Hello?

Kevin Rina! It's Kevin.

Rina Kevin, are you almost here?

Kevin No, actually I'm not sure how to get there from here.

Rina Huh? Did you get off the subway?

Kevin I came out of the subway exit, but I'm not sure what to do after that.

Rina What do you see around you right now?

Kevin There is a restaurant called 'Seoul' in front.

Rina 'Seoul Restaurant'? I do not know. Is there a building that's bigger than the restaurant? (lit. Not the restaurant, but is there not a bigger building?)

Kevin Um... there's a big bookstore on the other side of the street and there's also something that looks like a statue.

Rina Ah! I know where you are. You see the stairs at the entrance of the bookstore, right?

Kevin Yes, there are stairs.

Rina I'll come out to meet you. Cross the street and wait at the entrance of the bookstore.

New Vocabulary ▸P. 324

사실은 | 내리다 | 나오다 | 주변 | 말고 | 건너편 | 동상 | 마중 나가다 | 입구

New Expressions ▸P. 324

- 거의 다 왔어요?
- 어떻게 가는지 잘 모르겠어요.
- (A) 말고 (B) 없어요?

Tips

1 The Usage of 말고

말고 follows nouns and means "not this (noun), but" or "besides (noun)." The marker 도 or 는 may be attached to the end of 말고.

- 사과 **말고** 딸기 없어요? Besides apples, do you have strawberries?
- 빨간색 **말고** 다른 것으로 주세요.
  Please give me something besides red.
- 우유 **말고도** 커피도 샀어요. Besides milk, I also bought coffee.
- 동생 **말고는** 아무도 그 사실을 몰라요.
  No one knows about it besides my brother.

2 모르겠어요 vs. 몰라요

몰라요 is used when one does not know some information, whereas 모르겠어요 is used when one is not sure about or does not understand information.

- 마크는 선생님 전화번호를 **몰라요**. (O)
  Mark doesn't know the teacher's phone number.
  마크는 선생님 전화번호를 모르겠어요. (X)
- 이게 맞는지 몰라요. (X)
  이게 맞는지 **모르겠어요**. (O)
  I don't know if this is correct.

Actions Done on the Street

ⓐ 길을 건너다 to cross the street
ⓑ 길을 걷다 to walk on the street

ⓐ 버스를 타다 to get on the bus
ⓑ 버스를 내리다 to get off the bus

ⓐ 줄을 서다 to line up
ⓑ 신호를 기다리다 to wait for the (traffic) light

ⓐ 물건을 팔다 to sell goods
ⓑ 물건을 사다 to buy goods

ⓐ 쓰레기를 버리다 to throw away garbage
ⓑ 쓰레기를 줍다 to pick up garbage

ⓐ 동전을 넣다 to insert a coin
ⓑ 물건을 꺼내다 to take out an object

ⓐ 계단을 내려가다 to go downstairs
ⓑ 계단을 올라오다 to go upstairs

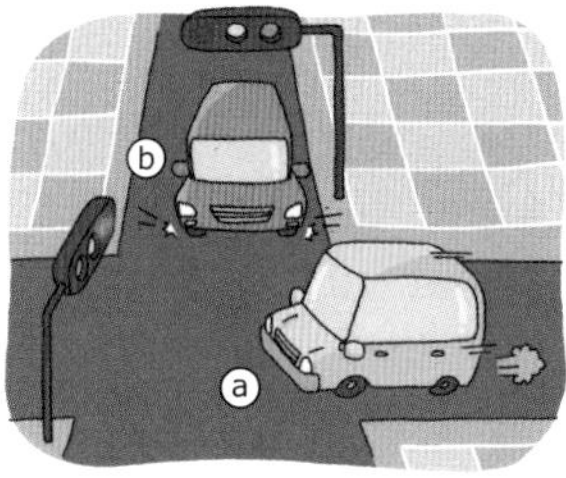

ⓐ 차가 출발하다 for a car to drive off
ⓑ 차가 멈추다 for a car to stop

Key Expressions

- 아직 멀었어요. I'm still far away.
- 반쯤 왔어요. I've come about halfway.
- 거의 다 왔어요. I'm almost there.
- 다 왔어요. I'm here.

Let's Talk!

Speaking Strategy — **Confirming Information**

- 몇 번 버스요? **Which number bus?**
- 몇 호선요? **Which (subway) line?**
- 몇 번 출구요? **Which exit?**
- 몇 번째 정거장요? **What number stop?**
- 언제요? **When?**
- 어디요? **Where?**

❶

이 곳에 가는 방법

- 친구들과 주말에 만나기 좋은 곳
- 혼자 산책하기 좋은 곳
- 쇼핑할 때 가는 단골 가게
- 데이트하기 좋은 곳
- 부모님께서 한국에 오셨을 때 같이 가고 싶은 곳
- 여행 가기 좋은 곳

❷ 교통수단

버스

- 버스를 타면 한번에 가요?
- 몇 번 버스를 타요?
- 버스가 자주 와요?
- 몇 정거장 가요?
- 어느 정류장에서 내려요?
- 버스비가 얼마예요?
- 시간이 얼마나 걸려요?

지하철

- 지하철을 타면 몇 번 갈아타요?
- 지하철 몇 호선을 타요?
- 지하철이 얼마나 자주 와요?
- 몇 정거장 가요?
- 무슨 역에서 내려요?
- 몇 번 출구로 나가요?
- 지하철 요금이 얼마예요?
- 시간이 얼마나 걸려요?

I wonder

첫 번째 정거장, 두 번째 정거장, 세 번째 정거장, 네 번째 정거장, 다섯 번째 정거장

❸ 주변 물건

그 근처에 가면 뭐가 있어요?

New Vocabulary

위치 location | 교통수단 transportation method | 한번에 at one go | 정거장 counter for stations | 정류장 bus station | 갈아타다 to transfer | 호선 (subway) line | 단골 regular (customer)

Word Web

Appendix P. 317

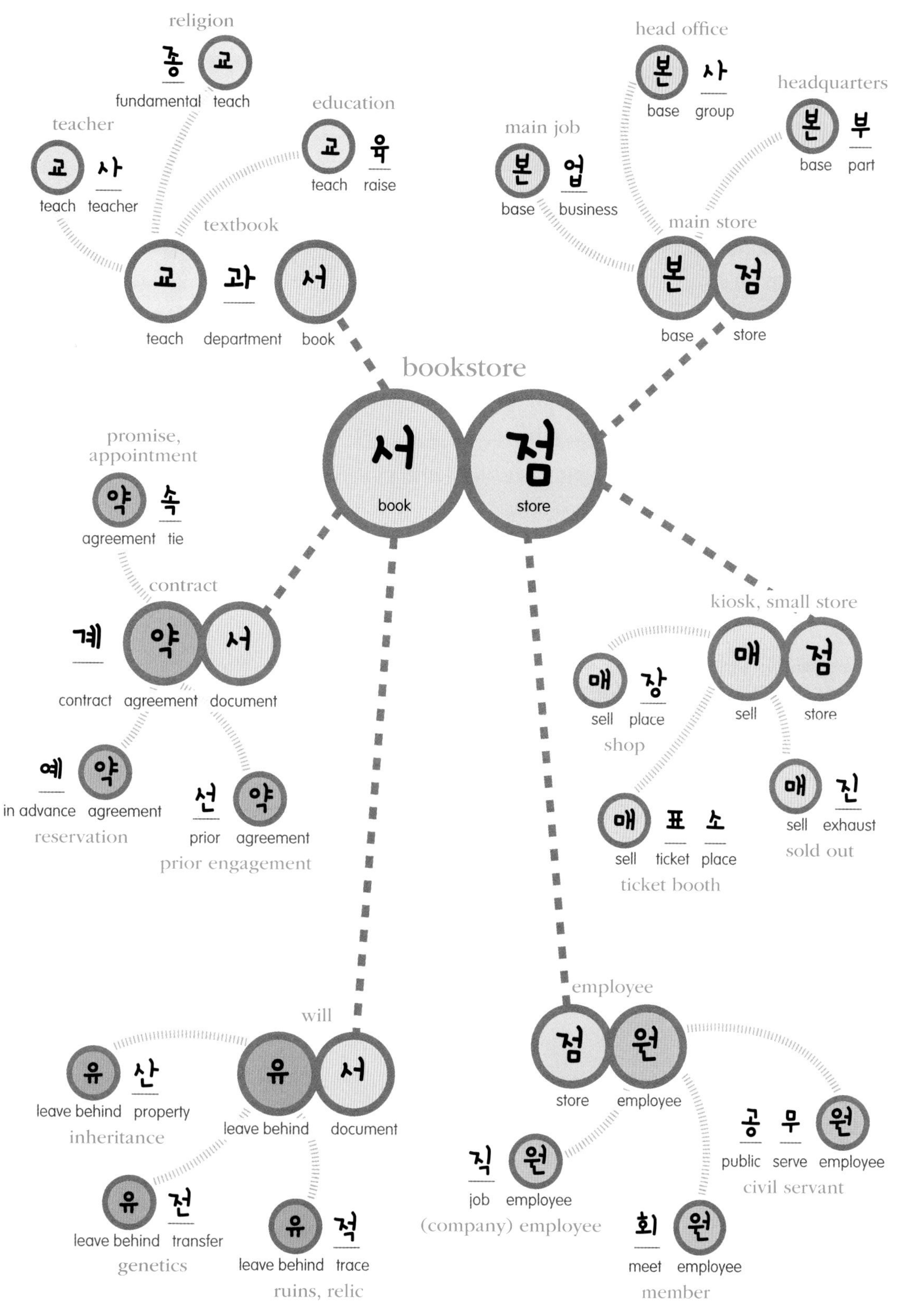

A Word on Culture

Let's Talk about People!

• 길치 directionally challenged, 음치 tone-deaf, 박치 bad sense of rhythm, 몸치 two-left feet

Whenever we walk around a familiar place, there is always someone who is lost. In Korea, these people are called 길치. 치 originally meant "to be immature" or "to be stupid," but it is now attached to words to playfully tease someone with no intention of demeaning them. Therefore, if someone has no sense of direction, they can call themselves 길치 and leave the directions to someone else. So what are some other words that use 치 that are often used by Koreans? 음치 refers to someone who is tone-deaf or off-key when singing, 박치 refers to someone bad at keeping rhythm, and 몸치 refers to someone clumsy, such as someone who takes three hours to learn a dance that should take one hour. In Korea, since meals with one's coworkers are a time to unwind in a relaxed environment, Koreans will teasingly call each other 음치, 박치, and 몸치 during these meals.

• 백수 a bum, 고수 a master

The literal meaning of 백수, based on the hanja, is "white hands." "White hands" refer to hands that have never done any work nor been exposed to sunlight, so 백수 means someone who does not have any particular job and who fools around all day. In contrast, 실업자 (unemployed person) is used in formal situations such as in newspapers or on the news but 백수 is used in everyday speech as a negative term. Another similar hanja word is 고수, in which 수 refers to not hands but a method or ability. Thus, 고수 means someone very skilled in a specific area.

• 술고래 a heavy drinker

술고래 refers to someone who drinks a lot. Just as 고래 (whales) does not seem to be bothered at all by ingesting much seawater, 술고래 refers to a person who can keep drinking without seeming to have any problem.

Chapter **05**

음식

Food

Goals
- Speaking about Foods You Like and Hate
- Speaking about What You Would Like to Do
- Ordering Food
- Describing Food
- Recommending Restaurants

Grammar

❶ -(으)려고 하다 "to intend to", "to be going to"

-(으)ㄴ/는데요 softening one's tone or expressing hesitation while explaining a situation

❷ -아/어 줄까요? "Shall I (do something for you)?"

-(으)ㄴ/는 대신에 "instead of"

❸ -(으)ㄴ 적이 있다 "having done something before"

-고 있다 "to be doing"

Grammar 1

-(으)려고 하다 "to intend to", "to be going to"

Appendix P. 267 

A 주말에 뭐 할 거예요?
What are you doing this weekend?

B 집에서 쉬려고 해요.
I am going to relax at home.

-(으)려고 하다 is used to express the speaker's intent to do something and to describe a situation that will soon change or take place (as in the third sentence below). It is attached to the stems of verbs.

- 이번 휴가 때 친구들하고 해외로 여행 가려고 해요. I'm going on a trip abroad with my friends this vacation.
- 이따가 갈비를 먹으려고 하는데 같이 갈 수 있어요? I'm going to eat galbi later, can you go with me?
- 기차가 출발하려고 해요. 빨리 기차 탑시다. The train is about to depart. Let's get on the train quickly.

-(으)ㄴ/는데요 softening one's tone or expressing hesitation while explaining a situation

Appendix P. 267 

A 오늘 저녁에 영화 볼까요?
Shall we watch a movie tonight?

B 오늘은 일이 많은데요.
I have a lot of work today.

This expression is used to indirectly explain one's situation in order to soften one's tone for the listener. In the above example, Rina refuses Minho's proposal in a roundabout manner by using -(으)ㄴ/는데요 to explain that she has much work to do rather than by directly saying "I can't watch a movie with you today." -는데요 is attached to verb stems, -(으)ㄴ데요 to adjective stems, and -았/었는데요 to both verb and adjective stems to express a past tense meaning.

- A 월요일까지 이 서류를 끝내세요. Please complete this document by Monday.
  B 저는 다른 서류를 만들고 있는데요. ("다른 사람에게 시키세요." is omitted.)
  I'm making another document.
- A 아까 왜 전화 안 했어요? Why didn't you call me earlier?
  B 배터리가 떨어졌는데요. ("그래서 전화 못 했어요." is omitted.)
  I ran out of battery.

▸Answers P. 313

1 그림을 보고 보기 와 같이 '-(으)려고 하다'를 사용하여 다음 대화를 완성하세요.

일요일 월요일 화요일 수요일 목요일 금요일 토요일
오늘

보기 A 다음 주 월요일에 뭐 할 거예요?
B 쇼핑하려고 해요.

(1) A 다음 주 화요일에 밖에서 친구를 만날 거예요?
B 아니요, 집에서 ______________.

(2) A 언제 영화를 볼 거예요?
B ______________ 는데 같이 갈까요?

(3) A 주말에 등산 갈 거예요?
B 아니요, 다음 주말에는 ______________.

2 알맞은 답을 고르세요.

(1) A 어제 일을 다 끝냈어요?
B 아니요, ⓐ 일을 끝내려고 하는데 / ⓑ 일을 끝내려고 했는데 갑자기 일이 생겨서 못 했어요.

(2) 시험 준비가 부족해서 이번에는 ⓐ 시험을 보려고 해요. / ⓑ 시험을 보지 않으려고 해요.

(3) 다이어트 때문에 초콜릿을 ⓐ 먹으려고 했지만 / ⓑ 먹지 않으려고 했지만 너무 맛있어 보여서 먹어 버렸어요.

(4) A ⓐ 회의가 시작하려고 하는데 / ⓑ 회의가 시작했는데 왜 안 와요? 곧 시작할 거예요.
B 입구에 도착했어요. 조금만 더 기다려 주세요.

3 대화를 완성하도록 알맞은 것끼리 연결하세요.

(1) 이따가 6시에 만날까요? •
(2) 직원한테 문제를 말해 보세요. •
(3) 전화 한 통만 할 수 있어요? •
(4) 한국어 공부 좀 도와주세요. •

• ⓐ 저도 핸드폰을 집에 놓고 왔는데요.
• ⓑ 저도 한국어 잘 못하는데요.
• ⓒ 벌써 말했는데요.
• ⓓ 저는 7시에 일이 끝나는데요.

Conversation 1

Track 13

링링 지금 어디에 가요?

마크 식당에 가요. 좀 일찍 밥을 먹으려고 해요.

링링 저도 지금 밥 먹으려고 하는데, 같이 갈까요?

마크 좋아요. 같이 가요.

링링 마크 씨는 무슨 음식 좋아해요?

마크 저는 한식 좋아해요.

링링 그럼, 김치찌개 먹으면 어때요?

마크 제가 매운 거 잘 못 먹는데요.

링링 그래요? 매운 거 빼고 다른 건 괜찮아요?

마크 네, 맵지 않으면 다 괜찮아요.

링링 그럼, 된장찌개는 어때요?

마크 그건 안 매워요?

링링 네, 안 매워요.

마크 그럼, 전 된장찌개 한번 먹어 볼게요.

Ling Ling Where are you going?

Mark To a restaurant. I'm going to eat a little early.

Ling Ling I'm also going to eat now. Shall we go together?

Mark Sure. Let's go together.

Ling Ling What kind of food do you like, Mark?

Mark I like Korean food.

Ling Ling Then why don't we eat kimchi jjigae?

Mark I can't handle spicy food though.

Ling Ling Really? Apart from spicy food, is everything else okay?

Mark Yes, as long as it is not spicy, it's okay.

Ling Ling Then how about doenjang jjigae?

Mark Is that not spicy?

Ling Ling Yes, it's not spicy.

Mark Then I'll try eating doenjang jjigae.

New Vocabulary ▸P. 325

일찍 | 한식 | 맵다 | 잘 | 다

New Expressions ▸P. 325

- (noun) 먹으면 어때요?
- (noun) 빼고 다른 건 괜찮아요?
- -(으)면 다 괜찮아요.

Tips

1 잘 못 vs 잘못

There is a difference between 잘 못, in which space indicates a pause when spoken, and 잘못 which has no pause. 잘 못 means that one cannot do something well, while 잘못 means that one has made a mistake.
In this conversation, 잘 and 못 are spaced to convey the meaning of not doing something well.

- 운동을 **잘 못하지만** 노래는 잘해요.
  I'm not good at sports, but I'm good at singing.
- 계산을 **잘못해서** 돈을 더 냈어요.
  I paid more because I made a mistake in the calculation.

2 Contractions Used in Speech

More contractions are used in speech than in writing. These contractions allow for more natural and better flowing speech. The following expressions are some examples of contractions.

게 (= 것이), 걸 (= 것을), 건 (= 것은), 그건 (= 그것은)
전 (= 저는), 널 (= 너를), 좀 (= 조금), 그럼 (= 그러면)

- **이건** 얼마예요?
  How much is this?
- **전** 그 얘기를 처음 들었어요.
  I heard about it for the first time.

❶ Flavors and Textures

❶  ❷  ❸  ❹  ❺  ❻ 

1. 달다 to be sweet
2. 맵다 to be spicy
3. 짜다 to be salty
4. 시다 to be sour
5. 쓰다 to be bitter
6. 느끼하다 to be greasy
7. 달콤하다 to be pleasantly sweet
8. 매콤하다 to be pleasantly spicy
9. 짭짤하다 to be pleasantly salty
10. 새콤하다 to be pleasantly sour
11. 고소하다 to be savory
12. 얼큰하다 to be spicy (in a tingling manner)
13. 싱겁다 to be bland
14. 담백하다 to be light (in flavor)
15. 부드럽다 to be soft
16. 쫄깃하다 to be chewy
17. 상큼하다 to be refreshing
18. 시원하다 to be warm and pleasant tasting

- **달고 짠** 음식은 건강에 안 좋으니까 조심하세요.
  Sweet and salty foods are not good for one's health, so be careful.
- 음식이 **싱거워도** 소금이나 후추를 너무 많이 넣지 마세요.
  Even if a dish is bland, do not add too much salt or pepper.

❷ States of Food

1. Freshness

- 과일이 **신선해요.**
  The fruit is fresh.
- 생선이 **싱싱해요.**
  The fish is fresh.

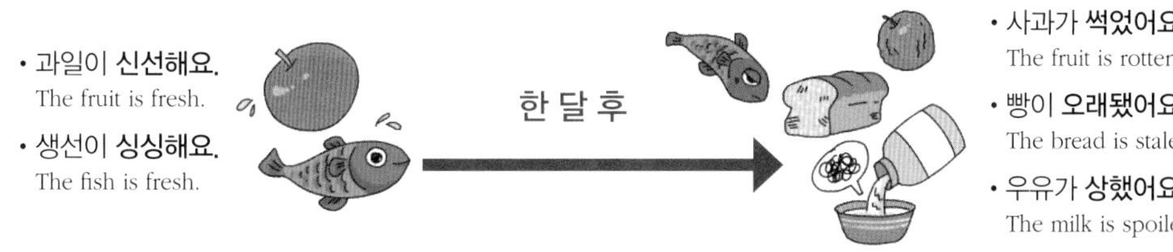

- 사과가 **썩었어요.**
  The fruit is rotten.
- 빵이 **오래됐어요.**
  The bread is stale.
- 우유가 **상했어요.**
  The milk is spoiled.

2. Doneness

- 새우가 **덜 익었어요.** The shrimp is undercooked.
- 새우가 **잘 익었어요.** The shrimp is well cooked.

3. Softness

- 케이크가 **부드러워요.** The cake is soft.
- 빵이 **딱딱해요.** The bread is hard.

4. Temperature of Liquids

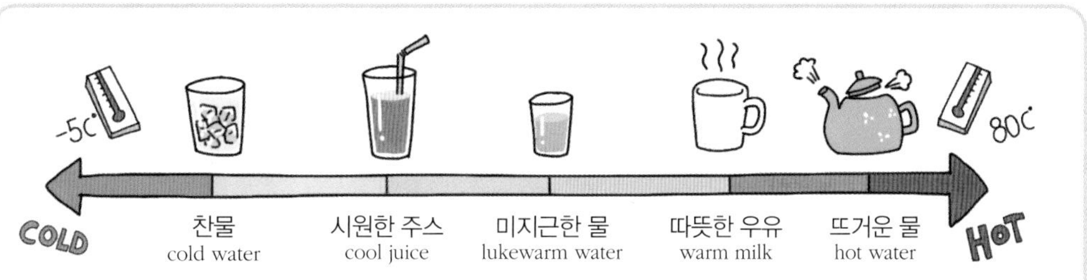

- 음식이 **따뜻해요.** 식기 전에 드세요.
  The food is warm. Please eat it before it gets cold.
- **찬** 머핀을 전자레인지에 데워 주세요.
  Please warm up the cold muffin in the microwave.

Key Expressions

- 저는 가리지 않고 다 좋아해요.
  I am not picky. I like everything.
- 저는 닭고기 빼고 다 괜찮아요.
  I am okay with everything except chicken.

Grammar 2

-아/어 줄까요? "Shall I (do something for you)?"

A 무겁죠? 짐 들어 줄까요?
It's heavy, right? Shall I take your luggage?

B 감사합니다. 문 앞까지만 들어 주세요.
Thank you. Just take it to the front of the door, please.

-아/어 줄까요? is used to ask a listener whether he/she would like a favor offered by the speaker. It is attached to verb stems. -아/어 드릴까요? is used if the listener is of higher status. If what is offered to the listener is an object rather than a favor, 줄까요? or 드릴까요? is attached to the object.

- A 마크 씨 전화번호 몰라요? 제가 아는데 알려 줄까요?
  You do not know Mark's phone number? I know it. Would you like me to share it?
  B 그래요? 그럼, 좀 알려 주세요. Really? Then, could you please let me know?
- A 박 선생님은 지금 안 계신데요. 메모 전해 드릴까요?
  Mr. Park is not in right now. Would you like me to pass him a note?
  B 네, 이 메모 좀 전해 주세요. Yes, please pass him this note.
- 따뜻한 물 드릴까요? 아니면 찬물 드릴까요? Can I get you some hot water? Or would you like some cold water?

-(으)ㄴ/는 대신에 "instead of"

▶ Appendix P. 268

A 배고픈데 간식 없어요?
I'm hungry. Do you have any snacks?

B 밤에는 간식을 먹는 대신에 물을 드세요.
At night, instead of eating a snack, you should drink water.

-(으)ㄴ/는 대신에 is used to express "instead of". -는 대신에 is used for present verbs while -(으)ㄴ 대신에 is used for past verbs and present adjectives. You can use "instead of" immediately after the noun.

- 주말에 여행 가는 대신에 집에서 책을 읽기로 했어요.
  Instead of going on a weekend trip, I decided to read a book at home.
- 이번 주에 많이 일하는 대신에 다음 주는 쉴 거예요. As I am working a lot this week, I'm taking a break next week.
- 지난 주말에 일한 대신에 내일은 쉴 거예요. Instead of working last weekend, I'll take a day off tomorrow.

1 그림을 보고 알맞은 답을 고르세요.

(1)

A 음식이 다 식었죠?
따뜻하게 ⓐ 데워 줄까요? / ⓑ 데워 주세요.

B 네, 감사합니다.

(2)

A 여기 젓가락 좀 ⓐ 갖다줄까요? / ⓑ 갖다주세요.

B 네, 알겠습니다.

(3)

A 저는 지하철역까지 걸어 가요.

B 제가 자동차가 있어요.
지하철역까지 ⓐ 태울까요? / ⓑ 태워 줄까요?

(4)

A 글자가 작아서 안 보이네.

B 할머니, 제가 읽어 ⓐ 줄까요? / ⓑ 드릴까요?

2 대화를 완성하도록 알맞은 것끼리 연결하세요.

(1) 잘 먹었습니다. •	• ⓐ 음악을 틀어 줄까요?
(2) 컴퓨터 선이 빠졌어요. •	• ⓑ 이따가 선생님께 전해 드릴까요?
(3) 선물을 살 시간이 없어요. •	• ⓒ 그럼, 그릇을 치워 드릴까요?
(4) 선생님께 메모를 남기고 싶은데요. •	• ⓓ 제가 선을 다시 연결해 드릴까요?
(5) 좋은 음악을 듣고 싶어요. •	• ⓔ 그럼, 제가 선물을 사다 줄까요?

3 다음에서 알맞은 답을 골라서 문장을 완성하세요.

분위기가 좋다　　얼굴이 예쁘다　　운전하다　　사다

(1) 그 여자는 ______________ 대신에 성격이 안 좋아요.

(2) 그 식당은 ______________ 대신에 너무 비싸요.

(3) 돈이 없어서 책을 ______________ 대신에 빌려서 읽어요.

(4) 운동할 시간이 없어서 ______________ 대신에 지하철을 자주 이용해요.

Conversation ❷

Track 14

직원 뭐 드시겠어요?

마크 된장찌개 하나 주세요.

직원 죄송합니다. 손님. 지금 된장이 떨어져서 된장찌개가 안 되는데요.

마크 그래요? 다른 건 돼요?

직원 네, 된장찌개만 빼고 다른 건 다 돼요.

마크 그럼, 이 중에서 안 매운 게 어떤 거예요?

직원 불고기하고 갈비탕이 안 매워요.

마크 갈비탕은 안 먹어 봤는데요. 뭘로 만들어요?

직원 소고기를 물에 넣고 끓인 거예요.

마크 고기 대신 채소로 만든 건 없어요?

직원 그럼, 비빔밥은 어떠세요? 여기에는 고기가 안 들어가요. 매운 거 안 좋아하시면 고추장을 넣지 말고 따로 드릴까요?

마크 네, 가능하면 맵지 않게 해 주세요.

직원 알겠습니다.

Waitress What would you like to eat?

Mark Please give me one order of doenjang jjigae.

Waitress Sorry, sir. We are out of bean paste so we cannot make doenjang jjigae.

Mark Really? Are other dishes available?

Waitress Yes, except doenjang jjigae, everything else is available.

Mark Then what is there among those dishes that are not spicy?

Waitress Bulgogi and galbitang are not spicy.

Mark I haven't tried galbitang yet. What is it made of?

Waitress It is made from beef boiled in water.

Mark Is there something made from vegetables instead of meat?

Waitress Then how about bibimbap? Here we don't add meat to it. If you don't like spicy food, I can put the gochujang on the side instead of having it added to the dish. (lit. shall I not add gochujang and give it to you separately?)

Mark Yes, if it is possible, please make it not spicy.

Waitress Okay.

New Vocabulary ▸ P. 325

된장 | 손님 | 떨어지다 | (음식이) 안 되다 | 이 중에서 | 뭘로 (= 무엇으로) | 넣다 | 끓이다 | 고기 | 채소 | 들어가다 | 따로 | 가능하면

New Expressions ▸ P. 325

- 뭐 드시겠어요?
- 다른 건 돼요?
- 가능하면 맵지 않게 해 주세요.

Tips

1 The Marker 만

The marker 만 means only and is used to refer to only what is written before it. The marker 만 is attached to nouns, while -기만 하다 is attached to adjectives and verbs.

- 저는 검정색 옷**만** 입어요. I only wear black clothes.
- 좀 피곤하**기만 해요**. 아프지는 않아요.
  I'm just a little tired. I'm not sick.
- 친구가 아무 말도 안 하고 울**기만 했어요**.
  My friend didn't say anything and just cried.

2 -(으)ㄴ/는 거예요: "It is a thing that"

In this conversation, -(으)ㄴ/는 거예요 is used to highlight the specific explanation of what the galbitang is made of. -는 거예요 is used for present verbs while -(으)ㄴ 거예요 is used for past verbs.

- 떡국은 한국 사람들이 설날 때 먹**는 거예요**.
  Tteokguk (rice cake soup) is what Koreans eat during the Lunar New Year.
- 이 목걸이는 할머니한테 받**은 거예요**.
  This necklace was given to me by my grandmother.

❶ 채소 Vegetables

- 오이 cucumber
- 마늘 garlic
- 무 radish
- 감자 potato
- 당근 carrot
- 고추 chili pepper
- 상추 lettuce
- 고구마 sweet potato
- 파 scallion
- 배추 napa cabbage
- 버섯 mushroom
- 시금치 spinach
- 양파 onion
- 양배추 cabbage
- 호박 pumpkin
- 콩 bean

❷ 과일 Fruits

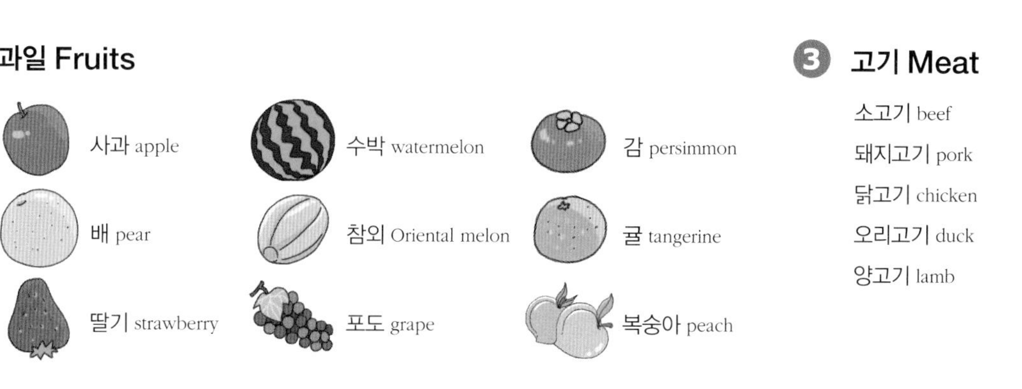

- 사과 apple
- 수박 watermelon
- 감 persimmon
- 배 pear
- 참외 Oriental melon
- 귤 tangerine
- 딸기 strawberry
- 포도 grape
- 복숭아 peach

❸ 고기 Meat

- 소고기 beef
- 돼지고기 pork
- 닭고기 chicken
- 오리고기 duck
- 양고기 lamb

❹ 해물 (= 해산물) Seafood

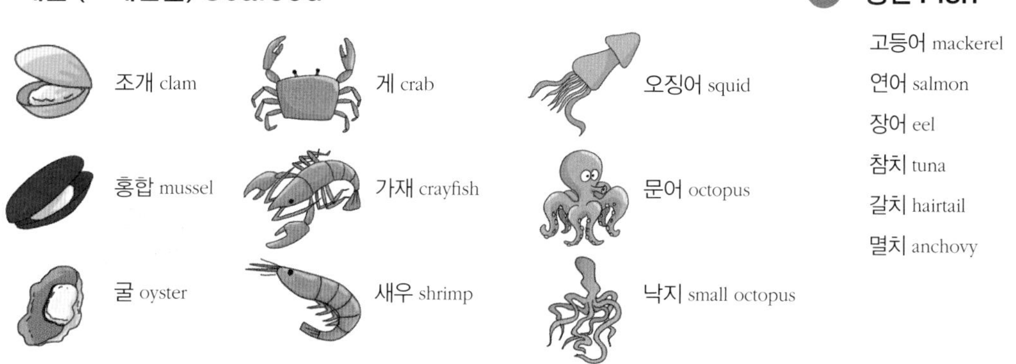

- 조개 clam
- 게 crab
- 오징어 squid
- 홍합 mussel
- 가재 crayfish
- 문어 octopus
- 굴 oyster
- 새우 shrimp
- 낙지 small octopus

❺ 생선 Fish

- 고등어 mackerel
- 연어 salmon
- 장어 eel
- 참치 tuna
- 갈치 hairtail
- 멸치 anchovy

❻ 기타 Other

- 쌀 uncooked rice
- 달걀/계란 egg
- 밀가루 flour
- 두부 tofu
- 면 noodles
- 인삼 ginseng

❼ 식재료 Ingredient States

- 날것 something raw/uncooked
- 말린 것 something dried
- 익힌 것 something well done
- 얼린 것 something frozen

Key Expressions

- (noun)만 빼 주세요. Please take out (noun).
- (A) 빼고 (B)만 넣어 주세요.
Please take out (A) and only put in (B).

Grammar ❸

(으)ㄴ 적이 있다 "having done something before"

Appendix P. 268

A 전에 지갑을 잃어버린 적이 있어요?
Have you lost your wallet before?

B 아니요, 그런 적 없어요.
No, that hasn't happened to me before.

-(으)ㄴ 적이 있다 is used to express one's experience. -(으)ㄴ 적이 있다 is attached to the stems of verbs, adjectives, and 이다. When expressing something one has not experienced, -(으)ㄴ 적이 없다 is used. The helping verb 보다 (which expresses trying something) may be added to form -아/어 본 적이 있다 to express an attempt at trying something.

- 전에 아프리카에 여행 간 적이 있어요. I've been to Africa before.
- 한 번도 해 본 적이 없어서 자신이 없어요. I've never done it before, so I'm not sure.
- 저 사람은 어디선가 본 적이 있는데, 이름이 기억 안나요.
  I've seen him somewhere, but I can't remember his name.

-고 있다 "to be doing"

Appendix P. 268

A 지금 잠깐 얘기할 수 있어요?
Can you talk for a little bit?

B 미안해요. 지금 회의하고 있어요.
Sorry, I am in a meeting now.

-고 있다 is used to express a continuing action in the present. It is also used to express a repeated action in a set time frame. -고 있다 is attached to verb stems. -고 있다 is used for the present, -고 있었다 for the past, -고 있을 것이다 for the future, and -고 있지 않다 for the negative.

- 지금 밥을 먹고 있으니까 제가 나중에 다시 전화할게요. I'm eating right now, so I'll call you back later.
- 지난달부터 운동하고 있는데 살이 빠지지 않아요. I've been exercising since last month, but I'm not losing weight.
- 요즘은 아르바이트를 하고 있지 않아요. I'm not working part-time these days.

▸ Answers P. 313

1 그림을 보고 알맞은 답을 고르세요.

(1)

ⓐ 여자가 전화하고 있어요.
ⓑ 여자가 전화하려고 해요.

(2)

ⓐ 여자가 운전하고 있어요.
ⓑ 여자가 운전하려고 해요.

(3)

ⓐ 남자가 샤워하고 있어요.
ⓑ 남자가 샤워하고 있지 않아요.

(4)

ⓐ 남자가 옷을 갈아입고 있어요.
ⓑ 남자가 옷을 갈아입고 있지 않아요.

2 알맞은 답을 고르세요.

(1) A 한국 음식을 지금 ⓐ 만들고 있는데 / ⓑ 만든 적이 없지만 우리 집에 와서 좀 도와주세요.
B 저는 한국 음식을 만들어 본 적이 없는데요.

(2) A 케빈 씨가 전에 부산에 살았어요?
B 잘 모르겠어요. 전에 어디에 ⓐ 살고 있는지 / ⓑ 산 적이 있는지 케빈 씨한테 물어볼까요?

(3) A 태권도를 배우고 싶어서 지금 학원을 ⓐ 알아보고 있어요. / ⓑ 알아본 적이 있어요.
B 저도 같이 하면 좋겠어요.

(4) A 대사관 전화번호 좀 가르쳐 주세요.
B 예전 전화번호만 알고 지금 전화번호는 ⓐ 갖고 있어요. / ⓑ 갖고 있지 않아요.

3 '-(으)ㄴ 적이 있다'나 '-(으)ㄴ 적이 없다'를 사용하여 문장을 완성하세요.

(1) 얼마 전에 경주에 ______________ 는데 정말 재미있었어요. (가다)
(2) 어렸을 때 피아노를 ______________ 지만 잘 못 쳐요. (배우다)
(3) 아직 ______________ 지만 기회가 있으면 해 보고 싶어요. (해 보다)
(4) 전에 삼계탕을 ______________ 는데 되게 맛있었어요. (먹다)
(5) 그런 얘기는 이제까지 ______________ 는데요. (듣다)
(6) 바다 근처에 ______________ 어서 해산물에 익숙하지 않아요. (살다)

Conversation ❸

Track 15

유키 뭐 하고 있어요?

케빈 맛집을 찾고 있어요.

유키 맛집은 왜요?

케빈 다음 주에 부모님이 한국에 오셔서 식당을 알아보고 있어요.

유키 그래요? 맛집은 찾았어요?

케빈 아니요, 어제부터 찾고 있는데, 아직 못 찾았어요.

유키 부모님이 한국에 오시니까 한정식 집을 찾고 있죠?

케빈 네, 맛도 좋고 분위기도 좋은 식당을 알면 추천해 주세요.

유키 혹시 '최고의 맛'이라는 식당에 가 본 적이 있어요?

케빈 아니요, 가 본 적이 없는데요.

유키 그럼, 거기에 한번 가 보세요.
며칠 전에 갔는데 맛있었어요.

케빈 그래요? 맛이 어때요?

유키 맵지도 않고 짜지도 않아서 외국인 입맛에 잘 맞을 거예요.

케빈 거기가 좋겠네요. 알려 줘서 고마워요.

Yuki What are you doing?

Kevin I'm looking for a good restaurant.

Yuki What for?

Kevin I'm looking for a restaurant because my parents are coming to Korea next week.

Yuki Really? Did you find a good restaurant?

Kevin No, I've been looking for one since yesterday, but I still haven't been able to find one.

Yuki Since your parents are coming to Korea, you are looking for a restaurant that serves hanjeongsik, right?

Kevin Yes, if you find a place that has good food and a good atmosphere, please recommend it to me.

Yuki Have you been to (the restaurant called) "최고의 맛" by any chance?

Kevin No, I haven't been there.

Yuki Then try going there. I went there a few days ago and it was good.

Kevin Really? What's the food like?

Yuki It's not spicy or salty so it should suit foreigners' tastes well.

Kevin That seems like a good place. Thank you for telling me.

New Vocabulary ▸P. 325

맛집 | 알아보다 | 한정식 집 | 맛이 좋다 | 분위기 | 추천하다 | 며칠 | 입맛에 맞다

New Expressions ▸P. 325

- 아직 못 찾았어요.
- (noun)에 가 본 적이 있어요?
- 알려 줘서 고마워요.

Tips

1 The Honorific -(으)시-

-(으)시- is added to a verb or adjective stem when expressing respect for the subject of the sentence. If -고 or -아/어서 is added, the form conjugates in the following way:

- 오고 (normal): 오**시고** (honorific) (← 오+시+고)
- 읽고 (normal): 읽**으시고** (honorific) (← 읽+으시+고)
- 와서 (normal): 오**셔서** (honorific) (← 오+시+어서)
- 읽어서 (normal): 읽**으셔서** (honorific) (← 읽+으시+어서)

2 Name + (이)라는

(이)라는 is attached to a noun when introducing a new name or title.

- '김진수'**라는** 학생을 알아요?
  Do you know a student named 'Kim Jinsu'?
- '아리랑'**이라는** 식당에 가 본 적이 있어요?
  Have you ever been to a restaurant called 'Arirang'?

❶ Cooking Methods

1.

끓이다 to boil

2.

찌다 to steam

3.
볶다 to sauté

4.

튀기다 to deep fry

5.
부치다 to fry (griddle)

6.
굽다 to grill

7. 삶다 to boil (Ex.: boiled egg, boiled noodles)
8. 데치다 to blanch, to parboil (Ex.: cooked vegetables)

❷ Eating Methods

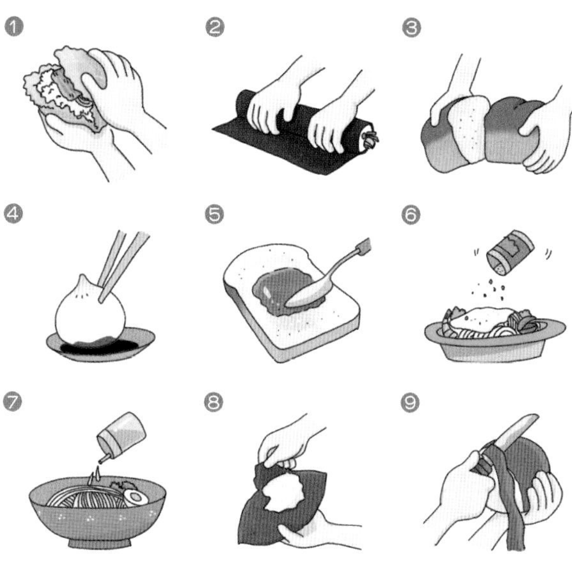

1. 채소를 싸다
 to wrap the vegetables (around something).
2. 김을 말다 to roll the dry laver.
3. 빵을 반으로 자르다 to cut the bread in half.
4. 간장을 찍다 to dip it in soy sauce.
5. 소스를 바르다 to spread the sauce on it.
6. 후추를 뿌리다 to sprinkle pepper on it.
7. 식초를 넣다 to add vinegar to it.
8. 껍질을 벗기다 to peel the skin off.
9. 사과(껍질)을 깎다
 to peel (the skin off) the apple.

Be careful

벗기다 to peel with your hands
깎다 to peel with a knife

❸ Describing a Restaurant

- 값이 싸다 to be cheap
- 맛있다 to be tasty
- 양이 많다 to be large in quantity
- 깨끗하다 to be clean
- 서비스가 좋다 to be of good service
- 손님이 많다 to have many customers
- 분위기가 좋다 to have a nice atmosphere
- 조용하다 to be quiet
- 유명하다 to be famous
- 메뉴가 다양하다 to have a diverse menu
- 젊은 사람들한테 인기가 많다
 to be popular among young peopl
- OO 전문점이다 (예: 두부 전문점)
 to spealize in OO (Ex. specialize in tofu)
- 입맛에 맞다 to suit one's taste
- 건강식이다 to be a healthy food
- 유기농 재료를 쓰다
 to use organic ingredients

Key Expressions

- 메뉴판 좀 갖다주세요. Please bring me the menu.
- 반찬 좀 더 주세요.
 Excuse me, please give me more side dishes.

Let's Talk!

Speaking Strategy — Agreeing

- **맞아요**. 한국 음식은 매운 편이죠. **You're right.** Korean food is pretty spicy.
- **그렇죠**? **맵죠**? **Right? Isn't** it spicy?
- 이거 좀 **맵지 않아요**? **Isn't** this a little spicy?

Eating Habits

❶ 평소 어떤 음식을 잘 먹어요?

❷ 보통 음식을 사 먹어요? 해 먹어요? 어떤 음식을 사 먹고 어떤 음식을 해 먹어요?
요리하는 것을 좋아해요? 어떤 음식을 잘 만들어요?

❸ 어떤 음식을 제일 좋아해요? 한국 음식 중에서 어떤 음식이 입에 잘 맞아요?
그 음식 맛이 어때요? 그 음식을 어디에서 먹었어요?

❹ 어떤 음식을 싫어해요? 한국 음식 중에서 못 먹는 음식이 있어요?
왜 그 음식을 못 먹어요? 혹시 음식 알레르기가 있어요?

❺ 자주 가는 식당이 있어요? 왜 거기에 자주 가요?

- ☐ 값에 비해 음식 맛이 좋은 편이에요.
- ☐ 싸고 양이 많아요.
- ☐ 가까워서 가기 편해요.
- ☐ 재료가 신선해요.
- ☐ 유기농 음식이에요.
- ☐ 집에서 만들 수 없는 맛이에요.
- ☐ 맛이 자극적이지 않아요.
- ☐ 기타

New Vocabulary

평소 as usual | 사 먹다 to buy food to eat | 해 먹다 to cook to eat | 알레르기 allergy | 양 amount | 에 비해 compared to | 유기농 음식 organic food | 자극적이다 to be pungent

Word Web

Appendix P. 317

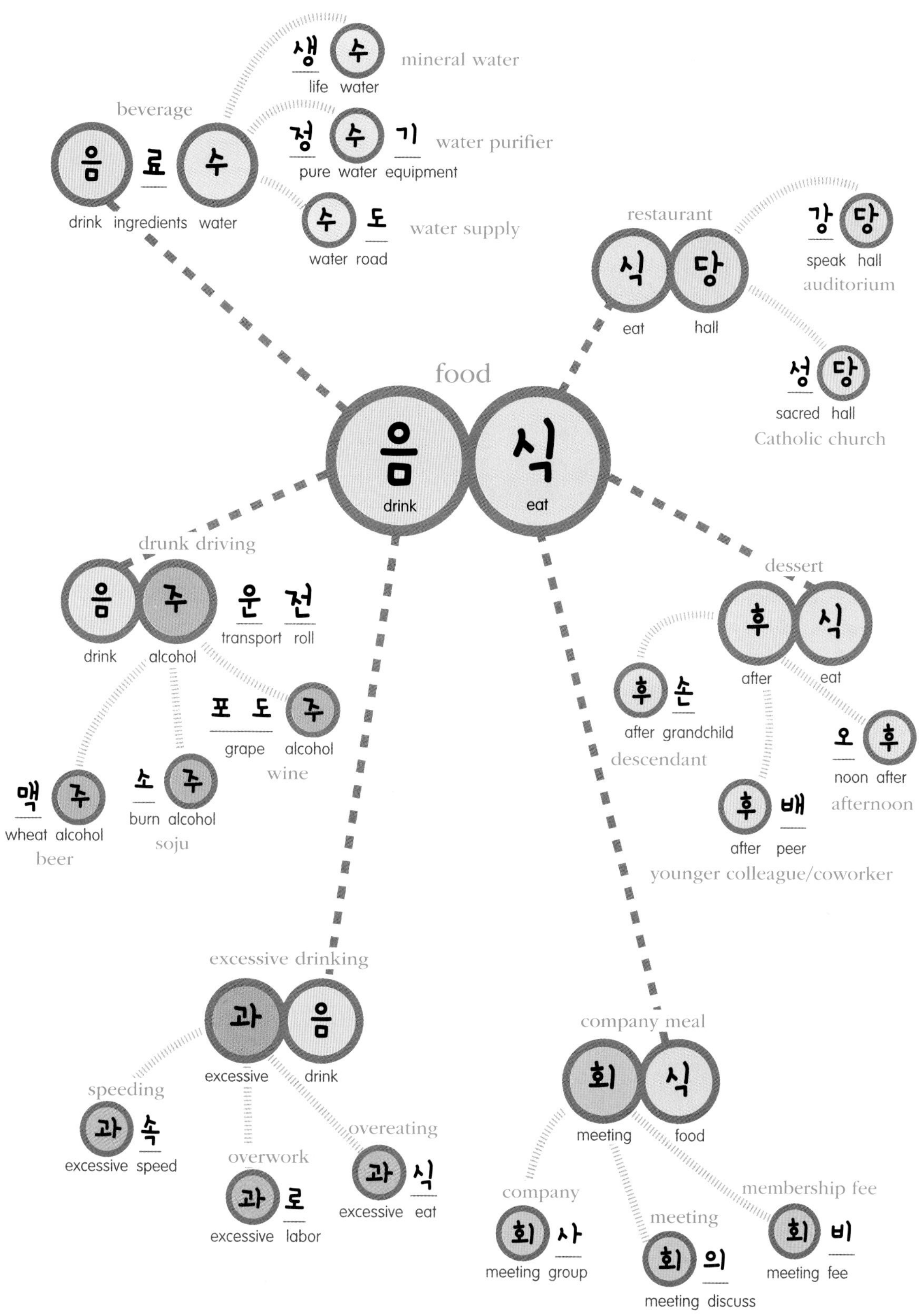

A Word on Culture

The Nuances of Describing Taste

• 시원하다 to feel refreshed, "hit the spot"

시원하다 originally means "a cool sensation," for example, a cold glass of juice provides coolness and refreshment. However, the use and meaning of 시원하다 have been greatly expanded.

Therefore, 시원하다 is not only used for cool beverages or cold soups but ironically hot soup and stews as well, since Koreans believe that hot soups and stews are refreshing and "hit the spot." Also, 시원하다 encompasses the refreshed feeling after a massage or sauna session or post-exercise.

In addition, the idea of 시원하다 is also used when someone solves a stressful problem, thereby being released from having the problem weigh heavily on one's mind.

Finally, 시원하다 may be used to describe a person who is not considered to be stuffy or overbearing, but rather straightforward and easy to get along with.

• 느끼하다 to be greasy

People who do not like oily foods describe greasy cuisine as 느끼하다. Also, instead of saying 싫다 about someone's sly action or way of speaking, one can say 느끼하다. In this context, it is often used as a negative expression to refer to men who crudely approach women.

• 고소하다 to be savory

고소하다 originally referred to the pleasant feeling of tasting something savory such as sesame oil or peanut butter. This word is also used to refer to the pleasant feeling one feels when something bad happens to a person you are not fond of. For example, one may use 고소하다 instead of 기분 좋다 to describe the slightly satisfying feeling of a selfish coworker getting caught by a superior for constantly evading work.

Chapter **06**

공공 규칙

Public Rules

Goals
- Asking Permission
- Talking about Rules
- Describing Objects in Detail
- Asking and Answering about Accommodations
- Making Appointments
- Asking and Answering about Company Rules
- Speaking about Appropriate Behavior in Company Culture
- Reacting to Something Someone Has Said

Grammar

❶ -아/어도 되다 "may"
-아/어야 되다 "must", "need to", "have to"

❷ -아/어 있다 expressing a resultant state that continues once an action is completed
-든지 "or"

❸ -(으)면 안 되다 "may not"
-네요 expressing realization

Grammar 1

-아/어도 되다 "may"

Appendix P. 269 

A 잠깐 들어가도 돼요?
May I come in for a second?

B 네, 들어오세요.
Yes, come in.

-아/어도 되다 is used as a question to ask permission to do an action or to ask whether a certain state is permissible. -아/어도 되다 is attached to verb stems. -(으)세요 may be used to grant permission. -아/어도 되다 is also used to express a general common sense rule or sociocultural norm. For these examples, -아/어도 되다 is attached to verbs, adjectives, and 이다.

- A 화장실 좀 써도 돼요? Could I use the bathroom?
  B 네, 그러세요. Yes, please go ahead.
- 회의는 끝났으니까 일찍 퇴근해도 돼요. The meeting is over, so you can leave work early.
- 녹차 물은 그렇게 뜨겁지 않아도 돼요. The water for the green tea doesn't have to be that hot.

-아/어야 되다 "must", "need to", "have to"

Appendix P. 270 

A 카드로 계산해도 돼요?
May I pay by card?

B 아니요, 현금으로 계산해야 돼요.
No, you must pay in cash.

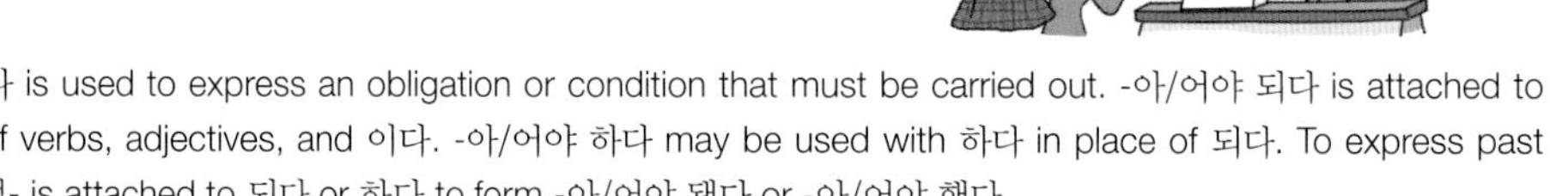

-아/어야 되다 is used to express an obligation or condition that must be carried out. -아/어야 되다 is attached to the stems of verbs, adjectives, and 이다. -아/어야 하다 may be used with 하다 in place of 되다. To express past tense, -았/었- is attached to 되다 or 하다 to form -아/어야 됐다 or -아/어야 했다.

- 한국에서는 신발을 벗고 집에 들어가야 돼요. In Korea, you have to take off your shoes and enter the house.
- 산에 가고 싶으면 지도가 꼭 있어야 해요. If you want to go to the mountains, you must have a map.
- 어제는 늦게까지 회사에서 일해야 했어요. Yesterday I had to work late at the company.

1 그림을 보고 '-아/어도 되다'를 사용하여 대화를 완성하세요.

(1)

A 화장실 좀 ______________ 돼요?

B 저쪽이에요. 쓰세요.

(2)

A 자리에 ______________ 돼요?

B 물론이죠. 앉으세요.

(3)

A 사진 좀 ______________ 돼요?

B 그러세요. 보세요.

(4)

A 이 옷을 ______________ 돼요?

B 그럼요. 입어 보세요.

2 다음에서 알맞은 답을 골라서 '-아/어야 되다'나 '-아/어야 하다'를 사용하여 문장을 완성하세요.

줄이다　　맡기다　　모으다　　지키다

(1) 여행 가고 싶으면 돈을 ______________ 돼요.

(2) 친구하고 비밀을 말하지 않기로 약속했으니까 비밀을 ______________ 해요.

(3) 살을 빼고 싶으면 매일 30분씩 운동하고 음식을 ______________ 돼요.

(4) 컴퓨터가 고장 났는데 혼자 고칠 수 없어요. 서비스 센터에 컴퓨터를 ______________ 돼요.

3 알맞은 답을 고르세요.

(1) 식당에서 밥 먹은 후 아직 돈을 안 냈어요. 집에 가기 전에 꼭
ⓐ 돈을 내도 돼요.
ⓑ 돈을 내야 돼요.

(2) 많이 바쁘면 저는 다른 사람하고 갈게요.
ⓐ 같이 안 가도 돼요.
ⓑ 같이 안 가야 돼요.

(3) 이건 중요한 얘기예요. 그러니까 엄마한테 반드시
ⓐ 얘기해도 돼요.
ⓑ 얘기해야 돼요.

(4) 아까 사무실 전화번호를 몰랐기 때문에 전화했는데 지금 알아요.
ⓐ 저한테 전화 안 해도 돼요.
ⓑ 저한테 전화 안 해야 돼요.

Conversation ❶

Track 16

유키 저기요, 뭐 좀 물어봐도 돼요?
직원 네, 말씀하세요.
유키 저 컴퓨터 좀 써도 돼요?
직원 쓰세요.
유키 이용료를 내야 돼요?
직원 아니요, 학생증이 있으면 무료예요.
유키 네. 아, 잠깐만요. 하나만 더 물어볼게요.
컴퓨터실이 몇 시에 문을 닫아요?
직원 평일에는 저녁 7시에 문을 닫아요.
유키 그럼, 주말에는요?
직원 토요일에는 오후 3시에 문을 닫고 일요일에는 문을 안 열어요.
유키 네. 여기 와이파이도 되죠?
직원 그럼요, 되죠.
유키 비밀번호가 뭐예요?
직원 이 비밀번호를 입력하면 돼요.
유키 감사합니다.

Yuki	Excuse me, may I ask you something?
Employee	Yes, go ahead.
Yuki	May I use that computer?
Employee	Please do.
Yuki	Do I need to pay a user fee?
Employee	No, it's free if you have a student ID.
Yuki	Okay. Ah, hold on. Let me ask you one more thing. What time does the computer room close?
Employee	On weekdays, we close at 7 PM.
Yuki	So, what about on weekends?
Employee	On Saturday, we close at 3 PM, and on Sundays, we are not open.
Yuki	Okay. Wireless Internet works here too, right?
Employee	Of course.
Yuki	How do I connect to the wireless Internet?
Employee	Just input this password.
Yuki	Thank you.

New Vocabulary ▸P. 325

말씀하다 | 이용료 | 내다 | 학생증 | 무료 | 평일 | 비밀번호 | 입력하다

New Expressions ▸P. 325

- 뭐 좀 물어봐도 돼요?
- 말씀하세요.
- 하나만 더 물어볼게요.

Tips

1 Honorific 말씀하시다 and 말씀드리다

말하다 becomes 말씀하시다 when the subject must be honored. In this conversation, 말씀하시다 is used by the employee to honor Yuki. Conversely, in the example below, 말씀드리다 is used to honor the object of the sentence (the one who is spoken to).

- 곧 사장님께서 **말씀하시겠습니다.** The president will speak soon.
- 제가 사장님께 **말씀드리겠습니다.** I will speak to the president.

2 Two Meanings of 그럼

In this conversation, the first 그럼요 expresses, in informal speech, that what was said is certain (of course). The second 그럼 is shortened from 그러면 and is used to introduce a new idea (if so, then).

- **그럼요**, 제가 정말 좋아하죠. Of course. I really like it.
- 피곤해요? **그럼**, 집에서 쉬세요.
Are you tired? If so, rest at home.

❶ Division of Time

1. 한 달 one month

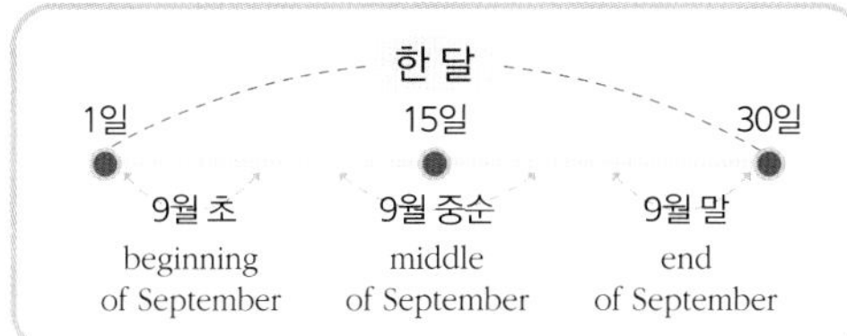

2. 1년 one year

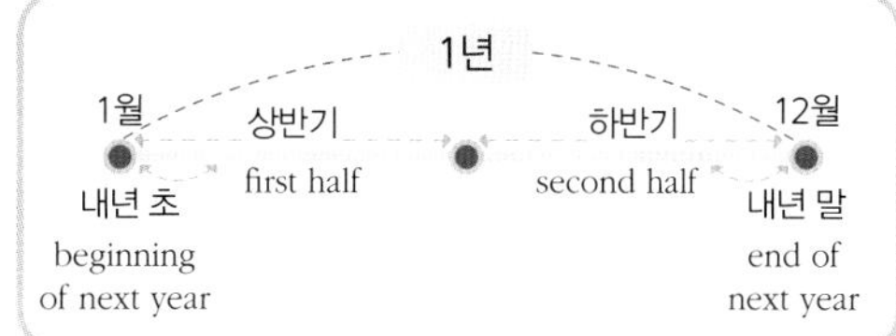

3. 10년 one decade

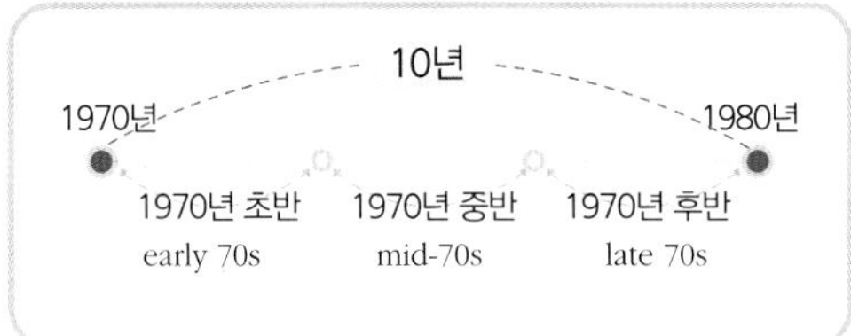

4. 100년 one century

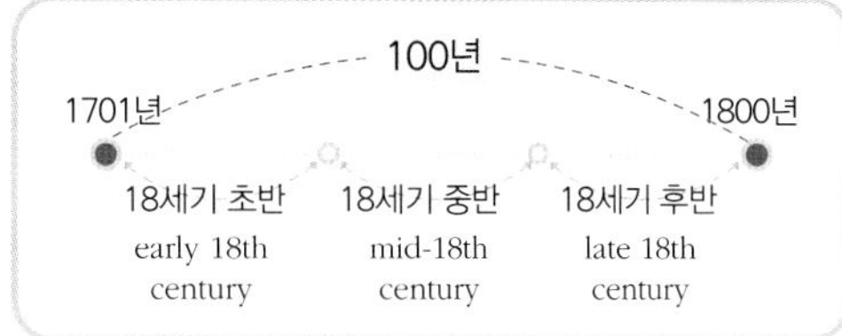

- 세금은 보통 **월말**에 내요. Tax is usually paid at the end of the month.
- **내년 초**에는 새 차를 사려고 해요. I plan to buy a new car at the beginning of next year.
- **1970년대 중반**에 이 노래가 유행했어요. This song was popular in the mid-70s.
- 이 건물은 **18세기 후반**에 만들어졌어요. This building was made at the end of the 18th century.

❷ Dates

1. 일 day (of the month)

3박 4일 3 nights 4 days
- 첫날 the first day
- 둘째 날 (= 그다음 날) the second day (= the next day)
- 셋째 날 the third day
- 넷째 날 (= 마지막 날) the fourth day (= the last day)

2. 주 week

한 달 one month
- 첫째 주 first week
- 둘째 주 second week
- 셋째 주 third week
- 넷째 주 (= 마지막 주) fourth week (= the last week)

- 입학 **첫날**에 긴장되기도 하고 설레기도 했어요. The first day I entered school, I was both nervous and excited.
- 매월 **첫째 주**와 **셋째 주** 일요일에 쉽니다. I rest on the first and third Sunday of every week.

❸ Reading Dates

- 2–3일: 이삼 일
  2 to 3 days
- 2–5일: 이 일에서 오 일
  2 to 5 days
- 2일–15일: 이 일부터 십오 일까지
  the 2nd to the 15th

- 이번 조사는 **3–4일(삼사 일)** 걸릴 거예요.
  This investigation will take 3 to 4 days.
- 시간이 **3–5일(삼 일에서 오 일)** 정도 더 필요해요.
  I need about 3 to 5 more days.
- 신청 기간은**15일–30일(십오 일부터 삼십 일까지)**예요.
  The application period is from the 15th to the 30th.

❹ Expressing Days

- 매주 **화, 목**은 3시에 수업이 끝나요.
  Class ends at 3 on Tuesday and Thursday every week.
- **월, 화** 드라마는 10시에 시작해요.
  On Monday and Tuesday, dramas start at 10.

Key Expressions
- 언제까지 해야 돼요?
  By when does this need to be done?
- 시간이 얼마나 더 필요해요?
  How much more time do you need?

Grammar 2

-아/어 있다 expressing a resultant state that continues once an action is completed

▶ Appendix P. 270

A 집에 불이 켜져 있어요.
The light in the house is turned on.

B 이상해요. 아까 불을 껐지요?
How strange. You just turned it off, right?

-아/어 있다 expresses a resultant state that continues once an action is completed. It is attached to verb stems. To express a state not continuing, -지 않다 is attached to the stem of 있다 in -아/어 있지 않다. -았/었- may also be attached to 있다 to form -아/어 있었다.

- 가방 안에 지갑하고 책이 들어 있어요. Inside the bag are a wallet and a book.
- 책에 이름이 쓰여 있지 않아요. There is no name written on the book.
- 조금 전에는 바닥에 아무것도 떨어져 있지 않았어요. Not long ago, nothing had fallen on the floor.

-든지 "or"

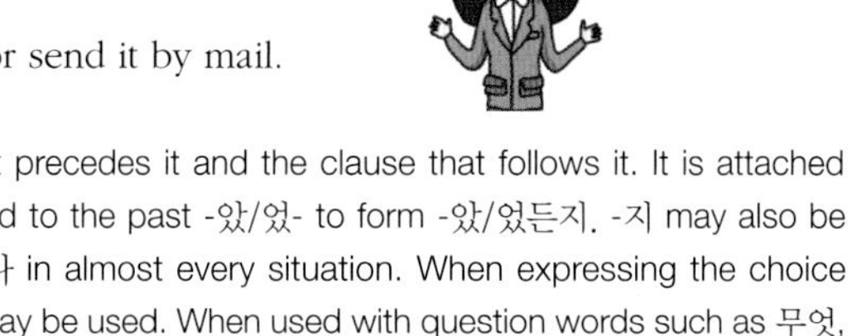

A 서류는 어떻게 내야 돼요?
How should I submit the document?

B 서류는 회사에 직접 내든지 우편으로 보내든지 하세요.
You can directly submit it to the company or send it by mail.

-든지 is used to offer a choice between the clause that precedes it and the clause that follows it. It is attached to verbs, adjectives, and 이다 and may also be attached to the past -았/었- to form -았/었든지. -지 may also be omitted, leaving -든. -든지 is interchangeable with -거나 in almost every situation. When expressing the choice between doing an action and not doing it, -든지 말든지 may be used. When used with question words such as 무엇, 누구, 언제, and 어디, it expresses that the choice does not matter.

- 남자든지 여자든지 상관없으니까 누구든지 오세요. It doesn't matter if you're male or female, so anyone can come.
- 미리 얘기했든 안 했든 지금 상황은 바뀌지 않아요.
  Whether we talked about it beforehand or not, the situation now doesn't change.
- 표를 이미 예약했으니까 가든지 말든지 마음대로 하세요.
  You've already booked your tickets, so feel free to go or not.
- 무엇을 먹든지 아무거나 잘 먹어요. It doesn't matter whatever we eat, since I'm not picky.

1 **그림을 보고 알맞은 답을 고르세요.**

(1)

ⓐ 의자에 남자가 앉고 있어요.
ⓑ 의자에 남자가 앉아 있어요.

(2)

ⓐ 공책에 글을 쓰고 있어요.
ⓑ 공책에 글이 쓰여 있어요.

(3)

ⓐ 조금 전에 책상 위에 노트북이 놓여 있어요.
ⓑ 조금 전에 책상 위에 노트북이 놓여 있었어요.

(4)

ⓐ 바지 주머니에 아무것도 들어 없어요.
ⓑ 바지 주머니에 아무것도 들어 있지 않아요.

2 보기 **와 같이 '-든지'를 사용하여 알맞게 바꿔 쓰세요.**

보기

- ☑ 매일 MP3로 듣기 연습해요.
- ☐ 한국 텔레비전을 많이 봐요.
- ☑ 한국 친구를 사귀어요.

➡ A 한국어 듣기는 어떻게 하면 잘해요?
B 매일 MP3로 듣기 연습하 든지
한국 친구를 사귀 든지 하면 돼요.

(1)

- ☑ 인터넷으로 사요.
- ☑ 여행사에 전화해요.
- ☐ 가족에게 부탁해요.

➡ A 이번 여행 비행기 표는 어떻게 살 거예요?
B ______________ 든지
______________ 든지 할 거예요.

(2)

- ☐ 극장에서 영화를 봐요.
- ☑ 공원에서 산책해요.
- ☑ 맛있는 음식을 먹어요.

➡ A 주말에 뭐 하고 싶어요?
B ______________ 든지
______________ 든지 하고 싶어요.

(3)

- ☑ 택시를 타요.
- ☑ 한국 사람에게 길을 물어봐요.
- ☐ 한국 친구에게 전화해요.

➡ A 길을 잃어버리면 어떻게 해요?
B ______________ 든지
______________ 든지 해요.

Conversation 2

Track 17

맥스 저, 이거 가져가도 돼요?

직원 물론이죠, 가져가세요.

맥스 지도도 있어요?

직원 여기 있어요.

맥스 여기에 숙박 시설도 나와 있어요?

직원 네, 어떤 숙박 시설을 찾으세요?

맥스 비싸지 않고 조용한 곳을 찾고 있어요.

직원 저기 탁자 위에 여러 가지 안내 책자가 놓여 있지요? 거기에 다양한 숙박 시설과 연락처가 나와 있어요.

맥스 여기에서 숙박 시설을 예약할 수 있어요?

직원 아니요, 여기에서는 예약이 안 돼요. 인터넷으로 예약하든지 직접 전화해서 물어보세요.

맥스 그럼, 여기에서 인터넷을 써도 돼요?

직원 그럼요, 이 컴퓨터를 쓰세요. 숙박 시설의 홈페이지에 들어가면 더 자세한 정보가 다양한 언어로 나와 있어요.

Max Excuse me, may I take this?

Employee Of course, please take it.

Max Do you also have a map?

Employee We have one here.

Max Is there also any information on accommodation?

Employee Yes, what kind of accommodation are you looking for?

Max I'm looking for a place that is inexpensive and quiet.

Employee You see all those information brochures on top of the table, right? There's a lot of information on accommodation and contact information in them.

Max Can I make lodging reservations here?

Employee No, you can't make them here. You can make a reservation on the Internet or call and ask about it.

Max Then may I use the Internet here?

Employee Sure. Use this computer. If you go on the website of the accommodation, there will be more detailed information in your respective language (lit. in various languages).

New Vocabulary ▸ P. 326

가져가다 | 물론 | 지도 | 숙박 시설 | 조용하다 | 곳 | 탁자 | 안내 책자 | 놓이다 | 예약하다 | 자세하다 | 정보

New Expressions ▸ P. 326

- 이거 가져가도 돼요?
- 물론이죠.
- 더 자세한 정보가 나와 있어요.

Tips

1 The Multiple Meanings of 되다

되다 has several meanings. First, it is used to express "possible" or "available" with words such as 시간, 돈, 예약. It is also used to express that a machine works. Generally, 되다 is used for the meaning "to be possible" and "to work" while 안 되다 is used for the opposite meaning "not to be possible" and "not to work".

- 오늘 배달**돼요**? Can it be delivered today?
- 어제부터 컴퓨터가 **안 돼요**.
  The computer has not been working since yesterday.

2 저기 over there vs. 거기 there

The main difference between 저기 and 거기 is that 저기 is used to indicate places that can be seen while 거기 is reserved for places that can't be seen.

- 내일 수업 후에 **저기**에서 만나요.
  Let's meet over there after class.
- 내일 콘서트가 있는데 **거기**에 가고 싶어요.
  There is a concert tomorrow, so I'd like to go there.

❶ Comparing Actions with Static States

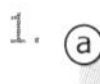

1. ⓐ

ⓑ

ⓐ 남자가 가고 있어요.
He is going.

ⓑ 남자가 가 있어요.
He is there.

2. ⓐ

ⓑ

ⓐ 여자가 창문을 닫고 있어요.
She is closing the window.

ⓑ 창문이 닫혀 있어요.
The window is closed.

3. ⓐ

ⓑ

ⓐ 남자가 이름을 쓰고 있어요.
He is writing a name.

ⓑ 이름이 쓰여 있어요.
The name is written.

4.

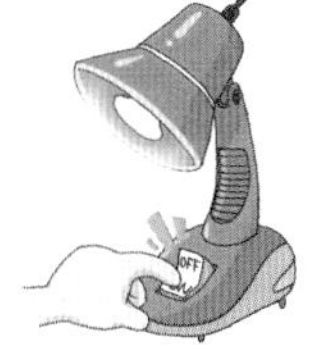

ⓐ 남자가 불을 켜고 있어요.
He is turning on the light.

ⓑ 불이 켜져 있어요.
The light is on.

5.

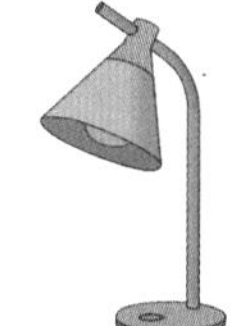

ⓐ 남자가 불을 끄고 있어요.
He is turning off the light.

ⓑ 불이 꺼져 있어요.
The light is off.

6.

ⓐ 남자가 책을 넣고 있어요.
He is putting the book in the bag.

ⓑ 책이 들어 있어요.
The book is inside the bag.

7.

ⓐ 여자가 컵을 놓고 있어요.
She is putting down the cup.

ⓑ 컵이 놓여 있어요.
The cup is on the table.

8.

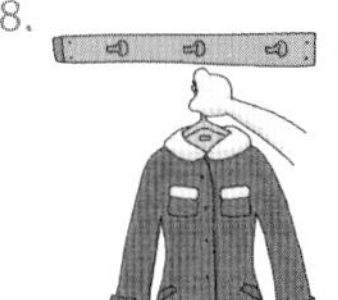

ⓐ 여자가 옷을 걸고 있어요.
She is hanging the clothes.

ⓑ 옷이 걸려 있어요.
The clothes are hanging.

9.

ⓐ 여자가 전화번호를 저장하고 있어요.
She is saving a phone number.

ⓑ 전화번호가 저장되어 있어요.
The phone number has been saved.

❷ Describing Static States

- 남자가 와 있어요. He is here.
- 얼굴이 그려져 있어요. The face is drawn.
- 이름표가 달려 있어요. The name tag is pinned on.
- 종이가 벽에 붙어 있어요. The paper is stuck on the wall.
- 종이가 떼어져 있어요. The paper is detached.
- 지갑이 떨어져 있어요. The wallet has fallen.
- 스마트폰이 물에 빠져 있어요. The smartphone is dropped in the water.
- 연필이 부러져 있어요. The pencil is broken.
- 창문이 깨져 있어요. The window is cracked.
- 표가 찢어져 있어요. The ticket is ripped.
- 종이가 구겨져 있어요. The paper is crumpled.

Key Expressions

- 어떤 상태예요?
  What kind of state is it in?
- 어떻게 되어 있어요?
  How is it?

Grammar ❸

-(으)면 안 되다 "may not"

A 여기에서는 사진을 찍으면 안 됩니다.
You may not take pictures here.

B 죄송합니다. 몰랐어요.
Sorry. I didn't know.

-(으)면 안 되다 is used to express the prohibition of an action or the limitation of a state. It is attached to the stems of verbs, adjectives, and 이다. The past tense -았/었- is attached to 되다 on -(으)면 안 되다. The negative is attached before -(으)면 안 되다, yielding -지 않으면 안 되다. In this negative usage, the obligation of the action is emphasized.

- 위험하니까 운전하면서 전화하면 안 돼요. It's dangerous, so you shouldn't call while driving.
- 환자니까 음식이 짜면 안 돼요. Since he is a patient, food should not be salty.
- 중학생이면 안 돼요. 고등학생부터 이 영화를 볼 수 있어요.
  Middle school students can't. Only high school students or older can watch this movie.
- 시험 때 신분증이 없으면 안 돼요. (= 신분증이 꼭 있어야 돼요.)
  You cannot do it without your ID at the time of the exam. (= ID is required.)

-네요 expressing realization

A 무선 인터넷이 잘 돼요?
Does the wireless Internet work well?

B 네, 진짜 빠르네요.
Yes, it's very fast.

-네요 is used to express the speaker's surprise at realizing a fact after directly experiencing something. It is especially used while looking at the listener to confirm that the listener has the same thought. -네요 is attached to the stems of verbs, adjectives, and 이다 when referring to a present fact. It is attached to -았/었- to form -았/었네요 to express a past fact.

- 외국인인데 한국어를 잘하시네요. You are a foreigner, but you speak Korean well.
- 벌써 7시네요. 퇴근할까요? It's already 7 o'clock. Should we call it a day?
- 오늘 멋지게 옷을 입었네요. 어디 가세요? You are dressed nicely today. Where are you going?

1 다음에서 알맞은 답을 골라서 '-(으)면 안 되다'를 사용하여 문장을 완성하세요.

늦게 오다	예약을 미루다	담배를 피우다	음악을 틀다

(1) 여기는 금연 구역이니까 여기에서 ______________________.

(2) 7시 정각에 출발하니까 이번에도 ______________________.

(3) 옆집에 방해가 되니까 밤늦게 큰 소리로 ______________________.

(4) 표가 몇 장 안 남았으니까 ______________________.

2 문장을 완성하도록 알맞은 것끼리 연결하세요.

(1) 예의가 아니니까 • • ⓐ 실수하면 안 돼요.

(2) 그날 전부 만나기로 했으니까 • • ⓑ 너무 빨리 말하면 안 돼요.

(3) 건강을 생각해야 하니까 • • ⓒ 이제부터 술을 마시면 안 돼요.

(4) 한국어를 잘 못하니까 • • ⓓ 고춧가루를 넣으면 안 돼요.

(5) 매운 것을 잘 못 먹으니까 • • ⓔ 어른에게 반말하면 안 돼요.

(6) 이번 발표는 아주 중요하니까 • • ⓕ 다른 약속을 잡으면 안 돼요.

3 알맞은 답을 고르세요.

(1) A 제 친구는 혼자 삼겹살 10인분을 먹어요.
B ⓐ 진짜 많이 먹네요.
ⓑ 삼겹살이 맛있네요.

(2) A 집에서 회사까지 5분밖에 안 걸려요.
B ⓐ 정말 가깝네요.
ⓑ 늦게 출발하네요.

(3) A 도서관이 3시에 문을 닫아요.
B ⓐ 일찍 닫네요.
ⓑ 책을 못 찾네요.

(4) A 지난주에 밤 12시까지 일했어요.
B ⓐ 힘드네요.
ⓑ 늦게까지 일했네요.

(5) A 어제 지갑을 잃어버렸어요.
B ⓐ 속상하시겠네요.
ⓑ 지갑을 찾았네요.

(6) A 드디어 운전 면허증을 땄어요.
B ⓐ 축하하네요.
ⓑ 차를 사야겠네요.

Conversation ❸

Track 18

리나 회사에 잘 다니고 있어요?

웨이 네, 회사 생활에 잘 적응하고 있어요.

리나 그런데 오늘은 정장을 안 입었네요. 회사에 안 갔어요?

웨이 갔다 왔어요. 그런데 우리 회사에서는 정장을 안 입어도 돼요.

리나 그래요? 회사 분위기가 자유롭네요.

웨이 네, 그런 편이에요. 특히 복장은 엄격하지 않아요.

리나 주중에도 청바지 같은 편한 옷을 입고 출근해도 돼요?

웨이 네, 마음대로 입어도 돼요. 하지만 회의 때에는 꼭 정장을 입어야 돼요.

리나 출퇴근 시간은 어때요?

웨이 정해진 시간은 없고 하루에 8시간 일하면 돼요.

리나 한국 회사는 회식도 자주 하는데, 회식에 빠져도 돼요?

웨이 회식에 빠지면 안 돼요. 하지만 술을 싫어하면 안 마셔도 돼요.

리나 좋네요. 자주 회식해요?

웨이 가끔 회식하는데, 회식 때 동료들과 얘기할 수 있어서 좋아요.

Rina Is your work going well?

Wei Yes, I'm adjusting well to company life.

Rina You're not wearing your suit today though. Did you not go to work?

Wei I already came back, but we don't have to wear suits at my company.

Rina Really? The office environment is quite relaxed, isn't it?

Wei Yes, it's somewhat relaxed. (lit. it's on the relaxed side.) The dress code is especially not strict.

Rina Even on weekdays, you can wear comfortable clothes like jeans to work?

Wei Yes, we can wear whatever we like (lit. as we please). However, we absolutely must wear a suit during meetings.

Rina How are the hours?

Wei There is no set time. We just have to work eight hours a day.

Rina In Korean companies, you have to eat out often with your coworkers. Are you allowed to skip company meals?

Wei We can't skip meals with our coworkers, but if someone doesn't like alcohol, they don't have to drink.

Rina Wow, that's nice. Do you have company meals often?

Wei We sometimes have company meals, but they are nice since I get to converse with my coworkers.

New Vocabulary ▸P. 326

다니다 | 적응하다 | 정장 | 갔다 오다 | 분위기 | 자유롭다 | 특히 | 엄격하다 | 출근하다 | 마음대로 | 꼭 | 정해진 시간 | 회식 | 빠지다 | 싫어하다 | 동료

New Expressions ▸P. 326

- (noun)에 잘 적응하고 있어요.
- 그런 편이에요.
- 마음대로 입어도 돼요.

Tips

1 Using -았/었- for Wearing Clothing

In Korean, both -고 있다 and the completion marker -았/었- are used to express wearing clothing. If the present tense is used, it expresses the action of putting on clothing.

- 민수는 지금 운동화를 **신고 있어요 (= 신었어요).**
  Minsu is putting on his shoes.
  ≠ 민수는 지금 운동화를 **신어요.**
  Minsu is wearing his shoes.

2 The Marker 대로

대로 is after nouns such as 사실 (fact), 약속 (promise), 마음 (heart), 규칙 (rule), and 법 (law) to express that the noun is the basis for action. When used after words such as 예상 (prediction), 생각 (thought), and 계획 (plan), it expresses that there is no change.

- 약속**대로** 제가 도와줄게요. As promised, I will help you.
- 예상**대로** 제주도는 정말 아름다웠어요.
  As expected, Jeju Island was very beautiful.

1 Before Finding a Job

- 일자리를 찾다 to search for a job
- 원서를 내다 to submit an application
- 면접을 보다 to have an interview
- 취직하다 to (succeed in) find(ing) a job

- 요즘 **일자리를 찾고** 있지만 **취직하기** 너무 어려워요.
  I'm looking for a job lately, but it's so hard to find one.
- 제 친구는 **원서**를 60번이나 냈지만 3번만 **면접**을 봤어요.
  My friend submitted sixty applications but only had three interviews.

2 Hanja Vocabulary Related to Work

근 (work)

- 출근하다 to go to work (out of home), to work
- 퇴근하다 to leave work
- 야근하다 to work overtime
- 결근하다 to be absent from work
- 근무하다 to be at work
- 교대 근무하다 to work a shift
- 재택근무하다 to work at home

직 (job)

- 취직하다 to (succeed in) find(ing) a job
- 휴직하다 to take a leave of absence
- 퇴직하다 to quit work
- 이직하다 to change jobs

3 Commonly Used Vocabulary in the Workplace

Meeting people

- 회의하다 to have a meeting
- 회식하다 to eat with coworkers

Making and giving reports

- 작성하다 to draw up (a report)
- 보고하다 to make a report
- 결재를 받다 to receive approval
- 발표하다 to give a presentation

Duties

- 일을 맡기다 to assign a job
- 일을 맡다 to take on a job
- (인사/재무/영업/홍보)을/를 담당하다 to be in charge of (human resources/finances/sales/publicity)

The work process

- 일이 잘되다 for work to be going well
- 일이 안되다 for work to not be going well

Expressions using 가다

- 휴가 가다 to go on vacation
- 출장 가다 to go on a business trip
- 연수 가다 to go training

Fortunate occurrences

- 월급을 받다 to receive a salary
- 월급이 오르다 for one's salary to be raised
- 승진하다 to be promoted

Unfortunate occurrences

- 일을 그만두다 to quit one's job
- 해고되다 to be fired
- 파업하다 to go on strike

- 이번에는 꼭 **승진해서 월급이 올랐으면** 좋겠어요. I hope that this time I will be promoted and my salary will be raised.
- 사업하고 싶어서 **일을 그만두고** 가게를 차렸어요. I quit my job and opened a store because I wanted to start a business.
- 부장님이 이번 프로젝트를 저에게 **일을 맡겨서** 어제부터 제가 **맡게** 됐어요.
  My boss assigned this project to me so starting yesterday, I began working on it (lit. took it on).
- 일을 잘하면 회사에서 인정받을 수 있을 거예요. **일이 잘되었으면** 좋겠어요.
  If you do your job well, you will receive recognition. I hope I do my job well (lit. my job goes well).

Key Expressions

- 큰 차이가 있네요.
  There's quite a big difference, isn't there?
- 별 차이가 없네요.
  There isn't much of a difference, is there?

Let's Talk!

Speaking Strategy **Comparing Korea with My Country**

- **우리 나라는 한국처럼** My country is **the same as** Korea in that...
- **우리 나라는 한국과 비슷하게** My country is **similar to** Korea in that...
- **우리 나라는 한국과 달리** My country is **different from** Korea in that...

❶ 한국 생활에서 필요한 정보는 어떻게 찾아요?
거기에 어떤 정보가 나와 있어요?

❷ 어떤 정보가 도움이 돼요?
어떤 정보가 도움이 안 돼요?

□ 날씨	□ 여행	□ 맛집	□ 뉴스
□ 대중문화	□ 문화	□ 쇼핑	□ 요리
□ 영화 리뷰	□ 길찾기	□ 패션	□ 역사

❸ 한국을 소개하는 웹사이트나 블로그를 만들 거예요. 한국에 대한 어떤 정보를 더 자세히 넣고 싶어요?
한국 생활에서 유용한 정보를 생각해 보세요.

좋은 점	안 좋은 점	신기한 점
1. ______	1. ______	1. ______
2. ______	2. ______	2. ______
3. ______	3. ______	3. ______

한국 지하철 요금이 정말 싼데 깨끗하기도 해서 정말 좋아요. 게다가 지하철에서 무선 인터넷이 되니까 정말 편리해요.

한국은 우리 나라와 달리 AS 센터의 서비스가 정말 빨라요. AS를 신청하면 그날이나 그다음 날에 결과가 나와요. 많이 기다리지 않아도 돼서 정말 편해요.

한국에서는 중국처럼 인터넷으로 할 수 있는 것이 많아서 좋아요. 또 인터넷이 빨라서 저는 인터넷으로 쇼핑도 하고 여러 가지 정보도 쉽게 찾아요. 인터넷을 못 하면 한국 생활이 불편할 거예요.

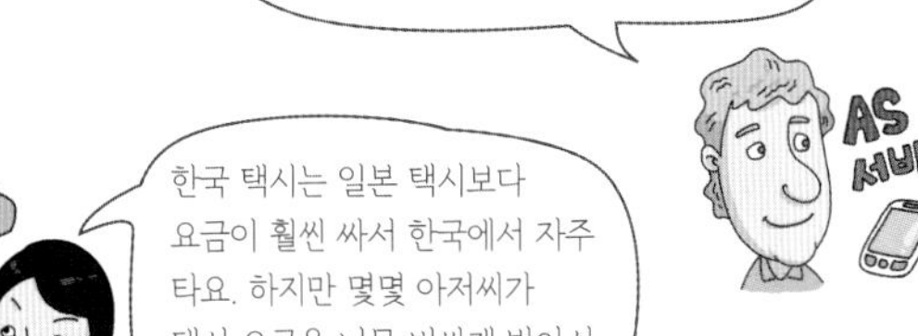

한국 택시는 일본 택시보다 요금이 훨씬 싸서 한국에서 자주 타요. 하지만 몇몇 아저씨가 택시 요금을 너무 비싸게 받아서 바가지를 썼어요.

New Vocabulary

도움이 되다 to be helpful | 유용하다 to be useful | 훨씬 much more | 바가지를 쓰다 to be ripped off | 신청하다 to apply

Word Web

Appendix P. 318

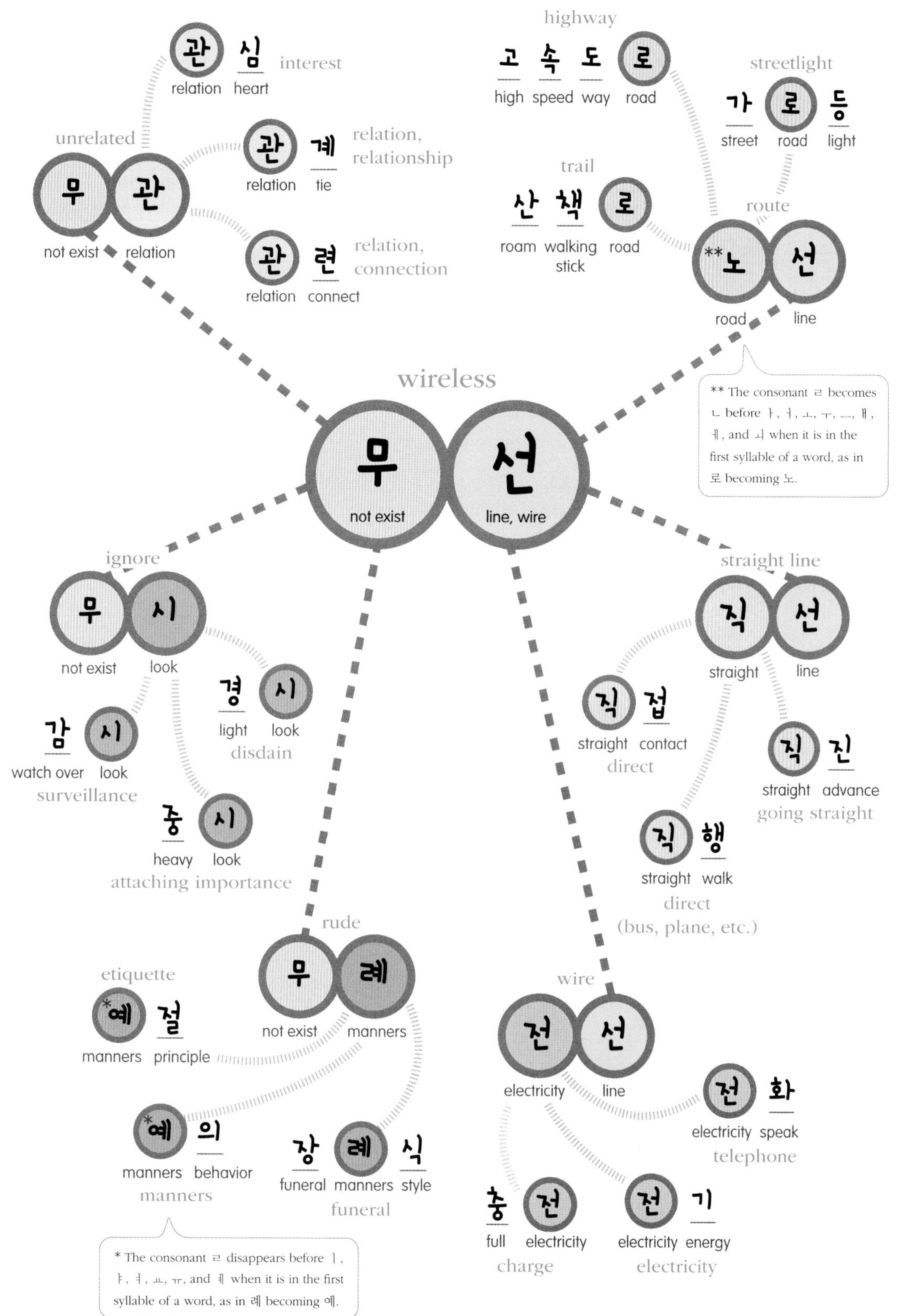

Korean Cultural Awareness

• 눈치가 없다 to be tactless, have no sense, be dull

눈치 is an essential skill that one must have in Korean society. 눈치 refers to the ability to tell how someone else is feeling even when they do not say anything. Because it has been a virtue in East Asia since ancient times not to express one's feelings, 눈치 has been considered a social skill. If one does not have 눈치, the situation generally becomes awkward. Because a person without 눈치 will be unable to read their superiors' feelings, they will experience difficulty in society. Conversely, a 눈치 빠른 (lit. fast sense) person will have a relatively easy time in the community as they will be able to understand their superiors' unsaid feelings.

• 눈치를 채다 to sense

눈치를 채다 expresses the action of understanding an event, situation, or atmosphere based only upon feeling and without words. Because a 눈치가 빠른 person can sense things right away, he/she can quickly find out secrets one means to hide or emotions one tries to conceal. Conversely, a 눈치가 느린 person is clueless as to what is going on even when hints are given.

• 눈치를 보다 to read one's expression

눈치를 보다 expresses the action of observing someone's mood or feelings. 눈치가 보이다 is the passive form and refers to a situation in which one must be sensible. For example, one can imagine a situation in which a husband senses that his wife is angry, so he decides not to go out to have a drink with his friend as he had planned. It is crucial to have 눈치, but someone who has too much 눈치 will go to lengths to please another person without regard for him/herself, giving a very undignified impression. 눈치를 준다 expresses trying to send a message to someone with one's eyes rather than saying something.

Chapter **07**

집

In the House

Goals
- Talking about the Pros of One's House
- Talking about the Cons of One's House
- Talking about Looking for a House
- Disagreeing with an Opinion
- Explaining Household Problems
- Giving Reasons
- Proposing Solutions

Grammar

❶ -기 쉽다/어렵다 "to be easy to/to be difficult to"
-게 되다 "to become", "to end up"

❷ -기 때문에 "because"
-기는요 expressing denial of a statement

❸ -거든요 expressing and emphasizing a reason
-지 그래요? expressing a gentle suggestion

Grammar 1

-기 쉽다/어렵다 (좋다/나쁘다/힘들다, 편하다/불편하다)

"to be easy to/to be difficult to"
("to be good to/to be bad to/to be hard to", "to be convenient to/to be inconvenient to")

C.C P. 298

A 깨지기 쉬운 물건이니까 조심하세요.
Be careful because it breaks easily (lit. it is a thing that breaks easily).

B 알겠습니다.
Okay.

This grammar pattern is used to express the possibility of an action or state by attaching -기 and words like 쉽다 (to be easy), 어렵다 (to be difficult), 좋다 (to be good), 나쁘다 (to be bad), 힘들다 (to be hard), 편하다 (to be convenient), 불편하다 (to be inconvenient). -았/었- may not be attached to -기, but the adjective following -기. Markers such as 가 and 도 may be attached to -기.

- 공원이 가깝고 교통도 편해서 살기 좋아요.
  It's close to the park and the transportation is convenient, so it's a good place to live.
- 초급 때 한국어 단어를 발음하기 어려웠어요. When I was a beginner, it was difficult to pronounce Korean words.
- 5층까지 계단으로 올라가기가 힘들 거예요. It will be difficult to take the stairs to the 5th floor.

-게 되다 "to become", "to end up"

C.C P. 297

A 왜 축구 경기를 보러 안 갔어요?
Why didn't you go see the soccer game?

B 비 때문에 못 가게 됐어요.
I ended up not being able to go because of the rain.

-게 되다 is used to express a resultant state coming about by external factors rather than the speaker's intent. If the state has already come about, -게 됐다 is often used. -게 되다 is attached to the stems of verbs and adjectives.

- 일찍 출발했는데 길이 막혀서 회의 시간에 늦게 됐어요.
  I left early, but the road was blocked so I ended up late for the meeting.
- 처음에는 매운 음식을 못 먹었는데 지금은 잘 먹을 수 있게 됐어요.
  At first, I couldn't eat spicy food, but now I can eat it well.
- 텔레비전을 너무 많이 보면 눈이 나쁘게 돼요. Watching too much TV can end up hurting your eyes.

Quiz Yourself

▸Answers P. 313

1 **알맞은 답을 고르세요.**

(1) 동료하고 사이가 좋아서
ⓐ 일하기 좋아요.
ⓑ 일하기 싫어요.

(2) 옷이 몸에 너무 딱 끼니까
ⓐ 입기 편해요.
ⓑ 입기 불편해요.

(3) 오늘은 날씨가 따뜻하니까
ⓐ 산책하기 좋아요.
ⓑ 산책하기 나빠요.

(4) 발음이 헷갈려서
ⓐ 외우기 쉬워요.
ⓑ 외우기 어려워요.

(5) 윗집의 소음 때문에
ⓐ 살기 좋아요.
ⓑ 살기 힘들어요.

(6) 매일 똑같은 잔소리는
ⓐ 듣기 좋아요.
ⓑ 듣기 싫어요.

2 **다음에서 알맞은 답을 골라서 '-게 되다'를 사용하여 문장을 완성하세요.**

짜다 잘하다 적응하다 그만두다

(1) 취직한 지 얼마 안 돼서 건강 때문에 회사를 ______________.

(2) 보통 음식을 싱겁게 하는데 이번에는 음식이 ______________.

(3) 처음에는 회사 생활이 너무 힘들었는데 동료들 덕분에 잘 ______________.

(4) 처음에는 누구나 듣기를 어려워하지만 많이 들으면 ______________.

3 **문장을 완성하도록 알맞은 것끼리 연결하세요.**

(1) 이 일을 혼자 하기 힘들면 •
(2) 일단 그 사람의 얘기를 들으면 •
(3) 요리책이 잘 설명되어 있어서 •
(4) 대학교 때 동아리에서 만나서 •
(5) 전에는 사람들과 쉽게 어울리지 못했는데 •

• ⓐ 한국 음식을 만들기 어렵지 않았어요.
• ⓑ 다른 사람에게 도움을 요청하세요.
• ⓒ 그때부터 사귀게 됐어요.
• ⓓ 지금은 잘 어울리게 됐어요.
• ⓔ 그 사람이 마음에 들게 될 거예요.

Conversation ❶

Track 19

유키 지금 어디에서 살아요?

케빈 이태원에 살아요.

유키 동네가 어때요?

케빈 조용하고 깨끗해서 살기 편해요.

유키 교통은 편리해요?

케빈 네, 지하철역도 가깝고 버스 정류장까지도 얼마 안 걸려요.

유키 집은 어때요?

케빈 방과 화장실이 두 개씩 있고 거실과 주방이 따로 있어요.

유키 집세는 싸요?

케빈 아니요, 집세는 좀 비싸요. 하지만 그거 빼고 나머지는 다 괜찮아요. 집 근처에 공원이 있어서 산책하기도 좋아요.

유키 집은 어떻게 찾았어요?

케빈 제 친구가 전에 이 집에 살았어요. 그 친구가 한국을 떠나면서 이 집을 소개해서 살게 됐어요.

유키 그랬군요.

Yuki Where do you live now?

Kevin I live in Itaewon.

Yuki How's the neighborhood?

Kevin It's convenient to live in because it's quiet and clean.

Yuki Is the commute convenient?

Kevin Yes, the subway station is close and the bus stop also doesn't take long to get to.

Yuki How's your house?

Kevin There are two rooms and two bathrooms, as well as a living room and kitchen.

Yuki Is the rent cheap?

Kevin No, the rent is a little expensive, but apart from that, the rest is fine. There's also a park near my house, so it's nice to take walks.

Yuki How did you find your house?

Kevin My friend lived in this house before. That friend left Korea so he showed it to me and I ended up living here.

Yuki I see.

New Vocabulary ▸ P. 326

동네 | 깨끗하다 | 편하다 | 교통 | 거실 | 주방 | 집세 | 나머지 | 떠나다

New Expressions ▸ P. 326

- (noun)이/가 어때요?
- 얼마 안 걸려요.
- 그거 빼고 나머지는 다 괜찮아요.

Tips

1 Markers Used Together with the Verb 살다

The markers 에 and 에서 may both be used with the verb 살다.

- 지금은 기숙사**에** 살아요. I live in a dormitory now.
- 한국을 떠날 때까지 우리 집**에서** 같이 살아요. Until you leave Korea, let's live together.

2 The Suffix 씩

씩 is used after quantity nouns and expresses splitting into certain quantities (each) or repetition (every).

- 빵과 우유를 하나**씩** 가져가세요. Take a piece of bread and a glass of milk.
- 매일 2시간**씩** 운동해요. I exercise for two hours every day.

1 Household Items

1. 방 Room

① 서랍장 dresser ② 옷장 closet ③ 이불 blanket
④ 침대 bed ⑤ 베개 pillow ⑥ 스탠드 desk lamp
⑦ 화장품 cosmetics ⑧ 화장대 vanity ⑨ 휴지통 wastebasket

2. 거실 Living Room

① 선반 shelf ② 벽 wall ③ 화분 flower pot ④ 그림 painting
⑤ 소파 sofa ⑥ 탁자 table ⑦ 천장 ceiling ⑧ 커튼 curtain
⑨ 텔레비전 television ⑩ TV장 TV cabinet

3. 서재 Study

① 책장 bookshelf ② 의자 chair ③ 블라인드 blinds
④ 책꽂이 bookcase ⑤ 시계 clock ⑥ 달력 calendar
⑦ 책상 desk

4. 화장실 Bathroom

① 욕조 bathtub ② 수도꼭지 faucet ③ 세면대 sink
④ 칫솔 toothbrush ⑤ 치약 toothpaste ⑥ 빗 comb ⑦ 비누 soap
⑧ 거울 mirror ⑨ 수건 washcloth ⑩ 변기 toilet ⑪ 휴지 tissue

5. 주방 Kitchen

① 정수기 water purifier ② 냉장고 refrigerator ③ 전자레인지 microwave
④ 냄비 pot ⑤ 주전자 kettle ⑥ 가스레인지 stove ⑦ 주방 후드 kitchen hood
⑧ 전기밥솥 electric rice cooker ⑨ 싱크대 sink ⑩ 찬장 cupboard
⑪ 식기세척기 dishwasher

2 Other Parts of the House

- 현관 entrance
- 계단 stairs
- 옥상 roof
- 창고 storage room
- 주차장 garage
- 베란다 veranda
- 정원 garden
- 마당 yard

Key Expressions

- 화장실을 각자/따로 써요.
  We each have our own bathroom.
  (lit. We use the bathroom separately.)
- 화장실을 공동으로 써요.
  We share the bathroom.
  (lit. We use the bathroom together.)

Grammar 2

-기 때문에 "because"

Appendix P. 271 

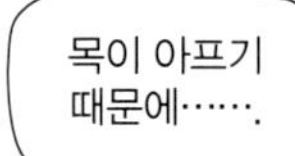

A 왜 음식을 안 먹어요?
Why aren't you eating?

B 목이 아프기 때문에 음식을 먹을 수 없어요.
I can't eat because my throat hurts.

-기 때문에 is used to express the reason for an event or situation. -기 때문에 is used after the reason, and the result follows. -기 때문에 is attached to the stem of verbs, adjectives, and 이다. If it is attached after -았/었-, it becomes -았/었기 때문에. -기 때문에 may not be used as the cause or reason for the command -(으)세요 or the proposal -(으)ㅂ시다.

- 이 일은 중요하기 때문에 먼저 끝내야 해요. This work is important, so we have to finish it first.
- 음식을 만들지 않기 때문에 밖에서 음식을 사 먹어요. We don't cook, so we buy food outside.
- 돈이 필요했기 때문에 학생 때부터 일하기 시작했어요.
  I started working when I was a student because I needed money.

-기는요 expressing denial of a statement

A 진수 씨, 노래 잘하죠?
Jinsu, you sing well, don't you?

B 노래를 잘하기는요. 정말 못해요.
I don't sing well. I really can't sing.

-기는요 is used to oppose someone's opinion politely. It is only used in speech and is also contracted to -긴요. -기는요 is attached to the stems of verbs and adjectives, while -은/는요 is attached to nouns. -기는요 may not be used with -았/었-. When opposing someone's opinion politely, -(으)ㄴ/는데요 is often attached, following the clause using -기는요, to what the speaker believes is true.

- A 한국어 발음이 쉽지요? It's easy to pronounce Korean, right?
  B 발음이 쉽긴요. 발음 때문에 자신이 없는데요.
  It's not easy to pronounce. I'm not confident about my pronunciation.
- A 어제 일 다 했어요? Did you finish all your work yesterday?
  B 다 하기는요. 아직 반도 못 했는데요. I didn't finish it all. I haven't even done half of it yet.

▸Answers P. 313

1 **알맞은 답을 고르세요.**

(1) ⓐ 배고프기 때문에 / ⓑ 배고프니까 먼저 밥부터 먹읍시다.

(2) 비가 와서 ⓐ 위험하니까 / ⓑ 위험하기 때문에 빠르게 운전하지 마세요.

(3) 한 달 전부터 여행 가고 ⓐ 싶기 때문에 / ⓑ 싶었기 때문에 미리 호텔을 알아봤어요.

(4) 그 사람은 ⓐ 학생 때문에 / ⓑ 학생이기 때문에 돈을 안 내도 돼요.

(5) 이상한 ⓐ 직장 상사 때문에 / ⓑ 직장 상사이기 때문에 어쩔 수 없이 회사를 그만뒀어요.

(6) 그냥 집에 돌아갔어요. 왜냐하면 친구가 갑자기 약속을 ⓐ 취소하기 / ⓑ 취소했기 때문이에요.

2 **'-기는요'를 사용하여 대화를 완성하세요.**

(1) A 저 남자가 멋있죠?
B ______________________. 옷도 이상하게 입었는데요.

(2) A 제가 요리를 못해요.
B ______________________. 아주 잘하시는데요.

(3) A 준비가 힘들죠?
B ______________________. 저는 별로 하는 것도 없는데요.

(4) A 숙제 안 했죠?
B ______________________. 일주일 전에 벌써 끝냈는데요.

(5) A 항상 저를 도와주셔서 고마워요.
B ______________________. 제가 오히려 도움을 많이 받았는데요.

(6) A 정말 미인이시네요.
B ______________________. 아니에요.

3 **밑줄 친 것을 고치세요.**

(1) 바람이 많이 <u>불기 때문에</u> 옷을 따뜻하게 입으세요. ➡

(2) 지난주에 전화를 <u>받기 때문에</u> 그 얘기를 알고 있어요. ➡

(3) 저 <u>친구들이기 때문에</u> 기분이 상했어요. ➡

(4) <u>피곤하기 때문에</u> 푹 쉬세요. ➡

Conversation 2

Track 20

새라 웨이 씨 동네는 어때요? 살기 좋아요?

웨이 살기 좋기는요. 여러 가지 불편해요.

새라 그래요? 뭐가 문제예요?

웨이 우선 집에서 직장까지 너무 멀기 때문에 출퇴근이 너무 불편해요.

새라 시간이 얼마나 걸려요?

웨이 두 시간이나 걸려요.

새라 시간이 너무 많이 걸리네요.

웨이 그리고 주변이 시끄럽기 때문에 집에서 일하기도 어려워요.

새라 문제네요. 집은 마음에 들어요?

웨이 아니요, 집도 너무 좁고 오래됐어요. 가끔 벌레가 나오기도 해요.

새라 그럼, 이사하면 어때요?

웨이 저도 지금 생각 중이에요.

새라 사실은 저도 집이 불편해서 이사를 생각하고 있어요.

웨이 그래요? 그럼, 우리 같이 좋은 집을 찾아봐요.

Sarah Wei, how is your neighborhood? Is it nice to live in?

Wei It isn't nice to live in at all. A lot of things are inconvenient.

Sarah Really? What's the problem?

Wei First, it's so inconvenient to commute to work because my house is so far.

Sarah How long does it take?

Wei It takes two hours.

Sarah Wow, it really does take a long time.

Wei It's also hard to work at home because the area is loud.

Sarah That's a real problem. Do you like your house?

Wei No, my house is also too small and old. Sometimes, there are even bugs.

Sarah Then what about moving?

Wei I'm thinking about that now, as well.

Sarah Actually, I'm thinking about moving, too, because my house is inconvenient.

Wei Really? Then let's look for a nice house together.

New Vocabulary ▸P. 326

여러 가지 | 불편하다 | 우선 | 직장 | 주변 | 마음에 들다 | 오래되다 | 벌레 | 이사하다 | 생각 중

New Expressions ▸P. 327

- 뭐가 문제예요?
- 집은 마음에 들어요?
- 저도 지금 생각 중이에요.

Tips

1 The Marker (이)나

The marker (이)나 is used after a noun to express that the number or extent is surprising because it is greater than one would expect.

- 혼자 고기 10인분**이나** 먹었어요.
  I ate ten orders of meat by myself.
- 벌써 반**이나** 끝냈어요.
  Half of it is already done.

2 The Expression of 중

중 is attached after nouns such as 생각 (thought), 고민 (worry), 통화 (call), 회의 (meeting), 식사 (meal), 외출 (going out), 공사 (construction), 수리 (repair), and 사용 (usage) to express that something is presently happening (similar to -고 있다).

- 친구한테 전화했는데 **통화 중**이에요.
  I called my friend but he is on the phone (with someone else).
- 1층 화장실이 **수리 중**이니까 2층으로 가세요.
  Go to the second floor because the bathroom on the first floor is under repair.

Describing Conditions at Home

1.

밝다 to be bright

어둡다 to be dark

2.

조용하다 to be quiet

시끄럽다 to be loud

3.

넓다 to be spacious

좁다 to be cramped

4.

따뜻하다 to be warm

춥다 to be cold

5.

깨끗하다
to be clean

더럽다 (지저분하다)
to be dirty (messy)

6.

새 집이다
to be a new house
지은 지 얼마 안 됐다
to have been recently built

오래되다
to be old

1. (월세가) 싸다 (for the monthly rent) to be cheap
   (월세가) 비싸다 (for the monthly rent) to be expensive
2. (동네가) 안전하다 (for the neighborhood) to be safe
   (동네가) 위험하다 (for the neighborhood) to be dangerous
3. 교통이 편리하다
   transportation (from this area) is convenient
   교통이 불편하다
   transportation (from this area) is inconvenient
4. 주변 환경이 좋다
   for the surrounding environment to be good
   주변 환경이 나쁘다
   for the surrounding environment to be bad
5. 최신식이다 to be the latest style
   구식이다 to be old-fashioned
6. 집 주변에 공기가 좋다
   for the air quality around the house to be good
   집 주변에 공기가 나쁘다
   for the air quality around the house to be bad
7. 전망이 좋다 for the view to be good
   전망이 안 좋다 for the view to not be good
8. 집주인이 친절하다 for the landlord to be kind
   집주인이 불친절하다 for the landlord to be unkind
9. 바람이 잘 통하다 to be well ventilated
   바람이 안 통하다 to be stuffy
10. 햇빛이 잘 들어오다 to be well-lit (by the sun)
    햇빛이 안 들어오다 to not be well-lit (by the sun)
11. 수납공간이 많다 for there to be a lot of storage space
    수납공간이 없다 for there not to be much storage space

Key Expressions

- 월세가 한 달에 (50만 원)쯤 해요.
  The monthly rent is about (500,000 won) a month.
- 월세가 한 달에 (50만 원) 좀 넘어요.
  The monthly rent is slightly more than (500,000 won) a month.
- 월세가 한 달에 (50만 원) 좀 안 돼요.
  The monthly rent is slightly less than (500,000 won) a month.

Grammar 3

-거든요 expressing and emphasizing a reason

A 왜 같이 안 가요?

Why aren't you going with me?

B 오늘 아르바이트가 있거든요.

I have my part-time job today.

-거든요 is used to express the speaker's thought or reason about a preceding statement or question. An action, situation, or question precedes the usage of -거든요 to express the reason or basis. It is only used in speech and not in writing. Because -거든요 gives the feeling of teaching the listener a fact that they were unaware of, it is generally used with close friends or someone who is younger and is not used with older people. -거든요 is attached to the stems of verbs, adjectives, and 이다. If the reason or basis has already been completed, -았/었- is attached in front of -거든요 to form -았/었거든요.

- 비빔밥을 드세요. 이 식당은 비빔밥이 제일 맛있거든요. Eat bibimbap. This restaurant has the best bibimbap.
- 제가 제임스를 잘 알아요. 제 친구거든요. I know James well. He's my friend.
- A 왜 이렇게 피곤해 보여요? Why do you look so tired?
  B 어제 잠을 못 잤거든요. I couldn't sleep yesterday.

-지 그래요? expressing a gentle suggestion

A 많이 아파요? 그럼 병원에 가 보지 그래요?

Are you very sick? Why don't you go to the hospital?

B 아니에요. 괜찮아요.

No, it's okay.

-지 그래요? is used to express a gentle suggestion or some advice for the listener. It is attached to the stems of verbs, and it is generally used in speech when one is in a comfortable atmosphere. When suggesting the listener not to do something, -지 말다 is added to make -지 말지 그래요? When asking someone why they did not do something, -지 그랬어요? may be used, but because there is a slight accusatory connotation, this form may only be used with younger people or of the same age.

- 배부르면 그만 먹지 그래요? Why don't you stop eating if you're full?
- 머리가 아프면 오늘 밖에 나가지 말지 그래요? If you have a headache, why not stay indoors?
- 늦었는데 택시를 타지 그랬어요? 그러면 늦지 않았을 거예요.
  Since it's late, why don't you take a taxi? Then you wouldn't be too late.

1 두 문장이 이어지도록 알맞은 것끼리 연결하세요.

(1) 좀 천천히 말해 주세요.	•	• ⓐ 밤에 늦게 자거든요.
(2) 담배를 꺼 주시겠어요?	•	• ⓑ 길이 많이 막히거든요.
(3) 제가 오늘 집까지 태워 줄게요.	•	• ⓒ 오늘 차를 가져왔거든요.
(4) 출근 시간에는 지하철을 타요.	•	• ⓓ 여기는 금연 구역이거든요.
(5) 보통 아침에 늦게 일어나는 편이에요.	•	• ⓔ 제가 아직 한국어를 잘 못하거든요.

2 다음에서 알맞은 답을 골라서 '-거든요'를 사용하여 문장을 완성하세요.

있다	살다	잘하다	다르다	오다

(1) 저 사람을 믿지 마세요. 저 사람은 거짓말을 ________________.

(2) 저는 독일로 자주 출장 가요. 독일에 우리 회사 지사가 ________________.

(3) 마크가 한자를 조금 읽을 수 있어요. 전에 중국에서 ________________.

(4) 내일 공항에 마중 나가야 해요. 친구가 한국에 ________________.

(5) 저는 이 빵집에서만 빵을 사요. 다른 빵집하고 맛이 ________________.

3 알맞은 답을 고르세요.

(1) A 보일러가 자꾸 고장 나요.

B 그럼, ⓐ 새 보일러로 바꾸지 그래요?
ⓑ 새 보일러로 바꾸지 말지 그래요?

(2) A 우산이 없어서 비를 맞았어요.

B 오는 길에 편의점에서 ⓐ 우산을 사지 그래요?
ⓑ 우산을 사지 그랬어요?

(3) A 친구가 기분이 안 좋아요.

B 그럼, 지금 ⓐ 얘기해 보지 그래요? 얘기는 나중에 하는 게 좋겠어요.
ⓑ 얘기하지 말지 그래요?

(4) A 어제 연락 못 해서 미안해요. 오늘 약속이 취소됐어요.

B ⓐ 미리 전화해 주지 그래요?
ⓑ 미리 전화해 주지 그랬어요?

Conversation ❸

Track 21

리나 얼굴이 안 좋아 보여요. 무슨 일 있어요?
마크 피곤해서 그래요. 어제 잠을 한숨도 못 잤거든요.
리나 왜요? 무슨 문제가 있어요?
마크 화장실에 문제가 생겨서 밤새 고쳤어요.
리나 그래요?
마크 게다가 창문 틈으로 바람이 많이 들어와서 방이 너무 추워요.
리나 집주인한테 얘기하지 그랬어요?
마크 얘기했어요. 집주인이 다음 주에 고쳐 주기로 했어요.
리나 다행이네요.
마크 그런데 문제가 또 있어요. 제 방에서 옆집 소리가 다 들리거든요.
리나 그래요? 옆집에 가서 얘기해 봤어요?
마크 아니요, 옆집 사람하고 아직 인사도 못 했어요.
리나 그러지 말고 옆집에 가서 직접 말하지 그래요? 이번 기회에 인사도 하세요.
마크 그게 좋겠네요.

Rina You don't look so well (lit. Your face doesn't look good). What's wrong?
Mark It's because I'm tired. I couldn't sleep even one wink (lit. one breath) last night.
Rina Why? Is there a problem?
Mark I stayed up all night fixing a problem in my bathroom.
Rina Really?
Mark And worse (lit. furthermore), my room is so cold because there's a small crack in my window that lets the wind in.
Rina Why didn't you speak to the landlady?
Mark I spoke to her. She said she would fix it for me next week.
Rina That's good (lit. fortunate).
Mark But I have another problem. I can hear all the sounds from next door in my room.
Rina Really? Have you tried going next door and telling your neighbors?
Mark No, I haven't even greeted them yet.
Rina (lit. Instead of doing that.) Shouldn't you speak to them directly? You can use that opportunity to introduce yourself to them too.
Mark I guess that would be good.

New Vocabulary ▸P. 327

숨 | 밤새 | 고치다 | 게다가 | 틈 | 들어오다 | 다행이다 | 옆집 | 소리 | 들리다 | 인사하다 | 기회

New Expressions ▸P. 327

- 다행이네요.
- 그러지 말고 …지 그래요?
- 그게 좋겠네요.

Tips

1 The Expression of Quantity

The expressions of quantity may be used in the following manner to emphasize something one is unable to do. It is used with a classifier, marker 도, and a negation.

- 어제 바빠서 빵 **한 입도 못 먹었어요.**
  I couldn't eat even one bite of bread because I was busy yesterday.
- 저는 술을 **한 모금도 못 마셔요.** I can't drink even one sip of alcohol.
- 너무 무서워서 말 **한 마디도 못 했어요.**
  I was so scared I couldn't say a single word.
- 돈이 **한 푼도 없어요.** I don't have even a single cent.

2 The Expression of Persuasion

When trying to convince someone to do something other than what they have said that they have done or will do, 그러지 말고 is used. It is followed by a command or proposal.

- A 오늘 영화 보는 게 어때요?
  Why don't we watch a movie today?
  B **그러지 말고** 쇼핑하러 가요.
  Let's not do that. Let's go shopping (instead).
- **그러지 말고** 내 얘기 좀 들어 보세요.
  Don't do that. Listen to what I have to say.

Commom Home Problems

1.

물이 새다
for water to leak

2.

수도꼭지가 고장 났다
for the faucet to be broken

3.

변기가 막혔다
for the toilet to be clogged

4.

하수구에서 냄새가 나다
for the drain to smell bad

5.

창문이 안 닫히다
for the window to not shut

6.
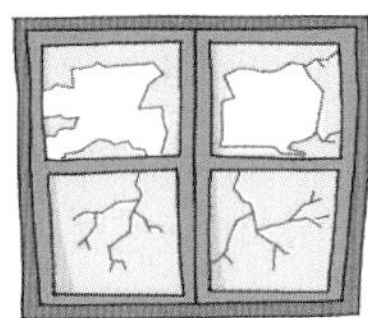
창문이 깨졌다
for the window to be broken

7.
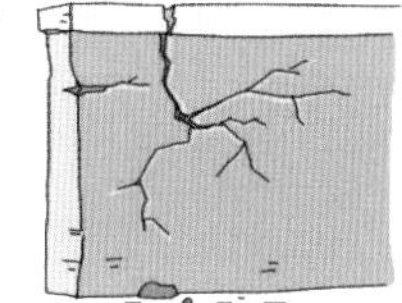
벽에 금이 갔다
for there to be a crack in the wall

8.
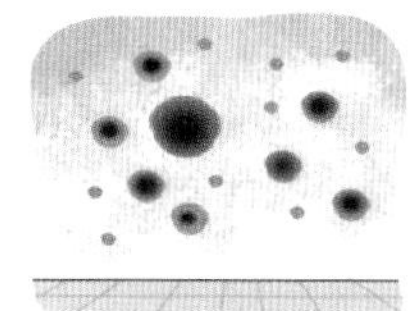
벽에 곰팡이가 생겼다
for mold to be growing on the wall

9.

불이 안 켜지다
for the light to not turn on

10.

가스가 안 켜지다
for the gas to not turn on

11.

난방이 안 되다
for the heat to not work

12.

더운 물이 안 나오다
for there not to be hot water

13.

문이 잠겼다
for the door to be locked

14.

손잡이가 망가지다
for the doorknob/door handle to not work

15.

소음이 심하다
for the noise to be loud (lit. extreme/harsh)

16.

벌레가 많다
for there to be many bugs

Key Expressions

- 직접 고쳤어요. I fixed it myself.
- 수리 기사를 불렀어요. I called a repairman.
- 문제를 그대로 내버려 뒀어요. I left the problem as is.

Let's Talk!

Speaking Strategy — Revising What One Has Said

- 사실은… **Actually,**
- 실제로는… **Actually,**
- 꼭 그런 건 아니에요. **That's not necessarily true.**
- 오히려 반대예요. **Actually it's the opposite.**

❶ 지금 어디에 살고 있어요?

- 어떻게 이 집을 알게 됐어요?
- 왜 이 집을 선택했어요?
- 어떤 점이 마음에 들었어요?

❷ 지금 살고 있는 집이 어때요?

- 지금 살고 있는 집의 장점이 뭐예요?
- 지금 살고 있는 집의 단점이 뭐예요?
- 집을 구할 때 어떤 점이 가장 중요해요?

□ 날씨	□ 시설	□ 가격
□ 크기	□ 집주인	□ 이웃
□ 주변 환경	□ 채광 (햇빛)	□ 통풍 (바람)
□ 방범	□ 편의 시설 (병원, 식당, 편의점 등)	

I wonder

여기 사무실의 반(1/2)쯤 돼요. This is about half (1/2) the office.
여기 사무실의 반의 반(1/4)쯤 돼요. This is about half of the half(1/4) of the office.
여기 사무실의 2배쯤 돼요. This is about twice the size of the office.

New Vocabulary

장점 pro (strong point) | 단점 con (weak point) | 구하다 to look for | 시설 facility | 크기 size | 이웃 neighbor | 채광 lighting | 통풍 ventilation | 방범 crime prevention | 편의 시설 amenities | 배 times | 월세 (monthly) rent | 부담되다 to be burdensome | 계약하다 to make a contract | 벽 wall | 곰팡이 mold

Word Web

Appendix P. 318

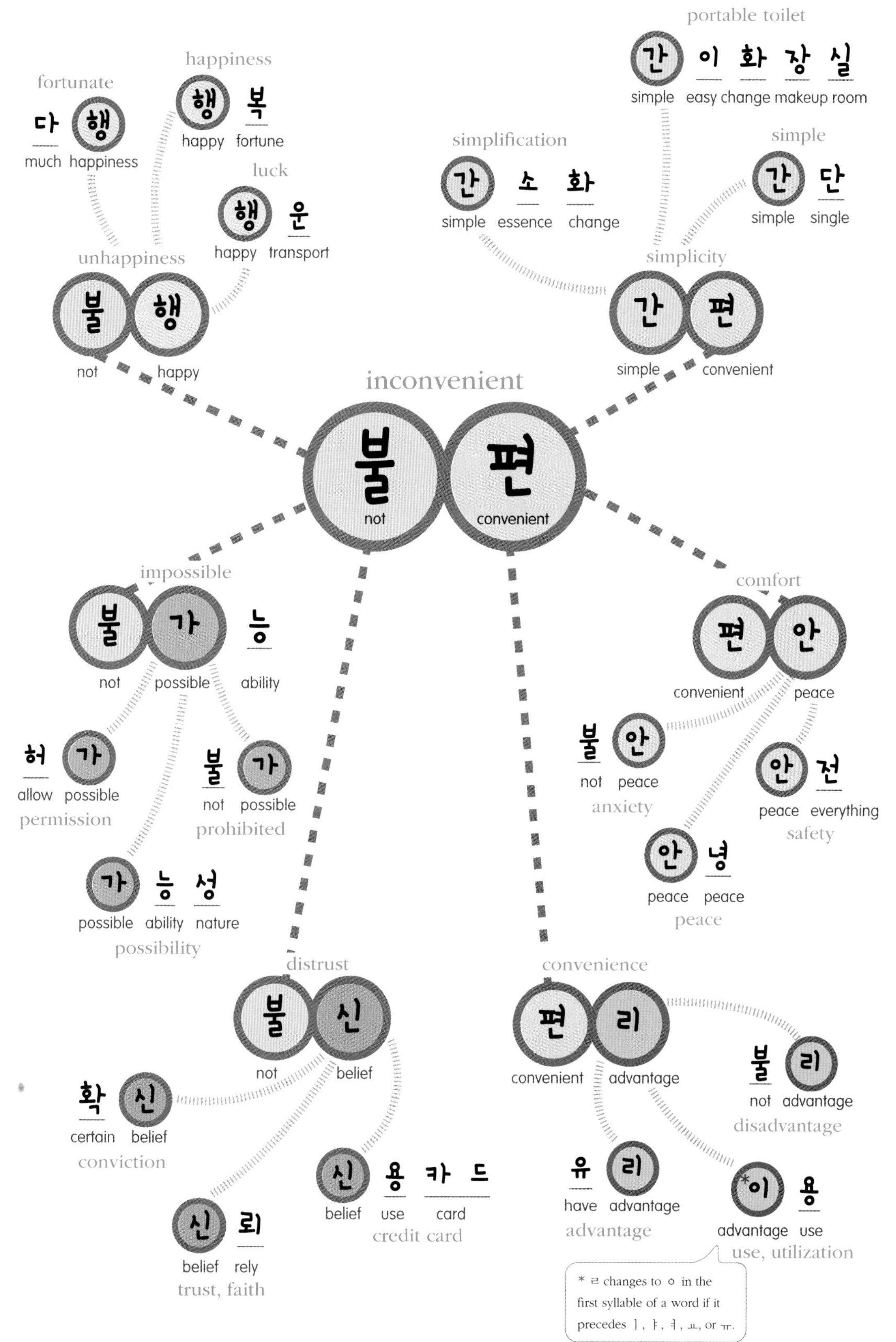

A Word on Culture

Let's Learn How to Use 방 (Room) and 집 (House)!

• Come to our cozy 방!

In Korea, the word 방 gives a warm, cozy image when attached to a word. While a similar word, the Sino-Korean syllable 실, expresses a place with a set size and purpose such as 교실 (classroom), 화장실 (bathroom), and 사무실 (office), words using 방 evoke a feeling of tidiness and thoughts of familiar scents.

The warm and cozy word 방 is used outside of the house as well, with representative examples being 노래방 (karaoke bar), 찜질방 (sauna), 만화방 (comic book store), and PC방 (Internet café). It is generally used for places that have separate rooms, such as 노래방 and 찜질방, but may also be used for places such as 만화방 and PC방, which do not consist of separate rooms but are, nonetheless, somewhat closed-off and small areas. However, it is essential to remember that the word 방 is unrelated to the size or arrangement of the actual place but is used, even by businesses, to express the intimacy and coziness of a place.

• Welcome to our 집!

집 refers to a space in which a family lives together. Beyond referring to one's private home, 집 may also be used to evoke the image of a warm and cozy place. In many cases, 집 refers to an incredibly small and welcoming store. The representative examples are 꽃집 (flower shop), 빵집 (bakery), 떡집 (rice cake shop), 술집 (bar), 고깃집 (meat restaurant, steakhouse), all of which are commonly seen in a neighborhood. 집 may be attached to whatever is sold at the store to express "a store that sells ___."

Furthermore, in everyday conversation, Koreans will often ask employees in the store "이 집에서 뭐가 제일 맛있어요? (What is the tastiest food in this store?)" or "이 집에서 뭐가 제일 잘 나가요? (What is the best-selling thing in this store?)". While there may be another word for the specific type of store (such as 식당 "restaurant"), 집 may be used to refer to the store once one is inside it. Here, the word 집 means "the place where I am at."

Chapter **08**

쇼핑

Shopping

Goals
- Asking and Answering about Products
- Talking about Pros and Cons of Products
- Making Comparisons
- Buying Products
- Requesting Product Exchanges
- Explaining Product Problems
- Asking about the Listener's Intent
- Explaining One's Reasons for Exchanging Products
- Explaining Item Return Procedures

Grammar

❶ -(으)ㄴ/는데 "but"; contrasting
-는 동안에 "during", "while"

❷ -(으)니까 expressing the realization of something after having done a certain action
-(으)시겠어요? "Would you…?"

❸ -(스)ㅂ니다 formal speech
-는 대로 "as soon as"

Grammar 1

-(으)ㄴ/는데 "but", contrasting

C.C P. 306

A 친구하고 어떻게 달라요?
How are you different from your friend?

B 저는 운동을 좋아하는데 제 친구는 운동을 안 좋아해요.
I like exercising, but my friend doesn't like exercising.

-(으)ㄴ/는데 is used to compare or contrast two ideas. The conjugation is the same as that of -(으)ㄴ/는데 in Chapter 4. It is common to attach the marker 은/는 to the topic of comparison to emphasize the contrast.

- 저 여자는 얼굴은 예쁜데 성격은 안 좋아요. (= 저 여자는 얼굴은 예뻐요. 그런데 성격은 안 좋아요.) That woman has a pretty face, but a bad personality (= That woman has a pretty face. But, she has a bad personality.)
- 열심히 준비했는데 시험을 잘 못 봤어요. I prepared diligently, but I didn't do well on the exam.
- 3년 전에는 학생이었는데 지금은 학생이 아니에요. I was a student 3 years ago, but I am not a student now.

-는 동안에 "during", "while"

Appendix P. 271

C.C P. 299

A 언제 어머니가 책을 읽어요?
When does the mother read a book?

B 아기가 자는 동안에 어머니는 아기 옆에서 책을 읽어요.
While her baby is sleeping, the mother reads next to her baby.

-는 동안에 is used to express an action or state occurring concurrently with another action or state. -는 동안에 connects to verb stems. -는 동안에 connects two actions occurring at the same time, while -(으)ㄴ 동안에 expresses a current state that is a result of an action that has already been completed. For example, in the final example below, the second action occurs after the action of "leaving" has been completed, and the state of "having left" is in place.

- 밥을 먹는 동안에 텔레비전을 보지 마세요. Do not watch TV while eating.
- 내가 옷을 구경하는 동안에 도둑이 내 지갑을 훔쳐 갔어요. A thief stole my wallet while I was shopping for clothes.
- 선생님이 교실에 없는 동안에 학생들이 장난을 쳤어요. (= 선생님이 교실을 나간 동안에 학생들이 장난을 쳤어요.) The students played around while the teacher was not in the classroom. (= The students played around while the teacher left the classroom.)

▸Answers P. 313

1 **문장을 완성하도록 알맞은 것끼리 연결하세요.**

(1) 그 식당은 음식이 맛있는데 •
(2) 제 친구가 밥은 많이 먹는데 •
(3) 10년 전에는 날씬했는데 •
(4) 제 친구는 돈을 많이 버는데 •
(5) 어제 친구들의 이름을 외웠는데 •

• ⓐ 값이 너무 비싸요.
• ⓑ 지금은 살이 쪘어요.
• ⓒ 돈을 쓰지 않아요.
• ⓓ 하나도 생각이 안 나요.
• ⓔ 운동은 전혀 안 해요.

2 **다음에서 알맞은 답을 골라서 '-는 동안에'를 사용하여 문장을 완성하세요.**

살다 다니다 외출하다 회의하다 공부하다

(1) 학교에 ________ 마크는 한 번도 결석하지 않았어요.
(2) 도서관에서 ________ 말 한 마디도 안 하고 책만 읽었어요.
(3) 친구하고 한 집에서 같이 ________ 작은 문제 때문에 많이 싸웠어요.
(4) 회사에서 ________ 전화를 진동으로 바꾸세요.
(5) 엄마가 ________ 아이가 컴퓨터 게임을 했어요.

2 **그림을 보고 알맞은 답을 고르세요.**

(1)

ⓐ 아기가 자면서 엄마가 집안일을 해요.
ⓑ 아기가 자는 동안에 엄마가 집안일을 해요.

(2)

ⓐ 낮에는 일하면서 밤에는 공부해요.
ⓑ 낮에는 일하는 동안에 밤에는 공부해요.

(3)

ⓐ 비가 온 동안에 운동을 못 했어요.
ⓑ 비가 오는 동안에 운동을 못 했어요.

(4)

ⓐ 여자가 화장실을 가면서 남자가 전화했어요.
ⓑ 여자가 화장실을 간 동안에 남자가 전화했어요.

Conversation ❶

Track 22

직원 뭐 찾으세요?
링링 노트북 보러 왔는데요.
직원 어떤 거 찾으세요?
링링 사용하기 편한 거 찾아요.
직원 이거 어떠세요? 요즘 이게 제일 잘 나가요.
링링 이게 어디 거예요?
직원 한국 거예요.
링링 디자인은 마음에 드는데 좀 비싸네요. 다른 거 없어요?
직원 그럼, 이거 어떠세요?
이건 좀 값이 싸서 젊은 사람들한테 인기가 있어요.
링링 음……, 값은 괜찮은데 색이 마음에 안 들어요.
다른 색 있어요?
직원 죄송합니다. 다른 색은 없는데요.
링링 그럼, 이 중에서 어떤 게 고장이 잘 안 나요?
직원 둘 다 튼튼해요. 사용하는 동안에 문제가 생기면 언제든지 가져오세요. 수리해 드릴게요.
링링 그럼, 이걸로 주세요.

Employee What are you looking for?
Ling Ling I came to look for a laptop.
Employee What kind are you looking for?
Ling Ling I'm looking for one that's easy to use.
Employee How about this one? It's the best-selling one lately.
Ling Ling Where is it from?
Employee It's from Korea.
Ling Ling I like the design but it's a little expensive. Do you have anything else?
Employee Then how about this one? It's popular with younger people because it's rather cheap.
Ling Ling Um... the price is fine, but I don't like the color. Do you have one in another color?
Employee Sorry, we don't have any other colors.
Ling Ling Then among these, which one is less likely to break?
Employee They're both sturdy. If there are any problems while you're using it, bring it in anytime. We'll get it fixed for you.
Ling Ling Then give me this one, please.

New Vocabulary ▸P. 327

사용하다 | 잘 나가다 | 젊다 | 인기가 있다 | 색 | 고장이 나다 | 둘 다 | 튼튼하다 | 가져오다 | 수리하다

New Expressions ▸P. 327

- 요즘 이게 제일 잘 나가요.
- 이게 어디 거예요?
- 이걸로 주세요.

Tips

1 Ways to Contract

In speech, forms of 이것 "this" with markers attached are often contracted.

이것이 → 이게/이거　　이것은 → 이건
이것을 → 이걸/이거　　이것으로 → 이걸로

- **이게** 제일 싸요. (= 이것이 제일 싸요.)
  This one is the cheapest.
- **이걸로** 보여 주세요. (= 이것으로 보여 주세요.)
  Show this one to me.

2 Two Meanings of 어떤

어떤 is a question word with two meanings. In this conversation, the first 어떤 is used to inquire about characteristics or states (what kind), while the second one is used to ask the listener to decide between choices (which).

- 사장님이 **어떤** 사람이에요?
  What kind of person is the president?
- 이 중에서 **어떤** 게 제일 맛있어요?
  Which is the best tasting out of these?

Describing Products

1. 재료 Material

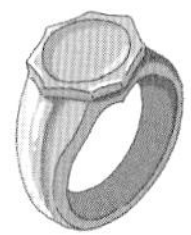

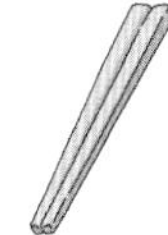

- 가죽 장갑
  leather gloves
- 금반지
  gold ring
- 은 목걸이
  silver necklace
- 유리 주전자
  glass kettle
- 털장갑
  fur/wool gloves
- 나무젓가락
  wooden chopsticks
- 천으로 만든 가방
  a cloth bag
- 나무로 만든 의자
  a wooden chair
- 흙으로 만든 도자기
  pottery made of soil

2. 가격 Price

- 값이 싸다 (= 저렴하다)
  to be cheap (= to be inexpensive)
- 값이 적당하다 to be just the right price
- 값이 비싸다 to be expensive

- 값이 적당해서 사려고 해요.
  I am going to buy it because the price is just right.

3. 디자인 Design

- 최신식이다 to be the newest model
  ↔ 구식이다 to be an old model
- 디자인이 마음에 들다 to like a design
- (사람) 한테 잘 어울리다
  to look good on/with (someone)

- 이 제품은 디자인이 독특해서 마음에 들어요.
  I like this product because its design is unique.

4. 품질 Quality

- 품질이 좋다 for the quality to be good
  ↔ 품질이 나쁘다 for the quality to be bad
- 정품이다 to be a genuine product
  ↔ 정품이 아니다 to not be a genuine product
- 튼튼하다 = 고장이 잘 안 나다
  to be sturdy = to not break easily

- 품질이 좋아요. The quality is good.
- 품질이 나빠요. The quality is bad.
- 정품이에요. It is a genuine product.
- 정품이 아니에요. It is not a genuine product.
- 튼튼해요. It is sturdy.
- 고장이 잘 안 나요. It does not break easily.

5. 무게 Weight

- 가볍다 → 들고 다니기 쉽다
  to be light → to be easy to carry
- 무겁다 → 들고 다니기 어렵다
  to be heavy → to be difficult to carry

- 이건 가벼워서 들고 다니기 쉬워요.
  It is easy to carry because it's light.
- 가죽 가방은 들고 다니기 어려울 거예요.
  The leather bag will be difficult to carry.

6. 부피 Volume

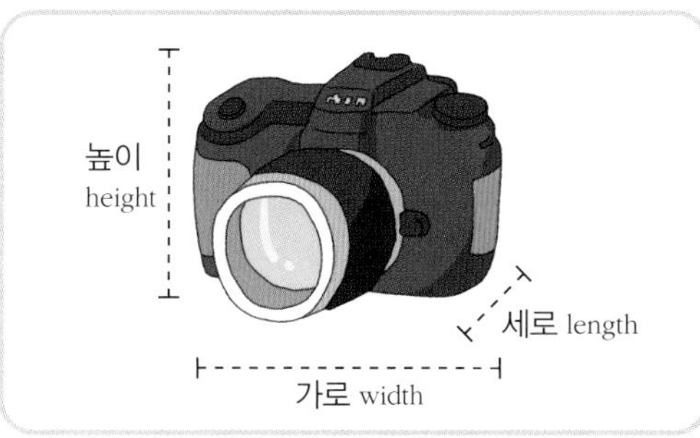

Key Expressions

- 어떻게 생겼어요? = 어떤 모양이에요?
  What does it look like?
- (디자인/색)이 어때요?
  How is the (design/color)?
- 값이 얼마나 해요?/크기가 얼마나 해요?
  How much is it?/How big is it?

Grammar 2

-(으)니까 expressing the realization of something after having done a certain action

▶ Appendix P. 272

A 빵을 안 사 왔어요?
Did you not buy the bread?

B 빵집에 가니까 문을 안 열었어요.
I went to the bakery and it wasn't open.

-(으)니까 is used to express the realization of a result after acting out an action or after a situation has occurred. It is attached to verb stems of the action that has been carried out or to that of the situation that has occurred, while the result that has been realized comes after. Though -(으)니까 expresses a past action or situation, it may not always combine with -았/었- when being used in the context of expressing a realization. It may, however, be used with -았/었- when explaining a reason. It may be attached to -아/어 보다 to form -아/어 보니까 to express a realization that occurs after having tried something new.

- 사무실에 전화하니까 민호 씨는 벌써 퇴근했어요. When I called the office, Minho had already left work.
- 어른이 되니까 부모님의 마음을 더 잘 이해할 수 있어요.
  As I become an adult, I better understand the feelings of my parents.
- 김치가 매워 보였는데 먹어 보니까 맵지 않고 맛있었어요.
  The kimchi looked spicy, but when I tried it, it was delicious and not spicy.

-(으)시겠어요? "Would you…?"

A 어떤 걸로 하시겠어요?
Which one would you like?

B 파란색으로 할게요.
I'll have the blue one.

어떤 걸로
하시겠어요?

-(으)시겠어요? is used to politely ask a person of higher status what he or she intends to do. -(으)시- is attached to honor the subject of the clause. For example, in order to ask about their intentions, it may be used by a child to their parents, by a student to a teacher, by a workplace employee to a superior, by a shop employee to a customer, or by someone to a stranger. -(으)시겠어요? is attached to verb stems. When asking someone who one does not need to honor, -겠어요? may be used instead. In responding to such a question, -(으)ㄹ게요 may be used to express one's intention.

- A 어디에서 기다리시겠어요? Where would you like to wait?
  B 1층에서 기다릴게요. I'll wait for you on the first floor.
- A 커피와 녹차가 있는데 뭐 드시겠어요? I have coffee and green tea. What would you like to have?
  B 저는 커피 마실게요. I'll drink coffee.

Quiz Yourself

▸Answers P. 313

1 알맞은 답을 고르세요.

(1) 집에 가니까 ⓐ 편지를 썼어요. / ⓑ 편지가 와 있었어요.

(2) 책을 보니까 ⓐ 어렸을 때를 생각했어요. / ⓑ 어렸을 때가 생각 났어요.

(3) 한국에 살아 보니까 ⓐ 지하철이 정말 편해요. / ⓑ 지하철을 안 타 봤어요.

(4) 회사에 도착하니까 ⓐ 아무도 없었어요. / ⓑ 일한 적이 있어요.

2 다음에서 알맞은 답을 골라서 '-아/어 보니까'를 사용하여 문장을 완성하세요.

전화하다	태권도를 배우다	지하철을 타다	차를 마시다	음악을 듣다

(1) ______________________ 이상한 노래였어요.

(2) ______________________ 아무도 전화를 받지 않았어요.

(3) ______________________ 기침에 효과가 있어요.

(4) ______________________ 생각보다 어렵지 않았어요.

(5) ______________________ 깨끗하고 편리했어요.

3 그림을 보고 '-(으)시겠어요?'를 사용하여 대화를 완성하세요.

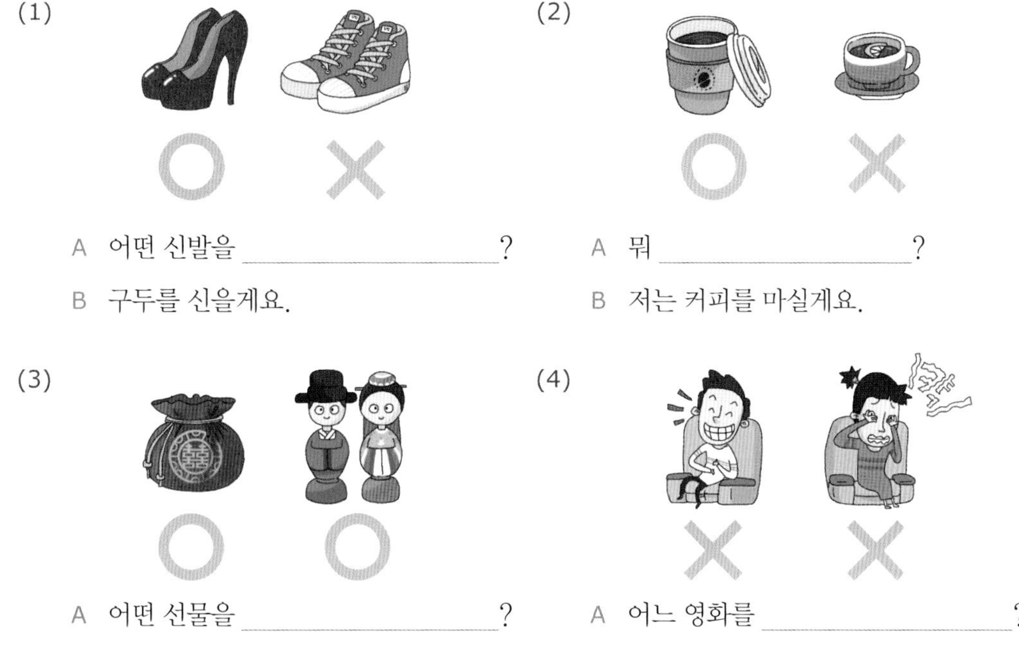

(1)

A 어떤 신발을 ______________?

B 구두를 신을게요.

(2)

A 뭐 ______________?

B 저는 커피를 마실게요.

(3)

A 어떤 선물을 ______________?

B 둘 다 사고 싶은데요.

(4)

A 어느 영화를 ______________?

B 저는 둘 다 보고 싶지 않아요.

Conversation 2

Track 23

직원 어떻게 오셨어요?

링링 며칠 전에 여기에서 노트북을 샀는데요. 집에 가서 보니까 전원이 안 켜져요.

직원 그러세요? 노트북 좀 보여 주시겠어요?

링링 여기 있어요.

직원 *(after checking the laptop)* 죄송합니다, 손님. 확인해 보니까 전원 버튼에 문제가 있네요.

링링 바꿔 줄 수 있어요?

직원 물론이죠. 새 제품으로 교환해 드릴게요. 같은 제품으로 하시겠어요?

링링 네, 같은 걸로 주세요.

직원 알겠습니다. 영수증 좀 보여 주시겠어요?

링링 여기 영수증요.

직원 *(after a while)* 여기 새 제품 있습니다. 확인해 보시겠어요?

링링 네, 확인해 볼게요. *(after checking the laptop)* 문제없네요. 이걸로 가져갈게요.

Employee May I help you? (lit. How did you come here?)

Ling Ling A few days ago I bought a laptop here. When I got home, I realized the power button didn't work.

Employee Is that so? Could you show me your laptop?

Ling Ling Here it is.

Employee *(after checking the laptop)* Sorry, ma'am. Now that I've checked it, I see that there is a problem with the power button.

Ling Ling Can you exchange it for me?

Employee Of course. I'll exchange it for a new product. Do you want the same product?

Ling Ling Yes, please give me the same product.

Employee Okay, could you please show me the receipt?

Ling Ling Here is the receipt.

Employee *(after a while)* Here is the new product. Would you like to take a look at it?

Ling Ling Yes, I'll take a look at it. *(after checking the laptop)* There's no problem with it. I'll take this.

New Vocabulary ▸P. 327

전원 | 켜지다 | 버튼 | 새 | 제품 | 교환하다 | 영수증

New Expressions ▸P. 327

- 어떻게 오셨어요?
- 전원이 안 켜져요.
- (noun) 좀 보여 주시겠어요?
- 물론이죠.

Tips

1 The Helping Verb -아/어 주다

The helping verb 주다 is used to express acting for someone else. In this conversation, 교환해 주다 is used to express that the action is being done for the customer. However, 드리다 was used instead of 주다 to express respect to the recipient of the action.

- 친구를 위해 이 사실을 말해 **줘야** 해요.
  You have to tell the truth for the sake of your friend.
- 부모님을 위해 스마트폰 사용법을 설명해 **드렸어요**.
  I explained to my parents how to use a smartphone.

2 Expressing a Direction of Change (으)로

The marker (으)로 is used to express the direction of a change. For example, when transferring from point A to point B, when changing item A to item B, or when moving from place A to place B, (으)로 is attached to B.

- 종로에서 3호선**으로** 갈아타세요.
  Transfer to line number three at Jongno.
- 명동**으로** 이사할 거예요. I'm going to move to Myeongdong.
- 원을 달러**로** 환전해 주세요. Please change this won to dollars.

1 Problems with Clothing

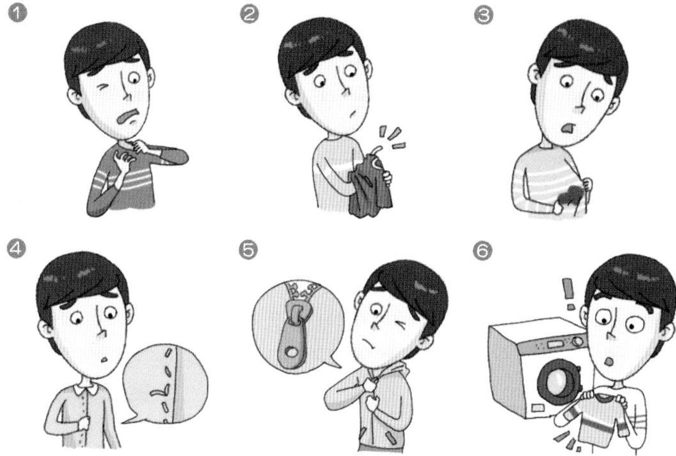

1. 사이즈가 안 맞아요.
   The size isn't right.
2. 옷에 구멍이 났어요.
   There's a hole in the clothing.
3. 옷에 얼룩이 있어요.
   There's a spot on the clothing.
4. 바느질이 엉망이에요.
   The stitching is off.
5. 지퍼가 고장 났어요.
   The zipper is broken.
6. 세탁 후에 옷이 줄어들었어요.
   The clothing shrank after I put it in the wash.

2 Problems with Electronics

1. 전원이 안 들어와요.
   There is no power.
2. 버튼이 망가졌어요.
   The button is broken.
3. 이상한 소리가 나요.
   It's making a strange sound.
4. 작동이 안 돼요.
   This function doesn't work.
5. 과열됐어요.
   It's overheated.
6. 배터리가 금방 떨어져요.
   The battery runs out quickly.

3 Problems with Furniture

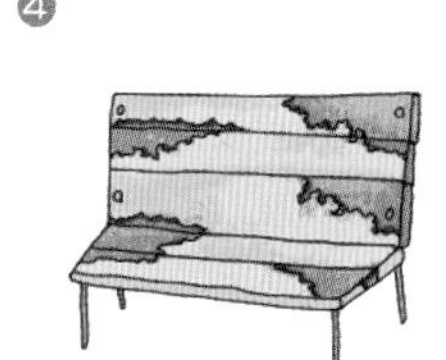

1. 흠집이 났어요. There's a chip.
2. 금이 갔어요. There's a crack.
3. 찌그러졌어요. It's dented.
4. 페인트가 벗겨졌어요.
   The paint is peeling.
5. 뭐가 묻었어요. It's stained.
6. 냄새가 나요. It smells bad.

Key Expressions

- 교환 가능하죠?
  I can exchange it, right?
- 다른 걸로 바꿔 주세요.
  Please change it for me.
- 환불하고 싶어요.
  I would like a refund.

Grammar ❸

(스)ㅂ니다 formal speech

▶ Appendix P. 272

A 죄송합니다. 지금 커피가 떨어졌습니다.
Sorry. The coffee just ran out.

B 그럼, 녹차 주세요.
Then give me green tea, please.

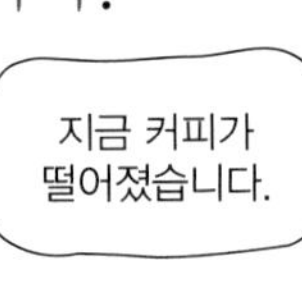

-(스)ㅂ니다 is a formal or official ending used in public speeches, presentations, or in situations when one must be formal, such as in business relations. For verbs and adjectives that end in a vowel and for 이다, -ㅂ니다 is used, while -습니다 is used for those that end with a consonant. When honoring the subject of the sentence, -(으)시- is attached, such that the ending becomes -십니다 if there is no final consonant and -으십니다 if there is a final consonant.

- 도시는 교통이 편리해서 살기 좋습니다. The city is a good place to live because of convenient transportation.
- 오늘은 회의가 있기 때문에 일이 늦게 끝납니다. I have a meeting today, so work will end late.
- 사장님께서 사무실에 오셔서 같이 회의하십니다.
  The president will come to the office and we will have a meeting together.

-는 대로 "as soon as"

A 언제 전화할 거예요?
When are you going to call me?

B 집에 도착하는 대로 연락할게요.
I'll call as soon as I arrive home.

-는 대로 is used to express an action occurring immediately after another action or situation occurs. -는 대로 is attached to verbs. -았/었- may not be attached in front of it.

- 회의가 끝나는 대로 출발합시다. Let's leave as soon as the meeting is over.
- 진수 소식을 듣는 대로 선생님께 알려 드렸어요. As soon as I heard about Jinsu's news, I informed the teacher.

Be careful

-는 대로 may be used interchangeably with -자마자 in most situations as the meanings are similar. However, -는 대로 may not be used for coincidental situations.

- 기차가 출발하는 대로 사고가 났어요. (X)
- 기차가 출발하자마자 사고가 났어요. (O) The accident happened as soon as the train left.

Quiz Yourself

▸Answers P. 313

1 보기 와 같이 '-(스)ㅂ니다'를 사용하여 문장을 완성하세요.

보기 제 친구에 대해 소개하겠습니다. (소개할게요)

친구의 직업은 (1) ________________.(변호사예요)
학생 때 그 친구와 많은 시간을 함께 (2) ________________.(보냈어요)
그런데 요즘은 친구가 바쁘니까 자주 못 (3) ________________.(만나요)
그래서 가끔 전화로 이야기를 (4) ________________.(주고받아요)
그 친구와 자주 못 보는 것이 (5) ________________.(아쉬워요)

우리 회사 사장님에 대해 (6) ________________.(말씀드릴게요)
사장님께서는 건강을 위해 운전하지 않고 지하철을
(7) ________________.(타세요) 평소에 사장님께서 우리를 가족처럼
(8) ________________.(대해 주세요) 어제도 사장님께서
회사 사람들과 함께 (9) ________________.(식사하셨어요)
우리 모두는 사장님을 (10) ________________.(존경하고 있어요)

2 밑줄 친 것을 '-(스)ㅂ니다'로 바꾸세요.

(1) A 혹시 경찰이세요? ➡
　　B 아니요, 저는 이 회사 직원이에요. ➡
(2) A 미국에서 오셨어요? ➡
　　B 그래요. ➡
(3) A 저한테 전화해 주세요. ➡
　　B 그렇게 할게요. ➡
(4) A 같이 식사부터 해요! ➡
　　B 그래요. ➡

3 다음에서 알맞은 답을 골라서 '-는 대로'를 사용하여 문장을 완성하세요.

읽다　　밝다　　받다　　끝나다

(1) 연락을 ________________ 제가 여기로 오겠습니다.
(2) 일이 ________________ 출발하세요.
(3) 날이 ________________ 여기를 떠나세요.
(4) 이 책을 다 ________________ 저한테도 빌려주세요.

Conversation ❸

Track 24

직원 '패션 쇼핑몰'입니다. 무엇을 도와드릴까요?

영주 인터넷으로 회색 바지를 샀는데, 바지를 입어 보니까 바지가 딱 껴서 불편해요. 더 큰 사이즈로 교환돼요?

직원 사이즈가 있으면 교환됩니다. 성함이 어떻게 되십니까?

영주 박영주예요.

직원 확인되었습니다. 그런데 죄송하지만, 같은 상품으로 더 큰 사이즈는 없습니다.

영주 그래요? 그럼, 반품은 돼요?

직원 네, 됩니다. 다만, 배송비는 고객님이 내셔야 합니다.

영주 할 수 없죠. 배송비 낼게요. 반품 접수해 주세요.

직원 반품 접수되었습니다. 상품을 상자에 넣어서 포장해 주십시오. 내일 오전 중에 택배 기사님이 방문할 겁니다.

영주 알겠어요. 언제 환불돼요?

직원 상품을 확인하는 대로 환불 처리해 드리겠습니다. 다른 문의 사항은 없으십니까?

영주 없어요. 감사합니다.

Employee This is Fashion Shopping Mall. What can I help you with?

Yeongju I bought gray pants on the Internet, but when I tried them on, I realized they were too tight (so it was uncomfortable). Could I exchange them for a larger size?

Employee You may change them if we have the size you need. May I ask your name?

Yeongju My name is Park Yeongju.

Employee Okay. (lit. I've confirmed your name). I'm sorry, but we don't have the same product in a larger size.

Yeongju Really? Then may I return it?

Employee Yes, you may. However, you must pay the shipping costs.

Yeongju I guess it can't be helped. I'll pay for it. Please confirm the return for me.

Employee We are confirming your return. Please package your product in a box for us. A deliveryman will be at your door tomorrow morning.

Yeongju Okay. When will I receive the refund?

Employee We will handle the refund as soon as we receive the product. Do you have any other questions?

Yeongju No. Thank you very much.

New Vocabulary ▸P. 327

딱 끼다 | 성함 | 반품 | 배송비 | 고객님 | 접수 | 상품 | 상자 | 포장하다 | 택배 기사님 | 환불 | 방문하다 | 처리하다 | 문의 사항

New Expressions ▸P. 328

- 무엇을 도와드릴까요?
- 성함이 어떻게 되십니까?
- 다른 문의 사항은 없으십니까?

Tips

1 -아/어 드릴까요?

-아/어 줄까요? is formed by attaching -(으)ㄹ까요? to the helping verb -아/어 주다 and is used to offer to do something for the listener. When honoring the listener, -아/어 드릴까요? is used. The proper answer is -아/어 주세요.

- 파전 먹고 싶어요? 제가 만들**어 줄까요**?
  Do you want to eat scallion pancakes? Shall I make them for you?
- A 길을 잃어버리셨어요? 제가 길을 가르쳐 **드릴까요**?
  Are you lost? Shall I show you the way?
  B 감사합니다. 좀 가르쳐 주세요.
  Thank you. Please show me the way.

2 오전 중에 vs. 오전 내내

When 중에 is used after a time expression such as 오전 (AM), the meaning is "sometime in the morning and no later." On the other hand, when 내내 is used in the same example, the meaning is "continuously throughout the morning."

- 비는 **오전 중에** 그치겠습니다.
  The rain should stop in the morning.
- **오전 내내** 전화했지만 그 사람이 전화를 안 받아요.
  I called all morning but that person didn't pick up.

❶ Verbs Related to Money

Opposite expressions	
• 돈을 벌다 to make money	↔ • 돈을 쓰다 to spend money
• 돈을 절약하다 to save money	↔ • 돈을 낭비하다 to waste money

Actions and results	
• 돈을 모으다 to save money	→ • 돈이 모이다 for money to be saved
• 돈을 들이다 to spend money	→ • 돈이 들다 to cost money
• 돈을 남기다 to leave behind money	→ • 돈이 남다 for money to remain

Money usage	The flow of money	Other
• 값을 깎다 to discount	• 돈을 빌려주다 to lend money	• 돈이 떨어지다 for money to run out
• 계산하다 to calculate	• 돈을 빌리다 to borrow money	• 환전하다 to exchange money
• 돈을 내다 (= 지불하다) to pay	• 돈을 돌려주다 to return money	
• 돈을 받다 to receive money	• 돈을 갚다 to payback money	

- 친구는 **돈을 벌지** 않고 **쓰기**만 해요. My friend makes no money and only spends it.
- **돈을 모으고** 있는데 **돈이 모이**면 여행 갈 거예요. I'm saving money. If I save enough, I'll go on vacation.
- **돈을 들여서** 집을 고쳤어요. 생각보다 **돈이** 많이 **들었어요.** I spent money to fix my house. It cost a lot more than I expected.
- **돈이 떨어지면** 저한테 연락하세요. If you run out of money, contact me.
- **돈을 빌려주세요.** 돈이 생기면 바로 **갚을게요.** Please lend me some money. I'll pay you back when I make some.
- 길에서 돈을 주워서 주인에게 **돌려줬어요.** I picked up some money on the street and returned it to the owner.

❷ Hanja Referring to Money

1. OO값 Price for a type of object	2. OO비 Money related to an expensive cost	3. OO금 Money for a specific purpose	4. OO료 Money related to a fee	5. OO세 Money related to taxes
옷값 clothing price 신발값 shoe price 가방값 bag price 가구값 furniture price	교통비 transportation fare 식비 food expenses 숙박비 room charge 수리비 repair cost	등록금 tuition 장학금 scholarship 벌금 fine, penalty 상금 prize money	수수료 commission 입장료 entrance fee 보험료 insurance fee 대여료 rental fee	소득세 income tax 재산세 property tax 주민세 residence tax 부가 가치세 value added tax (VAT)

❸ Payment Methods

1. 돈 Money

- 현금 cash
- 지폐 bill (paper money)
- 동전 coin
- 수표 check

2. 신용 카드 Credit Card

- 일시불 lump sum payment
- 할부 payment in installments
- 이자 interest
- 무이자 할부 installment plan with no interest
- 수수료 commission

3. Other

- 공짜 free (no cost)
- 거스름돈 (= 잔돈) change
- 영수증 receipt
- 사은품 freebie

Key Expressions

- 돈이 남아요.
  Amount of money remains.
- 돈이 모자라요.
  Amount of money is insufficient.

Let's Talk!

Speaking Strategy — Expressing Surprise

- When expressing a positive feeling
  우와! **Wow!**
  끝내준다! **Wonderful!**
- When expressing a negative feeling or incredulity
  진짜? **Really?**
  말도 안 돼! **No way!**

❶ 쇼핑할 때 주로 사는 게 뭐예요?

옷

신발

화장품

전자 제품

가전제품

가구

생활용품

식료품

❷ 물건을 살 때 뭐가 제일 중요해요?

□ 디자인 □ 가격 □ 품질 □ 크기 □ 상품평
□ 기능 □ 브랜드 □ 색 □ 무게 □ 보증기간

❸ 최근에 산 물건 중에 가장 마음에 드는 게 뭐예요?
어떤 점이 마음에 들어요? 그 물건값이 어때요? 정가예요?
할인받았어요? 바가지 썼어요?

❹ 단골 가게가 있어요? 그 가게가 어디에 있어요?
왜 단골이 됐어요? 얼마나 자주 가요?

❺ 최근에 산 물건 중에서 문제가 있는 것이 있었어요?
어떤 물건이에요?
어떤 문제가 있었어요?
문제를 어떻게 해결했어요?

New Vocabulary

전자 제품 electronics | 가전제품 home appliances | 생활용품 daily supplies | 식료품 groceries | 품질 product quality | 기능 function | 보증 기간 warranty period | 정가 fixed price | 할인 discount | 바가지 rip-off | 해결하다 to resolve

Word Web

▶ Appendix P. 318

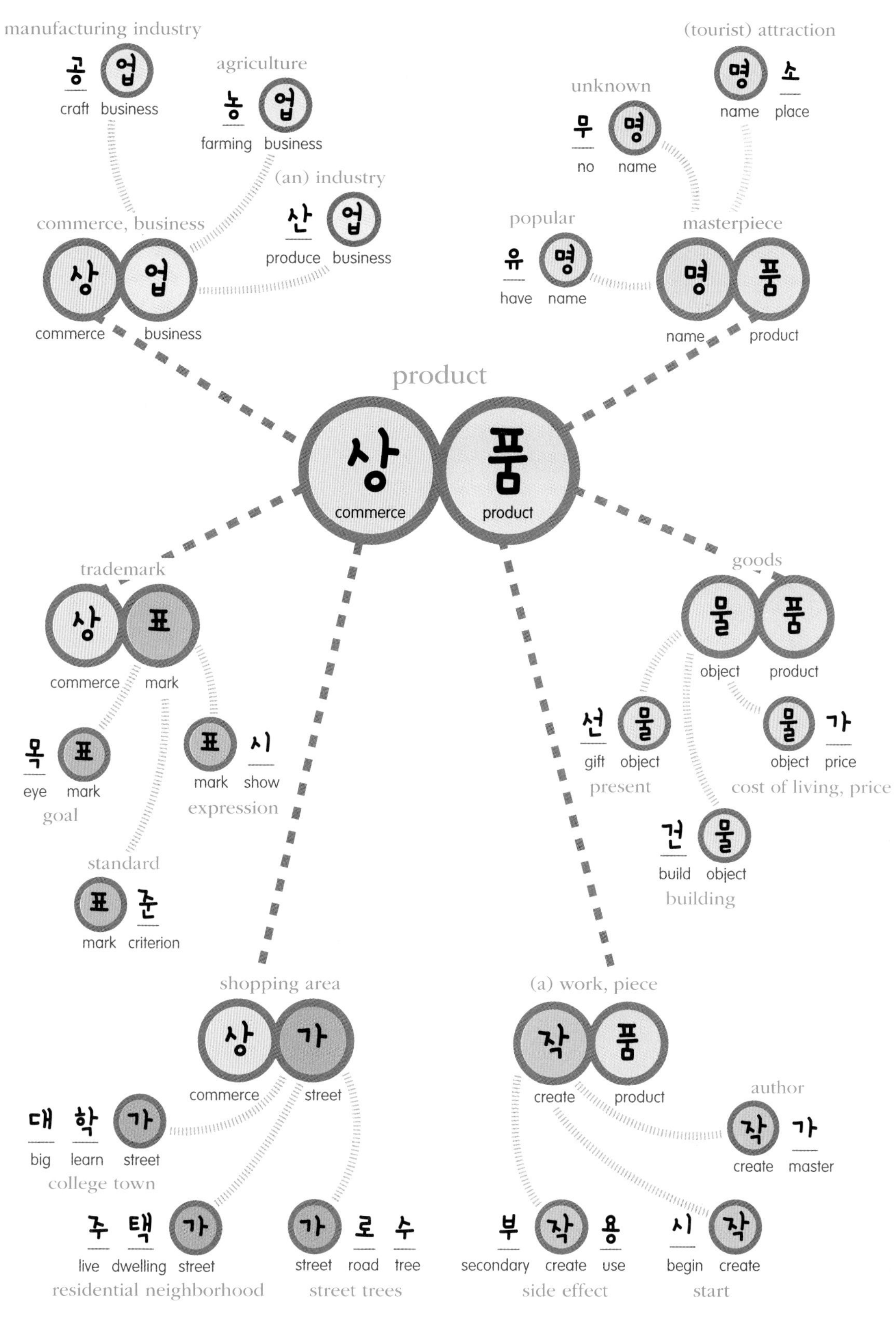

A Word on Culture

Expressions Used When Shopping

• 바가지 쓰다 Being ripped off

If you have ever unwittingly paid more for something than it was worth, then you can say 바가지를 썼다. This expression refers to the idea that you are unaware of the prices, even when it is written right in front of your eyes because you are wearing a 바가지 (large bowl) on your head. 바가지 씌운다 is used to express when someone rips a customer off by charging a higher price or fee. It would be best if you were exceptionally careful when there is no price tag attached or fee written because it is easy for you to be ripped off.

• 대박 Amazing!

대박 is used to refer to a good thing happening metaphorically. 대박 literally refers to a large gourd. From ancient times, gourds were considered to be treasure boxes, and thus, were associated with the idea of success. If you can buy a product for a low price, it can be called 대박. Also, if 대박 상품 is written in front of displayed items, it means that the product is being greatly discounted. Furthermore, if 대박 is used with a movie or play, it is a box office success. Thus, 대박 may be used for any surprising good thing that happens.

• 싸구려 Cheap merchandise and shameful actions

싸구려 refers to a cheap item or of poor quality. It is derived from 싸다 (to be cheap). It may also be used for indiscriminate or shameful actions. As 싸구려 means that the quality or level is low, it has a negative meaning, and therefore one should not use 싸구려 to refer to the clothing or possession of the listener. However, in traditional markets, 싸구려! is yelled at by touts to draw the customers' attention by emphasizing the low price of their products.

Chapter **09**

한국 생활

Living in Korea

Goals
- Comparing When You First Came to Korea with the Present
- Talking about Mistakes
- Expressing Feelings
- Expressing One's Difficulties in Studying Korean
- Asking and Giving Advice
- Talking about One's Current Job and Future Goals

Grammar

❶ -(으)ㄹ 때 "when"
-겠- the speculative suffix

❷ -아/어도 "even if", "even though"
-아/어지다 "to become", "to get more"

❸ -(으)려고 "in order to", "so that"
-(으)려면 "if one intends to", "if one wants to"

Grammar 1

-(으)ㄹ 때 "when"

▶ Appendix P. 279

A 한국에서는 사진을 찍을 때 뭐라고 말해요?
In Korea, what do you say when you take a picture?

B 사진을 찍을 때 '김치'라고 말해요.
When we take a picture, we say "kimchi."

-(으)ㄹ 때 is used to point to the time at which an action or event occurs or to the time during which it transpires. -(으)ㄹ 때 is attached to the stems of verbs, adjectives, and 이다. As a general rule, -(으)ㄹ 때 is used when the former and latter clauses occur at the same time, while if the former event has been completed, -았/었- is attached to form -았/었을 때.

- 밤에 잘 때 무서운 꿈을 꿨어요. I had a scary dream when I was sleeping at night.
- 저는 스트레스를 받을 때 많이 먹어요. I eat a lot when I'm stressed out.
- 그 사람을 처음 만났을 때 잠깐 얘기했어요. When I first met him, we talked for a while.

-겠- the speculative suffix

C.C P. 297

A 뭐 먹을까요?
What shall we eat?

B 저게 맛있겠네요. 저거 주문할까요?
That looks like it might be tasty. Shall we order that?

-겠- is used to make a guess based on the fact that one knows or sees or what the other person has said. It is attached to the stems of verbs, adjectives, and 이다. -았/었- may be attached to form -았/었겠- (must have been) if the action is surmised to have already happened.

- 아침을 안 먹었으니까 배고프겠어요. You might be hungry because you didn't eat breakfast.
- 음식을 많이 만들었어요. 혼자 다 먹을 수 없겠어요. I made a lot of food. I don't think I can eat it all by myself.
- 혼자 이사했으니까 힘들었겠어요. It must have been difficult because you moved alone.

Quiz Yourself

▸Answers P. 313

1 알맞은 것끼리 연결하세요.

(1) 회사에서 승진했을 때 •   • ⓐ 짜증 나요.

(2) 친구가 약속 때마다 늦게 올 때 •   • ⓑ 아쉬웠어요.

(3) 지하철에서 지갑을 잃어버렸을 때 •   • ⓒ 신기해요.

(4) 좋은 기회였는데 기회를 놓쳤을 때 •   • ⓓ 속상했어요.

(5) 어린 아이가 어려운 수학 문제를 풀 때 •   • ⓔ 신났어요.

2 다음에서 알맞은 답을 골라서 '-(으)ㄹ 때'를 사용하여 대화를 완성하세요.

처음 만나다   시간이 나다   회사를 그만두다   하기 싫은 일을 하다

(1) A 보통 언제 친구하고 문자를 주고받아요?

B ______________ 때마다 문자를 주고받아요.

(2) A 보통 언제 스트레스를 받아요?

B ______________ 때 스트레스를 많이 받아요.

(3) A 언제부터 그 사람이 마음에 들었어요?

B ______________ 때부터 마음에 들었어요.

(4) A 언제까지 한국에서 살 거예요?

B ______________ 때까지 한국에서 살 거예요.

3 알맞은 답을 고르세요.

(1) A 제 친구는 매일 하루에 2번씩 라면을 먹어요.

B 와! 진짜 많이 ⓐ 먹어요. / ⓑ 먹겠어요.

(2) A 제 집 바로 앞에 버스 정류장이 있어요.

B 정말 ⓐ 편해요. / ⓑ 편하겠어요.

(3) A 요즘 매일 야근하고 있어요.

B ⓐ 피곤해요. / ⓑ 피곤하겠어요.

(4) A 지난주에 3시간 동안 걸었어요.

B 많이 ⓐ 걸었어요. / ⓑ 걸었겠어요.

Conversation 1

Track 25

유키 마크 씨, 한국 생활이 어때요?

마크 지금은 괜찮지만, 처음에는 힘들었어요.

유키 언제 제일 힘들었어요?

마크 한국 사람하고 말이 안 통할 때 정말 힘들었어요.

유키 힘들었겠네요. 지금은 말이 잘 통해요?

마크 조금요. 말이 통하니까 한국 생활도 더 재미있어요.

유키 한국하고 미국은 생활 방식도 사고방식도 다른데 적응하기 쉬웠어요?

마크 아니요, 처음에는 문화 차이 때문에 적응이 안 됐어요. 또, 왜 그렇게 해야 하는지 모르니까 실수도 많이 했어요.

유키 지금은 적응했어요?

마크 완벽하게 적응하지 못했지만, 이제 많이 익숙해졌어요. 실수하면서 많이 배웠어요.

유키 예를 들면 어떤 실수를 했어요?

마크 전에 어떤 아줌마한테 반말을 해서 혼난 적도 있어요.

Yuki Mark, how is living in Korea?

Mark It's fine now but, at first, it was difficult.

Yuki When was it most difficult?

Mark It was really difficult when I couldn't communicate with Korean people.

Yuki It must have been difficult. Can you communicate well now?

Mark A little. Living in Korea is more fun, too, since I can communicate with people.

Yuki Koreans and Americans live different lifestyles and also have different ways of thinking. Was it easy to get used to that?

Mark No, I had trouble adapting at first because of the cultural differences. I also made many mistakes because I didn't know why I had to do things in certain ways.

Yuki Are you used to it now?

Mark I haven't been able to fully adapt to it, but I've become much more used to it. I learned a lot while making mistakes.

Yuki What kind of mistakes, for instance, did you make?

Mark I've been scolded by some middle-aged woman for speaking to her in banmal before.

New Vocabulary ▸ P. 328

말이 통하다 | 생활 방식 | 사고방식 | 차이 | 적응이 되다 | 실수 | 완벽하게 | 어떤 | 반말 | 혼나다

New Expressions ▸ P. 328

- 적응이 안 됐어요.
- 이제 많이 익숙해졌어요.
- 예를 들면

Tips

1 The Adverb 잘 vs. 안

The adverb 잘 may be added to emphasize the meaning of a phrase. When used with 안, it emphasizes the negation.

- 그 사람과는 말이 **잘** 안 통해요. (말이 통하다)
  I can't communicate well with that person.
- 이 음식은 제 입에 **잘** 맞아요. (입에 맞다)
  This food matches my tastes well.
- 사업은 제 적성에 잘 **안** 맞아요. (적성에 맞다)
  Business does not suit me well.

2 Expressions of Result Using 되다

Passive expressions are often used for the results of action verbs. The passive forms of many verbs formed by a noun and 하다 involve attaching the marker 이/가 to the noun and adding 되다. The negative form is 안 되다.

- 이 부분을 여러 번 읽으니까 **이해가 돼요.**
  After reading this part numerous times, I understand it.
- 집중하려고 했지만 너무 시끄러워서 **집중이 안 돼요.**
  I tried to concentrate, but I couldn't because it was too loud.

1 Expressions of Emotion from Hanja Attached to 하다

- 당황하다: 외국인이 저한테 외국어로 말을 걸었을 때 **당황했어요.**
  to panic, to be flustered (because of not knowing what to do): I panicked when a foreigner spoke to me in a foreign language.
- 창피하다: 사람들 앞에서 미끄러졌을 때 정말 **창피했어요.**
  to be embarrassed (because of making a mistake): It was really embarrassing when I slipped in front of people.
- 불안하다: 18살짜리 동생이 혼자 여행을 떠났을 때 걱정돼서 **불안했어요.**
  to be uneasy: I was uneasy because it worried me when my eighteen-year-old little brother went on a trip by himself.
- 실망하다: 친구가 저한테 거짓말을 한 것을 알았을 때 친구한테 **실망했어요.**
  to be disappointed: I was disappointed with my friend when I found out that she had lied to me.
- 좌절하다: 계속해서 시험에 다섯 번 떨어졌을 때 정말 **좌절했어요.**
  to be frustrated: I was really frustrated when I failed the test for the fifth time in a row.
- 우울하다: 돈도 없고 여자 친구도 없고 취직도 안 돼서 정말 **우울해요.**
  to be depressed: I am really depressed because I have no money, no girlfriend, and no job.
- 억울하다: 제가 잘못하지 않았는데 엄마가 저를 혼낼 때 **억울했어요.**
  to be unfair: It's unfair that my mother scolded me for not doing well.

2 Native Korean Expressions of Emotion with 하다

- 심심하다: 나는 약속도 없고 할 일이 없을 때 **심심해요.**
  to be bored: I am bored when I don't have appointments or things to do.
- 답답하다: 시험에서 공부한 단어가 생각 안 날 때 **답답해요.**
  to be frustrated (because of being unable to think of something (lit. to be stifling): I feel frustrated when I can't think of the vocabulary I studied while taking a test.
- 속상하다: 어머니께 선물 받은 소중한 목걸이를 잃어버렸을 때 **속상했어요.**
  to be upset: I was upset when I lost the precious necklace my mother gave me as a gift.
- 서운하다: 친한 친구가 제 생일을 잊어버리고 지나갔을 때 친구한테 **서운했어요.**
  to be disappointed (because of expectations for someone close): I was disappointed in my close friend when my birthday had passed, and he had forgotten it.

3 Expressing Feelings about a Person or Object

- 지겹다: 매일 똑같은 음식을 먹으면 그 음식이 **지겨울** 거예요.
  to get tired of: If you eat the same food every day, you'll get tired of it.
- 부럽다: 조금만 공부해도 잘 기억하는 사람이 **부러워요.**
  to be jealous: I'm jealous of people who can memorize a lot after only studying for a little while.
- 귀찮다: 주말에 집에서 쉴 때 집안일 하는 것이 **귀찮아요.**
  to be annoying: It's annoying to do housework when I rest at home on weekends.
- 그립다: 오랫동안 외국에서 사니까 고향 음식이 너무 **그리워요.**
  to miss: I really miss my hometown's food because I've been living abroad for a long time.
- 대단하다: 저 사람은 혼자 한국어를 공부했는데 정말 잘해요. 저 사람이 **대단해요.**
  to be impressive: That person speaks Korean really well, even though he studied it by himself. He's really impressive.
- 지루하다: 영화가 너무 **지루해서** 영화 보다가 잠이 들었어요.
  to be boring/bored: I fell asleep while watching the movie because it was so boring.
- 신기하다: 한국어를 잘 못하는데 한국 사람하고 말이 잘 통하는 것이 **신기해요.**
  to be amazing/excited: I can't speak Korean well, but it's amazing when I can communicate with Korean people.
- 불쌍하다: 부모가 없는 아이들이 어렵게 생활하는 것을 보면 아이들이 **불쌍해요.**
  to feel bad (lit. to be pitiful): I feel bad when I see children with no parents leading difficult lives.
- 끔찍하다: 뉴스에 나온 교통사고 장면이 정말 **끔찍했어요.**
  to be horrible: The scene on the news of the traffic accident was really horrible.
- 징그럽다: 큰 벌레가 정말 **징그러웠어요.**
  to be gross: Big bugs are really gross.

Be careful

When expressing feelings about a person or object, the speaker is omitted and 이/가 is added to the person or object that one has feelings about, treating it like a subject.

Ex. (저는) 이 음식이 지겨워요.
I'm tired of this food.

Key Expressions

- 신기한 느낌이 들어요.
  It feels amazing.
- 신기하게 생각하고 있어요.
  I'm thinking it's amazing.
- 신기하다고 생각해요.
  I think something is amazing.

Grammar 2

-이/어도 "even if", "even though"

A 그 사람 이름이 뭐예요?
What is that person's name?

B 아무리 생각해도 그 사람 이름이 생각 안 나요.
No matter how much I think about it, I can't remember his name.

-아/어도 is used to express an action or event that occurred differently from what one had hoped or expected. It is attached to the stems of verbs and adjectives. When it follows 이다, it becomes (이)라도. The adverb 아무리 (no matter how) may be added before the first clause for emphasis.

- 운동해도 살이 빠지지 않아요. Even if I exercise, I don't lose weight.
- 아무리 버스를 기다려도 버스가 오지 않아요. No matter how much I wait for the bus, the bus doesn't come.
- 동생이 똑똑하니까 걱정하지 않아도 잘할 거예요. Your younger sibling is smart, so don't worry as he will do well.
- 학생이라도 자기 잘못은 책임져야 해요. Even a student should be held accountable for his or her own mistakes.

-아/어지다 "to become", "to get more"

Appendix P. 274

A 날씨가 어때요?
How is the weather?

B 6월이 되니까 점점 더워져요.
It's gradually getting warmer since it's June.

점점 더워져요.

30℃
25℃
20℃
5월 6월 7월

-아/어지다 attaches to adjective stems and expresses a change of state. Adjectives with -아/어지다 attached act like verbs.

- 자주 만나면 그 사람과 더 친해져요. The more you see each other, the closer you get to that person.
- 텔레비전에 나온 후 그 가수가 유명해졌어요. After appearing on TV, the singer became famous.
- 새로 사업을 시작했으니까 앞으로 바빠질 거예요. I'm starting a new business, so I'll be busy going forward.

1 알맞은 답을 고르세요.

(1) 여러 번 전화해도 ⓐ 전화를 받았어요. / ⓑ 전화를 안 받았어요.

(2) 밥을 많이 먹어도 ⓐ 아직 배가 고파요. / ⓑ 벌써 배가 불러요.

(3) 아무리 얘기해도 ⓐ 제 말을 잘 들어요. / ⓑ 제 말을 듣지 않아요.

(4) ⓐ 열심히 일해서 / ⓑ 열심히 일해도 돈을 모았어요.

(5) ⓐ 물건값이 싸서 / ⓑ 물건값이 싸도 품질이 좋아요.

(6) ⓐ 음식이 싱거우니까 / ⓑ 음식이 싱거워도 소금을 넣지 마세요.

2 문장을 완성하도록 알맞은 것끼리 연결하세요.

(1) 봄이 되면 • • ⓐ 몸이 건강해져요.
(2) 운동을 하면 • • ⓑ 건강이 나빠질 거예요.
(3) 겨울이 되면 • • ⓒ 눈이 나빠져요.
(4) 담배를 피우면 • • ⓓ 더 예뻐질 거예요.
(5) 어두운 곳에서 책을 읽으면 • • ⓔ 날씨가 추워져요.
(6) 외모에 신경을 쓰면 • • ⓕ 날씨가 따뜻해져요.

3 다음에서 알맞은 답을 골라서 '-아/어도'나 '-아/어지다'를 사용하여 문장을 완성하세요.

춥다 편하다 비싸다 연습하다 한국인이다

(1) 그 음식은 값이 ________ 맛없어요.

(2) 컴퓨터 덕분에 옛날보다 생활이 ________.

(3) 아무리 ________ 한국어 발음이 쉽지 않아요.

(4) 가을이 되면 바람이 불어서 날씨가 ________.

(5) ________ 한국어 문법을 모를 때가 있어요.

Conversation 2

Track 26

리나 무슨 고민이 있어요? 왜 그래요?

케빈 요즘 한국어를 배우고 있는데, 열심히 공부해도 한국어 실력이 늘지 않아요. 말하기도 너무 어렵고요.

리나 한국어를 공부한 지 얼마나 됐어요?

케빈 한 6개월쯤 됐어요.

리나 얼마 안 됐네요.
실력이 늘 때까지 시간이 어느 정도 걸려요.

케빈 저도 알고 있지만 실력이 좋아지지 않아서 자신감이 점점 없어져요.

리나 보통 공부할 때 어떻게 해요? 한국 친구를 자주 만나요?

케빈 아니요, 일도 해야 되고 숙제도 많아서 친구 만날 시간이 없어요.

리나 혼자 열심히 공부해도 사람들하고 연습하지 않으면 실력이 늘지 않아요.

케빈 네, 저도 그렇게 생각해요.

리나 한국 친구를 최대한 많이 만나세요. 한국 친구하고 얘기할 때 한국어만 사용하고요.

케빈 알겠어요. 그렇게 해 볼게요.

리나 매일 꾸준히 연습하면 한국어 실력이 곧 좋아질 거예요.

Rina What's wrong? (lit. What problem do you have?) Why are you like this?

Kevin I've been learning Korean lately, but even though I study hard, my Korean proficiency isn't getting better. Speaking is so difficult too.

Rina How long have you been studying Korean?

Kevin It's been about six months.

Rina So it hasn't been very long. It takes a while until your proficiency improves.

Kevin I know that, but I'm slowly losing my confidence because my proficiency isn't getting better.

Rina How do you usually study? Do you meet with Korean friends often?

Kevin No, I have to work and also have a lot of homework, so I don't have time to meet friends.

Rina Even if you study hard by yourself, your proficiency won't get better if you don't practice with people.

Kevin Yes, I agree with you.

Rina Meet with Korean friends as much as possible. When you talk to them, only use Korean.

Kevin Okay. I'll try that.

Rina If you practice consistently every day, your Korean proficiency will improve in no time.

New Vocabulary ▸P. 328

고민 | 실력 | 한 | 어느 정도 | 자신감 | 점점 | 없어지다 | 최대한 | 꾸준히 | 곧

New Expressions ▸P. 328

- 무슨 고민이 있어요?
- 저도 그렇게 생각해요.
- 최대한 많이

Tips

1 -고요: "also", "too"

-고요 is attached to make an additional statement about a topic. In everyday speech, it is common to hear -구요.

- 채소를 많이 드세요. 그리고 매일 운동하세요.
  Eat a lot of vegetables. Also, exercise every day.
  → 채소를 많이 드세요. 매일 운동하**고요**.
- 혼자 문제를 푸세요. 그리고 사전을 보지 마세요.
  Solve the problem yourself. Also, don't look at the dictionary.
  → 혼자 문제를 푸세요. 사전을 보**지 말고요**.

2 The Infinitive -(으)ㄹ

-(으)ㄹ is used to modify a noun that has not yet occurred or that has a possibility of occurring in the future. In the above conversation, the speaker has not yet met his friend, but there is a possibility of meeting them in the future, so a 만날 시간 must be used rather than 만나는 시간.

- 어제 해야 **할 일**이 많아서 늦게 잤어요.
  I slept late last night because I had a lot of things to do.

1 Expressions of Emotion Attached to 나다

- 화나다 (= 화가 나다): 친구가 나를 무시했을 때 진짜 **화가 났어요.**
  to be angry: I was really angry when my friend ignored me.
- 짜증 나다 (= 짜증이 나다): 공부하는데 친구가 자꾸 말을 시켜서 **짜증 났어요.**
  to be annoyed: I got annoyed because my friend kept talking to me while I was studying.
- 신나다 (= 신이 나다): 사람들이 음악을 듣고 **신이 나서** 춤을 추기 시작해요.
  to be excited: People become excited and start to dance when they hear music.
- 겁나다 (= 겁이 나다): 사업에서 실패할 수 있다고 생각하니까 **겁이 났어요.**
  to be scared: I got scared because I think that my business might fail.
- 싫증 나다 (= 싫증이 나다): 공부에 **싫증 나서** 더 이상 공부하고 싶지 않아요.
  to be sick of: I don't want to study anymore because I'm sick of studying.

Be careful

이/가 나다 emotion expressions may be alternatively used as 을/를 내다, which implies the emotion is being expressed in action.

- 너무 많이 화가 나서 처음으로 친구에게 **화를 냈어요.**
  Because I was so angry, I got angry at (scolded, yelled at, etc.) my friend for the first time.

2 Expressions of Emotion Using 되다

- 긴장되다: 취업 면접을 앞두고 너무 **긴장돼요.**
  to be nervous: I am so nervous because of my upcoming job interview.
- 걱정되다: 내일이 시험인데 합격을 못 할까 봐 **걱정돼요.**
  to be worried: Tomorrow is my test, and I'm worried that I won't pass.
- 안심되다: 어두운 길을 걸을 때 친구와 함께 걸으면 **안심돼요.**
  to feel secure: I feel secure when I walk down a dark path with a friend.
- 기대되다: 새로운 곳에서 새로운 경험을 할 것이 **기대돼요.**
  to be expectant, to look forward to: I look forward to experiencing new things in a new place.
- 흥분되다: 우리 축구 팀이 이겼을 때 정말 **흥분됐어요.**
  to be excited: I was very excited when our soccer team won.
- 후회되다: 젊었을 때 더 많은 경험을 했으면 좋았을 텐데 **후회돼요.**
  to regret: I regret that I didn't have many experiences when I was young.

Be careful

When describing a feeling in a general statement/situation as opposed to an expression of a current feeling, 하다 is used.

- 저는 시험 전에는 항상 **긴장해서** 아무것도 먹지 않아요.
  I'm not eating anything because I am always nervous before a test. [general statement]
- 5분 후에 시험이 있어요. **긴장돼요.**
  There is a test in 5 minutes. I'm nervous. [current feeling]

3 Other Expressions of Emotion

- 즐겁다: 다른 사람을 도와주면, 몸은 힘들지만 마음이 **즐거워요.**
  to be happy/joyful/enjoyable: If you help other people, your body will be tired, but your heart will be happy.
- 기쁘다: 오랫동안 준비해 온 시험에 합격했을 때 정말 **기뻤어요.**
  to be happy: When I passed the test that I prepared for a long time, I was really happy.
- 무섭다: 밤에 집에 혼자 있을 때 이상한 소리가 나면 **무서워요.**
  to be scared: When I am alone at home at night, I get scared when there is a sound.
- 외롭다: 크리스마스에 외국에서 혼자 지내야 하니까 **외로운** 생각이 들었어요.
  to be lonely: I felt lonely because I had to spend Christmas alone in a foreign country.
- 괴롭다: 이상한 직장 상사 때문에 회사 생활이 너무 **괴로워요.**
  to be uncomfortable/unpleasant/stressful: It's stressful at work because of a strange superior of mine.
- 부끄럽다: 아이한테 한 약속을 내가 지키지 않았을 때 아이한테 **부끄러웠어요.**
  to be embarrassed: When I couldn't keep a promise I made to a child, I was embarrassed.
- 안타깝다: 친구가 열심히 노력했지만 시험에서 떨어져서 **안타까워요.**
  to be a shame (that something has happened to someone else): It's a shame that my friend tried so hard, yet failed the exam.
- 아깝다: 하루에 술값으로 100만 원을 쓰다니 정말 돈이 **아까워요.**
  to be a waste: It's really a waste of money to spend 1,000,000 won a day on alcohol.
- 아쉽다: 한국에서 더 있고 싶은데 내일 떠나야 해서 정말 **아쉬워요.**
  to be a shame (because of a missed opportunity): I want to stay in Korea longer. It's a shame that I have to leave tomorrow.

Key Expressions

- 언제 이런 느낌이 들어요?
  When do you feel this way?
- 언제 이런 느낌을 받아요?
  When do you get this feeling?

Grammar 3

-(으)려고 "in order to", "so that"

▶ Appendix P. 274 

A 왜 이 책을 샀어요?
Why did you buy this book?

B 지하철에서 읽으려고 이 책을 샀어요.
I bought this book so that I could read it on the subway.

-(으)려고 is used to express one's intent or goal. The intent or goal appears first in the clause with -(으)려고, and the action that is taken to reach the intent or goals follows thereafter. -(으)려고 is attached to verb stems. The subject on either side of the grammar point must be the same.

- 나중에 유학 가려고 외국어를 공부하고 있어요. I am studying a foreign language so that I study abroad later.
- 설날에 입으려고 한복을 준비했어요. I prepared a hanbok in order to wear it on New Year's Day.
- 약속에 늦지 않으려고 아침 일찍 출발했어요.
  I left early in the morning in order to avoid being late for my appointment.

-(으)려면 "if one intends to", "if one wants to"

C.C P. 304

A 명동에 어떻게 가요?
How do you get to Myeongdong?

B 명동에 가려면 여기에서 버스를 타세요.
If you want to get to Myeongdong, take the bus.

-(으)려면 is used to hypothesize a situation in which one intends to do something. The action taken to reach the goal follows -(으)려면 and may be a command, a suggestion, a situation that must take place, an intent, or action required to carry out the intent. -(으)려면 is attached to verb stems.

- 표를 사려면 일찍 가서 줄을 서야 돼요.
  If you want to buy a ticket, you have to go early and stand in line.
- 수업 시간에 졸지 않으려면 커피를 마셔야 돼요.
  I need to drink coffee so that I don't fall asleep in class.
- 건강해지려면 담배를 끊고 운동하세요.
  To be healthy, quit smoking and exercise.

Be careful

The above two grammar points both involve actions taken to fulfill a goal, but the forms of the following clauses differ.

- 한국어를 잘하**려고** 열심히 연습**했어요**.
- 한국어를 잘하**려면** 열심히 연습하**세요**.

▸Answers P. 314

1 **문장을 완성하도록 알맞은 것끼리 연결하세요.**

(1) 가방이 너무 무거워서 •	• ① 돈을 벌려고 •	• ⓐ 녹음해요.
(2) 선생님 말이 너무 빨라서 •	• ② 빨리 가려고 •	• ⓑ 새 노트북을 샀어요.
(3) 돈이 다 떨어져서 •	• ③ 가볍게 들고 다니려고 •	• ⓒ 택시를 타요.
(4) 약속에 늦어서 •	• ④ 나중에 다시 들으려고 •	• ⓓ 아르바이트를 시작했어요.

2 **다음에서 알맞은 답을 골라서 '-(으)려면'을 사용하여 대화를 완성하세요.**

타다　　잘하다　　후회하다　　거절하다　　화해하다

(1) A 한국어 공부가 어려운데 한국어를 ______________ 어떻게 해야 돼요?
　B 일단 한국 친구를 많이 사귀세요.

(2) A 고속버스를 ______________ 어느 쪽으로 가야 돼요?
　B 저기 매점에서 오른쪽으로 가면 터미널이 나와요.

(3) A 친구의 부탁을 ______________ 어떻게 해야 돼요?
　B 친구가 기분 나빠하지 않게 솔직하게 말하세요.

(4) A 친구와 싸웠는데 ______________ 어떻게 해야 돼요?
　B 먼저 친구에게 사과하세요.

(5) A 나중에 자기 인생을 ______________ 어떻게 해야 돼요?
　B 하고 싶은 일을 포기하지 말고 도전하세요.

3 **알맞은 답을 고르세요.**

(1) 시간 있으면 우리 집에 ⓐ 놀러 / ⓑ 놀려고 오세요.

(2) ⓐ 운동하러 / ⓑ 운동하려고 헬스장에 등록했어요.

(3) 시험을 잘 ⓐ 보려고 / ⓑ 보려면 수업에 빠지지 마세요.

(4) 서로 잘 ⓐ 이해하려고 / ⓑ 이해하려면 많이 노력했어요.

(5) 비행기 표를 싸게 ⓐ 사려고 / ⓑ 사려면 인터넷에서 사세요.

Conversation ❸

Track 27

유키 요즘 어떻게 지내요?

웨이 한국 요리를 배우고 있어요.

유키 재미있겠네요. 그런데 어렵지 않아요?

웨이 한국 사람처럼 잘하기는 어렵지만 생각보다 재미있어요.

유키 대단하네요. 그런데 왜 요리를 배워요?

웨이 저는 원래 한국 문화에 관심이 많이 있어요. 요리도 한국 문화를 더 잘 이해하려고 배워요.

유키 웨이 씨만큼 요리하려면 얼마나 배워야 돼요?

웨이 사람마다 다르죠. 익숙해지려면 적어도 6개월 이상 배워야 돼요.

유키 그렇군요. 저는 가요나 드라마 같은 것을 좋아해요. 특히 요즘에는 한국어 연습하려고 드라마를 잘 봐요.

웨이 드라마가 한국어 연습에 도움이 돼요?

유키 그럼요, 듣기 연습도 되고 문화도 배울 수 있어서 좋아요.

웨이 저는 드라마를 봤을 때 잘 못 알아들어서 금방 포기했어요.

유키 포기하지 말고 꾸준히 해 보세요. 자꾸 들으면 알아들을 수 있게 돼요.

Yuki What have you been up to lately?

Wei I'm learning to cook Korean food.

Yuki That must be fun. Isn't it difficult though?

Wei It's difficult to cook like a Korean person, but it's more fun than I expected.

Yuki That's impressive. But why are you learning to cook?

Wei I've always (lit. originally) been very interested in Korean culture. I'm also learning cooking in order to understand Korean culture better.

Yuki How much do I have to learn to be able to cook as well as you?

Wei It depends on the person. If you want to get used to it, you have to learn for at least six months.

Yuki That makes sense. I like songs and dramas, so lately, I've been especially watching a lot of dramas to practice Korean.

Wei Are dramas helpful for practicing Korean?

Yuki Of course. They're good for listening practice because you can learn about the culture.

Wei When I would watch dramas, I would give up right away because I couldn't understand much.

Yuki Don't give up. Keep trying. If you keep listening, you'll be able to understand.

New Vocabulary ▸P. 328

대단하다 | 원래 | 이해하다 | 만큼 | 적어도 | 이상 | 알아듣다 | 포기하다 | 자꾸

New Expressions ▸P. 328

- 요즘 어떻게 지내요?
- 사람마다 다르죠.
- (A) 이/가 (B) 에 도움이 돼요.

Tips

1 The Marker 만큼

The marker 만큼 is used to express the extent similar to the noun it is attached to.

- 그 사람도 가수**만큼** 노래해요.
  That person also sings as much as a singer does.
- 벌레가 손바닥**만큼** 커요.
  The bug is as big as my palm.

2 Two Meanings of 잘

The adverb 잘 has many meanings. In this conversation, the first 잘 in 잘 이해하다 expresses the meaning "in detail and accurately," while the second one in 잘 보다 is used to mean "a lot."

- 그 사람에 대해 **잘** 알고 있어요. I know a lot about that person.
- 아이들은 **잘** 울어요. Children cry often.

❶ Noun + 있다: "to be", "to have"

- 재미: 재미가 있다 to be interesting/funny
  ↔ 재미가 없다 to be uninteresting/not funny
- 인기: 인기가 있다 to be popular
  ↔ 인기가 없다 to not be popular
- 예의: 예의가 있다 to be polite
  ↔ 예의가 없다 to be impolite
- 실력: 실력이 있다 to be skilled
  ↔ 실력이 없다 to not be skilled
- 책임감: 책임감이 있다 to be responsible
  ↔ 책임감이 없다 to not be responsible
- 의미: 의미가 있다 to be meaningful
  ↔ 의미가 없다 to not be meaningful
- 관심: 관심이 있다 to be interested
  ↔ 관심이 없다 to not be interested
- 자신: 자신이 있다 to be confident
  ↔ 자신이 없다 to not be confident
- 매력: 매력이 있다 to be charming
  ↔ 매력이 없다 to not be charming
- 재능: 재능이 있다 to be talented
  ↔ 재능이 없다 to not be talented
- 효과: 효과가 있다 to be effective
  ↔ 효과가 없다 to not be effective
- 관련: 관련이 있다 to be related
  ↔ 관련이 없다 to not be related

- 언제나 **예의가 있는** 남자가 여자에게 **인기가 있어요.** Polite men are always popular with women.

❷ Noun + 많다: "for many/much to exist"

- 돈: 돈이 많다 ↔ 돈이 없다
  to have a lot of money ↔ to have no money
- 정: 정이 많다 ↔ 정이 없다
  to be very sympathetic ↔ to be unsympathetic
- 욕심: 욕심이 많다 ↔ 욕심이 없다
  to be very greedy ↔ to not be greedy
- 인내심: 인내심이 많다 ↔ 인내심이 없다
  to be very patient ↔ to be impatient

- 그 사람은 **돈이 없지만** 착하고 **정이 많은** 사람이에요. That person does not have money, but he is a nice and generous person.

❸ Noun + 나다: "to be emitted"

- 화: 화가 나다 ↔ 화가 안 나다
  to be angry ↔ to not be angry
- 힘: 힘이 나다 ↔ 힘이 안 나다
  to feel energized ↔ to have no energy
- 차이: 차이가 나다 ↔ 차이가 안 나다
  for there to be a difference ↔ for there to not be a difference
- 샘: 샘이 나다 ↔ 샘이 안 나다
  to be jealous ↔ to not be jealous

- 그 사람과 생각의 **차이가 나지만** 그 사람과 얘기하는 것이 재미있어요. My opinions differ from his, but it's fun to talk to him.

❹ Noun + 되다: "to become", "to happen"

- 이해: 이해가 되다 ↔ 이해가 안 되다
  to understand ↔ to not understand
- 적응: 적응이 되다 ↔ 적응이 안 되다
  to become used to ↔ to not become used to
- 도움: 도움이 되다 ↔ 도움이 안 되다
  to be helpful ↔ to not be helpful
- 해: 해가 되다 ↔ 해가 안 되다
  to be harmful ↔ to not be harmful

- 건강에 **해가 되는** 음식을 왜 먹는지 **이해가 안 돼요.**
  I don't understand why people eat food that is harmful to their health.

❺ Other

- 힘이 세다 to be strong ↔ 힘이 약하다 to be weak
- 키가 크다 to be tall ↔ 키가 작다 to be short
- 나이가 많다 to be old ↔ 나이가 적다 to be young
- 운이 좋다 to be lucky ↔ 운이 나쁘다 to be unlucky
- 기분이 좋다 to be in a good mood ↔ 기분이 나쁘다 to be in a bad mood
- 마음이 넓다 to be generous ↔ 마음이 좁다 to be stingy

Key Expressions

- 어떤 것에나 관심이 있어요.
  I am interested in everything.
- 어떤 것에도 관심이 없어요.
  I am not interested in anything.

Let's Talk!

Speaking Strategy — Reacting to Another's Feelings

- When sympathizing with the listener's current feelings **그렇겠네요. It must be (difficult/sad/etc.)**
- When sympathizing with the listener's past feelings **그랬겠네요. It must have been (difficult/sad/etc.)**

1 여러분은 언제 이런 느낌이 들어요?

Positive Emotions

신나요. It's exciting.
편해요. It's comfortable.
신기해요. It's exciting/amazing.
힘이 나요. I feel energized.
재미있어요. It's interesting/funny.
감동적이에요. It's touching.
흥미가 생겨요. I'm interested.
호기심이 생겨요. I'm curious.
자신감이 생겨요. I'm confident.

Negative Emotions

걱정돼요. I'm worried
긴장돼요. I'm nervous.
겁이 나요. I'm afraid.
불편해요. I'm uncomfortable.
힘들어요. It's difficult.
헷갈려요. I'm confused.
당황했어요. I was flustered.
황당했어요. It was ridiculous.
이해가 안 돼요. I don't understand.

영어에는 존댓말이 없어서 언제 존댓말을 쓰고 언제 반말을 써야 하는지 아직도 헷갈려요.

그렇겠네요.

2 한국 사람과 언제 사고방식의 차이를 느껴요? 여러분 나라와 한국이 어떤 문화 차이가 있어요?

한국에서는 회사에서 회의할 때 자기보다 나이가 많거나 지위가 높은 사람 앞에서 자신의 의견을 솔직하게 말하는 사람이 적은 것을 보고 깜짝 놀랐어요. 정말 사고방식이 달라요.

일본에서는 친구나 동료하고 같이 식사하면 반반씩 돈을 내지만, 한국에서는 돌아가면서 돈을 내는 경우가 많아요. 이럴 때 한국하고 일본이 사고방식이 다른 것을 느껴요.

한국에서는 나이가 많은 사람에게 이름을 부르는 경우가 적은데, 미국에서는 저보다 3-4살 많아도 이름을 부르는 것이 보통이에요. 나이가 많아도 친구니까 그냥 이름을 불러도 돼요.

3 한국에서 생활하면서 어떤 실수를 한 적이 있어요?

전에 실수로 아줌마한테 반말로 말한 적이 있는데 아줌마가 화를 내서 당황했어요. 그때 저는 왜 아줌마가 화가 났는지 이해가 안 됐어요. 그래서 …….

New Vocabulary

감동적이다 to be touching | 흥미 interest | 호기심 curiosity | 헷갈리다 to be confused | 지위 status | 솔직하게 frankly | 돌아가면서 while returning | 경우 circumstance

Word Web

▶ Appendix P. 319

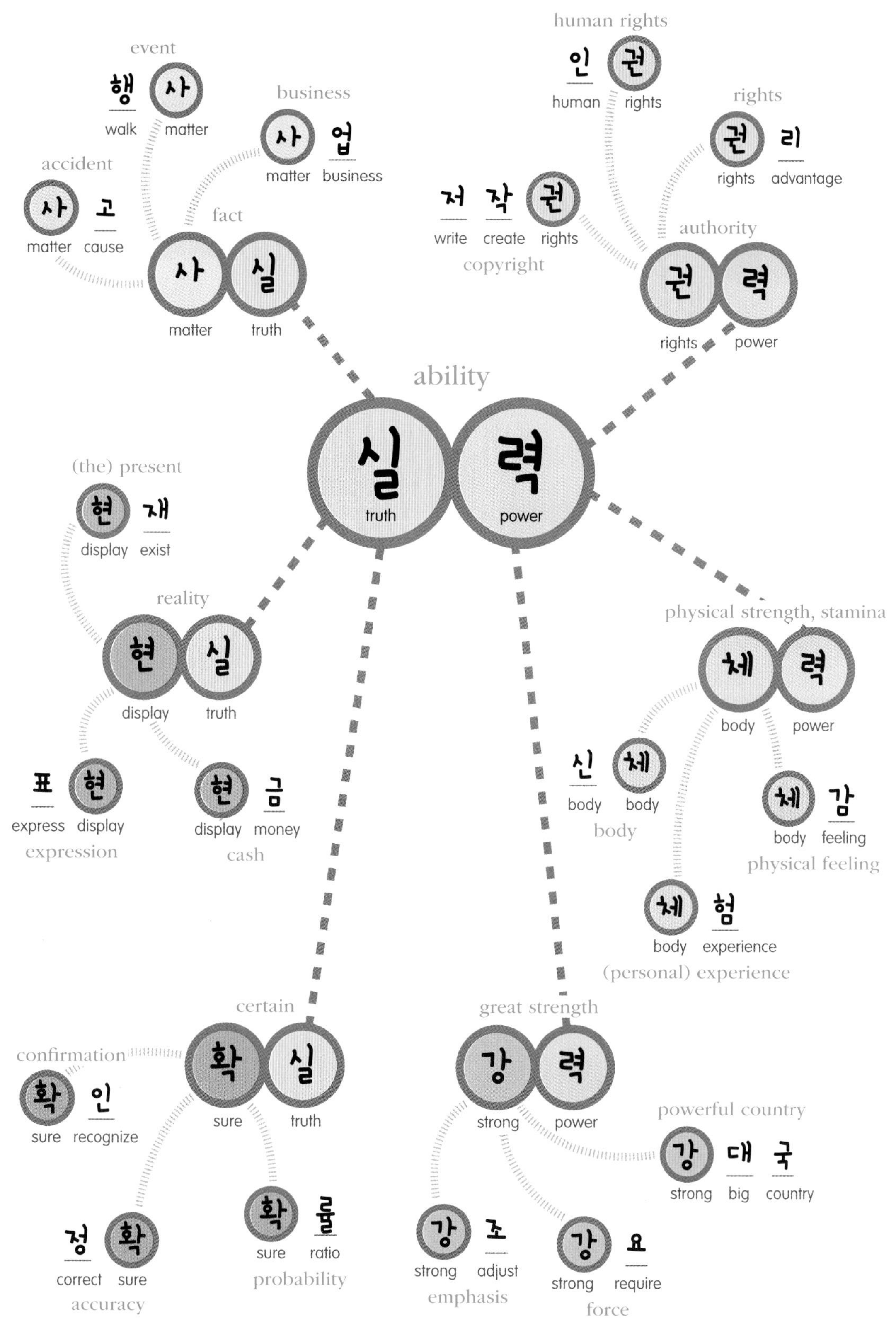

A Word on Culture

Interjections Commonly Used by Koreans

• 아이고! Ah!

Koreans often say 아이고! when in pain, when experiencing difficulty, or when slightly surprised or taken aback. It is often pronounced as [아이구] and is used by everyone: men, women, the old, and the young. Koreans often say 아이고, when they have accidentally dropped something, when bumping into something, when reacting to someone's bad news, or when suddenly realizing something.

• 깜짝이야! Oh my goodness!

깜짝 is an adverb used when one is suddenly startled, while 깜짝이야 is an exclamation used when one is surprised. For example, if you are daydreaming while sitting down and someone all of a sudden taps you on the shoulder, or if you are walking alone at night and a dark object suddenly appears out of nowhere, 깜짝어야 expresses a startling feeling. It has a stronger feeling than 아이고 and is used to surprise or express relief after finding out that some news was not as serious as one had thought.

• 맙소사! 세상에! Oh no!

맙소사! is used when one is dumbfounded. For example, it may be used as an exclamation in situations one never could have imagined would occur, such as if one were to learn that a family member or acquaintance has been in an accident or if one's invested money was swindled. In these cases, 세상에! may also be used, but 세상에! is also used when reacting to someone else's bad news. Both phrases are used when one has experienced a grave situation and exclaims in disbelief.

• 이야~! Wow!

이야 is used when one is surprised by how impressive something is or when one encounters a friend one has not seen for a long time. When used in real life, it is often stretched out and sounds similar to 이야~.

Chapter **10**

문제

Problems

Goals
- Asking and Replying about Problems
- Making Requests
- Accepting Requests
- Concerns about the Weather
- Suggesting New Ideas
- Bringing up Obligations
- Speaking about Decisions

Grammar

❶ 반말 "banmal" (casual speech)
-(으)ㄴ/는데요? Question ending asking more detail

❷ -(으)ㄹ 줄 알다 "to know how to"
-(으)ㄹ까 봐 "I'm afraid that..."

❸ -아/어야지요 "You should"
-아/어야겠다 "I think I should..."

Grammar 1

반말 "banmal" (casual speech)

▶ Appendix P. 275 U.U P. 311

A 지금 뭐 하고 있어요?
What are you doing?

B 책 읽고 있어요.
I'm reading a book.

Banmal is used when speaking to someone with whom one has a personal relationship, such as a younger family member (siblings, children, nephews, and nieces, etc.), a friend (from youth or school), a close younger colleague or classmate, or considerably younger people. It evokes a feeling of intimacy and is generally used in speech.

- A 어제 친구 만났어요? Did you meet your friend yesterday?
  B 아니요, 집에 있었어요. No, I was at home.
- 너한테 할 말이 있으니까 내 얘기 좀 들어 봐. (← 보세요) I have something to tell you, so listen to me.
- 이따가 나하고 같이 영화 보자. (← 봅시다) Watch a movie with me later.

-(으)ㄴ/는데요? Question ending asking more detail

C.C P. 306

A 배가 아파요.
My stomach hurts.

B 무슨 음식을 먹었는데요?
What did you eat?

-(으)ㄴ/는데요? is used to ask someone for more detail about something they have just said. These are questions involving question words. -(으)ㄴ/는데요? as a question may only be used in speech, and, as it is a reaction to a sentence, it may not be used at the beginning of a conversation. It is conjugated in the same manner as -(으)ㄴ/는데 in Chapter 4.

- A 나는 고기를 안 먹어. I don't eat meat.
  B 그럼, 무슨 음식을 좋아하는데? So, what kind of food do you like?
- A 어제 집에 있었어요. I was at home yesterday.
  B 집에서 뭐 했는데요? What did you do at home?

Be careful

-(으)ㄴ/는데요? may only be used in questions that contain a question word. It may not be used in yes/no questions.

- 한국 음식을 좋아하는데요? (X)
- 무슨 음식을 좋아하는데요? (O)
  What kind of food do you like?

1 그림을 보고 더 적절한 답을 고르세요.

(1)

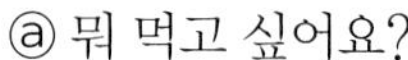

ⓐ 뭐 먹고 싶어요?
ⓑ 뭐 먹고 싶어?

(2)

ⓐ 회의가 언제 시작합니까?
ⓑ 회의가 언제 시작해?

(3)

ⓐ 몇 번 버스가 남산에 가요?
ⓑ 몇 번 버스가 남산에 가?

(4)

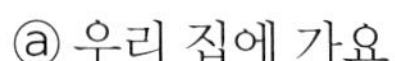

ⓐ 우리 집에 가요.
ⓑ 우리 집에 가자.

2 다음 대화를 반말로 바꾸세요.

	➡	
리나 진수 씨, 내일 시간 있어요?		리나 너, 내일 시간 (1) ______?
진수 네, 있어요. 왜요?		진수 (2) ______, 있어. (3) ______?
리나 내일 같이 영화 보러 가요.		리나 내일 같이 영화 보러 (4) ______.
진수 좋아요. 제가 표를 살게요.		진수 좋아. (5) ______ 표를 살게.
리나 아니에요. 표는 저한테 있어요. 진수 씨는 저녁을 사 주세요.		리나 (6) ______. 표는 (7) ______ 있어. (8) ______ 저녁을 (9) ______.
진수 알았어요. 내일 봐요.		진수 알았어. 내일 (10) ______.

3 밑줄 친 것을 고치세요.

(1) <u>저는</u> 요즘 건강을 위해 운동을 시작했어. ➡

(2) <u>네가</u> 이따가 전화할게. ➡

(3) 오늘 시간 있어요? 같이 밥 <u>먹자</u>. ➡

(4) A 지금 여권 있어?
B <u>네</u>, 있어. ➡

Conversation 1

Track 28

리나 진수야! 지금 뭐 하고 있어?
진수 아무것도 안 해. 그냥 쉬고 있어.
리나 그래? 그럼, 내 부탁 좀 들어줘.
진수 무슨 부탁인데?
리나 내 컴퓨터가 고장 났는데, 고치는 것 좀 도와줘.
진수 그래? 어떻게 안 되는데?
리나 갑자기 컴퓨터가 안 켜져. 왜 그런지 모르겠어.
진수 언제부터 그랬어?
리나 지금 막 고장 났어. 좀 전까지는 괜찮았는데…….
진수 선도 연결되어 있어?
리나 어, 그것도 확인했는데 선에는 아무 문제 없어.
진수 그럼, 이따가 저녁 먹은 후에 가서 고쳐 줄게.
리나 좀 급한데 지금 와서 도와주면 안 돼?
진수 알았어. 금방 갈게.

Rina Jinsu! What are you doing right now?
Jinsu I'm not doing anything. I'm just resting.
Rina Really? Then let me ask you a favor.
Jinsu What favor?
Rina My computer broke. Can you help me fix it?
Jinsu Really? What doesn't work?
Rina It suddenly stopped turning on and I don't know why.
Jinsu When did it start acting like this?
Rina It just broke. It was fine until just a little while ago...
Jinsu Is it plugged in? (lit. Is it connected?)
Rina Yes, I checked that and there's no problem with the plug.
Jinsu Then I'll go fix it for you later after eating dinner.
Rina I'm in a bit of a rush. Can't you come help me now?
Jinsu Okay, I'll be there in a moment.

New Vocabulary ▸P. 328

아무 | 부탁을 들어주다 | 고장 나다 | 고치다 | 갑자기 | 막 | 선 | 연결되다 | 문제 | 급하다

New Expressions ▸P. 329

- 아무것도 안 해.
- 지금 막 고장 났어.
- (noun)에는 아무 문제 없어.

Tips

1 Two Meanings of 좀

좀 has two meanings. In this conversation, the first and second 좀 mean "please" and are used to express politeness when asking favors. The third and fourth 좀 are contractions of 조금 used in speech.

- 이것 **좀** 도와주세요.
  Please help me with this.
- 저한테는 이 음식이 **좀** 매워요.
  This food is a little spicy for me.

2 The Usage of 아무

아무 is generally used with negative sentences to mean "no" or with positive sentences to mean "any (no particular one)."

- **아무도** 안 왔어요. No one came.
- **아무** 말**도** 안 했어요. I didn't say anything.

- **아무나** 들어가도 돼요. Anyone can enter.
- **아무거나** 얘기하세요. You can say anything.

Verbs Pertaining to Using Items

1.

불을 켜다 ↔ 불을 끄다
to turn on a light ↔ to turn off a light

2.

선풍기를 틀다 ↔ 선풍기를 끄다
to turn on a fan ↔ to turn off a fan

3.

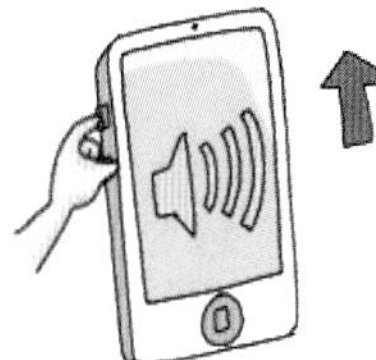

소리를 높이다 ↔ 소리를 줄이다
to raise the volume ↔ to lower the volume

4.

문을 밀다 ↔ 문을 당기다
to push a door ↔ to pull a door

5.

책을 꺼내다 ↔ 책을 넣다
to take out a book ↔ to put a book away

6.

가방을 들다 ↔ 가방을 놓다
to hold a bag ↔ to place a bag down

7.

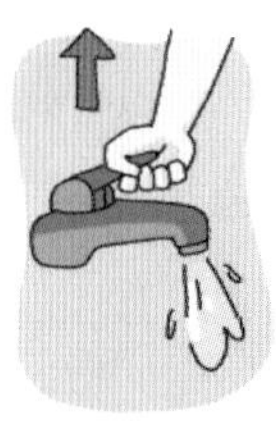

수도꼭지를 올리다 ↔ 수도꼭지를 내리다
to turn on a faucet ↔ to turn off a faucet

8.

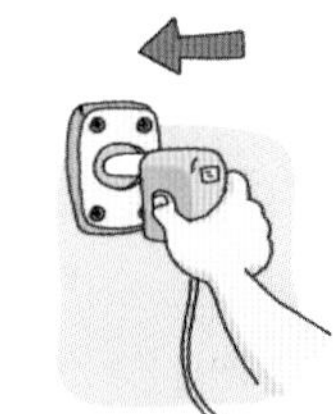

충전기를 꽂다 ↔ 충전기를 빼다
to plug in a charger ↔ to remove a charger

9. 창문을 열다 ↔ 창문을 닫다
to open a window ↔ to close a window

10. 문을 열다 ↔ 문을 잠그다
to open a door ↔ to lock a door

11. 뚜껑을 열다 ↔ 뚜껑을 덮다
to open a lid ↔ to close a lid

12. 책을 펴다 ↔ 책을 덮다
to open a book ↔ to close a book

13. 버튼을 누르다 to push a button
14. 채널을 돌리다 to change the channel
15. 카드를 대다 to tap a card
16. 손잡이를 잡다 to hold on to a handknob/strap/handle
17. 배터리를 충전하다 to charge a battery
18. 알람을 맞추다 to set an alarm

Key Expressions

- 컴퓨터가 망가졌어. My computer broke.
- 배터리가 떨어졌어. My battery ran out.
- 시계가 죽었어. My watch died.

Grammar 2

-(으)ㄹ 줄 알다 "to know how to"

A 수영할 줄 알아요?
Do you know how to swim?

B 아니요, 수영할 줄 몰라요.
No, I don't know how to swim.

-(으)ㄹ 줄 알다 is used to express if one has the ability or knowledge of how to do something. If one does not have this ability or knowledge of how to do something -(으)ㄹ 줄 모르다 is used. -(으)ㄹ 줄 알다 is attached to verb stems.

- 중국 사람이니까 한자를 읽을 줄 알아요.
  I'm Chinese, so I can read Chinese characters.
- 자전거를 탈 줄 몰라요. 가르쳐 주세요.
  I can't ride a bike. Please teach me.
- 전에는 독일어를 할 줄 알았는데, 지금은 다 잊어버렸어요.
  I could speak German in the past, but now I forgot.

Be careful

Because -(으)ㄹ 줄 알다 expresses one's learned knowledge, it may not be used for an innate ability or an ability one naturally knows without the need of learning.

- 저는 텔레비전을 볼 줄 알아요. (X)
- 저는 텔레비전을 볼 수 있어요. (O)
  I can watch TV.

-(으)ㄹ까 봐 "I'm afraid that..."

A 왜 아이스크림을 안 먹어요?
Why don't you eat ice cream?

B 살이 찔까 봐 안 먹어요.
I don't eat it because I'm afraid that I'll gain weight.

The clause after -(으)ㄹ까 봐 expresses an action taken because of worry that the clause before -(으)ㄹ까 봐 will happen. It is attached to the stems of verbs, adjectives, and 이다. If one is worried that an action has already happened, -았/었- may be attached to form -았/었을까 봐.

- 시험이 너무 어려워서 떨어질까 봐 걱정돼요.
  I am worried that I will fail because the exam is too difficult.
- 약속에 늦을까 봐 택시를 탔어요.
  I was afraid I would be late for my appointment, so I took a taxi.
- 기차가 벌써 출발했을까 봐 기차역까지 뛰어갔어요.
  I thought the train had already left, so I ran to the train station.

Be careful

As the action following -(으)ㄹ까 봐 has already taken place or is a regular action, -(으)세요, -(으)ㅂ시다, and -아/어야 하다, which imply future actions, may not be used.

- 비가 올까 봐 우산을 가져가세요. (X)
- 비가 올까 봐 우산을 가져왔어요. (O)
  I brought an umbrella in case it rains.

▸Answers P. 314

1 '-(으)ㄹ 줄 알다'나 '-(으)ㄹ 줄 모르다'를 사용하여 문장을 완성하세요.

(1) 저는 한국 요리를 좋아하지만 ______________. (만들다)

(2) 자전거를 ______________니까 저한테 자전거가 필요 없어요. (타다)

(3) 제가 컴퓨터를 ______________니까 문제 생기면 말씀하세요. (고치다)

(4) ______________면 저 대신에 운전 좀 해 주세요. (운전하다)

(5) 교통 카드를 ______________서 개찰구 앞에서 계속 서 있었어요. (사용하다)

2 문장을 완성하도록 알맞은 것끼리 연결하세요.

(1) 학생들이 이해 못 할까 봐 • • ⓐ 지도를 가져왔어요.

(2) 길을 헤맬까 봐 • • ⓑ 밤새 공부했어요.

(3) 아침에 못 일어날까 봐 • • ⓒ 선생님이 천천히 말했어요.

(4) 시험을 못 볼까 봐 • • ⓓ 가방에 신경 많이 썼어요.

(5) 물건을 도둑맞을까 봐 • • ⓔ 알람 시계를 두 개 맞췄어요.

3 알맞은 답을 고르세요.

(1) 한국 노래를 (ⓐ 부를 줄 아니까 / ⓑ 부를 줄 모르니까) 저는 미국 노래만 불렀어요.

(2) 친구 연락처를 (ⓐ 기억할까 봐 / ⓑ 잊어버릴까 봐) 핸드폰에 저장했어요.

(3) 아기가 침대에서 (ⓐ 떨어질까 봐 / ⓑ 떨어지지 않을까 봐) 엄마가 아기 옆에서 보고 있어요.

(4) 친구가 컴퓨터를 (ⓐ 사용할 줄 아니까 / ⓑ 사용할 줄 모르니까) 가르쳐 주고 있어요

(5) 건강이 더 (ⓐ 좋아질까 봐 / ⓑ 안 좋아질까 봐) 술과 담배를 끊었어요.

(6) 부모님이 핸드폰 사용법을 (ⓐ 이해할까 봐 / ⓑ 이해하지 못할까 봐) 다시 설명해 드렸어요.

Conversation ❷

Track 29

마크　새라야, 무슨 일 있어? 왜 그래?
새라　이번 주말에 비가 올까 봐 걱정이야.
마크　주말 날씨에 왜 신경을 쓰는데?
새라　이번 주말에 부모님 모시고 제주도로 여행 떠나거든.
마크　우산 가지고 가면 되지, 뭐.
새라　제주도의 유명한 '올레' 길을 걸으려고 하는데, 날씨 때문에…….
마크　그렇구나! 비가 오면 걷기 힘들겠다!
새라　그래서 어떻게 해야 할지 생각하고 있어.
마크　운전할 줄 알아?
새라　알지. 그건 왜?
마크　그럼, 제주도에서 자동차를 빌려서 드라이브하면 어때?
새라　그런데 제주도에 뭐가 있는지도 잘 모르는데…….
마크　제주도는 바다 경치가 유명하니까 바닷가 근처에 좋은 데가 있을 거야.
새라　그거 좋은 생각이다. 알려 줘서 고마워.
마크　고맙긴. 여행 잘 다녀와.

Mark　Sarah, what's wrong?
Sarah　I'm worried that it will rain this weekend.
Mark　Why are you worried about this weekend's weather?
Sarah　I'm taking my parents to Jeju Island this weekend.
Mark　Just bring an umbrella.
Sarah　I'm planning to walk down the famous "Olleh" road, but because of the weather...
Mark　Is that so? It'll be difficult if it rains!
Sarah　That's why I'm thinking about what to do.
Mark　Do you know how to drive?
Sarah　Of course I know. Why?
Mark　Why don't you rent a car and drive around Jeju Island?
Sarah　But I don't know what there is to see in Jeju Island...
Mark　There will be nice places by the sea since Jeju Island has famous ocean scenery.
Sarah　That's a good idea. Thank you for telling me.
Mark　No need to thank me. Have fun on your trip.

New Vocabulary ▸P. 329

날씨 | 모시고 | 걷다 | 빌리다 | 바닷가 | 경치 | 데 | 알리다

New Expressions ▸P. 329

- 무슨 일 있어?
- 그거 좋은 생각이다.
- 여행 잘 다녀와.

Tips

1 -(으)면 되지, 뭐: Informal Ways to Give Advice

This expression is used to give advice about a problem and imply that the problem is insignificant. It is generally used in informal situations between close friends. 뭐 may be attached to the end to emphasize the levity of the suggestion.

- 지금부터 공부하**면 되죠**, **뭐**.
  Just study from now on.

2 Question Word (what, how, where, etc.) + to do

-아/어야 할지 is used to express an action one must take.

- 무엇을 해**야 할지** 알려 주세요.
  Let me know what to do.
- 어디에 가**야 할지** 모르겠어요.
  I don't know where to go now.

❶ Weather Vocabulary

1. 나다

- 해가 나다 for the sun to come out

- 햇빛 sunlight
- 햇볕 sunray

2. 끼다

- 구름이 끼다 to be cloudy
- 안개가 끼다 to be foggy

- 먹구름 dark clouds

3. 오다/내리다

- 비가 오다/내리다 to rain
- 눈이 오다/내리다 to snow

- 소나기 shower
- 폭우 storm
- 폭설 blizzard

4. 불다

- 바람이 불다 for the wind to blow
- 태풍이 불다 for there to be a typhoon

- 비바람 rainstorm

5. 치다

- 번개가 치다 for lightning to strike
- 천둥이 치다 for there to be thunder

- 벼락 lightning bolt

- 소나기가 내린 후 **해가 났어요.** The sun came out after the shower.
- **바람이 불고 번개가 치는** 날에는 밖에 안 나가는 게 좋아요. It's good to not go outside on days the wind is blowing and when lightning is striking.

❷ Weather Descriptions

1.

맑다 to be clear → 흐리다 to be cloudy → 개다 to clear up

(비/눈/바람/태풍)이/가 그치다 (for the rain/snow/wind/typhoon) to stop

(구름/안개)이/가 걷히다 (for the clouds/fog) to clear

- 추위 cold
- 더위 heat

2.

춥다 to be cold

쌀쌀하다 to be chilly

시원하다 to be cool

따뜻하다 to be warm

덥다 to be hot

3.

건조하다 to be dry
습도가 높다 for the humidity to be high
후텁지근하다 to be sticky, stuffy
햇빛이 강하다 for the sunshine to be strong
(날씨가) 변덕스럽다 (for the weather) to be fickle
(날씨가) 포근하다 (for the weather) to be comfortable

- **비가 그치고 날씨가 갰으니까** 이따가 산책 가요. Let's go take a walk later because the rain has stopped and the weather has cleared up.
- 날씨가 **쌀쌀하니까** 밖에 나가려면 겉옷을 가져가야 해요. The weather is chilly, so you have to bring a jacket when you go outside.
- 겨울에는 너무 **건조해서** 크림을 바르는 게 피부에 좋아요. Because it's so dry in the winter, it's good to apply lotion to your skin.

Key Expressions

- 오전 내내 비가 오겠습니다. It will probably rain all morning.
- 오후에 비가 그치겠습니다. The rain will probably stop in the afternoon.

Grammar ❸

-아/어야지요 "You should"

▶ Appendix P. 278  C.C P. 300

A 물건이 잘못 배송되었는데 어떡하죠?
I received the wrong package. What should I do?

B 우선 고객 센터에 전화해야지요.
You should call the customer center first.

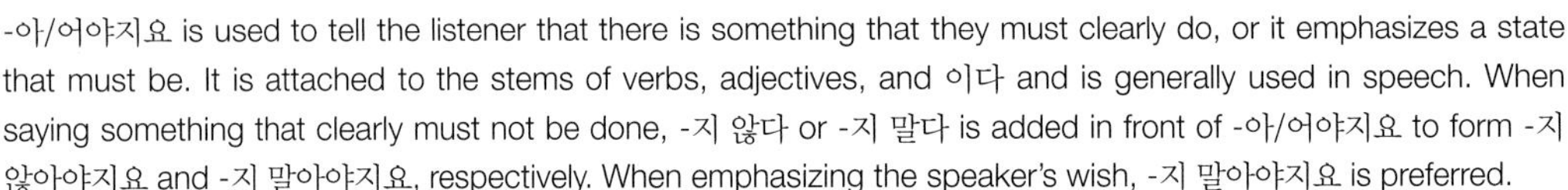

-아/어야지요 is used to tell the listener that there is something that they must clearly do, or it emphasizes a state that must be. It is attached to the stems of verbs, adjectives, and 이다 and is generally used in speech. When saying something that clearly must not be done, -지 않다 or -지 말다 is added in front of -아/어야지요 to form -지 않아야지요 and -지 말아야지요, respectively. When emphasizing the speaker's wish, -지 말아야지요 is preferred.

- 감기에 걸렸으면 푹 쉬어야지요. If you catch a cold, you should rest.
- 가게 직원은 손님에게 친절해야죠. Shopkeepers should be kind to customers.
- 어제 지각했으면 오늘은 늦지 말아야지요. If you were late yesterday, you shouldn't be late today.

-아/어야겠다 "I think I should..."

 C.C P. 301

A 벌써 8시네요.
Wow, it's already 8.

B 이제 집에 가 봐야겠어요.
I should go home now.

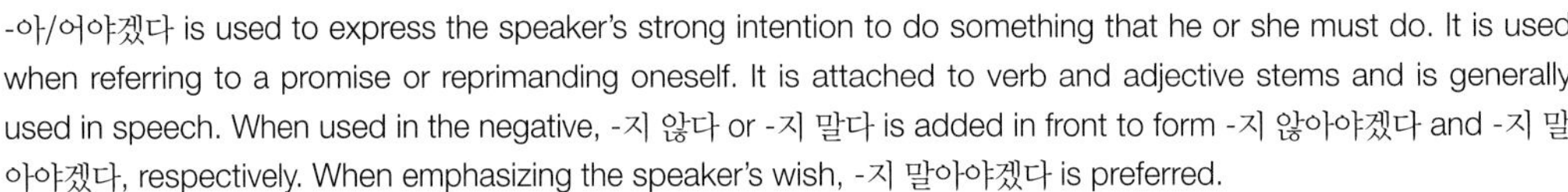

-아/어야겠다 is used to express the speaker's strong intention to do something that he or she must do. It is used when referring to a promise or reprimanding oneself. It is attached to verb and adjective stems and is generally used in speech. When used in the negative, -지 않다 or -지 말다 is added in front to form -지 않아야겠다 and -지 말아야겠다, respectively. When emphasizing the speaker's wish, -지 말아야겠다 is preferred.

- 요즘 친구가 연락이 안 돼요. 전화해 봐야겠어요. I can't get in touch with my friend these days. I should try calling.
- 행복하게 살려면 건강해야겠어요. If we want to live a happy life, we should be healthy.
- 이제부터 회사에 지각하지 말아야겠어. From now on, I should not arrive late to the company.

1 **알맞은 답을 고르세요.**

(1) 수영장에 가려면 ⓐ 수영복을 가져와야죠. ⓑ 수영복을 가져오지 않아야죠.

(2) 그 사람이 친구라면 ⓐ 거짓말을 해야죠. ⓑ 거짓말을 하지 말아야죠.

(3) 내일까지 일을 끝내려면 ⓐ 오늘 다른 약속을 잡아야죠. ⓑ 오늘 다른 약속을 잡지 않아야죠.

(4) 여권을 잃어버리면 ⓐ 경찰에게 숨겨야죠. ⓑ 경찰에게 신고해야죠.

2 **다음에서 알맞은 답을 골라서 '-아/어야겠다'를 사용하여 대화를 완성하세요.**

일하다　　피우다　　준비하다　　알아보다

(1) A 자주 길을 잃어버려서 걱정이에요.
B 맞아요. 다음부터는 꼭 지도를 ________________.

(2) A 사고를 예방하려면 왜 사고가 났는지 알아봐야죠.
B 맞아요. 먼저 사고 원인부터 ________________.

(3) A 이번에 승진이 안 됐어.
B 어, 내년에 승진하려면 더 열심히 ________________.

(4) A 요즘 건강이 안 좋아졌어요? 얼굴이 안 좋아 보여요.
B 네, 요즘 건강이 안 좋아요. 이제 담배를 ________________.

3 **문장을 완성하도록 알맞은 것끼리 연결하세요.**

(1) 비가 오니까 • 　　• ⓐ 재료부터 사 와야지.
(2) 여행을 가려면 • 　　• ⓑ 우산을 사야겠어요.
(3) 음식을 만들려면 • 　　• ⓒ 먼저 돈을 모아야죠.
(4) 친구가 오해할 수 있으니까 • 　　• ⓓ 계획을 잘 세워야지요.
(5) 실패하지 않으려면 • 　　• ⓔ 사실을 말해야겠어요.

Conversation ❸

Track 30

링링	지갑을 잃어버렸어. 어떡하지?
웨이	어디에서 잃어버렸는지 기억나?
링링	잘 모르겠어, 기억 안 나.
웨이	잘 생각해 봐. 마지막으로 언제 지갑을 봤는데?
링링	아까 식당에서 계산했을 때 지갑을 꺼냈어. 그 후에는 지갑을 못 봤어.
웨이	지갑 안에 뭐가 들어 있는데?
링링	카드하고 현금, 신분증이 들어 있어.
웨이	카드는 정지했어?
링링	아니, 깜빡 잊어버리고 아직 못 했어.
웨이	카드를 빨리 정지해야지. 그렇지 않으면 더 큰 문제가 생길 수도 있어.
링링	맞다! 은행에 전화해야겠다.
웨이	유실물 센터에는 가 봤어?
링링	아니, 아직 못 가 봤어.
웨이	유실물 센터에도 가 봐야지.
링링	알았어. 일단 유실물 센터부터 가 봐야겠다.

Ling Ling	I lost my wallet. What should I do?
Wei	Do you remember where you lost it?
Ling Ling	I'm not sure. I can't remember.
Wei	Think about it carefully. When was the last time you saw your wallet?
Ling Ling	I took out my wallet just now when I paid the bill at the restaurant. After that, I didn't see it.
Wei	What was inside it?
Ling Ling	A credit card, cash, and my ID were inside.
Wei	Did you cancel your credit card?
Ling Ling	No, I completely forgot and still haven't done it.
Wei	You have to cancel it quickly. Otherwise, you might have worse problems.
Ling Ling	That's right! I should call the bank.
Wei	Did you try going to the lost-and-found?
Ling Ling	No, I haven't been able to go yet.
Wei	You should also go to the lost-and-found.
Ling Ling	Okay. I guess I should go to the lost-and-found first.

New Vocabulary ▸P. 329

지갑 | 잃어버리다 | 기억나다 | 마지막으로 | 계산하다 | 꺼내다 | 들어 있다 | 현금 | 신분증 | 정지하다 | 깜빡 | 잊어버리다 | 유실물 센터 | 일단

New Expressions ▸P. 329

- 어떡하지?
- 기억 안 나.
- 깜빡 잊어버리고 아직 못 했어.

Tips

1 기억하다/생각하다 vs. 기억나다/생각나다

기억하다 and 생각하다 refer to the deliberate action of thinking about or trying to remember something, while 기억나다 and 생각나다 refer to suddenly and unintentionally remembering or being reminded of something. Thus, the marker 을/를 follows 기억하다 while 이/가 follows 기억나다.

- 그 사람의 이름을 **생각해도** 이름이 **생각** 안 **나요.**
  Although I'm trying to think of that person's name, I can't remember it.

2 일단 (noun)부터: "(noun) first"

When there are many things one must do, 일단 may be used before a noun to express the first and foremost thing that must be done, while 부터 follows the noun.

- **일단** 밥**부터** 먹읍시다. Let's eat first.
- **일단** 책**부터** 정리하죠.
  Let's arrange the books first.

Common Problems

1.

여권을 잃어버리다
to lose one's passport

2.

지갑을 도둑맞다
to have a wallet stolen

3.

중요한 서류가 없어지다
for an important document to disappear

4.

길을 헤매다
to be lost in the streets

5.

버스나 지하철을 잘못 타다
to take the wrong bus or subway

6.

차가 밀리다 (= 길이 막히다)
for there to be a traffic jam

7.

우산을 놓고 오다
to forget an umbrella (lit. to leave behind an umbrella and come)

8.

비밀번호를 잊어버리다
to forget a password

9.

시험에서 떨어지다
to fail a test

10.

전자 제품이 망가지다
for an electronic product to break

11.

다른 사람의 물건을 망가뜨리다
to break someone else's possession

12.

돈이 다 떨어지다
to run out of money

13. 거짓말이 들통나다 for a lie to be detected
14. 사업이 망하다 for a business to go bankrupt
15. 사기를 당하다 to be defrauded

Key Expressions

- 일단 신고부터 하세요. Report it first.
- 일단 전화부터 해 보세요. Call someone first.
- 일단 가방부터 다시 살펴보세요. Look for your bag again first.

Let's Talk!

Speaking Strategy — **Giving Advice**

- **제 경우에는** 혼자 생각해 보는 **것이 도움이 많이 됐어요.**
  In my case, it was very helpful to think about it alone.
- 다른 사람과 얘기할 시간을 갖는 **것이 좋겠어요.**
  It would be good to make some time to speak with someone.
- 먼저 그 사람과 얘기를 해 보는 **게 좋지 않을까요?**
  Wouldn't it be good to talk with that person first?

❶ 어떤 고민이 있었어요? 고민이 있을 때 어떻게 했어요? 고민이 해결됐어요?

어렸을 때

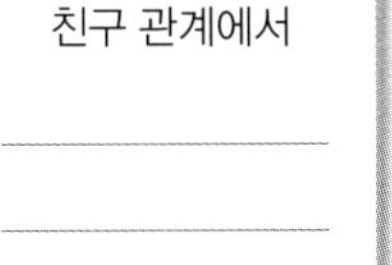

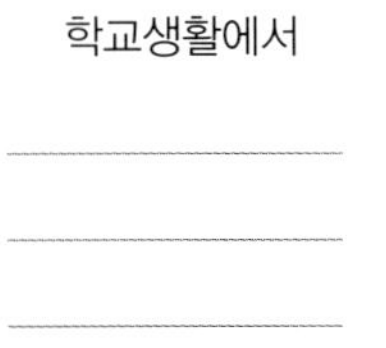

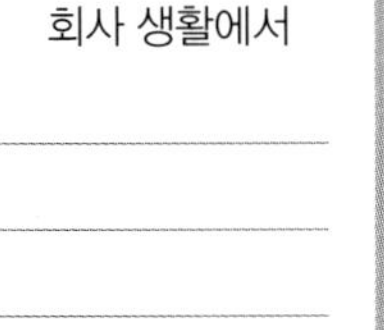

제 친구 중에 어떤 친구가 너무 자주 전화하고 문자해서 제 생활에 방해가 돼요.

그 친구에게 솔직하게 얘기하는 게 좋지 않을까요?

❷ 친구의 고민을 듣고 좋은 조언을 해 주세요.

- 친구가 자꾸 나를 오해해서 그 친구와 사이가 불편해졌어요.
- 직장 상사가 저를 싫어해요. 저는 매일 직장 상사에게 혼나요.
- 주변에 사람이 많아도 진짜 친구가 없어서 항상 외로워요.
- 아직 젊은데 머리가 자꾸 빠져요. 그래서 머리에 자꾸 신경이 쓰여요.
- 여러 가지 해 봐도 흥미가 없어요. 몸도 게을러져요.
- 열심히 공부하지만 단어를 외워도 자꾸 잊어버려요.
- 몸이 피곤하지만 밤에 잠이 안 와요.
- 외국어로 말할 때 너무 긴장해서 말이 안 나와요.
- 회사에서 언제 해고될지 몰라서 불안해요.
- 일을 그만두고 싶은데 돈이 없어서 계속 일해야 돼요.
- 아내가 낭비가 심해서 항상 돈이 부족해요.
- 하고 싶은 일이 있는데 부모님이 반대하세요.

New Vocabulary

해결되다 to be solved | 방해가 되다 to be an obstacle | 조언 advice | 오해하다 to misunderstand | 직장 상사 superior (at work) | 외롭다 to be lonely | 신경이 쓰이다 to pay attention, to worry | 흥미가 없다 to be uninteresting | 외우다 to memorize | 해고되다 to be fired | 낭비가 심하다 to be very wasteful | 부족하다 to be insufficient | 반대하다 to oppose

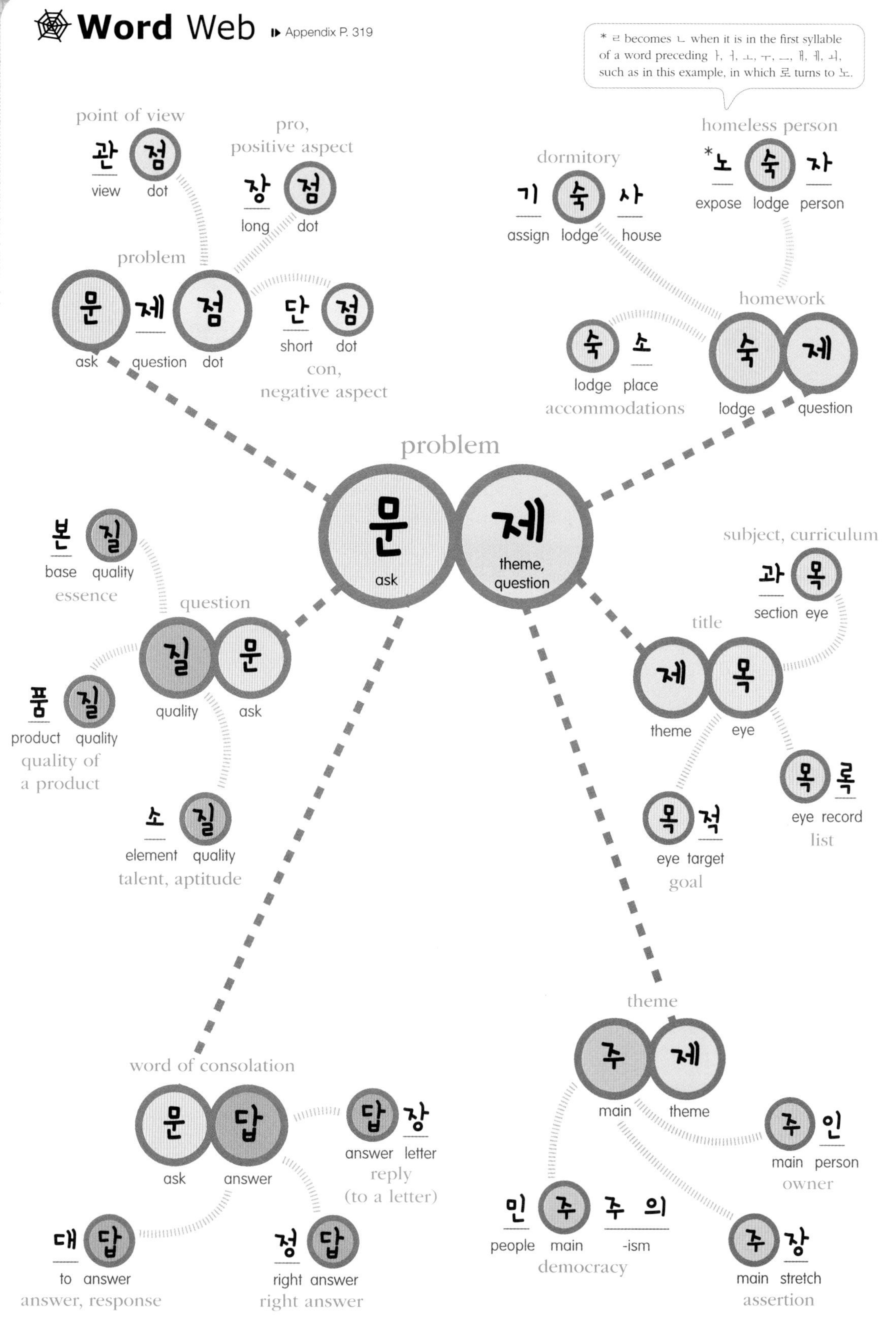

Word Web
▶ Appendix P. 319
* ㄹ becomes ㄴ when it is in the first syllable of a word preceding ㅏ, ㅓ, ㅗ, ㅜ, ㅡ, ㅐ, ㅔ, ㅚ, such as in this example, in which 로 turns to 노.
point of view
관 점
view dot
pro, positive aspect
장 점
long dot
problem
문 제 점
ask question dot
단 점
short dot
con, negative aspect
dormitory
기 숙 사
assign lodge house
homeless person
*노 숙 자
expose lodge person
homework
숙 제
lodge question
숙 소
lodge place
accommodations
problem
문 제
ask
theme, question
본 질
base quality
essence
question
질 문
quality ask
품 질
product quality
quality of a product
소 질
element quality
talent, aptitude
subject, curriculum
과 목
section eye
title
제 목
theme eye
목 적
eye target
goal
목 록
eye record
list
word of consolation
문 답
ask answer
답 장
answer letter
reply (to a letter)
대 답
to answer
answer, response
정 답
right answer
right answer
theme
주 제
main theme
주 인
main person
owner
민 주 주 의
people main -ism
democracy
주 장
main stretch
assertion

A Word on Culture

When Can You Say 너?

반말 is a form of speech that may be used in situations in which it is not required to be polite, such as with a sibling, a close friend, or a considerably younger person. It can be thought of as similar to the feeling of using a single short word to reply to a friend with whom one feels comfortable. However, it is, of course, difficult for a foreigner to understand what is exactly meant by a "comfortable relationship." When should 반말 be used?

If the listener is a seven-year-old child, it is acceptable to use 반말, even when first meeting him or her, so 너 may also be used. However, it is dangerous to thoughtlessly use 반말 with someone of similar age or who is only slightly younger when meeting him or her for the first time. It is especially possible to insult someone by using 반말 if they are only slightly younger and are already an adult. This is because 반말 expresses the lack of need to be polite, as such it can be interpreted as condescending if used with a stranger. Therefore, people do not use 반말 with people of the same age they are meeting for the first time, and it is mostly used once the two people have agreed upon using 반말. 반말 may be used once a close relationship has been forged.

For people living in the same community, the usage of 반말 can be a symbol of intimacy. For example, if an older college student uses 반말 to one younger student and not to another, it is implied that he or she feels closer to the student with whom he or she uses 반말. In other words, one may avoid using 반말 to maintain distance from an unfriendly person.

However, just because two people are close does not mean that 반말 may be unconditionally used. For example, even if one has forged a close relationship, 반말 is generally not used with coworkers, customers, store owners, or similar business-like situations. It is used between young classmates, particularly those with whom one feels comfortable sharing personal memories and thoughts. Thus, it is rude to use 반말 with a young part-time worker at a store one frequents. Furthermore, if one uses 너 with someone one has met in these situations, it is even ruder as it implies that the other person is beneath oneself. Therefore, relationships in which one may use 반말 depend on the level of intimacy and suggest an informal and close relationship.

Chapter 11
사람
People

Goals
- Describing People's Appearances
- Talking about Transitions and Changes of State
- Describing People's Outfits
- Expressing Vague Questions
- Confirming Information
- Talking about One's Wishes
- Talking about the Goals of One's Actions

Grammar

❶ -(으)ㄴ/는 noun modifier
-아/어 보이다 "to look like"

❷ -(으)ㄹ까요? expressing vague questions
-잖아요 reminding the listener of a fact he/she knows

❸ -았/었으면 좋겠다 "I wish", "I hope", "It would be nice if"
-도록 "such that", "so that"

Grammar 1

-(으)ㄴ/는 noun modifier

▶ Appendix P. 277

A 지금 뭐 해요?
What are you doing now?

B 학생들한테 받은 편지를 읽고 있어요.
I'm reading letters I received from my students.

The noun modifier is attached to relative clauses that give nouns more specificity. These relative clauses always precede the noun they modify. The noun modifier differs depending on whether it is attached to a verb, adjective, or 이다 and what the tense of the relative clause is. -는, -(으)ㄴ, and -(으)ㄹ can all be attached to verb stems. -는 expresses present tense modification. -(으)ㄴ expresses the past, and -(으)ㄹ expresses the future. -(으)ㄴ is also attached to adjective stems, but it expresses a present tense modification.

- 음악을 좋아하는 사람들이 이곳에 자주 가요. Music-loving people go here often.
- 아까 먹은 음식의 이름이 뭐예요? What's the name of the food eaten before?
- 내일 여행 갈 사람은 오늘까지 신청하세요. For those who will go on the trip tomorrow, please apply by today.

-아/어 보이다 "to look like"

A 그 사람의 첫인상이 어때요?
What's your first impression of that person?

B 정말 무서워 보여요.
He looks really scary.

-아/어 보이다 is used to guess at or express how a person or object may feel based on appearance. It describes one's impression of their appearance. -아/어 보이다 is attached to adjective stems.

- 옷을 그렇게 입으니까 젊어 보여요.
  You look younger because you dress like that.
- 이 음식이 정말 맛있어 보여. 이거 먹어 보자.
  This food looks so delicious. Let's eat this.
- 신발이 편해 보여서 샀는데 실제로 불편해요.
  I bought the shoes because they looked comfortable, but they are actually uncomfortable.

Be careful

보이다 is attached to adjective stems as -아/어 보이다 but to nouns as 처럼 보이다.

- 화장을 하니까 예뻐 보여요.
  You look pretty when you put on makeup.
- 화장을 하니까 배우처럼 보여요.
  You look like an actress when you put on makeup.

Quiz Yourself

▸Answers P. 314

1 알맞은 답을 고르세요.

(1) 몇 년 전에 ⓐ 졸업하는 / ⓑ 졸업한 학교에 다시 가 보려고 해요.

(2) 이 목걸이는 10년 전에 친구가 ⓐ 주는 / ⓑ 준 목걸이예요.

(3) 어렸을 때 키가 ⓐ 작은 / ⓑ 작았던 친구가 지금은 제일 키가 커요.

(4) ⓐ 할 / ⓑ 하는 말이 있는데 잠깐 얘기할 수 있어요?

(5) 지난주에 슈퍼에 가서 다음 주에 ⓐ 먹을 / ⓑ 먹은 음식을 사 왔어요.

(6) 어제 만난 사람 중에서 마음에 ⓐ 드는 / ⓑ 들 사람이 있었어요.

2 다음에서 알맞은 답을 골라서 '-(으)ㄴ/는'을 사용하여 대화를 완성하세요.

시설이 깨끗하다 친구하고 같이 보다 스트레스를 받지 않다 얘기를 잘 들어 주다

(1) A 어떤 집을 구하고 있어요?
B ________________ 집을 구하고 있어요.

(2) A 어떤 생활을 하고 싶어요?
B ________________ 생활을 하고 싶어요.

(3) A 어떤 사람을 좋아해요?
B ________________ 사람을 좋아해요.

(4) A 어떤 영화가 재미있었어요?
B 어제 ________________ 영화가 재미있었어요.

3 그림을 보고 다음에서 알맞은 답을 골라서 '-아/어 보이다'를 사용하여 문장을 완성하세요.

친하다 맛있다 나이 들다 피곤하다

(1) 케이크가 진짜 ____________ 보이네요. 저거 한번 먹어 봐요.

(2) 얼굴이 ____________ 보이네요. 어제 잠을 못 잤어요?

(3) 이런 옷을 입으면 ____________ 보여요.

(4) 두 사람이 정말 ____________ 보이네요. 오랜 친구 같아요.

Conversation ❶

Track 31

마크 이 중에서 네 남자 친구가 누구야?

새라 맨 오른쪽에 있는 사람이야.

마크 갈색 머리에 수염 있는 사람?

새라 어, 맞아.

마크 야~ 네 남자 친구 진짜 멋지다! 배우 같다!

새라 그치? 키도 크고 체격도 좋아.

마크 성격도 좋아 보이는데? 네가 딱 좋아하는 스타일이네.

새라 외모만이 아니야. 좋아하는 것도 나랑 비슷해.

마크 그래? 그나저나 처음에 어떻게 만났는데?

새라 전에 회사에서 같이 일한 적이 있는데 그때 얘기를 많이 하면서 친해졌어.

마크 첫눈에 반한 거야?

새라 아니야. 처음에는 그냥 그랬는데, 계속 만나니까 진짜 마음에 들어. 같이 얘기하면 마음이 되게 편해져.

마크 그렇구나. 좋겠다! 잘해 봐.

새라 나중에 기회가 되면 너한테 소개할게.

Mark Among these people, which one is your boyfriend?

Sarah He's the one at the far right.

Mark The person with brown hair and a beard?

Sarah Yes, that's right.

Mark Wow, your boyfriend is really good-looking! He looks like an actor!

Sarah Right? He's tall and is also fit. (lit. His physique is also good.)

Mark His personality seems good too. He's exactly your type. (lit. He's exactly the kind of style you like.)

Sarah It's not just his looks. His interests are also similar to mine.

Mark Really? By the way, how did you meet him in the first place?

Sarah We worked together at my company in the past. We talked a lot and got close.

Mark Was it love at first sight?

Sarah No. He was just okay at first, but I really got to like him as I kept getting to know him. I feel very comfortable when I talk to him.

Mark Is that so? That's great! I wish both of you the best.

Sarah I'll introduce him to you sometime when I get a chance.

New Vocabulary ▸P. 329

맨 | 갈색 | 수염 | 배우 | 체격 | 딱 | 그나저나 | 친하다 | 첫눈에 반하다 | 계속 | 되게 | 소개하다

New Expressions ▸P. 329

- 그치?
- 첫눈에 반한 거야?
- 잘해 봐.

Tips

1 Expressions Using 같다

When comparing something as a simile, 같다 may be attached to the comparison. The form of 같다 differs depending on where it is used.

- 그 사람이 영화 배우 **같아요**.
  That person looks like an actor. (as a predicate)
- 그 사람이 배우 **같은** 옷을 입었어요.
  That person is wearing what looks like an actor's costume. (in front of a noun, as a modifier)
- 그 사람이 배우 **같이** 말해요. (= 그 사람이 배우처럼 말해요.)
  That person speaks like an actor. (in front of a verb, as an adverb)

2 (이)랑: "and"

하고, 와/과, or (이)랑 may be used between nouns to mean "and." When speaking very colloquially with someone of similar status, (이)랑 is used to mean "and."

- 김치**와** 밥 = 밥**과** 김치 (formal)
- 김치**하고** 밥 = 밥**하고** 김치 (informal)
- 김치**랑** 밥 = 밥**이랑** 김치 (colloquial)
  kimchi and rice = rice and kimchi

1 Facial Features

- 얼굴이 둥글다 for one's face to be round
- 눈이 크다 for one's eyes to be big
- 눈썹이 짙다 for one's eyebrows to be thick
- 쌍꺼풀이 있다 to have double eyelids
- 코가 납작하다 for one's nose to be flat
- 입술이 두껍다 for one's lips to be thick
- 턱수염이 있다 to have a beard
- 콧수염이 없다 to not have a moustache
- 피부가 까무잡잡하다 for one's skin to be tan

- 얼굴이 갸름하다 for one's face to be slim
- 눈이 작다 for one's eyes to be small
- 눈썹이 가늘다 for one's eyebrows to be thin
- 쌍꺼풀이 없다 to not have double-eyelids
- 코가 오뚝하다 for one's nose to be high
- 입술이 얇다 for one's lips to be thin
- 턱수염이 없다 to not have a beard
- 콧수염이 있다 to have a moustache
- 피부가 하얀 편이다 for one's skin to be fairly white

2 Hair

- 검은색 머리 black hair
- 생머리 straight hair
- 단발머리 bobbed hair
- 핀을 꽂다 to insert a pin

- 갈색 머리 brown hair
- 곱슬머리 curly hair
- 커트 머리 short hair
- 머리띠를 하다 to wear a hair band

- 금발 머리 blonde hair
- 파마머리 permed hair
- 긴 머리 long hair
- 머리를 묶다 to tie one's hair

- 그 사람은 **이마가 넓고 눈썹이 짙고 수염이 있어서** 남자다워요.
  That person's forehead is wide, his eyebrows are thick, and he has facial hair, so he's very manly.
- 제 동생은 동양인인데 **피부가 까무잡잡한** 편이에요. My younger sister is East Asian, but her skin is fairly dark.
- 제 친구는 **긴 생머리를 묶고** 다녔는데, 요즘 머리를 짧게 잘랐어요.
  My friend used to tie her long, straight hair, but lately she has cut it short.

I wonder

- 갈색으로 염색한 머리 hair dyed brown
- 머리카락 = 머리 hair

Be careful

- 그 사람은 검은색 머리가 있어요. (X)
- 그 사람은 검은색 머리예요. (O)
  That person has black hair.

I wonder

- 흰머리가 있다 to have white hair
- 대머리이다 to be bald
- 가발을 쓰다 to wear a wig

3 Physique and Age

- 키가 크다 to be tall
- 마르다 to be thin
- 20대 초반이다 to be in one's early twenties

- 보통 키이다 to be of regular height
- 보통 체격이다 to be of regular body weight
- 30대 중반이다 to be in one's middle thirties

- 키가 작다 to be short
- 뚱뚱하다 to be fat
- 40대 후반이다 to be in one's late forties

4 First Impressions

- 아름답다 to be beautiful
- 귀엽다 to be cute
- 날씬하다 to be slim (for females)
- 잘생겼다 to be good looking
- 남성적이다 to be masculine
- 어려 보이다 to look young
- 예쁘다 to be pretty
- 멋지다 to be handsome
- 깔끔하다 to be neat
- 못생겼다 to be ugly
- 여성적이다 to be feminine
- 나이 들어 보이다 to look old

Key Expressions

- (noun)처럼 생겼어요.
  He/she looks like (noun).
- (noun)하고 닮았어요. (= 비슷해요.)
  He/she looks like (noun).
- (noun)하고 안 닮았어요.
  He/she does not look like (noun).

Grammar 2

-(으)ㄹ까요? expressing vague questions

C.C P. 302

A 두 팀 중에서 누가 이길까요?
Who do you think will win between the two teams?

B 글쎄요, 저도 잘 모르겠는데요.
Well, I'm not sure either.

-(으)ㄹ까요? expresses doubtfulness while asking a rhetorical question or asking the listener for his/her speculation. -(으)ㄹ까요? is often answered with -(으)ㄹ 거예요, which also expresses speculation. -(으)ㄹ까요? is attached to the stems of verbs, adjectives, and 이다. -았/었- is attached to form -았/었을까요? to express a guess about an event that has already finished.

- 공부하면 정말 시험을 잘 볼 수 있을까? Can I really do well on the exam if I study?
- A 내일 전시회에 사람들이 많이 올까요? Will a lot of people come to the exhibition tomorrow?
  B 아마 많이 올 거예요. There will probably be many.
- 누가 아침 일찍 와서 청소를 했을까요? Who would have come early in the morning to clean up?

-잖아요 reminding the listener of a fact he/she knows

A 어디가 좋을까요?
Where would be good?

B 남산이 제일 유명하잖아요. 거기로 가 보세요.
(You know that) Namsan (Mt. Nam) is the most famous.
Try going there.

-잖아요 is used to confirm that the listener knows the fact that he/she knows or to remind the listener of the fact that he/she knows. It is generally used in speech and not in writing. -잖아요 has a strong implication of "teaching" the listener, so it is generally only used with close friends or younger people, but not with older people. If it is used with older people, it should be accompanied by a cautious tone. -잖아요 is attached to the stems of verbs, adjectives, and 이다. If the fact being confirmed has already been completed, -았/었- is attached in front of -잖아요 to form -았/었잖아요.

- 내가 고기를 안 먹잖아. 그러니까 고기 말고 다른 것 먹자.
  (You know that) I don't eat meat. So let's eat something other than meat.
- 제가 요즘 시험 때문에 바쁘잖아요. 이해해 주세요.
  (You know that) I'm busy with exams these days. Please understand.
- 제가 전에 말했잖아요. 기억 안 나요? (You know that) I told you before. Don't you remember?

▸Answers P. 314

1 보기 와 같이 '-(으)ㄹ까요'를 사용하여 문장을 완성하세요.

그 사람에 대해 궁금한 게 많이 있어요.

보기 그 여자의 직업이 뭘까요? (뭐예요?)

(1) 나이가 ______? (몇 살이에요?)

(2) 어디에 ______? (살아요?)

(3) 남자 친구가 ______? (있어요?)

(4) 나에 대해 어떻게 ______? (생각해요?)

(5) 여기에 ______? (왜 왔어요?)

2 알맞은 답을 고르세요.

(1) A 높은 구두를 사고 싶어요.

B 왜요? ⓐ 키가 작잖아요. / ⓑ 키가 크잖아요. 높은 구두 안 신어도 돼요.

(2) A 운동 갔다 올게요.

B 지금 비가 ⓐ 오잖아요. / ⓑ 안 오잖아요. 운동은 나중에 하세요.

(3) A 진수한테도 이번 여행에 대해 말해야지.

B 어제 만나서 ⓐ 말했잖아. / ⓑ 말 안 했잖아. 생각 안 나?

(4) A 매튜한테 한자 책을 사 주면 어때요?

B 매튜가 오랫동안 중국에서 ⓐ 살았잖아요. / ⓑ 안 살았잖아요. 한자를 잘 알아요.

(5) A 자신이 없어서 너무 긴장돼요.

B 이제까지 ⓐ 잘했잖아요. / ⓑ 잘 못했잖아요. 이번에도 잘할 수 있을 거예요.

3 대화를 완성하도록 알맞은 것끼리 연결하세요.

(1) 그 사람이 나를 좋아할까요? •

(2) 이번 시험이 많이 어려울까요? •

(3) 영화가 벌써 시작했을까요? •

(4) 친구가 다른 사람에게 비밀을 말했을까요? •

• ⓐ 고민하지 말고 직접 물어보면 되잖아요.

• ⓑ 친구가 약속했잖아요. 친구를 믿어 보세요.

• ⓒ 선생님이 말했잖아요. 아마 어렵지 않을 거예요.

• ⓓ 시작 전에 광고를 하잖아요. 아직 시작 안 했을 거예요.

Conversation 2

Track 32

리나 아까 여기에 온 사람이 누구야?
진수 누구?
리나 회색 티셔츠에 청바지 입은 사람 말이야.
진수 누구지? 키가 크고 좀 마른 사람?
리나 어, 파란색 큰 우산을 들고 온 사람.
진수 내 친구의 친구 준기야. 근데 그건 왜?
리나 어디선가 봤는데 이름이 생각 안 나서.
진수 지난 수업 때 준기가 발표하는 거 같이 봤잖아.
리나 아! 맞다! 근데 머리 모양이 달라져서 못 알아봤어. 어쨌든 그 사람이 여기에 이 우산을 놓고 갔어.
진수 우산을? 그 사람이 우산을 찾으러 다시 올까?
리나 글쎄. 네가 그 사람 연락처를 알면 이것 좀 갖다줘.
진수 연락처는 나도 모르는데. 어떡하지?
리나 네 친구한테 물어보면 되잖아.
진수 맞다! 친구가 알겠구나! 그럼, 이거 내가 전해 줄게.

Rina Who was the person who just came here?
Jinsu Who?
Rina The person who was wearing a gray T-shirt and jeans.
Jinsu Who? The person who was tall and a little slim?
Rina Yeah, the one who was carrying a big blue umbrella.
Jinsu That's my friend's friend Jungi. But why do you ask? (lit. But why that?)
Rina Because I've seen him somewhere before, but I can't remember his name.
Jinsu It's because we saw Jungi's presentation last class.
Rina Ah! Right! I couldn't recognize him because his hair is different. Anyway, he left his umbrella here.
Jinsu His umbrella? Do you think he'll come back looking for it?
Rina Well, if you know his contact information, why don't you bring it to him?
Jinsu I don't know his contact information either. What should we do?
Rina Just ask your friend.
Jinsu Oh, right! My friend must know! I'll pass this (the umbrella) to him.

New Vocabulary ▸ P. 329

청바지 | 들다 | 그건 | 어디선가 | 생각나다 | 지난 | 발표하다 | 어쨌든 | 놓고 가다 | 갖다주다

New Expressions ▸ P. 330

- 어디선가 봤는데
- 아! 맞다!
- 글쎄.

Tips

1 (noun) 말이다: Emphasizing a Topic

말이다 may not be used alone. It is preceded by a noun or phrase and is used in speech in the following two situations. The second meaning was used in this conversation.

(1) When bringing up a new topic at the beginning of a conversation
- 어제 만난 사람 **말이야**. 그 사람 이름이 뭐지?
  The person I met yesterday. What was her name again?

(2) When clarifying a topic mentioned earlier
- A 그 영화 재미있었지요? That movie was interesting, wasn't it?
  B 무슨 영화요? Which movie?
  A 어제 본 영화 **말이에요**. The movie we watched yesterday.

2 The Negative 못

Generally, the meaning and usage of 안 (do not) and 못 (cannot) have different negative meanings. However, verbs related to perception such as 알다 (to know), 인식하다 (to recognize), 알아차리다 (to realize), and 알아보다 (to recognize by seeing) use 못 and not 안, even with the meaning of "do not."

- 그 사람이 누군지 알아차리**지 못했어요**.
  I didn't recognize who that person was.
- 안경을 안 써서 **못** 알아봤어요.
  I didn't recognize her because I wasn't wearing my glasses.

1 Wearing Clothing

1. 입다
Used when wearing an item on one's body

• 긴팔 티셔츠 long sleeve T-shirt

• 반팔 티셔츠 short sleeve T-shirt

• 정장 formal clothing

• 반바지 shorts

• 청바지 jeans

2. 신다
Used when wearing an item on one's feet

• 구두 shoes

• 운동화 sneakers

3. 쓰다
Used when wearing an item on one's head

• 모자 hat

• 안경 glasses

4. 하다
Used when wearing an accessory

• 목걸이 necklace

• 귀걸이 earrings

5. 끼다
Used when wearing an accessory that must be "inserted"

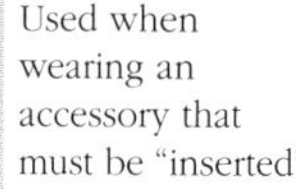

• 반지 ring

• 장갑 gloves

6. 차다
Used when wearing an item around a part of the body

• 시계 watch

• 벨트 belt

I wonder

Even with the same item, the verb may differ depending on the action used to wear the item.

- 넥타이: 하다 (by wearing it like an accessory)
  매다 (by tying it around one's neck)
- 안경: 쓰다 (by putting it on one's face)
  끼다 (by placing it on one's ears)
- 우산: 쓰다 (by holding it above one's head)
  들다 (by holding it in one's hand)
- 가방: 들다 (by holding it in one's hand)
  메다 (by putting it over one's shoulder)
  끌다 (by pulling it with wheels)

2 Describing Products

1. 모양 Shape

• 둥근 거울 a round mirror

• 네모난 안경 rectangular glasses

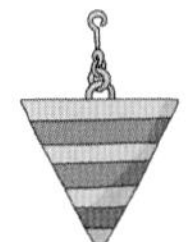
• 세모난 귀걸이 triangular earrings

• 사과 모양의 머리핀 an apple shaped hairpin

• 하트 모양의 목걸이 a heart-shaped necklace

• 별 모양의 귀걸이 star shaped earrings

2. 크기 Size

• 옷이 딱 끼다 for clothing to be tight
• 소매가 짧다 for sleeves to be short

• 옷이 딱 맞다 for clothing to fit perfectly

• 옷이 헐렁헐렁하다 for clothing to be baggy
• 소매가 길다 for sleeves to be long

3. 무늬 Pattern
- 줄무늬 셔츠 a striped shirt
- 체크무늬 셔츠 a checkered shirt
- 무늬 없는 셔츠 (= 민무늬 셔츠) a solid shirt

4. 색깔 Color
- 연한 보라색 light purple
- 진한 갈색 dark brown

Key Expressions
- 옷이 그 사람한테 잘 어울려요. ↔ 옷이 안 어울려요.
  Clothing suits him well. ↔ Clothing doesn't suit him well.
- 옷을 잘 입어요. ↔ 옷을 못 입어요.
  He is stylish. ↔ He is unstylish.
- 세련됐어요. ↔ 촌스러워요.
  He is polished/refined. ↔ He is tacky.

Grammar 3

-았/었으면 좋겠다 "I wish", "I hope", "It would be nice if"

▶ Appendix P. 277 

A 지금 제일 바라는 게 뭐예요?
What do you wish for most now?

B 한국어를 잘했으면 좋겠어요.
I wish that I could speak Korean well.

-았/었으면 좋겠다 is used when expressing a wish for something to happen to oneself or that the situation was contrary to present fact. -았/었으면 좋겠다 follows the desired situation and is attached to the stems of verbs, adjectives, and 이다. When expressing an undesired situation, -지 않다 or -지 말다 precedes -았/었으면 좋겠다. -지 말았으면 좋겠다 expresses the speaker's strong desire for the situation not to occur. In speech, 좋겠다 is often replaced with 하다 to form -았/었으면 하다.

- 부모님이 건강하셨으면 좋겠어요. I want my parents to be healthy.
- 사업이 잘됐으면 좋겠어요. I hope the business goes well.
- 여기에 쓰레기를 버리지 말았으면 좋겠어요. I hope you don't throw your garbage here.
- 후회할 일을 하지 않았으면 해요. I hope you don't do anything you'll regret.

-도록 "such that", "so that"

▶ Appendix P. 278 

A 잊어버리지 않도록 메모하세요.
Take notes so that you don't forget.

B 알겠어요. 메모할게요.
Alright. I'll take notes.

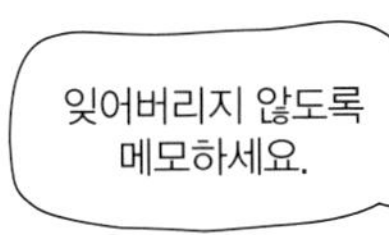

The clause attached to -도록 expresses the goal, criteria, or result of an action, while the following clause expresses the action. In the above example, the action of taking notes is done for the purpose of not forgetting. -도록 is attached to verb stems, and -았/었- may not be attached to it. The subjects of the clauses on either side of -도록 may be the same or different.

- 친구가 한국 생활에 쉽게 적응하도록 제가 도와줬어요.
  I helped my friend so that she easily adjusts to life in Korea.
- 다시는 회사에 늦지 않도록 조심하겠습니다. I will be careful so that I will not arrive late at the company again.
- 감기에 걸리지 않도록 손을 깨끗이 씻읍시다. Let's wash our hands thoroughly so that we avoid catching a cold.

1 그림을 보고 '-았/었으면 좋겠다'를 사용하여 문장을 완성하세요.

(1) 한국에서 일을 ________________. (구하다)

(2) 한국 친구를 많이 ________________. (사귀다)

(3) 아버지께서 ________________. (건강하다)

(4) 행복하게 ________________. (지내다)

(5) 집에 문제가 ________________. (생기다)

2 알맞은 답을 고르세요.

(1) 옆으로 [ⓐ 지나가도록 / ⓑ 지나가지 못하도록] 길 좀 비켜 주시겠어요?

(2) 눈이 오면 길이 미끄러우니까 [ⓐ 넘어지도록 / ⓑ 넘어지지 않도록] 조심하세요.

(3) 지하철역이 가까우니까 약속에 [ⓐ 늦도록 / ⓑ 늦지 않도록] 지하철을 타는 게 어때요?

(4) 비가 올 수도 있으니까 비를 맞지 않도록 우산을 [ⓐ 가져가세요. / ⓑ 집에 두고 가세요.]

(5) 날씨가 쌀쌀하니까 감기에 걸리지 않도록 [ⓐ 얇은 / ⓑ 두꺼운] 옷을 입는 게 좋겠어요.

3 문장을 완성하도록 알맞은 것끼리 연결하세요.

(1) 스트레스를 풀 수 있도록 •	• ⓐ 자동차가 있었으면 좋겠어요.
(2) 건강한 음식을 먹을 수 있도록 •	• ⓑ 한국어를 잘했으면 좋겠어요.
(3) 한국 사람과 말이 잘 통하도록 •	• ⓒ 요리를 배울 수 있었으면 좋겠어요.
(4) 편하게 이동할 수 있도록 •	• ⓓ 성격이 사교적이었으면 좋겠어요.
(5) 걸을 때 발이 아프지 않도록 •	• ⓔ 이번 주말에 여행 갔으면 좋겠어요.
(6) 많은 사람들과 어울릴 수 있도록 •	• ⓕ 가볍고 편한 신발을 샀으면 좋겠어요.

Conversation 3

Track 33

케빈 한국 친구를 사귀고 싶은데 어떻게 하면 좋을까요?

리나 동호회에 가입하지 그래요?

케빈 제가 수줍음이 많아서요. 괜찮은 한국 친구 있으면 좀 소개해 주세요.

리나 좋아요. 어떤 사람이 마음에 들어요?

케빈 제가 조용한 편이니까 좀 활발한 사람이었으면 좋겠어요.

리나 활발한 사람요. 그리고요?

케빈 같이 편하게 지낼 수 있도록 저하고 말이 잘 통했으면 좋겠어요.

리나 나이는요?

케빈 나이는 상관없어요. 하지만 성격이 중요해요. 전에 어떤 사람을 소개받았는데, 저하고 성격이 안 맞아서 힘들었거든요

리나 또 다른 건 뭐가 중요해요?

케빈 제 취미는 운동인데요. 함께 얘기도 하면서 운동할 수 있도록 그 사람이 운동을 좋아했으면 좋겠어요.

리나 알겠어요. 그런 사람으로 찾아볼게요.

Kevin I want to make Korean friends. What should I do?

Rina Why don't you join a club?

Kevin I'm quite shy. If you have any Korean friends, please introduce them to me.

Rina Okay. What kind of people do you like?

Kevin Since I'm rather quiet, it would be nice to meet someone who is somewhat outgoing.

Rina An outgoing person. And?

Kevin It would be good if we could communicate well so that we can get along well.

Rina What about age?

Kevin Age doesn't matter, but personality is important. I was introduced to someone once before, but it was difficult (to be friends with him) because our personalities clashed (lit. did not match).

Rina What else is important?

Kevin Exercising is a hobby of mine. It would be nice if the person liked to exercise so that we could exercise while talking to each other.

Rina Okay. I'll look for someone like that.

New Vocabulary ▸P. 330

사귀다 | 동호회 | 가입하다 | 수줍음이 많다 | 활발하다 | 상관없다 | 성격이 맞다

New Expressions ▸P. 330

- 어떻게 하면 좋을까요?
- 나이는 상관없어요.
- 또 다른 건 뭐가 …?

Tips

1 Common Contractions in Speech

In speech, it is common to omit and contract words based on what can be understood from the context. In this conversation, The question 그리고 어떤 사람이 마음에 들어요? can be shortened to 그리고 with 요 attached to form 그리고요? as the context makes the implied question clear.

2 The Impossibility of Omitting the Marker 이/가 after a Question

When asking questions, the object marker 을/를 attached to the question word is often omitted, but if the subject marker 이/가 is attached, it may not be omitted.

- 뭐**가** 마음에 안 들어요? What do you not like?
- 뭐를 제일 좋아해요? What do you like the most?

❶ Contrasting Personality Traits

1. 착하다 ↔ 못됐다 to be good ↔ to be mean	• 옛날 이야기에서 **착한** 사람은 복을 받고 **못된** 사람은 벌을 받아요. In old stories, good people receive happiness and bad people receive punishments.
2. 겸손하다 ↔ 거만하다 to be modest ↔ to be arrogant	• **겸손한** 사람은 자기 자랑을 하지 않는데 **거만한** 사람은 다른 사람을 무시해요. Modest people do not brag about themselves, while arrogant people look down on others.
3. 활발하다 ↔ 조용하다 to be outgoing ↔ to be quiet	• **활발한** 사람과 함께 있으면 힘이 생기고, **조용한** 사람과 있으면 차분해져요. If I am with outgoing people, I become energized, and if I'm with quiet people, I become calm.
4. 부지런하다 ↔ 게으르다 to be diligent ↔ to be lazy	• **부지런한** 사람은 항상 열심히 일하는 반면에, **게으른** 사람은 항상 일을 미뤄요. Diligent people always work hard, while lazy people always procrastinate.
5. 예의 바르다 ↔ 예의 없다 to be polite ↔ to be impolite	• **예의 바른** 사람은 예의 있게 행동하는데, **예의 없는** 사람은 자기 마음대로 행동해요. Polite people act politely, while impolite people act however they want.
6. 다정하다 ↔ 냉정하다 to be tender ↔ to be cold-hearted	• **다정한** 사람은 정이 많아서 따뜻한데, **냉정한** 사람은 차가워요. Tender people care a lot, so they are warm, but cold-hearted people are cold.
7. 보수적이다 ↔ 개방적이다 to be conservative ↔ to be open-minded	• **보수적인** 사람은 새로운 것보다 전통을 좋아하는 반면에, **개방적인** 사람은 새로운 것을 좋아해요. Conservative people like traditional things more than new things, while open-minded people like new things.
8. 적극적이다 ↔ 소극적이다 to be assertive ↔ to be passive	• **적극적인** 사람은 문제가 생겼을 때 열심히 해결하는 반면에, **소극적인** 사람은 문제를 피해요. Assertive people actively solve problems when they arise, while passive people avoid problems.
9. 자신감이 있다 ↔ 자신감이 없다 to be confident ↔ to not be confident	• **자신감이 있는** 사람은 자신의 능력을 믿는데, **자신감이 없는** 사람은 자신의 능력을 믿지 않아요. Confident people believe in their own ability, while people who lack confidence do not believe in their own ability.
10. 책임감이 있다 ↔ 책임감이 없다 to be responsible ↔ to be irresponsible	• **책임감이 있는** 사람은 맡은 일을 끝까지 하는데, **책임감이 없는** 사람은 금방 포기해요. Responsible people do the work they are assigned until it is finished, but irresponsible people give up right away.
11. 인내심이 많다 ↔ 인내심이 없다 to be very patient ↔ to be impatient	• **인내심이 많은** 사람은 힘들어도 참을 수 있는데, **인내심이 없는** 사람은 참을 수 없어요. Patient people can endure even when things are difficult, while impatient people cannot endure.
12. 고집이 세다 ↔ 고집이 없다 to be stubborn ↔ to not be stubborn	• **고집이 센** 사람은 자신의 생각을 잘 바꾸지 않는데, **고집이 없는** 사람은 다른 사람의 의견을 잘 들어요. Stubborn people do not often change their own opinions, while people who are not stubborn often listen to other people's opinions.

❷ Other Personality Traits

- 이기적이다: **이기적인** 사람은 자기만 생각하고 다른 사람을 배려하지 않아요.
  to be selfish: Selfish people only think of themselves and do not consider others.
- 변덕스럽다: **변덕스러운** 사람은 기분이 자꾸 바뀌어서 옆에 있는 사람이 힘들어요.
  to be fickle: Fickle people's moods change often, so it is difficult for people around them.
- 욕심이 많다: **욕심이 많은** 사람은 자기가 갖고 있는 것에 만족하지 못해요.
  to be greedy: Greedy people are unsatisfied with what they have.
- 사교적이다: **사교적인** 사람은 쉽게 친구를 사귈 수 있어요.
  to be sociable: Sociable people can easily make friends.
- 성실하다: **성실한** 사람은 자기가 맡은 일을 열심히 해요.
  to be earnest: Earnest people diligently work on the jobs they are assigned.
- 솔직하다: **솔직한** 사람은 거짓말을 하지 않아요.
  to be frank: Frank people do not lie.

Key Expressions

- 우리는 공통점이 많아요.
  We have much in common.
- 우리는 공통점이 하나도 없어요.
  We have nothing in common.

Let's Talk!

Speaking Strategy **Describing People**

- 얼굴은 ______________ **을/를 닮았어요.** His/her face **looks like** that of __________.
- 스타일은 ______________ **같아요.** His/her style is **like** __________'s.
- 키는 ______________ **만 해요.** He is **as** tall **as** __________.
- ______________ **처럼** 행동해요. He acts **like** __________.

❶ 주변 인물을 소개해 보세요.

> 대학교 친구인데 4년 동안 항상 같이 다녔어요. 갸름한 얼굴에 눈이 크고 입이 작아서 귀엽게 생겼어요. 편한 옷을 즐겨 입는데, 특히 신발에 신경을 많이 쓰는 편이었어요. 우리는 둘 다 솔직하고 활발해서 마음이 잘 맞아요. 요즘에는 친구가 바빠서 자주 못 보지만 이메일로 연락해요.

어렸을 때 친구

대학교 친구

예전 남자 친구

남자 친구

동료

직장 상사

(1) 누구
- 이름이 뭐예요?
- 어떤 관계예요?
- 언제 처음 만났어요? 어떻게 친하게 됐어요?

(2) 외모
- 어떻게 생겼어요? (얼굴, 머리 모양, 체격 등)
- 첫인상이 어땠어요?

(3) 옷차림
- 평소 옷차림이 어때요?
- 무엇에 신경 쓰는 편이에요? (옷, 머리 스타일, 피부, 말투 등)

(4) 성격
- 성격이 어때요?
- 어떤 점이 비슷해요? 어떤 점이 달라요?
- 그 친구 성격의 장점과 단점이 뭐예요?

(5) 현재
- 지금 그 친구는 어떻게 지내요?
- 얼마나 자주 연락해요?

❷ 어떤 사람이에요?

- 이성에게 매력적인 사람 (남자/여자)
- 회사 면접 때 인기가 좋은 사람 (남자/여자)
- 스트레스를 주는 사람 (남자/여자)
- 제일 존경하는 사람 (남자/여자)

New Vocabulary

즐기다 to be enjoyable | 관계 relationship | 옷차림 outfit | 매력적이다 to be charming | 존경하다 to respect

Word Web ▶ Appendix P. 320

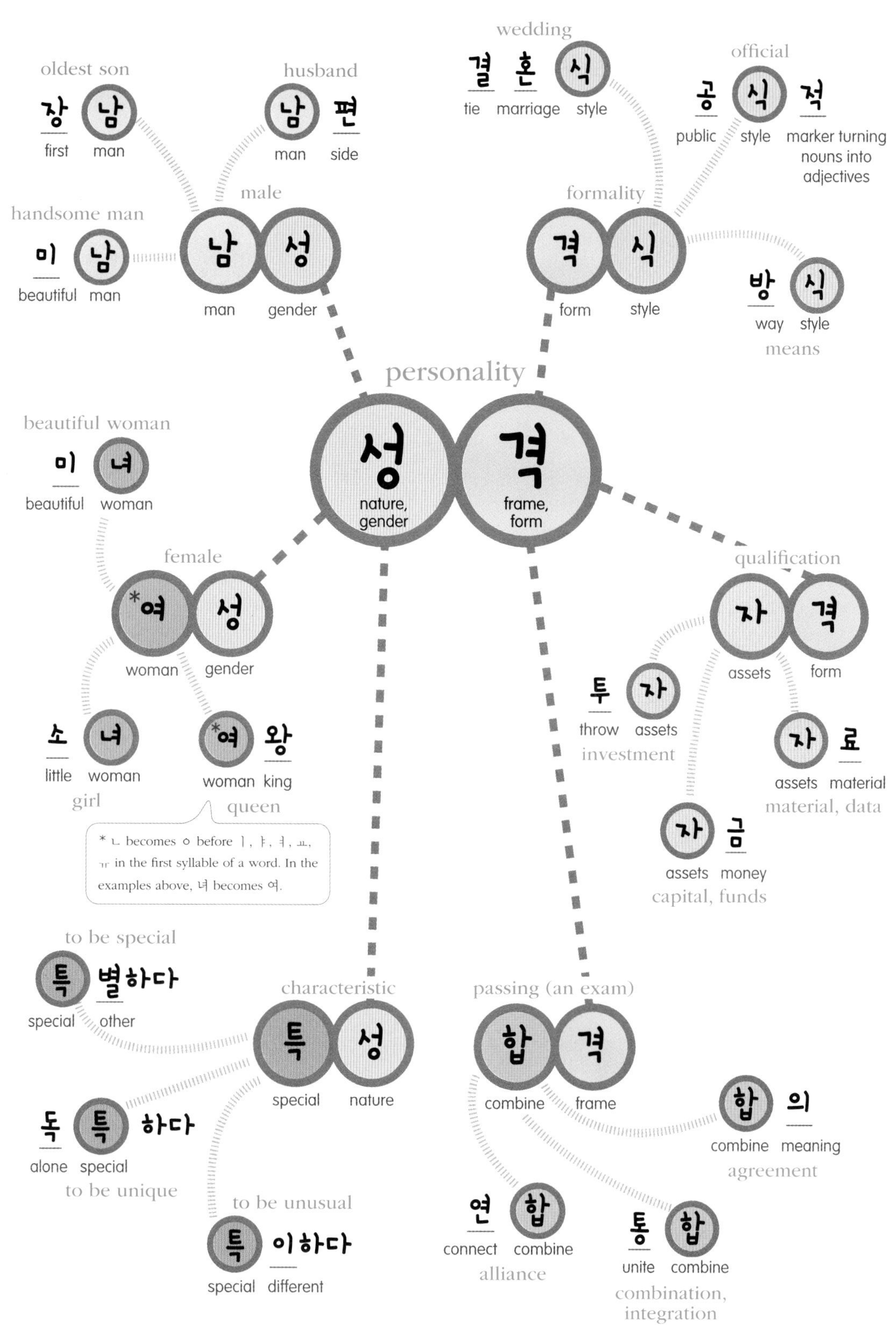

A Word on Culture

Let's Talk About Personality!

• 통이 크다 Generosity vs. 통이 작다 Stinginess

Originally, 통 referred to the width of the inside of pants or sleeves, but it also refers to how generous or lenient one is. Thus, 통이 크다 refers to one being generous and lenient while not paying attention to unimportant matters. For example, when donating money, if one donates not 1,000 won or 10,000 won, but 100,000,000 or 1,000,000,000 won, the act may be described as 통이 크게. When paying for someone, 통 크게 한턱내다 may refer to treating someone to a rare and expensive meal. Conversely, 통이 작다 refers to being stingy or fastidious, thus paying close attention to unimportant problems.

In Korean culture, where generosity is considered an important trait, 통이 큰 people are naturally favored. Men, in particular, must be 통이 크다. This is because if one always tries to pay and receive change to the exact won, it is seen as stingy. The culture of older people and men paying for meals is somewhat related to the preference for 통이 큰 people.

• 뒤끝이 있다 Resentment vs. 뒤끝이 없다 Forgiveness

뒤끝 refers to the sore feeling that still exists even after something is over. For example, even after fighting and reconciling, 뒤끝 있다 may be used to describe the negative feeling that may still linger after a fight. On the contrary, 뒤끝 없다 refers to one's ability to settle an issue and forget about it. In Korea, 뒤끝 없다 is a positive characteristic in people, just as 통이 큰 people are seen favorably.

Chapter 12

건강

Health

Goals
- Relating News
- Confirming What One Has Just Heard
- Making Conjectures
- Making Vague Guesses
- Confirming Rumors
- Inquiring After and Saying Hello to People
- Explaining Reasons for Injuries and Illnesses

Grammar

❶ -다고 하다 indirect quotations
-다고요? "Did you say…?"

❷ -(으)ㄴ/는 것 같다 "to seem"
-(으)ㄹ지도 모르다 "might"

❸ -다면서요? "I heard…. Is that true?"
-(으)ㄹ 뻔하다 "almost"

Grammar 1

-다고 하다 indirect quotations

Appendix P. 278

A 진수가 "오늘은 시간이 없어."라고 했어요.

Jinsu said, "I don't have time today."

→ 진수가 오늘은 시간이 없다고 했어요.

Jinsu said he does not have time today.

The indirect quotation -다고 하다 is used to express what someone has said. -다고 하다 is attached to the quoted content. -다고 하다 conjugates differently depending on whether the quoted content is in the present or the past, whether the predicate is a verb, adjective, or 이다, and whether the sentence is a statement, question, proposal, or command. 하다 may be replaced by verbs such as 말하다 (to say), 얘기하다 (to tell), or 듣다 (to hear).

- 진수가 "매일 12시에 자요."라고 했어요. → 진수가 매일 12시에 잔다고 했어요.
  Jinsu said, "I go to bed at 12 every day." → Jinsu said he sleeps at 12:00 every day.
- 리나가 "보통 아침을 먹지 않아요."라고 말했어요. → 리나가 보통 아침을 먹지 않는다고 말했어요.
  Rina said, "I usually don't eat breakfast." → Rina said she doesn't usually eat breakfast.
- 민호가 "저한테 얘기하세요."라고 했어요. → 민호가 자기한테 얘기하라고 했어요.
  Minho said, "Talk to me." → Minho told me to talk to him.

-다고요? "Did you say…?"

A 어제 여권을 잃어버렸어요.

I lost my passport yesterday.

B 여권을 잃어버렸다고요?

Did you say that you lost your passport?

-다고요? is used to confirm what someone has said or to report by forcing someone to reflect on what he or she has said. After the quoted content, -다고 하다 is used with 하다 omitted and a question mark inserted to express a confirmatory question. -요 is attached to -다고 if the other speaker must be respected. This form conjugates the same way as the indirect quotation.

- A 나는 한국 친구가 한 명도 없어. I don't have any Korean friends.
  B 한국 친구가 한 명도 없다고? Did you say you don't have any Korean friends?
- A 내일 여행 갈까요? Shall we go on a trip tomorrow?
  B 네? 내일 여행 가자고요? Excuse me? Did you say that we are going on a trip tomorrow?

▸Answers P. 314

1 보기 와 같이 '-다고 하다'를 사용하여 문장을 완성하세요.

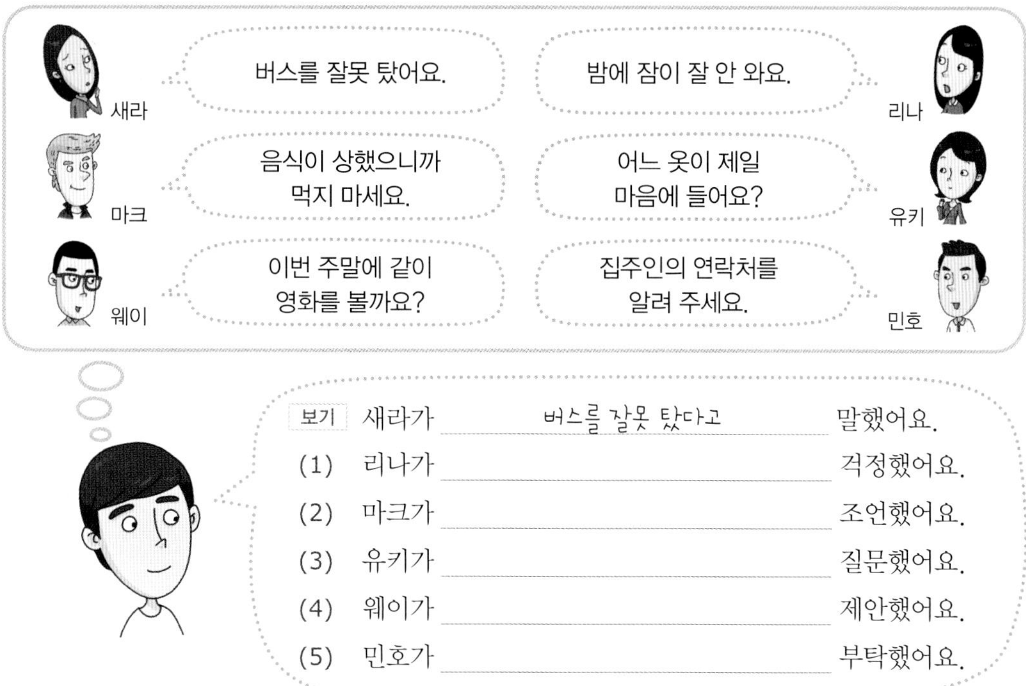

보기 새라가 버스를 잘못 탔다고 말했어요.
(1) 리나가 ______ 걱정했어요.
(2) 마크가 ______ 조언했어요.
(3) 유키가 ______ 질문했어요.
(4) 웨이가 ______ 제안했어요.
(5) 민호가 ______ 부탁했어요.

2 '-다고요?'를 사용하여 대화를 완성하세요.

(1) A 친구를 사귀기 어려워요.
B 친구를 사귀기 ______? 맞아요. 저도 그래요.

(2) A 한국 노래를 하나도 몰라요.
B 한국 노래를 하나도 ______? 그럼, 제가 가르쳐 줄까요?

(3) A 다른 친구에게 비밀을 말하지 마세요.
B 다른 친구에게 비밀을 ______? 걱정하지 마세요.

(4) A 조금 후에 다시 전화할게.
B 조금 후에 다시 ______? 그럼, 전화 기다릴게.

3 밑줄 친 것을 고치세요.

(1) 친구가 네라고 대답했어요. ➡
(2) 리나는 제 지갑이 갈색이라고 말했어요. ➡
(3) 피터는 보통 편지를 쓰지 않다고 들었어요. ➡
(4) 동생이 한국 음식을 먹고 싶는다고 자주 말했어요. ➡
(5) 하숙집이 불편하면 원룸에서 살으라고요? ➡

Conversation ❶

Track 34

케빈 진수 씨 얘기 들었어요?

유키 아니요, 못 들었어요. 무슨 얘기요?

케빈 진수 씨가 어제 교통사고가 났다고 해요.

유키 뭐라고요? 어디를 다쳤대요?

케빈 다리를 다쳐서 병원에 입원했다고 들었어요.

유키 병원이라고요? 수술했대요?

케빈 그건 잘 모르겠어요. 저도 오늘 아침에 연락받았거든요.

유키 그렇군요. 많이 안 다쳤으면 좋겠네요.

케빈 저도 그러길 바라고 있어요.

유키 우리도 병원에 가야죠?

케빈 그럼요, 친구들한테 연락해서 같이 병문안 가요. 제가 다른 친구들한테 연락해 볼게요.

유키 그 전에 병원에 전화해서 면회 시간을 알아보는 게 좋겠어요.

케빈 그게 좋겠네요.

Kevin Did you hear what happened to Jinsu?

Yuki No, I didn't hear. What happened?

Kevin I heard he got in a car accident yesterday.

Yuki What did you say? Where did you hear he was injured?

Kevin I heard he was admitted to the hospital because he hurt his leg.

Yuki The hospital? Did you hear if he had to get an operation?

Kevin I don't know about that. I too was only contacted this morning.

Yuki I see. I hope he wasn't too hurt.

Kevin I also hope so. (lit. I also wish that.)

Yuki We should go to the hospital too, shouldn't we?

Kevin Of course. Let's contact our friends and make a visit. I'll try contacting them.

Yuki It would be good to call the hospital and ask about the visiting hours before that.

Kevin That's a good idea.

New Vocabulary ▸P. 330

교통사고 | 사고가 나다 | 다치다 | 입원하다 | 수술하다 | 바라다 | 병문안 | 면회

New Expressions ▸P. 330

- 뭐라고요?
- 그건 잘 모르겠어요.
- 저도 그러길 바라고 있어요.

Tips

1 The Negative 못

안 (do not) and 못 (cannot) are differentiated. However, for verbs referring to senses such as sight (보다 "to see") and hearing (듣다 "to hear"), 못 is more natural to use even with the meaning of "do not," unless one purposely tries not to see or hear something.

- 조금 전에 여기서 흰색 자동차 **못 봤어요**?
  Did you not see the white car that was here a little while ago?
- 그런 얘기는 **못 들었는데요**.
  I didn't hear that story.

2 -기 바라다: "to wish/hope..."

-기 바라다 is used to express one's wish or hope that an action will succeed or that a situation will be brought about. The marker 를 may be attached to form -기를 바라다, which may also be contracted to -길 바라다. It is generally used in formal speech and writing.

- 이번에 꼭 승진하**길 바라고 있어요**.
  I hope that I will be promoted this time.
- 올해도 하시는 일이 잘되시**길 바랍니다**.
  I wish you success in this coming year.

❶ Parts of the Body

- 머리 head
- 머리카락 hair
- 눈 eye
- 눈썹 eyebrow
- 쌍꺼풀 double eyelids
- 귀 ear
- 턱 chin
- 점 mole
- 얼굴 face
- 이마 forehead
- 볼 cheek
- 보조개 dimple
- 코 nose
- 입 mouth
- 입술 lips
- 이 tooth
- 혀 tongue

- 목 neck
- 가슴 chest
- 팔 arm
- 팔뚝 forearm
- 어깨 shoulder
- 배 belly
- 배꼽 navel
- 팔꿈치 elbow

- 등 back
- 엉덩이 buttocks
- 허리 waist, lower back
- 옆구리 side, flank

- 다리 leg
- 허벅지 thigh
- 무릎 knee
- 발꿈치 heel

- 피부 skin
- 피 blood
- 털 body hair
- 근육 muscle
- 뼈 bone
- 지방 fat

- 손 hand
- 발 foot
- 손목 wrist
- 발목 ankle
- 손가락 finger
- 발가락 toe
- 손톱 fingernail
- 발톱 toenail
- 손바닥 palm
- 발바닥 sole
- 손등 back of the hand
- 발등 top of the foot

❷ Verbs Related to Body Parts

눈 eye

- 눈을 감다 to shut one's eyes
- 눈을 뜨다 to open one's eyes
- 눈을 깜빡이다 to blink
- 눈을 찡그리다 to frown

코 nose

- 냄새를 맡다 to smell
- 코를 골다 to snore
- 코를 막다 to hold one's nose
- 코를 풀다 to blow one's nose

입 mouth

- 하품하다 to yawn
- 숨을 쉬다 to take a breath
- 한숨을 쉬다 to sigh
- 말하다 to speak
- 소리를 지르다 to scream
- 소리치다 to scream, to shout
- 입을 다물다 to keep quiet
- 입을 벌리다 to open one's mouth
- 씹다 to chew
- 삼키다 to swallow
- 뱉다 to spit
- 토하다 to vomit

손 hand

- 들다 to hold
- 잡다 to grab
- 놓다 to place down
- 악수하다 to shake someone's hand
- 박수를 치다 to applaud
- 만지다 to touch
- 대다 to touch; to put up against something
- 머리를 쓰다듬다 to stroke someone's hair

몸 body

- 몸을 떨다 to shiver, shudder, tremble
- 몸을 흔들다 to shake one's body (ex. to a beat)
- 땀을 흘리다 to sweat
- 앉다 to sit
- 서다 to stand up
- 기대다 to lean
- 눕다 to lay down

발 foot

- 걷다 to walk
- 뛰다 to run
- 달리다 to race
- 밟다 to step on

Key Expressions

- 어디가 아파요? Where does it hurt?
- 아픈 데가 어디예요? Where does it hurt?
- 다친 데 없어요? Are you hurt somewhere?

Grammar 2

-(으)ㄴ/는 것 같다 "to seem"

Appendix P. 281

A 밖에 날씨가 어때요?
How is the weather outside?

B 비가 오는 것 같아요.
사람들이 우산을 쓰고 있어요.
It seems like it is raining. People are using umbrellas.

-(으)ㄴ/는 것 같다 is used to guess that an action, state, or event has happened or is happening based on what one has observed. If the conjecture is about something in the present, -(으)ㄴ 것 같다 is attached to adjective stems, while -는 것 같다 is attached to verb stems. -(으)ㄴ/는 것 같다 is also used to express one's subjective thought. In this situation, the usage of -(으)ㄴ/는 것 같다 expresses the speaker's opinion in a polite, soft, and roundabout manner.

- 어제 마크 씨가 늦게 잔 것 같아요. 피곤해 보여요. I think Mark went to bed late yesterday. He looks tired.
- 요즘 진수가 일이 많은 것 같아. 주말에도 회사에 출근해.
  Jinsu seems to have a lot of work these days. He goes to work even on weekends.
- 한국어를 공부해 보니까 생각보다 어렵지 않은 것 같아요. Studying Korean is not as difficult as I thought.

-(으)ㄹ지도 모르다 "might"

A 야구 경기 보러 가요!
Let's go watch a baseball game!

B 주말이니까 표가 없을지도 몰라요.
It's the weekend, so there might not be any tickets.

-(으)ㄹ지도 모르다 is used to express a vague guess. It is especially used when the conjecture has no particular basis or the speaker has little conviction. It is attached to the stems of verbs, adjectives, and 이다. If it is guessed that the situation has already been completed, -았/었을지도 모르다 is used.

- 그런 얘기를 하면 진수가 기분 나빠할지도 몰라. If you say things like that, Jinsu might feel offended.
- 바닷가는 저녁에 추울지도 모르니까 겉옷을 가져가세요.
  The beach might be cold in the evening, so bring your outerwear.
- 리나는 영화를 좋아하니까 벌써 그 영화를 봤을지도 몰라요.
  Rina likes movies, so she might have already seen that movie.

1 알맞은 답을 고르세요.

(1) 이 영화가 [ⓐ 재미있는 / ⓑ 재미없는] 것 같아. 평일에 가도 표가 없어.

(2) 마크 씨가 전에 중국에서 [ⓐ 산 / ⓑ 살은] 것 같아요. 중국어를 잘해요.

(3) 리나 씨가 이 책을 [ⓐ 읽지 않는 / ⓑ 읽지 않은] 것 같아요. 이 책을 선물합시다!

(4) 미리 준비하면 시험이 그렇게 [ⓐ 어렵지 않은 / ⓑ 어렵지 않는] 것 같아요.

(5) 알람 시계가 없으면 내일도 늦게 [ⓐ 일어나는 / ⓑ 일어날] 것 같아.

(6) 여행을 가기 전에 더 많은 정보가 [ⓐ 필요한 / ⓑ 필요하는] 것 같아요.

2 두 문장이 이어지도록 알맞은 것끼리 연결하세요.

(1) 방에 불이 켜져 있어요. •	• ⓐ 정말 똑똑한 것 같아요.
(2) 아이가 세 살인데 책을 읽어요. •	• ⓑ 약속 시간 안에 못 갈 것 같아요.
(3) 길에 차가 너무 많아요. •	• ⓒ 무슨 일이 생긴 것 같아요.
(4) 민호가 회사에 안 왔대요. •	• ⓓ 변호사인 것 같아요.
(5) 한국어를 못해서 말이 안 통해요. •	• ⓔ 아직 안 자는 것 같아요.
(6) 법에 대해 잘 알아요. •	• ⓕ 한국에서 살기 힘들 것 같아요.

3 다음에서 알맞은 답을 골라서 '-(으)ㄹ지도 모르다'를 사용하여 문장을 완성하세요.

알다　　받다　　가다　　늦다　　싸다　　말하다

(1) 그 사람은 항상 지각하니까 오늘도 ________________ 몰라요.

(2) 친구가 요즘 바쁘니까 전화를 안 ________________ 몰라.

(3) 유키 씨가 마크 씨하고 친하니까 마크 씨 전화번호를 ________________ 모르잖아요.

(4) 그 물건을 사기 전에 값을 물어보세요. 비싸 보이지만 실제로 ________________ 몰라요.

(5) 리나 씨가 교실에서 일찍 나갔으니까 벌써 집에 ________________ 몰라.

(6) 진수 씨가 민호 씨하고 친하니까 그 얘기를 민호 씨한테 벌써 ________________ 몰라요.

Conversation ❷

Track 35

마크 약속 시간이 지났는데, 새라는 왜 안 와요?

리나 아까 새라한테서 전화 왔는데 연락 못 받았어요?

마크 아니요, 새라가 뭐라고 했어요?

리나 오늘 사정이 있어서 약속에 못 온다고 했어요.

마크 그래요? 왜요?

리나 잘 모르겠지만, 몸이 안 좋은 것 같아요.

마크 어디가 아프대요?

리나 그런 말은 안 했는데, 목소리를 들어 보니까 감기에 걸린 것 같아요.

마크 감기에 걸렸다고요? 많이 아픈 것 같아요?

리나 그런 것 같아요. 평소와 달리 힘이 너무 없었어요.

마크 새라한테 전화해 봐야겠네요.

리나 전화는 나중에 해 보세요. 지금 자고 있을지도 몰라요.

마크 낮인데요?

리나 몸이 안 좋잖아요. 전화는 내일 하는 게 좋을 것 같아요.

Mark It's past the time we agreed to meet. Why hasn't Sarah come?

Rina Sarah just called me. Were you not contacted?

Mark No. What did Sarah say?

Rina She said that she can't make it because something came up.

Mark Really? Why?

Rina I don't know, but it seems like she's not feeling well.

Mark What did she say was wrong? (lit. Where did she say it hurts?)

Rina She didn't say, but listening to her voice, it seems like she caught a cold.

Mark She caught a cold? Does she seem very sick?

Rina It seems so. She really had no energy compared to her usual self (lit. differently from usual).

Mark I think I should give Sarah a call.

Rina Try calling her later. She might be sleeping now.

Mark But it's daytime.

Rina She's sick though. It will probably be better to call her tomorrow.

New Vocabulary ▸P. 330

(시간이) 지나다 | 아까 | 전화가 오다 | 사정이 있다 | 몸이 안 좋다 | 그런 | 목소리 | 감기에 걸리다 | 힘이 없다 | 낮

New Expressions ▸P. 330

- 뭐라고 했어요?
- 그런 것 같아요.
- 평소와 달리

Tips

1 Using 어디 to Ask about an Area or Part of Something

어디 is used to ask about a certain part of something or an area. In this conversation, 어디가 아프대요? is used to ask about what part of Sarah's body hurts.

- **어디** 좀 봅시다. Let's take a look.
- **어디**가 문제가 있어요? Which part has a problem?

2 -(으)ㄴ/는데요?: "But..."

-(으)ㄴ/는데요? is used to express some doubt about what the other speaker has said. In the above conversation, 낮인데요? implies "It's daytime, but she's sleeping?" The meaning is similar to that of -아/어도 learned in chapter 9.

- A 밖에 나가서 운동해요. I'm going out to exercise.
  B 지금 비가 오**는데요**? But it's raining now.

1 Expressions Using 아프다 with Body Parts

- 허리가 아프다 for one's lower back to hurt
- 어깨가 아프다 for one's shoulder to hurt
- 목이 아프다 for one's throat to hurt

2 Expressions Using the Hanja 통 (pain) with Body Parts

- 두통이 있다 (= 머리가 아프다)
  to have a headache (= for one's head to hurt)
- 치통이 있다 (= 이가 아프다)
  to have a toothache (= for one's tooth to hurt)
- 통증이 있다 to have pain

3 Expressions of Body Ailments and Injuries Using the Verb 나다

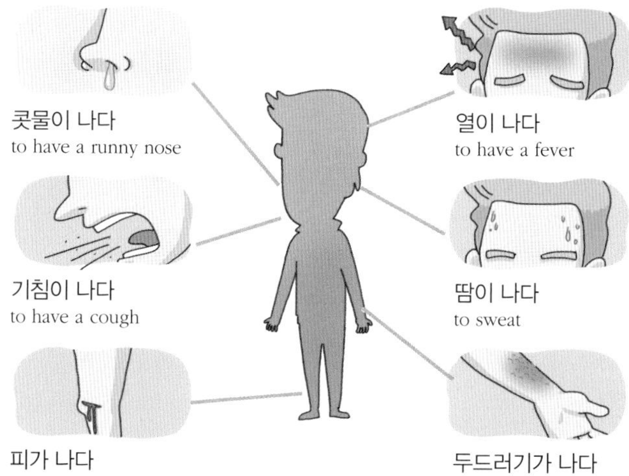

- 재채기가 나다 to sneeze
- 눈물이 나다 to well up with tears
- 수염이 나다 for facial hair to grow
- 털이 나다 for body hair to grow
- 흰머리가 나다 for white hair to grow
- 여드름이 나다 to have acne
- 상처가 나다 to be injured
- 혹이 나다 to get a bump on one's head
- 멀미가 나다 to feel motion sickness
- 몸살이 나다 to experience aching all over one's body
- 배탈이 나다 to have an upset stomach
- 설사가 나다 to have diarrhea

4 Expressions Using 걸리다 or 있다 to Describe Specific Conditions

1. 걸리다

- 감기에 걸리다 to catch a cold
- 눈병에 걸리다 to have an eye disease
- 치매에 걸리다 to have Alzheimer's disease
- (폐암/위암/간암)에 걸리다
  to have (lung cancer/stomach cancer/liver cancer)
- (위염/장염)에 걸리다 to have gastritis (stomach inflammation)/ enteritis (intestinal inflammation)

2. 있다

- 우울증이 있다 to have depression
- 불면증이 있다 to have insomnia
- 건망증이 있다 to be forgetful
- 변비가 있다 to have constipation
- 알레르기가 있다 to have allergies

5 Other

- 소화가 안되다 (= 체했다)
  to have indigestion
- 어지럽다 to be dizzy
- 가렵다 to be itchy
- 매스껍다 to be nauseous
- 목이 부었다
  to have a swollen throat
- 어깨가 쑤시다
  for one's shoulders to be sore
- 눈이 충혈됐다
  to have bloodshot eyes

Key Expressions

- 평소처럼 목소리가 밝았어요.
  She is energetic as usual.
  (lit. Her voice is light as usual.)
- 평소와 달리 목소리가 힘이 없었어요.
  She's not as energetic as usual.
  (lit. Usually, she does not have energy in her voice.)

Grammar ❸

-다면서요? "I heard… is that true!"

A 시험에 합격했다면서요? 축하해요.
I heard you passed your test, right? Congratulations.

B 고마워요.
Thank you.

-다면서요? is used to confirm the news that one has heard. The news may be about the listener or another person. This ending uses the indirect quotation -다고 하다, replacing -고 하다 with -면서요? to form -다면서요? When speaking with a friend in banmal (casual speech), one may use -다면서? or even reduce it to -다며? The conjugation is equivalent to that of the indirect quotation.

마신다~~고 했어요~~. + 면서요? → 마신다면서요?
읽으라~~고 했어요~~. + 면서요? → 읽으라면서요?

- 내일 학교에 일찍 오라면서? 무슨 일이야?
  I heard we are supposed to come to school early tomorrow? What's the problem?
- 매일 아침 8시에 회의 시작한다면서요? 정말이에요? I heard that meetings start at 8 AM every morning? Is it true?
- 발표 준비를 같이 하자며? 잘 생각했어! I heard you want to prepare a presentation together? Good thinking!

-(으)ㄹ 뻔하다 "almost"

C.C P. 304

A 무슨 일 있었어?
What happened?

B 길이 미끄러워서 넘어질 뻔했어.
I almost fell on the street because it was slippery.

-(으)ㄹ 뻔하다 is used to express an event that almost happened. It is attached to verb stems. The past form -(으)ㄹ 뻔했다 is always used to refer to these events.

- 오늘 출근할 때 교통사고가 날 뻔했어요. 다행히 안 다쳤어요.
  I almost had a car accident on my way to work today. Fortunately, I wasn't hurt.
- 약속을 잊어버릴 뻔했는데 메모를 확인하고 약속에 나갔어요.
  I almost forgot my appointment, but I checked my notes and went to the appointment.
- 이번 시험에서 떨어질 뻔했는데 운이 좋아서 겨우 합격했어요. I almost failed this exam, but luckily I barely passed.

Quiz Yourself

▶ Answers P. 314

1 보기 와 같이 '-다면서요?'를 사용하여 문장을 완성하세요.

준기 씨가 지난주에 회사를 그만뒀어요.

준기 씨가 다음 달에 결혼할 거예요.

준기 씨의 집이 크고 집세도 싸요.

준기 씨가 회사에 갈 때 버스로 2시간 걸려요.

준기 씨가 바빠서 시간이 없어요.

준기 씨의 양복이 백만 원이에요.

보기 준기 씨가 지난주에 회사를 그만뒀다면서요? 그러면 앞으로 뭐 할 거라고 했어요?

(1) ______________________? 저도 그런 집에서 살고 싶어요.

(2) ______________________? 언제 시간이 날까요?

(3) ______________________? 자동차를 사는 게 좋겠어요.

(4) ______________________? 왜 그렇게 비싸요?

(5) ______________________? 어디에서 결혼하는지 알아요?

2 알맞은 답을 고르세요.

(1) 어제 길에서 ⓐ 넘어졌어요. / ⓑ 넘어질 뻔했어요. 그래서 다리를 심하게 다쳤어요.

(2) 친구에게 실수로 사실을 ⓐ 말했어요. / ⓑ 말할 뻔했어요. 다행히 말하지 않았어요.

(3) 배고파서 ⓐ 죽었어요. / ⓑ 죽을 뻔했어요. 그래서 밥을 많이 먹었어요.

(4) 학교에 ⓐ 갔어요. / ⓑ 갈 뻔했어요. 그런데 학교에 아무도 없었어요.

(5) 오늘 회사에 ⓐ 늦었어요. / ⓑ 늦을 뻔했어요. 뛰어가서 늦지 않게 도착했어요.

(6) 친구 생일을 ⓐ 잊어버렸어요. / ⓑ 잊어버릴 뻔했어요. 다행히 생각나서 선물을 샀어요.

3 밑줄 친 것을 고치세요.

(1) 그 사람이 사장님이다면서요? 저는 직원이라고 생각했어요. ➡

(2) 1시간 더 기다려라면서요? 진짜 그렇게 말했어요? ➡

(3) 시험을 못 봐서 떨어질 뻔해요. 다행히 떨어지지 않았어요. ➡

(4) 오늘 회식이 있는다면서요? 언제 모여요? ➡

Conversation 3

Track 36

새라 지난주에 다리를 다쳤다면서요?

진수 얘기 들었어요?

새라 네, 케빈한테서 들었어요. 많이 다쳤어요?

진수 교통사고가 나서 다리가 부러질 뻔했는데 다행히 괜찮아요. 다리는 안 부러졌고 그냥 약간 삐었어요.

새라 큰일 날 뻔했네요. 병원에는 갔어요?

진수 지금도 병원에 왔다 갔다 하면서 치료받고 있어요. 곧 괜찮아질 거예요.

새라 그렇군요. 많이 다쳤을까 봐 걱정 많이 했어요.

진수 걱정해 줘서 고마워요. 새라 씨도 감기에 심하게 걸렸다면서요? 괜찮아요?

새라 지난주에 많이 고생했는데, 지금은 다 나았어요.

진수 다행이네요. 요즘에 감기에 걸린 사람이 많은 것 같아요.

새라 그런 것 같아요. 건강에 더 신경 써야겠어요.

진수 저도요. 새라 씨, 몸조리 잘하세요.

새라 고마워요. 진수 씨도 빨리 낫기를 바랄게요.

Sarah Is it true that you hurt your leg last week?

Jinsu You heard?

Sarah Yes, I heard it from Kevin. Are you very hurt?

Jinsu I almost broke my leg in a car accident, but fortunately, it was okay. I didn't break it and only sprained it a little.

Sarah That was a close call! (lit. Something bad almost happened). Did you go to the hospital?

Jinsu I'm going to the hospital every now and then to receive treatment. It will be okay soon.

Sarah Wow. I was very worried that you might have really hurt yourself.

Jinsu Thanks for worrying. I also heard that you caught a serious cold. Is that true? Are you okay?

Sarah I was having a lot of trouble last week, but I've completely recovered now.

Jinsu That's fortunate. It seems like a lot of people are catching colds lately.

Sarah It seems so. I guess I should watch my health more carefully.

Jinsu Me too. Sarah, take good care of your health.

Sarah Thank you. I hope that you get well soon too.

New Vocabulary ▸P. 330

부러지다 | 다행히 | 약간 | 큰일(이) 나다 | 왔다 갔다 하다 | 치료받다 | 걱정하다 | 심하게 | 고생하다 | 낫다

New Expressions ▸P. 330

- 큰일 날 뻔했네요.
- 몸조리 잘하세요.
- 빨리 낫기를 바랄게요.

Tips

1 왔다 갔다 하다: "to go back and forth (doing an action)"

This phrase expresses repeatedly carrying out two opposite but related actions. -다 -다 하다 is attached to these actions.

- 아이가 불을 **켰다 껐다 하면서** 장난을 쳐요.
  The child fooled around by turning the lights off and on.
- 다리 운동을 위해 계단을 **올라갔다 내려갔다 하는** 운동을 하고 있어요.
  I'm exercising my legs by going up and down the stairs.

2 Passive Expressions with 받다

Korean has various ways of expressing a passive. One way is to use 받다 in place of 하다 with certain nouns. In this conversation, the patient receives treatment, which is expressed by 치료받다.

- 수술**받으면** 병을 고칠 수 있어요.
  If you receive surgery, you can cure your sickness.
- 사장님께 칭찬**받아서** 정말 기분이 좋았어요.
  I'm in a good mood because I was praised by the company president.

❶ Injuries

불에 데다
to be burned

칼에 베다
to be cut by a knife

가시에 찔리다
to be pricked by a thorn

이마가 찢어지다
to get a gash on one's forehead

팔이 긁히다
for one's arm to be scratched

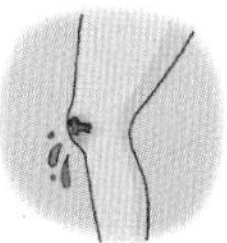

무릎이 까지다
for one's knee to be scraped

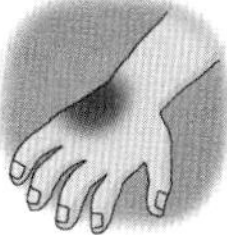

멍이 들다
to get bruised

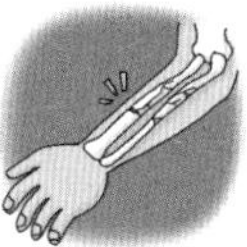

뼈에 금이 가다
for one's bone to be fractured

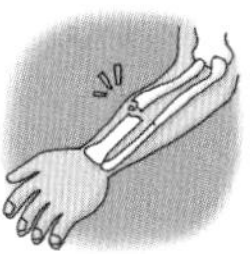

뼈가 부러지다
for one's bone to be broken

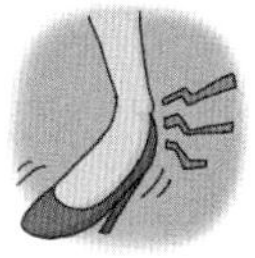

발목이 삐다
for one's ankle to be sprained

눈에 뭐가 들어가다
for something to be caught in one's eye

얼굴에 뭐가 나다
for something to appear on one's face

❷ Reasons for Injuries

- 넘어지다 to fall
- 미끄러지다 to slip
- 다른 사람과 부딪치다 to be bumped into someone
- 차에 치이다 to be hit by a car
- 사고가 나다 for an accident to happen
- 공에 맞다 to be hit by a ball
- 무리해서 운동하다 to overexert oneself by exercising
- 고양이가 할퀴다 to be scratched by a cat
- 개에게 물리다 to be bitten by a dog
- 기절하다 to faint

❸ Treating an Injury or Sickness

1. 약 medicine

- 소독하다
  to disinfect
- 약을 바르다
  to apply medicine
- 약을 뿌리다
  to spray medicine
- 약을 먹다
  to take medicine
- 약을 넣다
  to use (lit. insert) medicine (such as eyedrops)

2. 붙이다, 감다
to stick, to wrap

- 파스를 붙이다
  to stick a medicine patch on
- 밴드를 붙이다
  to stick a bandaid on
- 붕대를 감다
  to wrap a bandage around
- 깁스하다
  to wear a cast

3. 맞다, 받다
to be hit, to receive

- 주사를 맞다
  to get a shot
- 링거를 맞다
  to receive an IV injection
- 침을 맞다
  to receive acupuncture
- 응급 치료를 받다
  to receive emergency care
- 물리 치료를 받다
  to receive physical therapy

4. Other

- 수술하다
  to get surgery
- 꿰매다
  to stitch
- 입원하다
  to be admitted into the hospital
- 찜질하다
  to apply a hot pack
- 얼음찜질하다
  to apply an ice pack

❹ Types of Medicine

- 소화제 digestive aid
- 해열제 fever remedy
- 진통제 painkiller
- 수면제 sleeping pill
- 소염제 anti-inflammatory medicine
- 감기약 cold medicine
- 멀미약 motion sickness medicine
- 소독약 disinfectant
- 구급약 emergency medicine
- 안약 eyedrop

Key Expressions

- 빨리 나으세요. Get well soon.
- 몸조리 잘하세요.
  Take good care of your health.

Let's Talk!

Speaking Strategy — Expressing One's Opinions in a Roundabout Manner

- **제가 보기에… -(으)ㄴ/는 것 같아요. In my opinion**, it seems that…
- **제가 알기에… From my knowledge…**
- **제가 듣기에… From what I have heard…**
- **제가 느끼기에… I feel that…**

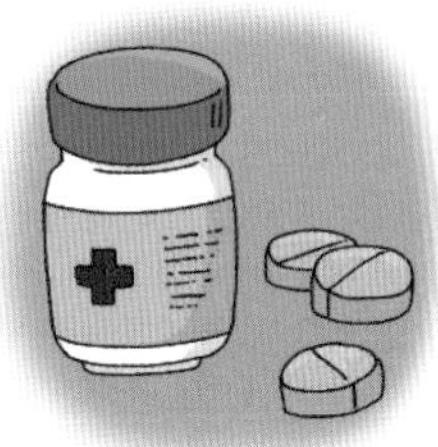

❶ 보통 아프면 어떻게 해요?

- 병원에 자주 가요? 약을 자주 먹는 편이에요?
- 자주 먹는 약이 있나요?

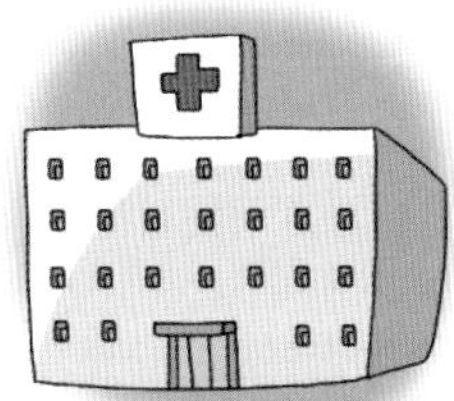

❷ 어렸을 때 심하게 아프거나 다친 적이 있어요?

- 언제 그랬어요? 왜 그랬어요?

❸ 병원에 일주일 이상 입원한 적이 있어요?

- 무슨 일로 입원했어요?
- 어떻게 치료했어요? 치료가 얼마나 걸렸어요?

❹ 건강을 위해 특별히 운동하고 있어요?

- 어떤 운동을 했어요?
- 효과가 있었어요?

❺ 보통 이럴 때 어떻게 해요?

- 효과적인 방법을 소개해 주세요.
- 실제로 해 봤어요?

잠이 안 올 때

감기에 걸렸을 때

스트레스를 심하게 받을 때

어깨가 아플 때

New Vocabulary

(noun)을/를 위해 in order for (noun) | 효과가 있다 for there to be an effect | 효과적이다 to be effective

Word Web ▶ Appendix P. 320

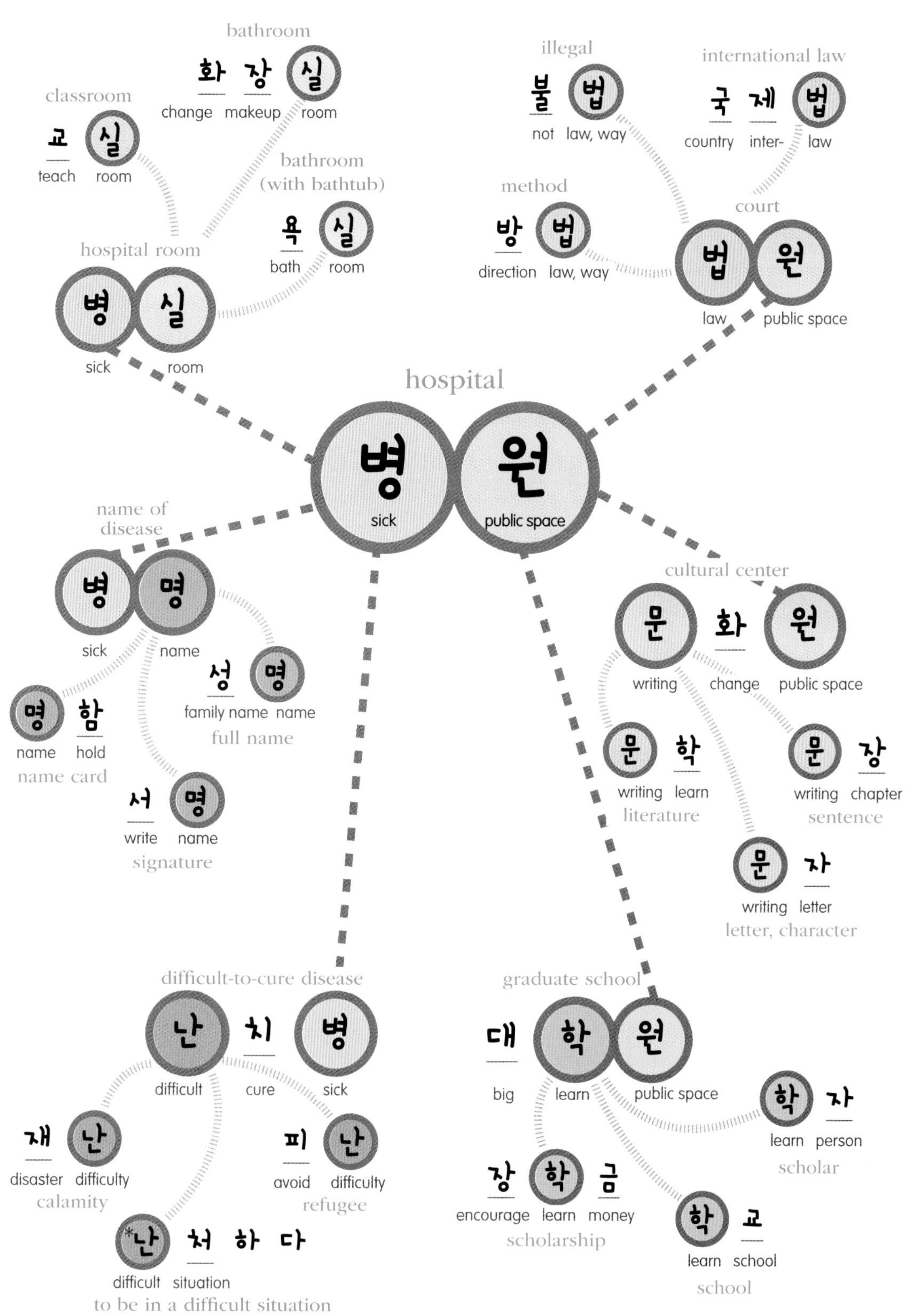

A Word on Culture

Idioms Involving the Body Part 애

• 애타다 (= 애가 타다) to be anxious

애 originally meant "entrails" in the past. In the present day, it refers to the inside of one's anxious heart filling with worry. 애가 타다 is used to worrying until one's entrails have burned idiomatically. For example, 애가 탄다 may be said if one is anxiously waiting while one's family member is receiving emergency surgery after a severe accident.

• 애태우다 (= 애를 태우다) to cause worry

애를 태우다 refers to making another person 애가 타다, that is, extremely worried. For example, when parents wait anxiously for their child who has run away from home, it can be said that the child is 애를 태운다 (worrying) his or her parents.

• 애쓰다 (= 애를 쓰다) to make an effort

애를 쓰다 refers to painstakingly giving all one's heart or using all one's energy. It means "trying with all one's might" or "to be painstaking" or "to have much trouble." 애쓰고 있다 may be used for someone who is diligently trying to study in order to pass a difficult exam, and 애썼다 may be said to someone who has solved a problem, finished a difficult job, or gone through a stressful period.

• 애먹다 (= 애를 먹다) to undergo hardship

애를 먹다 refers to someone enduring hardship. It can be understood as making an effort to the point of "eating one's intestines." For example, while travelling abroad, an airline loses your luggage, causing you unforeseen hardship. Your difficult situation can be described as 애 먹었다. Another instance in which 애 먹고 있다 may be used is when an employee must work for an insufferable and persnickety boss who is difficult to please, causing hardship to the employee.

Chapter 13

관심사

Interests

Goals
- Speaking about One's Plans
- Making Proposals
- Expressing Worries
- Giving Encouragement
- Expressing One's Opinions Politely
- Giving Advice

Grammar

❶ -(으)ㄹ 테니까 "since (someone) will probably...", "I will, so..."
-(으)ㄹ래요 "I will", "I want"

❷ -(으)ㄹ까 하다 "I might", "I am thinking of"
-(으)ㄹ수록 "The more..."

❸ -기는 하지만 "It is..., but"
-군요 expressing recognition and understanding of a newly learned fact

Grammar 1

-(으)ㄹ 테니까 "since (someone) will probably…", "I will, so…"

C.C P. 302

A 다녀올게요.
Goodbye (lit. I'll go and come back).

B 이따가 비가 올 테니까 우산을 가져가세요.
Take an umbrella, since it will probably rain later.

-(으)ㄹ 테니까 is used to express an action to be taken on the basis that something will happen as one surmises. In this usage, -(으)ㄹ 테니까 is attached to the stems of verbs, adjectives, and 이다, and the subject of the clause may be any person. If something is surmised to have already finished, -았/었- is attached to form -았/었을 테니까. Another usage of -(으)ㄹ 테니까 is to express a promise or intention that one will act so that, in turn, the speaker may seek favor from or give advice to the listener. In this usage, -(으)ㄹ 테니까 is attached to verb stems, and the subject of the first clause must be the speaker.

- 너도 그 사람을 보면 알 테니까 나중에 서로 인사해.
  You'll know when you see that person, so greet each other later.
- 이제 회의가 끝났을 테니까 전화해도 될 거예요. Now the meeting should be over, so you can call.
- 이 책을 빌려줄 테니까 다음 주에 돌려주세요. I will lend you this book, so please return it next week.

-(으)ㄹ래요 "I will", "I want"

▶ Appendix P. 282

A 지금 점심 먹으러 가는데 같이 갈래요?
I'm going to eat lunch now. Do you want to join me?

B 좋아요. 같이 가요.
Great. Let's go together.

-(으)ㄹ래요 expresses the speaker's intention or desire and is attached to verb stems. If it is used in question form as -(으)ㄹ래요?, it asks the listener his or her intention, or for a favor, or to make a proposal. It is generally used in speech, and it is used when the speaker and listener have a comfortable relationship, so it evokes an air of informality and intimacy.

- 시간이 오래 걸릴 테니까 먼저 갈래요? It will take a long time, so would you like to go first?
- 이 일이 힘들어도 이번에는 혼자 할래요. Even if this job is difficult, I will do it alone this time.
- 가방을 잃어버렸는데 도와줄래요? I lost my bag, could you help me?

▶Answers P. 314

1 **다음에서 알맞은 답을 골라서 '-(으)ㄹ 테니까'를 사용하여 대화를 완성하세요.**

짜다	말하다	돌보다	막히다	도착하다

(1) 소금을 더 넣으면 ______________ 그만 넣는 게 좋겠어요.

(2) 내가 아이를 잠깐 ______________ 밖에 나갔다 오세요.

(3) 지금은 길이 ______________ 지하철로 가는 게 어때요?

(4) 나도 그 사람에게 ______________ 너도 말하지 마.

(5) 지금쯤 집에 ______________ 한번 전화해 보세요.

2 **알맞은 답을 고르세요.**

(1) A 뭐 먹을래요?
B 비빔밥 ⓐ 먹을게요. / ⓑ 먹어 줄게요.

(2) A 잠깐만 기다려 줄래?
B 여기에서 ⓐ 기다릴게. / ⓑ 기다리자.

(3) A 내일부터 같이 운동할래?
B ⓐ 그럴래. / ⓑ 그러자.

(4) A 내 부탁 좀 들어줄래?
B ⓐ 들어줄게. / ⓑ 들어주자. 말해 봐.

(5) A 커피와 녹차 중에서 어떤 거 드실래요?
B 커피 ⓐ 마실래요. / ⓑ 마셔 줄래요.

(6) A 우리 계획 같이 세울래요?
B 좋아요. 같이 ⓐ 세울게요. / ⓑ 세웁시다.

3 **문장을 완성하도록 알맞은 것끼리 연결하세요.**

(1) 지난번보다 어려울 테니까 • • ⓐ 내 차에 탈래?

(2) 날씨 때문에 고생할 테니까 • • ⓑ 난 좀 더 연습할래요.

(3) 내가 먹을 것을 사 올 테니까 • • ⓒ 여기에서 잠깐 기다릴래?

(4) 채소가 건강에 좋을 테니까 • • ⓓ 소풍을 다른 날로 연기할래?

(5) 내가 집까지 데려다줄 테니까 • • ⓔ 이제부터 꾸준히 먹어 볼래요.

Conversation 1

Track 37

민호 한국어를 배운 다음에 뭐 할 거예요?
유키 일을 찾으려고 해요.
민호 무슨 일을 하고 싶은데요?
유키 한국어를 사용해서 하는 일을 했으면 좋겠어요.
민호 혹시 한국에서 일을 찾고 있어요?
유키 네, 고향에 돌아가기 전에 한국에서 경험을 쌓고 싶어요.
민호 좋은 경험이 되겠네요.
유키 그런데 요즘 일자리가 별로 없어서 걱정이에요.
민호 그렇긴 하죠. 전에 아르바이트로 번역해 본 적이 있죠?
유키 네, 몇 번 해 봤어요.
민호 통역에도 관심 있다고 했죠?
유키 관심 있죠. 그런데 그건 왜요?
민호 제가 통역 아르바이트 소개해 줄 테니까 한번 해 볼래요?
유키 통역요? 통역은 해 본 적이 없는데 괜찮을까요?
민호 지금부터 준비하면 되죠. 잘할 수 있을 테니까 걱정하지 마세요.
유키 그렇게 얘기해 줘서 고마워요.

Minho What will you do after you finish studying Korean?
Yuki I intend to look for a job.
Minho What kind of job do you want?
Yuki It would be nice if I could find a job in which I can use Korean.
Minho Are you looking for work in Korea, by any chance?
Yuki Yes, before returning to my hometown, I want to gain a lot of experience in Korea.
Minho I'm sure you'll have a great experience.
Yuki But lately there aren't many available positions, so I'm worried.
Minho That's true. You've tried translating as a part-time job, right?
Yuki Yes, I tried it a few times.
Minho You also said you're interested in oral translation, right?
Yuki I'm interested. But why?
Minho I'll introduce you to a part-time oral translation job. Want to try it?
Yuki Oral translation? I've never done oral translation before. Do you think I can do it?
Minho Just start preparing now. Don't worry. You'll be able to do well.
Yuki Thanks for saying that. (lit. Thanks for speaking like that.)

New Vocabulary ▸P. 331

고향 | 경험을 쌓다 | 일자리 | 번역하다 | 통역

New Expressions ▸P. 331

- 그렇긴 하죠.
- 몇 번 해 봤어요.
- 그렇게 얘기해 줘서 고마워요.

Tips

1 Expressions of Partial Agreement

After listening to what the other speaker has said, if one has a differing opinion, -긴 하죠 may be used to express half-hearted agreement. -긴 하죠 is attached to the stems of verbs, adjectives, and 이다. If the content is in the past, -긴 했죠 may be used.

- 그건 그래요. 주말에는 보통 늦잠을 자**긴 하죠.**
  You're right. I usually sleep in on weekends.
- 맞아요. 저도 어렸을 때 노는 것을 좋아하**긴 했죠.**
  You're right. I also liked playing around when I was little.

2 Expressions of Gratitude

-아/어 줘서 or -아/어 주셔서 may be used to express the reason for thanking someone when using 고맙다 or 감사합니다.

- 제 얘기를 들었으니까 고마워요. (X)
- 제 얘기를 들어서 고마워요. (X)
- 제 얘기를 들**어 줘서** 고마워요. (O)
  Thanks for listening to me.

● Fields of Interest

- 모으다 (= 수집하다) to collect
- 만들다 to make
- 글을 쓰다 to write
- 인터넷을 검색하다 to search the Internet
- 악기를 배우다 to learn an instrument
- 수리하다 to repair
- 뜨개질을 하다 to knit
- 맛집을 찾아다니다 to look for good restaurants

- 취미 활동으로 다음 달부터 **악기를 배워** 보려고 해요.
  I plan to learn an instrument starting next month as a regular hobby (lit. as a hobby activity).
- 제 친구는 **여행하는** 것을 정말 좋아해요. 여러 나라의 **기념품을 모으고** 있어요.
  My friend really likes to travel. She is collecting souvenirs from various countries.
- 저는 음식에 **관심이 많이 있어서** 요즘에는 **맛집을 찾아다니고** 있어요.
  Lately, I've been looking for restaurants because I'm very interested in food.

Key Expressions

- 시간이 날 때마다
  Every time one has time
- 여유가 있을 때마다
  Whenever one is free
- 기회가 생길 때마다
  Whenever an opportunity comes up

Grammar 2

-(으)ㄹ까 하다 "I might", "I am thinking of"

Appendix P. 283

A 주말에 뭐 할 거예요?

What are you going to do this weekend?

B 날씨가 더워지니까 여름 옷을 살까 해요.

I am thinking of buying summer clothing since the weather is getting hot.

-(으)ㄹ까 하다 expresses the speaker's plans or ideas. The plan or idea is not yet concrete and is rather only vaguely formed in one's head. As the speaker must be the subject, -(으)ㄹ까 하다 is only used in the first person. It attaches to verb stems.

- 올해에는 태권도를 배워 볼까 해요. I am thinking of learning Taekwondo this year.
- 이따가 산책할지도 모르니까 운동화를 신을까 해요. I might go for a walk later, so I think I'll wear sneakers.
- 이번 휴가 때 여행을 갈까 말까 고민하고 있어요.
  I'm debating whether or not to go on a trip this upcoming vacation.

-(으)ㄹ수록 "The more..."

A 또 먹고 싶어요?

Do you want to eat again?

B 네, 먹을수록 더 먹고 싶어져요.

Yes. The more I eat, the more I want to eat.

-(으)ㄹ수록 expresses that as the situation in the first clause progresses or happens more often, so does the second clause. It is attached to the stems of verbs, adjectives, and 이다. -(으)ㄹ수록 may be preceded by -(으)면 to emphasize the repetitive nature of the first action.

- 많이 연습할수록 실력이 늘겠죠. The more you practice, the better your skills will be.
- 친구는 많으면 많을수록 좋아요. The more friends, the better.
- 나이가 들수록 기억력이 안 좋아요. The older you get, the worse your memory gets.

▸Answers P. 315

1 **알맞은 답을 고르세요.**

(1) 한국 요리 수업이 주말에 있대요.
저도 주말에 그 수업을 ⓐ 들을까 해요. / ⓑ 듣지 말까 해요.

(2) 돈이 좀 부족하니까 이번 달에는 ⓐ 쇼핑할까 해요. / ⓑ 쇼핑하지 말까 해요.

(3) 건강에 좋다고 하니까 운동을 ⓐ 시작할까 해요. / ⓑ 시작하지 말까 해요.

(4) 혼자 여행하는 것은 위험하니까 앞으로 혼자 ⓐ 여행할까 해요. / ⓑ 여행하지 말까 해요.

2 **그림을 보고 다음에서 알맞은 답을 골라서 '-(으)ㄹ까 하다'를 사용하여 문장을 완성하세요.**

가다	먹다	배우다	사다

(1) 한국 노래를 하나도 몰라요.
내년부터 한국 노래를 조금씩 ______________.

(2) 전에 제주도에 가 봤어요.
그러니까 이번에는 제주도에 ______________.

(3) 오늘 점심은 국수를 ______________는데 너도 같이 갈래?

(4) 가방이 너무 비싸서 ______________ 말까 고민하고 있어요.

3 **'-(으)ㄹ수록'을 사용하여 문장을 완성하세요.**

(1) 물이 부족하면 건강에 안 좋아요. 물을 많이 ______________ 몸에 좋아요. (마시다)

(2) 돈이 없을 때는 욕심이 없었어요. 그런데 돈이 ______________ 욕심이 더 생겨요. (많다)

(3) 그 사람은 항상 함부로 말해요. 그래서 그 사람의 말을 ______________ 화가 나요. (듣다)

(4) 어렸을 때는 매일 친구하고만 놀았어요.
그런데 나이가 ______________ 가족이 소중하게 느껴져요. (들다)

Conversation ❷

Track 38

마크 다음 달부터 한자를 공부할까 하는데, 같이 할래?

새라 글쎄, 난 수영을 시작할까 해. 수영을 하나도 못하거든.

마크 왜 갑자기 수영을 시작하는데?

새라 요즘 살이 많이 쪘어. 그리고 나이 들수록 운동이 중요한 것 같아서.

마크 그건 그렇지!

새라 그런데 내가 보기에 수영이 어려운 것 같아서 걱정이야.

마크 아니야. 어렵지 않아. 너도 실제로 해 보면 생각이 바뀔걸.

새라 그럴까? 사실은 전에 수영을 배우려고 했는데 어려워 보여서 포기했거든.

마크 처음에는 어렵지. 그래도 연습하면 좋아져.

새라 많이 연습해야겠지? 잘하려면 얼마나 해야 돼?

마크 많이 연습할수록 좋지. 일주일에 2-3일씩 최소한 6개월 이상 해야 돼.

새라 내가 할 수 있을까? 자신이 없는데…….

마크 일단 시작해 봐. 내가 조금씩 가르쳐 줄게.

새라 알았어. 고마워.

Mark Starting next month, I might start studying hanja. Do you want to study together?

Sarah Well, I might start learning to swim. I don't know how to at all.

Mark Why have you suddenly decided to learn how to swim?

Sarah I've gained a lot of weight lately. Also, exercise seems increasingly important as one gets older.

Mark That's true!

Sarah But I'm worried because from what I've seen, swimming looks difficult.

Mark No, it's not difficult. If you really start doing it, your opinion might change.

Sarah Will it? Actually, I planned to learn to swim before, but I quit because it seemed hard.

Mark At first it's difficult. Even so, if you practice, you'll get better.

Sarah I guess I have to practice a lot, right? If I want to get good at it, how much do I have to practice?

Mark The more you exercise, the better you'll get. You have to do it for two to three days a week for at least six months.

Sarah Will I be able to do it? I'm not very confident…

Mark Just start it first. I'll teach you a little by little at a time (lit. a little each).

Sarah Okay. Thanks.

New Vocabulary ▸P. 331

한자 | 살이 찌다 | 실제로 | 바뀌다 | 씩 | 최소한 | 조금씩

New Expressions ▸P. 331

- 그건 그렇지!
- 내가 보기에
- 최소한 … 이상

Tips

1 -(으)ㄹ걸요: "might" (speculations)

-(으)ㄹ걸요 is used to express a guess that the speaker is unsure of. It has the feeling of taking on responsibility for one's guess, so it is not used with people of higher status and is mainly used with those of the same or lower status in informal situations. It is attached to the stems of verbs, adjectives, and 이다. It is not a question, but the intonation rises at the end.

- 리나는 아마 집에 있**을걸**. Rina might be at home.
- 진수가 친구들한테 벌써 말**했을걸요**. Jinsu might have already told his friends.

2 The Usage of -아/어야겠지?

-아/어야겠지? is a question that is used to confirm the fact that the speaker assumes the listener takes for granted. The listener may answer this question by using the ending -지, which we learned in Chapter 4.

- A 내가 잘못했으니까 먼저 사과해**야겠지**?
  Should I apologize first because I was wrong?
  B 그럼, 먼저 사과하면 좋**지**.
  Well, it would be better if you apologize first.

1 Opposite Adverbs

1. 최대한 ↔ 최소한
   at most ↔ at least (under certain conditions)
   - 보고서는 **최소한** 3페이지 이상 써야 해요.
     At least 3 pages must be written for this report.
2. 많아도 ↔ 적어도
   at most ↔ at least (limited in quantity)
   - 표는 **적어도** 일주일 전에는 예매해야 돼요.
     You have to reserve tickets at least a week in advance.
3. 빨라도 ↔ 늦어도
   at the earliest ↔ at the latest
   - 2시에 시작하니까 **늦어도** 1시 50분까지 오세요.
     Please come by 1:50 at the latest because it starts at 2:00.
4. 오래 ↔ 잠깐
   for a long time ↔ for a moment
   - 친구와 **오래** 얘기하고 싶었지만 **잠깐** 얘기했어요.
     I wanted to speak with my friends for a long time, but we only spoke for a moment.
5. 더 ↔ 덜
   more ↔ less
   - 채소는 **더** 먹고 고기는 **덜** 먹어야 돼요.
     You have to eat more vegetables and less meat.
6. 일찍 ↔ 늦게
   early ↔ late
   - **일찍** 도착하려고 했는데 **늦게** 도착했네요.
     I planned to arrive early but I ended up arriving late.
7. 같이 ↔ 따로
   together ↔ separately
   - 항상 식사비를 **같이** 계산했는데 이번에는 **따로** 계산했어요.
     We always paid for food together, but this time we paid separately.
8. 함께 ↔ 혼자
   together ↔ alone
   - **함께** 먹으면 **혼자** 먹을 때보다 음식이 더 맛있어요.
     A meal tastes better when eaten together rather than when eaten alone.
9. 먼저 ↔ 나중에
   first ↔ later
   - **먼저** 시작하세요. 전 **나중에** 해도 돼요.
     Please start first. I can do it later.
10. 전에 ↔ 나중에
    before ↔ later
    - **전에** 만난 적이 있죠? **나중에** 또 만나요.
      We've met before right? Let's meet again later.
11. 아까 ↔ 이따가
    just before ↔ later
    - **아까** 얘기 못했어요. **이따가** 얘기할게요.
      I wasn't able to tell you before. I'll tell you later.
12. 처음 ↔ 마지막으로
    first ↔ last
    - **처음** 만났을 때 첫인상이 정말 좋았어요.
      When I met him for the first time, his first impression was very good.
13. 처음에 ↔ 마지막에
    at first ↔ in the end
    - 영화 **처음에**는 재미있었는데 **마지막에**는 지루했어요.
      The movie was interesting at first, but it was boring at the end.
14. 아직 ↔ 벌써
    not yet ↔ already
    - **아직** 안 왔어요? **벌써** 영화가 시작했어요.
      She hasn't come yet? The movie started already.
15. 계속 ↔ 그만
    continuously (keep) ↔ stopped
    - 음식을 **계속** 먹을 수 있었지만 **그만** 먹었어요.
      I could have kept eating, but I stopped.
16. 실수로 ↔ 일부러
    accidentally ↔ on purpose
    - **실수로** 잘못 말했어요. **일부러** 그런 건 아니에요.
      I misspoke. It wasn't on purpose.
17. 대충 ↔ 자세히
    roughly ↔ in detail, thoroughly
    - 보통 뉴스를 **대충** 보지만 오늘 뉴스는 **자세히** 봤어요.
      I usually skim through (lit. read roughly) the news, but today I read it carefully.
18. 충분히 ↔ 부족하게
    fully ↔ insufficiently
    - 뭐든지 **충분히** 연습해야 돼요.
      One has to thoroughly practice everything.

2 Common Expressions

1. **이상** or more ↔ **이하** or less
   - 이 영화는 19세 **이상**만 볼 수 있습니다. 19세 **미만**은 볼 수 없습니다.
     Only people 19 years or older can watch this movie. People younger than 19 may not watch it.
2. **초과** more than ↔ **미만** less than
   - 이 엘리베이터는 700kg을 **초과**하면 안 됩니다. 700kg 이하는 괜찮습니다.
     This elevator cannot withstand a weight more than 700kg. 700kg or lower is permissible.

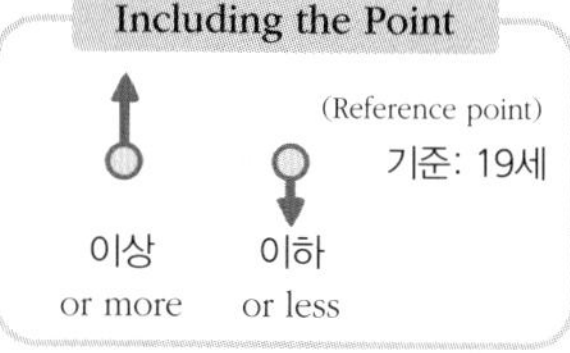

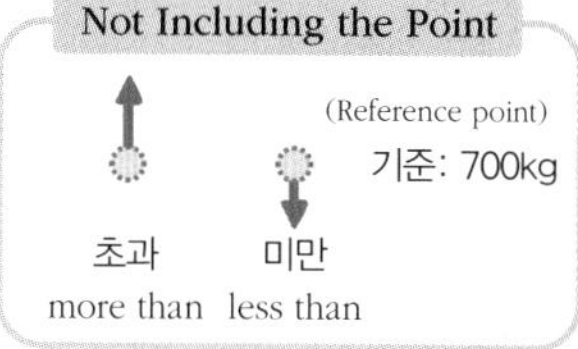

Key Expressions

- 일주일에 최소한 세 번 이상
  at least three times a week
- 적어도 30분 이상 at least 30 minutes
- 늦어도 잠자기 한 시간 전에
  at the latest one hour before sleeping

Grammar 3

-기는 하지만 "It is..., but"

Appendix P. 283 

A 이 구두 정말 예쁘죠?
These shoes are really beautiful, right?

B 구두가 예쁘긴 하지만 값이 너무 비싸네요.
The shoes are beautiful, but the price is too expensive.

-기는 하지만 acknowledges the first clause but follows it up with a clause with contrastive content. It is softer than -지만. -기는 하지만 is attached to the stems of verbs, adjectives, and 이다. -기는 may be shortened to -긴. If the content is in the past, -기는 했지만 is used. Instead of -지만, -(으)ㄴ/는데 may be used. However, when -(으)ㄴ/는데 is used, -기는 하는데 is attached if it is a verb, while -기는 한데 is attached if it is an adjective.

- 한국어가 어렵기는 하지만 재미있어요. (= 한국어가 어렵기는 해요. 하지만 재미있어요.)
  Korean is difficult but fun. (= Korean is difficult. But, it's fun.)
- 텔레비전을 보긴 하는데 무슨 말인지 이해할 수 없어요. I watch TV, but I don't understand what is being said.
- 친구를 만나긴 했지만 그 얘기를 하지 못했어요. I met a friend, but I couldn't talk about that.

-군요 expressing recognition and understanding of a newly learned fact

Appendix P. 284 

A 매워서 먹을 수 없어요.
I can't eat it because it's spicy.

B 매운 음식을 못 먹는군요.
Ah, so you can't eat spicy food.

-군요 is used after seeing a situation or hearing a piece of information and learning something new. It also implies that the speaker did not know the fact until now. It is generally used only in speech. -는군요 is attached to present verb stems, while -군요 is attached to the stems of adjectives and 이다. When referring to a present fact, -았/었- or -겠- may also be attached to form -았/었군요 and -겠군요, respectively. The banmal (casual form) of -군요 is -구나.

- 한국어를 배워 보니까 발음이 어렵군요. I'm learning Korean, but it's difficult to pronounce.
- 혼자 살면 한국 생활이 외롭겠군요. If you live alone, life in Korea will be lonely.
- 아파서 학교에 안 나왔구나! You didn't come to school because you were sick!

▸Answers P. 315

1 **알맞은 답을 고르세요.**

(1) 맛있긴 하지만 생각보다 ⓐ 비싸요. / ⓑ 안 비싸요.

(2) 그 사람에 대해 알긴 하지만 말해 줄 수 ⓐ 있어요. / ⓑ 없어요.

(3) ⓐ 마음에 들긴 한데 / ⓑ 마음에 들긴 하는데 너무 비싸서 못 샀어요.

(4) 한국에 온 지 ⓐ 오래되긴 하지만 / ⓑ 오래되긴 했지만 아직 한국어를 잘 못해요.

(5) 그 사람을 곧 ⓐ 만나긴 하겠지만 / ⓑ 만나긴 했지만 이번 주말에는 안 만날 거예요.

2 **다음 대답 중에서 틀린 것 하나를 고르세요.**

(1) A 집에서 회사까지 2시간이나 걸려요.

B ⓐ 시간이 많이 걸리는군요.
ⓑ 집에서 회사까지 멀군요.
ⓒ 아침마다 고생하겠군요.
ⓓ 집에서 일찍 출발하는군요.

(2) A 저녁에 운동하러 체육관에 가요.

B ⓐ 건강해지는군요.
ⓑ 살이 빠지겠군요.
ⓒ 저녁에 집에 없겠군요.
ⓓ 집에서 운동 안 하는군요.

(3) A 내일 아침에 여행 떠나요.

B ⓐ 신나겠군요.
ⓑ 오늘 짐을 싸야겠군요.
ⓒ 스트레스가 풀리는군요.
ⓓ 내일 오후에 만날 수 없군요.

(4) A 어제 감기 때문에 너무 많이 아팠어.

B ⓐ 많이 아팠구나.
ⓑ 힘들었겠구나.
ⓒ 감기에 걸렸겠구나.
ⓓ 약이 필요했겠구나.

3 **'-군요'를 사용하여 대화를 완성하세요.**

(1) A 이 노래를 들어 보세요. 좋죠?
B 가수의 목소리가 듣기 ________________. (좋다)
가수 이름이 뭐예요?

(2) A 한국에 온 지 1년 됐어요.
B 1년 전에 한국에 ________________. (오다)
저보다 일찍 왔네요.

(3) A 몇 년 전에 부산에서 살았어요.
B 부산에 대해 잘 ________________. (알다)
부산 여행 때 안내 좀 부탁해요.

(4) A 저는 어렸을 때하고 지금이 얼굴이 똑같아요.
B 그러면 어렸을 때도 ________________. (귀엽다)
어렸을 때의 사진을 보고 싶네요.

Conversation ❸

Track 39

리나 대학교를 졸업한 후에 뭐 할 거야?

진수 취직할까 대학원에 갈까 고민 중이야.

리나 아직 못 정했구나! 대학원에 갈 거라고 생각했는데.

진수 더 공부하고 싶긴 한데 사회에서 경험을 쌓는 것도 좋을 것 같아.

리나 그래도 계속 공부하는 게 낫지 않을까?

진수 그렇긴 하지만 공부하려면 돈이 필요해서 취직도 생각하고 있어.

리나 장학금을 받아서 공부하면 되잖아. 네 생각은 어때?

진수 그러면 좋지. 하지만 장학금 받는 게 쉽지 않잖아.

리나 하긴. 그런데 대학원에 가게 되면 뭐 전공하려고?

진수 국제 관계를 전공하려고 해.

리나 그렇구나! 같은 분야를 전공하는 사람과 얘기해 봤어?

진수 아니, 적당한 사람이 없어서 아직 얘기 못 해 봤어.

리나 그래? 내 친구 중에 국제 관계를 전공하는 친구가 한 명 있는데, 만나 볼래?

진수 정말? 만나면 도움이 많이 될 것 같아. 고마워.

리나 알았어. 그 친구한테 연락해 보고 말해 줄게.

Rina What will you do after you graduate college?

Jinsu I'm thinking about whether to find a job or go to graduate school.

Rina Oh, you haven't decided yet! I thought you were going to go to graduate school.

Jinsu I do want to study more, but it also seems like it would be good to get some work experience (lit. pile up some experience in society).

Rina Even so, wouldn't it be better to keep studying?

Jinsu That's true. But, if you end up going to graduate school, what do you want to specialize in?

Rina Just get a scholarship to study. What do you think?

Jinsu That would be good if I could do that. But it's not easy to get a scholarship, you know.

Rina That's true. If you end up going to graduate school, what do you want to specialize in?

Jinsu I want to specialize in international relations.

Rina Really? Have you spoken to people who specialize in the same field?

Jinsu No, I haven't spoken to anyone because I haven't found someone (lit. because there isn't someone suitable).

Rina Really? Among my friends, there's someone who specializes in international relations. Do you want to meet him?

Jinsu Really? I think it would be helpful to meet him. Thanks.

Rina Okay. I'll try to contact him and let you know.

New Vocabulary ▸P. 331

졸업하다 | 취직 | 대학원 | 사회 | 낫다 | 장학금 | 전공하다 | 국제 관계 | 분야

New Expressions ▸P. 331

- 네 생각은 어때?
- 그러면 좋지.
- 하긴.

Tips

1 하긴: "That's true."

하긴 is used when you end up agreeing with another person upon an initial difference in opinion or position. It is used in situations in which one may be informal.

- A 백화점은 너무 비싸지 않아요? Aren't department stores too expensive?
  B 비싸긴 하지만 품질이 좋잖아요.
  They are expensive, but the quality of their products is good.
  A **하긴** 품질은 좋지요. That's true, the quality is good.

2 Contractions in Speech

When speaking in certain cases, portions of grammar patterns may be omitted. In the above conversation, "뭐 전공하려고 해?" may be contracted to "뭐 전공하려고?". In this case, the phrase can be pronounced as "뭐 전공하려구?".

1 Demographics

1. 
전부, 모든 N (100%)
completely, all

2. 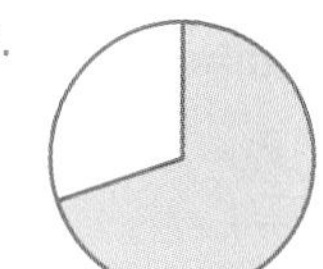
대부분 (70-80%)
mostly, most

3. 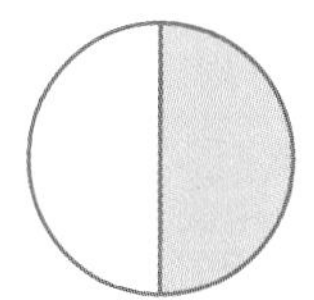
절반 (50%)
half (of)

4. 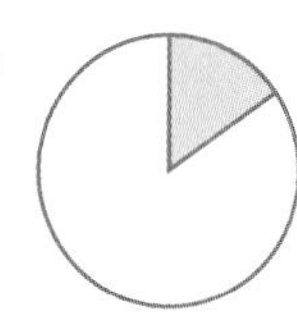
일부 (10-20%)
partially, part of

5. 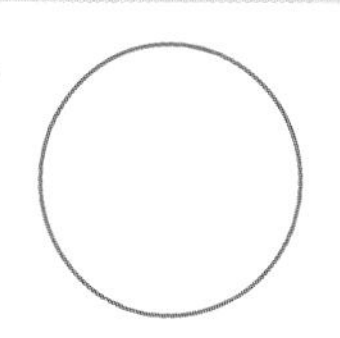
어떤 N도 … 안/못 (0%)
no one / none

- 20대 남자 **전부**가 건강해요.
  All men in their twenties are healthy.
- 20대 남자 **대부분**이 운동을 좋아해요.
  Most men in their twenties like to exercise.
- 20대 남자 **절반**이 모임에 왔어요.
  Half of the men in their twenties came to the meeting.
- 20대 남자 **일부**가 졸업하지 않았어요.
  Some of the men in their twenties did not graduate.
- 20대 남자 중 **어떤** 사람**도** 취직하지 **못했**어요.
  None of the men in their twenties were able to find a job.

- **모든** 20대 남자가 건강해요.
  All men in their twenties are healthy.
- **대부분**의 20대 남자가 운동을 좋아해요.
  Most men in their twenties like to exercise.
- **절반**의 20대 남자가 모임에 왔어요.
  Half of the men in their twenties came to the meeting.
- **일부** 20대 남자가 졸업하지 않았어요.
  Some of the men in their twenties did not graduate.
- **어떤** 20대 남자**도** 취직하지 **못했**어요.
  None of the men in their twenties were able to find a job.

2 Comparing Metrics

1. 1/2: 이 분의 일 one half
   1/3: 삼 분의 일 one third
   1/4: 사 분의 일 one fourth
2. 만큼 as much as
3. 2(두) 배 two times
   3(세) 배 three times
   1.5(일점오) 배 1.5 times

- 우리 반 학생들의 **1/3**이 일본 사람이에요. 1/3 of our class' students are Japanese.
- 이 사무실은 내 방**만큼** 좁아요. This office is as small as my room.
- 이 가방은 내 가방보다 **두 배** 비싸요. This bag is two times more expensive than my bag.

3 Reading Graphs

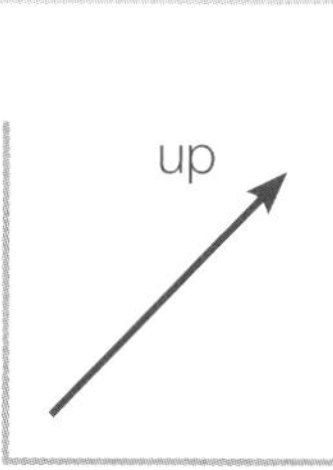

- 값이 올라가다 for the price to go up ↔ 값이 내려가다 for the price to go down
- 실력이 늘다 for one's skill to improve ↔ 실력이 줄다 for one's skill to worsen
- 돈이 늘어나다/증가하다 for money to increase ↔ 돈이 줄어들다/감소하다 for money to decrease
- 수가 늘다/늘어나다/증가하다 for a number to rise/increase ↔ 수가 줄다/줄어들다/감소하다 for a number to fall/decrease

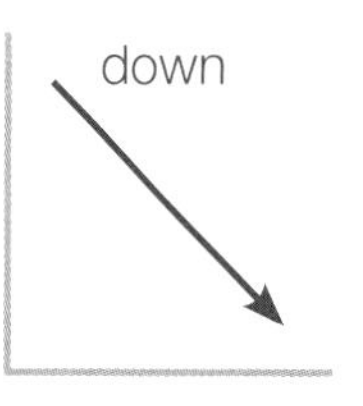

- 지난 10년 동안 집세가 점점 **올라가고** 있어요.
  During the last ten years, rent gradually went up.
- 한국어 실력이 많이 **늘었어요**.
  Your Korean ability improved a lot.
- 이번 휴가 때 관광객이 크게 **늘어났어요**.
  During this vacation, the number of tourists greatly increased.

Key Expressions

- (noun)이/가 서서히 늘어났어요.
  (noun) gradually increased.
- (noun)이/가 급격히 줄어들었어요.
  (noun) sharply decreased.
- (noun)이/가 그대로예요. (noun) is the same.

Let's Talk!

Speaking Strategy — Recalling Information

- 그 사람 이름이 뭐**더라**? What was that person's name **again**?
- 얼마**더라**? How much was it **again**?
- 언제 봤**더라**? When did I see that **again**?

❶ 무엇에 관심이 있어요? 왜 그것에 관심이 생겼어요?

	나	친구
• 좋아하는 책		
• 하고 싶은 운동		
• 자주 듣는 음악		
• 자주 보는 텔레비전 프로그램		
• 하기 싫은 일		
• 잘하는 음식		
• 배우고 싶은 것		
• 일하고 싶은 분야		
• 한국에 대해 제일 관심 있는 것		
• 한국어를 배운 후 계획		

❷ 시간이 있을 때 주로 어떤 것을 해요?

책

- 무엇에 관한 책을 주로 읽어요?
- 좋아하는 작가가 누구예요? 왜 좋아해요?
- 한국에 대한 책을 읽은 적이 있어요?

영화

- 어떤 영화를 좋아해요?
(액션 영화, 드라마, 공포 영화, 코미디 영화, 스릴러 ……)
- 어떤 영화가 제일 좋았어요? 왜요?
- 그 영화에 어떤 배우가 나와요? 영화감독이 누구예요?

공연이나 콘서트

- 어떤 공연을 좋아해요? 얼마나 자주 가요?
- 최근에 어떤 공연을 봤어요? 어디에서 했어요?
- 누구하고 같이 갔어요?

운동 경기

- 어떤 운동 경기를 자주 봐요?
- 최근에 언제 경기를 봤어요?
- 응원하는 팀이 이겼어요? 누가 이겼어요? 누가 졌어요?

New Vocabulary

작가 author | 감독 director | 응원하다 to cheer for, to support | 이기다 to win | 지다 to lose

Word Web ▸ Appendix P. 320

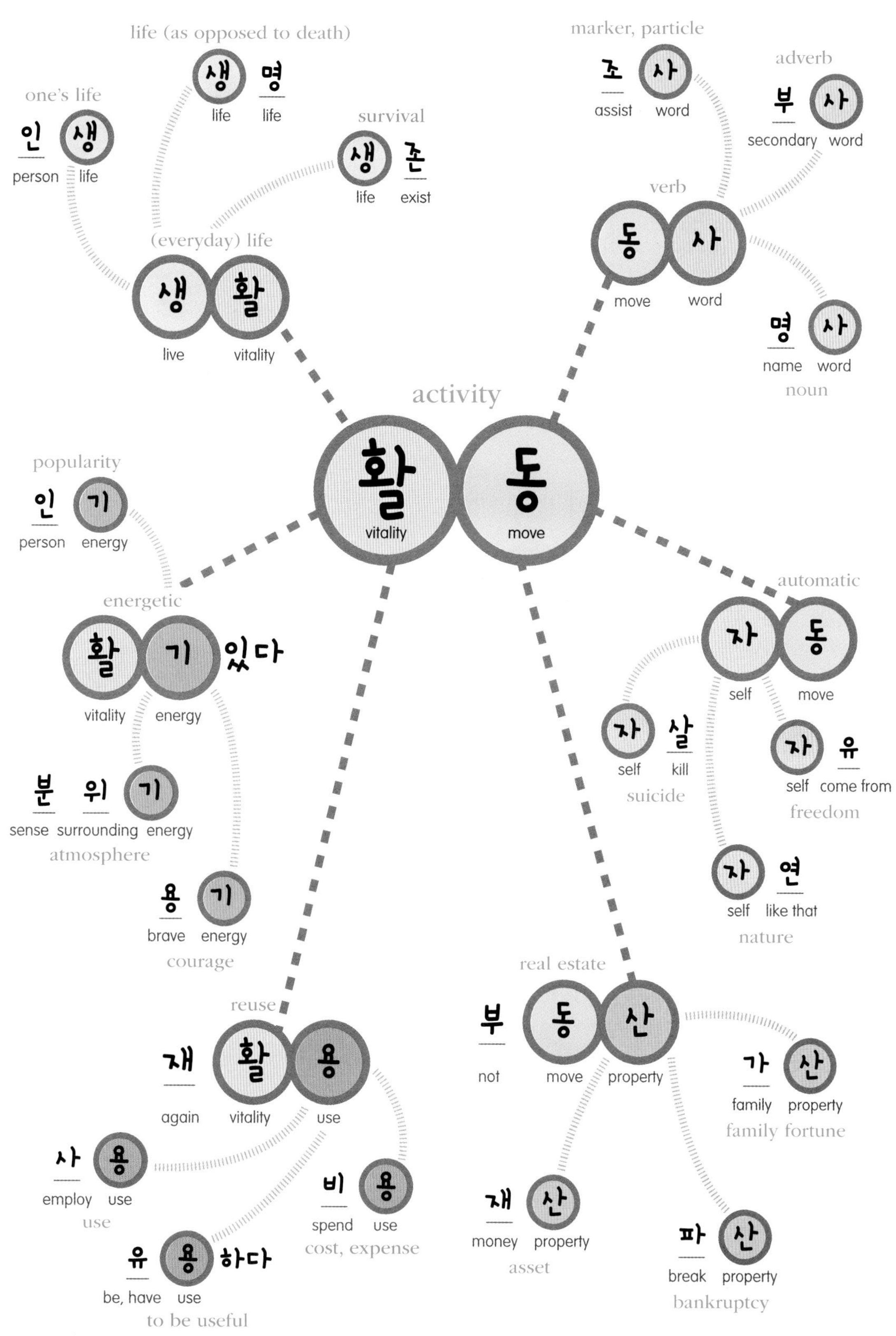

A Word on Culture

Let's Talk About People!

• 괴짜 He's a little…eccentric!

괴짜 refers to an eccentric. "Eccentric" here refers to people who carry out actions that most people do not often do. It can be seen as a positive trait in that the person has a fascinating perception of themselves, but it can also be seen as a negative trait in that the person carries out actions that are poorly understood by ordinary people. There was a notion that it is difficult for a 괴짜 to survive in traditional Korean society, in which it is essential to read what other people are thinking, but nowadays, a 괴짜 may be considered unique, as creativity is regarded as a critical trait in the modern generation.

• 왕따 Don't leave me out!

왕따 refers to the act of ostracizing someone or alienating someone as a pariah. The 따 comes from 따돌림 (ostracizing), while the 왕 in front means "to do seriously" or "to do often." Every society is united to the extent that people with similar interests have gathered together, but in Korean society, which has developed based upon a communal culture, 왕따 undergo much psychological stress as they are unable to join any group. 왕따 face many societal problems, particularly in school, the military, and companies, in which group mentality is strong.

• 컴맹 Do you know how to use a computer?

Recently, as computers have become an essential part of life, a lack of computer skills is particularly noticeable. 컴맹 refers to those who are not technologically savvy. It is formed from the combination of 컴, which comes from 컴퓨터, and 맹, which refers to ignorance. As computers have become a regular part of life, this word has also become common. The term 컴맹 is generally used by people who have difficulty using computers to refer to themselves, particularly when asking someone who knows more about computers for help or to repair a computer.

• 몸짱 What a body!

몸짱 is used to refer to people who diligently exercise and keep good care of their bodies. It is formed with 몸 (body) and 짱, which means "the best." Thus, 몸짱 refers to people who have a body that everyone would wish to have. It is used as a term of admiration for the hard work that one has put into taking care of one's body, particularly in today's society, where good health is valued.

Chapter 14
여행
Travel

Goals
- Making Conjectures
- Talking about Misunderstandings
- Talking about Trip Memories
- Asking and Answering about Travel Experiences
- Talking about Habitual Actions
- Making Excuses
- Talking about Regrets

Grammar
❶ -나 보다 "to look (like)"
-(으)ㄴ/는 줄 알았다 "to have thought that"

❷ -던 the retrospective modifier
-곤 하다 "usually", "used to"

❸ -느라고 "because (of doing something at the time)"
-(으)ㄹ 걸 그랬다 "should have"

Grammar 1

-나 보다 "to look (like)"

Appendix P. 284

A 저 식당에 많은 사람들이 줄을 서 있어요.
A lot of people are standing in line at that restaurant.

B 저 식당 음식이 맛있나 봐요.
That restaurant looks like it has tasty food.

-나 보다 is used to conjecture an action or state based on what one has witnessed. If the conjecture is about the present, -(으)ㄴ가 보다 is attached to the stems of adjectives or 이다, while -나 보다 is attached to the verb stems. If the conjecture is about the past, -았/었나 보다 is attached to the stems of verbs, adjectives, and 이다.

- 민호는 요즘 바쁜가 봐. 연락이 안 되네. It looks like Minho is busy these days. I can't get in touch with him.
- 많은 사람들이 모여 있어요. 유명한 사람이 왔나 봐요.
  A lot of people are gathering. It looks like a famous person must have come.
- 저 사람이 리나의 남자 친구인가 봐. 리나하고 손을 잡고 걸어가네.
  I think that person is Rina's boyfriend. He is holding hands and walking with Rina.

-(으)ㄴ/는 줄 알았다 "to have thought that"

Appendix P. 285

A 저는 한국 음식이 다 매운 줄 알았어요. 그런데 이건 안 매워요.
I thought that all Korean food was spicy, but this isn't spicy.

B 안 매운 음식도 있지요.
There's food that isn't spicy too.

-(으)ㄴ/는 줄 알았다 is used to express a factual or situational misunderstanding. The clause preceding it is the misunderstood content. If the misunderstanding is about the present, -는 줄 알았다 is attached to the stems of verbs, while -(으)ㄴ 줄 알았다 is attached to the stems of adjectives and 이다. If the misunderstanding is about the past, -(은) 줄 알았다 is attached to the stems of verbs. -(으)ㄹ 줄 알았다 is attached to the stems of verbs, adjectives, and 이다 when expressing the future or a conjecture.

- 진수가 농담하는 줄 알았어요. 그런데 진심이었어요. I thought Jinsu was joking. But he was sincere.
- 처음에는 한국 물가가 싼 줄 알았는데 와 보니까 생각보다 비싸요.
  At first, I thought Korean prices were cheap, but when I came, it was more expensive than I thought.
- 영어를 잘해서 미국 사람인 줄 알았는데 독일 사람이에요.
  I thought he was American because he spoke English well, but he is German.

▸Answers P. 315

1 알맞은 답을 고르세요.

(1) 우리 선생님이 오늘 옷을 예쁘게 입었어요. ⓐ 배우인가 봐요. / ⓑ 데이트하나 봐요.

(2) 마크가 어제부터 아무것도 못 먹었대요. ⓐ 배가 아픈가 봐요. / ⓑ 배가 고픈가 봐요.

(3) 가게에 사람들이 줄을 서 있어요. ⓐ 음식이 맛있나 봐요. / ⓑ 돈을 많이 버나 봐요.

(4) 원래 집까지 30분 걸리는데 오늘은 2시간 걸렸대요. ⓐ 피곤한가 봐요. / ⓑ 길이 막혔나 봐요.

2 다음에서 알맞은 답을 골라서 '-나 보다'를 사용하여 문장을 완성하세요.

멀다	자다	오다	있다	유명하다

(1) 마크 씨 옷이 다 젖었어요. 밖에 비가 ____________.

(2) 오늘 피곤해 보여요. 어제 잠을 못 ____________.

(3) 사람들이 모두 저 사람의 이름을 알아요. 저 사람이 ____________.

(4) 리나가 요즘에 항상 학교에 늦게 와요. 집이 학교에서 ____________.

(5) 민호가 요즘 얼굴 표정이 밝아요. 민호에게 좋은 일이 ____________.

3 '-(으)ㄴ/는 줄 알았다'를 사용하여 문장을 완성하세요.

(1) A 케빈은 전에 중국에서 살았나 봐요.
B 아니요, 그런 적이 없는데요.
A 그래요? 중국어를 잘해서 전에 중국에서 ____________.

(2) A 리나는 영화 보러 자주 가나 봐요.
B 아니요, 시간이 없어서 자주 못 가요.
A 그래요? 영화에 대해 잘 알아서 영화 보러 자주 ____________.

(3) A 오랫동안 여기에서 일했나 봐요.
B 아니요, 저도 일한 지 얼마 안 되는데요.
A 그래요? 회사 사람들하고 친해 보여서 오랫동안 ____________.

(4) A 찌개가 매운가 봐요.
B 아니요, 하나도 안 매워요. 왜 그렇게 생각했어요?
A 사람들이 찌개를 먹으면서 땀을 많이 흘려서 ____________.

Conversation 1

Track 40

새라 이게 언제 찍은 사진이에요?

진수 초등학교 때 찍은 사진이에요.

새라 어렸을 때 정말 귀여웠네요.
어디에서 이 사진을 찍었어요?

진수 어디더라? 부산에 여행 갔을 때 찍은 것 같아요.

새라 오른쪽 옆에 있는 사람이 동생인가 봐요. 얼굴이 닮았네요.

진수 아니요, 그 애는 어렸을 때 제 친구예요.

새라 그래요? 저는 얼굴이 비슷해서 동생인 줄 알았어요.

진수 그런 얘기 많이 들었어요.

새라 같이 여행도 다닌 것을 보니까 많이 친했나 봐요.

진수 방학 때 이 친구네 가족이랑 바닷가에 자주 놀러 갔어요.

새라 그랬군요. 지금도 이 친구를 자주 만나요?

진수 아니요, 제가 이사 가면서 친구하고 연락이 끊겼어요.

새라 안타깝네요.

Sarah When did you take this picture?

Jinsu I took it in elementary school.

Sarah You were really cute when you were young! Where did you take this picture?

Jinsu Where could it have been? I think it was when I traveled to Busan.

Sarah The person to your right looks like your little brother. Your faces look really alike.

Jinsu No, that kid was my friend when I was young.

Sarah Really? I thought it was your little brother because your faces were similar.

Jinsu I've heard that a lot.

Sarah Seeing that you traveled together, it seems like you were close.

Jinsu During vacation, I went to the beach often with this friend's family.

Sarah I see. Do you still see this friend often?

Jinsu No. I lost contact with my friend when I moved.

Sarah That's a shame.

New Vocabulary ▸ P. 331

초등학교 | 어렸을 때 | 귀엽다 | 여행 다니다 | 지금도 | 이사 가다 | 연락이 끊기다

New Expressions ▸ P. 331

- 어디더라?
- 그런 얘기 많이 들었어요.
- 안타깝네요.

Tips

1 Recalling Information

-더라? is used when searching for a memory. As it is considered talking to oneself (혼잣말), there is no formal form. -더라 is attached to the stems of verbs, adjectives, 이다, and also to question words.

- 이름이 뭐**더라?** 생각이 안 나네.
  What was his name again? I can't remember.
- 언제 여행 **갔더라?** 기억이 안 나네요.
  When did I go on vacation? I can't remember.

2 네: Person's Family/Person's House

네 is attached to a noun that refers to a person in order to refer to the group to which the person belongs. In this conversation as well, 친구네 가족 means the same thing as 친구의 가족. 가족 or 집 may be used or omitted.

- 지난 주말에 동생**네**에 갔다 왔어요.
  Last weekend I went to my younger sibling's home.
- 민수**네** 얘기를 들었어요?
  Did you hear what happened to Minsu's family?

❶ Identifying a Person's Location

• 뒷줄 (세 번째 줄)
back row (third row)

• 가운데 줄 (두 번째 줄)
middle row (second row)

• 앞줄 (첫 번째 줄)
front row (first row)

❶ 마지막 줄의 맨 왼쪽에서 두 번째
second from the left in the last row

❷ 뒷줄의 중앙 (= 가운데)
middle of the back row

❸ 두 번째 줄의 맨 왼쪽
far left in the second row

❹ 앞줄의 왼쪽에서 두 번째
second from the left in the front row

❺ 가운데 줄의 오른쪽에서 세 번째
third from the right in the middle row

❻ 첫 번째 줄의 맨 오른쪽
far right in the first row

❷ Pointing Out a Location in a Photograph

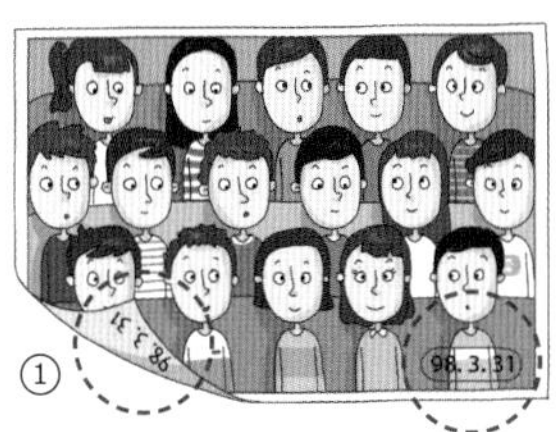

❶ 사진의 **뒷면**에 날짜를 써서 친구에게 줬어요.
I wrote the date on the back of the photograph and sent it to my friend.

❷ 사진의 **오른쪽 아래**에 사진 찍은 날짜가 나와 있어요.
The date that the photo was taken is at the bottom right of the picture.

❸ Common Descriptions of Photographs

1. 사진이 잘 나왔어요. = 사진이 뚜렷하게 나왔어요.
The photo came out well. = The photo came out clearly.

2. 사진이 잘 안 나왔어요.
The photo did not come out well.

• 사진이 흐리게 나왔어요.
The photo came out blurry.

• 사진이 초점이 안 맞아요.
The focal point in the photo is wrong.

• 사진이 흔들렸어요.
The photo is shaky.

• 얼굴이 잘렸어요.
His face is cut off.

3. 사진을 거꾸로 들고 있어요.
The photo is held upside-down.

4. 사진을 뒤집어서 들고 있어요.
The photo is held with the back side facing forward.

Key Expressions

• 언제 찍은 사진이에요? When was this picture taken?
• 어디서 찍었어요? Where did you take this picture?
• 옆에 있는 사람이 누구예요? Who is the person next to you?

Grammar 2

-던 the retrospective modifier

Appendix P. 288

A 예전 집에 가 봤어요?
Have you been to your old house (lately)?

B 어릴 때 살던 집이 지금은 없어졌어요.
The house I used to live in when I was young no longer exists.

-던 is used in front of nouns as a modifier referring to a recollection of a past state or event. It is attached to the stems of verbs, adjectives, and 이다. -던 refers to an action or habit that was repeated over a set time or to a state that continued over a set period of time. -았/었- may be attached to form -았/었던, implying that the action or state occurred once or only a few times in the past.

- 항상 웃던 친구의 얼굴이 지금도 기억나요. I still remember the face of my friend who always smiled.
- 내가 지난번에 말했던 얘기 생각나? Do you remember what I said last time?
- 3년 전까지 야구 선수였던 사람이 지금은 가수가 됐어요.
  The person who was a baseball player three years ago is now a singer.

-곤 하다 "usually", "used to"

A 그 공원에 가 본 적이 있어요?
Have you been to that park?

B 어렸을 때 가족과 같이 공원에 놀러 가곤 했어요.
When I was young, I used to go to that park with my family.

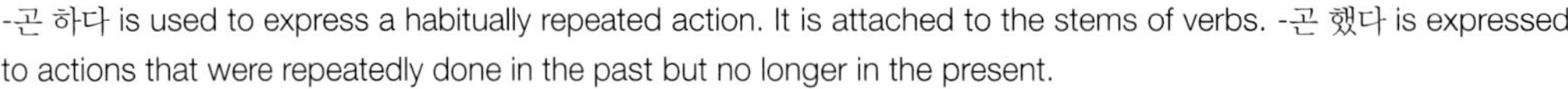

-곤 하다 is used to express a habitually repeated action. It is attached to the stems of verbs. -곤 했다 is expressed to actions that were repeatedly done in the past but no longer in the present.

- 피곤하면 음악을 듣곤 해요. When I'm tired, I usually listen to music.
- 어렸을 때 심하게 장난쳐서 엄마한테 혼나곤 했어요.
  When I was a kid, my mother used to scold me for rough-and-tumble play.
- 전에는 친구와 가끔 점심을 먹곤 했는데 요즘은 바빠서 못 해요.
  I used to have lunch with my friends occasionally before, but I can't because I'm busy these days.

▸Answers P. 315

1 그림을 보고 '-던'을 사용하여 문장을 완성하세요.

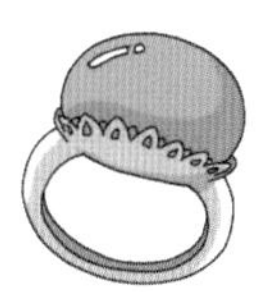

몇 년 전에
할머니께서 주셨어요.

5년 전에
제 회사 동료였어요.

어렸을 때
가지고 놀았어요.

70년대에
유행했어요.

전에 친구하고
갈비를 먹었어요.

학교 다닐 때
키가 작았어요.

(1) ________________ 노래를 다시 들어 보고 싶어요.
(2) ________________ 인형을 창고에서 발견했어요.
(3) ________________ 식당이 어디에 있는지 생각 안 나요.
(4) ________________ 친구가 지금은 우리 중에서 키가 제일 커요.
(5) ________________ 사람이 우리 옆집에 살아요.
(6) ________________ 반지를 어제 길에서 잃어버려서 너무 속상해요.

2 알맞은 답을 고르세요.

(1) 10년 동안 ⓐ 쓰는 / ⓑ 쓰던 자동차를 지난달에 바꿨어요.
(2) 1년 전에 ⓐ 결혼한 / ⓑ 결혼했던 부부가 지금도 잘 살고 있대요.
(3) 지난주에 ⓐ 보내던 / ⓑ 보냈던 편지가 아직도 도착 안 했나 봐요.
(4) 다 ⓐ 읽은 / ⓑ 읽었던 책은 책상 위에 놓아 주세요. 제가 나중에 정리할게요.
(5) 전화 끊었어? 그럼 아까 ⓐ 먹던 / ⓑ 먹었던 밥 계속 먹어.

3 '-곤 하다'를 사용하여 문장을 완성하세요.

(1) 평소에는 밖에서 사 먹지만 가끔 도시락을 싸 와서 ________________. (먹다)
(2) 혼자 영화 보는 것을 좋아해서 평일에 가끔 혼자 영화를 ________________. (보다)
(3) 지금은 동생하고 사이가 좋지만 어렸을 때는 가끔 ________________. (싸우다)
(4) 요즘에는 시간이 없어서 산책을 못 하지만 예전에는 시간이 날 때마다 한강에서 ________________. (산책하다)

Conversation ❷

Track 41

마크 이건 태국에 여행 가서 찍었던 사진이에요.

리나 네? 이 사람이 마크 씨예요?
머리 모양이 달라서 다른 사람인 줄 알았어요.

마크 그렇죠? 다른 사람들도 다 그렇게 말해요.

리나 그런데 전부 혼자 찍은 사진이네요. 혼자 여행 갔나 봐요.

마크 네, 전에는 혼자 여기저기 돌아다니면서 여행하곤 했어요.

리나 요즘에도 혼자 여행 가요?

마크 아니요, 이제는 친구랑 같이 편하게 다니는 게 좋아요.

리나 저도 그래요.
여행할 때 먹었던 음식 중에서 뭐가 제일 생각나요?

마크 거기에서 먹었던 팟타이 맛을 지금도 잊을 수 없어요.

리나 그렇게 맛있었어요?

마크 네, 관광객이 찾는 식당 말고 현지인들이 가는 식당이 더 싸고 맛있었어요.

리나 그렇군요.

Mark This is the picture I took when I traveled to Thailand.

Rina Huh? Is this person you?
I thought it was someone else because your hairstyle was different.

Mark Right? Other people say that too.

Rina So you took all the pictures yourself. It looks like you went alone.

Mark Yes, I used to travel around (lit. here and there) by myself before.

Rina Do you travel alone lately too?

Mark No, now I like to travel comfortably with my friends.

Rina So do I.
Among the foods you have tasted when traveling, what do you remember best?

Mark Even now, I still can't forget the taste of the Pad Thai I had there.

Rina It was that tasty?

Mark Yes. Restaurants that locals go to are cheaper and tastier than those that tourists go to.

Rina I see.

New Vocabulary ▸P. 332

모양 | 전부 | 잊다 | 관광객 | 현지인

New Expressions ▸P. 332

- 다른 사람들도 다 그렇게 말해요.
- 뭐가 제일 생각나요?
- 지금도 잊을 수 없어요.

Tips

1 Expressions of Nonspecific Things and Places

- **여기저기** 찾아봤지만 지갑이 없어요.
  I looked here and there, but I couldn't find my wallet.
- 오랜만에 쇼핑해서 **이것저것** 많이 샀어요.
  I bought this and that because I hadn't shopped for so long.
- 친구를 만나서 **이런저런** 얘기를 했어요.
  I met up with my friend and spoke about all kinds of things.
- 친구는 변덕스러워서 항상 **이랬다 저랬다** 해요.
  My friend is fickle, so he always flip-flops.

2 The Usage of 저도 그래요

It is used to express that one shares the same feeling or situation or experience as the speaker. It may be shortened to 저도요. In Korean, this may be used for both positive and negative sentences.

- A 여행할 때는 기차를 자주 타요.
  When I travel, I often take trains.
  B **저도 그래요.** So do I.
- A 오늘 기분이 안 좋아. I'm not in a good mood today.
  B **나도 그래.** Neither am I.

❶ Packing for Trips

1. 의류 Clothing
- 옷 clothing
- 속옷 underwear
- 양말 socks
- 잠옷 pajamas
- 겉옷 outerwear
- 수영복 swimwear
- 스키복 ski gear
- 등산복 hiking gear

2. 세면도구 Toiletries
- 수건 towel/washcloth
- 칫솔 toothbrush
- 치약 toothpaste
- 비누 soap
- 샴푸 shampoo
- 린스 conditioner

3. 소지품 Personal Belongings
- 핸드폰 mobile phone
- 충전기 charger
- 카메라 camera
- 여권 passport
- 지갑 wallet
- 돈 money
- 화장품 cosmetics
- 휴지 tissue
- 지도 map
- 선글라스 sunglasses
- 모자 hat
- 비상약 emergency medication

4. 기타 Other
- 노트북 laptop
- 책 book
- 사전 dictionary
- 필기도구 writing utensils
- 모기약 mosquito repellent
- 컵라면 cup ramen
- 통조림 canned food
- 부채 fan
- 우산 umbrella
- 장갑 glove
- 물병 water bottle

❷ Travel Preparations

- 여행 정보를 찾다 to look for travel information
- 여행 일정을 짜다 to set a travel date
- (비행기/기차/버스) 표를 사다 to buy (plane/train/bus) tickets
- 숙소를 예약하다 to reserve lodging
- 환전하다 to exchange money
- 비자를 받다 to receive a visa
- 예약을 확인하다 to confirm a reservation
- 여행자 보험에 들다 to obtain travel insurance
- 비상약을 준비하다 to prepare emergency medication
- 예방 주사를 맞다 to receive travel vaccinations

❸ Travel Destinations

1. 도시 City Terms

- 시내 downtown
- 관광지 sight
- 맛집 tasty restaurant
- 전시회 exhibition
- 백화점 department store
- 면세점 duty-free shop
- 박물관 museum
- 전통적인 건물 traditional building
- 광장 plaza
- 야경 명소 sight with a good view at night

2. 시골 Countryside Terms

- 바다 sea
- 강 river
- 호수 lake
- 시내 stream
- 연못 pond
- 바닷가 beach
- 섬 island
- 산 mountain
- 계곡 valley
- 폭포 waterfall
- 숲 forest
- 동굴 cave
- 들 field
- 논 rice paddy
- 역사 유적지 historic site
- 절 Buddhist temple
- 교회 church
- 성당 Catholic church
- 밭 field
- 일출 (일몰) 명소 sunrise (sunset) viewing site

❹ Travel Duration

- 당일 여행 one-day trip
- 1박 2일 one night two days
- 2박 3일 two nights three days
- 무박 2일 overnight trip

❺ Types of Trips

- 국내 여행 domestic trip
- 해외여행 overseas trip
- 단체 여행 group trip
- 개별 여행 solitary trip
- 단기 여행 short-term trip
- 장기 여행 long-term trip

❻ Traveling Expenses

- 숙박비 room charge
- 교통비 transportation fee
- 식비 food expenses
- 입장료 (박물관, 공연 등) admission fee (museum, park, etc.)

Key Expressions

- 최대한 빨리 as fast/soon as possible
- 되도록 일찍 as early as possible
- 가능하면 미리 in advance, if possible

Grammar ❸

-느라고 "because (of doing something at the time)"

▶ Appendix P. 287

A 왜 전화를 안 받았어요?
Why didn't you pick up your phone?

B 음악을 듣느라고 전화 소리를 못 들었어요.
I couldn't hear the telephone ring because I was listening to music.

-느라고 is used when describing an unintended negative outcome that arises from carrying out a particular action. The reason for the negative consequence is expressed in the clause preceding -느라고, while the consequence is stated in the following clause. The subject of both clauses must be the same, and this grammar point is often used when giving an excuse for why the unintended negative situation occurred to the subject. -느라고 may also be used, however, to thank someone for the work he/she has done. In this usage, -느라고 is used to express the gratitude the speaker feels for everything the subject has done and gone through. In both cases, -느라고 is attached to verb stems, but -았/었- and the negative -지 않다 may not be attached.

- 우리 아이는 밖에서 노느라고 공부는 안 해요. My child doesn't study because he plays outside.
- 돈을 모으느라고 한동안 여행을 못 갔어요. I couldn't travel for a while because I was saving money.
- 이렇게 많은 음식을 준비하느라고 수고하셨습니다. You worked hard to prepare so many dishes.

-(으)ㄹ 걸 그랬다 "should have"

▶ Appendix P. 288

A 기차를 놓쳤네요.
I see you missed your train.

B 집에서 1시간 일찍 나올 걸 그랬어요.
I should have left my house an hour earlier.

-(으)ㄹ 걸 그랬다 is used when regretting not having made another choice in the past. It expresses a feeling of remorse. The clause preceding -(으)ㄹ 걸 그랬다 describes the action that one regrets not doing. -(으)ㄹ 걸 그랬다 is generally used in speech and is attached to verb stems. When expressing regret, the negative -지 않을 걸 그랬다 or -지 말 걸 그랬다 is used.

- 시험을 잘 못 본 것 같아요. 열심히 공부할 걸 그랬어요.
  I think I didn't do well on the exam. I should've studied harder.
- 약을 좀 더 일찍 먹을 걸 그랬어요. 그러면 지금쯤은 열이 내렸을 거예요.
  I should've taken the medicine sooner. The fever would have gone down by now.
- 담배를 피우지 말 걸 그랬어요. 그러면 건강이 이렇게 나빠지지 않았을 거예요.
  I shouldn't have smoked. My health wouldn't have gotten as bad as it is.

▸Answers P. 315

1 다음에서 알맞은 답을 골라서 '-느라고'를 사용하여 문장을 완성하세요.

사다 참다 찾다 나오다 돌보다 공부하다

(1) 시험 때문에 어제 ______________ 밤을 새웠어요.

(2) 웃음을 ______________ 얼굴이 빨개졌어요.

(3) 이것저것 선물을 ______________ 돈을 다 썼어요.

(4) 아이를 ______________ 일을 그만뒀어요.

(5) 시간이 있을 때마다 정보를 ______________ 정신이 없어요.

(6) 집에서 급하게 ______________ 지갑을 집에 두고 왔어요.

2 밑줄 친 것을 고치세요.

(1) 비가 오느라고 오늘은 운동 못 해요. ➡

(2) 바쁘느라고 친구한테 연락 못 했어요. ➡

(3) 갑자기 회의가 있느라고 전화를 못 받았어요. ➡

(4) 동생이 음악을 듣느라고 제가 공부하지 못했어요. ➡

(5) 여자 친구가 생기느라고 요즘 열심히 공부하지 않아요. ➡

3 알맞은 답을 고르세요.

(1) 표를 사려고 하는데 다 팔렸어요.
ⓐ 미리 표를 살 걸 그랬어요.
ⓑ 미리 표를 사지 말 걸 그랬어요.

(2) 결혼하니까 정말 행복해요.
ⓐ 일찍 결혼할 걸 그랬어요.
ⓑ 일찍 결혼하지 말 걸 그랬어요.

(3) 길에서 지갑을 잃어버렸어요.
ⓐ 집에서 지갑을 가지고 올 걸 그랬어요.
ⓑ 집에서 지갑을 가지고 오지 말 걸 그랬어요.

(4) 아침에 늦게 일어나서 회사에 늦었어요.
ⓐ 알람 시계를 맞추고 잘 걸 그랬어요.
ⓑ 알람 시계를 맞추고 자지 않을 걸 그랬어요.

(5) 중고 자동차가 자꾸 고장 나요.
ⓐ 중고 자동차를 살 걸 그랬어요.
ⓑ 중고 자동차를 사지 말 걸 그랬어요.

Conversation 3

Track 42

유키 지난 휴가 때 여행 갔다 왔다면서요?
케빈 얘기 들었어요? 친구들하고 동해에 갔다 왔어요.
유키 그래요? 여행이 어땠어요?
케빈 서울하고 분위기가 진짜 달라서 재미있었어요.
유키 좋았겠네요. 동해는 해산물이 유명한데 먹어 봤어요?
케빈 당연히 먹었죠. 정말 싱싱해서 서울에서 먹은 것보다 훨씬 맛있었어요.
유키 그럼, 일출은 봤어요?
케빈 아니요, 원래 일출을 보려고 했는데 자느라고 못 봤어요. 그 전날 설악산을 등산했거든요. 정말 아쉬워요.
유키 일출을 본 다음에 설악산에 가지 그랬어요?
케빈 맞아요. 먼저 일출부터 볼 걸 그랬어요.
유키 너무 아쉬워하지 마세요. 다음에 또 가면 되죠, 뭐.
케빈 그렇긴 해요.
유키 그럼, 다음에 같이 가는 게 어때요?
케빈 그래요. 시간 맞춰서 같이 가요.

Yuki I heard you went on a trip last vacation?
Kevin You heard? I went with my friends to Donghae.
Yuki Really? How was the trip?
Kevin It was fun because the atmosphere was completely different from Seoul.
Yuki It must have been nice. The seafood in Donghae is famous. Did you get to eat some?
Kevin Of course, I ate some. It was really fresh so it was much tastier than what I've eaten in Seoul.
Yuki Did you see the sunrise?
Kevin No, I originally planned to see the sunrise, but I couldn't see it because I was sleeping. The day before we hiked Seorak-san. It is really a shame (that I was unable to see the sunrise).
Yuki Why didn't you climb Seorak-san (Mt. Seorak) after seeing the sunrise?
Kevin Yeah, we should have seen the sunrise first.
Yuki Don't feel too bad. You can see it next time you go.
Kevin That's true.
Yuki So, how about we go together next time?
Kevin Okay. Let's set a time and go together.

New Vocabulary ▸P. 332

해산물 | 당연히 | 싱싱하다 | 일출 | 전날 | 등산하다 | 아쉽다

New Expressions ▸P. 332

- 당연히 먹었죠.
- 너무 아쉬워하지 마세요.
- 시간 맞춰서 같이 가요.

Tips

1 The Usage of 그

A period of time relative to another specific day is referred to using "그", which, in conversation, refers to the day that is used as a reference. "전" or "다음", followed by the time being addressed, is attached afterward.

- 그 전날 / 그다음 날
  the day before / the day after
- 그 전주 / 그다음 주
  the week before / the week after
- 그 전달 / 그다음 달
  the month before / the month after
- 그 전해 / 그다음 해
  the year before / the year after

2 아쉽다 vs. 아쉬워하다

In Korean, while emotion adjectives are used to describe feelings, one cannot know exactly what another person is feeling. Since all we can do is guess about emotions from someone else's behavior, -아/어하다 is attached to emotion adjectives to describe another person's emotional state/behavior. When -아/어하다 is added, it becomes a verb.

- (제가) 지갑을 잃어버려서 **속상해요**.
  I'm upset because I lost my wallet.
- 너무 **속상해하**지 마세요. 지갑을 곧 찾을 거예요.
  Don't be too upset. You'll find your wallet soon.
  (-지 마세요 requires a verb so -아/어하다 must be attached to adjectives.)

1 Adverbial Expressions

1. **대로**

- 계획대로 according to plan
- 생각대로 according to what one thought
- 예상대로 as expected

2. **와/과 달리**

- 계획과 달리 differently from planned
- 생각과 달리 differently from what one thought
- 예상과 달리 differently from expected

3. **보다**

- 계획보다 more than planned
- 생각보다 more than one thought
- 예상보다 more than one expected

- 계획**대로** 되지 않아서 걱정돼요. I'm worried because it didn't go according to plan.
- 예상**과 달리** 숙소가 너무 좁았어요. The rooms were very small, unlike what I expected.
- 생각**보다** 날씨가 더웠어요. The weather was much hotter than I thought it would be.

4. **없이**

- 계획 없이 without plans
- 생각 없이 without thinking
- 돈 없이 without money

5. **외로**

- 예상 외로 unexpectedly (from one's expectation)
- 생각 외로 unexpectedly (from one's thought)
- 상상 외로 unimaginably

6. **Other**

- 일반적으로 (= 흔히, 보통) generally (= commonly, usually)
- 예외적으로 as an exception

- 생각 **없이** 말했는데 친구가 기분 나빠했어요. I spoke without thinking, upsetting my friend.
- 예상 **외로** 여행비가 많이 들었어요. The trip was unexpectedly very expensive.
- **일반적으로** 실내에서는 사진을 찍을 수 없어요. Generally, photos may not be taken indoors.
- 그런데 여기에서는 **예외적으로** 사진을 찍을 수 있어요. However, pictures maybe taken here (as an exception).

2 Travel Issues

1. **사람들** People

- 말이 안 통하다 to not communicate well
- 문화가 다르다 for culture to be different
- 사람들이 불친절하다 for people to be unkind
- 아는 사람이 없다 to not know anyone

2. **음식** Food

- 음식이 입에 안 맞다 the taste of the cuisine does not suit the diner
- 배탈이 나다 to get indigestion

3. **숙소** Lodging

- 숙소가 예약이 안 되어 있다 for reservations to not have been made
- 숙소에 빈방이 없다 for there to be no vacant rooms

4. **쇼핑** Shopping

- 물가가 너무 비싸다 for the prices to be too expensive
- 바가지를 쓰다 to get ripped off

5. **교통** Transportation

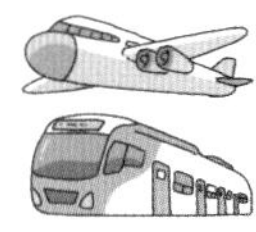

- 기차를 놓치다 to miss the train
- 비행기가 늦게 도착하다 (= 연착하다) for the airplane to arrive late
- 멀미가 나다 to get motion sickness

6. **사고** Accidents

- 여권을 잃어버리다 to lose one's passport
- 가방을 도둑맞다 for one's bag to be stolen

7. **날씨** Weather

- 날씨가 너무 덥다 for the weather to be too hot
- 날씨가 너무 춥다 for the weather to be too cold

8. **Other**

- 여행지가 위험하다 for the travel destination to be dangerous
- 관광지가 공사 중이다 for the sight to be under construction
- 길을 헤메다 to be lost
- 비행기가 결항하다 for a flight to be cancelled
- 표가 매진되다 for tickets to be sold

Key Expressions

- 바가지를 쓰는 것이 보통이에요. Being ripped off is normal.
- 빈방이 있을 때가 드물어요. It is rare to have vacant rooms.

Let's Talk!

Speaking Strategy **Hesitating in Speech**

- 음……. Um...
- 글쎄요. Well...
- 그게 말이에요. About that...

❶ 자주 여행 가요? 어떤 여행을 좋아해요?

❷ 제일 기억에 남는 여행 장소를 소개해 주세요.

	어디예요?	언제 갔어요?	어떤 느낌?	주의 사항?
• 흥미로운 장소				
• 야경이 아름다운 곳				
• 음식이 색다른 곳				
• 다시 가고 싶지 않은 곳				
• 말이 안 통했던 곳				
• 문화가 많이 달랐던 곳				
• 경치가 좋았던 곳				
• 물가가 쌌던 곳				
• 바가지 썼던 곳				
• 혼자 여행하기 좋은 곳				

- 뭐가 인상적이었어요?
- 뭐 때문에 힘들었어요?
- 여행할 때 알면 좋은 정보가 뭐예요?

음……, 제 경우에는 여행지에 아는 사람이 없으면 숙소 서비스를 먼저 확인해요. 어떤 숙소는 예약하면 그 숙소에서 공항까지 저를 마중 나와서 편하거든요.

글쎄요. 여행지가 좋아도 밤늦게 혼자 돌아다니는 게 위험하니까 어두워진 후에 혼자 돌아다니지 마세요. 낮에도 위험한 곳이 있을 수 있어요.

New Vocabulary

휴양지 resort | 유적지 historical site | 흥미롭다 to be interesting | 야경 night scenery | 색다르다 to be unusual | 물가 price | 인상적이다 to be memorable, to be impressive | 숙소 lodging | 마중 나오다 to come out to meet

Word Web

Appendix P. 321

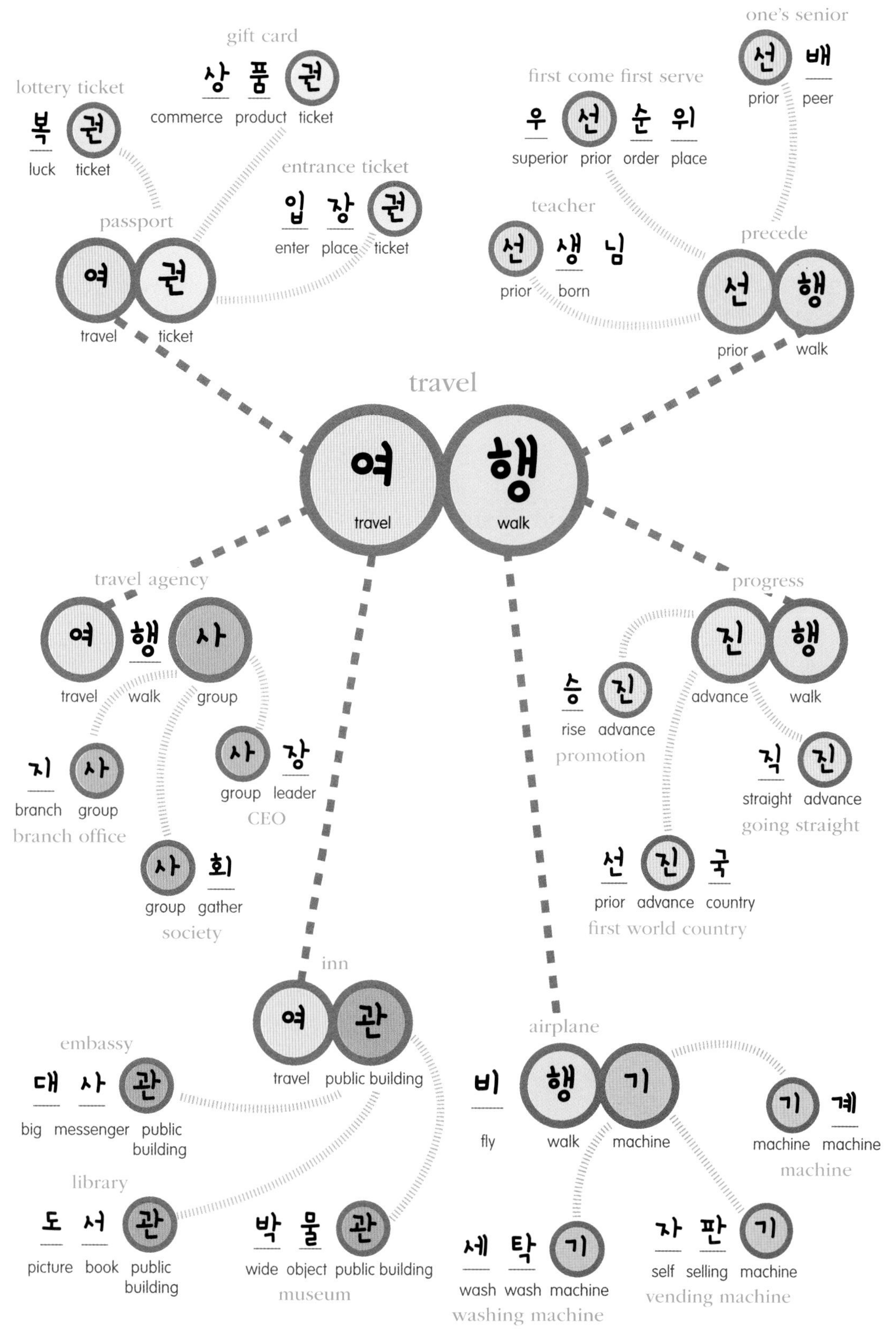

A Word on Culture

Let's Talk About Food!

• 파전 Scallion Pancakes and 막걸리 Unrefined Rice Wine

On wet, rainy days, Koreans like to eat certain foods. These are 파전 (scallion pancakes) and 막걸리 (unrefined rice wine). Koreans believe that when the temperature is slightly lower than usual, eating pan-fried 파전, which can be seen as the Korean version of pizza while drinking a glass of 막걸리, which is made from rice, matches the atmosphere of the falling rain well. Koreans believe that greasy foods are also a good match for slightly cooler rainy days. Of course, some people will think of 찌개 and other soupy dishes, but those who were born and raised in Korea think of 파전 and 막걸리 on rainy days.

• 김밥 Gimbap (Korean-Style Sushi)

When schoolchildren go on picnics, they pack 김밥 (Korean-style sushi) in lunch boxes. Today it can be bought inexpensively, but in the 90s, 김밥 was a food that was very looked forward to as it could only be eaten at picnics. The ingredients that went into 김밥 differed depending on each mother's preference. When Koreans think of picnics, they think of 김밥.

• 짜장면 Black-Bean Noodles

When there is little time to cook on days in which one is moving or cleaning the house, Koreans generally order and eat 짜장면 (Korean version of Chinese black bean noodles). 짜장면 is often ordered and eaten not because 짜장면 provides fond memories of homecooked meals or enjoying a dish on a rainy day, but rather because it is cheap, convenient, and makes one full. 짜장면 has become the standard delivery food, to the point that there is no Chinese restaurant that does not deliver 짜장면. Whether you're at the beach, park, or Han River, 짜장면 can be quickly delivered anywhere, at any time of the day, with a short call.

• 치맥 Chicken and Beer

When watching a sport, such as baseball or soccer, or when spending time outdoors, Koreans eat fried chicken and drink cold beer. This is the so-called 치맥 (a combination of the first part of 치킨 (chicken) and 맥주 (beer). Just as people think of popcorn when watching movies, Koreans think of 치맥 watching baseball or soccer, or when outdoors. In particular, 치맥 is by far the most popular food ordered by company men at night.

Chapter 15

관계

Relationships

Goals
- Explaining One's Actions
- Asking One's Opinion
- Reprimanding Someone for Not Doing Something They Should Have Done
- Making Excuses
- Making Official Apologies
- Rejecting Requests
- Guessing Future Events
- Describing Another Person

Grammar

❶ -다가 "while …ing", "in the middle of …ing"
-(으)ㄴ/는데도 "even though", "even if"

❷ -았/었어야지요 "You should have…"
-았/었어야 했는데 "should have…, but…"

❸ -(으)ㄹ 텐데 expressing conjectures, hopes, and hypothetical situations: "will probably…", "I hope", "I wish"
-(으)려던 참이다 "to be about to"

Grammar 1

-다가 "while ...ing", "in the middle of ...ing"

Appendix P. 288

A 왜 전화 안 했어요?

Why didn't you call?

B 텔레비전을 보다가 잠이 들었어요.

I fell asleep while watching TV.

-다가 expresses the interruption of an action by another action or state. It is attached to the stems of verbs and adjectives that describe the changing action or state, and the subject of both the preceding and following clauses must be the same. -다가 may also be used when an unexpected situation, usually negative, arises in the middle of another action. In this case, the subject of the latter clause may not be the same as that of the first, but the situation of the second clause must pertain to or have happened to the subject of the first clause.

- 회의하다가 전화를 받았어요. I answered a phone call in the middle of the meeting.
- 집에 가다가 편의점에 잠깐 들렀어요. On my way home, I stopped by a convenience store for a while.
- 옷을 입다가 옷이 찢어졌어요. My clothes were torn while I was wearing them.

-(으)ㄴ/는데도 "even though", "even if"

C.C P. 306

A 아까 커피를 안 마셨어요?

Didn't you just drink coffee?

B 커피를 세 잔이나 마셨는데도 계속 졸려요.

I drank three cups of coffee, but I'm still sleepy.

-(으)ㄴ/는데도 expresses that the clause following it occurs despite what happened in the clause preceding it. In the above example, one would expect someone not to be sleepy if they had drunk coffee, but the speaker still feels sleepy despite drinking coffee. If the preceding clause is in the present, -는데도 is attached to verb stems and -(으)ㄴ데도 to the stems of adjectives and 이다. If it is in the past, -았/었는데도 is attached to the stems of verbs, adjectives, and 이다. The conjugation is the same as that of -(으)ㄴ/는데 in Chapter 4.

- 내 동생은 키가 작은데도 저보다 힘이 세요.
  My younger brother is stronger than me even though he is shorter.
- 그 사람의 얼굴을 아는데도 이름이 생각이 안 나요.
  I know the person's face, even though I can't remember his name.
- 몇 번이나 설명했는데도 그 사람은 제 말을 이해 못 해요.
  Even though I explained it numerous times, the person doesn't understand what I'm saying.

Be careful

The usage of -(으)ㄴ/는데도 is similar to that of -아/어도 in Chapter 9. However, while -아/어도 is used for hypothetical situations, -(으)ㄴ/는데도 may not be.

- 앞으로 무슨 일이 있어도 저만 믿으세요. (O)
  Trust me no matter what happens in the future.
- 앞으로 무슨 일이 있는데도 저만 믿으세요. (X)

1 문장을 완성하도록 알맞은 것끼리 연결하세요.

(1) 영화를 보다가 •	• ① 친구가 안 와서 •	• ⓐ 돈을 더 찾았어요.
(2) 친구를 기다리다가 •	• ② 소리가 너무 커서 •	• ⓑ 영화관 밖으로 나갔어요.
(3) 쇼핑하다가 •	• ③ 재미없어서 •	• ⓒ 비를 맞았어요.
(4) 음악을 듣다가 •	• ④ 돈이 떨어져서 •	• ⓓ 친구한테 전화했어요.
(5) 친구하고 얘기하다가 •	• ⑤ 갑자기 비가 와서 •	• ⓔ 전화 받으러 나갔어요.
(6) 길을 걷다가 •	• ⑥ 전화가 와서 •	• ⓕ 소리를 줄였어요.

2 그림을 보고 다음에서 알맞은 답을 골라서 '-다가'를 사용하여 문장을 완성하세요.

걷다　　들다　　졸다　　놀다

(1) 무거운 물건을 ________ 허리를 다쳤어요.

(2) 친구하고 ________ 공에 맞아서 얼굴에 멍이 들었어요.

(3) 지하철에서 ________ 정류장을 지나쳤어요.

(4) 높은 구두를 신고 ________ 발목을 삐었어요.

3 알맞은 답을 고르세요.

(1) 여러 번 전화했는데도 전화를 ⓐ 받아요. / ⓑ 안 받아요.

(2) 저는 친구가 많은데도 항상 ⓐ 외로워요. / ⓑ 외롭지 않아요.

(3) 전화번호를 바꿨는데도 계속 전화가 ⓐ 와요. / ⓑ 안 와요.

(4) 제 친구는 매일 ⓐ 노는데도 / ⓑ 놀지 않는데도 시험을 잘 봐요.

(5) 이 가게 물건은 값이 ⓐ 싼데도 / ⓑ 비싼데도 품질이 안 좋아요.

(6) 제 동생은 ⓐ 운동선수인데도 / ⓑ 운동선수가 아닌데도 운동을 잘해요.

Conversation ❶

Track 43

리나 저 리나인데요. 지금 통화 괜찮아요?

케빈 네, 잠깐이면 괜찮아요. 그런데 무슨 일이에요?

리나 영화 표 예매하다가 문제가 생겨서 전화했어요.

케빈 무슨 문제요?

리나 토요일에 보기로 한 영화 말이에요.
예매하려고 하는데 표가 다 팔렸어요.

케빈 다른 영화관에도 표가 없어요?

리나 이 영화가 인기가 많은가 봐요. 다른 영화관을 찾았는데도 자리가 없어요. 아무래도 다른 영화를 봐야 할 것 같아요.

케빈 저는 어떻게 하든지 상관없어요.
리나 씨 마음대로 하세요. 그럼, 얘기 다 끝난 거예요?

리나 잠깐만요. 하나만 더 물어볼게요.
영화가 좀 늦게 끝나도 괜찮아요?
아까 문자 몇 번이나 보냈는데도 답장이 없어서요.

케빈 미안해요. 제가 일하느라고 답장 못 보냈어요.
저는 몇 시든지 괜찮아요. 리나 씨! 제가 일하다가 전화 받아서 통화 오래 못 할 것 같아요.

리나 알겠어요. 그럼, 영화 표 예매하면 문자 보낼게요.

Rina This is Rina. Can you speak right now (on the phone)?

Kevin Yes, I can if it's short. What's wrong?

Rina I'm calling because I ran into a problem while reserving tickets.

Kevin What problem?

Rina I meant to reserve for the movie that we decided to watch on Saturday, but they were all sold out.

Kevin Are there no tickets in any other movie theaters?

Rina It seems like this movie is popular. I even looked at other movie theaters but there aren't any seats! In any case, it seems like we'll have to watch another movie.

Kevin I'm fine with whatever you decide. Do what you want to do, Rina. So, is that all?

Rina Hold on. I have one more question. Is it okay even if the movie ends a little late? I just sent you a few texts but you didn't respond.

Kevin Sorry. I couldn't respond while working. Any time is okay. (I'm sorry) Rina! I don't think I can speak for long, since I'm at work.

Rina Okay. I'll send you a text when I reserve the tickets.

New Vocabulary ▸P. 332

표가 팔리다 | 영화관 | 자리 | 아무래도

New Expressions ▸P. 332

- 무슨 일이에요?
- 상관없어요.
- 하나만 더 물어볼게요.

Tips

1 Confirming Completion: -(으)ㄴ 거예요?

This expression is used to confirm that an action has been completed. -(으)ㄴ 거예요 is connected to verb stems.

- 얘기 다 끝난 **거예요**? Are we done speaking?
- 밥이 다 된 **거예요**? Is the rice all ready?
- 다 말한 **거예요**? Have you said everything?

2 Two Meanings of 몇

몇 may be used as a question word in front of a counter noun to mean "how many," and it can also refer to an indefinite amount. In this conversation, the first usage in 몇 번이나 means "several times," while the second usage in 몇 시든지 means "no matter what time."

- 우리 집에 **몇** 명 왔어요? How many people came to our home?
- **몇** 명 왔어요. A few people came.

❶ Making Reservations

1. Reserving Tickets

- 표를 예매하다 to reserve tickets
- 주차비가 무료이다
  for parking to be free
  팝콘이 공짜다
  for popcorn to be free
- 표가 많이 남아 있다
  for there to be many tickets left
  표가 얼마 남아 있지 않다
  for there to not be many tickets left
- 표가 다 팔렸어요. (= 매진이 됐어요.)
  All the tickets are sold out
- 지정석 / 자유석
  reserved seat / unreserved seat
- 입장하다 / 퇴장하다
  to enter (a place) / to exit (a place)
- 예매가 안 됐어요. No reservations were made.

2. Reservations

- 방을 예약하다 to reserve a room
- 조식이 포함되어 있다
  for breakfast to be included
  조식이 포함되어 있지 않다
  for breakfast to not be included
- 빈방이 많다
  for there to be many available rooms
  빈방이 얼마 남아 있지 않다
  for there to not be many available rooms left
- 방이 다 찼어요. (= 빈방이 없어요)
  All the rooms are full. (= There are no vacant rooms.)
- 1인실 / 2인실
  single room / double room
- 체크인(입실)하다 / 체크아웃(퇴실)하다
  to check in / to check out
- 예약이 안 됐어요. No reservations were made.

- 영화 표를 인터넷으로 **예매하려고** 했는데, 보고 싶은 영화 **표가 다 팔렸어요**. 그래서 다른 시간도 알아봤지만 **표가 얼마 남아 있지 않았어요**. I planned to reserve tickets on the Internet, but all the tickets for the movie I wanted to see were sold out, so I checked the other times, but there weren't many tickets left.
- 호텔 방을 인터넷으로 **예약하려고** 했는데, 가고 싶은 호텔에는 **빈방이 없었어요**. 그래서 다른 호텔에도 알아봤지만 성수기라서 **빈방이 얼마 남아 있지 않았어요**. I planned to reserve a hotel room on the Internet, but all the hotels I wanted to go to had no vacant rooms, so I checked other hotels, but because it's peak season, there weren't many free rooms left.

❷ Using the Telephone

1. 전화하다 to call

- 전화를 걸다 to call
- 전화를 받다 to answer the phone
- 통화하다 to talk on the phone
- 전화를 끊다 to hang up the phone

2. 메시지 Message

- 문자/음성/영상 메시지를 보내다 to send a text/audio/video message
- 문자/음성/영상 메시지를 받다 to receive a text/audio/video message
- 문자/음성/영상 메시지를 확인하다 to check a text/audio/video message

★ When speaking, 문자 메시지 is abbreviated as 문자, 음성 메시지 is abbreviated as 음성, and 영상 메시지 is abbreviated as 영상.

3. 전화 표현 Expressions when using the phone

- 통화 중이에요. (Someone) is in the middle of a phone call.
- 외출 중이에요. (Someone) is outside.
- 회의 중이에요. (Someone) is in the middle of a meeting.
- 전화 잘못 걸었어요. You called the wrong number.
- 전화를 안 받아요. (Someone) isn't picking up.
- 신호가 약해요. The signal is weak.
- 전원이 꺼져 있어요. The phone is turned off.
- 배터리가 떨어졌어요. The battery ran out.

Key Expressions

Saying goodbye on the phone

- 안녕히 계세요. Goodbye.
- 들어가세요. Goodbye. (lit. Go inside.)
- 전화 끊을게요. Goodbye. (lit. I'll hang up the phone)

Grammar 2

-았/었어야지요 "You should have…"

C.C P. 300

A 그렇게 많이 아프면 병원에 갔어야죠.
왜 안 갔어요?

If you're that sick, you should have gone to the hospital.
Why didn't you go?

B 어제까지 이렇게 안 아팠어요.

I wasn't that sick yesterday.

-았/었어야지요 is used to reproach the listener for not carrying out an action they should have done or for not maintaining a state that they should have kept. It is generally used in speech. The preceding clause -았/었어야지요 is neither carried out in the past nor a connective ending. -았/었어야지요 is attached to the stems of verbs, adjectives, and 이다. -지 않았어야지요 or -지 말았어야지요 are attached to reproach someone for an action that should not have been carried out. -지요 is also contracted as -죠.

- 약속을 했으면 약속을 지켰어야죠. 안 지키면 어떡해요?
  If you make a promise, you should keep it. Why did you not keep your word?
- 그런 일이 있으면 나한테 미리 말했어야지. 왜 말 안 했어?
  If that's the case, you should have told me in advance. Why don't you tell me?
- 그 사람의 비밀을 말하지 말았어야죠. 얘기하면 어떡해요?
  You shouldn't have told him her secret. Why did you tell him?

-았/었어야 했는데 "should have…, but…"

A 생일 선물을 미리 준비했어야 했는데 미안해.

I should have prepared your birthday gift in advance. Sorry.

B 괜찮아. 선물 안 해도 돼.

It's okay. You don't have to give me a gift.

-았/었어야 했는데 is used to express regret for not having carried out an action one should have done or for a situation that should have occurred but did not. The action that should have been carried out precedes -았/었어야 했는데, while the result that one regrets follows. It is attached to the stems of verbs, adjectives, and 이다. When regretting having done an action, -지 않다 or -지 말다 are used to create -지 않았어야 했는데 and -지 말았어야 했는데, respectively. If the clause following -았/었어야 했는데 is omitted, the sentence evokes a feeling of the speaker's regret.

- 미리 말했어야 했는데 걱정할까 봐 얘기 못 했어요.
  I should have told you in advance, but I didn't say anything because I was afraid you would worry.
- 모델을 하려면 키가 더 컸어야 했는데 아쉽네요. I should have been taller to model. It's a pity.
- 무거운 짐을 혼자 들지 말았어야 했는데 결국 허리를 다쳤어요.
  I shouldn't have lifted a heavy load by myself. I ended up hurting my back.
- 내가 더 신경 썼어야 했는데……. I should have paid more attention...

▸Answers P. 315

1 다음에서 알맞은 답을 골라서 '-았/었어야지요'나 '-지 말았어야지요'를 사용하여 문장을 완성하세요.

받다	참다	나가다	확인하다	예약하다

(1) 여름에 휴가 가려면 미리 호텔을 ______________. 지금은 방이 없잖아요.

(2) 아무리 화가 나도 끝까지 ______________. 그렇게 화를 내면 어떡해요?

(3) 중요한 회의 시간에는 전화를 ______________. 사장님이 화가 나셨잖아요.

(4) 감기에 걸렸으면 밖에 ______________. 감기가 낫지 않았잖아요.

(5) 그렇게 중요한 서류는 내기 전에 ______________. 확인도 안 하면 어떡해?

2 '-았/었어야 했는데'를 사용하여 대화를 완성하세요.

(1) A 어제 모임에 늦게라도 갔어야죠. 왜 안 갔어요?
B ______________ 갑자기 집에 일이 생겨서 못 갔어요.

(2) A 잘못했으면 먼저 사과했어야죠. 왜 사과 안 해요?
B ______________ 사과할 기회가 없어서 못 했어요.

(3) A 어제까지 책을 돌려준다고 약속했으면 돌려줬어야죠. 왜 안 돌려줘요?
B ______________ 집에 책을 놓고 와서 못 돌려줬어요.

(4) A 사장님이 심각하게 말씀하실 때 웃지 말았어야죠. 웃으면 어떡해요?
B ______________ 갑자기 다른 일이 생각나서 웃었어요. 미안해요.

3 알맞은 답을 고르세요.

(1) 아프면 미리 (ⓐ 말했어야죠. / ⓑ 말하지 말았어야죠.) 그냥 숨기면 어떻게 해요?

(2) 친구가 유학을 떠나기 전에 (ⓐ 만났어야 했는데 / ⓑ 만나지 말았어야 했는데) 결국 못 만났어요.

(3) 친구가 부탁하면 그 부탁을 (ⓐ 잊어버렸어야죠. / ⓑ 잊어버리지 말았어야죠.) 잊어버리면 어떡해요?

(4) 아이에게 위험한 물건을 (ⓐ 줬어야죠. / ⓑ 주지 말았어야죠.) 혹시 아이가 다치면 어떡해요?

(5) 어제까지 보고서를 (ⓐ 냈어야 했는데 / ⓑ 내지 않았어야 했는데) 결국 못 냈어요.

Conversation ❷

Track 44

민호	늦어서 죄송합니다.
상사	왜 이렇게 늦었어요? 회의에 1시간이나 늦게 오면 어떡합니까?
민호	교통사고 때문에 길이 너무 많이 막혀서 늦었습니다.
상사	차가 밀리는 시간을 생각해서 일찍 출발했어야죠.
민호	더 일찍 출발했어야 했는데 죄송합니다.
상사	박민호 씨를 기다리다가 회의가 늦어졌잖아요.
민호	죄송합니다.
상사	전화는 왜 안 했어요? 늦으면 미리 전화를 했어야죠.
민호	미리 연락을 했어야 했는데 마침 배터리가 떨어져서 못 했습니다.
상사	박민호 씨, 요즘 왜 이렇게 정신이 없어요?
민호	죄송합니다. 앞으로 다시는 이런 일이 생기지 않도록 조심하겠습니다.
상사	다음부터는 회의 시간에 늦지 않도록 하세요.
민호	네, 알겠습니다.
상사	그리고 다음 회의 때 문제가 생기지 않도록 자료 준비는 미리 하세요.
민호	그렇게 하겠습니다.

Minho	Sorry for being late.
Senior Coworker	Why were you so late? What are we supposed to do when you're an hour late for the meeting?
Minho	I'm late because there was a traffic accident. There was a lot of traffic.
Senior Coworker	You should have thought about the traffic (lit. the time when cars pile up) and left early.
Minho	I should have left earlier. I'm sorry.
Senior Coworker	The meeting was delayed because we were waiting for you.
Minho	I'm sorry.
Senior Coworker	Why didn't you call? If you were late, you should have called in advance.
Minho	I should have called in advance, but just then my battery died and I couldn't call.
Senior Coworker	Mr. Park, why are you so out of it lately?
Minho	I'm sorry. I will be careful not to let this happen again from now on.
Senior Coworker	Next time don't be late.
Minho	I understand.
Senior Coworker	And next time prepare (lit. prepare data) in advance so there isn't a problem.
Minho	I will do that.

New Vocabulary ▸P. 332

죄송하다 | 길이 막히다 | 차가 밀리다 | 출발하다 | 마침 | 정신이 없다 | 조심하다 | 자료

New Expressions ▸P. 332

- 늦어서 죄송합니다.
- 다음부터는 …지 않도록 하세요.
- 그렇게 하겠습니다.

Tips

1 The Usage of 왜 이렇게

왜 이렇게 is used in front of an adverb or adjective to emphasize not being able to understand or being surprised about a situation or action.

- **왜 이렇게** 더워요? Why is it so hot?
- **왜 이렇게** 많이 싸워요? Why do you fight so much?

2 The Formal Expression: -도록 하세요

-도록 하세요 is used instead of -(으)세요 at the end of a sentence in formal situations when the speaker is ordering or urging the listener to do something. It attaches to verb stems.

- 내일까지 서류를 준비하**도록 하세요**. (= 준비하세요.) Prepare the documents by tomorrow.
- 이 일을 잊지 않**도록 하세요**. (= 잊지 마세요.) Don't forget this.

받다: Encoding the Passive Meaning

1. 질문하다 – 질문받다 to ask a question – to be asked a question	• **질문받은** 것 중에서 이해 안 되는 게 있으면 **질문하세요.** If there is anything you don't understand in the questions you are asked, please ask.
2. 초대하다 – 초대받다 to invite – to be invited	• 이 모임에는 **초대받은** 사람만 올 수 있어요. Only people who were invited may come to this gathering.
3. 부탁하다 – 부탁받다 to ask – to be asked	• **부탁받은** 것 중에서 친구가 **부탁한** 것을 먼저 할까 해요. Among the things I was asked to do, I'm thinking that I will do what my friend asked first.
4. 조언하다 – 조언받다 to advise – to be advised	• 친구가 **조언해** 준 것을 실천해 보려고 해요. I plan to do what my friend advised me.
5. 허락하다 – 허락받다 to permit – to receive permission	• 결혼하기 전에 부모님께 결혼을 **허락받고** 싶어요. Before getting married, I want to receive permission from my parents.
6. 명령하다 – 명령받다 to order – to be ordered	• **명령하는** 사람은 그것에 대한 책임도 져야 해요. The person who ordered this also has to take responsibility for it.
7. 지시하다 – 지시받다 to give orders – to receive orders	• 어제 본부에서 **지시받았는데** 왜 시작도 안 했어요? I received orders from headquarters yesterday. Why haven't we started?
8. 요구하다 – 요구받다 to request – to receive a request	• 인터넷으로 산 물건의 반품을 **요구했지만** 결국 반품 못 했어요. I requested a product return on the Internet but, in the end, I wasn't able to return it.
9. 신청하다 – 신청받다 to apply – to receive an application	• 이 프로그램을 하고 싶은 사람은 내일까지 사무실에 **신청하세요.** Everyone who wants to join this program should apply at the office by tomorrow.
10. 사과하다 – 사과받다 to apologize – to receive an apology	• 잘못한 일을 **사과하는** 것은 용기 있는 행동이야. It is courageous to apologize for something you have done wrong.
11. 추천하다 – 추천받다 to recommend – to receive a recommendation	• 이번에는 **추천받은** 사람 중에서 뽑으려고 해요. This time, we plan to choose someone from among those who were recommended.
12. 소개하다 – 소개받다 to introduce – to be introduced	• **소개받은** 사람이 별로 마음에 들지 않아요. I don't really like the person I was introduced to.
13. 칭찬하다 – 칭찬받다 to praise – to be praised	• 잘 **칭찬하지** 않는 사장님께 **칭찬받아서** 정말 기분이 좋아요. I'm in a really good mood because I was praised by my boss, who doesn't give praise often.
14. 비판하다 – 비판받다 to criticize – to be criticized	• 정부를 **비판하는** 여론이 요즘 심해졌어요. The public opinion criticizing the government recently worsened.
15. 인정하다 – 인정받다 to recognize – to be recognized	• 회사에서 **인정받지** 못한 사람은 승진할 수 없어요. Those who are not recognized at a company cannot be promoted.
16. 무시하다 – 무시받다 to ignore – to be ignored	• 다른 사람을 **무시하는** 것은 예의 없는 행동이에요. Ignoring other people is rude.
17. 위로하다 – 위로받다 to console – to receive consolation	• 안 좋은 일이 있는 친구를 **위로하느라고** 집에 못 갔어요. I couldn't go home because I was consoling my friend who had something bad happen to her.
18. 격려하다 – 격려받다 to encourage – to be encouraged	• 선생님이 **격려해** 주셔서 다시 자신감을 찾았어요. I was able to find my confidence again because my teacher encouraged me.
19. 방해하다 – 방해받다 to hinder – to be hindered	• 어른이 됐으니까 다른 사람에게 **방해받고** 싶지 않아요. I don't want to be hindered by other people because I'm an adult.
20. 간섭하다 – 간섭받다 to interfere – to be interfered with	• 이건 제 일이에요. 남의 일에 **간섭하지** 마세요. This is my job. Don't interfere with other people's jobs.
21. 용서하다 – 용서받다 to forgive – to be forgiven	• 너무 크게 잘못해서 이번에는 **용서받기** 어려울 것 같아. It will probably be difficult for you to be forgiven this time because you made a really big mistake.
22. 제안하다 – 제안받다 to suggest – to receive a suggestion	• 같이 일하자고 **제안했지만** 그 사람은 받아들이지 않았어요. I suggested that we work together, but he refused.

Key Expressions

- 반드시(= 꼭) 질문하세요.
  Definitely ask questions.
- 절대로 방해하지 마세요.
  Do not hinder us, by any means.

Grammar ❸

-(으)ㄹ 텐데 expressing conjectures, hopes, and hypothetical situations: "will probably…", "I hope", "I wish"

Appendix P. [illegible]

A 비 오는 날에 운전하면 위험할 텐데.
It is probably dangerous to drive on rainy days.

B 그러게 말이에요.
Exactly.

-(으)ㄹ 텐데 is used to express a conjectured situation. If a clause follows -(으)ㄹ 텐데, it may be related to or contrast with the content preceding -(으)ㄹ 텐데. -(으)ㄹ 텐데 is attached to the stems of verbs, adjectives, and 이다. Just like -(으)ㄴ/는데, the content following -(으)ㄹ 텐데 may be omitted.

- 아침부터 아무것도 안 먹었으니까 배고플 텐데 이것 좀 드세요.
  You will probably be hungry because you haven't eaten anything since the morning, so eat some of this.
- 옷을 그렇게 두껍게 입으면 오늘 더울 텐데 괜찮겠어요?
  It will probably be hot today if you wear such thick clothes. Will you be alright?
- 조금만 더 열심히 하면 잘할 텐데 (아쉽네요). If you work a little harder, you will do well. (It is a pity.)

-(으)려던 참이다 "to be about to"

A 지금 뭐 해요?
What are you doing now?

B 막 자려던 참이었어요.
I was just about to sleep.

-(으)려던 참이다 expresses the moment at which an intended action was about to be carried out. It is attached to verb stems.

- 마침 너한테 전화하려던 참인데, 전화 잘 했어. I was just about to call you, but it is good that you called.
- 명동에 간다고? 나도 명동에 가려던 참인데 같이 가자.
  Are you going to Myeongdong? I was about to go to Myeongdong, but let's go together.
- 잘 왔네요. 지금 점심을 먹으려던 참인데 같이 먹어요.
  It's good that you came. I was about to have lunch right now, but we can eat together.

1 **알맞은 답을 고르세요.**

(1) 밖에 비가 오니까 [ⓐ 더울 텐데 / ⓑ 추울 텐데] 겉옷을 가져가는 게 어때요?

(2) 아이들이 많이 오면 음식이 [ⓐ 부족할 텐데 / ⓑ 충분할 텐데] 더 만들까요?

(3) 중요한 일이니까 [ⓐ 잘할 텐데 / ⓑ 잘해야 할 텐데] 너무 긴장돼요.

(4) 아무 일도 [ⓐ 없을 텐데 / ⓑ 없어야 할 텐데] 실수할까 봐 자꾸 걱정돼요.

(5) 친구한테 말하면 친구가 [ⓐ 도와줄 텐데 / ⓑ 도와줘야 할 텐데] 왜 말 안 해요?

(6) 어제 늦게 자지 않았으면 오늘 이렇게 [ⓐ 피곤했을 텐데 / ⓑ 피곤하지 않았을 텐데] 후회돼요.

2 **다음에서 알맞은 답을 골라서 '-(으)ㄹ 텐데'를 사용하여 문장을 완성하세요.**

비싸다 아니다 예쁘다 심심하다 화가 나다

(1) 웃으면서 인사하면 더 ________________ 왜 저한테는 웃지 않을까요?

(2) 백화점이 시장보다 ________________ 왜 백화점에 가요?

(3) 혼자 여행하면 ________________ 나하고 같이 가자!

(4) 일부러 그런 것은 ________________ 직접 얘기를 들어 보면 어때요?

(5) 그 사람도 분명히 ________________ 겉으로 화를 내지 않았어요.

3 **문장을 완성하도록 알맞은 것끼리 연결하세요.**

(1) 저도 식사하러 나가려던 참인데 • • ⓐ 같이 드실래요?

(2) 이제 막 일을 끝내려던 참인데 • • ⓑ 재활용하면 더 좋지요.

(3) 그 얘기를 하려던 참이었는데 • • ⓒ 무슨 일이 또 있어요?

(4) 이 종이를 버리려던 참이었는데 • • ⓓ 친구가 먼저 그 얘기를 꺼냈어요.

Conversation ❸

Track 45

민호	안녕하세요? 새라 씨. 저 민호예요.
새라	민호 씨? 저도 민호 씨한테 전화하려던 참이었는데 잘됐네요.
민호	그래요? 무슨 일 있어요?
새라	사실은 지난주에 부탁했던 번역 말이에요. 제가 못 하게 될 것 같아요.
민호	네? 왜요?
새라	이번에 회사에서 다른 일을 맡게 됐어요. 미안해요.
민호	그랬군요. 새라 씨한테 잘된 일이네요. 그런데 갑자기 다른 사람을 구하기 힘들 텐데 걱정이네요.
새라	저 말고 부탁할 사람이 없어요?
민호	글쎄요, 좀 더 시간이 있으면 찾을 수 있을 텐데 지금은 모르겠어요.
새라	그럼, 제가 다른 사람을 소개하면 어떨까요?
민호	어떤 사람인데요?
새라	제 친구를 통해 아는 사람인데요, 다른 데서 번역했던 경험이 많아요. 번역한 것을 보니까 실력도 좋은 것 같아요.
민호	그래요? 한번 만나 보면 좋겠네요.

Minho	Hello? Sarah, it's Minho.
Sarah	Minho? I was just about to call you. Good timing.
Minho	Really? What's wrong?
Sarah	Actually it's about the translation you asked me to do last week. I don't think I'll be able to do it.
Minho	What? Why not?
Sarah	I was put in charge of another job at the company. Sorry.
Minho	I see. That's good for you. But I'm worried because it will probably be difficult to suddenly find another person now.
Sarah	You don't have anyone else to ask other than me?
Minho	Well, I'd probably be able to find someone if I had more time, but I don't know now.
Sarah	Then what if I introduce you to someone?
Minho	Who?
Sarah	It's someone I know through a friend. She's had a lot of experience translating elsewhere. I've looked at her translations, and she seems very skilled.
Minho	Really? It would be good if I could meet her.

New Vocabulary ▸P. 332

잘되다 | 부탁하다 | 맡다 | 을/를 통해

New Expressions ▸P. 332

- 전화하려던 참이었는데 잘됐네요.
- 저 말고 부탁할 사람이 없어요?
- 제가 다른 사람을 소개하면 어떨까요?

Tips

1 Revealing One's Name on the Phone

When revealing one's name on the phone, 저 is used in front of one's name, as in this conversation. Be careful not to use 저는. In particular, if the person on the other end of the line already knows your name, it is better only to use 저.

- 기억 안 나세요? **저** 민수예요.
  Do you not remember? It's Minsu.

2 (noun) 말고: "not", "other than"

말고 is used to express that one is not looking for a certain object, but rather a different one. It is generally used in speech and follows nouns.

- 빨간색 **말고** 파란색 없어요?
  Not red. Do you not have blue?
- 이 영화 **말고** 다른 영화 봐요.
  Not this movie. Let's watch another movie.

Describing Conversations

1. **물어보다** to ask

이 문법은 언제 사용해요?

자세히 대답하다
to answer in detail

이 문법은 나이가 많은 사람에게 …….

간단하게 대답하다
to answer briefly

이 문법은 부탁할 때 사용해요.

2. **허락을 구하다** to ask permission

노트북 좀 써도 돼요?

허락하다
to allow, permit

그럼요, 쓰세요.

허락하지 않다
to not allow,
to not permit

미안하지만, 저도 지금 써야 하는데요.

3. **설명하다** to explain

이 문법은 주로 나이가 어린 …….

이해가 되다
to understand

그렇군요. 알겠어요.

이해가 잘 안 되다
to not really understand

잘 모르겠는데요.

4. **초대하다** to invite

이번 주말에 우리 집에서
집들이하는데 올래요?

초대를 받아들이다
to accept an invitation

좋아요. 갈게요.

초대를 거절하다
to turn down an invitation

미안해요. 다른 일이 있어요.

5. **제안하다** to suggest

이번 주말에 같이
영화 보는 게 어때요?

제안을 받아들이다
to accept a suggestion

좋아요. 같이 봐요.

제안을 거절하다
to turn down a suggestion

미안해요. 다음에 같이 가요.

6. **부탁하다** to ask/request (a favor)

다음 주말에 이사하는데
좀 도와줄래요?

부탁을 받아들이다
to grant a request

그래요. 몇 시까지 가면 돼요?

부탁을 거절하다
to reject a request

미안해요. 그날은 다른 약속이 있어요.

7. **사과하다** to apologize

늦어서 미안해요.

사과를 받아들이다
to accept an apology

아니에요. 별로 오래 기다리지 않았어요.

8. **변명하다** to give an excuse

길이 너무 많이 막혀서 늦었어요.

Key Expressions

- 글쎄요. Well… I'm not sure.
- 잠시만요. Hold on.
- 생각 좀 해 볼게요. I'll think about it.

Let's Talk!

Speaking Strategy — Agreeing and Disagreeing

Agreeing
- 저도 그렇게 생각해요. **I think so too.**
- 제 생각도 같아요. **My thoughts exactly.**
- 저도 마찬가지예요. **I'm the same.**

Disagreeing
- 저는 그렇게 생각하지 않아요. **I don't think so.**
- 제 생각은 달라요. **My opinion is different.**

❶ 친구나 아는 사람에게 이렇게 해 본 적이 있어요?

	나	친구 1	친구 2
• 친구에게 어려운 부탁을 하다			
• 추천받은 것에 실망하다			
• 친구의 부탁을 거절하다			
• 친구의 충고를 무시하다			
• 잘못했는데 사과 안 하다			
• 다른 사람이 기분 나빠할까 봐 거짓말하다			
• 잘 모르는 사람을 다른 사람에게 소개하다			
• 이해 못 했는데 이해한 척하다			
• 사람들 앞에서 칭찬받다			
• 다른 사람의 일에 간섭하다			

언제 이런 일이 있었어요?

그래서 어떻게 됐어요?

저는 친구의 부탁을 거절 못 하는 편이에요. 그래서 하기 싫어도 어쩔 수 없이 친구의 부탁을 들어줘요. 친구의 부탁을 거절하면 친구하고 관계가 멀어질 것 같아요.

저는 그렇게 생각하지 않아요. 하기 싫은데 억지로 부탁을 들어주면 그건 친구 사이가 아니라고 생각해요. 친구라면 솔직하게 말해야 해요.

❷ 사람들과 좋은 관계를 유지하려면 어떻게 해야 해요?

New Vocabulary

실망하다 to be disappointed | 거절하다 to reject | 무시하다 to ignore | 잘못하다 to make a mistake | 사과하다 to apologize | -는 척하다 to pretend to... | 칭찬받다 to be praised | 간섭하다 to interfere | 어쩔 수 없이 unable to do anything else

Word Web

▸ Appendix P. 321

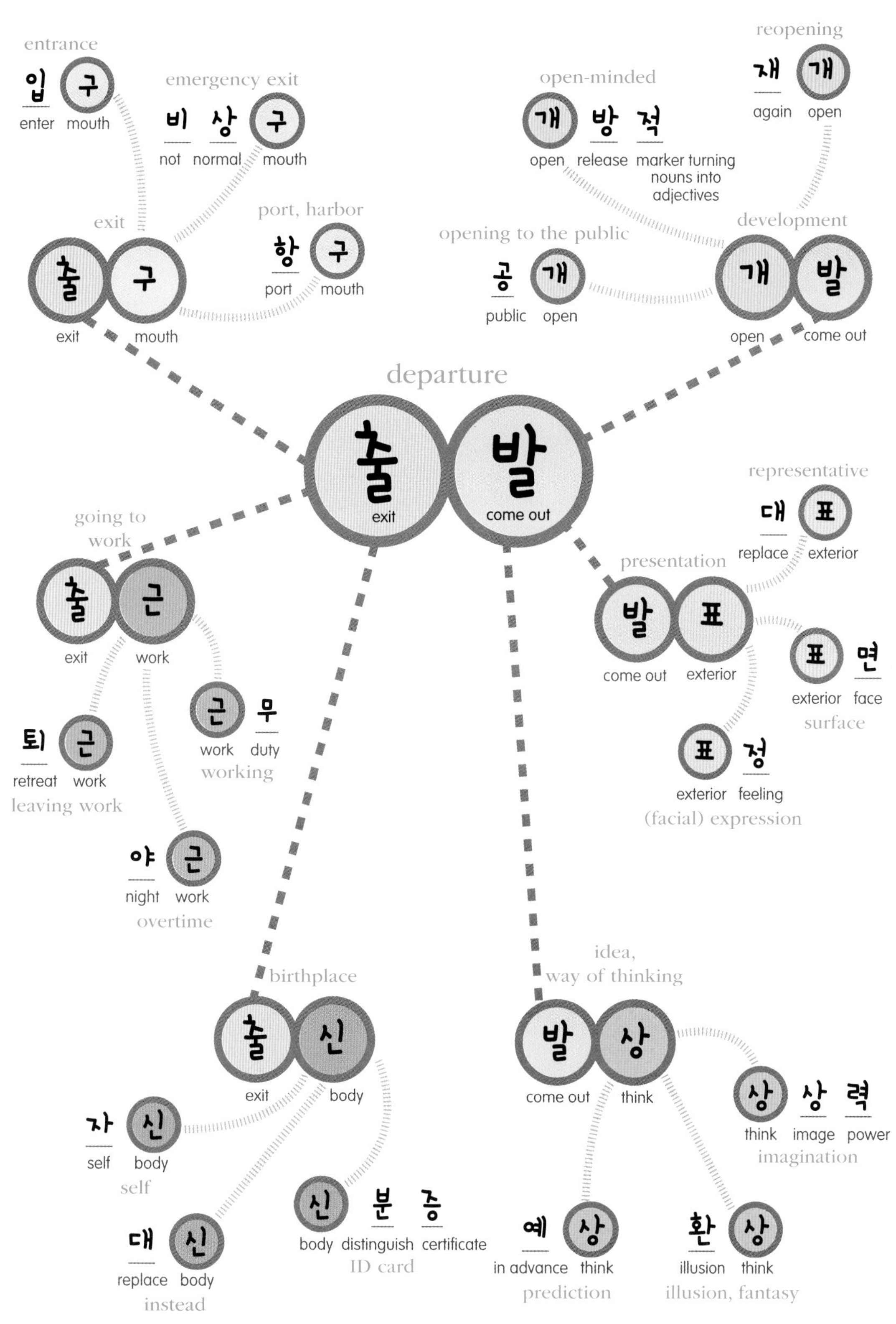

A Word on Culture

Let's Learn Some Contractions!

Let's get used to the contractions commonly used by the SMS text-loving generation! Words more than three syllables long are shortened to increase typing speed while maintaining a mutual understanding with the younger generation. Among the countless contractions, there are commonly used words in everyday life that do not appear in the dictionary and are thus not standard, regardless of the generation. Let's try to familiarize ourselves with some of the more popular expressions.

• Contractions using the first parts of each word

Among words that are three, four, or more syllables, there are many phrases that are shortened by taking only the first part of each word. The representative examples are 남친 (boyfriend) and 여친 (girlfriend). 남친 is from the first parts of 남자 and 친구 while 여친 is from the first parts of 여자 and 친구. There are a fair number of these words in everyday life, such as 자판기 (vending machine) from 자동판매기 and the beloved 소맥 (soju and beer mix), from 소주 and 맥주.

남친 여친

• Contractions formed from shortening the word

The three-syllable word 선생님 is shortened to 샘. As these informal words can only be used in close relationships, 샘 expresses intimacy, but remember that it does not express much respect or politeness. If one is in a formal situation, it is better not to use this contraction.

It is common to shorten the foreign word 아르바이트 (part-time job) to 알바. It is also common to call students who work part-time jobs 알바생. 알바 is used not only in informal conversation but even in advertisements searching for part-time workers. It is shortened because it is a long foreign word.

Besides these words, there is also the representative example of 욜, which is used not in conversation, but often in texts. It is shortened from 요일 (day of the week). Thus, 화요일 is shortened to 화욜 and 금요일 to 금욜.

선생님 → 샘

아르바이트 → 알바

화요일 → 화욜

APPENDIX

Grammar Appendix •
Korean Conjugation •
Conjugation Charts •
Answers •
Word Web Appendix with Hanja •
New Vocabulary & New Expressions •

Grammar Appendix

Chapter 1

Question Words

1 Using question words

In Korean, markers have the grammatical function of marking roles such as subject and object. As such, word order is not as important as in English. The predicate must be at the end, but apart from that, there is no set word order. When asking questions, the sentence does not always have to start with a question word as in English, but rather a marker follows the question word to mark its role in the sentence.

A 동생이 누구에게 책을 줬어요?
Who did your younger brother give the book to?

B 동생이 선생님에게 책을 줬어요.
My younger brother gave the teacher the book.

People	누가 Who (subject)	누가 밥을 먹어요? Who is eating rice?
	누구 Who	진수 씨가 누구를 좋아해요? Who does Jinsu like?
		조금 전에 누구하고 얘기했어요? Who were you speaking to just now?
Objects	뭐 What (informal)	뭐가 건강에 좋아요? What is healthy?
		보통 저녁에 뭐 먹어요? What do you usually eat at night?
		뭐에 관심이 있어요? What are you interested in?
	무엇 What (formal)	이름이 무엇입니까? What is your name?
		무엇을 도와드릴까요? What can I help you with?
Characteristics / Types	무슨 Which/What	무슨 일을 해요? What kind of work do you do?
	어떤 What kind	어떤 사람이에요? What kind of person is she?
	어느 Which	어느 건물에서 일해요? Which building do you work in?
Time	언제 When	언제 여행을 떠나요? When are you going on vacation?
	며칠 What day	며칠에 파티를 해요? What day are you having the party?
Duration	얼마나 How long	집에서 회사까지 시간이 얼마나 걸려요? How long does it take for you to get to work from your house?
	얼마 동안 How long	얼마 동안 한국에 살았어요? How long did you live in Korea?
Place	어디 Where	화장실이 어디에 있어요? Where is the bathroom?
		어디에서 친구를 만났어요? Where did you meet your friend?
Reason	왜 Why	왜 늦게 왔어요? Why did you come late?
Method	어떻게 How	어떻게 그 사실을 알았어요? How did you find this out?
Price	얼마 How much	그 가방을 얼마에 샀어요? How much did you buy that bag for?
	얼마나 How much	돈이 얼마나 들었어요? How much did it cost?
Degree	얼마나 How	집이 얼마나 커요? How big is your house?
Frequency	얼마나 자주 How often	얼마나 자주 운동해요? How often do you exercise?
Counting Numbers	몇 How many	모자가 몇 개 있어요? How many hats do you have?
		친구가 몇 명 집에 왔어요? How many friends came to your house?
		부산에 몇 번 가 봤어요? How many times have you been to Busan?
Reading Numbers	몇 What	몇 번에 전화했어요? What number did you dial?

I wonder

The question word 무엇 takes different forms depending on if the conversation is informal or formal.

- 뭐 (informal): 이름이 뭐예요?
  What's your name?
- 무엇 (formal): 이름이 무엇입니까?
  What is your name?

In speech, the marker 을/를 may be omitted after question words, but other markers may not be omitted.

- 어제 시장에서 뭐 샀어요?
  What did you buy at the market yesterday?
  = 어제 시장에서 뭐를 샀어요?
- 인사동은 뭐가 유명해요? (○)
  What is Insadong famous for?
  인사동은 뭐 유명해요? (×)

2 Using question words with 이다

When a question word (what, who, when, where, etc.) stands in for a piece of information (for example, names, people, objects, time, place, price, etc.), the question word with 이다 appears at the very end of the sentence.

- 집이 어디예요? Where is your house?
- 졸업식이 언제예요? When is the graduation ceremony?

3 누가 and 누구

누가 and 누구 are the Korean words corresponding to "who." When asking for the subject of an action (any predicate other than 이다), 누가 (think of 가 as standing in for the subject marker) is used, while 누구 is used in all other cases.

- 누가 일찍 왔어요? (O) Who came early?
  누구 일찍 왔어요? (×)
- 지금 누구를 기다려요? Who are you now waiting for?
- 누구하고 같이 일했어요? Who did you work with?
- 마이클 씨가 누구예요? (O) Who is Michael?
  마이클 씨가 누가예요? (×)

4 The usage of 몇

몇 is used when counting numbers and also when reading numbers. 몇 cannot be used by itself. It must be followed by a classifier, which differs depending on the noun.

- 모임에 사람들이 몇 명 왔어요?
  How many people came to the gathering?
- 나이가 몇 살이에요? How old are you?
- 어제 삼겹살을 몇 인분 먹었어요?
  How many servings of pork belly did you eat yesterday?

In response to 몇 번, the number is read differently depending on whether the answer is a number or a frequency.

Reading a number

A 몇 번 문제를 몰라요?
Which problem number do you not know?

B 3(삼) 번이에요. The third.
(read as the Sino-Korean number)

Expressing frequency

A 제주도에 몇 번 갔어요?
How many times have you been to Jeju Island?

B 3(세) 번 갔어요. I went three times.
(read as the native Korean number)

-(으)ㄴ 지 "It has been (length of time) since"

-(으)ㄴ 지 is used to express how long an action or situation has been occurring. -(으)ㄴ 지 attaches to verb stems, and a noun describing the length of time follows. 동안, which expresses the length of time, cannot be used alongside -(으)ㄴ 지.

- 한국에 산 지 2년 됐어요. (O)
  It has been two years since I started living in Korea.
  한국에 산 지 2년 동안 됐어요. (×)

Be careful

The following time nouns differ in whether they take Sino-Korean numbers or native Korean numbers.

3초 (3 seconds)	3분 (3 minutes)	3시간 (3 hours)	3일 (3 days)	3주일 (3 weeks)	3개월/3달 (3 months)	3년 (3 years)
삼 초	삼 분	세 시간	삼 일	삼 주일	삼 개월 /세 달	삼 년

얼마나 is used to ask how much time has passed.

A 태권도를 배운 지 얼마나 됐어요?
How long have you been learning Taekwondo?

B 한 달 됐어요. It's been a month.

After -(으)ㄴ 지, a noun expressing a specific amount of time or a noun or adverb describing a vague amount of time, such as 한참 (for a while) or 오래 (for a long time), can be used. 쯤 or 정도 may be attached to the length of time to express approximation. The verb 되다, 지나다, or 넘다 may be used after -(으)ㄴ 지.

- 이 회사에 다닌 지 3년 정도 됐어요.
  I've been with this company for about 3 years.
- 결혼한 지 벌써 10년이 넘었어요.
  We've been married for over 10 years.
- 그 사람하고 헤어진 지 한참 지났어요.
  It's been a while since I broke up with that person.

The marker (이)나 may be attached to the noun expressing a length of time if the speaker feels that the length of time is incredibly long, while "밖에 + 안 + verb" may be attached if the speaker feels that it is exceptionally short.

- 이 컴퓨터가 고장 난 지 일주일이나 지났어요.
  It's been a week since this computer broke.
- 한국어 공부를 시작한 지 1년밖에 안 됐어요. 하지만 한국어를 잘해요.
  It has only been 1 year since I started studying Korean. But I can speak Korean well.
- 이 선풍기를 산 지 얼마 안 됐어요. 그런데 벌써 고장 났어요.
  I recently bought this fan. But it's already broken.

-(으)러 "in order to"

-(으)러 is followed by movement verbs such as 가다, 오다, and 다니다 and expresses the purpose of moving somewhere. -(으)러 may be attached to the stem of a verb to express this purpose. The destination of the movement is followed by the marker 에 and may be before or after -(으)러.

- 우리 집에 집을 구경하러 한번 오세요.
  Please come to take a look around my home.
- 다음 주에 친구 만나러 제주도에 갈 거예요.
  I'm going to Jeju Island next week to see my friend.
- 어제 저녁 먹으러 친구 집에 갔어요.
  I went to a friend's house for dinner yesterday.

Be careful

A movement verb may follow but not precede -(으)러. -(으)려고 may be used if the movement is the goal.

- 고향에 가러 공항에 갔어요. (×)
  고향에 가려고 공항에 갔어요. (○)
  I went to the airport in order to go home.

Be careful

The marker 에 is attached to the destination of the verb movement used after -(으)러; the marker 에서 may not be used. In the following examples, 식당 is not the place in which "eating" is done, but rather the destination toward which the subject is headed to eat. Thus, the marker 에 is used.

- 식당에 밥을 먹으러 갑시다. (○)
  Let's go to a restaurant to eat.
  식당에서 밥을 먹으러 갑시다. (×)

Reading Native Korean Numbers

When reading numbers, such as a telephone number, password, room number, or page number, Sino-Korean numbers are used. In contrast, native Korean numbers are used after classifiers to count things or people. The numbers from 1 to 4 (as well as from 11 to 14, 21 to 24, 31 to 34, etc.), and 20 differ slightly in shape when followed by classifiers.

	Native Korean number	Forms preceding classifiers
1	하나	한 개
2	둘	두 개
3	셋	세 개
4	넷	네 개
5	다섯	다섯 개
6	여섯	여섯 개
7	일곱	일곱 개
8	여덟	여덟 개
9	아홉	아홉 개
10	열	열 개
11	열하나	열한 개
12	열둘	열두 개
13	열셋	열세 개
14	열넷	열네 개
15	열다섯	열다섯 개
20	스물	스무 개
21	스물하나	스물한 개
22	스물둘	스물두 개
23	스물셋	스물세 개
24	스물넷	스물네 개
25	스물다섯	스물다섯 개

There are different classifiers depending on the type of noun. The following are commonly used classifiers.

개 (objects)	명 (people)	분 (honorific people)	마리 (animals)	장 (paper)
한 개	두 명	세 분	네 마리	다섯 장
잔 (cups)	병 (glasses of liquid)	대 (electronics)	송이 (flowers)	켤레 (pairs)
여섯 잔	일곱 병	여덟 대	아홉 송이	열 켤레
살 (age)	번 (frequency)	통 (letters, texts)	끼 (meals)	곡 (songs)
한 살	두 번	세 통	네 끼	다섯 곡
군데 (places)	마디 (words)	방울 (drops)	모금 (gulps of liquid or gas)	입 (bites of food)
한 군데	한 마디	한 방울	한 모금	한 입

- 보통 하루에 전화 열 통쯤 해요.
  I usually make about ten calls a day.

- 말 한 마디도 못 했어요.
  I didn't say a word.
- 매장 여러 군데를 가 봤지만 물건이 없었어요.
  I went to several stores, but the product was not there.

Originally native Korean numbers were used to count objects, but Sino-Korean numbers generally express large numbers (such as hundreds, thousands, tens of thousands, etc.) are generally expressed by Sino-Korean numbers. The native Korean numbers are usually used up to 20, while the Sino-Korean numbers are usually used for numbers more than 20.

- 교실에 의자가 18(열여덟) 개 있어요.
  There are 18 chairs in the classroom.
- 편의점은 24(이십사) 시간 영업해요.
  The convenience store is open 24 hours.
- 이 체육관은 한번에 50(오십) 명씩 운동할 수 있어요.
  50 people at a time can work out at this gym.

However, Native Korean Numbers are always used before 살 for all ages. 살 can be omitted, and the native Korean number may be used alone if expressing the age of an elderly person (elderly based on the view of the speaker). In speech, the native Korean number is used with 살, while in official documents, 세 is used with the Sino-Korean number.

10	20	30	40	50	60	70	80	90	100
열	스물	서른	마흔	쉰	예순	일흔	여든	아흔	백

- 제 동생은 30(서른) 살이 안 됐어요.
  My brother is not yet 30.
- 우리 할머니는 90(아흔)이 다 되셨지만 건강하세요.
  My grandmother is 90 now, but she's healthy.
- 23(이십삼) 세 이상 지원할 수 있습니다.
  Those 23 or older can apply.

Be careful

Unlike English, the age of people and objects is expressed with different words.

- 그 아이는 10살이에요. (human's age: 살)
  The child is 10 years old.
- 이 건물은 10년 됐어요. (object's age: 년)
  This building is 10 years old.

Along with other exceptions such as 킬로미터 (kilometers) and 킬로그램 (kilograms), 인분 (a classifier expressing food portion) also use Sino-Korean numbers.

- 요즘 3(삼) kg 살이 빠졌어요.
  I lost 3 kgs lately.
- 저 사람은 혼자 삼겹살 5(오) 인분을 먹을 수 있어요.
  That person can eat five portions of pork belly.

Be careful

Depending on the usage of nouns like 동, either the native Korean number or the Sino-Korean number is used.

(when counting the number of apartment buildings)
- 한강아파트는 모두 3(세) 동이 있어요.
  There are 3 buildings in Hangang Apartments.

(when reading an apartment building's number)
- 우리 집은 3(삼) 동 101호예요.
  Our house is unit 101 in the third building.

The Possessive Marker 의

The marker 의 expresses possession and appears between the possessor and the possessed object. In speech, the marker 의 is often pronounced as [에] or is omitted.

- 그 사람의 목소리 = 그 사람 목소리 That person's voice.

When the marker 의 is attached to pronouns, the resulting word is contracted as 내 (나의: my) and 네 (너의: your). to maintain a clear distinction.

- 나의 얘기 = 내 얘기 My story
- 너의 계획 = 네 계획 (= 니 계획) Your plan
- 저의 연락처 = 제 연락처 My contact information

If the possessor or possessed object is modified by a noun or adjective, the possessive marker 의 may not be omitted.

- 친구의 빨간색 지갑 (○) ≠ 친구 빨간색 지갑 (×)
  My friend's red wallet
- 우리 가족의 생활 (○) ≠ 우리 가족 생활 (×)
  Our family's life

However, if the possessor is a pronoun, it must be contracted.

- 내 친구의 책 (O) ≠ 나의 친구의 책 (X)
  My friend's book

Chapter 2

-고 "and"

C.C P. 296

1 Connecting two actions or states

-고 is used to express two actions or states that are not chronologically ordered. If the clauses before and after -고 are switched, there is no change in meaning. -고 attaches to the stem of verbs, adjectives, and 이다, and it may also be preceded by -았/었-.

- 그 여자는 키가 커요. 그리고 머리가 길어요.
  That lady is tall. And, she has long hair.
  → 그 여자는 키가 크고 머리가 길어요.
  (= 그 여자는 머리가 길고 키가 커요.)
- 지난 휴가 때 친구도 만났고 책도 많이 읽었어요.
  Last vacation, I met friends and read a lot of books.
  (= 지난 휴가 때 친구도 만나고 책도 많이 읽었어요.)
- 그 사람은 국적이 미국인이고 직업이 운동선수예요.
  That person is American and is an athlete by profession.

Be careful

"and" changes form depending on what it follows.

그리고 (used between sentences)	저녁을 먹어요. 그리고 책을 읽어요. I eat dinner. And, I read a book.
-고 (used between verbs and adjectives)	밥을 먹고 커피를 마셔요. I eat my meal and drink coffee.
-하고 (used between nouns)	밥하고 반찬을 먹어요. I eat rice and side dishes.

2 Expressing the chronological order of two actions

1) -고

-고 is also used to connect two actions that happen in a sequence. In this case, the temporal order is important, so the meaning differs depending on which action is stated first. This usage of -고 attaches to verbs but may not be preceded by -았/었- or -겠-. The subject of both clauses may be different.

- 수업이 끝나고 학생들이 자리에서 일어났어요.
  After the class ended, the students got up from their seats.
  (≠ 학생들이 자리에서 일어나고 수업이 끝났어요.)
- 어젯밤에 샤워하고 잤어요. (○)
  I showered last night and slept.
  어젯밤에 샤워했고 잤어요. (×)

2) -아/어서

-아/어서 is used instead of -고 if two sequential actions are related, whereas -고 is used to express two unrelated sequential actions.

- 친구를 만나서 저녁을 먹었어요.
  I met a friend and had dinner (with her).
  (The speaker met a friend and ate dinner with him/her.)
- 친구를 만나고 저녁을 먹었어요.
  I met a friend and had dinner (without that friend).
  (The speaker did not eat with the friend he/she met, rather he/she ate alone or with another friend.)

The subject of the two clauses in -아/어서 must be the same if it is used with the meaning "and."

- 동생이 돈을 모아서 여행을 가고 싶어 해요.
  My younger sibling wants to save money and go on a trip.
- 제가 생선을 사서 요리할 거예요.
  I'm going to buy some fish and cook it.
  ≠ 제가 생선을 사서 엄마가 요리할 거예요.
  I'm going to buy some fish and my mother will cook it.

Be careful

-고 changes form in a negative sentence depending on what it follows.

Following a noun	Statement	저 사람은 일본 사람이 아니고 한국 사람이에요. That person is not Japanese, he's Korean. (= 일본 사람이 아니에요. 그리고 ……)
	Command / Proposition	저 사람에게 커피 말고 녹차를 주세요. Give him green tea, not coffee. (= 저 사람에게 커피 주지 마세요. 그리고 ……)
Following a verb	Statement	친구는 제 얘기를 듣지 않고 밖으로 나갔어요. My friend didn't listen to me and went outside. (= 친구는 제 얘기를 듣지 않았어요. 그리고 ……)
	Command / Proposition	담배를 피우지 말고 운동을 시작하세요. Stop smoking and start exercising. (= 담배를 피우지 마세요. 그리고 ……)

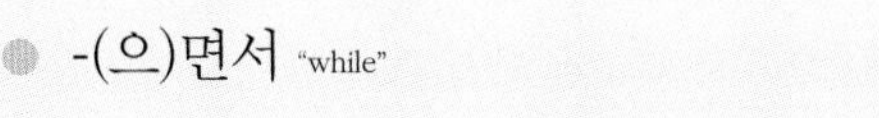

-(으)면서 "while"

C.C P. 303

1 Expressing two simultaneous actions or states

-(으)면서 is used to express two actions or states that occur simultaneously. It attaches to the stems of verbs, adjectives, and 이다 and cannot attach to -았/었- or -겠-.

- 운전하면서 전화하면 위험해요.
  It is dangerous to call while driving.
- 품질이 좋으면서 싼 물건은 많지 않아요.
  There are not many things that are cheap and of good quality.
- 제 친구는 대학생이면서 작가예요.
  My friend is a college student and a writer.

-(으)면서 is generally used in speech, while -(으)며 is used in writing.

- 책을 읽으면서 친구를 기다려요. (speech)
  I wait for my friend while reading a book.
  책을 읽으며 친구를 기다린다. (writing)

The subject of the clauses before and after -(으)면서 must be the same.

- 친구가 운동하면서 전화가 왔어요. (×)
  친구가 운동하면서 전화를 받았어요. (○)
  My friend picked up the phone while exercising.

2 Expressing a Contrast

-(으)면서 is also used to express a contrast between two actions or states. In these instances, it may not be exchanged with -(으)며.

- 그 여자는 그 남자를 좋아하면서 싫어하는 척해요.
  That woman likes that man but pretends to hate him.
- 그 사람은 다 알면서 거짓말했어요.
  That man knew everything, yet lied.
- 이 식당은 비싸지 않으면서 음식 맛이 좋아요.
  This restaurant is not expensive, but the food tastes good.

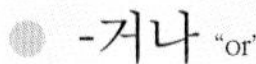

-거나 "or"

C.C P. 296

-거나 is used to express a choice between two actions or states. -거나 attaches to the stems of verbs and adjectives, as well as to -았/었-.

- 바쁘지 않거나 관심이 있는 사람은 저한테 연락해 주세요.
  Please contact me if you are not busy or are interested.
- 그 돈은 벌써 썼거나 다른 사람에게 줬을 거예요.
  They have either already paid the money or they have given it to someone else.

Be careful

"or" changes form depending on what it follows.

아니면/또는 (used between sentences)	커피 드릴까요? 아니면 녹차를 드릴까요? Can I get you some coffee? Or, would you like some green tea? 음식을 해 먹어요. 또는 밖에서 사 먹어요. I eat home-cooked meals. Or, I buy my meals outside.
-거나 (used between verbs or adjectives)	쉬거나 자요. I rest or sleep. 방이 작거나 추우면 얘기하세요. Talk to me if the room is small or cold.
Marker (이)나 (used between nouns)	버스나 지하철로 가요. I go by bus or subway. 금요일이나 토요일에 시간 있어요. I have time on Friday or Saturday.

-(으)ㄴ/는 편이다 "relatively", "sort of"

C.C P. 305

-(으)ㄴ/는 편이다 is used to express relativity rather than an absolute judgment about the degree of some quality.

- 우리 동네는 조용해요. (absolute)
  Our neighborhood is quiet.
- 우리 동네는 조용한 편이에요. (relative)
  Our neighborhood is on the quieter side.
  (The neighborhood is on the quiet side.)

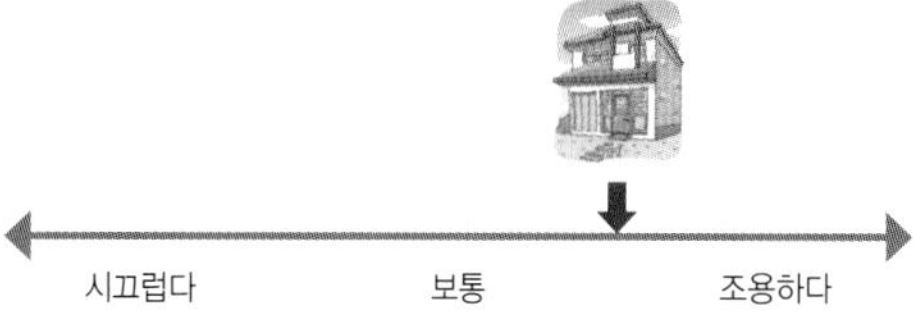

-는 편이다 attaches to verbs, while -(으)ㄴ 편이다 attaches to adjectives.

- 저는 노래는 못하는 편이니까 노래방에 가고 싶지 않아요.
  I'm relatively poor at singing, so I don't want to go to the Noraebang.
- 저는 음악을 즐겨 듣는 편이 아니에요.
  I'm not a fan of music, relatively speaking.
- 어렸을 때는 조용한 편이었는데 지금은 아니에요.
  I used to be relatively quiet when I was younger, but not now.

Be careful

When -는 편이다 is attached to verbs, an adverb expressing degree must be added, as a verb by itself does not imply degree.

- 저는 물을 마시는 편이에요. (×)
  저는 물을 (많이/조금/자주/가끔) 마시는 편이에요. (○)
  I tend to drink water (a lot/a little/often/sometimes).

When the negative -지 않다 attaches to -(으)ㄴ/는 편이다, its form changes depending on whether it follows a verb or adjective.

	동사 Verb	형용사 Adjective
Positive	일찍 일어나는 편이에요. I tend to get up early.	키가 큰 편이에요. I am relatively tall.
Negative	일찍 일어나지 않는 편이에요. I tend to not get up early.	키가 크지 않은 편이에요. I am not tall, relatively speaking.

Be careful

-(으)ㄴ/는 편이다 cannot be used with certain adjectives, such as 아프다 "to be sick," which are not considered to have varying degrees of severity in Korean.

- 저는 머리가 아픈 편이에요. (×)
  저는 머리가 아파요. (○)
  I have a headache.

Chapter 3

-(으)ㄴ/는 것 changing verbs and to nouns ("...ing") C.C P. 305

-(으)ㄴ/는 것 has the function of changing a verb, adjective, or phrase into a noun like gerund in positions where a noun can appear. Therefore, it could replace a position in a sentence where there could be a subject or object.

- 저는 한국 사람하고 얘기하는 것을 좋아해요.
  (a noun position)
  I like to talk to Koreans.

When expressing the present tense of a verb, -는 것 attaches to the verb stem. -(으)ㄴ 것 is attached to adjective stems.

- 한국어를 듣는 것은 괜찮지만 말하는 것이 어려워요.
  Listening to Korean is fine, but speaking Korean is difficult.
- 한국 생활에서 제일 재미있는 것은 한국 친구를 사귀는 것이에요.
  The most fun thing about living in Korea is making Korean friends.
- 한국 회사에서는 일을 잘하는 것도 중요하지만 성실한 것이 더 중요해요.
  In a Korean company, it is important to do a good job, but it is more important to be sincere.

When markers are added to 것, the resulting form is shortened in speech. 것이 becomes 게, 것을 becomes 걸, 것은 becomes 건, and 것이에요 becomes 거예요.

- 것을 → 걸 (= 거): 저는 운동하는 걸 좋아해요.
  I like to exercise.
- 것이 → 게 (= 거): 요리를 잘하는 게 정말 부러워요.
  I'm really envious that you are good at cooking.
- 것은 → 건: 친구들에게 연락하는 건 제가 할게요.
  I'll take care of contacting our friends.
- 것이에요 → 거예요: 인생에서 중요한 것은 좋은 친구를 찾는 거예요.
  The important thing in life is to find good friends.

-(으)니까 "because" C.C P. 303

-(으)니까 is used when providing the reason or grounds for an event or situation. -(으)니까 is attached to the reason clause, which must always appear before the clause expressing the result. -(으)니까 attaches to the stems of verbs, adjectives, and 이다. It can also attach to -았/었-.

- 우리 집에 김치가 있으니까 제가 김치를 가져올게요.
  I have kimchi at my home, so I'll bring kimchi.
- 오늘 일을 다 끝냈으니까 이제 퇴근해도 돼요.
  I finished all my work today, so I can call it a day.

-(으)니까 plays a similar role to -아/어서, which expresses a reason or cause. However, -아/어서 may not attach to -았/었-, while -(으)니까 may.

- 어제 늦게 집에 들어갔으니까 피곤할 거예요.
  = 어제 늦게 집에 들어가서 피곤할 거예요.
  You will be tired as you went home late yesterday.

If a sentence ends in a command or proposal, -(으)니까 may be used to express the reason, but -아/어서 may not.

- 제가 옆에 있으니까 언제든지 저를 불러 주세요. (○)
  I'm by your side, so please call me anytime.
  제가 옆에 있어서 언제든지 저를 불러 주세요. (×)
- 오늘은 시간이 있으니까 같이 영화 볼까요? (○)
  Since I have some free time today, shall we watch a movie together?
  오늘은 시간이 있어서 같이 영화 볼까요? (×)

-는 게 patterns using -는 것 

-는 것, followed by the marker 이 (contracted to -는 게), is attached to a verb if in a position where a subject noun would occur. The predicate may then be, for example, 어때요? or 좋겠다, as in the following sentence structures.

1 -는 게 어때요? "How about...?"

-는 게 어때요? is used to ask the listener his or her thoughts about doing a specific action. -는 게 어때요? attaches to verb stems, and the intonation rises at the end. -는 게 (= 것이) 어때요? can be replaced with -는 건 (= 것은) 어때요? The conjugation is the same as -는 것.

A 제주도는 작년에 가 봤으니까 이번에는 부산에 가는 게 어때요?
I went to Jeju Island last year, so how about going to Busan this time?

B 좋아요. 부산에 가요.
Sounds good. Let's go to Busan.

2 -는 게 좋겠다 "It would be good to..."

-는 게 좋겠다 is used to politely express a subjective opinion to the listener. It is usually used to say or suggest one's personal idea to the listener. -는 게 좋겠다 attaches to verb stems. Because it expresses an opinion, the sentence is often preceded by 제 생각에는 (I think) or 제가 보기에는 (In my opinion).

- 오늘은 늦게 일이 끝나니까 내일 만나는 게 좋겠어요.
  I'm going to finish work late today, so it would be good to see you tomorrow.
- 제 생각에는 혼자 지내는 것보다 사람들하고 함께 어울리는 게 좋겠어요.
  I think it would be good to hang out with people rather than to be alone.

이/가 좋겠다 is used if the suggested action is a noun.

- 밤에 잠을 못 자니까 커피보다는 우유가 좋겠어요.
  I can't sleep at night, so I prefer milk over coffee.

Chapter 4

-(으)면 "if"

C.C P. 303

1 Expressing conditions

-(으)면 is used to express a condition. -(으)면 attaches to verbs, adjectives, and 이다. -(으)면 may be attached to -았/었-.

- 열심히 준비하세요. 그러면 좋은 결과가 있을 거예요.
  Prepare it well. Then, there will be a good result.
  → 열심히 준비하면 좋은 결과가 있을 거예요.
  If you prepare it well, you will receive a good result
- 학생이면 무료예요. 그냥 들어가세요.
  It's free if you're a student. Just go in.
- 이 일을 시작했으면 끝까지 책임지세요.
  If you've started it, take responsibility for it until the end.

Be careful

In Korean, 그러면 and 그래서 are both used to mean "so." Remember that 그러면 is used when expressing a condition-result and 그래서 is used when describing cause and effect.

- (condition) 날씨가 추워요. 그러면 두꺼운 옷을 입으세요.
  The weather is cold. So, dress warm.
- (cause) 날씨가 추워요. 그래서 감기에 걸렸어요.
  The weather is cold. So, I caught a cold.

I wonder

그러면 is also shortened to 그럼 in speech.

2 Expressing suppositions

-(으)면 is used to hypothesize about uncertain, impossible, or unfulfilled actions or situations. The first clause expresses the supposition, followed by the result in the second clause.

- 돈을 많이 벌면 여행을 떠나고 싶어요.
  When I earn a lot of money, I want to go on a trip.
- 복권에 당첨되면 그 돈으로 뭐 하고 싶어요?
  If you won the lottery, what would you like to do with that money?
- 그 사실을 미리 알았으면 그 일을 하지 않았을 거예요.
  Had I known that in advance, I wouldn't have done it.

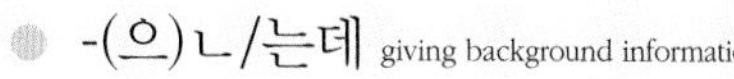

-(으)ㄴ/는데 giving background information

C.C P. 306

-(으)ㄴ/는데 is used to provide the background for a question, request, proposal, or order. It is also used to provide a backdrop or to describe a rough situation before giving specific information or relaying the speaker's feelings or thoughts. The first clause expresses the situation or background and is followed by -(으)ㄴ/는데.

- 운동을 시작하고 싶은데, 가르쳐 주시겠어요?
  I want to start exercising. Can you teach me?
  (before making a request)
- 한국학을 전공하고 있는데, 특히 한국 역사에 관심이 있어요.
  I am majoring in Korean Studies, and I am particularly interested in Korean history.
  (before stating specific information)
- 요즘 태권도를 배우고 있는데, 생각보다 어렵지 않아요.
  I'm learning Taekwondo these days, and I find it's not as difficult as I thought.
  (before stating one's thoughts or feelings)

If the clause explaining the situation or background ends in a present verb, -는데 is attached; if it ends in an adjective, -(으)ㄴ데 is attached; if it ends in 이다, 인데 is attached. If the clause ends in a past verb or adjective, -았/었는데 is attached.

- 오늘은 좀 바쁜데, 내일 만나는 게 어때요?
  I'm a little busy today, how about meeting tomorrow?
- 여기는 남산인데, 야경이 아름다워요.
  This is Namsan, and the night view is beautiful.
- 집에 들어갔는데, 아무도 없었어요.
  I went into the house, but no one was there.

Be careful

-아/어서 is used instead of -(으)ㄴ/는데 to express the background or situation of a direct cause or reason.

- 시간이 없는데 오늘 만날 수 없어요. (×)
  시간이 없어서 오늘 만날 수 없어요. (○)
  I can't meet you today because I don't have time.

-(으)려고 하는데 is used to express the future background for a subject's intent, while -(으)ㄹ 건데 is often used to express a future event that is not of the speaker's own volition. -(으)ㄹ 텐데 is used to express the background of a guess.

- 내일 친구하고 부산에 여행 가려고 하는데 아직 표를 못 샀어요.
  I'm going on a trip to Busan with my friend tomorrow, but I haven't bought a ticket yet.
- 다음 주에 프로젝트가 끝날 건데, 그다음에 뭐 할까요?
  The project will be finished next week, what should we do next?
- 지금 출발하면 약속에 늦을 텐데 택시를 타는 게 좋겠어요.
  If I leave now, I'll be late for my appointment. So, I'd better take a taxi.

Be careful

-(으)ㄴ/는데 should be used only once in a sentence.

- 이번 주에 시험이 있는데 공부를 안 했는데 걱정돼요. (×)
  이번 주에 시험이 있는데 공부를 안 해서 걱정돼요. (○)
  I have a test this week, but I'm worried because I haven't studied.

-(으)ㄴ/는지 indirect questions

-(으)ㄴ/는지 expresses a speaker's indirect question. It can occur in a subject or object position.

- 이 제품이 왜 인기가 많아요? + 알고 싶어요.
  Why is this product so popular? + I want to know.
  이 제품이 왜 인기가 많은지 알고 싶어요.
  I want to know why this product is so popular.
  (The question appears in the place of the object of 알다.)

If the question ends in the present form of a verb, -는지 is attached, while -(으)ㄴ지 is attached if it is a present tense adjective or 이다, -았/었는지 if it is a past tense verb or adjective, and -(으)ㄹ지 if it is a future tense verb or adjective.

- 한국 음식을 어떻게 만드는지 배울 거예요.
  You will learn how to cook Korean food.
- 신청자가 얼마나 많은지 미리 알아보세요.
  You should look up in advance how many applicants there are.
- 그 사람 나이가 몇 살인지 궁금해요.
  I wonder how old that person is.
- 사장님이 왜 화가 났는지 잘 모르겠어요.
  I don't know why my president was angry.
- 앞으로 어떻게 할지 생각해 봐야겠어요.
  I'll have to think about what to do next.

If the question is in the negative, the form -지 않다 differs depending on whether it follows an adjective or verb.

- 왜 일하지 않는지 그 이유를 모르겠어요. (verb)
  I don't know the reason why he's not working
- 어떤 것이 맵지 않은지 알려 주세요. (adjective)
  Please let me know which ones are not spicy.

If the question word is followed by 이다, it conjugates as follows:

(formal) (informal)
뭐예요? → 무엇인지 / 뭔지
누구예요? → 누구인지 / 누군지
언제예요? → 언제인지 / 언젠지
어디예요? → 어디인지 / 어딘지

- 저 사람의 이름이 뭔지 아세요?
  Do you know what that person's name is?
- 저 사람이 누군지 확인한 다음에 알려 주세요.
  Let me know after you confirm who that person is.

-(으)ㄴ/는지 can also be used with yes/no questions (without a question word).

- 그 사람이 한국 음식을 좋아하는지 알고 싶어요.
  I want to know if he likes Korean food.
- 친구에게 이 책을 읽어 봤는지 물어볼 거예요.
  I will ask my friend if he has read this book.

-(으)ㄴ/는지 may be repeated, as in the following examples.

- 몇 명이 가는지, 언제 출발하는지 확인하세요.
  Please see how many people are going and when they will leave.
- 키가 큰지 작은지는 중요하지 않아요.
  It doesn't matter if you are tall or short.
- 이따가 영화를 볼지 저녁을 먹을지 같이 정해요.
  Let's decide whether to watch a movie or have dinner together later.

-(으)ㄴ/는지 can be used with the following negatives to express "or not."

- 이게 사실인지 아닌지 솔직하게 말해 주세요.
  Please be honest with me if this is true or not.
- 이 일이 중요한지 중요하지 않은지 제가 말할 수 없어요.
  I can't say if this is important or not.
- 이 사실을 친구에게 말해야 할지 말지 아직 못 정했어요.
  I haven't decided yet whether I should tell this fact to my friend or not.

Chapter 5

-(으)려고 하다 "to intend to", "to be going to" 

1 Expressing the subject's intention or purpose

-(으)려고 하다 is used to express a speaker's intention or goal to do something. It is attached to the stems of action verbs. -았/었- may only be attached to 하다.

- 내년에는 꼭 취직하려고 해요.
  I intend to get a job next year no matter what.
- 주말에 등산하려고 하는데 같이 가면 어때요?
  I'm going to go hiking on the weekend. How about going together?
- 이제부터 담배를 피우지 않으려고 해요.
  I'm trying not to smoke from now on.
- 어제 전화하려고 했는데 시간이 없어서 못 했어요.
  I intended to call you yesterday, but I couldn't because didn't have time.

In colloquial speech, -(으)려고 해요 is often shortened to -(으)려고요 when responding to a question about one's future intention. Sometimes it is pronounced as -(으)려구요.

A 언제 숙제 시작할 거예요?
When are you going to start your homework?

B 조금 후에 시작하려고요.
I'm going to start it a little later.

Be careful

ㄹ is often attached to -(으)려고 하다, even though this is not "standard."

- 이거 살려고 해요. I plan to buy this.
  (이거 사려고 해요 is the standard form.)

I wonder

-(으)려고 하다 expresses the intent of the subject of the sentence, while -(으)ㄹ 거예요 expresses an expected future.

- 내년에 미국에 유학 가려고 해요. 그래서 지금 열심히 영어를 공부해요.
  I'm planning to go to the US next year to study. So now I am studying English hard.
- 열심히 공부하면 시험을 잘 볼 거예요.
  If you study hard, you will do well on the exam.

2 Describing a situation that will soon take place

-(으)려고 하다 is also used to describe a situation that will soon take place or that will change.

- 영화가 시작하려고 해요. 빨리 들어갑시다.
  The movie is about to start. Let's get in quickly.
- 아기가 울려고 하는데 어떡해요?
  The baby is about to cry. What should I do?
- 단추가 떨어지려고 하니까 다른 옷으로 갈아입으세요.
  The button is about to fall off, so change into a different outfit.

-(으)ㄴ/는데요 softening one's tone or expressing hesitation while explaining a situation 

In Korean, there are often cases where speakers will omit the main point and indirectly express a situation in order to attenuate a listener's reaction. Koreans use this phrase often when speaking carefully to be polite.

A 오늘 같이 저녁 먹을까요?
Shall we have dinner together tonight?

B 다른 약속이 있는데요. (It means "같이 저녁 못 먹어요.")
I have another appointment. (It means "We can't have dinner together.")

In these situations, -(으)ㄴ/는데요 is added to the end of the situational description. In the following example, B softly refuses A's proposal to take a walk by speaking only of the hot weather and not directly saying that he/she does not want to go. -(으)ㄴ/는데요 conjugates depending on whether it is following a verb, adjective, or 'to be'. The conjugation is the same as -(으)ㄴ/는데 in Chapter 4.

A 잠깐 밖에 산책하러 가는 게 어때요?
How about going for a walk outside for a while?

B 지금 더운데요. (It means "산책하러 가고 싶지 않아요.")
It's hot right now. (It means "I don't want to go for a walk.")

A 이 모임을 계속할 거예요?
Are you going to continue with this gathering?

B 아직 못 정했는데요. (It means "왜 물어보세요?")
I haven't decided yet. (It means, "Why are you asking?")

-(으)ㄴ/는데 is also used to imply a proposal or a favor and to wait for the listener's response without asking outright. In the following example, the speaker only describes the situation of there being many good movies nowadays in order to propose that the listener goes with him/her to see a movie.

- 요즘 재미있는 영화가 많은데…….
  ("같이 영화 봅시다." is omitted.)
  There are a lot of interesting movies these days...
  ("Let's watch a movie together." is omitted.)
- 소금이 다 떨어졌는데…….
  ("소금 좀 사다 주세요." is omitted.)
  I ran out of salt. ("Buy some salt, please." is omitted.)

-(으)ㄴ/는 대신에 "instead of"

-(으)ㄴ/는 대신에 is used to express the action of the first clause being replaced with that of the second clause. -는 대신에 is attached to the stems of verbs while -(으)ㄴ 대신에 is attached to the stems of adjectives if the former and latter clauses take place at the same time, while -(으)ㄴ 대신에 is attached to the stems of both verbs and adjectives if the first clause ends before the second one takes place. -(으)ㄴ 대신에 is attached to present adjectives.

- 제가 이 일을 하는 대신에 제 부탁 좀 들어주세요.
  I will do this work for you, but please do me a favor in exchange.
- 음식을 만드는 대신에 사 가려고 해요.
  Instead of making food, I'm going to buy it.

-(으)ㄴ/는 대신에 is also used to describe a situation that is a better alternative to the action in the first clause.

- 월급을 많이 받는 대신에 늦게까지 일해야 돼요.
  I receive a high salary, but I have to work until late.
- 동생에게 장난감을 양보하는 대신에 엄마에게 칭찬을 받았어요.
  Since I shared my toys with my sister, I received compliments from my mom.
- 칼로리 높은 음식을 많이 먹은 대신에 운동을 많이 해야 돼요.
  Since you ate a lot of high-calorie foods, you should exercise a lot.

-(으)ㄴ/는 대신에 is also used to describe a situation that is contrary to a situation in the first phrase.

- 그 아이는 공부에 소질이 있는 대신에 운동에 소질이 없어요.
  The child is not good at sports but is instead good at studying.
- 그 가게는 비싼 대신에 품질이 더 좋아요.
  The store has better quality than expensive products.

대신에 by itself is attached to nouns.

- 아침에 시간이 없어서 밥 대신에 사과를 먹어요.
  I don't have time in the morning, so I eat an apple instead of rice.

-(으)ㄴ 적이 있다 "having done something before"

-(으)ㄴ 적이 있다 is used to express one's experience. -(으)ㄴ 적이 있다 is attached to the stems of verbs, adjectives, and 이다. -(으)ㄴ 적이 없다 is used to express the lack of experience of having done something. 적 may be replaced with 일. Because -(으)ㄴ already expresses the past, there is no need to say -(으)ㄴ 적이 있었다.

- 어렸을 때 팔을 다친 적이 있어요.
  I injured my arm when I was young.
- 이제까지 행복한 적이 없어요.
  I've never been happy before.
- 잃어버린 물건을 찾은 일이 한 번도 없어요.
  I've never found a lost item before.

Be careful

일 may be used in place of 적 to express experience, but 것 may not be used.

- 주차장에서 일한 적이 있어요. (○)
  I used to work in a parking place.
  = 주차장에서 일한 일이 있어요. (○)
  ≠ 주차장에서 일한 것이 있어요. (×)

-아/어 보다 is attached to form -아/어 본 적이 있다 in order to express the meaning of having attempted or tried something. However, the verb 보다 is the only one to which the verb 보다 may not be attached. 본 적이 있다 is used in this situation.

- 몽골 음식을 먹어 본 적이 없으니까 한번 먹어 보고 싶어요.
  I have never eaten Mongolian food before, so I want to try it.
- 한국 영화를 본 적이 있어요.
  I've seen a Korean movie before.
  ≠ 한국 영화를 봐 본 적이 있어요. (×)

-(으)ㄴ 적이 있다 is used to seek a yes/no answer, as in the following example. After confirming this answer, the concrete details must be discussed in the simple past tense rather than with -(으)ㄴ 적이 있다.

A 삼계탕을 먹은 적이 있어요?
Have you ever eaten samgyetang?

B 네, 한 번 있어요.
Yes, I tried it once.

A 언제 먹었어요? ('언제 먹은 적이 있어요?' may not be used.)
When did you try it? ('When did you try it before?' may not be used.)

B 1년 전에 처음 먹었어요.
I ate it for the first time a year ago.

-고 있다 "to be doing"

1 Describing an action in progress

-고 있다 is used to express continuing action in the present. It also expresses a repeated action occurring in a set time frame. 이다 is conjugated to express tense or negation. -고 있었다 expresses the past, -고 있을 것이다 the future, and -고 있지 않다 the negative.

- 요즘 일자리를 알아보고 있지만 좋은 일자리가 없어요.
  I'm looking for a job these days, but I can't find a good one.
- 어제 저녁 7시에 집에서 밥을 먹고 있었어요. 회사에 없었어요.
  Yesterday evening at 7 PM, I was eating at home. I wasn't at the company.
- 이사는 지금 생각하고 있지 않아요. 지금 집에 만족하고 있어요.
  The director is not thinking right now. He is happy at his home now.

I wonder

-고 있다 can be replaced with -고 계시다 to honor the subject.

- (normal) 동생이 책을 읽고 있어요.
  My brother is reading a book.
- (honorific) 할아버지 책을 읽고 계세요.
  Grandpa is reading a book.

Be careful

-고 있었다 is only used to express an action occurring in a specific time frame in the past.

- 3년 전에 백화점에서 아르바이트를 하고 있었어요. (×)
  3년 전에 백화점에서 아르바이트를 했어요. (○)
  I worked part-time at a department store three years ago.
- 어제 친구의 전화를 받았을 때 청소하고 있었어요. (○)
  I was cleaning when I received a call from a friend yesterday.

2 Describing states

-고 있다 is also used to express the state of possessing something with some verbs, such as 갖다 (to hold, to have) or 보관하다 (to keep).

- 유실물 센터에서 잃어버린 물건을 보관하고 있어요.
  The Lost and Found Center stores lost items.
- 저는 그 책을 갖고 있지 않아요. 다른 사람에게 물어보세요.
  I don't have that book. Please ask someone else.
- 5년 전에 저는 자동차를 갖고 있었어요.
  Five years ago I had a car.

-고 있다 is also used to describe one's attire. While there is a single expression 'wearing' in English, Korean has different verbs depending on how the article of clothing or accessory is worn and where it is worn on the body.

- 저는 검은색 옷에 청바지를 입고 있어요.
  I'm wearing black clothes and jeans.
  (입다: to wear on the body (regardless of whether it is worn on the upper body or lower body))
- 친구는 운동화를 신고 있어요.
  My friend is wearing running shoes.
  (신다: to wear on one's feet: shoes, sneakers, socks, pantyhose)
- 할머니가 모자를 쓰고 계세요.
  Grandma is wearing a hat.
  (쓰다: to wear on one's head: hats, glasses, toupee, mask)
- 선생님이 목걸이를 하고 있어요.
  The teacher is wearing a necklace.
  (하다: to wear an accessory: scarf, earrings, ties)
- 저는 시계를 안 차고 있어요.
  I don't wear a watch.
  (차다: to wear by wrapping around: watch, belt)
- 친구는 반지를 끼고 있지 않아요.
  My friend is not wearing a ring.
  (끼다: to wear by inserting: ring, gloves, contact lenses)

Chapter 6

-아/어도 되다 "may"

C.C P. 300

1 Asking permission

-아/어도 되다 is used in questions to ask the listener for permission for an action or state. -아/어도 되다 attaches to verb stems. -(으)세요 can be attached to the relevant verb to give permission to someone. If permission may not be given, -(으)ㄴ/는데요 may be used to politely decline rather than the more direct -지 마세요.

A 이 옷 좀 입어도 돼요? Can I wear this dress?

B 그럼요. 저기 탈의실에서 입어 보세요.
Of course. Try it on in the changing room over there.

A 이 물 마셔도 돼요? Can I drink this water?

B 이건 물이 아닌데요. This is not water.

괜찮다 or 좋다 may replace 되다 in -아/어도 되다. -(으)ㄹ까요? may also be attached to become -아/어도 될까요? to express greater politeness.

A 옆 자리에 앉아도 괜찮아요?
Is it okay if I sit next to you?

B 물론이죠. 앉으세요. Sure. Have a seat.

A 음악 소리를 좀 크게 틀어도 될까요?
Can I turn up the music a little louder?

B 마음대로 하세요. Do as you please.

Be careful

When permitting an action, -(으)세요 is used instead of -(으)ㄹ 수 있다.

A 이 옷 좀 입어 봐도 돼요? Can I try this on?

B 네, 입어 봐도 돼요. (X)
입어 볼 수 있어요. (X)
→ 입어 보세요. (O) Try it on.

2 Expressing permission

-아/어도 되다 is used to express that an action or state is allowed based on general knowledge about societal or cultural norms or rules. In this usage, -아/어도 되다 is attached to the stems of verbs, adjectives, and 이다. 좋다 and 괜찮다 may also be substituted for 되다 in this usage.

- 냉장고의 음식은 아무거나 먹어도 돼요.
  You can eat anything from the refrigerator.
- 이번 숙제는 하지 않아도 돼요.
  You don't have to do the homework this time.
- 음식이 이 정도 매워도 괜찮아요. 먹을 수 있어요.
  It's okay if the food is this spicy. I can eat it.
- A 회사 지원 자격은 꼭 한국인만 돼요?
  Do you have to be Korean to apply for the company?
  B 아니요, 외국인이어도 돼요. 상관없어요.
  No. You can be a foreigner. It (nationality) does not matter.

-았/었- is attached to -아/어도 되다 to express that an action or state was allowed in the past.

- 전에는 신분증만 있으면 들어가도 됐는데, 요즘에는 들어갈 수 없어요.
  In the past, you could only enter with an ID, but these days you cannot regardless.
- 실수로 불을 껐어도 괜찮아요. 다시 불을 켜면 돼요.
  It's okay if you accidentally turn off the light. Just turn the light back on.

-아/어야 되다 "must", "need to", "have to"

C.C P. 300

-아/어야 되다 is used to express an obligation or duty in a situation, a state, or a condition that must take place. -아/어야 되다 is attached to the stems of verbs, adjectives, and 이다.

- 학교에서는 모든 학생이 교복을 입어야 돼요.
  At school, all students must wear a uniform.
- 시험을 볼 때 꼭 신분증이 있어야 돼요.
  You must have your ID when taking the exam.

되다 in -아/어야 되다 can be replaced with 하다 with little change in meaning. -아/어야 되다 is generally used in speech, while -아/어야 하다 is usually used in writing.

- 나이가 많은 사람에게 존댓말을 사용해야 돼요.
  You should use respectful words for older people.
- 밤 10시까지 기숙사에 들어와야 합니다.
  You must enter the dormitory by 10 PM.

되다 may be conjugated to express tense. In negative sentences, -아/어야 되다 attaches to -지 않다 to form -지 않아야 되다. -지 말아야 되다 is also used to express the speaker's hope or wish.

- 학생 때 낮에 일하고 밤에 공부해야 됐어요 (= 해야 했어요).
  When I was a student, I had to work during the day and study at night.
- 내일은 평소보다 더 일찍 출발해야 될 거예요.
  Tomorrow you will have to leave earlier than usual.
- 이번 회의에는 절대로 늦지 않아야 돼요.
  You must not be late for this meeting.
  = 이번 회의에는 절대로 늦지 말아야 돼요.

Be careful

-아/어야 되다 may not be used in every situation where "should" in English may be used. -아/어야 되다 is used for obligations and conditions, whereas -아/어 보세요 is used for recommendations and advice.

- 회사에는 늦어도 9시까지 와야 돼요. (duty)
  You have to come to work by 9 o'clock at the latest.
- 제주도에 한번 가 보세요. 정말 좋아요. (recommendation)
  Please visit Jeju Island. It is really nice.

-아/어 있다 expressing a resultant state that continues once an action is completed

C.C P. 301

-고 있다 expresses an action in progress, while -아/어 있다 expresses the continuation of the state of action having been completed.

ⓐ  ⓑ 

ⓐ 진수가 문을 열고 있어요. Jinsu is opening the door.
ⓑ 문이 열려 있어요. The door is open.

-아/어 있다 is generally used with intransitive verbs, which do not have an object. It attaches to the stem of verbs. -아/어 있지 않다 is attached to the verb stem to express that the state does not continue. -아/어 있었다 is attached to express a past state.

- 저는 약속 장소에 벌써 와 있어요.
  I'm already at the meeting point.
- 회사 전화번호가 핸드폰에 저장되어 있지 않아요.
  The company phone number is not saved on my mobile phone.
- 아까 탁자 위에 열쇠가 놓여 있었어요.
  There was a key on the table earlier.

Be careful

Because intransitive verbs attach to -어 있다, the marker 이/가 is attached to the subject of the verb.

- 문을 열려 있어요. (×)
  문이 열려 있어요. (○) The door is open.

Be careful

The negative of -아/어 있다 is not -아/어 없다, but rather -아/어 있지 않다.

- 사람들이 의자에 앉아 없어요. (×)
  사람들이 의자에 앉아 있지 않아요. (○)
  People are not sitting on the chairs.

Chapter 7

-기 때문에 "because"

-기 때문에 expresses the reason for an action or state. -기 때문에 is attached to the clause with the reason, while the result follows. -기 때문에 attaches to the stems of verbs, adjectives, and 이다. -았/었- can also precede -기 때문에 to form -았/었기 때문에.

- 텔레비전이 없기 때문에 드라마를 볼 수 없어요.
  I can't watch the drama because I don't have a TV.
- 저는 외국인이기 때문에 빨리 말하면 알아들을 수 없어요.
  I'm a foreigner, so I can't understand if you speak quickly.
- 주말에 일하지 않기 때문에 보통 주말 오전에는 시간이 있어요.
  I don't work on weekends, so I usually have time on the weekend mornings.
- 지갑을 잃어버렸기 때문에 돈이 없어요.
  I have no money because I lost my wallet.

-기 때문에 may not be used to express the reason for a command (which ends in -(으)세요) or a suggestion (which ends in -(으)ㅂ시다). In these cases, -(으)니까 must be used for the reason.

- 배가 고프기 때문에 밥 먼저 드세요. (×)
  배가 고프니까 밥 먼저 드세요. (○)
  You are hungry, so eat first.

-기 때문에 attaches to the stem of 이다 after nouns. This meaning differs from when 때문에 is attached directly to the noun, which implies that the noun is the direct cause of a negative result.

- 아기이기 때문에 혼자 걷지 못해요.
  He can't walk alone because he's a baby.
- 아기 때문에 제가 잠을 못 잤어요.
  I couldn't sleep because of the baby.

Be careful

There are situations in which 이기 때문에 and 때문에 may be confused. Remember that it is similar to "because (subject) is (noun)" in English as opposed to "because of (noun)."

- 금요일이기 때문에 시내에 사람이 많아요. (○)
  There are a lot of people in the city because it's Friday.
  금요일 때문에 시내에 사람이 많아요. (×)

If the result appears before the reason, the sentences must be split into two in the following manner.

- 그 사람은 학생이기 때문에 오전에 학교에 가야 해요.
  He has to go to school in the morning because he is a student.
  = 그 사람은 오전에 학교에 가야 해요. 왜냐하면 학생이기 때문이에요.
  He has to go to school in the morning. It is because he is a student.

Chapter 8

-는 동안에 "during", "while"

-는 동안에 expresses the continuation of an action or state. -는 동안에 attaches to verb stems.

- 아내가 집안일을 하는 동안에 남편이 아이를 돌봐요.
  The husband takes care of the children while the wife does the housework.
- 제가 없는 동안에 무슨 일이 있었어요?
  What happened while I was away?
- 한국에서 사는 동안에 많은 경험을 하고 싶어요.
  I want to experience many things while living in Korea.

-(으)면서 can replace -는 동안에 for a similar meaning. However, while the subject of both clauses in a sentence with -(으)면서 must be the same, the subject of each clause in a sentence with -는 동안에 may differ.

- 운전하는 동안에 전화를 받지 마세요. (○)
  Do not answer the phone while driving.
  = 운전하면서 전화를 받지 마세요. (○)
- 비가 오는 동안에 실내에서 커피를 마셨어요. (○)
  I had coffee indoors while it was raining.
  ≠ 비가 오면서 실내에서 커피를 마셨어요. (×)

The actions in either clause of -는 동안에 take place at the same time. -(으)ㄴ 동안에 is used if the second action takes place after the first is done.

- 남편은 지하철을 타고 가는 동안에 책을 읽어요.
  The husband reads a book on the way to work by subway.

• 남편은 회사에 간 동안에 아내는 집안일을 해요.
The wife does household chores after the husband leaves for work.

-(으)니까 expressing the realization of something after having done a certain action

-(으)니까 expresses the new realization of a fact after having carried out an action. -(으)니까 is attached to the first clause's action, while the realized fact is expressed in the second clause. -(으)니까 is attached to verb stems. The conjugation is the same as that of -(으)니까, which expresses a reason, discussed in Chapter 3.

• 집에 가니까 집에 아무도 없었어요.
When I got home, no one was home.

• 이 책을 보니까 한국어 문법 설명이 잘 나와 있어요.
This book explains Korean grammar well.

-아/어 보다 can attach to -(으)니까 to form -아/어 보니까 to express trying out experience and having a subsequent realization. For the verb 보다 (to see), 보니까 must be used instead of 봐 보니까.

• 가방 안을 확인해보니까 지갑이 없어요.
I looked inside the bag and there was no wallet.

• 한국에서 살아 보니까 한국 문화가 저하고 잘 맞아요.
Living in Korea, I have realized that Korean culture suits me well.

• 한국 텔레비전을 보니까 드라마가 다양했어요.
When I watched Korean TV, I realized there were various dramas.

Be careful

As the realization of a fact or result after an action appears after -(으)니까, a verb expressing the speaker's intent cannot appear in the second clause.

• 제주도에 가 보니까 바다에서 수영했어요. (×)
제주도에 가 보니까 바다에서 수영하고 싶었어요. (O)
I wanted to swim in the sea when I went to Jeju Island.
제주도에 가 보니까 바다가 아름다웠어요. (O)
The sea was beautiful when I went to Jeju Island.

The action and realization take place in temporal order when -(으)니까 is used. Even if the action was in the past, -았/었- cannot attach to -(으)니까.

• 그 사람을 만나 봤으니까 좋은 사람이에요. (×)
그 사람을 만나 보니까 좋은 사람이에요. (O)
I met him and felt he is a good person.

While the usage of -(으)니까 to express an action and subsequent realization may not be combined with -았/었-, the usage to express a reason may utilize it.

• 어제 회사에 일찍 갔으니까 아침에 서류를 다 끝낼 수 있었어요. (reason)
I went to work early yesterday to finish all the paperwork by the morning.

• 어제 회사에 일찍 가니까 사람들이 아무도 없었어요. (realization)
I went to work early yesterday and no one was there.

-(스)ㅂ니다 formal speech

-(스)ㅂ니다 is used in official or formal situations, such as when giving a speech to the public or when needing to be formal with someone from work. It is generally used by newscasters, service people such as flight attendants, or department store employees who must wear uniforms and speak politely to customers. It is also used by the military. Compared to -아/어요, -(스)ㅂ니다 is more formal.

• 저는 항상 8시에 회사에 도착해요. (informal)
I always get to work at 8 o'clock.
저는 항상 8시에 회사에 도착합니다. (formal)
I always get to work at 8 o'clock.

If the verb, adjective, or 이다 ends in a vowel, -ㅂ니다 is attached. If there is a final consonant, -습니다 is attached. -았/었습니다 attaches to the stem to form the past, while -(으)ㄹ 것입니다 attaches to the stem to form the future.

• 채소와 과일이 건강에 좋습니다.
Vegetables and fruits are good for one's health.

• 요즘에는 종이 신문을 많이 읽지 않습니다.
I don't read a lot of paper newspapers these days.

• 제가 표를 사 오겠습니다.
I'll go and buy a ticket.

• 지난주에 일을 그만뒀습니다.
I quit my job last week.

• 다음 주부터 일을 찾을 것입니다.
I will be looking for work from next week.

I wonder

것입니다 is often shortened to 겁니다 when speaking in the future form.

• 다음 주에 신제품을 발표할 겁니다. (= 발표할 것입니다.)
We will be announcing a new product next week.

• 사장님께서 내일 여기에 오실 겁니다. (= 오실 것입니다.)
The president will come here tomorrow.

-(으)시- is attached to form -(으)십니다 in order to honor the subject of the sentence. -(으)셨습니다 is attached to the stem to form the past tense while -(으)실 것입니다 is attached to the stem to form the future tense.

- 사장님께서 들어오십니다.
  The president is coming in.
- 부장님이 자리에 앉으셨습니다.
  The manager sat down.
- 이제부터 사장님께서 발표하시겠습니다.
  From now on, the president will be presenting.
- 회장님이 10분 후에 도착하실 것입니다.
  The Chairman will arrive in 10 minutes.

Be careful

In formal situations, certain verbs such as 먹다/마시다, 있다, 자다, and 말하다 must be changed to their honorific forms 드시다 (잡수시다), 계시다, 주무시다, and 말씀하시다.

- 직원이 1층에 있습니다. (formal)
  The staff is on the first floor.
- 사장님께서 10층에 계십니다. (formal honorific)
  The president is on the 10th floor.

When using honorifics in formal speech, the honorific form may attach to grammar patterns, just as -(으)시- may attach to a sentence ending.

Grammar beginning with consonants		Grammar beginning with -(으)		Grammar beginning with -아/어	
Normal	Honorific	Normal	Honorific	Normal	Honorific
-고	-(으)시고	-(으)면	-(으)시면	-아/어서	-(으)셔서
-지만	-(으)시지만	-(으)려고	-(으)시려고	-아/어도	-(으)셔도
-기 전에	-(으)시기 전에	-(으)니까	-(으)시니까	-아/어야	-(으)셔야

- 사장님께서 일찍 출근하시지만 늦게 퇴근하십니다.
  The president goes to work early but leaves work late.
- 사장님께서 먼저 시작하시면 저희도 함께 하겠습니다.
  If the president starts first, we will follow in suit.
- 사장님께서 바쁘셔서 오늘 모임에 오지 못하셨습니다.
  The president was busy and couldn't come to today's gathering.

When asking a question in formal speech, the -다 in -(스)ㅂ니다 is replaced with -까? to form -(스)ㅂ니까. If the listener is of higher status or is a stranger and the speaker must use honorific speech, the -다 in -(으)십니다 is replaced with -까? to form -(으)십니까? A positive answer to such a question is 네 or 그렇습니다, while the negative answer is 아닙니다.

A 회의가 오후1시부터 시작합니까?
Does the meeting start at 1 PM?

B 그렇습니다. That's right.

A 이번에 발표를 하십니까?
Are you presenting this time?

B 아닙니다. 저는 다음에 발표할 것입니다.
No. I will announce it next time.

In formal speech -(으)십시오 is attached to verbs to form a command, while -(으)ㅂ시다 is attached to verbs to form a proposal.

- 질문이 있으면 손을 들고 질문하십시오.
  If you have any questions, raise your hand and ask a question.
- 잠깐 쉬었다가 다시 회의 시작합시다.
  Let's take a short break and start the meeting again.

Be careful

The informal 그래요 has the following different forms depending on the context.

- (answer) 그래요. → (formal) 그렇습니다.
- (question) 그래요? → (formal) 그렇습니까?
- (command) 그래요. → (formal) 그러십시오.
- (proposal) 그래요! → (formal) 그럽시다.

Chapter 9

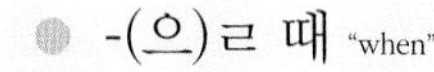

-(으)ㄹ 때 "when"

C.C P. 302

-(으)ㄹ 때 is used to refer to a specific time or period of time during which an event or state takes place. -(으)ㄹ 때 attaches to the stems of verbs, adjectives, and 이다.

- 피곤할 때 집에서 쉬는 것이 좋아요.
  It is best to rest at home when one is tired.
- 길에 자동차가 많을 때 지하철이 택시보다 더 빨라요.
  When there are many cars on the road, the subway is faster than a taxi.
- 10년 전에 외국에 살 때 기숙사에서 지냈어요.
  When I was living abroad 10 years ago, I lived in a dormitory.

As a general rule, the events in the two clauses on either side of -(으)ㄹ 때 take place at the same time. In other words, even if the event in the second clause took place in the past, -(으)ㄹ 때 is used if the event in the first clause took place at the same time. However, if the event in the first clause took place in the past, -았/었- may be used before -(으)ㄹ 때 to form -았/었을 때. As in the following example, if 그 친구를 처음 만났다 (meeting the friend for the first time) happened at the same time as 대학교에 다녔다 (attending college), then 다닐 때 may be used while 다녔을 때 may be used if the speaker wishes to express the completion of having attended college. There is no difference between these two sentences.

- 대학교에 다닐 때 그 친구를 처음 만났어요.
  I first met him when I was in college.
  = 대학교에 다녔을 때 그 친구를 처음 만났어요.
- 아르바이트로 일할 때 많이 고생했어요.
  I experienced hardships while working part-time.
  = 아르바이트로 일했을 때 많이 고생했어요.

However, if the action in the first clause is instantaneous such as 보다 (to see), 다치다 (to become injured), and 죽다 (to die), -았/었을 때 must be used if it took place and already done in the past.

- 전에 다리를 다쳤을 때 그 친구가 많이 도와줬어요. (○)
  When I injured my leg before, he helped me a lot.
  ≠ 전에 다리를 다칠 때 그 친구가 많이 도와줬어요. (×)
- 그 사람을 처음 봤을 때 첫눈에 사랑에 빠졌어요. (○)
  When I first saw her, I fell in love at first sight.
  ≠ 그 사람을 처음 볼 때 첫눈에 사랑에 빠졌어요. (×)

The meanings of -(으)ㄹ 때 and -았/었을 때 also differ for movement verbs such as 가다 (to go) and 오다 (to come). 갈 때/올 때 implies that the second action takes place during the state of going or coming, while 갔을 때/왔을 때 implies that the second action takes place during the state of completion, that is, after having arrived.

- 회사에 갈 때 지하철에서 책을 읽어요. (while moving)
  I read a book on the subway when I go to work.
- 회사에 갔을 때 사무실에 아무도 없었어요.
  (after having completed the movement)
  When I went to work, no one was in the office.

Be careful

때 may also follow some nouns that express time, such as 생일 (birthday), 방학 (vacation), 휴가 (vacation), and 명절 (holiday), However, 에, rather than 때, follows other time nouns such as 오전 (morning), 오후 (afternoon), 주말 (weekend), and 주중 (weekdays)

- 생일 때 책 선물을 받고 싶어요. (○)
  I want to receive a book as a gift on my birthday.
- 주말 때 친구를 만날 거예요. (×)
  주말에 친구를 만날 거예요. (○)
  I'm going to meet a friend over the weekend.

-아/어지다 "to become", "to get more"

C.C P. 301

Both -아/어지다 and -게 되다 may be attached to the stems of adjectives that express a change in state. There is little difference in meaning, but -게 되다 emphasizes that the result came about without the speaker's intention. However, while -아/어지다 can only attach to adjectives, -게 되다 may attach to both verbs and adjectives.

- 텔레비전에 자주 나와서 그 식당이 유명해졌어요.
  The restaurant became famous because it appeared frequently on TV.
- 텔레비전에 자주 나와서 그 식당이 유명하게 됐어요.
  The restaurant appeared frequently on TV so it became famous.

Verbs such as 있다/없다 (as in -(으)ㄹ 수 있다/없다) or 않다 (as in -지 않다) must be used with -게 되다 to express change and not with -아/어지다.

- 처음에는 매운 음식을 못 먹었는데 지금은 먹을 수 있게 됐어요. (○)
  At first, I couldn't eat spicy food, but now I can eat it.
  처음에는 매운 음식을 못 먹었는데 지금은 먹을 수 있어졌어요. (×)
- 전에는 밤늦게 음식을 많이 먹었는데 지금은 먹지 않게 됐어요. (○)
  I used to eat a lot late at night, but now I don't.
  전에는 밤늦게 음식을 많이 먹었는데 지금은 먹지 않아졌어요. (×)

Be careful

Specific grammar patterns, such as -고 싶다 (to want to), -지 마세요 (do not), and -(으)려면 (if you want to), may be used with only verbs, and not adjectives. In these cases, -아/어지다 can be attached to turn the adjective into a verb.

- 저 친구와 더 친해지고 싶어요. (○)
  I want to get to know that friend more.
  저 친구와 더 친하고 싶어요. (×)

-(으)려고 "in order to", "so that"

C.C P. 304

-(으)려고 is used to express the intent or purpose of an action. The subject of the clauses before and after -(으)려고 is the same.

- 나중에 아이에게 보여 주려고 어릴 때 사진을 모으고 있어요.
  I'm collecting childhood pictures to show my kids later.
- 아기가 엄마하고 떨어지지 않으려고 계속 울어요.
  The baby keeps crying so as not to be separated from his mother.

Because -(으)려고 expresses the intention or goal of the action or state of the subject, adjectives may not be used. -(으)려고 attaches to verb stems.

- 피곤하지 않으려고 커피를 마셔요. (×)
  → 피곤해서 자지 않으려고 커피를 마셔요. (○)
  I'm tired so I am drinking coffee to prevent myself from sleeping.

-(으)려고 and -(으)러 both express a goal or intention, but the verbs that may follow each one are different. -(으)러 may only be used with verbs expressing movement such as 가다, 오다, and 다니다, while -(으)려고 may be followed by any verb.

• 한국에 일하러 왔어요. (○)
I came to Korea to work.
한국에 일하려고 왔어요. (○)
I came to Korea to work.

• 한국에서 일하러 한국어를 배워요. (×)
한국에서 일하려고 한국어를 배워요. (○)
I am learning Korean to work in Korea.

However, verbs preceding -(으)러 may not be negative, even with movement verbs.

• 늦지 않으러 택시로 집에 가요. (×)
늦지 않으려고 택시로 집에 가요. (○)
In order not to arrive too late, I am going home by taxi.

Furthermore, -(으)러 may be followed by a command -(으)세요 or proposal -(으)ㅂ시다, but -(으)려고 may not.

• 밥을 먹으러 식당에 갈까요? (○)
Shall we go to a restaurant to eat?
밥을 먹으려고 식당에 갈까요? (×)

Chapter 10

반말 "banmal" (casual speech)

C.C P. 311

1 The usage of "banmal"

"Banmal" (casual speech) is used with younger family members (siblings or children, nephews and nieces), friends (from one's youth or school years), younger classmates, young children, or those with whom one has a close relationship. As it expresses a sense of closeness and informality, it is rude to use with those with whom one is not close. Banmal is formed by removing the polite marker -요. Furthermore, the subject marker 이/가 and object marker 을/를 are often omitted.

A 보통 주말에 뭐 해요?
What do you usually do on the weekend?

B 집에서 쉬거나 친구를 만나요.
I rest at home or meet friends.

"Yes" and "no" are shortened as follows.

네 → 어/응
아니요 → 아니

A 밥 먹었어요?
Did you eat?

B 아니요, 아직 못 먹었어요.
No. I haven't eaten yet.

2 The various conjugations in "banmal"

"Banmal" is generally formed by removing -요 from the -아/어요 form, but there are some other forms as well.

	Conjugation	Example
Future	-(으)ㄹ 거예요 → -(으)ㄹ 거야	다음 주에 여행 갈 거야. I'm going on a trip next week. 조금 후에 점심 먹을 거야. I'll have lunch in a little bit.
The Verb 이다	예요/이에요 → 야/이야	남자야. He's a man. 미국 사람이야. She's American.
Commands	-(으)세요 → -아/어	이것 좀 봐. (보세요 → 봐요) Take a look at this. 기다려 줘. (주세요 → 줘요) Wait for me.
Proposals	-(으)ㅂ시다 → -자	집에 가자. Let's go home. 밥 먹자. Let's eat.

3 Personal pronouns in banmal

Just as there is no need to honor the listener in banmal (casual speech), there is also no need to be humble when referring to oneself. The personal pronouns in casual speech are laid out below.

1st person		2nd person	
Humble	Normal	Honorific	Normal
저는	나는	OO 씨는 (or the proper title)	너는
저를	나를	OO 씨를	너를
저한테	나한테	OO 씨한테	너한테
제가	내가	OO 씨가	네가
제	내	OO 씨	네

• 저는 마크예요. → 나는 마크야. I'm Mark.

• 데니 누가 저한테 전화할 거예요? → 누가 나한테 전화할 거야?
Who's going to call me?
리나 제가 데니 씨한테 전화할게요. → 내가 너한테 전화할게.
I'll call you.

• 제 책을 돌려주세요. → 내 책을 돌려줘.
Give me back my book.

• (to Jinsu) 진수 씨 말을 믿을 수 없어요.
→ 네 말을 믿을 수 없어.
I can't believe what you're saying.

4 Commands and requests in "banmal"

In "banmal" sentences, -아/어 is combined between verb stems, and -자 is combined between verb stems in the case of requests. In banmal, the -아/어 in commands and declarations share the same form.

"Banmal" commands	"Banmal" requests
• 내일 일찍 오세요. → 내일 일찍 와. Please come early tomorrow. → Come early tomorrow.	• 밥부터 먹읍시다. → 밥부터 먹자. Let's eat first. → Let's eat first.
• 저한테 얘기해 주세요. → 나한테 얘기해 줘. Please tell me. → Tell me.	• 내일 봐요! → 내일 보자. See you tomorrow! → See you tomorrow.
• 이거 먹어 보세요. → 이거 먹어 봐. Please try this. → Try this.	• 그래요! → 그러자. Sounds good! → Sounds good.

Be careful

Avoid adding the honorific '-요' to '-자' in declarative sentences, and instead apply the honorific '-요' to '-아/어'.

- 같이 여행 가자요! (×) → 같이 여행 가요! (○)
  Let's travel together!
  같이 여행 갑시다. (○)
  Let's travel together.

5 Calling someone's name in "banmal"

When using "banmal" and calling someone's name, 야! is attached if the name ends in a vowel. If it ends in a consonant, 아! is attached.

- 진수야! 밥 먹자! Jinsu! Let's eat!
- 민정아! 놀자! Minjung! Let's play!

Be careful

Banmal is used for informal purposes with those with whom one is close. However, even if one is among friends -(으)시- should be attached to any subject that must be honored. Because the following example is among friends, it is in banmal, but -(으)시- is attached to honor the listeners' parents and a company's president.

- 부모님께서 무슨 일 하셔?
  What do your parents do (for a living)?
  (= 하 + -시- + -어)
  (honoring parents) (banmal ending)
- 사장님께서 지난달에 한국에 오셨어.
  The president came to Korea last month.
  (= 오 + -시- + -었- + -어)
  (honoring president of company) (past) (banmal ending)
- 내일도 부모님께서 연락하실 거야.
  Tomorrow, my parents will call me too.
  (= 연락하 + -시- + -ㄹ 거야)
  (honoring parents) (future, banmal ending)

-아/어야지요 "You should" 

1 Emphasizing the obviousness of an action

-아/어야지요 emphasizes that the listener should clearly do something or that a state must be a certain way. Because it has a tone of urgency or of reprimanding an action, it is not used with those of higher status but rather with those of lower status. It is usually used in speech, with -지요 shortened to -죠. It is not used in writing. -아/어야지요 attaches to the stems of verbs, adjectives, and 이다.

- 건강하게 살려면 매일 조금씩이라도 운동해야죠.
  To live a healthy life, you need to exercise at least a little every day.
- 사업이 잘되기 위해서는 바빠야죠.
  In order for a business to do well, it has to be busy.
- 지난번에는 남자였으니까 이번에는 여자여야죠.
  Last time it was a man, so this time it must be a woman.

To express that something should not be done, -지 않다 or -지 말다 is attached before -아/어야지요 to form -지 않아야지요 or -지 말아야지요. When emphasizing the speaker's strong wish, -지 말아야지요 is used.

- 옆에 아기가 있으면 담배를 피우지 않아야죠. 그렇죠?
  If you have a baby next to you, you shouldn't smoke. Right?
- 친구 사이인데 거짓말을 하지 말아야죠. 친구를 속이면 어떡해요?
  We're friends, so don't lie. Why would one hide from a friend?

2 When expressing the speaker's determination or intention

-아/어야지 with -요 removed is also used when expressing to oneself one's determination or intent to do something. Because it is considered talking to oneself, there is no formality required, so -요 can be omitted. -아/어야지 is attached to verb stems. In these instances, -아/어야겠다 may be used as well.

- 이제부터 열심히 공부해야지.
  I should study hard from now on.
  = 이제부터 열심히 공부해야겠다.
  I will study hard from now on.
- 다음에는 저 공연을 꼭 봐야지.
  I must see that show next time.
  = 다음에는 저 공연을 꼭 봐야겠다.
  I will definitely watch that show next time.

When remarking to oneself both -아/어야겠다 and -아/어야지 can be used, but with a different nuance, -아/어야겠다 is usually used after a new realization, while -아/어야지 is used for generally known truths.

- 건강해지려면 운동해야지. (generally known truths)
  I must exercise in order to be healthy.
- 건강이 안 좋아졌다. 이제부터 운동해야겠다. (new realization)
  My health has deteriorated. I have to exercise from now on.

Chapter 11

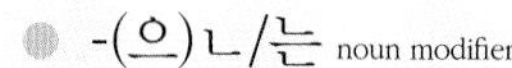 -(으)ㄴ/는 noun modifier 

C.C P. 305

The modifier ending -(으)ㄴ/는 must be used at the end of relative clauses modifying nouns. In Korean, the modifying element must always precede the modified one. The ending is attached to the stem of the verb, adjective, or 이다, which ends the relative clause, giving the noun a concrete description. The modifier ending form differs depending on the tense and whether it follows a verb, adjective, or 이다.

- 제일 늦게 퇴근하는 사람이 창문을 닫으세요.
  The person the last to leave work closes the window.
- 심한 운동은 약을 먹는 사람에게 위험해요.
  Heavy exercise is dangerous for people who take medicine.
- 가을에는 단풍이 유명한 곳에 가고 싶어요.
  In autumn, I want to go to a place famous for autumn foliage.
- 직업이 화가인 내 친구는 항상 밤에 일해요.
  My friend who is a painter always works at night.

Words ending in 있다/없다 have -는 attached to the stem rather than -(으)ㄴ.

- 재미있는 책이 없어요. (O)
  There are no interesting books.
  재미있은 책이 없어요. (×)

If a relative clause modifying a noun ends in a verb in the present tense, -는 is attached to the verb stem. The ending -는 implies that the verb in the relative clause occurred at the same time as that of the main sentence.

- 그 사람은 제가 잘 아는 사람이에요.
  That person is a person I know well.
- 어젯밤에 친구가 전화하는 소리 때문에 잠을 못 잤어요.
  I couldn't sleep last night because of the sound that came from my friend on the phone.
  (-는 is used because the phone call was made at the same time as when the speaker was unable to sleep.)

-(으)ㄴ or -았/었던 at the end of the relative clause expresses that the verb in the relative clause happened before that in the main clause.

- 지난주에 본 영화가 재미있었어요.
  The movie I watched last week was fun.
- 예전에 착했던 친구가 성격이 이상해졌어요.
  The friend used to be kind has a strange personality.
- 한때 야구 선수였던 그 남자는 지금은 회사원이에요.
  The man who was once a baseball player is now an office worker.

-(으)ㄹ at the end of the relative clause expresses that the action in the relative clause will happen in the future or is an action that has not yet occurred.

- 다음 주에 먹을 음식 재료를 어제 시장에서 샀어요.
  I bought ingredients for us to eat next week at the market yesterday.
  (While the action of buying took place in the past, the action of eating will take place in the future.)
- 어제 해야 할 일이 많아서 늦게 잤어요.
  Yesterday I slept late because I had a lot of work to do.
  (The errands were not yet carried out as of yesterday.)
- 할 말이 있었지만 결국 말 못 했어요.
  There was something I wanted to say but, in the end, I couldn't say it
  (What was to be said was not spoken after all.)

The conjugation differs for -지 않다 depending on whether it follows a verb or adjective and what tense it is in.

	Past	Present	Future/ Supposition
Verb	여행 가지 않은 사람	여행 가지 않는 사람	여행 가지 않을 사람
Adjective	필요하지 않았던 물건	필요하지 않은 물건	필요하지 않을 물건

Be careful

It is unnatural to use the topic marker 은/는 with the subject inside a relative clause.

- 저는 이번에 여행 가는 곳이 부산이에요. (×)
  제가 이번에 여행 가는 곳이 부산이에요. (O)
  The place I am going to travel to this time is Busan.

-았/었으면 좋겠다 "I wish", "I hope", "It would be nice if" 

C.C P. 303

The speaker's wish for a specific situation is conveyed in front of -았/었으면 좋겠다. Thus, -고 싶다 may not be used in front of -았/었으면 좋겠다.

- 한국어를 잘했으면 좋겠어요. (O)
  I hope I can speak Korean well.
- 한국어를 잘하고 싶었으면 좋겠어요. (×)

In speech, -았/었으면 하다 is often used instead of -았/었으면 좋겠다.

• 다른 집으로 이사했으면 해요 (= 좋겠어요).
I want to move to another house.

Be careful

When expressing someone's own desires, -았/었으면 좋겠다 and -(으)면 좋겠다 may be used interchangeably. However, while -았/었으면 is used to express the speaker's strong wish for an unlikely situation, a situation that is different from that of the present, or an impossible situation, -(으)면 좋겠다 is generally used to express a condition or choice.

• 언젠가 세계 여행을 했으면 좋겠어요.
I wish I could travel around the world someday.
(speaking about a wish)

• 이번에는 제주도로 여행 가면 좋겠어요.
This time, I would like to travel to Jeju Island.
(speaking about a choice)

-도록 "such that", "so that"

C.C P. 298

1 The usage of -도록

-도록 is used to express the goal, criterion, or result for the action that follows it.

• 사람들이 지나가도록 길을 비켜 줬어요.
They cleared the way for people so that they can pass by.
(I moved so that people could pass.)

• 손님이 만족할 수 있도록 정성껏 음식을 만들어요.
We make food with sincerity so that we satisfy our customers.
(I make food sincerely so that the customers will be happy.)

-도록 is attached to verb stems. -았/었- may not be attached in front of -도록 but a negative ending such as -지 않다 may. The subject in the clause preceding -도록 and the one after it may be the same or different.

• 나중에 가족이 놀라지 않도록 미리 얘기하세요.
You should speak to your family about it in advance so that they don't get surprised later.

• 아이들도 쉽게 따라 할 수 있도록 요리 책을 쉽게 만들었어요.
I made a cookbook that is easy for children to follow.

2 Comparing -도록 and -게

-게 is used with the same meaning as -도록 and is also attached to verb stems. -도록 is more formal, while -게 is more informal.

• 나중에 문제가 생기지 않도록 지금 확인하는 게 좋겠습니다.
It's better to check now in order to avoid problems later.
= 나중에 문제가 생기지 않게 지금 확인하는 게 좋겠어요.

3 Comparing -도록 and -(으)려고

-도록 has a similar meaning to -(으)려고, which expresses the subject's intention, but there are cases in which they are used differently. -(으)려고 emphasizes the speaker's intention so the subject must be the same in the clauses preceding and following -(으)려고. When the subject is the same in both clauses, either -도록 or -(으)려고 can be used with no change in meaning.

• 회사에 늦지 않으려고 택시를 탔어요. (O)
I took a taxi to avoid being late for work.
= 회사에 늦지 않도록 택시를 탔어요. (O)
I took a taxi so I wouldn't be late for work.

However, when the subjects are different in both clauses as in the following example, -(으)려고 may not be used and only -도록 may.

• 학생들이 쉽게 이해하려고 선생님이 그림을 그려서 설명했어요. (×)
학생들이 쉽게 이해하도록 선생님이 그림을 그려서 설명했어요. (O)
The teacher drew pictures and explained them to the students so that they could easily understand.

Also, when the second clause is in the command form -(으)세요 or the proposal for -(으)ㅂ시다, -(으)려고 may not be used and only -도록 may.

• 늦지 않으려고 일찍 출발하세요. (×)
늦지 않도록 일찍 출발하세요. (O)
Leave early so that you won't be late.

Chapter 12

-다고 하다 indirect quotations

C.C P. 308

Indirect quotations are used to express what someone else has said. The form is either -다고 하다, -(으)라고 하다, -자고 하다, or -냐고 하다 depending on whether it is a statement, command, proposal, or question, respectively. Verbs such as 말하다 (to speak), 얘기하다 (to say), 제안하다 (to propose), 조언하다 (to suggest), or 질문하다 (to ask) may be used in place of 하다.

1 Indirectly quoting a statement

-다고 하다 is attached to statements. If the indirectly quoted statement is in the present, -ㄴ/는다고 is attached to verb stems, -다고 하다 to adjective stems, and (이)라고 하다 to 이다. If the indirectly quoted statement is in the past, -았/었다고 하다 is attached to the stem of the verb, adjective, or 이다. If the indirectly quoted statement is in the future or is a supposition, -(으)ㄹ 거라고 하다 is attached to the stem of the verb, adjective, or 이다. -(으)ㄹ 것이라고 하다 is used in writing.

- 진수가 "보통 아침에 7시에 일어나요."라고 했어요.
  Jinsu said, "I usually get up at 7 in the morning."
  → 진수가 보통 아침에 7시에 일어난다고 했어요.
  Jinsu said that he usually wakes up at 7 in the morning.
- 리나가 "일주일에 한 권씩 책을 읽어요."라고 말했어요.
  Rina said, "I read one book a week."
  → 리나가 일주일에 한 권씩 책을 읽는다고 말했어요.
  Rina said that she reads one book a week.
- 케빈이 "갑자기 배가 아파요."라고 소리 질렀어요.
  "Suddenly my stomach hurts," shouted Kevin.
  → 케빈이 갑자기 배가 아프다고 소리 질렀어요.
  Kevin suddenly shouted that he had a stomachache.
- 웨이가 "회사원이에요."라고 대답했어요.
  Wei replied, "I'm an office worker."
  → 웨이가 회사원이라고 대답했어요.
  Wei replied that he was an office worker.
- 민호가 "어제 회사에 갑자기 일이 생겼어요."라고 얘기했어요.
  Minho said, "Something suddenly came up at work yesterday."
  → 민호가 어제 회사에 갑자기 일이 생겼다고 얘기했어요.
  Minho told me that something suddenly came up at work yesterday.
- 마크가 "다음 주에 미국에 갔다 올 거예요."라고 했어요.
  Mark said, "I'm going to America next week."
  → 마크가 다음 주에 미국에 갔다 올 거라고 했어요.
  Mark told me that he was going to America the next week.

In Korean, events that take place in the near future may use the present tense.

- 친구들이 다음 주에 휴가 갈 거라고 말했어요.
  My friends told me that they would be going on vacation next week.
  = 친구들이 다음 주에 휴가 간다고 말했어요.

-(으)ㄹ게요, which expresses a promise to the listener or oneself, is indirectly quoted in the following ways:

- 진수가 "이따가 연락할게요."라고 말했어요.
  Jinsu said, "I'll call you later."
  → 진수가 이따가 연락하겠다고 말했어요.
  Jinsu said he would call me later.
  = 진수가 이따가 연락한다고 말했어요.

The reply 네 is indirectly quoted as 그렇다고 하다 or 맞다고 하다, while 아니오 is indirectly quoted as 아니라고 하다.

- 진수가 "네."라고 했어요. Jinsu said "Yes."
  → 진수가 그렇다고 했어요. Jinsu said yes.
- 새라가 "아니요."라고 말했어요. Sarah said "No."
  → 새라가 아니라고 말했어요. Sarah said no.

2 Remember the following points when using the indirect quotation

Statements that end in the negative -지 않다 or -지 못하다 take different forms depending on whether a verb or adjective follows it. The negative becomes -지 않다고 하다 when following an adjective, while it becomes -지 않는다고 하다 or -지 못한다고 하다 when following a verb.

- 리나가 "바쁘지 않아요."라고 했어요.
  "I'm not busy," said Rina.
  → 리나가 바쁘지 않다고 했어요.
  Rina said she wasn't busy.
- 리나가 "운동하지 않아요."라고 했어요.
  "I don't exercise," said Rina.
  → 리나가 운동하지 않는다고 했어요.
  Rina said she doesn't exercise.
- 리나가 "수영하지 못해요."라고 말했어요.
  "I can't swim," said Rina.
  → 리나가 수영하지 못한다고 했어요.
  Rina said she couldn't swim.

The conjugation of compound phrases such as -고 싶다 and -아/어야 하다 in indirect quotations differs depending on if the compound phrase ends in a verb or adjective. For example, because -고 싶다 ends in the adjective 싶다, -다고 하다 is attached. On the other hand, because -아/어야 하다 ends in the verb 하다, -ㄴ다고 하다 is attached. -(으)ㄴ/는 편이다 ends in the noun 편, so -(이)라고 하다 is attached.

Adjectival Compound Phrases	Verbal Compound Phrases
"먹고 싶어요." "I want to eat." → 먹고 싶다고 했어요. I said I wanted to eat.	"먹어야 해요." "You have to eat." → 먹어야 한다고 했어요. I said you had to eat it.
"먹을 수 있어요." "I can eat it." → 먹을 수 있다고 했어요. I said I could eat it.	"먹으면 안 돼요." "You can't eat." → 먹으면 안 된다고 했어요. I said you couldn't eat it.
"볼 수 없어요." "I can't see." → 볼 수 없다고 했어요. I said I couldn't see.	"먹으려고 해요." "I'm trying to eat it." → 먹으려고 한다고 했어요. I said that I was trying to eat it.
"맛있나 봐요." "Looks delicious." → 맛있나 보다고 했어요. I said it looked delicious.	"먹을 줄 알아요." "I know how to eat it." → 먹을 줄 안다고 했어요. I said that I knew how to eat it.

Endings such as -네요, -군요, -거든요, and -잖아요 may not be reflected in indirect quotations. Honorifics are also not reflected in indirect quotations.

- 리나가 "비빔밥이 정말 맛있네요."라고 했어요.
  Rina said, "The bibimbap is really good."
  → 리나가 비빔밥이 정말 맛있다고 했어요.
  Rina told me that the bibimbap was really good.

- 웨이가 "처음에 회사에서 많이 고생했군요."라고 말했어요.
  Wei said, "You had a lot of hardships with the company at first."
  → 웨이가 처음에 회사에서 많이 고생했다고 말했어요.
  Wei told me that I had a lot of hardships with the company at first.
- 가게 직원이 "손님들이 이 음식을 많이 주문하세요."라고 했어요.
  The worker at the store said, "Customers order a lot of this food."
  → 가게 직원이 손님들이 이 음식을 많이 주문한다고 했어요.
  The worker at the store told me that customers ordered a lot of this food.

The first person pronouns 저, 나, or 우리 are quoted as 자기 (oneself) except when quoting one's own words.

- 마크가 "직원이 저한테 전화했어요."라고 했어요.
  Mark said, "The employee called me."
  → 마크가 직원이 자기한테 전화했다고 했어요.
  Mark said that the employee called him.
- 에릭이 "내 친구의 이름은 박준수야."라고 말했어요.
  Eric said, "My friend's name was Junsu Park."
  → 에릭이 자기 친구의 이름은 박준수라고 말했어요.
  Eric said that his friend's name was Junsu Park.
- 피터가 "우리 회사 사람은 전부 남자예요."라고 했어요.
  Peter said, "All the people in our company were men."
  → 피터가 자기 회사 사람은 전부 남자라고 했어요.
  Peter said all the people in his company were men.
- 저는 "제가 한국 사람이에요."라고 말했어요.
  I said, "I'm Korean."
  → 저는 제가 한국 사람이라고 했어요. (○)
  → 저는 자기가 한국 사람이라고 했어요. (×)

-고 했다 is used if the indirect quotation was spoken by a person, while -고 하다 is used if it is a commonly said statement.

- 마크가 한국 음식이 건강에 좋다고 했어요.
  Mark said Korean food is good for one's health.
- 사람들이 한국 음식이 건강에 좋다고 해요.
  People say that Korean food is good for one's health.

Verbs such as 생각하다, 보다, and 느끼다 can be used in place of 하다 in -고 하다 to express the subject's opinions or feelings.

- 마크는 "한국어를 공부할 때 단어가 제일 중요해요."라고 생각해요.
  Mark thinks that "words are the most important thing when studying Korean."
  → 마크는 한국어를 공부할 때 단어가 제일 중요하다고 생각해요.
  Mark thinks that words are the most important thing when studying Korean.
- 진수가 "요즘은 취직하기 어려워요."라고 느껴요.
  Jinsu feels that "it's hard to find a job these days."
  → 진수가 요즘은 취직하기 어렵다고 느껴요.
  Jinsu feels that it's hard to find a job these days.

3 Expressing indirect commands, proposals, and questions

If the indirect quotation is a command, -(으)라고 하다 is used. If it is a proposal, -자고 하다 is used. If it is a negative, 말다 is used to form -지 말라고 하다 for commands and -지 말자고 하다 in proposals.

- 진수가 "지하철 3호선을 타세요."라고 했어요.
  Jinsu said, "Take subway line 3."
  → 진수가 지하철 3호선을 타라고 했어요.
  Jinsu said to take subway line 3.
- 리나가 "걱정하지 마세요."라고 얘기했어요.
  Rina said, "Don't worry."
  → 리나가 걱정하지 말라고 얘기했어요.
  Rina said not to worry about it.
- 민호가 "다음에 만나서 얘기합시다."라고 말했어요.
  Minho said, "Let's meet next time and talk about it."
  → 민호가 다음에 만나서 얘기하자고 말했어요.
  Minho said to meet next time and talk about it.
- 웨이가 "더 이상 걱정하지 맙시다."라고 했어요.
  Wei said, "Don't worry about it anymore."
  → 웨이가 더 이상 걱정하지 말자고 말했어요.
  Wei said not to worry about it anymore.

When quoting -아/어 주세요, there are two different forms to express "to give." If the action is done for someone else, -아/어 주라고 했어요 is used, while if the action is done for oneself, -아/어 달라고 했어요 is used instead.

- 진수가 "이 책을 리나에게 전해 주세요."라고 말했어요.
  Jinsu said, "Please give this book to Rina."
  → 진수가 이 책을 리나한테 전해 주라고 했어요. (for Rina)
  Jinsu told me to give this book to you, Rina.
- 진수가 "이 책을 저한테 전해 주세요."라고 말했어요.
  Jinsu said, "Give me this book."
  → 진수가 이 책을 자기한테 전해 달라고 했어요. (for Jinsu himself)
  Jinsu told me to give this book to him.

If the indirect quotation is a question, -냐고 하다 is attached. In the present, it is -냐고 하다, in the past, it is -았/었냐고 하다, and in the future, it is -(으)ㄹ 거냐고 하다.

- 진수가 마크에게 "언제 한국에 왔어요?"라고 물어봤어요.
  Jinsu asked Mark, "When did you come to Korea?"
  → 진수가 마크에게 언제 한국에 왔냐고 물어봤어요.
  Jinsu asked Mark when he came to Korea.
- 리나가 유키에게 "한국 생활이 어때요?"라고 질문했어요.
  Rina asked Yuki, "How is life in Korea?"
  → 리나가 유키에게 한국 생활이 어떠냐고 질문했어요.
  Rina asked Yuki how her life was in Korea.
- 마크가 민호에게 "휴가 때 뭐 할 거예요?"라고 질문했어요.
  Mark asked Minho, "What are you going to do during the vacation?"
  → 마크가 민호에게 휴가 때 뭐 할 거냐고 질문했어요.
  Mark asked Minho what he was going to do during the vacation.

Be careful

Question marks are not used after indirectly quoted questions.

- 진수가 "어디에 가요?"라고 물어봤어요.
  Jinsu asked, "Where are you going?"
  → 진수가 어디에 가냐고 물어봤어요? (×)
  → 진수가 어디에 가냐고 물어봤어요. (○)
  Jinsu asked where he was going.

4 Shortened Indirect Quotations (Colloquial Abbreviation)

The forms of indirect quotations vary greatly in Korean, and it is very common to shorten them in banmal or informal conversation. -다고 했어요 becomes -대요, -라고 했어요 becomes -래요, -자고 했어요 becomes -재요, and -냐고 했어요 becomes -냬요.

- 진수가 어제 잠을 못 자서 피곤하다고 했어요.
  Jinsu said he was tired yesterday because he couldn't sleep.
  → 피곤하대요
- 리나가 날씨가 안 좋으니까 우산을 가져가라고 했어요.
  Rina told me to bring an umbrella because the weather was bad.
  → 가져가래요
- 새라가 주말에 같이 영화 보자고 제안했어요.
  Sarah suggested that we see a movie together over the weekend.
  → 보재요
- 유키가 내일 시간이 있냐고 물어봤어요.
  Yuki asked if I had time tomorrow.
  → 있냬요

5 Expressing two co-occurring quotations or actions alongside a quotation

-(으)면서 is used to connect two co-occurring actions. In the same manner, it can also be attached to -고 하다 to form -고 하면서 in order to express the co-occurrence of one statement with another or with a separate action.

- 케빈이 피곤하냐고 하면서 커피를 줬어요.
  Kevin asked if I was tired and gave me coffee.
- 리나가 음악을 듣고 싶다고 하면서 좋은 노래가 있냐고 물어봤어요.
  Rina said she wanted to listen to music and asked if I knew of any good songs.

-(으)ㄴ/는 것 같다 "to seem"

C.C P. 305

1 Making suppositions

-(으)ㄴ/는 것 같다 is used to form a supposition about an action, state, or event. If the supposition is in the present, -(으)ㄴ 것 같다 follows adjective stems while -는 것 같다 follows verb stems. If the supposition is in the past, -았/었던 것 같다 follows adjective stems while -(으)ㄴ 것 같다 follows verb stems. If the supposition is in the future or is a guess, -(으)ㄹ 것 같다 follows both adjective and verb stems.

- 사람들이 두꺼운 옷을 입고 있어요. 밖이 추운 것 같아요.
  People are wearing thick clothes. I think it's cold outside.
- 리나 씨가 답을 아는 것 같아요. 자신 있게 웃고 있어요.
  I think Rina knows the answer. She's smiling in confidence.
- 케빈한테 여자 친구가 생긴 것 같아. 시간이 날 때마다 전화하러 나가.
  I think Kevin has a girlfriend. He goes out when calling on the phone.
- 내 친구가 이 책을 읽은 것 같아. 여러 가지 물어봤는데 다 대답을 잘해.
  I think my friend read this book. I asked a lot of questions, and my friend answered everything well.
- 발음을 들어 보니까 미국 사람인 것 같아.
  Listening to his pronunciation, it seems that he is an American.
- 하늘이 어두워요. 비가 올 것 같아요.
  The sky is dark. I think it will rain.
- 밥을 안 먹고 산에 올라가면 배가 고플 것 같아요.
  If I go up the mountain without eating, I think I will be hungry.

However, adjectives that end in 있다/없다 (ex. 재미있다, 맛있다, etc.) are followed not by -(으)ㄴ 것 같다 but by -는 것 같다.

- 저 음식이 제일 맛있는 것 같아요. 제일 많이 팔려요. (○)
  I think that food is the best. It sells the best.
- 저 음식이 제일 맛있은 것 같아요. 제일 많이 팔려요. (×)

Be careful

There is a slight difference if the future or present is used with adjectives.

- 주말에는 사람이 많은 것 같아.
  It seems to be crowded on weekends.
  (Expressing a supposition, based on the observation that there are generally many people on the weekends.)
- 주말에는 사람이 많을 것 같아.
  (Making a guess that there will be many people on the weekend without any prior knowledge or information.)

When the negative -지 않다 precedes -(으)ㄴ/는 것 같다, the form differs depending on whether it follows an adjective or a verb. If it follows an adjective, it is -지 않은 것 같다, while if it follows a verb, it is -지 않는 것 같다.

- 오늘 날씨가 춥지 않은 것 같아요. 사람들이 옷을 얇게 입었어요.
  I don't think the weather will be cold today. People aren't wearing much.
- 저 사람은 영화를 자주 보지 않는 것 같아요. 요즘 영화에 대해 잘 몰라요.
  I don't think he watches movies very often. He doesn't know much about movies these days.

Be careful

In speech, -는 것 같아요 is also pronounced -는 거 같아요. While it is not standard, 같아요 is also pronounced as 같애요.

2 When expressing one's subjective opinion in a roundabout manner

-(으)/는 것 같다 is not only used for conjectures but also to express one's subjective opinion. In these cases, it does not express the speaker's strong opinion about an issue but provides a more roundabout tone.

- 가격표를 보세요. 여기가 다른 가게보다 비싼 것 같아요.
  Look at the price list. I think this place is more expensive than other stores.
  (The person expresses an opinion, rather than a guess because he is looking at the price and is stating what he thinks based on what he directly observed or experienced.)
- 작년에 산 바지가 작아. 내가 요즘 살이 찐 것 같아.
  The pants I bought last year are small. I think I've gained weight these days.
  (The person did not directly measure his or her weight, but rather is expressing a thought based on how he or she feels.)

Chapter 13

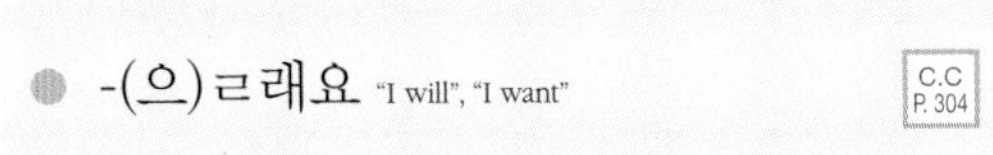

1 Expressing the speaker's intent

-(으)ㄹ래요 is used to express the speaker's intent and is attached to verb stems. It is generally used in speech. -지 않다 is attached to form the negative -지 않을래요. -(으)ㄹ래요 expresses informality and comfortability, so it should only be used with those of equal or lower status.

- 오늘 좀 피곤하니까 운동은 쉴래요.
  I'm a little tired today, so I'll take a break from exercising.
- 나는 이거 안 먹을래.
  I don't want to eat this.

2 Asking the listener's intent or making a request or proposal

The question -(으)ㄹ래요? is used to ask the listener's intent or to make a request or proposal. In this case, one must be careful to respond to the question according to one's intent. Let us look at the following situations.

(1) Asking intent

A 진수 씨, 뭐 마실래요? (= 먹고 싶어요?)
Jinsu, what would you like to drink?
(= Do you want to eat?)

B 전 커피 마실게요.
I'll drink coffee.

Be careful

One may answer the question -(으)ㄹ래요? with -(으)ㄹ래요, but in responding that way, it implies that the intention has been made without regard to the person who asked the question. As such, the implied message seems rude and impolite. In contrast, -(으)ㄹ게요 expresses the speaker's careful consideration of the choice and is, therefore, more polite. -(으)ㄹ래요 should be used with those with whom one feels close and with whom one wants to show one's intent, while -(으)ㄹ게요 should be used with those to whom one must show respect.

- 엄마: 밥 먹을래? Do you want to eat?
  아이 1: 싫어, 밥 안 먹을래. No. I won't eat.
  (expresses childlike grumbling)
  아이 2: 저는 밥 안 먹을게요. I don't want to eat.
  (expresses a polite declination)

(2) Request

A 사무실 연락처 좀 알려 줄래요? (= 알려 주시겠어요?)
Could you give me your office contact information?
(= Can you tell me?)

B 알려 줄게요. I'll let you know.

(3) Suggestion

A 제가 밥을 살 테니까 같이 식사할래요? (= 식사할까요?)
I'll buy some food, so would you like to have a meal together? (= Shall we eat?)

B 좋아요, 같이 식사해요.
Sounds good. Let's eat together.

In the negative, -지 않다 or -지 말다 are used in front to form -지 않을래요 or -지 말래요.

- 오늘 점심은 시원하게 국수로 먹지 않을래요?
  Why don't we refresh ourselves by having some noodles for lunch today?
- 오늘 모임에 가지 말래요? 우리끼리 영화나 봐요.
  Why don't we not go to the gathering today? Let's watch a movie together.

-(으)ㄹ래요? is used in informal situations in which one does not need to express politeness. But in cases where one must show respect, the honorific -(으)시- should be attached to form -(으)실래요? It may be used with close older coworkers, school friends, or relatives with whom there is a close rapport.

- 뭐 드실래요?
  What do you want to eat?
  (to a close older school friend)
- 저하고 같이 준비하실래요?
  Would you like to prepare with me?
  (to a close older coworker)

-(으)ㄹ래? 말래? can be used with close friends with whom one does not need to be polite to ask about intent to do or not to do something.

- 오늘 쇼핑하러 가는데 같이 갈래? 말래?
  I'm going shopping today, would you like to go with me? Or not?
- 도시락 싸 왔어. 너도 같이 먹을래? 말래?
  I brought a lunch box. Would you like to eat it together? Or not?

-(으)ㄹ까 하다 "I might", "I am thinking of"

-(으)ㄹ까 하다 is used to express the speaker's thoughts about carrying out an action. In these cases, the thought is vague and not yet concrete, so it implies that the action is one of many choices and can be easily changed. Because the speaker must be the subject, only the first person can be used. -(으)ㄹ까 하다 attaches to verb stems.

- 일이 끝났으니까 오랜만에 친구를 만날까 해요.
  Since I finished my work, I'm thinking of meeting a friend as it has been a long time.
- 오늘 점심은 냉면을 먹을까 하는데 어때요?
  I would like to have naengmyeon for lunch today. How about it?

I wonder

Both -(으)ㄹ까 하다 and -(으)려고 하다 express the speaker's thoughts, but -(으)ㄹ까 하다 does not express an already made decision, rather it indicates a vague idea about what to do. In contrast, -(으)려고 하다 is generally used to express an intention to take any action to carry out a plan.

- 이번 방학 때 제주도로 여행 갈까 해요.
  I'm thinking of going on a trip to Jeju Island this vacation.
  (a vague idea that could change)
- 이번 방학 때 제주도로 여행 가려고 해요.
  I'm going on a trip to Jeju Island this vacation.
  (implies that the decision to go is set)

-(으)ㄹ까 -(으)ㄹ까 is used repeatedly to show hesitation in making a decision between multiple choices. If one is deciding whether to do something or not -(으)ㄹ까 말까 can be used.

- 주말에 동창 모임에 갈까 집에서 쉴까 고민하고 있어요.
  I am debating whether to go to a class reunion on the weekend or to rest at home.
- 물건은 마음에 드는데 비싸서 살까 말까 생각하고 있어요.
  I like the item, but it is expensive, so I am thinking about whether to buy it or not.

Be careful

Because -(으)ㄹ까 in -(으)ㄹ까 하다 implies a question to oneself, it can only be used in the first person. Therefore, the second or third person may not be used, and -(으)ㄹ까 하다 may not be used as a question to someone else.

- 친구는 일을 그만둘까 해요. (×)
  → 친구는 일을 그만두려고 해요. (○)
  My friend is about to quit his job.
- 언제 일하기 시작할까 해요? (×)
  → 언제 일하기 시작할 거예요? (○)
  When will you start working?

-기는 하지만 "It is..., but"

-기는 하지만 is used to partially concede the first clause and to follow up with a contrasting one. It is used primarily during debates to concede the other speaker's point while expressing a separate opinion. Compared to -지만, it is more polite. It attaches to the stems of verbs, adjectives, and 이다. In speech, -기는 may be shortened to -긴.

- 그 영화가 재미있기는 하지만 너무 길어요.
  The movie is fun, but it's too long.
  (= 그 영화가 재미있기는 해요. 하지만 너무 길어요.)
- 고기를 먹을 수 있긴 하지만 좋아하지 않아요.
  I can eat meat, but I don't like it.

Instead of -지만, -(으)ㄴ/는데 may be used. However, when -(으)ㄴ/는데 is used, -기는 하는데 is attached if it is a verb, while -기는 한데 is attached if it is an adjective.

- 이 식당은 비싸긴 한데 맛있어요.
  This restaurant is expensive, but it is delicious.
- 이 옷이 저한테 딱 맞기는 하는데 색이 마음에 안 들어요.
  This dress fits me perfectly, but I don't like the color.

-았/었- or -겠- can attach to 하다 in -기는 하다.

- 여행이 힘들긴 했는데 재미있었어요.
  The trip was tiresome, but it was fun.
- 제가 음식을 만들긴 하겠지만 맛이 없을 거예요.
  I'll make the food, but it won't taste good.

When -기는 하지만 is used, the speaker's strong opinion is always expressed in the second clause, so it is natural, as well as polite, to omit the second clause and only imply it in speech.

- 그 식당이 맛있긴 해요.
  That restaurant is delicious. (But...)
  〔The speaker concedes that the restaurant is tasty but implies a complaint, such as unsatisfactory service or high prices.〕
- 그 사람의 이름을 듣기는 했어요.
  I did hear his name. (But...)
  〔The speaker admits that he/she has heard the name before but implies that he/she does not know what the person looks like.〕

-군요 expressing recognition and understanding of a newly learned fact 

By expressing recognition and understanding of a newly learned fact, -군요 is used by a speaker to express surprise at a new realization from seeing or hearing something. If the realized piece of information occurs in the present, -는군요 is attached to verb stems, while -군요 is attached to the stems of adjectives and 이다. If the realized piece of information occurred in the past, -았/었군요 is attached to the stems of verbs, adjectives, and 이다. When speaking to oneself, -구나 can be used instead of -군요.

- 어제 집에 일이 있었군요. 몰랐어요.
  Something came up at your home yesterday. I did not know.
- 케빈은 정말 좋은 사람이구나!
  Kevin's such a nice guy!

-겠- can be attached to -군요 to form -겠군요 if the speaker is making a conjecture based on a situation at the current time. -았/었- may be attached in front to form -았/었겠군요 if the conjecture is based on a situation that has already been completed.

- 하루에 열 시간씩 일하면 힘들겠군요.
  It must be hard working ten hours a day.
- 여행할 때 가방을 도둑맞아서 고생했겠군요.
  You must have experienced hardship because your bag was stolen while traveling.

I wonder

-네요 and -군요 may both be used to express the speaker's thoughts or feelings. The two are used similarly, but there is a small key difference.

- 이 길이 맞네요. 제가 전에 말했잖아요.
  This way is the right way. I told you before.
  〔The speaker emphasizes that what is being said is in accord with his/her expectation.〕
- 이 길이 맞군요. 몰랐어요.
  This is the right way. I did not know.
  〔The speaker expresses realization of a fact that he/she did not know before.〕

Chapter 14

-나 보다 "to look (like)" 

1 Making a conjecture

-나 보다 is used to make a guess about an action, state, or situation. Because -나 보다 involves the speaker looking at something and making a guess, it may not be used in the first person. Since this grammar point involves making a guess about something uncertain, it is formed with the question ending -나, followed by 보다 (with the meaning of "to think"), to form -나 보다. If the conjectured clause takes place in the present, -(으)ㄴ가 보다 is attached to the stems of adjectives and to 이다, while -나 보다 is attached to verb stems. If it takes place in the past, -았/었나 보다 is attached to the stems of verbs, adjectives, and 이다.

- 저 집은 과일을 많이 먹나 봐요. 매일 과일을 많이 사 가요.
  That household seems to eat a lot of fruit. They buy a lot of fruit every day.

- 역사에 관심이 많은가 봐요. 집에 역사책이 많이 있네요.
  You must be interested in history. You have a lot of history books at home.
- 어젯밤에 잠을 못 잤나 봐요. 얼굴이 피곤해 보여요.
  It looks like you didn't sleep much last night. Your face looks tired.

However, adjectives formed with 있다/없다 have -나 보다 attached to the stem instead of -(으)ㄴ가 보다.

- 저 영화가 제일 재미있나 봐요. 표가 매진됐어요. (O)
  I think that movie is the funnest. The tickets are sold out.
  저 영화가 제일 재미있은가 봐요. 표가 매진됐어요. (×)

2 Comparing -나 보다 and -(으)ㄴ/는 것 같다

Similar to the use of -나 보다 to express the speaker's conjecture from observing a situation, -(으)ㄴ/는 것 같다 expresses the same meaning. However, while -(으)ㄴ/는 것 같다 includes the speaker's thought or evaluation based on prior experience, -나 보다 cannot be used if the statement is being made based on direct experience.

- 식당에 사람들이 많은 것을 보니까 이 식당 음식이 맛있나 봐요. (O)
  The food at this restaurant must be delicious as there are many people in the restaurant.
  (The speaker has had no experience eating at this restaurant but is guessing that the food is tasty based on his/her observation that there are many patrons at the restaurant.)
  = 식당에 사람들이 많은 것을 보니까 이 식당 음식이 맛있는 것 같아요. (O)
  I think the food at this restaurant is delicious since there are many people in the restaurant.
- 전에 먹어 보니까 이 식당 음식이 맛있는 것 같아요. (O)
  Having eaten here before, I think the food at this restaurant is delicious.
  (The speaker is evaluating the restaurant based on prior experience.)
  = 전에 먹어 보니까 이 식당 음식이 맛있나 봐요. (×)

Thus, subjective adverbial clauses, such as 제 생각에 (I think) or 제가 보기에 (in my opinion), may not be used together with -나 보다. It is more natural to use them with -(으)ㄴ/는 것 같다.

- 제 생각에 한국어 공부는 어려운가 봐요. (×)
  제 생각에 한국어 공부는 어려운 것 같아요. (O)
  I think studying Korean is difficult.

Also because the speaker cannot make a conjecture about his/her own state, -나 보다 may not be used in the first person.

(after hearing one's stomach growl)

- 제가 배고픈가 봐요. (×)
  제가 배고픈 것 같아요. (O) I think I'm hungry.

However, if the speaker has a delayed realization about something that was unbeknownst to him or her before, -나 보다 may be used within the first person. Because this usage is often made without a listener, it is common to drop -요 and use banmal.

- 내가 저 사람을 좋아하나 봐. I think I like him.
- 그 사실을 나만 몰랐나 봐.
  I guess I was the only one who didn't know that.

3 Note the following points for -나 보다

There are many grammatical restrictions on -나 보다, but it may combine with tense markers such as -았/었- or the negative -지 않다. These must come before -나 보다 and be attached to the supposition.

- 여행이 재미있나 봤어요. (×)
  → 여행이 재미있었나 봐요. (O)
  The trip must have been fun.
- 오늘 날씨가 추운가 보지 않아요 (×)
  → 오늘 날씨가 춥지 않은가 봐요. (O)
  I guess it's not cold today.

-(으)ㄴ/는 줄 알았다 "to have thought that"

C.C P. 305

-(으)ㄴ/는 줄 알았다 is used to express a mistaken thought about a fact or state. Because it is an expression of a mistaken thought, 알았다 must be used. If the mistaken thought ends in a verb and is in the present, -는 줄 알았다 is attached to the stem, and if it is in the past, -(으)ㄴ 줄 알았다 is attached. -(으)ㄴ 줄 알았다 is also attached to the stems of adjectives and to 이다 in the present tense. If the mistaken thought takes place in the future or is a supposition, -(으)ㄹ 줄 알았다 is attached to the stems of verbs, adjectives, and 이다.

- 처음에는 한국 사람이 영어를 못하는 줄 알았어요.
  At first, I thought Koreans couldn't speak English.
  (= 처음에는 한국 사람이 영어를 못한다고 생각했는데 그렇지 않았어요.)
  (= At first, I thought Koreans couldn't speak English, but they could.)
- 어제 회사에 간 줄 알았는데 사실은 가지 않았대요.
  I thought he went to work yesterday, but he said he didn't.
- 얼굴이 어려 보여서 학생인 줄 알았는데 선생님이래요.
  He looked young, so I thought he was a student, but he is a teacher.

I wonder

The grammar pattern -(으)ㄹ 줄 알다, which expresses the ability to do something, may be confused with the past form of this grammar pattern, -(으)ㄹ 줄 알았다, which expresses a mistaken thought. The form is the same but the meanings differ, so the correct meaning must be gleaned from the context.

- 전에는 피아노를 칠 줄 알았어요. 그런데 지금은 다 잊어버렸어요.
  Before, I knew how to play the piano. But now I've forgotten it all.
  (knowing how to do something)
- 전에는 다른 사람이 피아노를 칠 줄 알았어요. 그런데 아니었어요.
  Before, I thought someone else could play the piano. But I was wrong.
  (a mistaken thought)

-(으)ㄴ/는 줄 몰랐다 is used to express the speaker's lack of prior realization about a fact. While -(으)ㄴ/는 줄 알았다 is used to emphasize a mistaken thought, -(으)ㄴ/는 줄 몰랐다 is used to emphasize one's lack of knowledge about something. The conjugation is the same as -(으)ㄴ/는 줄 알았다.

- 그 사람이 결혼한 줄 알았어요.
  I thought he was married.
  = 그 사람이 결혼 안 한 줄 몰랐어요.
  I didn't know he wasn't married.

Be careful

While -(으)ㄴ/는 줄 알았다 expresses a mistaken thought, -ㄴ/는다는 것을 알았다 expresses a realization about a fact or state.

- 그 사람이 나를 좋아하는 줄 알았다.
  I thought that person liked me.
  (mistaken thought)
- 그 사람이 나를 좋아한다는 것을 알았다.
  I knew he liked me.
  (the realized fact)

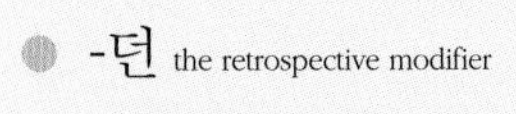

1 The retrospective modifier -던

-던 is a modifier ending that precedes nouns and is used to express a recollection of a past situation or state. -던 expresses a recollection of a past situation that no longer occurs in the present.

the period in the past that can be used with -던

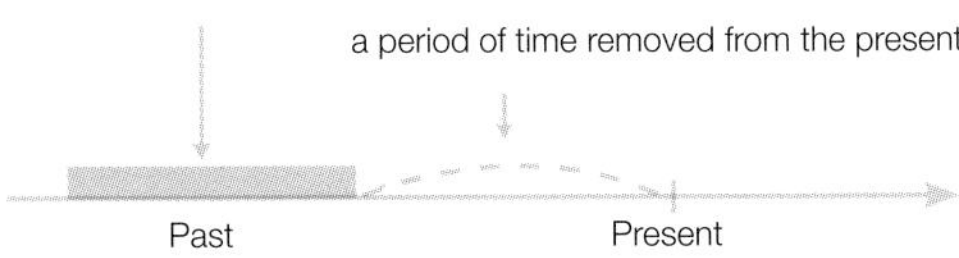

-던 is attached to the stems of verbs, adjectives, and 이다. When -던 is attached, it is implied that the action took place or continued for a set period of time in the past or that it happened repeatedly or habitually. -았/었- may be attached to form -았/었던- to emphasize that the action occurred once or only a few times and does not continue into the present.

- 어렸을 때 같이 놀던 친구하고 지금 연락이 안 돼요.
  I lost contact with a friend I used to play with when I was young.
- 전에는 활발하던 아이가 지금은 조용하네요.
  The child who was active before is now quiet.
- 사랑했던 사람을 잊을 수가 없어요.
  I can't forget the person I loved.
- 학생 때 다리를 다쳤던 경험이 있어요.
  I experienced a leg injury when I was a student.

2 Comparing -던 with -았/었던

-던 is attached to verb stems to express a repeated or habitual action in the past, while -았/었던 is attached to verb stems to express an action that occurred only once or a few times.

- 학교 다닐 때 자주 가던 식당이 지금은 없어졌어요.
  The restaurant I used to go to when I was in school is now gone.
- 그 공원은 옛날에 학교 다닐 때 한 번 갔던 곳이에요.
  That park is a place I went to once when I was in school.

However, verbs such as 살다 (to live), 다니다 (to attend), 사귀다 (to make friends, go out with), and 좋아하다 (to like), which do not express a single action but a continuous state, can take either -던 or -았/었던 with almost no difference in meaning.

- 어렸을 때 내가 살던 동네에는 놀이터가 없었어요.
  When I was a kid, there was no playground in the neighborhood where I lived.
  = 어렸을 때 내가 살았던 동네에는 놀이터가 없었어요.

In the same way, verbs such as 죽다 (to die), 다치다 (to hurt), and 결혼하다 (to marry), which happen in an instant, take -았/었던 and do not take -던.

- 10년 전에 죽었던 개가 지금도 생각나요. (○)
  I still remember the dog that died 10 years ago.
  10년 전에 죽던 개가 지금도 생각나요. (×)

If an adjective describes a state that exists over a set amount of time in the past, there is no difference in using -던 or -았/었던.

- 예전에는 뚱뚱하던 친구가 지금은 날씬해졌어요.
  My friend who used to be fat is now skinny.
  = 예전에는 뚱뚱했던 친구가 지금은 날씬해졌어요.

3 Comparing -았/었던 with -(으)ㄴ

There are many cases in which -(으)ㄴ and -았/었던 are interchangeable when talking about a past event or state.

- 전에 길에서 만난 친구 이름이 뭐예요?
  What's the name of the friend you met on the street before?
  = 전에 길에서 만났던 친구 이름이 뭐예요?

-았/었던 points to an action or state occurring during a set time in the past and implies it does not continue into the present.

- 그 사람은 3년 전에 결혼한 사람이에요.
  That person married three years ago and is still married.
  그 사람은 3년 전에 결혼했던 사람이에요.
  That person married three years ago but is no longer married.

Furthermore, because -았/었던 generally refers to a recollection or memory, it cannot be used for a witnessed action that was immediately completed.

- 식사를 다 한 사람은 교실로 돌아가세요. (○)
  When you're done eating, go back to the classroom.
  식사를 다 했던 사람은 교실로 돌아가세요. (×)

4 Using -던 for interrupted actions

-던 can also refer to a past action or situation that did not end but was interrupted in the middle. In these cases where the action is incomplete, -았/었-, which implies completion, cannot be attached.

- 아까 내가 마시던 커피가 어디 있지? 반도 안 마셨는데.
  Where's the coffee I drank earlier? I didn't even drink half of it.
- 회의가 끝났으니까 아까 하던 얘기 계속합시다.
  Now that the meeting is over, let's continue what we were talking about earlier.

In situations where an action is interrupted, there is a clear distinction between -던 and -(으)ㄴ. As -았/었- expresses completion, -았/었던 and -(으)ㄴ can only refer to completed actions.

- (an eaten but unfinished snack)
  아까 먹던 과자는 책상 위에 있으니까 먹어.
  The cookies you ate earlier are on the desk, so feel free to eat them.
- (an entirely eaten snack)
  아까 먹은 (= 먹었던) 과자가 이상한 것 같아. 배가 아파.
  I think there is something wrong with the cookies I ate. my stomach hurts.

-느라고 "because (of doing something at the time)"

C.C P. 299

1 The usage of -느라고

-느라고 is used to express a negative result occurring from an action. It is generally used to give an excuse for a negative consequence. -느라고 is attached to the verb stem of the action.

- 주말에 집안일 하느라고 쉬지 못했어요.
  I couldn't take a break because I was doing housework on the weekend.
- 재미있는 책을 읽느라고 밤을 새웠어요.
  I stayed up all night reading an interesting book.
- 요즘 아르바이트하느라고 바빠요.
  I'm busy working part-time these days.

Verbs like 수고하다 (to try hard) or 애쓰다 (to make an effort) have a similar meaning as 고생하다 (to have trouble) where the implied meaning does not denote an excuse, but rather gratitude for the listener's diligence.

- 그동안 많은 일을 혼자 하느라고 수고하셨습니다.
  You worked hard to do many things by yourself up to now.
- 발표 준비하느라고 애쓰셨어요.
  You put in a lot of effort preparing the presentation.

2 Incorrect usages of -느라고

-느라고 refers to a negative result occurring from an action taken by the subject; the subjects of both clauses around -느라고 must be the same.

- 갑자기 일이 생기느라고 전화 못 했어요. (×)
  → 갑자기 일이 생겨서 그 일을 하느라고 전화 못 했어요. (○)
  I couldn't call because I had to do something that came up all of a sudden.

As the clause before -느라고 expresses an action leading to a negative result, -느라고 may not attach to adjectives.

- 춥느라고 감기에 걸렸어요. (×)
  → 추워서 감기에 걸렸어요. (○)
  It was cold and I caught a cold.

As -느라고 expresses a negative result brought about by a decision to take any action, negative forms cannot precede -느라고.

- 전화 안 하느라고 친구가 화가 났어요. (×)
  → 전화 안 해서 친구가 화가 났어요. (○)
  My friend got angry because I didn't call.

Even if the action preceding -느라고 refers to the past, -았/었- may not precede it.

- 친구하고 놀았느라고 숙제를 못 했어요. (×)
  → 친구하고 노느라고 숙제를 못 했어요. (○)
  I couldn't do my homework because I was playing with my friends.

-(으)ㄹ 걸 그랬다 "should have"

1 Expressing regret with -(으)ㄹ 걸: "I should have"

-(으)ㄹ 걸 그랬다 expresses regret for not having done something. 그랬다 refers to a regrettable inaction in the past, while the lack of accomplishment of the action is expressed by the ending -(으)ㄹ. In speech, 그랬다 may be omitted, leaving only -(으)ㄹ걸. When expressing the feeling of regret, the intonation does not rise. When speaking to oneself, -요 is not attached to -(으)ㄹ걸. Conversely, -지 않을 걸 그랬다 or -지 말 걸 그랬다 expresses regret for having done something in the past. In these instances, 그랬다 may also be omitted to leave -지 않을걸 or -지 말걸.

- 미리 전화해 볼 걸 그랬다. 그러면 오늘 퇴근이 늦는 것을 알았을 것을.
  I should've called first. Then I would've known that you will end work late today.
- 아까 소금을 더 넣지 말 걸 그랬어요. 먹어 보니까 음식이 좀 짜네요.
  I shouldn't have added more salt earlier. The food is a bit salty when I eat it.

Be careful

As the action was not carried out, the ending -(으)ㄹ, which represents the lack of accomplishment of an action, is used.

- 친구에게 미리 전화한 걸 그랬어요. (×)
- 친구에게 미리 전화할 걸 그랬어요. (○)
  I should've called my friend ahead of time.

2 The conjectural meaning of -(으)ㄹ걸: "might"

In the second conversation of Chapter 13, the conjectural -(으)ㄹ걸, which looks identical to the shortened form of the regretful -(으)ㄹ 걸 그랬다, is used, but with a completely different meaning. The conjectural -(으)ㄹ걸 form expresses the speaker's uncertainty or lack of confidence in making a conjecture. It is not used in formal situations but is rather used in informal situations with those with whom one is close. In this usage, -(으)ㄹ걸 attaches to the stems of verbs, adjectives, 이다, and -요. The intonation also rises at the end. If the conjectured action has already been completed, -았/었- is attached before -(으)ㄹ걸 to form -았/었을걸요.

- 글쎄요, 아마 진수도 그 사실을 모를걸요.
  I do not know. Jinsu probably doesn't even know about it.
- 두고 봐. 내가 너보다 더 잘할걸.
  Just wait. I'll do better than you.
- 이미 표가 다 팔렸을걸. 그 영화가 얼마나 인기가 많은데.
  I'm sure all of the tickets have already been sold out. That movie is incredibly popular.

Be careful

Remember that the expression of regret and conjecture -(으)ㄹ걸 look the same, but the intonation at the end of the sentence differs for each.

- 미리 준비할걸. 그러면 실수하지 않았을 거야.
  I should've prepared in advance. Then I wouldn't have made a mistake.
  (regret)
- 미리 준비할걸. 리나는 항상 미리 하는 성격이잖아.
  Rina will prepare it in advance. She is the type to always be ahead of time.
  (conjecture)

Chapter 15

-다가 "while …ing", "in the middle of …ing"

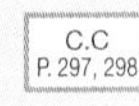

1 When switching actions or states in the middle of another

-다가 expresses a switch to a different action or state while in the middle of a parti cular action or state. Because -다가 expresses a change of action or state, the subject in both clauses must be the same. -다가 attaches to verb and adjective stems.

- 그 책을 읽다가 어려워서 그만뒀어요.
  I stopped reading that book because it was difficult.
- 친구가 자동차를 5년 동안 쓰다가 저에게 줬어요.
  A friend gave me his car after using it for 5 years.
- 오늘 오전에는 흐리다가 오후에는 개겠습니다.
  Cloudy this morning and clear in the afternoon.

-았/었- may be attached in front of -다가 to express the completion of an action or state and a switch to another one.

- 열이 났다가 약을 먹고 열이 떨어졌어요.
  I had a fever then took medicine, and my fever went down.
- 여자 친구에게 반지를 선물했다가 헤어진 후 다시 가져갔어요.
  I gave the ring to my girlfriend and took it back after we broke up.
- 그 사람은 원래는 군인이었다가 경찰이 됐어요.
  He was originally a soldier and then became a police officer.

-았/었- is not attached in front of -다가 if the action is not carried out to completion and is interrupted. -았/었다가 expresses that the second action does not happen until the first is finished.

- 집에 가다가 우연히 친구를 만났어요.
  On the way home, I met a friend by chance.
  (The friend was met on the way home.)
- 집에 갔다가 우연히 친구를 만났어요.
  I met a friend by chance after arriving home.
  (The friend was met after arriving home.)

Be careful

The subject on either side of -다가 must be the same.

- 친구가 샤워하다가 전화가 왔어요. (×)
  → 친구가 샤워하다가 전화를 받았어요. (○)
  A friend was showering and answered a phone call.

2 Expressing an unexpected situation

-다가 can also express an unexpected, unintentional situation arising in the middle of another action. In this usage, the unexpected situation is often negative.

- 버스를 타고 가다가 지갑을 잃어버린 것 같아요.
  I think I lost my wallet while riding the bus.
- 뛰어가다가 (돌에 걸려서) 넘어졌어요.
  I fell (stumbled on a stone) while running.
- 샤워하다가 (미끄러져서) 허리를 다쳤어요.
  I hurt my back (slipped) while showering.
- 친구하고 얘기하다가 그 사실을 알게 됐어요.
  I found out about it while talking to a friend.

While -다가 expresses the occurrence of an unintentional and unexpected situation, -아/어서 expresses an intentional or expected situation.

- 편의점에 들렀다가 친구를 만났어요.
  I met a friend while dropping by the convenience store.
  (While carrying out an errand at the convenience store, the speaker suddenly saw his/her friend.)
- 편의점에 들러서 친구를 만났어요.
  I stopped by a convenience store and met a friend.
  (The speaker intended to meet his/her friend at the store.)

3 Expressing the repeated occurrence

-다가 may be used on each verb (followed by 하다 at the end of the entire clause) to show the repeated occurrence of two or more situations. -가 can be dropped from -다가 to form -다 -다 하다.

- 공부하다가 텔레비전을 보다가 하면 집중할 수 없잖아.
  If you watch TV while studying, you won't be able to concentrate.
- 한국하고 일본을 왔다 갔다 하면서 사업하려고 해요.
  I'm trying to do business by going back and forth between Korea and Japan.
- 스위치를 껐다 켰다 하지 마.
  Don't turn the switch on and off.

-(으)ㄹ 텐데

expressing conjectures, hopes, and hypothetical situations
"will probably…", "I hope", "I wish"

C.C P. 303

1 Expressing conjectures with -(으)ㄹ 텐데

-(으)ㄹ 텐데 is used to express a conjectured situation made by the speaker. Similarly to -(으)ㄴ/는데 in Chapter 4, the following clause is related to or is in contrast to the clause preceding -(으)ㄹ 텐데. -(으)ㄹ 텐데 attaches to the stems of verbs, adjectives, and 이다. Just like -(으)ㄴ/는데, the clause following -(으)ㄹ 텐데 can be omitted and simply implied.

- 이미 소금을 많이 넣어서 짤 텐데 또 소금을 넣으려고 해요?
  I already put in a lot of salt to make it, but are you going to add salt again?
- 매일 운동하면 건강이 좋아질 텐데 실제로 매일 운동하기 어려워요.
  If you exercise every day, your health will improve, but it is actually difficult to exercise every day.
- 넘어져서 꽤 아플 텐데 아이가 울지 않네요.
  The fall must be quite painful, but the child is not crying.
- 어린아이가 혼자 유학 가는 것이 쉽지 않을 텐데.
  It must not be easy for a child to go study abroad alone.

If it is conjectured that a situation has already been completed, -았/었- may be attached beforehand to form -았/었을 텐데.

- 회의가 이미 시작했을 텐데 어떻게 하죠?
  The meeting must have already started. What should we do?
- 3시 비행기니까 벌써 출발했을 텐데 전화를 해 볼까요?
  It's a 3 o'clock flight, so it must have already departed. Shall we call?

I wonder

While -(으)ㄹ 텐데 expresses the speaker's conjecture, -(으)ㄹ 건데 expresses a future intended action.

- 저 일은 혼자 하기 어려울 텐데 신입 사원이 혼자 맡았어요.
  It would be difficult to do that job alone, but the new employee was given the task.
- 내일 출장을 갈 건데 일이 아직 다 준비가 안 됐어요.
  I'm going on a business trip tomorrow, but things aren't ready yet.

2 Expressing hopes with -아/어야 할 텐데

-아/어야 하다 can be attached before -(으)ㄹ 텐데 to form -아/어야 할 텐데 to express that the speaker strongly wishes for a situation to occur.

- 이번에는 꼭 취직해야 할 텐데 걱정이에요.
  I'm worried because I must get a job this time around.

- 다음 주에 여행 가려면 날씨가 좋아야 할 텐데…….
  If I go on a trip next week, I hope the weather will be nice...

3 Expressing hypothetical situations with -(으)면 (으)ㄹ 텐데

-(으)면 and -(으)ㄹ 텐데 may be used together to express a hypothetical situation.

- 친구에게 사과하면 우리 사이가 다시 좋아질 텐데.
  If I apologized to my friend, we would have gotten along again.
  (Because the friend did not apologize, the relationship has not improved yet.)
- 가족과 함께 있지 않으면 외로울 텐데.
  I'd be lonely if I wasn't with my family.
  (Because the speaker is with his/her family, he/she is not lonely.)

When referring to a hypothetical situation that would have occurred in the past, -았/었- can be attached beforehand to form -았/었으면 았/었을 텐데.

- 내가 좀 더 참았으면 친구하고 싸우지 않았을 텐데 (실제로 친구하고 싸워서) 후회돼요.
  If I had been more patient, I wouldn't have fought with my friend. I regret it (because I fought with my friend).
  (expresses that the speaker fought with a friend because he/she was unable to control his/her temper)
- 그때 친구가 나를 도와주지 않았으면 나는 그 일을 포기했을 텐데 (친구가 도와줘서) 다행이에요.
  If my friend hadn't helped me then I would have given up on the job. Thank goodness (he helped me).
  (expresses that the speaker did not give up because a friend helped him/her)

Korean **Conjugation**

1 What is conjugation?

In Korean, conjugation is the process by which various endings are added to inflecting words, specifically, verbs, adjectives, and the copula 이다, to change the meaning.

There are three types of endings for inflecting word stems: pre-final endings (these express tense, honorific, etc.); final endings (these express the type of sentence: statement, question, command, and proposal); and conjunctive endings (these connect two clauses and express the relationship between the clauses). For example, when 읽다 is conjugated as 읽어요/읽었어요, one can tell which tense it is; if it is conjugated as 읽습니다/읽습니까/읽으십시오/읽읍시다, one can tell what type of sentence it is; and if it is conjugated as 읽고/읽지만/읽어서/읽으면, one can tell the relationship between the clause and the following clause. Therefore, conjugating a verb, adjective, and 이다 by altering the grammatical endings of inflecting word stems significantly changes the meaning of a sentence.

> **stem:** the form of a verb, adjective, or 이다; identified by removing the 다 from the infinite form
>
> | Ex | 마시다 (to drink) : 마시 (stem) + 다
> 먹다 (to eat) : 먹 (stem) + 다
> 좋다 (to be good): 좋 (stem) + 다
> 이다 (to be) : 이 (stem) + 다

2 How do you conjugate?

When conjugating, careful attention must be paid to whether the inflecting word is a regular or irregular word.

Conjugation of Regular Inflecting Words

When endings are added to the stems of regular inflecting words, they are attached in a fixed manner.

1. The ending -아/어 is attached to stems in the following ways:

❶ The ending -여:

-여 is attached to stems that end in 하 to form 해.

| Ex. | **하다** (to do): 하 (verb stem) + -여 (ending) → 해

❷ The ending -아:

-아 is attached to stems whose final vowel is ㅏ or ㅗ.

| Ex. | **찾다** (to look for, to find): 찾 (verb stem) + -아 (ending) → 찾아
만나다 (to meet): 만나 (verb stem) + -아 (ending) → 만나
(When ㅏ and ㅏ are connected, they are contracted to a single ㅏ.)
좋다 (to be good): 좋 (adjective stem) + -아 (ending) → 좋아
오다 (to come): 오 (verb stem) + -아 (ending) → 와
(When ㅗ and ㅏ are connected, the vowel is contracted to ㅘ.)

❸ The ending -어:

-어 is attached to stems that do not end in 하 or whose final vowels are not ㅏ or ㅗ.

| Ex. | **먹다** (to eat): 먹 (verb stem) + -어 (ending) → 먹어
입다 (to wear): 입 (verb stem) + -어 (ending) → 입어
마시다 (to drink): 마시 (verb stem) + -어 (ending) → 마셔
(When ㅣ and ㅓ are connected, the vowel is contracted to ㅕ.)
줄다 (to decrease): 줄 (verb stem) + -어 (ending) → 줄어
주다 (to give): 주 (verb stem) + -어 (ending) → 줘
(When ㅜ and ㅓ are connected, the vowel is contracted to ㅝ.)

2. If the inflecting word ends in ㅡ or ㄹ, the ㅡ or ㄹ is omitted when followed by the following endings:

❶ ㅡ omission:

ㅡ is omitted when followed by -아/어.

| Ex. | **바쁘다** (to be busy): 바쁘 (adjective stem) + -아 (ending) → 바빠 (ㅡ is omitted.)
cf.) 바쁘 (adjective stem) + -고 (ending) → 바쁘고
(ㅡ is not omitted before consonants.)
쓰다 (to write): 쓰 (verb stem) + -어 (ending) → 써 (ㅡ is omitted.)
cf.) 쓰 (verb stem) + -면 (ending) → 쓰면 (ㅡ is not omitted before consonants.)

❷ ㄹ omission:

ㄹ is omitted when followed by endings beginning in ㄴ, ㅂ, or ㅅ.

| Ex. | **살다** (to live): 살 (verb stem) + -는 (ending) → 사는 (ㄹ is omitted.)
살 (verb stem) + -ㅂ니다 (ending) → 삽니다 (ㄹ is omitted.)
살 (verb stem) + -세요 (ending) → 사세요 (ㄹ is omitted.)
cf.) 살 (verb stem) + -고 (ending) → 살고
(ㄹ is not omitted before endings beginning in consonants other than ㄴ, ㅂ, or ㅅ.)
살 (verb stem) + -아요 (ending) → 살아요 (ㄹ is not omitted before vowels.)

★ Stems that end in ㄹ cannot combine with those that begin with -으-.

| Ex. | **살다** (to live): 살 (verb stem) + -면 (ending) → 살면 (O)
살 (verb stem) + -으면 (ending) → 살으면 (X)
(으 cannot follow 살.)
살 (verb stem) + -ㄴ (ending) → 산 (O)
살 (verb stem) + -은 (ending) → 살은 (X)
(으 cannot follow 살.)

Conjugation of Irregular Inflecting Words

When an irregular inflecting word stem and an ending are connected, the word is conjugated differently than the conjugation of regular inflecting verbs. The following are examples of the general patterns by which irregular inflecting words are conjugated.

1. Examples showing pairs of inflecting words that have the same ending in the stem but as irregular words are conjugated differently:

	Regular Conjugations	Irregular Conjugations
When the final letter of the stem is ㄷ	**닫다** (to close): 문을 닫아요. **받다** (to receive): 선물을 받아요. (The final letter ㄷ does not change when conjugating.)	**듣다** (to listen): 음악을 들어요. **걷다** (to walk): 길을 걸어요. (The final letter ㄷ changes to ㄹ when conjugating and both the spelling and pronunciation change.)
When the final letter of the stem is ㅂ	**입다** (to wear): 옷을 입어요. **좁다** (to be narrow): 길이 좁아요. (The final letter ㅂ does not change when conjugating.)	**줍다** (to pick up): 길에서 돈을 주웠어요. **쉽다** (to be easy): 한국어 공부가 쉬워요. (The final letter ㅂ changes to 우 when conjugating and both the spelling and pronunciation change.)
When the final letter of the stem is ㅅ	**웃다** (to smile): 크게 웃어요. **씻다** (to wash): 손을 씻어요. (The final letter ㅅ does not change when conjugating.)	**짓다** (to build): 건물을 지어요. **낫다** (to be cured): 감기가 나았어요. (The final letter ㅅ is dropped when conjugating and both the spelling and pronunciation change.)
When the final letter of the stem is 르	**들르다** (to stop by): 친구 집에 잠깐 들렀어요. **따르다** (to follow): 친구를 따라 갔어요. (ㄹ is not added to the stem when conjugating and only ㅡ is dropped.)	**누르다** (to press): 버튼을 눌러요. **다르다** (to be different): 성격이 달라요. (The ㅡ part of the stem is dropped when conjugating and ㄹ is added and both the spelling and pronunciation change.)
When the final letter of the stem is ㅎ	**넣다** (to insert): 물건을 가방에 넣어요. **좋다** (to be good): 날씨가 좋아요. (The final letter ㅎ does not change when conjugating.)	**그렇다** (to be that way): 정말 그래요. **하얗다** (to be white): 눈이 하얘요. (The final letter ㅎ drops out and the ending vowel becomes ㅐ or ㅒ and both the spelling and pronunciation change.)

2. Either the stem or the ending of irregular inflecting words change in the following ways:

❶ ㄷ irregular conjugation:

The ㄷ at the end of the stem is changed to ㄹ when followed by a vowel.

| Ex. | 듣다 (to listen)

(1) before a consonant	(2) before the vowels -아/어	(3) before the vowel -으
듣 + -고 → 듣고 듣 + -지 → 듣지 듣 + -니 → 듣니	듣 + -어요 → 들어요 듣 + -어서 → 들어서 듣 + -어도 → 들어도	듣 + -은 → 들은 듣 + -을 → 들을 듣 + -으면 → 들으면

Changed only before vowels

❷ ㅂ irregular conjugation:

The ㅂ at the end of the stem is changed to 우 when followed by a vowel.

| Ex. | **덥다** (to be hot)

(1) before a consonant	(2) before the vowels -아/어	(3) before the vowel -으
덥 + -고 → 덥고	덥 + -어요 → 더워요	덥 + -은 → 더운
덥 + -지 → 덥지	덥 + -어서 → 더워서	덥 + -을 → 더울
덥 + -니 → 덥니	덥 + -어도 → 더워도	덥 + -으면 → 더우면

Changed only before vowels

| Exception | The verb 돕다 and the adjective 곱다 conjugate with 오 instead of 우 in front of -아/어.

(1) before a consonant	(2) before the vowels -아/어	(3) before the vowel -으
돕 + -고 → 돕고	돕 + -아요 → 도와요	돕 + -은 → 도운
돕 + -지 → 돕지	돕 + -아서 → 도와서	돕 + -을 → 도울
돕 + -니 → 돕니	돕 + -아도 → 도와도	돕 + -으면 → 도우면

Changed only before -아/어

❸ ㅅ irregular conjugation:

The ㅅ at the end of the stem is omitted when followed by a vowel.

| Ex. | **짓다** (to build)

(1) before a consonant	(2) before the vowels -아/어	(3) before the vowel -으
짓 + -고 → 짓고	짓 + -어요 → 지어요	짓 + -은 → 지은
짓 + -지 → 짓지	짓 + -어서 → 지어서	짓 + -을 → 지을
짓 + -니 → 짓니	짓 + -어도 → 지어도	짓 + -으면 → 지으면

Changed only before vowels

❹ 르 irregular conjugation:

In front of a vowel, the ㅡ of the final 르 of the stem is omitted and another ㄹ is attached to the stem.

| Ex. | **모르다** (to not know): 모르 (verb stem) + -아요 (ending)

→ 모ㄹ (ㅡ is omitted) + ㄹ (ㄹ is added) + -아요 (ending) → 몰라요

(1) before a consonant	(2) before the vowels -아/어	(3) before the vowel -으
모르 + -고 → 모르고	모르 + -아요 → 몰라요	
모르 + -지 → 모르지	모르 + -아서 → 몰라서	
모르 + -니 → 모르니	모르 + -아도 → 몰라도	

Changed only in front of -아/어

Because there is no final consonant in the 르 irregular verbs, it cannot combine with endings beginning with -으-.

❺ ㅎ irregular conjugation:

The ㅎ at the end of the stem is omitted before endings beginning with vowels, ㄴ, or ㅁ. However, if the following ending is -아/어, ㅎ is omitted and the conjugated vowel changes to ㅐ or ㅒ.

| Ex. | **그렇다** (to be that way)

(1) before a consonant	(2) before the vowels -아/어	(3) before the vowel -으
그렇 + -고 → 그렇고 그렇 + -지 → 그렇지 그렇 + -니 → 그러니	그렇 + -어요 → 그래요 그렇 + -어서 → 그래서 그렇 + -어도 → 그래도	그렇 + -은 → 그런 그렇 + -을 → 그럴 그렇 + -으면 → 그러면
Changed only in front of endings beginning with ㄴ	Changed only in front of the vowels -아/어	Changed only before vowels and endings beginning with ㅁ

★ Short Irregular Word List

ㄷ irregular	ㅂ irregular	ㅅ irregular	르 irregular	ㅎ irregular
듣다 (to listen)	**돕다** (to help)	**짓다** (to build)	**모르다** (to not know)	**파랗다** (to be blue)
걷다 (to walk)	**줍다** (to pick up)	**낫다** (to be cured)	**고르다** (to choose)	**빨갛다** (to be red)
묻다 (to ask)	**굽다** (to roast)	**붓다** (to swell up)	**부르다** (to call)	**노랗다** (to be yellow)
싣다 (to load)	**덥다** (to be hot)	**잇다** (to connect)	**흐르다** (to flow)	**까맣다** (to be black)
깨닫다 (to realize)	**어렵다** (to be difficult)	**긋다** (to draw)	**빠르다** (to be fast)	**하얗다** (to be white)

Conjugation Charts

In Korean, verbs, adjectives, and 이다 change form when grammatical endings are attached to the stem. This is known as conjugation. The conjugations are laid out below. There are grammatical endings that do not change regardless of whether what precedes is a verb or adjective. On the other hand, some endings do change.

I. Grammatical endings that do not change form based on whether what precedes is a verb or adjective

There are three main types of grammatical endings that do not change form based on whether what precedes is a verb or adjective.

- Grammatical endings beginning with ㄱ, ㄷ, ㅈ that are attached to the stems of verbs, adjectives and 이다

	Condition	Example	-지만 P. 22		-고 P. 34		-거나 P. 38		-든지 P. 102		-기 때문에 P. 118		-기는 하지만 P. 218	
			Present	-았/었-	Present	-았/었-	Present	-았/었-	Present	-았/었-	Present	-았/었-	Present	-았/었-
Verbs	Vowel ending	보다	보지만	봤지만	보고	봤고	보거나	봤거나	보든지	봤든지	보기 때문에	봤기 때문에	보기는 하지만	보기는 했지만
	Consonant ending	먹다	먹지만	먹었지만	먹고	먹었고	먹거나	먹었거나	먹든지	먹었든지	먹기 때문에	먹었기 때문에	먹기는 하지만	먹기는 했지만
	으 omission	쓰다	쓰지만	*썼지만	쓰고	*썼고	쓰거나	*썼거나	쓰든지	*썼든지	쓰기 때문에	*썼기 때문에	쓰기는 하지만	쓰기는 했지만
	ㄹ omission	살다	살지만	살았지만	살고	살았고	살거나	살았거나	살든지	살았든지	살기 때문에	살았기 때문에	살기는 하지만	살기는 했지만
	ㄷ irregular	듣다	듣지만	*들었지만	듣고	*들었고	듣거나	*들었거나	듣든지	*들었든지	듣기 때문에	*들었기 때문에	듣기는 하지만	듣기는 했지만
	ㅂ irregular	돕다	돕지만	*도왔지만	돕고	*도왔고	돕거나	*도왔거나	돕든지	*도왔든지	돕기 때문에	*도왔기 때문에	돕기는 하지만	돕기는 했지만
	ㅅ irregular	짓다	짓지만	*지었지만	짓고	*지었고	짓거나	*지었거나	짓든지	*지었든지	짓기 때문에	*지었기 때문에	짓기는 하지만	짓기는 했지만
	르 irregular	모르다	모르지만	*몰랐지만	모르고	*몰랐고	모르거나	*몰랐거나	모르든지	*몰랐든지	모르기 때문에	*몰랐기 때문에	모르기는 하지만	모르기는 했지만
	있다/없다 to exist/not exist	있다	있지만	있었지만	있고	있었고	있거나	있었거나	있든지	있었든지	있기 때문에	있었기 때문에	있기는 하지만	있기는 했지만
Adjectives	Vowel ending	편하다	편하지만	편했지만	편하고	편했고	편하거나	편했거나	편하든지	편했든지	편하기 때문에	편했기 때문에	편하기는 하지만	편하기는 했지만
	Consonant ending	좋다	좋지만	좋았지만	좋고	좋았고	좋거나	좋았거나	좋든지	좋았든지	좋기 때문에	좋았기 때문에	좋기는 하지만	좋기는 했지만
	으 omission	바쁘다	바쁘지만	*바빴지만	바쁘고	*바빴고	바쁘거나	*바빴거나	바쁘든지	*바빴든지	바쁘기 때문에	*바빴기 때문에	바쁘기는 하지만	바쁘기는 했지만
	ㄹ omission	길다	길지만	길었지만	길고	길었고	길거나	길었거나	길든지	길었든지	길기 때문에	길었기 때문에	길기는 하지만	길기는 했지만
	ㅂ irregular	어렵다	어렵지만	*어려웠지만	어렵고	*어려웠고	어렵거나	*어려웠거나	어렵든지	*어려웠든지	어렵기 때문에	*어려웠기 때문에	어렵기는 하지만	어렵기는 했지만
	르 irregular	다르다	다르지만	*달랐지만	다르고	*달랐고	다르거나	*달랐거나	다르든지	*달랐든지	다르기 때문에	*달랐기 때문에	다르기는 하지만	다르기는 했지만
	'이다' to be	남자(이)다	남자지만	남자였지만	남자고	남자였고	남자거나	남자였거나	남자든지	남자였든지	남자기 때문에	남자였기 때문에	남자기는 하지만	남자기는 했지만
	'이다' to be	사람이다	사람이지만	사람이었지만	사람이고	사람이었고	사람이거나	사람이었거나	사람이든지	사람이었든지	사람이기 때문에	사람이었기 때문에	사람이기는 하지만	사람이기는 했지만

* See pages 293~295 for more detailed explanations of irregular verb conjugations.
** -게 되다 attaches to both verb and adjective stems. 'Nouns+이다' become 'Noun이/가 되다'.

1. Endings beginning with consonants

❶ Grammatical endings beginning with ㄱ, ㄷ, ㅈ

Grammatical endings that begin with ㄱ, ㄷ, or ㅈ are attached to the stem of the verb, regardless of whether it ends in a vowel or consonant. They do not change even after irregular verbs. However, there are many irregularities if -았/었- is attached.

I wonder

Grammatical endings marked with -다 (ex. -게 되다, -고 있다, etc.) can be used in both speech and writing.

Grammatical endings ending in -요 (ex. -거든요, -지요, etc.) can only be used in speech.

Be careful

Keep in mind which endings can be attached to verbs, adjectives, and 이다; and, which can be attached exclusively to verbs.

Keep in mind which endings can and cannot be attached to -았/었-; and, if they can, to where they attach.

-던 P. 230		-다가 P. 242		-지요 P. 74		-거든요 P. 122		-겠- P. 146		-잖아요 P. 182		-게 되다 P. 114	
Present	'-았/었-'	Present	'-았/었-'	Present	'-았/었-'	Present	'-았/었-'	Present	'-았/었-'	Present	'-았/었-'	Present	'-았/었-'
보던	봤던	보다가	봤다가	보지요	봤지요	보거든요	봤거든요	보겠어요	봤겠어요	보잖아요	봤잖아요	보게 돼요	보게 됐어요
먹던	먹었던	먹다가	먹었다가	먹지요	먹었지요	먹거든요	먹었거든요	먹겠어요	먹었겠어요	먹잖아요	먹었잖아요	먹게 돼요	먹게 됐어요
쓰던	★썼던	쓰다가	*썼다가	쓰지요	*썼지요	쓰거든요	*썼거든요	쓰겠어요	*썼겠어요	쓰잖아요	*썼잖아요	쓰게 돼요	쓰게 됐어요
살던	살았던	살다가	살았다가	살지요	살았지요	살거든요	살았거든요	살겠어요	살았겠어요	살잖아요	살았잖아요	살게 돼요	살게 됐어요
듣던	*들었던	듣다가	*들었다가	듣지요	*들었지요	듣거든요	*들었거든요	듣겠어요	*들었겠어요	듣잖아요	*들었잖아요	듣게 돼요	듣게 됐어요
돕던	*도왔던	돕다가	*도왔다가	돕지요	*도왔지요	돕거든요	*도왔거든요	돕겠어요	*도왔겠어요	돕잖아요	*도왔잖아요	돕게 돼요	돕게 됐어요
짓던	★지었던	짓다가	*지었다가	짓지요	*지었지요	짓거든요	*지었거든요	짓겠어요	*지었겠어요	짓잖아요	*지었잖아요	짓게 돼요	짓게 됐어요
모르던	★몰랐던	모르다가	*몰랐다가	모르지요	*몰랐지요	모르거든요	*몰랐거든요	모르겠어요	*몰랐겠어요	모르잖아요	*몰랐잖아요	모르게 돼요	모르게 됐어요
있던	있었던	있다가	있었다가	있지요	있었지요	있거든요	있었거든요	있겠어요	있었겠어요	있잖아요	있었잖아요	있게 돼요	있게 됐어요
편하던	편했던	편하다가	편했다가	편하지요	편했지요	편하거든요	편했거든요	편하겠어요	편했겠어요	편하잖아요	편했잖아요	편하게 돼요	편하게 됐어요
좋던	좋았던	좋다가	좋았다가	좋지요	좋았지요	좋거든요	좋았거든요	좋겠어요	좋았겠어요	좋잖아요	좋았잖아요	좋게 돼요	좋게 됐어요
바쁘던	★바빴던	바쁘다가	*바빴다가	바쁘지요	*바빴지요	바쁘거든요	*바빴거든요	바쁘겠어요	*바빴겠어요	바쁘잖아요	*바빴잖아요	바쁘게 돼요	바쁘게 됐어요
길던	길었던	길다가	길었다가	길지요	길었지요	길거든요	길었거든요	길겠어요	길었겠어요	길잖아요	길었잖아요	길게 돼요	길게 됐어요
어렵던	★어려웠던	어렵다가	*어려웠다가	어렵지요	*어려웠지요	어렵거든요	*어려웠거든요	어렵겠어요	*어려웠겠어요	어렵잖아요	*어려웠잖아요	어렵게 돼요	어렵게 됐어요
다르던	★달랐던	다르다가	*달랐다가	다르지요	*달랐지요	다르거든요	*달랐거든요	다르겠어요	*달랐겠어요	다르잖아요	*달랐잖아요	다르게 돼요	다르게 됐어요
남자던	남자였던	남자다가	남자였다가	남자지요	남자였지요	남자거든요	남자였거든요	남자겠어요	남자였겠어요	남자잖아요	남자였잖아요	**남자가 돼요	**남자가 됐어요
사람이던	사람이었던	사람이다가	사람이었다가	사람이지요	사람이었지요	사람이거든요	사람이었거든요	사람이겠어요	사람이었겠어요	사람이잖아요	사람이었잖아요	**사람이 돼요	**사람이 됐어요

- Grammatical endings beginning with ㄱ, ㄷ, ㅈ that are attached to the stems of verbs, adjectives, and 이다, but are not attached to -았/었-

	Condition	Example	-기는요 P. 118
Verbs	Vowel ending	보다	보기는요
	Consonant ending	먹다	먹기는요
	으 omission	쓰다	쓰기는요
	ㄹ omission	살다	살기는요
	ㄷ irregular	듣다	듣기는요
	ㅂ irregular	돕다	돕기는요
	ㅅ irregular	짓다	짓기는요
	르 irregular	부르다	부르기는요
	있다/없다 to exist/not exist	있다	있기는요
Adjectives	Vowel ending	편하다	편하기는요
	Consonant ending	좋다	좋기는요
	으 omission	바쁘다	바쁘기는요
	ㄹ omission	길다	길기는요
	ㅂ irregular	어렵다	어렵기는요
	르 irregular	다르다	다르기는요
	'이다' to be	남자(이)다	남자기는요
	'이다' to be	사람이다	사람이기는요

- Grammatical endings beginning with ㄱ, ㄷ, ㅈ that are attached only to verb stems

	Condition	Example	-기로 하다 P. 54		-고 있다 P. 90		-기 쉽다/어렵다 P. 114		-지 그래요? P. 122		-곤 하다 P. 230	
			Present	'-았/었-'	Present	'-았/었-'	Present	'-았/었-'	Present	'-았/었-'	Present	'-았/었-'
Verbs	Vowel ending	보다	보기로 해요	보기로 했어요	보고 있어요	보고 있었어요	보기 쉬워요	보기 쉬웠어요	보지 그래요?	보지 그랬어요?	보곤 해요	보곤 했어요
	Consonant ending	먹다	먹기로 해요	먹기로 했어요	먹고 있어요	먹고 있었어요	먹기 쉬워요	먹기 쉬웠어요	먹지 그래요?	먹지 그랬어요?	먹곤 해요	먹곤 했어요
	으 omission	쓰다	쓰기로 해요	쓰기로 했어요	쓰고 있어요	쓰고 있었어요	쓰기 쉬워요	쓰기 쉬웠어요	쓰지 그래요	쓰지 그랬어요?	쓰곤 해요	쓰곤 했어요
	ㄹ omission	살다	살기로 해요	살기로 했어요	살고 있어요	살고 있었어요	살기 쉬워요	살기 쉬웠어요	살지 그래요?	살지 그랬어요?	살곤 해요	살곤 했어요
	ㄷ irregular	듣다	듣기로 해요	듣기로 했어요	듣고 있어요	듣고 있었어요	듣기 쉬워요	듣기 쉬웠어요	듣지 그래요?	듣지 그랬어요?	듣곤 해요	듣곤 했어요
	ㅂ irregular	돕다	돕기로 해요	돕기로 했어요	돕고 있어요	돕고 있었어요	돕기 쉬워요	돕기 쉬웠어요	돕지 그래요?	돕지 그랬어요?	돕곤 해요	돕곤 했어요
	ㅅ irregular	짓다	짓기로 해요	짓기로 했어요	짓고 있어요	짓고 있었어요	짓기 쉬워요	짓기 쉬웠어요	짓지 그래요?	짓지 그랬어요?	짓곤 해요	짓곤 했어요
	르 irregular	부르다	부르기로 해요	부르기로 했어요	부르고 있어요	부르고 있었어요	부르기 쉬워요	부르기 쉬웠어요	부르지 그래요?	부르지 그랬어요?	부르곤 해요	부르곤 했어요

- Grammatical endings beginning with ㄱ, ㄷ, ㅈ that are attached only to verb stems, but are not attached to -았/었-

	Condition	Example	-기 전에 P. 42	-자마자 P. 70	-도록 P. 186	-다가 P. 242
Verbs	Vowel ending	보다	보기 전에	보자마자	보도록	보다가
	Consonant ending	먹다	먹기 전에	먹자마자	먹도록	먹다가
	으 omission	쓰다	쓰기 전에	쓰자마자	쓰도록	쓰다가
	ㄹ omission	살다	살기 전에	살자마자	살도록	살다가
	ㄷ irregular	듣다	듣기 전에	듣자마자	듣도록	듣다가
	ㅂ irregular	돕다	돕기 전에	돕자마자	돕도록	돕다가
	ㅅ irregular	짓다	짓기 전에	짓자마자	짓도록	짓다가
	르 irregular	부르다	부르기 전에	부르자마자	부르도록	부르다가

❷ Grammatical endings that begin with ㄴ

When grammatical endings that begin with ㄴ follow stems that end in ㄹ, ㄹ is omitted under the influence of ㄴ (Ex. 살 + 네요 → 사네요).

- Grammatical endings beginning with ㄴ that are attached to the stems of verbs, adjectives, and 이다

	Condition	Example	-네요 P. 106	
			Present	'-았/었-'
Verbs	Vowel ending	보다	보네요	봤네요
	Consonant ending	먹다	먹네요	먹었네요
	으 omission	쓰다	쓰네요	*썼네요
	ㄹ omission	살다	*사네요	살았네요
	ㄷ irregular	듣다	듣네요	*들었네요
	ㅂ irregular	돕다	돕네요	*도왔네요
	ㅅ irregular	짓다	짓네요	*지었네요
	르 irregular	부르다	부르네요	*불렀네요
Adjectives	Vowel ending	편하다	편하네요	편했네요
	Consonant ending	작다	작네요	작았네요
	으 omission	바쁘다	바쁘네요	*바빴네요
	ㄹ omission	길다	*기네요	길었네요
	ㅂ irregular	어렵다	어렵네요	*어려웠네요
	르 irregular	다르다	다르네요	*달랐네요
	'이다' to be	남자(이)다	남자네요	남자였네요
	'이다' to be	사람이다	사람이네요	사람이었네요

* See pages 293–295 for more detailed explanations of irregular verb conjugations.

- Grammatical endings beginning with ㄴ that are attached only to verb stems, but are not attached to -았/었-

	Condition	Example	-는 게 어때요? P. 58	-는 게 좋겠다 P. 58	-는 동안에 P. 130	-는 대로 P. 138	-느라고 P. 234
Verbs	Vowel ending	보다	보는 게 어때요?	보는 게 좋겠어요	보는 동안에	보는 대로	보느라고
	Consonant ending	먹다	먹는 게 어때요?	먹는 게 좋겠어요	먹는 동안에	먹는 대로	먹느라고
	으 omission	쓰다	쓰는 게 어때요?	쓰는 게 좋겠어요	쓰는 동안에	쓰는 대로	쓰느라고
	ㄹ omission	살다	*사는 게 어때요?	*사는 게 좋겠어요	*사는 동안에	*사는 대로	*사느라고
	ㄷ irregular	듣다	듣는 게 어때요?	듣는 게 좋겠어요	듣는 동안에	듣는 대로	듣느라고
	ㅂ irregular	돕다	돕는 게 어때요?	돕는 게 좋겠어요	돕는 동안에	돕는 대로	돕느라고
	ㅅ irregular	짓다	짓는 게 어때요?	짓는 게 좋겠어요	짓는 동안에	짓는 대로	짓느라고
	르 irregular	부르다	부르는 게 어때요?	부르는 게 좋겠어요	부르는 동안에	부르는 대로	부르느라고

* See pages 293–295 for more detailed explanations of irregular verb conjugations.

2. Grammatical endings beginning with -아/어-

Grammatical endings that begin with -아/어- conjugate the same as -아/어요. If the verb or adjective stem ends in 하, 하 becomes 해. Furthermore, if the final vowel in the stem is ㅏ or ㅗ, -아- is what attaches, otherwise -어- is what attaches. Keep the irregularity of verbs ending in 르 before -았/었- in mind!

- **Grammatical endings beginning with -아/어- are attached to the stems of verbs, adjectives, and 이다**

	Condition	Example	-아/어도 P. 150		-아/어도 되다 P. 98		-아/어야 되다 P. 98		-아/어야지요 P. 170, P. 246		-아/어야 했는데 P. 246	
			Present	-았/었-	Present	-았/었-	Present	-았/었-	Present	-았/었-	Present	-았/었-
Verbs	Stem ends in 하	일하다	일해도	일했어도	일해도 돼요	일해도 됐어요	일해야 돼요	일해야 됐어요	일해야지요	일했어야 지요	일해야 했는데	일했어야 했는데
	***ㅏ	만나다	만나도	만났어도	만나도 돼요	만나도 됐어요	만나야 돼요	만나야 됐어요	만나야지요	만났어야 지요	만나야 했는데	만났어야 했는데
	***ㅗ	보다	봐도	봤어도	봐도 돼요	봐도 됐어요	봐야 돼요	봐야 됐어요	봐야지요	봤어야 지요	봐야 했는데	봤어야 했는데
	***ㅓ	먹다	먹어도	먹었어도	먹어도 돼요	먹어도 됐어요	먹어야 돼요	먹어야 됐어요	먹어야지요	먹었어야 지요	먹어야 했는데	먹었어야 했는데
	***ㅣ	마시다	마셔도	마셨어도	마셔도 돼요	마셔도 됐어요	마셔야 돼요	마셔야 됐어요	마셔야지요	마셨어야 지요	마셔야 했는데	마셨어야 했는데
	***ㅜ	주다	줘도	줬어도	줘도 돼요	줘도 됐어요	줘야 돼요	줘야 됐어요	줘야지요	줬어야 지요	줘야 했는데	줬어야 했는데
	으 omission	쓰다	*써도	*썼어도	*써도 돼요	*써도 됐어요	*써야 돼요	*써야 됐어요	*써야지요	*썼어야 지요	*써야 했는데	*썼어야 했는데
	ㄹ omission	살다	살아도	살았어도	살아도 돼요	살아도 됐어요	살아야 돼요	살아야 됐어요	살아야지요	살았어야 지요	살아야 했는데	살았어야 했는데
	ㄷ irregular	듣다	*들어도	*들었어도	*들어도 돼요	*들어도 됐어요	*들어야 돼요	*들어야 됐어요	*들어야 지요	*들었어야 지요	*들어야 했는데	*들었어야 했는데
	ㅂ irregular	돕다	*도와도	*도왔어도	*도와도 돼요	*도와도 됐어요	*도와야 돼요	*도와야 됐어요	*도와야지 요	*도왔어야 지요	*도와야 했는데	*도왔어야 했는데
	ㅅ irregular	짓다	*지어도	*지었어도	*지어도 돼요	*지어도 됐어요	*지어야 돼요	*지어야 됐어요	*지어야 지요	*지었어야 지요	*지어야 했는데	*지었어야 했는데
	르 irregular	모르다	*몰라도	*몰랐어도	*몰라도 돼요	*몰라도 됐어요	*몰라야 돼요	*몰라야 됐어요	*몰라야 지요	*몰랐어야 지요	*몰라야 했는데	*몰랐어야 했는데
Adjectives	Ends in 하	편하다	편해도	편했어도	편해도 돼요	편해도 됐어요	불편해야 돼요	불편해야 됐어요	편해야지요	편했어야 지요	편해야 했는데	편했어야 했는데
	***ㅏ	비싸다	비싸도	비쌌어도	비싸도 돼요	비싸도 됐어요	비싸야 돼요	비싸야 됐어요	비싸야 지요	비쌌어야 지요	비싸야 했는데	비쌌어야 했는데
	***ㅗ	많다	많아도	많았어도	많아도 돼요	많아도 됐어요	많아야 돼요	많아야 됐어요	많아야지요	많았어야 지요	많아야 했는데	많았어야 했는데
	으 omission	바쁘다	*바빠도	*바빴어도	*바빠도 돼요	*바빠도 됐어요	*바빠야 돼요	*바빠야 됐어요	*바빠야 지요	*바빴어야 지요	*바빠야 했는데	*바빴어야 했는데
	ㄹ omission	길다	길어도	길었어도	길어도 돼요	길어도 됐어요	길어야 돼요	길어야 됐어요	길어야지요	길었어야 지요	길어야 했는데	길었어야 했는데
	ㅂ irregular	어렵다	*어려워도	*어려웠어도	*어려워도 돼요	*어려워도 됐어요	*어려워야 돼요	*어려워야 됐어요	*어려워야 지요	*어려웠어야 지요	*어려워야 했는데	*어려웠어야 했는데
	르 irregular	다르다	*달라도	*달랐어도	*달라도 돼요	*달라도 됐어요	*달라야 돼요	*달라야 됐어요	*달라야 지요	*달랐어야 지요	*달라야 했는데	*달랐어야 했는데
	'이다' to be	남자(이)다	*남자라도	남자였어도	**남자라도 돼요	**남자라도 됐어요	남자여야 돼요	남자여야 됐어요	남자여야 지요	남자였어야 지요	남자여야 했는데	남자였어야 했는데
	'이다' to be	사람이다	*사람이라도	사람이었어도	**사람이라 도 돼요	**사람이라 도 됐어요	사람이어야 돼요	사람이어야 됐어요	사람이어야 지요	사람이었어야 지요	사람이어야 했는데	사람이었어야 했는데

★ See pages 293-295 for more detailed explanations of irregular verb conjugations.

★★ If 아/어도 is attached to a noun+이다, it becomes noun+(이)라도. However, if -았/었- is attached, it becomes -였어도/이었어도.

★★★ Each vowel refers to the vowel of the final letter in the stem. For example, the verb 마시다 has two vowels ㅏ and ㅣ in the stem (마시), but the vowel of the final letter in the stem is ㅣ.

● Grammatical endings beginning with -아/어- are attached to verb stems, but are not to -았/었-

	Condition	Example	-아/어서 P. 54	-아/어 줄까요? P. 86	-아/어 주시겠어요? P. 66	-아/어야겠다 P. 170
Verbs	Stem ends in 하	일하다	일해서	일해 줄까요?	일해 주시겠어요?	일해야겠어요
	*** ㅏ	가다	가서	가 줄까요?	가 주시겠어요?	가야겠어요
	*** ㅗ	보다	봐서	봐 줄까요?	봐 주시겠어요?	봐야겠어요
	*** ㅓ	읽다	읽어서	읽어 줄까요?	읽어 주시겠어요?	읽어야겠어요
	*** ㅣ	기다리다	기다려서	기다려 줄까요?	기다려 주시겠어요?	기다려야겠어요
	*** ㅜ	춤을 추다	춤을 춰서	춤을 춰 줄까요?	춤을 춰 주시겠어요?	춤을 춰야겠어요
	으 omission	쓰다	*써서	*써 줄까요?	*써 주시겠어요?	*써야겠어요
	ㄹ omission	놀다	놀아서	놀아 줄까요?	놀아 주시겠어요?	놀아야겠어요
	ㄷ irregular	듣다	*들어서	*들어 줄까요?	*들어 주시겠어요?	*들어야겠어요
	ㅂ irregular	돕다	*도와서	*도와 줄까요?	*도와 주시겠어요?	*도와야겠어요
	ㅅ irregular	짓다	*지어서	*지어 줄까요?	*지어 주시겠어요?	*지어야겠어요
	르 irregular	부르다	*불러서	*불러 줄까요?	*불러 주시겠어요?	*불러야겠어요

* See pages 293-295 for more detailed explanations of irregular verb conjugations.

*** Each vowel refers to the vowel of the final letter in the stem.

● Grammatical endings beginning with -아/어- that are attached only to adjective stems

	Condition	Example	-아/어지다 P. 150		-아/어 보이다 P. 178	
			Present	'-았/었-'	Present	'-았/었-'
Verbs	Stem ends in 하	유명하다	유명해져요	유명해졌어요	유명해 보여요	유명해 보였어요
	*** ㅏ	비싸다	비싸져요	비싸졌어요	비싸 보여요	비싸 보였어요
	*** ㅗ	많다	많아져요	많아졌어요	많아 보여요	많아 보였어요
	으 omission	바쁘다	*바빠져요	*바빠졌어요	*바빠 보여요	*바빠 보였어요
	ㄹ irregular	길다	길어져요	길어졌어요	길어 보여요	길어 보였어요
	ㅂ irregular	어렵다	*어려워져요	*어려워졌어요	*어려워 보여요	*어려워 보였어요
	르 irregular	다르다	*달라져요	*달라졌어요	*달라 보여요	*달라 보였어요

* See pages 293-295 for more detailed explanations of irregular verb conjugations.

*** Each vowel refers to the vowel of the final letter in the stem.

● The Resultative -아/어 있다: Expressing the continuation of a state after a change or an action

-아/어 있다 P. 102							
살다 to live	살아 있다 to be alive	켜지다 to be turned on	불이 켜져 있다 to be turned on	쓰이다 to be written	책에 이름이 쓰여 있다 to be written	떨어지다 to fall	바닥에 쓰레기가 떨어져 있다 to have fallen
죽다 to die	죽어 있다 to be dead	꺼지다 to be turned off	불이 꺼져 있다 to be turned off	그려지다 to be drawn	종이에 그림이 그려져 있다 to be drawn	빠지다 to be dropped	물 속에 젓가락이 빠져 있다 to be dropped
가다 to go	가 있다 to be gone	열리다 to be opened	문이 열려 있다 to be opened	걸리다 to hang	벽에 시계가 걸려 있다 to be hung	부러지다 (for something sticklike) to break	연필이 부러져 있다 (for something sticklike) to be dropped
오다 to come	와 있다 to have arrived	닫히다 to be closed	문이 닫혀 있다 to be closed	달리다 to hang	옷에 단추가 달려 있다 to be hung	깨지다 (for something glass or ceramic) to break	컵이 깨져 있다 (for something glass or ceramic) to be broken
앉다 to sit	앉아 있다 to be sitting	놓이다 to be put down	책상 위에 책이 놓여 있다 to be put down	붙이다 to be stuck on	벽에 종이가 붙어 있다 to be stuck on	찢어지다 to be ripped	옷이 찢어져 있다 to be ripped
서다 to stand	서 있다 to be standing		*가방 안에 책이 들어 있다 to be placed in	새겨지다 to be engraved	반지에 글자가 새겨져 있다 to be engraved	구겨지다 to be crumpled	종이가 구겨져 있다 to be crumpled

3. Grammatical endings beginning with -(으)-

When grammatical endings beginning with -(으)- follow stems that end with vowels, -으- is omitted.

- **Grammatical endings beginning with -(으)- that are attached to the stems of verbs, adjectives, and 이다**

	Condition	Example	-(으)ㄹ 때 P. 146		-(으)ㄹ까 봐 P. 166		-(으)ㄹ까요? P. 50 Conjecture		-(으)ㄹ지도 모르다 P. 198		-(으)ㄹ 테니까 P. 210	
			Present	'-았/었-'	Present	'-았/었-'	Present	'-았/었-'	Present	'-았/었-'	Present	'-았/었-'
Verbs	Vowel ending	보다	볼 때	봤을 때	볼까 봐	봤을까 봐	볼까요?	봤을까요?	볼지도 몰라요	봤을지도 몰라요	볼 테니까	봤을 테니까
	Consonant ending	먹다	먹을 때	먹었을 때	먹을까 봐	먹었을까 봐	먹을까요?	먹었을까요?	먹을지도 몰라요	먹었을지도 몰라요	먹을 테니까	먹었을 테니까
	으 omission	쓰다	쓸 때	*썼을 때	쓸까 봐	*썼을까 봐	쓸까요?	*썼을까요?	쓸지도 몰라요	*썼을지도 몰라요	쓸 테니까	*썼을 테니까
	ㄹ omission	살다	살 때	살았을 때	살까 봐	살았을까 봐	살까요?	살았을까요?	살지도 몰라요	살았을지도 몰라요	살 테니까	살았을 테니까
	ㄷ irregular	듣다	*들을 때	*들었을 때	*들을까 봐	*들었을 까 봐	*들을까요?	*들었을까요?	*들을지도 몰라요	*들었을지도 몰라요	*들을 테니까	*들었을 테니까
	ㅂ irregular	돕다	*도울 때	*도왔을 때	*도울까 봐	*도왔을 까 봐	*도울까요?	*도왔을까요?	*도울지도 몰라요	*도왔을지도 몰라요	*도울 테니까	*도왔을 테니까
	ㅅ irregular	짓다	*지을 때	*지었을 때	*지을까 봐	*지었을 까 봐	*지을까요?	*지었을까요?	*지을지도 몰라요	*지었을지도 몰라요	*지을 테니까	*지었을 테니까
	르 irregular	모르다	모를 때	*몰랐을 때	모를까 봐	*몰랐을 까 봐	모를까요?	*몰랐을까요?	모를지도 몰라요	*몰랐을지도 몰라요	모를 테니까	*몰랐을 테니까
Adjectives	Vowel ending	불편하다	불편할 때	불편했을 때	불편할까 봐	불편했을 까 봐	불편할까요?	불편했을 까요?	불편할지도 몰라요	불편했을지도 몰라요	불편할 테니까	불편했을 테니까
	Consonant ending	많다	많을 때	많았을 때	많을까 봐	많았을까 봐	많을까요?	많았을까요?	많을지도 몰라요	많았을지도 몰라요	많을 테니까	많았을 테니까
	으 omission	바쁘다	바쁠 때	*바빴을 때	바쁠까 봐	*바빴을 까 봐	바쁠까요?	*바빴을까요?	바쁠지도 몰라요	*바빴을지도 몰라요	바쁠 테니까	*바빴을 테니까
	ㄹ omission	길다	길 때	길었을 때	길까 봐	길었을까 봐	길까요?	길었을까요?	길지도 몰라요	길었을지도 몰라요	길 테니까	길었을 테니까
	ㅂ irregular	어렵다	*어려울 때	*어려웠을 때	*어려울까 봐	*어려웠을 까 봐	어려울까요?	*어려웠을 까요?	*어려울지도 몰라요	*어려웠을지 도 몰라요	*어려울 테니까	*어려웠을 테니까
	르 irregular	다르다	다를 때	*달랐을 때	다를까 봐	*달랐을 까 봐	다를까요?	*달랐을까요?	다를지도 몰라요	*달랐을지도 몰라요	다를 테니까	*달랐을 테니까
	'이다' to be	남자(이)다	남자일 때	남자였을 때	남자일까 봐	남자였을 까 봐	남자일까요?	남자였을 까요?	남자일지도 몰라요	남자였을지도 몰라요	남자일 테니까	남자였을 테니까
	'이다' to be	사람이다	사람일 때	사람이었을 때	사람일까 봐	사람이었을 까 봐	사람일까요?	사람이었을 까요?	사람일지도 몰라요	사람이었을지 도 몰라요	사람일 테니까	사람이었을 테니까

* See pages 293-295 for more detailed explanations of irregular verb conjugations.

-(으)ㄹ걸?: Conjecture P. 234		(으)ㄹ 텐데 P. 250		-(으)니까 P. 134 Reason P. 58		-(으)면 P. 66		-(으)면 좋겠다 P. 186		-(으)면 안 되다 P. 106	
Present	'-았/었-'	Present	'-았/었-'	Present	'-았/었-'	Present	'-았/었-'	Present	'-았/었-'	Present	'-았/었-'
볼걸?	봤을걸?	볼 텐데	봤을 텐데	보니까	봤으니까	보면	봤으면	보면 좋겠어요	봤으면 좋겠어요	보면 안 돼요	보면 안 됐어요
먹을걸?	먹었을걸?	먹을 텐데	먹었을 텐데	먹으니까	먹었으니까	먹으면	먹었으면	먹으면 좋겠어요	먹었으면 좋겠어요	먹으면 안 돼요	먹으면 안 됐어요
쓸걸?	*썼을걸?	쓸 텐데	*썼을 텐데	쓰니까	*썼으니까	쓰면	*썼으면	쓰면 좋겠어요	*썼으면 좋겠어요	쓰면 안 돼요	쓰면 안 됐어요
살걸?	살았을걸?	살 텐데	살았을 텐데	*사니까	살았으니까	살면	살았으면	살면 좋겠어요	살았으면 좋겠어요	살면 안 돼요	살면 안 됐어요
*들을걸?	*들었을걸?	*들을 텐데	*들었을 텐데	*들으니까	*들었으니까	*들으면	*들었으면	*들으면 좋겠어요	*들었으면 좋겠어요	*들으면 안 돼요	*들으면 안 됐어요
*도울걸?	*도왔을걸?	*도울 텐데	*도왔을 텐데	*도우니까	*도왔으니까	*도우면	*도왔으면	*도우면 좋겠어요	*도왔으면 좋겠어요	*도우면 안 돼요	*도우면 안 됐어요
*지을걸?	*지었을걸?	*지을 텐데	*지었을 텐데	*지으니까	*지었으니까	*지으면	*지었으면	*지으면 좋겠어요	*지었으면 좋겠어요	*지으면 안 돼요	*지으면 안 됐어요
모를걸?	*몰랐을걸?	모를 텐데	*몰랐을 텐데	모르니까	*몰랐으니까	모르면	*몰랐으면	모르면 좋겠어요	*몰랐으면 좋겠어요	모르면 안 돼요	모르면 안 됐어요
불편할걸?	불편했을걸?	불편할 텐데	불편했을 텐데	불편하니까	불편했으니까	불편하면	불편했으면	불편하면 좋겠어요	불편했으면 좋겠어요	불편하면 안 돼요	불편하면 안 됐어요
많을걸?	많았을걸?	많을 텐데	많았을 텐데	많으니까	많았으니까	많으면	많았으면	많으면 좋겠어요	많았으면 좋겠어요	많으면 안 돼요	많으면 안 됐어요
바쁠걸?	*바빴을걸?	바쁠 텐데	*바빴을 텐데	바쁘니까	*바빴으니까	바쁘면	*바빴으면	바쁘면 좋겠어요	*바빴으면 좋겠어요	바쁘면 안 돼요	바쁘면 안 됐어요
길걸?	길었을걸?	길 텐데	길었을 텐데	*기니까	길었으니까	길면	길었으면	길면 좋겠어요	길었으면 좋겠어요	길면 안 돼요	길면 안 됐어요
*어려울걸?	*어려웠을걸?	*어려울 텐데	*어려웠을 텐데	*어려우니까	*어려웠으니까	*어려우면	*어려웠으면	*어려우면 좋겠어요	*어려웠으면 좋겠어요	어려우면 안 돼요	*어려우면 안 됐어요
다를걸?	*달랐을걸?	다를 텐데	*달랐을 텐데	다르니까	*달랐으니까	다르면	*달랐으면	다르면 좋겠어요	*달랐으면 좋겠어요	다르면 안 돼요	다르면 안 됐어요
남자일걸?	남자였을걸?	남자일 텐데	남자였을 텐데	남자니까	남자였으니까	남자(이)면	남자였으면	남자(이)면 좋겠어요	남자였으면 좋겠어요	남자(이)면 안 돼요	남자(이)면 안 됐어요
사람일걸?	사람이었을걸?	사람일 텐데	사람이었을 텐데	사람이니까	사람이었으니까	사람이면	사람이었으면	사람이면 좋겠어요	사람이었으면 좋겠어요	사람이면 안 돼요	사람이면 안 됐어요

- Grammatical endings beginning with -(으)- that are attached to the stems of verbs, adjectives, and 이다, but are not attached to -았/었-

	Condition	Example	-(으)ㄴ 적이 있다 P. 90	-(으)ㄹ수록 P. 214
Verbs	Vowel ending	일하다	일한 적이 있어요	일할수록
	Consonant ending	읽다	읽은 적이 있어요	읽을수록
	으 omission	쓰다	쓴 적이 있어요	쓸수록
	ㄹ omission	놀다	*노 적이 있어요	놀수록
	ㄷ irregular	걷다	*걸은 적이 있어요	*걸을수록
	ㅂ irregular	돕다	*도운 적이 있어요	*도울수록
	ㅅ irregular	짓다	*지은 적이 있어요	*지을수록
	르 irregular	부르다	부른 적이 있어요	부를수록

	Condition	Example	-(으)ㄴ 적이 있다 P. 90	-(으)ㄹ수록 P. 214
Adjectives	Vowel ending	불편하다	불편한 적이 있어요	불편할수록
	Consonant ending	많다	많은 적이 있어요	많을수록
	으 irregular	바쁘다	바쁜 적이 있어요	바쁠수록
	ㄹ omission	길다	*긴 적이 있어요	길수록
	ㅂ omission	어렵다	*어려운 적이 있어요	*어려울수록
	르 irregular	다르다	다른 적이 있어요	다를수록
	'이다' to be	가수(이)다	가수인 적이 있어요	가수일수록
	'이다' to be	학생이다	학생인 적이 있어요	학생일수록

★ See pages 293-295 for more detailed explanations of irregular verb conjugations.

- Grammatical endings beginning with -(으)- that are attached only to verb stems

	Condition	Example	-(으)려고 하다 P. 82		-(으)ㄹ 줄 알다 P. 166		-(으)ㄹ까 하다 P. 214	
			Present	'-았/었-'	Present	'-았/었-'	Present	'-았/었-'
Verbs	Vowel ending	하다	하려고 해요	하려고 했어요	할 줄 알아요	할 줄 알았어요	할까 해요	할까 했어요
	Consonant ending	읽다	읽으려고 해요	읽으려고 했어요	읽을 줄 알아요	읽을 줄 알았어요	읽을까 해요	읽을까 했어요
	으 omission	쓰다	쓰려고 해요	쓰려고 했어요	쓸 줄 알아요	쓸 줄 알았어요	쓸까 해요	쓸까 했어요
	ㄹ omission	놀다	놀려고 해요	놀려고 했어요	놀 줄 알아요	놀 줄 알았어요	놀까 해요	놀까 했어요
	ㄷ irregular	듣다	*들으려고 해요	*들으려고 했어요	*들을 줄 알아요	*들을 줄 알았어요	*들을까 해요	*들을까 했어요
	ㅂ irregular	돕다	*도우려고 해요	*도우려고 했어요	*도울 줄 알아요	*도울 줄 알았어요	*도울까 해요	*도울까 했어요
	ㅅ irregular	짓다	*지으려고 해요	*지으려고 했어요	*지을 줄 알아요	*지을 줄 알았어요	*지을까 해요	*지을까 했어요
	르 irregular	부르다	부르려고 해요	부르려고 했어요	부를 줄 알아요	부를 줄 알았어요	부를까 해요	부를까 했어요

★ See pages 293-295 for more detailed explanations of irregular verb conjugations.

- Grammatical endings that are attached only to verb stems, but not to -았/었-

	Condition	Example	-(으)ㄴ 지 P. 18	-(으)ㄴ 후 P. 42	-(으)니까: Sequence of events P. 134	-(으)러 P. 22	-(으)려고 P. 154	-(으)려면 P. 154	-(으)ㄹ까요?: Proposal P. 50	-(으)ㄹ 뻔하다 P. 202	-(으)ㄹ래요 P. 210	-(으)ㄹ 걸 그랬다: Regret P. 234	-(으)려던 참이다 P. 250	-(으)시겠어요? P. 134
Verbs	Vowel ending	보다	본 지	본 후	보니까	보러	보려고	보려면	볼까요?	볼 뻔했어요	볼래요	볼 걸 그랬어요	보려던 참이에요	보시겠어요?
	Consonant ending	읽다	읽은 지	읽은 후	읽으니까	읽으러	읽으려고	읽으려면	읽을까요?	읽을 뻔했어요	읽을래요	읽을 걸 그랬어요	읽으려던 참이에요	읽으시겠어요?
	으 omission	쓰다	쓴 지	쓴 후	쓰니까	쓰러	쓰려고	쓰려면	쓸까요?	쓸 뻔했어요	쓸래요	쓸 걸 그랬어요	쓰려던 참이에요	쓰시겠어요?
	ㄹ omission	놀다	*논 지	*논 후	*노니까	놀러	놀려고	놀려면	놀까요?	놀 뻔했어요	놀래요	놀 걸 그랬어요	놀려던 참이에요	*노시겠어요?
	ㄷ irregular	듣다	*들은 지	*들은 후	*들으니까	*들으러	*들으려고	*들으려면	*들을까요?	*들을 뻔했어요	*들을래요	*들을 걸 그랬어요	*들으려던 참이에요	*들으시겠어요?
	ㅂ irregular	돕다	*도운 지	*도운 후	*도우니까	*도우러	*도우려고	*도우려면	*도울까요?	*도울 뻔했어요	*도울래요	*도울 걸 그랬어요	*도우려던 참이에요	*도우시겠어요?
	ㅅ irregular	짓다	*지은 지	*지은 후	*지으니까	*지으러	*지으려고	*지으려면	*지을까요?	*지을 뻔했어요	*지을래요	*지을 걸 그랬어요	*지으려던 참이에요	*지으시겠어요?
	르 irregular	부르다	부른 지	부른 후	부르니까	부르러	부르려고	부르려면	부를까요?	부를 뻔했어요	부를래요	부를 걸 그랬어요	부르려던 참이에요	부르시겠어요?

★ See pages 293-295 for more detailed explanations of irregular verb conjugations.

II. Grammatical endings that change form depending on whether what precedes is a verb or adjective

The following charts display grammatical endings that conjugate differently depending on if they follow verbs or nouns.

1. Grammatical endings beginning with -(으)ㄴ/는

Grammatical endings that begin with -는 attach to verb stems; -(으)ㄴ attach to adjective stems; and 이다 combines to form -인. The past forms, however, differ as follows:

- The noun modifier ending: Nouns such as 것, 게 (= 것이), 대신, 편, and 줄 cannot stand alone and rely on a modifying clause

	Condition	Example	-(으)ㄴ/는 + 명사 P. 178		-(으)ㄴ/는 것 P. 50		-(으)ㄴ/는 것 같다 P. 198		-(으)ㄴ/는 편이다 P. 38		-(으)ㄴ/는 줄 알았다 P. 226		-(으)ㄴ/는 대신에 P. 86	
			Present	Past	Present	Past	Present	Past	Present	Past	Present	Past	Present	Past
Verbs	Vowel ending	만나다	만나는	만난	만나는 것	만난 것	만나는 것 같아요	만난 것 같아요	만나는 편이에요	만난 편이에요	만나는 줄 알았어요	만난 줄 알았어요	만나는 대신에	만난 대신에
	Consonant ending	읽다	읽는	읽은	읽는 것	읽은 것	읽는 것 같아요	읽은 것 같아요	읽는 편이에요	읽은 편이에요	읽는 줄 알았어요	읽은 줄 알았어요	읽는 대신에	읽은 대신에
	으 omission	쓰다	쓰는	쓴	쓰는 것	쓴 것	쓰는 것 같아요	쓴 것 같아요	쓰는 편이에요	쓴 편이에요	쓰는 줄 알았어요	쓴 줄 알았어요	쓰는 대신에	쓴 대신에
	ㄹ omission	놀다	*노는	*논	*노는 것	*논 것	*노는 것 같아요	*논 것 같아요	*노는 편이에요	*논 편이에요	*노는 줄 알았어요	*논 줄 알았어요	*노는 대신에	*논 대신에
	ㄷ irregular	걷다	걷는	*걸은	걷는 것	*걸은 것	걷는 것 같아요	*걸은 것 같아요	걷는 편이에요	*걸은 편이에요	걷는 줄 알았어요	*걸은 줄 알았어요	걷는 대신에	*걸은 대신에
	ㅂ irregular	돕다	돕는	*도운	돕는 것	*도운 것	돕는 것 같아요	*도운 것 같아요	돕는 편이에요	*도운 편이에요	돕는 줄 알았어요	*도운 줄 알았어요	돕는 대신에	*도운 대신에
	ㅅ irregular	짓다	짓는	*지은	짓는 것	*지은 것	짓는 것 같아요	*지은 것 같아요	짓는 편이에요	*지은 편이에요	짓는 줄 알았어요	*지은 줄 알았어요	짓는 대신에	*지은 대신에
	르 irregular	부르다	부르는	부른	부르는 것	부른 것	부르는 것 같아요	부른 것 같아요	부르는 편이에요	부른 편이에요	부르는 줄 알았어요	부른 줄 알았어요	부르는 대신에	부른 대신에
	있다/없다 to exist/ not exist	있다	*있는	있었던	*있는 것	있었던 것	*있는 것 같아요	있었던 것 같아요	*있는 편이에요	있었던 편이에요	*있는 줄 알았어요		*있는 대신에	
Adjectives	Vowel ending	유명하다	유명한	유명했던	유명한 것	유명했던 것	유명한 것 같아요	유명했던 것 같아요	유명한 편이에요	유명했던 편이에요	유명한 줄 알았어요		유명한 대신에	
	Consonant ending	많다	많은	많았던	많은 것	많았던 것	많은 것 같아요	많았던 것 같아요	많은 편이에요	많았던 편이에요	많은 줄 알았어요		많은 대신에	
	있다/없다 to be/ not be	맛있다	**맛있는	맛있었던	**맛있는 것	맛있었던 것	**맛있는 것 같아요	맛있었던 것 같아요	**맛있는 편이에요	맛있었던 편이에요	**맛있는 줄 알았어요		**맛있는 대신에	
	으 omission	바쁘다	바쁜	*바빴던	바쁜 것	*바빴던 것	바쁜 것 같아요	*바빴던 것 같아요	바쁜 편이에요	*바빴던 편이에요	바쁜 줄 알았어요		바쁜 대신에	
	ㄹ omission	길다	*긴	*길었던	*긴 것	*길었던 것	*긴 것 같아요	*길었던 것 같아요	*긴 편이에요	*길었던 편이에요	*긴 줄 알았어요		*긴 대신에	
	ㅂ irregular	어렵다	*어려운	*어려웠던	*어려운 것	*어려웠던 것	*어려운 것 같아요	*어려웠던 것 같아요	*어려운 편이에요	*어려운 편이에요	*어려운 줄 알았어요		*어려운 대신에	
	르 irregular	다르다	다른	*달랐던	다른 것	*달랐던 것	다른 것 같아요	*달랐던 것 같아요	다른 편이에요	*달랐던 편이에요	다른 줄 알았어요		다른 대신에	
	'이다' to be	남자(이)다	남자인	남자였던	남자인 것	남자였던 것	남자인 것 같아요	남자였던 것 같아요	남자인 편이에요	남자였던 편이에요	남자인 줄 알았어요		남자인 대신에	
	'이다' to be	사람이다	사람인	사람이었던	사람인 것	사람이었던 것	사람인 것 같아요	사람이었던 것 같아요	사람인 편이에요	사람이었던 편이에요	사람인 줄 알았어요		사람인 대신에	

** Adjectives that take 있다 or 없다 (ex. 맛있다) take -는.

● -(으)ㄴ/는데 and -(으)ㄴ/는지

	Condition	Example	-(으)ㄴ/는데(요) P. 70, P. 82, P. 130, P. 162			-(으)ㄴ/는데도 P. 242			-(으)ㄴ/는지 P. 74		
			Present	Past	Future/ Conjecture	Present	Past	Future/ Conjecture	Present	Past	Future/ Conjecture
Verbs	Vowel ending	만나다	만나는데	만났는데	만날 건데 / 만날 텐데	만나는데도	만났는데도	만날 건데도 / 만날 텐데도	만나는지	만났는지	만날지
	Consonant ending	읽다	읽는데	읽었는데	읽을 건데 / 읽을 텐데	읽는데도	읽었는데도	읽을 건데도 / 읽을 텐데도	읽는지	읽었는지	읽을지
	으 omission	쓰다	쓰는데	*썼는데	쓸 건데 / 쓸 텐데	쓰는데도	*썼는데도	쓸 건데도 / 쓸 텐데도	쓰는지	*썼는지	쓸지
	ㄹ omission	놀다	*노는데	놀았는데	놀 건데 / 놀 텐데	*노는데도	놀았는데도	놀 건데도 / 놀 텐데도	*노는지	놀았는지	놀지
	ㄷ irregular	걷다	걷는데	*걸었는데	*걸을 건데 / 걸을 텐데	걷는데도	*걸었는데도	*걸을 건데도 / 걸을 텐데도	걷는지	*걸었는지	*걸을지
	ㅂ irregular	돕다	돕는데	*도왔는데	*도울 건데 / 도울 텐데	돕는데도	*도왔는데도	*도울 건데도 / 도울 텐데도	돕는지	*도왔는지	*도울지
	ㅅ irregular	짓다	짓는데	*지었는데	*지을 건데 / 지을 텐데	짓는데도	*지었는데도	*지을 건데도 / 지을 텐데도	짓는지	*지었는지	*지을지
	르 irregular	부르다	부르는데	*불렀는데	부를 건데 / 부를 텐데	부르는데도	*불렀는데도	부를 건데도 / 부를 텐데도	부르는지	*불렀는지	부를지
	있다/없다 to exist/not exist	있다	있는데	있었는데	있을 건데 / 있을 텐데	있는데도	있었는데도	있을 건데도 / 있을 텐데도	있는지	있었는지	있을지
Adjectives	Vowel ending	유명하다	유명한데	유명했는데	유명할 건데 / 유명할 텐데	유명한데도	유명했는데도	유명할 건데도 / 유명할 텐데도	유명한지	유명했는지	유명할지
	Consonant ending	많다	많은데	많았는데	많을 건데 / 많을 텐데	많은데도	많았는데도	많을 건데도 / 많을 텐데도	많은지	많았는지	많을지
	있다/없다 to be/not be	맛있다	**맛있는데	맛있었는데	맛있을 건데 / 맛있을 텐데	**맛있는데도	맛있었는데도	맛있을 건데도 / 많있을 텐데도	**맛있는지	맛있었는지	맛있을지
	으 omission	바쁘다	바쁜데	*바빴는데	바쁠 건데 / 바쁠 텐데	바쁜데도	*바빴는데도	바쁠 건데도 / 바쁠 텐데도	바쁜지	*바빴는지	바쁠지
	ㄹ omission	길다	*긴데	길었는데	길 건데 / 길 텐데	긴데도	길었는데도	길 건데도 / 길 텐데도	*긴지	길었는지	길지
	ㅂ irregular	어렵다	*어려운데	*어려웠는데	*어려울 건데 / 어려울 텐데	*어려운데도	*어려웠는데도	*어려울 건데도 / 어려울 텐데도	*어려운지	*어려웠는지	*어려울지
	르 irregular	다르다	다른데	*달랐는데	다를 건데 / 다를 텐데	다른데도	*달랐는데도	다를 건데도 / 다를 텐데도	다른지	*달랐는지	다를지
	'이다' to be	남자(이)다	남자인데	남자였는데	남자일 건데 / 남자일 텐데	남자인데도	남자였는데도	남자일 건데도 / 남자일 텐데도	남자인지	남자였는지	남자일지
	'이다' to be	사람이다	사람인데	사람이었는데	사람일 건데 / 사람일 텐데	사람인데도	사람이었는데도	사람일 건데도 / 사람일 텐데도	사람인지	사람이었는지	사람일지

★ See pages 293-295 for more detailed explanations of irregular verb conjugations.
★★ Adjectives that take 있다 or 없다 (ex. 맛있다) take -는데 or -는지.

● -(는)군요: Expressing recognition

	Condition	Example	-(으)ㄴ/는군요 P. 218		
			Present	Past	Future/ Conjecture
Verbs	Vowel ending	만나다	만나는군요	만났군요	만날 거군요
	Consonant ending	읽다	읽는군요	읽었군요	읽을 거군요
	ㅡ omission	쓰다	쓰는군요	*썼군요	쓸 거군요
	ㄹ omission	놀다	*노는군요	놀았군요	놀 거군요
	ㄷ irregular	걷다	걷는군요	*걸었군요	걸을 거군요
	ㅂ irregular	돕다	돕는군요	*도왔군요	*도울 거군요
	ㅅ irregular	짓다	짓는군요	*지었군요	*지을 거군요
	르 irregular	부르다	부르는군요	*불렀군요	부를 거군요
	있다/없다 to exist/not exist	있다	*있군요	있었군요	있을 거군요
Adjectives	Vowel ending	유명하다	유명하군요	유명했군요	유명할 거군요
	Consonant ending	많다	많군요	많았군요	많을 거군요
	있다/없다 to be/not be	맛있다	**맛있군요	맛있었군요	맛있을 거군요
	ㅡ omission	바쁘다	바쁘군요	*바빴군요	바쁠 거군요
	ㄹ omission	길다	길군요	길었군요	길 거군요
	ㅂ irregular	어렵다	어렵군요	*어려웠군요	*어려울 거군요
	르 irregular	다르다	다르군요	*달랐군요	다를 거군요
	'이다' to be	남자(이)다	남자군요	남자였군요	남자일 거군요
	'이다' to be	사람이다	사람이군요	사람이었군요	사람일 거군요

★ See pages 293-295 for more detailed explanations of irregular verb conjugations.
★★ Adjectives that take 있다 or 없다 (ex. 맛있다) take -는데 or -는지.

● -(으)ㄴ가/나 보다: Expressing a conjecture

	Condition	Example	-나 봐요 P. 226		
			Present	Past	Future/ Conjecture
Verbs	Vowel ending	만나다	만나나 봐요	만났나 봐요	만날 건가 봐요
	Consonant ending	읽다	읽나 봐요	읽었나 봐요	읽을 건가 봐요
	ㅡ omission	쓰다	쓰나 봐요	*썼나 봐요	쓸 건가 봐요
	ㄹ omission	놀다	*노나 봐요	놀았나 봐요	놀 건가 봐요
	ㄷ irregular	걷다	걷나 봐요	*걸었나 봐요	*걸을 건가 봐요
	ㅂ irregular	돕다	돕나 봐요	*도왔나 봐요	*도울 건가 봐요
	ㅅ irregular	짓다	짓나 봐요	*지었나 봐요	*지을 건가 봐요
	르 irregular	부르다	부르나 봐요	*불렀나 봐요	부를 건가 봐요
	있다/없다 to exist/not exist	있다	*있나 봐요	있었나 봐요	있을 건가 봐요
Adjectives	Vowel ending	유명하다	유명한가 봐요	유명했나 봐요	
	Consonant ending	많다	많은가 봐요	많았나 봐요	
	있다/없다 to be/not be	맛있다	**맛있나 봐요	맛있었나 봐요	
	ㅡ omission	바쁘다	바쁜가 봐요	*바빴나 봐요	
	ㄹ omission	길다	*긴가 봐요	길었나 봐요	
	ㅂ irregular	어렵다	*어려운가 봐요	*어려웠나 봐요	
	르 irregular	다르다	다른가 봐요	*달랐나 봐요	
	'이다' to be	남자(이)다	남자인가 봐요	남자였나 봐요	
	'이다' to be	사람이다	사람인가 봐요	사람이었나 봐요	

★ See pages 293-295 for more detailed explanations of irregular verb conjugations.
★★ Adjectives that take 있다 or 없다 (ex. 맛있다) take -나 보다.

2. Indirect quotations

The indirect quotation grammatical endings, whose infinitive is -다고, conjugate in the following manner.

	Condition	Example	Statement -다고 하다 P. 194			Question -냐고 하다 P. 194			Command -(으)라고 하다 P. 194		Proposal -자고 하다 P. 194	
			Present	Past	Future	Present	Past	Future	Positive	Negative	Positive	Negative
Verbs	Vowel ending	만나다	만난다고 했어요	만났다고 했어요	만날 거라고 했어요	만나냐고 했어요	만났냐고 했어요	만날 거냐고 했어요	만나라고 했어요	만나지 말라고 했어요	만나자고 했어요	만나지 말라고 했어요
	Consonant ending	읽다	읽는다고 했어요	읽었다고 했어요	읽을 거라고 했어요	읽냐고 했어요	읽었냐고 했어요	읽을 거냐고 했어요	읽으라고 했어요	읽지 말라고 했어요	읽자고 했어요	읽지 말자고 했어요
	으 omission	쓰다	쓴다고 했어요	*썼다고 했어요	쓸 거라고 했어요	쓰냐고 했어요	*썼냐고 했어요	쓸 거냐고 했어요	쓰라고 했어요	쓰지 말라고 했어요	쓰자고 했어요	쓰지 말자고 했어요
	ㄹ omission	놀다	*논다고 했어요	놀았다고 했어요	놀 거라고 했어요	*노냐고 했어요	놀았냐고 했어요	놀 거냐고 했어요	놀라고 했어요	놀지 말라고 했어요	놀자고 했어요	놀지 말자고 했어요
	ㄷ irregular	걷다	걷는다고 했어요	*걸었다고 했어요	*걸을 거라고 했어요	걷냐고 했어요	*걸었냐고 했어요	*걸을 거냐고 했어요	*걸으라고 했어요	걷지 말라고 했어요	걷자고 했어요	걷지 말자고 했어요
	ㅂ irregular	돕다	돕는다고 했어요	*도왔다고 했어요	*도울 거라고 했어요	돕냐고 했어요	*도왔냐고 했어요	*도울 거냐고 했어요	*도우라고 했어요	돕지 말라고 했어요	돕자고 했어요	돕지 말자고 했어요
	ㅅ irregular	짓다	짓는다고 했어요	*지었다고 했어요	*지을 거라 고 했어요	짓냐고 했어요	*지었냐고 했어요	*지을 거냐고 했어요	*지으라고 했어요	짓지 말라고 했어요	짓자고 했어요	짓지 말자고 했어요
	르 irregular	부르다	부른다고 했어요	*불렀다고 했어요	부를 거라고 했어요	부르냐고 했어요	*불렀냐고 했어요	부를 거냐고 했어요	부르라고 했어요	부르지 말라고 했어요	부르자고 했어요	부르지 말자고 했어요
	있다/없다 to exist/not exist	있다	*있다고 했어요	있었다고 했어요	있을 거라고 했어요	있냐고 했어요	있었냐고 했어요	있을 거냐고 했어요	있으라고 했어요	있지 말라고 했어요	있자고 했어요	있지 말자고 했어요
Adjectives	Vowel ending	유명하다	유명하다고 했어요	유명했다고 했어요	유명할 거라고 했어요	유명하냐고 했어요	유명했냐고 했어요	유명할 거냐고 했어요				
	Consonant ending	많다	많다고 했어요	많았다고 했어요	많을 거라고 했어요	많냐고 했어요	많았냐고 했어요	많을 거냐고 했어요				
	있다/없다 to be/not be	맛있다	**맛있다고 했어요	맛있었다고 했어요	맛있을 거라고 했어요	**맛있냐고 했어요	맛있었냐고 했어요	맛있을 거냐고 했어요				
	으 omission	바쁘다	바쁘다고 했어요	*바빴다고 했어요	바쁠 거라고 했어요	바쁘냐고 했어요	*바빴냐고 했어요	바쁠 거냐고 했어요				
	ㄹ omission	길다	길다고 했어요	길었다고 했어요	길 거라고 했어요	*기냐고 했어요	길었냐고 했어요	길 거냐고 했어요				
	ㅂ irregular	어렵다	어렵다고 했어요	*어려웠다고 했어요	*어려울 거라고 했어요	어렵냐고 했어요	*어려웠냐고 했어요	어려울 거냐고 했어요				
	르 irregular	다르다	다르다고 했어요	*달랐다고 했어요	다를 거라고 했어요	다르냐고 했어요	*달랐냐고 했어요	다를 거냐고 했어요				
	'이다' to be	남자(이)다	*남자라고 했어요	남자였다고 했어요	남자일 거라고 했어요	남자냐고 했어요	남자였냐고 했어요	남자일 거냐고 했어요				
	'이다' to be	사람이다	*사람이라고 했어요	사람이었다고 했어요	사람일 거라고 했어요	사람이냐고 했어요	사람이었냐고 했어요	사람일 거냐고 했어요				

* See pages 293-295 for more detailed explanations of irregular verb conjugations.
** Adjectives that take 있다 or 없다 (ex. 맛있다) take -다고 to form 있다고/없다고.

3. Korean speech style and honorifics

- -(으)시- : Honorifics in informal style

	Condition	Example	Normal			Honorific		
			Present -아/어요	Past -았/었어요	Future / Conjecture -(으)ㄹ 거예요	Present -(으)세요	Past -(으)셨어요	Future / Conjecture -(으)실 거예요
Verbs	Vowel ending	보다	봐요	봤어요	볼 거예요	보세요	보셨어요	보실 거예요
	Consonant ending	읽다	읽어요	읽었어요	읽을 거예요	읽으세요	읽으셨어요	읽으실 거예요
	으 omission	쓰다	*써요	*썼어요	쓸 거예요	쓰세요	쓰셨어요	쓰실 거예요
	ㄹ omission	살다	살아요	살았어요	살 거예요	*사세요	*사셨어요	*사실 거예요
	ㄷ irregular	듣다	*들어요	*들었어요	*들을 거예요	*들으세요	*들으셨어요	*들으실 거예요
	ㅂ irregular	돕다	*도와요	*도왔어요	*도울 거예요	*도우세요	*도우셨어요	*도우실 거예요
	ㅅ irregular	짓다	*지어요	*지었어요	*지을 거예요	*지으세요	*지으셨어요	*지으실 거예요
	르 irregular	모르다	*몰라요	*몰랐어요	모를 거예요	모르세요	모르셨어요	모르실 거예요
	Exceptional verds	먹다	먹어요	먹었어요	먹을 거예요	*드세요	*드셨어요	*드실 거예요
		자다	자요	잤어요	잘 거예요	*주무세요	*주무셨어요	*주무실 거예요
		말하다	말해요	말했어요	말할 거예요	*말씀하세요	*말씀하셨어요	*말씀하실 거예요
		있다 (existance)	있어요	있었어요	있을 거예요	*계세요	*계셨어요	*계실 거예요
Adjectives	있다 to be possessive	있다 (possession)	있어요	있었어요	있을 거예요	*있으세요	*있으셨어요	*있으실 거예요
	Vowel ending	편하다	편해요	편했어요	편할 거예요	편하세요	편하셨어요	편하실 거예요
	Consonant ending	좋다	좋아요	좋았어요	좋을 거예요	좋으세요	좋으셨어요	좋으실 거예요
	으 omission	바쁘다	*바빠요	*바빴어요	바쁠 거예요	바쁘세요	바쁘셨어요	바쁘실 거예요
	ㄹ omission	길다	길어요	길었어요	길 거예요	*기세요	*기셨어요	*기실 거예요
	ㅂ irregular	어렵다	*어려워요	*어려웠어요	*어려울 거예요	*어려우세요	*어려우셨어요	*어려우실 거예요
	르 irregular	다르다	*달라요	*달랐어요	다를 거예요	다르세요	다르셨어요	다르실 거예요
	'이다' to be	남자(이)다	남자예요	남자였어요	남자일 거예요	남자세요	남자셨어요	남자실 거예요
	'이다' to be	사람이다	사람이에요	사람이었어요	사람일 거예요	사람이세요	사람이셨어요	사람이실 거예요

★ See pages 293-295 for more detailed explanations of irregular verb conjugations.

● Formal speech -(스)ㅂ니다: Honorifics in formal style

	Condition	Example	Statement						Command		Proposal	
			Formal Speech			Formal Honorific Speech			Positive	Negative	Positive	Negative
			Present -(스)ㅂ니다	Past -았/었습니다	Future / Conjecture -(으)ㄹ 것입니다	Present -(으)십니다	Past -(으)셨습니다	Future / Conjecture -(으)실 것입니다	-(으) 십시오	-지 마십시오	-(으)ㅂ시다	-지 맙시다
Verbs	Vowel ending	보다	봅니다	봤습니다	볼 것입니다	보십니다	보셨습니다	보실 것입니다	보십시오	보지 마십시오	봅시다	보지 맙시다
	Consonant ending	읽다	읽습니다	읽었습니다	읽을 것입니다	읽으십니다	읽으셨습니다	읽으실 것입니다	읽으십시오	읽지 마십시오	읽읍시다	읽지 맙시다
	으 omission	쓰다	씁니다	*썼습니다	쓸 것입니다	쓰십니다	쓰셨습니다	쓰실 것입니다	쓰십시오	쓰지 마십시오	씁시다	쓰지 맙시다
	ㄹ omission	살다	*삽니다	살았습니다	살 것입니다	*사십니다	*사셨습니다	*사실 것입니다	*사십시오	살지 마십시오	*삽시다	살지 맙시다
	ㄷ irregular	듣다	듣습니다	들었습니다	*들을 것입니다	*들으십니다	*들으셨습니다	*들으실 것입니다	*들으십시오	듣지 마십시오	*들읍시다	듣지 맙시다
	ㅂ irregular	돕다	돕습니다	*도왔습니다	*도울 것입니다	*도우십니다	*도우셨습니다	*도우실 것입니다	*도우십시오	돕지 마십시오	*도웁시다	돕지 맙시다
	ㅅ irregular	짓다	짓습니다	*지었습니다	*지을 것입니다	*지으십니다	*지으셨습니다	*지으실 것입니다	*지으십시오	짓지 마십시오	*지읍시다	짓지 맙시다
	르 irregular	부르다	부릅니다	*불렀습니다	부를 것입니다	부르십니다	부르셨습니다	부르실 것입니다	부르십시오	부르지 마십시오	부릅시다	부르지 맙시다
	Consonant ending	먹다	먹습니다	먹었습니다	먹을 것입니다	*드십니다	*드셨습니다	*드실 것입니다	*드십시오	*드시지 마십시오	먹읍시다	먹지 맙시다
	Consonant ending	자다	잡니다	잤습니다	잘 것입니다	*주무십니다	*주무셨습니다	*주무실 것입니다	*주무십시오	*주무시지 마십시오	잡시다	자지 맙시다
	Consonant ending	말하다	말합니다	말했습니다	말할 것입니다	*말씀하십니다	*말씀하셨습니다	*말씀하실 것입니다	*말씀하십시오	*말씀하시지 마십시오	말합시다	말하지 맙시다
	있다 to exist	있다	있습니다	있었습니다	있을 것입니다	*계십니다	*계셨습니다	*계실 것입니다	*계십시오	*계시지 마십시오	*있읍시다	*있지 맙시다
Adjectives	있다 to be possessive	있다	있습니다	있었습니다	있을 것입니다	*있으십니다	*있으셨습니다	*있으실 것입니다				
	Vowel ending	편하다	편합니다	편했습니다	편할 것입니다	편하십니다	편하셨습니다	편하실 것입니다				
	Consonant ending	좋다	좋습니다	좋았습니다	좋을 것입니다	좋으십니다	좋으셨습니다	좋으실 것입니다				
	으 omission	바쁘다	바쁩니다	*바빴습니다	바쁠 것입니다	바쁘십니다	바쁘셨습니다	바쁘실 것입니다				
	ㄹ omission	길다	깁니다	길었습니다	길 것입니다	*기십니다	*기셨습니다	*기실 것입니다				
	ㅂ irregular	어렵다	어렵습니다	*어려웠습니다	*어려울 것입니다	*어려우십니다	*어려우셨습니다	*어려우실 것입니다				
	르 irregular	다르다	다릅니다	*달랐습니다	다를 것입니다	다르십니다	다르셨습니다	다르실 것입니다				
	'이다' to be	남자(이)다	남자입니다	남자였습니다	남자일 것입니다	남자십니다	남자셨습니다	남자실 것입니다				
	'이다' to be	사람이다	사람입니다	사람이었습니다	사람일 것입니다	사람이십니다	사람이셨습니다	사람이실 것입니다				

★ See pages 293-295 for more detailed explanations of irregular verb conjugations.

I wonder

The honorific ending -(으)시- conjugates in the following ways when it follows conjunctive endings.

Normal	Honorific	Normal	Honorific	Normal	Honorific
-고	-(으)시고	-(으)면	-(으)시면	-아/어서	-(으)셔서
-지만	-(으)시지만	-(으)려고	-(으)시려고	-아/어도	-(으)셔도
-기 전에	-(으)시기 전에	-(으)니까	-(으)시니까	-아/어야	-(으)셔야

• Casual speech: Informal speech without honorifics

	Condition	Example	Statement			Command		Proposal	
			Present	Past	Future/ Conjecture	Positive	Negative	Positive	Negative
Verbs	Vowel ending	보다	봐	봤어	볼 거야	봐	보지 마	보자	보지 말자
	Consonant ending	먹다	먹어	먹었어	먹을 거야	먹어	먹지 마	먹자	먹지 말자
	으 omission	쓰다	*써	*썼어	쓸 거야	*써	쓰지 마	쓰자	쓰지 말자
	ㄹ omission	놀다	놀아	놀았어	놀 거야	놀아	놀지 마	놀자	놀지 말자
	ㄷ irregular	듣다	*들어	*들었어	*들을 거야	*들어	듣지 마	듣자	듣지 말자
	ㅂ irregular	돕다	*도와	*도왔어	*도울 거야	*도와	돕지 마	돕자	돕지 말자
	ㅅ irregular	짓다	*지어	*지었어	*지을 거야	*지어	짓지 마	짓자	짓지 말자
	르 irregular	부르다	*불러	*불렀어	부를 거야	*불러	부르지 마	부르자	부르지 말자
	있다/없다 to exist/not exist	있다	있어	있었어	있을 거야	있어	있지 마	있자	있지 말자
Adjectives	Vowel ending	편하다	편해	편했어	편할 거야				
	Consonant ending	좋다	좋아	좋았어	좋을 거야				
	으 omission	바쁘다	*바빠	*바빴어	바쁠 거야				
	ㄹ omission	길다	길어	길었어	길 거야				
	ㅂ irregular	어렵다	*어려워	*어려웠어	*어려울 거야				
	르 irregular	다르다	*달라	*달랐어	다를 거야				
	'이다' to be	남자(이)다	*남자야	*남자였어	남자일 거야				
	'이다' to be	사람이다	*사람이야	*사람이었어	사람일 거야				

★ See pages 293-295 for more detailed explanations of irregular verb conjugations.

Answers

Chapter 1

Quiz Yourself 1 ····· P. 10

1 (1) ⓑ (2) ⓑ (3) ⓑ (4) ⓐ (5) ⓐ (6) ⓑ (7) ⓐ (8) ⓐ

2 (1) 얼마나 (2) 어떻게 (3) 누가 (4) 어때요 (5) 왜 (6) 얼마예요

3 (1) 기다린 지 (2) 먹은 지 (3) 산 지 (4) 다닌 지

Quiz Yourself 2 ····· P. 23

1 (1) ⓑ (2) ⓑ (3) ⓐ (4) ⓐ (5) ⓑ (6) ⓐ

2 (1) 어렵지만 (2) 없지만 (3) 했지만 (4) 재미없었지만

3 (1) 영화를 보러 (2) 밥을 먹으러 (3) 음료수를 사러 (4) 선물을 찾으러 (5) 친구를 만나러 (6) 약을 사러

Quiz Yourself 3 ····· P. 27

1 (1) ⓑ (2) ⓐ (3) ⓑ (4) ⓑ (5) ⓑ (6) ⓐ

2 (1) 마리가 (2) 곡을 (3) 마디 (4) 군데

3 (1) 세 잔을 (2) 세 장을 (3) 한 켤레 (4) 두 봉지를 (5) 한 상자를

Chapter 2

Quiz Yourself 1 ····· P. 35

1 (1) 비가 오고/왔고 바람이 불었어요
(2) 체육관에 가서 운동할 거예요
(3) 값이 싸고 맛있어요

2 (1) ⓐ (2) ⓑ (3) ⓑ (4) ⓐ (5) ⓑ (6) ⓑ

3 (1) 일하면서 (2) 좋으면서 (3) 운전하면서 (4) 낮으면서

Quiz Yourself 2 ····· P. 39

1 (1) 타거나 (2) 내거나 (3) 많거나

2 (1) 많이 자는 (2) 늦게 일어나는 (3) 자주 요리하는 (4) 거의 영화를 안 보는/보지 않는

3 (1) ⓑ (2) ⓑ (3) ⓑ (4) ⓐ

Quiz Yourself 3 ····· P. 43

1 (1) 세수한 후에/다음에/뒤에 (2) 면도한 후에 (3) 닦기 전에 (4) 집에서 나가기

2 (1) 일을 시작하기 전에
(2) 친구하고 싸운 후에/다음에/뒤에
(3) 고향에 돌아가기 전에
(4) 한국어를 배운 후에/다음에/뒤에

3 (1) 비가 온 (2) 식기 (3) 사기 (4) 끝난

Chapter 3

Quiz Yourself 1 ····· P. 51

1 (1) 여행 갈까요 (2) 식사할까요 (3) 예매할까요 (4) 들을까요

2 (1) 쉬는 (2) 사용하는 (3) 필요한 (4) 전화하는

3 (1) ⓑ (2) ⓐ (3) ⓐ (4) ⓐ (5) ⓑ

Quiz Yourself 2 ····· P. 55

1 (1) ⓑ (2) ⓑ (3) ⓐ (4) ⓐ (5) ⓐ (6) ⓐ

2 (1) 갑자기 다른 일이 생겨서 (2) 자판기가 고장 나서
(3) 배터리가 다 돼서 (4) 성격이 안 맞아서
(5) 문법 질문이 있어서

3 (1) 운동하기로 (2) 공부하기로 (3) 늦지 않기로 (4) 여행 가기로

Quiz Yourself 3 ····· P. 59

1 (1) ⓑ (2) ⓐ (3) ⓑ (4) ⓑ (5) ⓐ (6) ⓑ

2 (1) 맛있으니까 (2) 불편하니까 (3) 봤으니까
(4) 잠이 들었으니까 (5) 안 끝났으니까/끝나지 않았으니까

3 (1) ⓑ (2) ⓓ (3) ⓐ (4) ⓒ

Chapter 4

Quiz Yourself 1 ····· P. 67

1 (1) 물어보면 (2) 늦으면 (3) 읽으면 (4) 마시면

2 (1) ⓑ (2) ⓐ (3) ⓐ (4) ⓑ

3 (1) ⓒ (2) ⓐ (3) ⓓ (4) ⓑ

Quiz Yourself 2 ····· P. 71

1 (1) ⓔ (2) ⓓ (3) ⓐ (4) ⓕ (5) ⓑ (6) ⓒ

2 (1) ⓑ (2) ⓑ (3) ⓐ (4) ⓑ

3 (1) 대학교를 졸업하자마자 (2) 소식을 듣자마자
(3) 핸드폰을 사자마자 (4) 숙소를 찾자마자
(5) 집에 들어가자마자

Quiz Yourself 3 ····· P. 75

1 (1) 언제 일을 시작하는지 (2) 어떻게 그 사실을 알았는지
(3) 어디로 여행 가고 싶은지 (4) 고향이 어딘지/어디인지
(5) 어른에게 어떻게 말해야 하는지
(6) 왜 친구의 얘기를 듣지 않는지

2 (1) ⓑ (2) ⓑ (3) ⓑ (4) ⓐ

3 (1) 싸지요 (2) 덥지요 (3) 쉽지 않지요 (4) 먹었지요 (5) 읽지요 (6) 부산이지요

Chapter 5

Quiz Yourself 1 ······ P. 83

1 (1) 책을 읽으려고 해요
(2) 다음 주 수요일에 보려고 하
(3) 등산 안 가려고 해요/등산 가지 않으려고 해요

2 (1) ⓑ (2) ⓑ (3) ⓑ (4) ⓐ

3 (1) ⓓ (2) ⓒ (3) ⓐ (4) ⓑ

Quiz Yourself 2 ······ P. 87

1 (1) ⓐ (2) ⓑ (3) ⓑ (4) ⓑ

2 (1) ⓒ (2) ⓓ (3) ⓔ (4) ⓑ (5) ⓐ

3 (1) 얼굴이 예쁜 (2) 분위기가 좋은 (3) 사는 (4) 운전하는

Quiz Yourself 3 ······ P. 91

1 (1) ⓑ (2) ⓐ (3) ⓑ (4) ⓐ

2 (1) ⓐ (2) ⓑ (3) ⓐ (4) ⓑ

3 (1) 간 적이 있 (2) 배운 적이 있 (3) 해 본 적이 없
(4) 먹은 적이 있 (5) 들은 적이 없 (6) 산 적이 없어서

Chapter 6

Quiz Yourself 1 ······ P. 99

1 (1) 써도 (2) 앉아도 (3) 봐도 (4) 입어 봐도

2 (1) 모아야 (2) 지켜야 (3) 줄여야 (4) 맡겨야

3 (1) ⓑ (2) ⓐ (3) ⓑ (4) ⓐ

Quiz Yourself 2 ······ P. 103

1 (1) ⓑ (2) ⓐ (3) ⓑ (4) ⓑ

2 (1) 인터넷으로 사, 여행사에 전화하
(2) 공원에서 산책하, 맛있는 음식을 먹
(3) 택시를 타, 한국 사람에게 길을 물어보

Quiz Yourself 3 ······ P. 107

1 (1) 담배를 피우면 안 돼요 (2) 늦게 오면 안 돼요
(3) 음악을 틀면 안 돼요 (4) 예약을 미루면 안 돼요

2 (1) ⓔ (2) ⓕ (3) ⓒ (4) ⓑ (5) ⓓ (6) ⓐ

3 (1) ⓐ (2) ⓐ (3) ⓐ (4) ⓑ (5) ⓐ (6) ⓑ

Chapter 7

Quiz Yourself 1 ······ P. 115

1 (1) ⓐ (2) ⓑ (3) ⓐ (4) ⓑ (5) ⓑ (6) ⓑ

2 (1) 그만두게 됐어요 (2) 짜게 됐어요 (3) 적응하게 됐어요
(4) 잘하게 돼요/잘하게 될 거예요

3 (1) ⓑ (2) ⓔ (3) ⓐ (4) ⓒ (5) ⓓ

Quiz Yourself 2 ······ P. 119

1 (1) ⓑ (2) ⓐ (3) ⓑ (4) ⓑ (5) ⓐ (6) ⓑ

2 (1) 멋있기는요 (2) 못하기는요 (3) 힘들기는요
(4) 안 하기는요 (5) 고맙기는요 (6) 미인은요

3 (1) 부니까 (2) 받았기 때문에 (3) 친구들 때문에
(4) 피곤하니까

Quiz Yourself 3 ······ P. 123

1 (1) ⓔ (2) ⓓ (3) ⓒ (4) ⓑ (5) ⓐ

2 (1) 잘하거든요 (2) 있거든요 (3) 살았거든요
(4) 오거든요 (5) 다르거든요

3 (1) ⓐ (2) ⓑ (3) ⓑ (4) ⓑ

Chapter 8

Quiz Yourself 1 ······ P. 131

1 (1) ⓐ (2) ⓔ (3) ⓑ (4) ⓒ (5) ⓓ

2 (1) 다니는 동안에 (2) 공부하는 동안에 (3) 사는 동안에
(4) 회의하는 동안에 (5) 외출한 동안에

3 (1) ⓑ (2) ⓐ (3) ⓑ (4) ⓑ

Quiz Yourself 2 ······ P. 135

1 (1) ⓑ (2) ⓑ (3) ⓐ (4) ⓐ

2 (1) 음악을 들어 보니까 (2) 전화해 보니까
(3) 차를 마셔 보니까 (4) 태권도를 배워 보니까
(5) 지하철을 타 보니까

3 (1) 신으시겠어요 (2) 드시겠어요 (3) 사시겠어요
(4) 보시겠어요

Quiz Yourself 3 ······ P. 139

1 (1) 변호사입니다 (2) 보냈습니다 (3) 만납니다
(4) 주고받습니다 (5) 아쉽습니다 (6) 말씀드리겠습니다
(7) 타십니다 (8) 대해 주십니다 (9) 식사하셨습니다
(10) 존경하고 있습니다

2 (1) 이십니까? 아닙니다, 입니다
(2) 오셨습니까? 그렇습니다 (3) 주십시오, 하겠습니다
(4) 합시다! 그럽시다

3 (1) 받는 대로 (2) 끝나는 대로 (3) 밝는 대로
(4) 읽는 대로

Chapter 9

Quiz Yourself 1 ······ P. 147

1 (1) ⓔ (2) ⓐ (3) ⓓ (4) ⓑ (5) ⓒ

2 (1) 시간이 날 (2) 하기 싫은 일을 할 (3) 처음 만났을
(4) 회사를 그만둘

3 (1) ⓐ (2) ⓑ (3) ⓑ (4) ⓐ

Quiz Yourself 2 P. 151

1 (1) ⓑ (2) ⓐ (3) ⓑ (4) ⓐ (5) ⓑ (6) ⓑ

2 (1) ⓕ (2) ⓐ (3) ⓔ (4) ⓑ (5) ⓒ (6) ⓓ

3 (1) 비싸도 (2) 편해졌어요 (3) 연습해도 (4) 추워져요
(5) 한국인이라도

Quiz Yourself 3 P. 155

1 (1) ③ⓑ (2) ④ⓐ (3) ①ⓓ (4) ②ⓒ

2 (1) 잘하려면 (2) 타려면 (3) 거절하려면
(4) 화해하려면 (5) 후회하지 않으려면

3 (1) ⓐ (2) ⓑ (3) ⓑ (4) ⓐ (5) ⓑ

Chapter 10

Quiz Yourself 1 P. 163

1 (1) ⓑ (2) ⓐ (3) ⓐ (4) ⓑ

2 (1) 있어 (2) 어/응 (3) 왜 (4) 가자 (5) 내가 (6) 아니야
(7) 나한테 (8) 너는 (9) 사 줘 (10) 보자/봐

3 (1) 나는 (2) 내가 (3) 먹어요/먹읍시다 (4) 어/응

Quiz Yourself 2 P. 167

1 (1) 만들 줄 몰라요 (2) 탈 줄 모르 (3) 고칠 줄 아
(4) 운전할 줄 알 (5) 사용할 줄 몰라

2 (1) ⓒ (2) ⓐ (3) ⓔ (4) ⓑ (5) ⓓ

3 (1) ⓑ (2) ⓑ (3) ⓐ (4) ⓑ (5) ⓑ (6) ⓑ

Quiz Yourself 3 P. 171

1 (1) ⓐ (2) ⓑ (3) ⓑ (4) ⓑ

2 (1) 준비해야겠어요 (2) 알아봐야겠어요 (3) 일해야겠어
(4) 피우지 않아야겠어요/피우지 말아야겠어요

3 (1) ⓑ (2) ⓒ (3) ⓐ (4) ⓔ (5) ⓓ

Chapter 11

Quiz Yourself 1 P. 179

1 (1) ⓑ (2) ⓑ (3) ⓑ (4) ⓐ (5) ⓐ (6) ⓐ

2 (1) 시설이 깨끗한 (2) 스트레스를 안 받는/받지 않는
(3) 얘기를 잘 들어 주는 (4) 친구하고 같이 본

3 (1) 맛있어 (2) 피곤해 (3) 나이 들어 (4) 친해

Quiz Yourself 2 P. 183

1 (1) 몇 살일까요 (2) 살까요 (3) 있을까요
(4) 생각할까요 (5) 왜 왔을까요

2 (1) ⓑ (2) ⓐ (3) ⓐ (4) ⓐ (5) ⓐ

3 (1) ⓐ (2) ⓒ (3) ⓓ (4) ⓑ

Quiz Yourself 3 P. 187

1 (1) 구했으면 좋겠어요 (2) 사귀었으면 좋겠어요
(3) 건강했으면 좋겠어요/건강하셨으면 좋겠어요
(4) 지냈으면 좋겠어요
(5) 생기지 않았으면 좋겠어요/생기지 말았으면 좋겠어요

2 (1) ⓐ (2) ⓑ (3) ⓑ (4) ⓐ (5) ⓑ

3 (1) ⓔ (2) ⓒ (3) ⓑ (4) ⓐ (5) ⓕ (6) ⓓ

Chapter 12

Quiz Yourself 1 P. 195

1 (1) 밤에 잠이 잘 안 온다고
(2) 음식이 상했으니까 먹지 말라고
(3) 어느 옷이 제일 마음에 드냐고
(4) 이번 주말에 같이 영화를 보자고
(5) 집주인의 연락처를 알려 달라고

2 (1) 어렵다고요 (2) 모른다고요 (3) 말하지 말라고요
(4) 전화하겠다고/전화한다고

3 (1) 그렇다고 (2) 자기 지갑이 (3) 쓰지 않는다고
(4) 먹고 싶다고 (5) 살라고요?

Quiz Yourself 2 P. 199

1 (1) ⓐ (2) ⓐ (3) ⓑ (4) ⓐ (5) ⓑ (6) ⓐ

2 (1) ⓔ (2) ⓐ (3) ⓑ (4) ⓒ (5) ⓕ (6) ⓓ

3 (1) 늦을지도 (2) 받을지도 (3) 알지도 (4) 쌀지도
(5) 갔을지도 (6) 말했을지도

Quiz Yourself 3 P. 203

1 (1) 준기 씨의 집이 크고 집세도 싸다면서요
(2) 준기 씨가 바빠서 시간이 없다면서요
(3) 준기 씨는 회사에 갈 때 버스로 2시간 걸린다면서요
(4) 준기 씨 양복이 백만 원이라면서요
(5) 준기 씨가 다음 달에 결혼할 거라면서요

2 (1) ⓐ (2) ⓑ (3) ⓑ (4) ⓐ (5) ⓑ (6) ⓑ

3 (1) 사장님이라면서요? (2) 기다리라면서요?
(3) 떨어질 뻔했어요 (4) 있다면서요?

Chapter 13

Quiz Yourself 1 P. 211

1 (1) 짤 테니까 (2) 돌볼 테니까 (3) 막힐 테니까
(4) 말하지 않을 테니까/말 안 할 테니까 (5) 도착했을 테니까

2 (1) ⓐ (2) ⓐ (3) ⓑ (4) ⓐ (5) ⓐ (6) ⓑ

3 (1) ⓑ (2) ⓓ (3) ⓒ (4) ⓔ (5) ⓐ

Quiz Yourself 2 .... P. 215

1 (1) ⓐ (2) ⓑ (3) ⓐ (4) ⓑ

2 (1) 배울까 해요 (2) 안 갈까 해요/가지 말까 해요
(3) 먹을까 하 (4) 살까

3 (1) 마실수록 (2) 많을수록 (3) 들을수록 (4) 들수록

Quiz Yourself 3 .... P. 219

1 (1) ⓐ (2) ⓑ (3) ⓑ (4) ⓑ (5) ⓐ

2 (1) ⓓ (2) ⓐ (3) ⓒ (4) ⓒ

3 (1) 좋군요 (2) 왔군요 (3) 알겠군요 (4) 귀여웠겠군요

Chapter 14

Quiz Yourself 1 .... P. 227

1 (1) ⓑ (2) ⓐ (3) ⓐ (4) ⓑ

2 (1) 오나 봐요 (2) 잤나 봐요 (3) 유명한가 봐요
(4) 먼가 봐요 (5) 있나 봐요

3 (1) 산 줄 알았어요 (2) 가는 줄 알았어요
(3) 일한 줄 알았어요 (4) 매운 줄 알았어요

Quiz Yourself 2 .... P. 231

1 (1) 70년대에 유행했던/유행하던
(2) 어렸을 때 가지고 놀았던/놀던
(3) 전에 친구하고 갈비를 먹었던
(4) 학교 다닐 때 키가 작았던/작던
(5) 5년 전에 회사 동료였던/동료이던
(6) 몇 년 전에 할머니께서 주셨던

2 (1) ⓑ (2) ⓐ (3) ⓑ (4) ⓐ (5) ⓐ

3 (1) 먹곤 해요 (2) 보곤 해요 (3) 싸우곤 했어요
(4) 산책하곤 했어요

Quiz Yourself 3 .... P. 235

1 (1) 공부하느라고 (2) 참느라고 (3) 사느라고
(4) 돌보느라고 (5) 찾느라고 (6) 나오느라고

2 (1) 비가 와서 (2) 바빠서
(3) 회의를 하느라고/회의가 있어서
(4) 제가 음악을 듣느라고/동생이 음악을 들어서
(5) 여자 친구를 만나느라고/여자 친구가 생겨서

3 (1) ⓐ (2) ⓐ (3) ⓑ (4) ⓐ (5) ⓑ

Chapter 15

Quiz Yourself 1 .... P. 243

1 (1) ③ⓑ (2) ①ⓓ (3) ④ⓐ (4) ②ⓕ
(5) ⑥ⓔ (6) ⑤ⓒ

2 (1) 들다가 (2) 놀다가 (3) 졸다가 (4) 걷다가

3 (1) ⓑ (2) ⓐ (3) ⓐ (4) ⓐ (5) ⓑ (6) ⓑ

Quiz Yourself 2 .... P. 247

1 (1) 예약했어야지요 (2) 참았어야지요
(3) 받지 말았어야지요/받지 않았어야지요
(4) 나가지 말았어야지요/나가지 않았어야지요
(5) 확인했어야지

2 (1) 갔어야 했는데 (2) 사과했어야 했는데
(3) 돌려줬어야 했는데 (4) 웃지 말았어야 했는데

3 (1) ⓐ (2) ⓐ (3) ⓑ (4) ⓑ (5) ⓐ

Quiz Yourself 3 .... P. 251

1 (1) ⓑ (2) ⓐ (3) ⓑ (4) ⓑ (5) ⓐ (6) ⓑ

2 (1) 예쁠 텐데 (2) 비쌀 텐데 (3) 심심할 텐데
(4) 아닐 텐데 (5) 화가 났을 텐데

3 (1) ⓐ (2) ⓒ (3) ⓓ (4) ⓑ

Word Web Appendix with Hanja

Chapter 1

한국 (韓[Korea]國[Country]): The Republic of Korea

대한민국 (大[big]韓[Korea]民[people]國[country]): The Republic of Korea

- 대학 (大[big]學[learn]): college
- 최대 (最[most]大[big]): biggest
- 대부분 (大[big]部[part]分[separate]): most

한복 (韓[Korea]服[clothing]): hanbok (traditional Korean clothing)

- 교복 (校[school]服[clothing]): school uniform
- 운동복 (運[transport]動[move]服[clothing]): gym clothing
- 수영복 (水[water]泳[swim]服[clothing]): swimsuit

한류 (韓[Korea]流[flow]): Korean wave (spread of Korean pop culture)

- 교류 (交[exchange]流[flow]): exchange
- 상류 (上[up]流[flow]): upper class, upstream
- 주류 (主[main]流[flow]): mainstream

국어 (國[country]語[language]): Korean language

- 단어 (單[simple]語[language, word]): vocabulary
- 언어 (言[speak]語[language, word]): language
- 어학 (語[language, word]學[study]): language study

외국 (外[outside]國[country]): foreign country

- 외출 (外[outside]出[exit]): going outside
- 외교 (外[outside]交[exchange]): diplomacy
- 해외 (海[sea]外[outside]): overseas

국내 (國[country]內[inside]): domestic

- 실내 (室[room]內[inside]): indoors
- 시내 (市[city]內[inside]): downtown, in the city
- 내용 (內[inside]容[contain]): contents

Chapter 2

주말 (週[week]末[end]): weekend

매주 (每[every]週[week]): every week

- 매일 (每[every]日[day]): every day
- 매월 (每[every]月[month]): every month
- 매년 (每[every]年[year]): every year

일주일 (一[one]週[week]日[day]): one week

- 생일 (生[birth]日[day]): birthday
- 휴일 (休[rest]日[day]): day off
- 기념일 (紀[historical record]念[think]日[day]): Memorial Day

주급 (週[week]給[provide]): weekly salary

- 월급 (月[month]給[provide]): monthly salary
- 시급 (時[hour]給[provide]): hourly wage
- 급식 (給[provide]食[eat]): provision of meals (Ex. at school)

월말 (月[month]末[end]): end of the month

- 월세 (月[month]貰[rent]): monthly rent
- 월초 (月[month]初[beginning]): beginning of the month
- 월간지 (月[month]刊[inscribe]誌[record]): monthly subscription

연말 (年[year]末[end]): end of the year

- 작년 (昨[last]年[year]): last year
- 내년 (來[come]年[year]): next year
- 연금 (年[year]金[money]): pension

결말 (結[tie]末[end]): ending

- 결국 (結[tie]局[situation]): eventually
- 결과 (結[tie]果[result]): result
- 결론 (結[tie]論[discussion]): conclusion

Chapter 3

시간 (時[time]間[interval]): time

동시 (同[same]時[time]): at the same time

- 동료 (同[same]僚[colleague]): colleague, coworker
- 동창 (同[same]窓[window]): classmate
- 동의 (同[same]意[meaning]): agreement

일시적 (一[one]時[time]的[marker turning nouns into adjectives]): temporary

일부 (一[one]部[part]): one part

일방적 (一[one]方[side]的[marker turning nouns into adjectives]): one sided

통일 (統[unite] 一[one]): unification

시계 (時[time]計[calculate]): clock

온도계 (溫[warm]度[degree]計[calculate]): thermometer

계산 (計[calculate] 算[count]): calculation

계획 (計[calculate]劃[(pen) stroke]): plan

중간 (中[middle]間[interval]): middle

중심 (中[middle]心[heart]): center

중순 (中[middle]旬[ten days]): 10 days in a month (the 11th-20th of a month)

집중 (集[collect]中[middle]): concentrate

기간 (期[period]間[interval]): period (of time)

단기 (短[short]期[period]): short period (of time)

장기 (長[long]期[period]): long period (of time)

초기 (初[beginning]期[period]): the beginning part of a period (of time)

인간 (人[person]間[interval]): human

개인 (個[piece]人[person]): individual

본인 (本[origin]人[person]): oneself

군인 (軍[military]人[person]): soldier

Chapter 4

서점 (書[book]店[store]): bookstore

교과서 (敎[teach]科[department]書[book]): textbook

교사 (敎[teach]師[teacher]): teacher

종교 (宗[fundamental]敎[teach]): religion

교육 (敎[teach]育[raise]): education

계약서 (契[contract]約[agreement]書[document]): contract

약속 (約[agreement]束[tie]): promise, appointment

예약 (豫[in advance]約[agreement]): reservation

선약 (先[prior]約[agreement]): prior engagement

유서 (遺[leave behind]書[document]): will

유산 (遺[leave behind]産[property]): inheritance

유전 (遺[leave behind]傳[transfer]): genetics

유적 (遺[leave behind]跡[trace]): ruins, relic

본점 (本[base]店[store]): main store

본업 (本[base]業[business]): main job

본사 (本[base]社[group]): head office

본부 (本[base]部[part]): headquarters

매점 (賣[sell]店[store]): kiosk, small store

매장 (賣[sell]場[place]): shop

매표소 (賣[sell]票[ticket]所[place]): ticket booth

매진 (賣[sell]盡[exhaust]): sold out

점원 (店[store]員[employee]): employee

직원 (職[job]員[employee]): (company) employee

회원 (會[meet]員[employee]): member

공무원 (公[public]務[serve]員[employee]): civil servant

Chapter 5

음식 (飮[drink]食[eat]): food

음료수 (飮[drink]料[ingredients]水[water]): beverage

생수 (生[life]水[water]): mineral water

정수기 (淨[pure]水[water]器[equipment]): water purifier

수도 (水[water]道[road]): water supply

음주 운전 (飮[drink]酒[alcohol]運[transport]轉[roll]): drunk driving

맥주 (麥[wheat]酒[alcohol]): beer

소주 (燒[burn]酒[alcohol]): soju

포도주 (葡萄[grape]酒[alcohol]): wine

과음 (過[excessive]飮[drink]): excessive drinking

과속 (過[excessive]速[speed]): speeding

과로 (過[excessive]勞[labor]): overwork

과식 (過[excessive]食[eat]): overeating

식당 (食[eat]堂[hall]): restaurant

강당 (講[speak]堂[hall]): auditorium

성당 (聖[sacred]堂[hall]): Catholic church

후식 (後[after]食[eat]): dessert

후손 (後[after]孫[grandchild]): descendant

후배 (後[after]輩[peer]): younger colleague/coworker

오후 (午[noon]後[after]): afternoon

회식 (會[meeting]食[food]): company meal

회사 (會[meeting]社[group]): company

회의 (會[meeting]議[discuss]): meeting

회비 (會[meeting]費[fee]): membership fee

Chapter 6

무선 (無[not exist]線[line, wire]): wireless

무관 (無[not exist]關[relation]): unrelated
- 관심 (關[relation]心[heart]): interest
- 관계 (關[relation]係[tie]): relation, relationship
- 관련 (關[relation]聯[connect]): relation, connection

무시 (無[not exist]視[look]): ignore
- 감시 (監[watch over]視[look]): surveillance
- 경시 (輕[light]視[look]): disdain
- 중시 (重[heavy]視[look]): attaching importance

무례 (無[not exist]禮[manners]): rude
- 예절 (禮[manners]節[principle]): etiquette
- 예의 (禮[manners]儀[behavior]): manners
- 장례식 (葬[funeral]禮[manners]式[style]): funeral

노선 (路[road]線[line]): route
- 고속도로 (高[high]速[speed]道[way]路[road]): highway
- 산책로 (散[roam]策[walking stick]路[road]): trail
- 가로등 (街[street]路[road]燈[light]): streetlight

직선 (直[straight]線[line]): straight line
- 직접 (直[straight]接[contact]): direct
- 직진 (直[straight]進[advance]): going straight
- 직행 (直[straight]行[walk]): direct (bus, plane, etc.)

전선 (電[electricity]線[line]): wire
- 충전 (充[full]電[electricity]): charge
- 전기 (電[electricity]氣[energy]): electricity
- 전화 (電[electricity]話[speak]): telephone

Chapter 7

불편 (不[not]便[convenient]): inconvenient

불행 (不[not]幸[happy]): unhappiness
- 다행 (多[much]幸[happiness]): fortunate
- 행복 (幸[happy]福[fortune]): happiness
- 행운 (幸[happy]運[transport]): luck

불가능 (不[not]可[possible]能[ability]): impossible
- 허가 (許[allow]可[possible]): permission
- 불가 (不[not]可[possible]): prohibited
- 가능성 (可[possible]能[ability]性[nature]): possibility

불신 (不[not]信[belief]): distrust
- 확신 (確[certain]信[belief]): conviction
- 신뢰 (信[belief]賴[rely]): trust, faith
- 신용 (信[belief]用[use])카드: credit card

간편 (簡[simple]便[convenient]): simplicity
- 간단 (簡[simple]單[single]): simple
- 간이 화장실 (簡[simple]易[easy]化[change]粧[makeup]室[room]): portable toilet
- 간소화 (簡[simple]素[essence]化[change]): simplification

편안 (便[convenient]安[peace]): comfort
- 불안 (不[not]安[peace]): anxiety
- 안녕 (安[peace]寧[peace]): peace
- 안전 (安[peace]全[everything]): safety

편리 (便[convenient]利[advantage]): convenience
- 유리 (有[have]利[advantage]): advantage
- 이용 (利[advantage]用[use]): use, utilization
- 불리 (不[not]利[advantage]): disadvantage

Chapter 8

상품 (商[commerce]品[product]): product

상업 (商[commerce]業[business]): commerce, business
- 공업 (工[craft]業[business]): manufacturing industry
- 농업 (農[farming]業[business]): agriculture
- 산업 (産[produce]業[business]): (an) industry

상표 (商[commerce]標[mark]): trademark
- 목표 (目[eye]標[mark]): goal
- 표시 (標[mark]示[show]): expression
- 표준 (標[mark]準[criterion]): standard

상가 (商[commerce]街[street]): shopping area
- 대학가 (大[big]學[learn]街[street]): college town
- 주택가 (住[live]宅[dwelling]街[street]): residential neighborhood
- 가로수 (街[street]路[road]樹[tree]): street trees

명품 (名[name]品[product]): masterpiece
유명 (有[have]名[name]): popular
무명 (無[no]名[name]): unknown
명소 (名[name]所[place]): (tourist) attraction

물품 (物[object]品[product]): goods
선물 (膳[gift]物[object]): present
물가 (物[object]價[price]): cost of living, prices
건물 (建[build]物[object]): building

작품 (作[create]品[product]): (a) work, piece
시작 (始[begin]作[create]): start
작가 (作[create]家[master]): author
부작용 (副[secondary]作[create]用[use]): side effect

Chapter 9

실력 (實[truth]力[power]): ability

사실 (事[matter]實[truth]): fact
사고 (事[matter]故[cause]): accident
행사 (行[walk]事[matter]): event
사업 (事[matter]業[business]): business

현실 (現[display]實[truth]): reality
현재 (現[display]在[exist]): (the) present
표현 (表[express]現[display]): expression
현금 (現[display]金[money]): cash

확실 (確[sure]實[truth]): certain
확인 (確[sure]認[recognize]): confirmation
정확 (正[correct]確[sure]): accuracy
확률 (確[sure]率[ratio]): probability

권력 (權[rights]力[power]): authority
저작권 (著[write]作[create]權[rights]): copyright
인권 (人[human]權[rights]): human rights
권리 (權[rights]利[advantage]): rights

체력 (體[body]力[power]): physical strength, stamina
신체 (身[body]體[body]): body
체험 (體[body]驗[experience]): (personal) experience
체감 (體[body]感[feeling]): physical feeling

강력 (强[strong]力[power]): great strength
강조 (强[strong]調[adjust]): emphasis
강요 (强[strong]要[require]): force
강대국 (强[strong]大[big]國[country]): powerful country

Chapter 10

문제 (問[ask]題[theme, question]): problem

문제점 (問[ask]題[question]點[dot]): problem
관점 (觀[view]點[dot]): point of view
장점 (長[long]點[dot]): pro, positive aspect
단점 (短[short]點[dot]): con, negative aspect

질문 (質[quality]問[ask]): question
본질 (本[base]質[quality]): essence
품질 (品[product]質[quality]): quality of a product
소질 (素[element]質[quality]): talent, aptitude

문답 (問[ask] 答[answer]): question and answer
대답 (對[to] 答[answer]): answer, response
정답 (正[right] 答[answer]): right answer
답장 (答[answer] 狀[letter]): reply (to a letter)

숙제 (宿[lodge]題[question]): homework
기숙사 (寄[assign]宿[lodge]舍[house]): dormitory
노숙자 (露[expose]宿[lodge]者[person]): homeless person
숙소 (宿[lodge]所[place]): accommodations

제목 (題[theme]目[eye]): title
과목 (科[section]目[eye]): subject, curriculum
목록 (目[eye]錄[record]): list
목적 (目[eye]的[target]): goal

주제 (主[main]題[theme]): theme
주인 (主[main]人[person]): owner
주장 (主[main]張[stretch]): assertion
민주주의 (民[people]主[main]主義[-ism]): democracy

Chapter 11

성격 (性[nature, gender]格[frame, form]): personality

남성 (男[man]性[gender]): male
장남 (長[first]男[man]): oldest son
남편 (男[man]便[side]): husband
미남 (美[beautiful]男[man]): handsome man

여성 (女[woman]性[gender]): female
미녀 (美[beautiful]女[woman]): beautiful woman
소녀 (少[little]女[woman]): girl
여왕 (女[woman]王[king]): queen

특성 (特[special]性[nature]): characteristic
특별 (特[special]別[other])하다: to be special
독특 (獨[alone]特[special])하다: to be unique
특이 (特[special]異[different])하다: to be unusual

합격 (合[combine]格[frame]): passing (an exam)
연합 (聯[connect]合[combine]): alliance
통합 (統[unite]合[combine]): combination, integration
합의 (合[combine]意[meaning]): agreement

자격 (資[assets]格[form]): qualification
투자 (投[throw]資[assets]): investment
자금 (資[assets]金[money]): capital, funds
자료 (資[assets]料[material]): material, data

격식 (格[form]式[style]): formality
결혼식 (結[tie]婚[marriage]式[style]): wedding
공식적 (公[public]式[style]的[marker turning nouns into adjectives]): official
방식 (方[way]式[style]): means

Chapter 12

병원 (病[sick]院[public space]): hospital

병실 (病[sick]室[room]): hospital room
교실 (教[teach]室[room]): classroom
욕실 (浴[bath]室[room]): bathroom (with bathtub)
화장실 (化[change]粧[makeup]室[room]): bathroom

병명 (病[sick]名[name]): name of disease
명함 (名[name]銜[hold]): name card
서명 (署[write]名[name]): signature
성명 (姓[family name]名[name]): full name

난치병 (難[difficult]治[cure]病[sick]): a disease that is difficult to cure
재난 (災[disaster]難[difficulty]): calamity
난처 (難[difficulty]處[situation])하다: to be in a diffcult situation
피난 (避[avoid]難[difficulty]): refugee

법원 (法[law]院[public space]): court
방법 (方[direction]法[law, way]): method
불법 (不[not]法[law]): illegal
국제법 (國[country]際[inter-]法[law]): international law

문화원 (文[writing]化[change]院[public space]): cultural center
문학 (文[writing]學[learn]): literature
문장 (文[writing]章[chapter]): sentence
문자 (文[writing]字[letter]): letter, character

대학원 (大[big]學[learn]院[public space]): graduate school
장학금 (奬[encourage]學[learn]金[money]): scholarship
학교 (學[learn]校[school]): school
학자 (學[learn]者[person]): scholar

Chapter 13

활동 (活[vitality]動[move]): activity

생활 (生[live]活[vitality]): (everyday) life
인생 (人[person]生[life]): one's life
생명 (生[life]命[life]): life (as opposed to death)
생존 (生[life]存[exist]): survival

활기 (活[vitality]氣[energy])있다: energetic
인기 (人[person]氣[energy]): popularity
분위기 (雰[sense]圍[surrounding]氣[energy]): atmosphere
용기 (勇[brave]氣[energy]): courage

재활용 (再[again]活[vitality]用[use]): reuse
사용 (使[employ]用[use]): use
유용 (有[be, have]用[use])하다: to be useful
비용 (費[spend]用[use]): cost, expense

동사 (動[move]詞[word]): verb

조사 (助[assist]詞[word]): marker, particle

부사 (副[secondary]詞[word]): adverb

명사 (名[name]詞[word]): noun

자동 (自[self]動[move]): automatic

자살 (自[self]殺[kill]): suicide

자유 (自[self]由[come from]): freedom

자연 (自[self]然[like that]): nature

부동산 (不[not]動[move]產[property]): real estate

재산 (財[money]產[property]): asset

가산 (家[family]產[property]): family fortune

파산 (破[break]產[property]): bankruptcy

Chapter 14

여행 (旅[travel]行[walk]): travel

여권 (旅[travel]券[ticket]): passport

복권 (福[luck]券[ticket]): lottery ticket

상품권 (商[commerce]品[product]券[ticket]): gift card

입장권 (入[enter]場[place]券[ticket]): entrance ticket

여행사 (旅[travel]行[walk]社[group]): travel agency

지사 (支[branch]社[group]): branch office

사장 (社[group]長[leader]): CEO

사회 (社[group]會[gather]): society

여관 (旅[travel]館[public building]): inn

대사관 (大[big]使[messenger]館[public building]): embassy

도서관 (圖[picture]書[book]館[public building]): library

박물관 (博[wide]物[object]館[public building]): museum

선행 (先[prior]行[walk]): precede

선생 (先[prior]生[born])님: teacher

우선순위 (優[superior]先[prior]順[order]位[place]): first come first serve

선배 (先[prior]輩[peer]): one's senior

진행 (進[advance]行[walk]): progress

승진 (昇[rise]進[advance]): promotion

직진 (直[straight]進[advance]): going straight

선진국 (先[prior]進[advance]國[country]): first world country

비행기 (飛[fly]行[walk]機[machine]): airplane

세탁기 (洗[wash]濯[wash]機[machine]): washing machine

자판기 (自[self]販[selling]機[machine]): vending machine

기계 (機[machine]械[machine]): machine

Chapter 15

출발 (出[exit]發[come out]): departure

출구 (出[exit]口[mouth]): exit

입구 (入[enter]口[mouth]): entrance

비상구 (非[not]常[normal]口[mouth]): emergency exit

항구 (港[port]口[mouth]): port, harbor

출근 (出[exit]勤[work]): going to work

퇴근 (退[retreat]勤[work]): leaving work

근무 (勤[work]務[duty]): working

야근 (夜[night]勤[work]): overtime

출신 (出[exit]身[body]): birthplace

자신 (自[self]身[body]): self

대신 (代[replace]身[body]): instead

신분증 (身[body]分[distinguish]證[certificate]): ID card

개발 (開[open]發[come out]): development

개방적 (開[open]放[release]的[marker turning nouns into adjectives]): open-minded

공개 (公[public]開[open]): opening to the public

재개 (再[again]開[open]): reopening

발표 (發[come out]表[exterior]): presentation

대표 (代[replace]表[exterior]): representative

표면 (表[exterior]面[face]): surface

표정 (表[exterior]情[feeling]): (facial) expression

발상 (發[come out]想[think]): idea, way of thinking

예상 (豫[in advance]想[think]): prediction

환상 (幻[illusion]想[think]): illusion, fantasy

상상력 (想[think]像[image]力[power]): imagination

New Vocabulary & New Expressions

Chapter 1

Conversation 1 P. 20

| New Vocabulary |

지난달	last month
반갑다	to be nice to meet (someone)
시	city
서쪽	west
얼마나	how long
앞으로	from now on
지내다	to get along with

| New Expressions |

만나서 반가워요.
Nice to meet you.

그렇군요.
Is that so?

우리 앞으로 잘 지내요.
I look forward to seeing you again.
(lit. Let's get along well from now on.)

Conversation 2 P. 24

| New Vocabulary |

가르치다	to teach
생활	living in (a place), daily life
언어	language
때문에	because of
힘들다	to be difficult
아직	still
못하다	to be unable to
잘하다	to do well
연락처	contact information

| New Expressions |

무슨 일 하세요?
What kind of work do you do?

한국 생활은 어떠세요?
How is living in Korea?

아직 잘 못해요.
I can't do it well yet.

Conversation 3 P. 28

| New Vocabulary |

이거	this
모두	all, everything
(나이) 차이가 나다	to be (length of time) apart (in age), for there to be a difference (in age)
빼고	except, aside from
함께	together
여기저기	in different places
떨어져 살다	to live apart

| New Expressions |

가족이 모두 몇 명이에요?
How many members are in your family?

오빠하고 나이가 세 살 차이가 나요.
My older brother and I are three years apart.

여기저기 떨어져 살아요.
We all live apart in different places.

Chapter 2

Conversation 1 P. 36

| New Vocabulary |

돌아가다	to return
쉬다	to rest
확인하다	to check
관심이 있다	to be interested
주로	generally, mainly, usually
에 대한	about
주중	weekday
이것저것	all kinds of, this and that
다양하게	various
가요	pop song

| New Expressions |

저는 여행에 관심이 있어요.
I'm interested in travel.

토요일 아침마다 운동해요.
I exercise every Saturday morning.

이것저것 다양하게 들어요.
I listen to all kinds of music.

Conversation 2

P. 40

| New Vocabulary |

밖	outside
정도	extent, approximately, about
반반씩	half each
집안일	chores
소설	novel
역사	history
게으르다	to be lazy
가끔씩	sometimes

| New Expressions |

한 달에 2-3(두세) 번 정도 만나요.
I meet them about two or three times a month.

영어하고 한국어로 반반씩 해요.
We talk half of the time in English and half of the time in Korean.

집안일은 가끔 해요.
I only occasionally do chores.

Conversation 3

P. 44

| New Vocabulary |

씻다	to wash
바로	just, right
새벽	dawn, hours from midnight to sunrise
때	when
쭉	straight through, ever since
불규칙하다	to be irregular
해가 뜨다	for the sun to rise
푹	(sleep) soundly
평일	weekday
하루 종일	all day
건강	health
습관	habit
고쳐지다	to become fixed

| New Expressions |

학생 때부터 쭉 그랬어요.
I've been doing that ever since becoming a student.

그때그때 달라요.
It depends on the day.

그렇긴 해요.
That's true.

Chapter 3

Conversation 1

P. 52

| New Vocabulary |

직접	oneself, directly, firsthand
경기	sporting event, competition
시간 맞추다	to time one's arrival
경기장	stadium
출구	exit
예매하다	to reserve tickets

| New Expressions |

야구나 축구 같은 거 좋아해요.
I like sports such as baseball or soccer.

오후 2시 어때요?
How's at 2 PM?

그때 봐요.
See you then.

Conversation 2

P. 56

| New Vocabulary |

그날	that day
일이 생기다	for something to come up
혹시	maybe, perhaps
(약속을) 미루다	to postpone (an appointment)
벌써	already
바꾸다	to change
안부	greetings
전하다	to pass on

| New Expressions |

웬일이에요?
What's up?, What are you doing here?, What's going on?

안부 전해 주세요.
Please say hi to the others for me.

끊을게요.
Goodbye. (lit. I'll hang up.)

Conversation 3 P. 60

| New Vocabulary |

뭐 what
한정식 hanjeongsik (traditional Korean meal consisting of many side dishes)
값 price, cost
적당하다 to be just right
넘어서 past, after
언제든지 anytime, whenever
이후 from 〔time〕 on
넉넉하게 amply
가지고 오다 to bring (an object)
데리러 가다 to take (a person)
연락하다 to contact, to call
서두르다 to rush, to hurry

| New Expressions |

저는 언제든지 괜찮아요.
Any time is fine for me.

그러면 좋지요.
That would be great if you could do that.

서두르지 마세요.
Please don't rush.

Chapter 4

Conversation 1 P. 68

| New Vocabulary |

이쪽 this way
저쪽 that way
건너다 to cross
자세히 in detail, specifically
설명하다 to explain, to tell
처음 first
횡단보도 crosswalk
보이다 to be seen
끼고 돌다 to turn at (a landmark)
또 also, again
물어보다 to ask

| New Expressions |

저, 실례합니다.
Excuse me.

이쪽이 아니라 저쪽이에요.
It's not this way. It's that way.

좀 자세히 설명해 주시겠어요?
Could you tell me more specifically?

Conversation 2 P. 72

| New Vocabulary |

휴지 toilet paper, tissue
지하 basement
복잡하다 to be confusing/complicated/crowded
내려가다 to go down
계단 stairs
음료수 beverage
코너 section
맞은편 opposite side
이제 now

| New Expressions |

더 자세히 말해 주시겠어요?
Could you tell me more specifically?

저기 〔noun〕 보이죠?
You see 〔noun〕 over there, right?

또 필요한 거 없으세요?
Is there anything else you need?
(lit. Is there nothing else you need?)

Conversation 3 P. 76

| New Vocabulary |

사실은 actually
내리다 to go down, to get off
나오다 to come out, to get out
주변 surroundings
말고 not… (but)
건너편 opposite side
동상 statue
마중 나가다 to go out to meet
입구 entrance

| New Expressions |

거의 다 왔어요?
Are you almost here?

어떻게 가는지 잘 모르겠어요.
I'm no t sure how to get there.

〔A〕 말고 〔B〕 없어요?
Besides 〔A〕, is there 〔B〕?

Chapter 5

Conversation 1

P. 84

| New Vocabulary |

일찍	early
한식	Korean food
맵다	to be spicy
잘	well
다	all

| New Expressions |

(noun) 먹으면 어때요?
Why don't we eat (noun)?

(noun) 빼고 다른 건 괜찮아요?
Except for (noun), is everything else okay?

-(으)면 다 괜찮아요.
As long as it is … it's okay.

Conversation 2

P. 88

| New Vocabulary |

된장	doenjang
손님	customer
떨어지다	to put in
(음식이) 안 되다	(for food) to not be available
이 중에서	among these
뭘로 (= 무엇으로)	from what, of what
넣다	to put in
끓이다	to be boiled
고기	meat
채소	vegetable
들어가다	to put in
따로	separately
가능하면	if possible

| New Expressions |

뭐 드시겠어요?
What would you like to eat?

다른 건 돼요?
Is everything else available?

가능하면 맵지 않게 해 주세요.
If it is possible, please make it not spicy.

Conversation 3

P. 92

| New Vocabulary |

맛집	good restaurant
알아보다	to find out
한정식 집	restaurant serving hanjeongsik (traditional Korean meal consisting of many small dishes)
맛이 좋다	for taste to be good
분위기	atmosphere
추천하다	to recommend
며칠	a few days
입맛에 맞다	to suit one's taste

| New Expressions |

아직 못 찾았어요.
I still haven't been able to find one.

(noun)에 가 본 적이 있어요?
Have you been to (noun)?

알려 줘서 고마워요.
Thank you for telling me.

Chapter 6

Conversation 1

P. 100

| New Vocabulary |

말씀하다	to speak (honorific)
이용료	user fee
내다	to pay
무료	free, no cost
학생증	student ID
평일	weekdays
비밀번호	password
입력하다	to input

| New Expressions |

뭐 좀 물어봐도 돼요?
May I ask you something?

말씀하세요.
Go ahead. (lit. Speak.)

하나만 더 물어볼게요.
Let me ask you one more thing.
(lit. I will ask you one more thing.)

Conversation 2 P. 104

| New Vocabulary |

가져가다	to go (and come back)
물론	of course
지도	map
숙박 시설	accommodation
조용하다	to be quiet
곳	place
탁자	table
안내 책자	information brochure
놓이다	to be on top of (the passive of 놓다 "to put on")
예약하다	to reserve
자세하다	to be detailed
정보	information

| New Expressions |

이거 가져가도 돼요?
May I take this?

물론이죠.
Of course.

더 자세한 정보가 나와 있어요.
There will be more detailed information.

Conversation 3 P. 108

| New Vocabulary |

다니다	to attend work/school, to go to work/school
적응하다	to adjust to
정장	suit
갔다 오다	to go (and come back)
분위기	environment, atmosphere
자유롭다	to be relaxed
특히	especially
엄격하다	to be strict
출근하다	to go to work
마음대로	as one pleases, whatever one likes
꼭	absolutely
정해진 시간	set time
회식	meal with coworkers, company meal
빠지다	to skip
싫어하다	not to like
동료	coworker

| New Expressions |

(noun)에 잘 적응하고 있어요.
I'm adjusting well to (noun).

그런 편이에요.
It's somewhat relaxed. (lit. It's on the relaxed side.)

마음대로 입어도 돼요.
We can wear whatever we like (lit. as we please).

Chapter 7

Conversation 1 P. 116

| New Vocabulary |

동네	neighborhood
깨끗하다	to be clean
편하다	to be convenient
교통	traffic
거실	living room
주방	kitchen
집세	rent
나머지	the rest
떠나다	to leave

| New Expressions |

(noun)이/가 어때요?
How's (noun)?

얼마 안 걸려요.
It doesn't take long.

그거 빼고 나머지는 다 괜찮아요.
Apart from that, the rest is fine.

Conversation 2 P. 120

| New Vocabulary |

여러 가지	a lot of things
불편하다	to be inconvenient
우선	first
직장	work(place)
주변	neighborhood
마음에 들다	to like
오래되다	to be old (for an object)
벌레	bug
이사하다	to move
생각 중	in the middle of thinking

| New Expressions |

뭐가 문제예요?
What's the problem?

집은 마음에 들어요?
Do you like your house?

저도 지금 생각 중이에요.
I'm thinking about that now as well.

Conversation 3

P. 124

| New Vocabulary |

숨	breath
밤새	all night
고치다	to fix
게다가	moreover rhclek ekdmadp sjgdj wntpdy.
틈	crack
들어오다	to come in
다행이다	to be fortunate
옆집	next door
소리	sound
들리다	to be heard
인사하다	to greet
기회	opportunity

| New Expressions |

다행이네요.
That's good (lit. fortunate).

그러지 말고 …지 그래요?
Instead… why don't you…?

그게 좋겠네요.
I guess that would be good.

Chapter 8

Conversation 1

P. 132

| New Vocabulary |

사용하다	to use
잘 나가다	to sell well
젊다	to be young
인기가 있다	to be popular
색	color
고장이 나다	to break
둘 다	both
튼튼하다	to be sturdy
가져오다	to take, to bring
수리하다	to get 〔noun〕 fixed

| New Expressions |

요즘 이게 제일 잘 나가요.
It's the best-selling one lately.

이게 어디 거예요?
Where is it from?

이걸로 주세요.
Give me this one, please.

Conversation 2

P. 136

| New Vocabulary |

전원	power
켜지다	to turn on
버튼	button
새	new
제품	product
교환하다	to exchange
영수증	receipt

| New Expressions |

어떻게 오셨어요?
May I help you? (lit. How did you come here?)

전원이 안 켜져요.
The power button didn't work.

〔noun〕 좀 보여 주시겠어요?
Could you show me 〔noun〕?

물론이죠.
Of course.

Conversation 3

P. 140

| New Vocabulary |

딱 끼다	to be too tight
성함	name 〔honorific〕
반품	return
배송비	delivery fee
고객님	customer 〔honorific〕
접수	receipt
상품	goods
상자	box
포장하다	to package
택배 기사님	deliveryman
환불	refund
방문하다	to be at someone's door, to visit
처리하다	to handle
문의 사항	question

| New Expressions |

무엇을 도와드릴까요?
What can I help you with?

성함이 어떻게 되십니까?
May I ask your name?

다른 문의 사항은 없으십니까?
Do you have any other questions?

Chapter 9

Conversation 1

P. 148

| New Vocabulary |

말이 통하다	to be able to communicate
생활 방식	lifestyle
사고방식	way of thinking
차이	difference
적응이 되다	to get used to
실수	mistake
완벽하게	perfectly, fully
어떤	what kind/a certain 〔noun〕, some
반말	banmal (casual speech)
혼나다	to be scolded

| New Expressions |

적응이 안 됐어요.
I had trouble adapting, I didn't get used to it.

이제 많이 익숙해졌어요.
I've become much more used to it., Now I have adapted a lot.

예를 들면
for example, for instance

Conversation 2

P. 152

| New Vocabulary |

고민	worry, problem
실력	proficiency
한	approximately, about
어느 정도	to an extent, awhile
자신감	confidence
점점	gradually
없어지다	to disappear
최대한	as much as possible
꾸준히	consistently
곧	soon

| New Expressions |

무슨 고민이 있어요?
What's wrong? (lit. What problem do you have?)

저도 그렇게 생각해요.
I think so too., I agree with you.

최대한 많이
As much as possible

Conversation 3

P. 156

| New Vocabulary |

대단하다	to be impressive
원래	originally
이해하다	to understand
만큼	as much as
적어도	at least
이상	at least
알아듣다	to understand (from listening)
포기하다	to quit, to give up
자꾸	continuously, keep (...ing)

| New Expressions |

요즘 어떻게 지내요?
What have you been up to lately?

사람마다 다르죠.
It depends on the person.

〔A〕이/가 〔B〕에 도움이 돼요.
〔A〕 is helpful for 〔B〕.

Chapter 10

Conversation 1

P. 164

| New Vocabulary |

아무	any
부탁을 들어주다	to accept a favor
고장 나다	to be broken
고치다	to get fixed
갑자기	suddenly
막	just
선	wire
연결되다	to be connected
문제	problem
급하다	to be in a rush

| New Expressions |

아무것도 안 해.
I'm not doing anything.

지금 막 고장 났어.
It just broke.

(noun)에는 아무 문제 없어.
There is no problem with (noun).

Conversation 2

P. 168

| New Vocabulary |

날씨	weather
모시고	taking someone (honorific)
걷다	to walk
빌리다	to borrow, to rent
바닷가	beach, seaside
경치	scenery
데	place
알리다	to tell, to inform

| New Expressions |

무슨 일 있어?
What's wrong?

그거 좋은 생각이다.
That's a good idea.

여행 잘 다녀와.
Have fun on your trip.

Conversation 3

P. 172

| New Vocabulary |

지갑	wallet
잃어버리다	to lose
기억나다	to remember
마지막으로	the last time, finally
계산하다	to calculate, to pay a bill
꺼내다	to take out
들어 있다	to be inside
현금	cash
신분증	ID
정지하다	to cancel (a credit card)
깜빡	completely
잊어버리다	to forget
유실물 센터	lost-and-found
일단	first

| New Expressions |

어떡하지?
What should I do?

기억 안 나.
I can't remember.

깜빡 잊어버리고 아직 못 했어.
I completely forgot and still haven't done it.

Chapter 11

Conversation 1

P. 180

| New Vocabulary |

맨	most
갈색	brown
수염	beard
배우	actor
체격	physique
딱	exactly
그나저나	by the way
친하다	
첫눈에 반하다	to fall in love at first sight
계속	countinuously
되게	very
소개하다	to introduce

| New Expressions |

그치?
Right?

첫눈에 반한 거야?
Was it love at first sight?

잘해 봐.
Good luck.

Conversation 2

P. 184

| New Vocabulary |

청바지	jeans
들다	to carry
그건	that (thing)
어디선가	somewhere
생각나다	to think of, to recall
지난	last
발표하다	to present
어쨌든	anyway
놓고 가다	to leave (behind and go)
갖다주다	to bring (for someone)

| New Expressions |

어디선가 봤는데
I've seen him somewhere, but…

아! 맞다!
Ah! Right!

글쎄.
Well. (I'm not sure.)

Conversation 3

P. 188

| New Vocabulary |

사귀다	to make a friend, to date
동호회	club
가입하다	to join
수줍음이 많다	to be shy
활발하다	to be outgoing
상관없다	to not matter
성격이 맞다	to have matching personalities

| New Expressions |

어떻게 하면 좋을까요?
What should I do?

나이는 상관없어요.
Age doesn't matter.

또 다른 건 뭐가 …?
What else is …?

Chapter 12

Conversation 1

P. 196

| New Vocabulary |

교통사고	traffic(car) accident
사고가 나다	for an accident to happen, (for a person) to have an accident
다치다	to hurt, to injure
입원하다	to be admitted to a hospital
수술하다	to have an operation/an surgery
바라다	to wish
병문안	visit (to a hospital)
면회	visiting (hours)

| New Expressions |

뭐라고요?
What did you say?

그건 잘 모르겠어요.
I don't know about that.

저도 그러길 바라고 있어요.
I also hope so. (lit. I also wish that.)

Conversation 2

P. 200

| New Vocabulary |

(시간이) 지나다	(for time) to pass
아까	just now
전화가 오다	to receive a call
사정이 있다	for something to come up
몸이 안 좋다	to not feel well
그런	that kind of
목소리	voice
감기에 걸리다	to catch a cold
힘이 없다	to have no energy
낮	daytime

| New Expressions |

뭐라고 했어요?
What did 〔person〕 say?

그런 것 같아요.
It seems so; It seems that way.

평소와 달리
Compared to one's usual self (lit. differently from usual)

Conversation 3

P. 204

| New Vocabulary |

부러지다	to break (a bone)
다행히	fortunately
약간	a little
큰일(이) 나다	for something serious to happen
왔다 갔다 하다	to go back and forth
치료받다	to receive treatment
걱정하다	to worry
심하게	seriously
고생하다	to have trouble/hardship
낫다	to heal, to get better

| New Expressions |

큰일 날 뻔했네요.
That was a close call.

몸조리 잘하세요.
Take good care of your health.

빨리 낫기를 바랄게요.
I hope that you will get well soon.

Chapter 13

Conversation 1 P. 212

| New Vocabulary |

고향	hometown
경험을 쌓다	to gain much experience (lit. to pile experience)
일자리	job position
번역하다	to translate
통역	oral translation

| New Expressions |

그렇긴 하죠.
That's true.

몇 번 해 봤어요.
Just start preparing now.

그렇게 얘기해 줘서 고마워요.
Thanks for saying that.
(lit. Thanks for speaking like that.)

Conversation 2 P. 216

| New Vocabulary |

한자	hanja (Chinese characters)
살이 찌다	to gain weight
실제로	actually
바뀌다	to change
씩	each, apiece
최소한	at least
조금씩	little by little

| New Expressions |

그건 그렇지!
That's true!

내가 보기에
From what I've seen; In my opinion

최소한 … 이상
At least ... or more

Conversation 3 P. 220

| New Vocabulary |

졸업하다	to graduate
취직	to find a job
대학원	graduate school
사회	society
낫다	to be better
장학금	scholarship
전공하다	to specialize, to major
국제 관계	international relations
분야	field

| New Expressions |

네 생각은 어때?
What do you think?

그러면 좋지.
That'll be great.

하긴.
That's true.

Chapter 14

Conversation 1 P. 228

| New Vocabulary |

초등학교	elementary school
어렸을 때	when someone was young
귀엽다	to be cute
여행 다니다	to travel
지금도	still
이사 가다	to move
연락이 끊기다	to end contact

| New Expressions |

어디더라?
Where was that?

그런 얘기 많이 들었어요.
I've heard that a lot.

안타깝네요.
That's a shame.

Conversation 2 P. 232

| New Vocabulary |

모양	shape, style
전부	all
잊다	to forget
관광객	tourist
현지인	local

| New Expressions |

다른 사람들도 다 그렇게 말해요.
Other people say that too.

뭐가 제일 생각나요?
What do you remember best?

지금도 잊을 수 없어요.
Even now, I still can't forget it.

Conversation 3 P. 236

| New Vocabulary |

해산물	seafood
당연히	of course
싱싱하다	to be fresh
일출	sunrise
전날	the day before
등산하다	to hike (a mountain)
아쉽다	to be a shame, to be regretful

| New Expressions |

당연히 먹었죠.
Of course I ate it.

너무 아쉬워하지 마세요.
Don't feel too bad. (lit. Don't regret it too much.)

시간 맞춰서 같이 가요.
Let's set a time and go together.

Chapter 15

Conversation 1 P. 244

| New Vocabulary |

표가 팔리다	for tickets to be sold
영화관	movie theater
자리	seat
아무래도	in any case

| New Expressions |

무슨 일이에요?
What's the matter?

상관없어요.
I'm fine with whatever you decide.

하나만 더 물어볼게요.
Let me ask one more question.

Conversation 2 P. 248

| New Vocabulary |

죄송하다	to be sorry (honorific)
길이 막히다	for there to be a blocked road
차가 밀리다	to be stuck in traffic
출발하다	to leave, to depart
마침	just (then)
정신이 없다	to be out of it
조심하다	to be careful
자료	data

| New Expressions |

늦어서 죄송합니다.
Sorry for being late.

다음부터는 …지 않도록 하세요.
Next time try not to ...

그렇게 하겠습니다.
I will do that.

Conversation 3 P. 252

| New Vocabulary |

잘되다	to go well
부탁하다	to ask, to request
맡다	to be put in charge
을/를 통해	through

| New Expressions |

전화하려던 참이었는데 잘됐네요.
I was just about to call you. Good timing.

저 말고 부탁할 사람이 없어요?
You don't have anyone else to ask other than me?

제가 다른 사람을 소개하면 어떨까요?
What if I introduce you to someone?

Memo

Memo

Memo